CREOLE CHIPS AND OTHER WRITINGS

"To Jobi

Hoping you'll be enspired!

Juanita Cox

ALSO BY EDGAR MITTELHOLZER

Creole Chips
Corentyne Thunder
A Morning at the Office
Shadows Move Among Them
Children of Kaywana
The Weather in Middenshot
The Life and Death of Sylvia
The Adding Machine
The Harrowing of Hubertus
My Bones and My Flute
Of Trees and the Sea
A Tale of Three Places
With a Carib Eye (nf)
Kaywana Blood
The Weather Family
A Tinkling in the Twilight
The Mad MacMullochs (as H. Austin Woodsley)
Eltonsbrody
Latticed Echoes
The Piling of Clouds
Thunder Returning
The Wounded and the Worried
A Swarthy Boy (nf)
Uncle Paul
The Aloneness of Mrs Chatham
The Jilkington Drama

EDGAR MITTELHOLZER

CREOLE CHIPS AND OTHER WRITINGS:

SHORT FICTION, DRAMA, POETRY, AND ESSAYS

EDITED BY

JUANITA COX

PEEPAL TREE

This Compendium Published by
Peepal Tree Press Ltd
17 King's Avenue
Leeds LS6 1QS
England
2018

Printed & bound by ImprintDigital.com, UK

Creole Chips was self-published in New Amsterdam,
British Guiana in 1937.
The Adding Machine was first published by
The Pioneer Press, Kingston, Jamaica, 1954
See "Sources" for the origins of other material.

ISBN13: 9781845233006

Supported by
ARTS COUNCIL
ENGLAND

CONTENTS

INTRODUCTION

The prolific Guyanese[1] writer, Edgar Mittelholzer (1909-1965) is best known for his many novels, all of which were published with the notable exception of *Corentyne Thunder* (1941) between 1950 and 1965. Several of his early novels received international acclaim and were translated into European languages including Dutch, French, Italian and German. Less well known among today's readers is the range and scope of Mittelholzer's shorter works: from his collection of self-published skits, *Creole Chips* (1937) to his anti-capitalist novella, *The Adding Machine* (1954), over 20 short stories, poems, and plays as well as non-fictional essays and personal writings. While a few of the stories and poems have been anthologised, most can only be obtained from back copies of Caribbean journals such as *BIM* and *Kyk-Over-Al* or the BBC's *Caribbean Voices* archives, and the two published works, *Creole Chips* and *The Adding Machine* can only be found in specialist libraries. No attempt has been made, until now, to bring this body of work together as one collection.

The material that has been included in *Creole Chips and Other Writings* came to my attention as the result of background research for a PhD thesis: *Edgar Mittelholzer (1909-1965) and the Shaping of his Novels*. As the lapse of time between the writing and publication of his shorter pieces was generally a matter of months[2], rather than several years, as in the case of novels like *The Aloneness of Mrs. Chatham* (1965), they provided useful insights into the emergence and development of the novelist's key but complexly interlinked and often abstruse themes (e.g., religion/oriental occultism, sex, death, crime); his literary, philosophical and other influences, and sociological preoccupation with dynamics of race, colour and class. My initial interest in these pieces was thus on the usefulness of their content rather than their literary qualities. It was nevertheless obvious that as a body of work, they deserved greater exposure and warranted fresh critical attention.

This collection attempts to be, but is not, a comprehensive compendium of Mittelholzer's uncollected and fugitive output as a writer. For one thing, research into Mittelholzer's previously published and unpublished works continues to throw up new leads. Peepal Tree was approached with the offer of a 1930s Mittelholzer novel whose title was wholly unknown to me.

There is mention too of a radio play in a letter Mittelholzer wrote to one of his brothers in 1953 that I am yet to locate:

> During the past two or three weeks I have been doing [...] a radio play commissioned by the B. B. C. for the Third Programme in their series "Imaginary Conversations". [...]. It is entitled SÉANCE IN GUIANA and it is a satire on the new Communist government in B. G., with many digs at the English and Americans.[3]

Perhaps given the political sensitivities of the time and the suspension of British Guiana's constitution in October 1953, the BBC withdrew its decision to broadcast the play? Perhaps the recording no longer exists? A similar situation applies to some of the stories he wrote. Writing to Carl van Vechten on 23rd June 1954, Mittelholzer stated:

> Yes, I did tell you of a children's tale I'd done last December entitled MOMENTS IN MAGIC LAND. Unfortunately, I'm beginning to doubt whether it will ever be published. [4]

Perhaps one day this tale will be found in the archives of a publishing house, or was destroyed like many of Mittelholzer's earlier works. Frances Williams reminds: "We must remember [...] that he left us only the tip of the iceberg, as he systematically destroyed all the manuscripts returned by the publishing houses between 1928 and 1941 [...]."[5] The other factor is, as Patrick Guckhian and A J Seymour have respectively pointed out, that Mittelholzer published a significant number of short essays in local newspapers during the early days of his literary career in British Guiana, and wrote short stories for annuals like the *Christmas Tide*; these are yet to be found or collated as my primary focus was on the periods between Mittelholzer's first and last novel (1941-1965).[6] Various letters, moreover, report that Mittelholzer sent material to the *Caribbean Post*, a Jamaican monthly[7]; a 'one-act play' to a W I Radio Newspaper in Washington[8], and a story called "Forest Scene" to *Life and Letters* (a UK based journal whose editor, Robert Herring, published the work of several West Indian writers).[9] These archives, and others, remain unexplored. One final point of note is that Mittelholzer by his own admission published some of his material in British Guiana under an unspecified pen name.[10] It would thus take careful research and a considerable amount of time to positively identify these.

Furthermore, due to the already swelling size of the collection, the section – *"Essays and Personal Writing"* – offers only some of the available material in this genre. It is nevertheless hoped that these pieces will help to increase, and inform a better understanding of Mittelholzer – man and writer – while perhaps stimulating further research into his contribution to the canon of Anglophone Caribbean literature. For the benefit of literary scholars and other curious researchers, it should be mentioned that Mittel-holzer wrote over seventy reviews of fiction and non-fiction books for the *Barbados Advocate*'s weekend edition (the *Sunday Advocate*) between 1953 and 1956. He also wrote several interesting pieces on art and culture for the *Trinidad Guardian* during his residence in Trinidad (1941-1948). As a broadcaster and editor for the BBC *Caribbean Voices* programmes between 1956 and 1958 Mittelholzer spoke on various literary topics such as the "Torment of Technique" (26 August 1956) and offered interesting overviews as an editor of the material that was broadcast. These pieces are included. He also wrote a wide variety of more personal writing, including recollec-tions of his early life in British Guiana in journals, newspapers and magazines as varied as the *Daily Chronicle, Kyk-Over-Al, Books and Bookmen, The Nation* and the *Times Literary Supplement*. This body of writing acts as an extremely useful primary source of material, providing insights into Mittelholzer, the man: his religious standpoint, he view of the West, his attitudes to women, race, sexuality, creative writing and so forth. Only some of this material has been included here.

So what about what is in this collection? The eponymous *Creole Chips* (1937) is a collection of twenty-five skits, seven of which first appeared in the *Daily Chronicle*. In the absence of a local publishing house, Mittelholzer arranged for the collection to be printed by the Lutheran Press in New Amsterdam, and took on the responsibility of selling them at a cost of 4 cents from door-by-door. The publication of the collection highlights Mittelholzer's determination to become a professional writer – the practice of hawking his own booklets conflicted with the mores of his middle class counterparts and earned him the title of 'madman' – but it also offers today's readers a different view of the author. As described by Frances Williams in "Colonial Literature or Caribbean Orature?" (2001) (and republished in the forthcoming companion volume to this one, *In the Eye of the Storm: Edgar Mittelholzer: Critical Perspectives*), the skits are: "frank, caustic but amusing, born of the colony, for the colony"[11] and importantly capture, for the most part, the dialect of the local people. Most critics have viewed Mittelholzer, on the basis of his novels as Anglo-centric without appreciating the complexity of his sense of identity or the impact that his reliance on Western publishers would have on the shaping of his novels.

Mittelholzer's 20,000-word modern-day fable, *The Adding Machine* (1954), sets a similarly different tone from his novels. Mr Hedge, the miserly and mean owner of a failing coconut plantation, receives a visit (in a dream) from a thin grey man, Mr Lesort. Lesort (or 'fate' if we translate the French name into English) presents an adding machine that will help improve Hedge's business fortunes but only on the proviso that he is honest, kind to his workers, charitable to his fellowmen and does not exceed profits of $25,000. After waking up the next morning, Hedge discovers to his surprise that an adding machine has appeared on a table in his veranda. The remainder of the novella follows the fate of Hedge based on his use of the adding machine and the decisions he makes. This vehemently anti-capitalist novella is in keeping with the views he is known to have held in the 1940s, the period (1942/1943) in which he wrote the fable and complicates latter-day views of Mittelholzer as a straightforwardly right-wing novelist.[12] Like *Creole Chips* it was published within the Caribbean (this time by Pioneer Press in Jamaica), and seemingly expressed a view that was unacceptable to Mittelholzer's European and American publishers, with one single exception: in 1961 it was published by Edizioni KKK, under the title 'Il Prezzo Del Demonio' and under the Italian spelling of his name, Edgard Mittelholzer. Here, we may note Mittelholzer as a pioneer in the genre of speculative fiction in Caribbean writing, as recognised by one of the leading contemporary exponents in this field, Karen Lord, in her essay on *The Adding Machine* in *The Eye of the Storm*.

The vast majority of short stories contained in this collection were published in *BIM*; a Barbados-based journal founded in 1942 by E. L. Cozier, and edited for the most part by Frank Collymore. Mittelholzer first came across *BIM* during a visit to Collymore's Free Library in Barbados circa 1944 and soon established a close friendship based on their mutual love of literature. Believing strongly in the need to develop and contribute to regional literature, Mittelholzer later suggested that he try selling copies of *BIM* in Trinidad (where he lived, 1941-1948) and found an enthusiastic readership: "Here am I again with another *BIM* sales campaign at an end. *BIM* went off so fast and seems to have met with such a favourable reception here [in Trinidad] – I've heard many compliments – the next time I suggest definitely that you send 75 copies."[13] Impressed by the regional ethos of *BIM*, Mittelholzer made regular contributions to the journal, submitting at least one story, drama, poem or essay to nearly every single issue published between Feb 1945 and June 1961. He also contributed a couple of short stories –" Jasmine and the Angels" (1946/47), and "West Indian Rights" (1947/48) – and at least one poem, "Epithalamium" (1945), to British Guiana's *Caribia*, a journal that was published by Mittelholzer's friend Clement Gomes[14] in collaboration with B. G. Litho[15]. The other key platform for the publication of his short stories was for him, as with many, the BBC's *Caribbean Voices* Programme. One aspect of Mittelholzer's short fiction worth noting is its variety of generic forms, its overt determination to entertain and its focus on the Caribbean reader. Unlike the novels, published in London, the stories appeared in places that had a predominantly Caribbean readership or listenership. Again, in a period when contemporary Caribbean writers have been exploring "popular" generic fictional forms, in distinction to the "literary" and the "realist" that has dominated the output of the Caribbean novel, Mittelholzer's practice can be seen as pioneering.

A versatile writer, Mittelholzer also turned his hand to poetry. As a genre that offered little or no financial reward, Mittelholzer's output appears to have been driven largely by mood rather than by disciplined endeavour. There is also a sense that he did not always feel like a particularly talented poet, as exemplified by the final line of a poem – 'Oh These Girls' – that appeared in the *New Daily Chronicle* on 26 June 1932.

> Oh, these girls with their fickle ways.
> That cause such anguish to their days,
> Why do they their precious moments waste
> In planning to marry in such haste
> (with apologies to all real poets)

All of the previously unpublished poems that appear in this collection were amongst some letters that Mittelholzer had sent to his close friend, Ruth Wilkinson and were written between 1941 and 1942. Some of these poems are uneven in quality, as exemplified here by jarring lines from "Poet Creating":

> Until the very wracked timbre of my being
> Reels and quivers like a noisy mint,
> Coining words and dreams and potent jellies…

But are nevertheless interesting, particularly if read from a historical or biographical perspective. In "Poet Creating" Mittelholzer's compulsion to "create and create" is powerfully conveyed through the evocation of a "Lernian [sic] Hydra", whose many mouths need feeding. Another poem written on 13th March 1941 acts as an elegy to "The Memory of Ken Johnson"[16] (b. 1914): a black British Guianese jazz musician whose band, The West Indian Orchestra, had become popular residents of London's elite nightclub, Café de Paris; been featured on television, and broadcast by BBC radio. Johnson's death, during the bombing of Café de Paris (8th March 1941) appears to have had a profound effect on Mittelholzer, and prompted him to reflect on the role of the colonial artist in wartime.

Colonial Artist in War-time is one of the longest of Mittelholzer's poems. In order to make money from it, or to at least break even, Mittelholzer arranged for it to be printed as an A5 booklet of 20 pages by the Argosy, around half of which was dedicated advertising space. As he remarked to Ruth Windebank in 1941[17]: "I launched my offensive against various firms in Water Street, and in two days have collected $35.00 worth of advertisements – over the amount required to produce the booklet (the Argosy's charge is $30.00)." The front cover of the booklet was also designed and drawn by Mittelholzer and features two falling bombs, a palm tree and submarine in tropical sea. It is worth noting that the structure of this wartime poem is influenced by orchestral music and opens with an "overture"

– this perhaps being an nod to the daring of artists like Johnson, who strode "through the yellowed flashing night" with defiant laughter and dance. The war for Mittelholzer notably reinforced question marks he had long had about the existence of an orthodox Christian God and the function of war: "You there in the Saxon north, / Tell me if to silt your bodies in putrescent hate, / […] / Will give you joy… and sate / Your spirits…". When he signed up to the Trinidad Royal Naval Volunteer Reserve (TRNVR) in December 1941 as a naval rating, he did so more out of a desire to leave the "backwaters" of British Guiana, than to join the war effort.

While in Trinidad, Mittelholzer became a member of a literary circle headed by the colonial administrator and judge, Eric Hallinan and appears to have used his successes with *Creole Chips* and *Colonial Artist in War-Time*, to help initiate the production of another booklet, *Papa Bois*. While direct credit for the production of *Papa Bois* is not given to Mittelholzer in the booklet (one might more likely assume that it was the idea of Hallinan), a letter to Collymore dated 13th May 1947 suggests otherwise. Mittelholzer noted that he was in the process of gathering material for a literary magazine in Trinidad that would be funded by Judge (Eric) Hallinan.[18] The small booklet, *Papa Bois* (1947) appears, however to have been a one-off, perhaps a result of Mittelholzer's decision to move to the UK on 9th February 1948. It is nevertheless an important contribution to Trinidad's literary scene and contains submissions from Gaston Lorre, B. Ramon-Fortune, C. Arnold Thomasos, A. C. Farrell, Ernest Carr, Neville Giuseppi, Seepersad Naipaul, alongside two poems, "Dove on Gasparee" and "Island Tints" by Mittel-holzer. As Lawrence Breiner has observed "Island Tints" is the most "ambitious and rewarding poem"[19] in *Papa Bois*, and offers a cutting yet playful sociological exposition on the myriad dynamics of race and colour in the Caribbean. The remainder of the poems in this collection have been pooled from submissions to British Guianese journals: A J Seymour's, *Kyk-Over-Al*[20], Gomes's *Caribia*, the *Chronicle Xmas Album,* as well as the anthology edited by A. M. Clarke, *Best Poems of Trinidad* (1943).

While Mittelholzer had an interest in writing and producing theatre plays, the dearth of surviving material makes it difficult to assess the extent of that interest. His first known attempt at producing a play dates back to 1941 when he wrote a drama that he hoped to put on at the Assembly Rooms in Georgetown. Nothing, however, seemingly materialised despite many hours of rehearsal:

> Rehearsals on play being held up by inability to cast two parts – very important parts, too. Manly, Rodrigues, Goring, Mrs Cookson, all let me down in the long run. Gerard de Freitas and Miss Hunt only two I'm sure of. Seems as if the play is going to be shelved. Me alone versus Philistine Georgetown.[21]

It is known that he wrote radio plays and dramas like "The Sub-

Committee" (1951) and "Before the Curtain Rose" (1959) – both published in BIM – and as an regular theatre goer reviewed plays including those that were put on at the Green Room in Barbados during his three years resident (1953-1956) in that country: e.g., *Caesar and Cleopatra* (1953), *Ten Little Indians* (1954), and *The Winslow Boy* (1953). That aside, the only other direct contact with theatre to my knowledge, relates to Moss Hart's dramatization of Mittelholzer's novel *Shadows Move Among Them* (1951), and in that instance, Mittelholzer was involved only as a consultant on the storyline. The play, *The Climate of Eden*, opened at Broadway's Martin Beck Theatre on 6th November 1952 and won, despite its short run of 20 performances, the 1953 Theatre World Award. The recently discovered and previously unpublished theatre plays: "The Twisted Man" and "Borderline Business" are thereby exciting finds and warrant close critical attention. "Borderline", in particular, as Jeremy Poynting has noted, "is a revelation and genuinely funny". It as interestingly highlights how rapidly Mittelholzer tapped into "elements of the theatre of the absurd with its references to Eugène Ionescu and N. F. Simpson's *A Resounding Tinkle*."[22] In terms of sophistication it is on a par with anything that was written in the Caribbean around the same time. Another recent find, "Village in Guiana", was written as short radio play and offers an amusing sketch relating to the wily production of illicit bush rum in the village of Sandvoort on the lower reaches of the Canje creek.

Mittelholzer's novels have been residing too long on the margins of the canon of Caribbean literature as a result of acts of "selection, exclusion and preference"[23] that have in recent years been questioned by critics like Alison Donnell, Belinda Edmondson and Raphael Dalleo. Given the reality that much of the material in this collection has been subject to low visibility / accessibility; and in some cases completely hidden from public gaze, there is undoubtedly an urgent need for scholars to revisit his wide-ranging body of work. That aside, my hope is that this collection will be enjoyed by a wide range of readers, add to the already diverse range of Caribbean short stories, poetry and plays, and be recognised as an important contribution to the canon of Caribbean literature.

Acknowledgements

This collection would not have been possible without access to the personal archives of several families. My particular thanks go to the late Lucille Mittelholzer, Herman Mittelholzer and Gail Calthrop; to the late Ruth Wilkinson and her daughter, Jean Henser; and to Ann Seymour for invaluable access to her collection of *Kyk-Over-Al*. I am indebted to the Department of Archives in Barbados for access to the Mittelholzer letters held in the Frank Collymore Collection and to the University of Birmingham for the material held in the Henry Swanzy (Caribbean Voices) collection, and the University of the West Indies (Cave Hill) for access to BIM. I am grateful too, to Dr Klaus Stuckert for proofreading and making corrections to the German phrases in "Herr Pfangle". My heartfelt thanks also goes to Jeremy Poynting for making this publication possible, and for writing the first major critical review of Mittelholzer's short stories which appears in *The Eye of the Storm*.

Endnotes

1. I will refer to Guyana in the remainder of this paper as British Guiana as it is important to remember that Mittelholzer died before the colony achieved its independence from the United Kingdom on 26 May 1966 and before becoming a republic on 23 February 1970.

2. There are notable exceptions to this. Mittelholzer had for instance sent a short story, "Something Fishy", to the *Sunday Graphic* (British Guiana) in August 1944. Thinking that it had been consigned to the "wpb", Mittelholzer gave it to Collymore for publication in the 6th issue of *BIM* (December 1945). Mittelholzer then discovered that the *Sunday Graphic* had published it around the same time as *BIM* for their Xmas issue, 1945. See letter dated 12th February 1946 from Mittelholzer to Collymore in the Frank Collymore collection.

3. See letter from Edgar Mittelholzer to his brother, Arthur Mittelholzer dated 28th June 1953 courtesy of the late Lucille Mittelholzer and now held in private collection of Juanita Cox.

4. See letter dated 23rd June 1954 in Beinecke Rare Books & Manuscript Library (Ref: Carl Van Vechten Correspondence) at Yale University.

5. Williams, F, "Colonial Literature or Caribbean Orature? *Creole Chips* by Edgar Mittelholzer" in Bardolph, J (ed.) *Telling Stories: Postcolonial Short Fiction in English* (Amsterdam / Atlanta: Rodolphi, 2001) p. 130; and reprinted in *Edgar Mittelholzer, 1909-1965: In the Eye of the Storm* (Leeds: Peepal Tree Press, 2018).

6. Refer to 'Abstract' in Guckhian, P. *Failure in Exile: A Critical Study of the Works of Edgar Mittelholzer* (University of West Indies: Barbados, 1970). Guckhian's assertions are sadly unsupported by bibliographical references so interested researches would need to do the painstaking work of trawling British Guiana's newspapers of the time: e.g., *Daily Chronicle* and the *Daily Argosy*. Further corroborative research is therefore required. In Seymour, A. J. *The Making of Guyanese Literature* (Georgetown: Guyana, 1978) p. 70, readers are informed that

Mittelholzer wrote a piece that was included in the 1937 edition of Christmastide.

7. See letter dated 12th February 1946 – Letter from Mittelholzer to Collymore (Frank Collymore Collection).

8. See letter dated 26th April 1945 – Letter from Mittelholzer to Collymore (Frank Collymore Collection).

9. See letter dated 21st October 1948 – Letter from Mittelholzer to Collymore (Frank Collymore Collection).

10. See undated letter circa 1941 to Ruth Wilkinson in Jean Henser's private collection of Mittelholzer letters.

11. Williams, F "Colonial Literature or Caribbean Orature? *Creole Chips* by Edgar Mittelholzer" in Bardolph, J (ed.) *Telling Stories: Postcolonial Short Fiction in English* (Amsterdam / Atlanta: Rodolphi, 2001) p. 133.

12. In the early 1940s Mittelholzer referred to himself as a communist (see letter dated 30 July 1941 to Ruth Wilkinson in Jean Henser's private collection). It is evident that Mittelholzer had rejected communism as a failed ideology by the early 1950s. This does not infer however that he did not continue to hold anti-capitalist views.

13. See letter dated 14th February 1947 – Letter from Mittelholzer to Collymore (Frank Collymore Collection).

14. See letter dated 29th January 1946 – Letter from Mittelholzer to Collymore (Frank Collymore Collection).

15. See A J Seymour, *The Making of Guyanese Literature* (Georgetown: Guyana, 1978) p. 72.

16. Ken Johnson was more popularly known as 'Snakehips' Johnson.

17. The letter is undated but forms part of a collection of letters that were written to Ruth Wilkinson in the first half of 1941.

18. See letter dated 13th May 1947 – Letter from Mittelholzer to Collymore (Frank Collymore Collection).

19. Breiner, L. A. *An Introduction to West Indian Poetry* (University Press: Cambridge, 1998) p. 73.

20. While *Kyk-Over-Al* published 37 short stories (between 1945-1961), its main emphasis was on poetry and criticism.

21. See letter dated 24th May 1941 from Mittelholzer to Ruth Wilkinson. The Wilkinson collection of Mittelholzer letters is currently in the possession of Jean Henser.

22. Email from Jeremy Poynting dated 17th October 2017 to Juanita Cox.

23. See Alison Donnell's critique of canon building in *Twentieth-Century Caribbean Literature* (2006).

CREOLE CHIPS

CREOLE CHIP NO. 1

The bus called Sweet Muchacha came to a stop at the corner of Lamaha and Cummings Streets, and Bill, the stevedore, and Jim, the shovel-man, got in.

BILL: But man, is wha' you know? Me tell you deh ain' got one star fo' beat Norma Shearah.
JIM: Aw! You talkin' ——! (censored) Norma Shearah! Who is Norma Shearah! You din see Kat'rine Hepburn in "Marnin' Glory"? Oh gaad! Man, dah is wha' you call acting!
BILL: Eh-h-h-h! But look you now! Kat'rine Hepburn in "Marnin' Glory"? Wha' 'bout Norma Shearah in "De Barrets o' Wimpole Street"? Man you ain' begin talk, man.
JIM: (laughing and lighting a cigarette stump) Man, you is a joke. You don' read dem film-magazine, na? Look! Lemme tell you! Kat'rine Hepburn win de prize fo' de BES' performance –
BUS CONDUCTOR: Fare!
JIM: Eh-eh! Well is wha' man? We jus' come in you' bus.
BUS CONDUCTOR: Fare, Ah seh!
BILL: Eh-eh! (looking at Jim) But wha' wrang wid 'e?
JIM: You t'ink we na go pay you?
BUS CONDUCTOR: Fare, Ah seh, man! Hurry up.
BILL: (looking at Jim) But is why coolie stan' suh, na?
JIM: Eh-eh! Tek you' jill! Heh! Tek you' jill!
BILL: Eh-heh! Tek you' jill, man! Look! Tek am! Oh, me gaad! Well, me meet money-shark in dis worl', but dis beat all string-ban'!

★

CREOLE CHIP NO. 2

Mr. Bond, bachelor and retired customs clerk, of 9990, Middle Street, said to Mr. Bard, his neighbour, that his (Mr. Bond's) terrier, Moghams, had been missing now for two days, and that his sister, Miss Bond, was greatly worried because she was inordinately fond of dear little Moghams. Little Moghams had always been such a good companion for Larty-pops (Miss Bond's bull-dog) and Tarty-pops (Miss Bond's tabby-cat). Ramnaraine, the gardener, Mr Bond explained, had searched everywhere in the neighbourhood for little Moghams – but without success, and today Mr. Bond had thought it necessary to report the matter to Brickdam because Moghams had never before stayed away for so long a period

(forgetting, of course, last year when Mr. Bard's mongrel bitch, Norah, had proven so diverting an influence – hee, hee! And kept poor Moghams away from his master and mistress. "Ah well, but these things will happen. Yes yes.")

Throughout this "over-the-fence" conversation, Mr. Bard (unlike his neighbour a married man) had expressed no comment, save a nod or a grunting noise. Mr. Bard had no canine worries, and, moreover, possessed a family (and other families) who occupied his thoughts to such an extent that whenever he listened to Mr. Bond across the fence he did so with a markedly preoccupied air, puffing slowly at his pipe.

As Mr. Bond came to the end of his tale, Mr. Bard hawked and spat, and then remarked irrelevantly that he had noticed that a new cook-shop had been opened "around the corner". "Fellow named Loo Kow Hoo," he added abstractedly – and it was not until getting into bed that night that Mr. Bard thought he saw why Mr. Bond had uttered such a terrible exclamation of desolation at this remark.

★

CREOLE CHIP NO. 3

Mr. Beake, the Magistrate, looked keenly from the face of the infant to the face of George Benn, the chauffeur, and said there seemed to him a striking resemblance between the two faces, so striking a resemblance that he (Mr. Beake) saw no reason why he should not award three shillings a week to Matilda Greaves.

George, who was conducting his own defence, protested that his brother Charlie and he resembled each other closely and that Charlie had also had dealings with Matilda Greaves. How then was the court to know that the child was not Charlie's?

The Magistrate frowned and scratched his head, admitting to himself that this was certainly a poser.

But at this point, Charlie, who happened to be in the court, rose and said that his brother was lying, that he had never had anything to do with Matilda, whereupon Matilda exclaimed: "Ow, Charlie! You lie!" and the Marshal called for order in court.

When the confusion had abated somewhat, George said that the child had a mole on its neck exactly the same as the one which Charlie had on his neck. Charlie was called and examined an, sure enough, a mole was found on the neck of the child, too, which corresponded exactly.

But Charlie protested that the child had a mole on the part which he (the child) would one day use for sitting on and that George also had a mole on the same part. So George was taken out of the court-room and examined, and sure enough, the mole came to light.

"One and six a week from you, George," said the Magistrate. "And one and six a week from you, Charlie. Next case!"

CREOLE CHIP NO. 4

A paw-paw tree in Mrs. Jones's yard was leaning well over the fence and dropping dead leaves and (when rain fell) long trickles of water on to the delicate limbs of a rose-plant in Mrs. Smith's yard. Mrs. Smith, who was very proud of her rose-plants and extremely painstaking over them, wrote a friendly little note to Mrs. Jones. The note read: "Dear Mrs. Jones, I hope I'm not worrying you too much, but won't you try to get that paw-paw tree cut down? It keeps dropping leaves and water on my Marshall Neil rose-plant, and I notice it's only a male paw-paw tree and doesn't bear. I trust you are well. Yours kindly, Maisie Smith."

Mrs. Jones, on reading this, made an acid sound and crumpled up the note, telling the bedpost that she would see Mrs. Smith between the hinges before she cut down her paw-paw tree. "A male paw-paw tree, is it? Well just for that reason it'll remain where it is. Confound her Marshall Neil rose-plant!" So taking writing-pad and pen, Mrs. Jones wrote back to Mrs. Smith as follows:

"Dear Mrs. Smith. I think you are quite right about the paw-paw tree, my dear. It really seems so useless. I'm terribly sorry if it has damaged your Marshall Neil rose-plant in any way. I'm going to see and have it cut down as soon as I can."

Of course, the paw-paw tree has not been cut down. It still leans over the fence. But it no more drops leaves or water on Mrs. Smith's Marshall Neil rose-plant, because Mrs. Smith's Marshall Neil rose-plant died two months ago.

★

CREOLE CHIP NO. 5

One bright morning in February last, Sergeant Strypes of Alfredtown Police Station said to Constable Batton that word had come to him that P-c Batton was in the habit, while on night-beat, of calling in at the cottages of various young ladies of doubtful repute. This was a serious matter, Sergeant Strypes pointed out, and if the truth of it could be proved it would mean instant dismissal for P-c Batton. Wilful neglect of duty while on beat! Did P-c Batton realise what this meant? Ha!

P-c Batton strenuously denied the charge, and Sergeant Strypes, with an ominous wave of his hand, said "Awright, awright" and told P-c Batton to go.

Two days later P-c Batton was allotted the nine to midnight beat in Regent Street. At ten-fifteen P-c Batton, with a sharp glance up and down the deserted street, made his way bravely into a yard and knocked on the door of a small two-roomed cottage.

A voice from within the cottage said, "Who dah?" the voice of Matilda Lesperance, the housemaid of Mrs. Jeeves of Camp Street.

P-c Batton replied: "Is me Charlie. Open de door, man. Is wha' wrong wid you?"

The door opened to reveal Matilda and a kerosene lamp. Matilda expressed pleasure at seeing P-c Batton and told him to "Come in, sweetie. Ah didn' know was you."

P-c Batton entered, but before the door could be closed again a voice from Outer Darkness rapped: "Hold there, Batton!"

It was the voice of Sergeant Strypes – Sergeant Strypes disguised as a ragged mendicant. The Sergeant was accompanied by Sub-Inspector Nancy, also disguised as a ragged mendicant.

★

CREOLE CHIP NO. 6

In New Amsterdam, at 12.15 a.m. one Tuesday, the rat-trap placed on a high ledge in the dining-room of Mrs. Shrew, caught a rat, and in doing do fell from the ledge on to the glassware on the dinner-wagon beneath.

The crash roused the whole household, and lights were switched on. Voices emanated from the bedrooms, followed by footsteps and investigation. Two glasses were discovered broken and a soup-plate cracked. The blood of the dead rat (for it was one of those vicious "catch-quick" traps) had ruined the cloth on the upper shelf of the dinner-waggon, and Mrs. Shrew and her daughter, Catherine, set about to remove it. The broken glass was also collected and taken into the kitchen, and then Mrs. Shrew and her daughter went back to bed.

The following day, Mrs. Mouthley (Mrs. Shrew's next door neighbour) told Mrs. Whispry of King Street that Mrs. Shrew and her husband had a fight last night. "Me dear, you shoulda hear the breaking glass. He cut her with a razor and wash away the table-cloth with blood. Oh, it was *disgraceful!*"

Two days later Mrs. Waits of Pope Street was told by Mrs. Bizzy of St. Magdalen Street that "two nights ago Mr. Shrew chopped his wife with an axe. He broke two of her ribs, smashed up a wardrobe. I hear she's in hospital in a *terrible* condition, poor thing."

★

CREOLE CHIP NO. 7

One Wednesday, in the course of their usual matutinal quarrel, Mrs. Reynolds of Albouystown said to Mrs. Peters that she "gwine do" for her. "You wait," added Mrs. Reynolds, arms akimbo, "Ah gwine *praper* do fo' you! Call me a ugly jumbie, eh? Awright! Wait good! Me gwine do fo' you. You wait! Me gwine *do* fo' you."

Mrs. Peters cut short the third stanza of "Jerusalem the golden" in order that she might raise her face to a mango tree and utter a prolonged laugh. Something like this: "Hay-hay-Hay! Ow me laad! Hay-hay-Hay! A-you look 'tory, na! Hay-hay-Hay!"

The following morning, on awakening, Mrs. Peters found that a boil had appeared on her right elbow. She took no notice of it (save to wash it with three different lotions, show it to all the neighbours, apply cobweb to it and bandage it up with strips from an old pillow-case.)

Four days later the boil had developed into a very painful abscess – an abscess which became the leading theme of every discussion in the neighbourhood.

Mrs. Peters took herself to a dispenser for treatment and while that gentleman dressed the abscess the afflicted lady wagged her head and said: "Ow me gaad! Ow! De wickedness in dis worl', eh? You see how dah woman do fo' me, doctah? Eh? You see how dah woman do fo' me? Ow me laad!"

★

CREOLE CHIP NO. 8

Young Tommy would not desist from throwing crumpled paper balls on top the bed-tester, so Nana said to him in an ominous voice that if he didn't stop she would go and bring "de ol' hye-g" for him.

Tommy desisted at once and accompanied Nana to the bath-room like a good little boy.

That afternoon on the way to the sea-wall, Tommy saw an old bent-backed negress, a beggar, hobbling slowly on her way on the side-walk of Camp Street. Tommy started, pointed furtively, and, glancing at Nana, asked in an awed voice, "Nana, is she an ol' hye-g?"

Nana glanced in the direction of the old woman, then opened her eyes in mock fear, nodded impressively and said in a low voice: "Y-e-s. Dah is de ol' hye-g. If you don' behave you'self she going come to-night and suck you' blood."

Tommy drew nearer to Nana's skirts.

And then another afternoon, in Regent Street, Tommy happened to ask in childish curiosity: "Who lives in that little house there, Nana?"

"Susan is live dere," said Nana.

"Susan? You mean Susan who works at Mrs. Jones-Jones?"

"Yes. De same Susan."

"Oh! And why has she marked exes with chalk on the walls near the windows, Nana?"

"Ah-h-h-h!" said Nana, her eyes widening. "Dah is to keep off de ol' hye-g. De ol' hye-g caan' pass in through de window if you chalk up exes on de wall."

"Oh-h-h-h!" said Tommy, nodding slowly.

CREOLE CHIP NO. 9

Soon after Cousin John had arrived back from Nickerie, the residents of St. Ann Street, New Amsterdam, began to hear strange wailing sounds proceeding from the residence of the Benjamins. These sounds only made themselves heard in the still of the night, and the neighbours wagged their heads and told each other that they "thought so". Ha! That man, eh? They had always known that he dealt with bacoos. This proved it beyond doubt.

Good gracious! Hear how the thing wailed at nights! The evil in this world, eh? And he a professing Christian.

Mrs. Singer was of the opinion that he didn't feed it on raw beef; that was why it wailed.

But Mrs. Tawker thought it was because it had got out of his control. "Ha! You can't go dabbling in the Dark and get off scot-free, my dear."

Mrs. Whistknot held the theory that he kept it in the kitchen and the rats disturbed it. "You have to know how to treat these creatures," she said wisely. "You can't make fun with them. Huh!"

Two days later the Benjamins' cook had received a livid brand on her bare arm. Who had branded her? Nobody knew.

But Mrs. Singer said to Mrs. Tawker: "Ha! You see that, my dear. What did I tell you? I knew it was coming. I knew. Ha! You can't play with baccoo and get off."

★

CREOLE CHIP NO. 10

A cat belonging to Mrs. Reynolds of Albouystown one day happened to stray into the outdoor kitchenette of Mrs. Peters, her neighbour. The cat made off with a half-a-pound of raw steak, and Mrs. Peters, returning from a nearby vat with a bucket of water, arrived just in time to see the animal gliding off, steak in mouth, back into the muddy gloom of an alley way.

Mrs. Reynolds, frying salt-fish and onions and singing "Jesu, lover of my soul", heard a loud scream of "Oh me gaad!" from Mrs. Peters, so what was wrong? Mrs. Peters, in a voice of great fury, told her to look what her so-and-so (censored) cat had gone and done. Run off with a whole half-pound of steak!

Now Mrs. Reynolds was not particularly in love with Mrs. Peters, and this fact coupled with the fact of Mrs. Peters calling her cat a "so-and-so" cat annoyed Mrs. Reynolds so much that this lady informed Mrs. Peters in a rather sarcastic voice that she had not told her to leave her steak where the cat could get it.

Mrs. Peters, putting her arms akimbo, lifted up her voice to the whole neighbour-hood and asked the neighbourhood to look at her cross this good morning, where-upon Mrs. Reynolds, unperturbed, broke forth once more into a lusty rendering of "Jesu, lover of my soul". This was more than Mrs. Peters could stand, so taking up her bucket of water she strode rapidly forward and drenched Mrs. Reynolds from head to filarial foot.

The matter was finally settled in the Magistrate's Court, and the newspapers referred to the case in a short paragraph headed "Three Cats and a Steak."

★

CREOLE CHIP NO. 11

Argument in the Green Tiger Spirit Shop was assuming the nature of a *crescendo assai*, as a musician might say. In other words, the tone was rising to great heights. Invigorated by several rounds of Green Tiger Special, the debaters bawled and gesticulated without the slightest thought of restraint. Indeed, as Thomas Babb had remarked not a moment ago, when Abyssinia was the subject of any discussion, nobody was going to restrain him from "talking his mind". James Ball and James Green concurred heartily, the latter adding aggressively that "nat Mussulooni 'eself gwine stap" him from expressing his views.

Mention of "Mussulooni" seemed to act as the proverbial red rag to the proverbial bull, and James Ball and Thomas Babb immediately launched forth an attack on the Dictator in Italy, stating what they would do to various parts of the Duce's anatomy if they were given the opportunity.

Jose Freheiro and Manoel Pumeiro, who were definitely pro-Duce, added their voices to the fracas, declaring that Haile Selassie was a coward and a deserter, and that were they given the opportunity they would do so-and-so to his so-and-so so-and-so.

Thomas Babb, jerking his head pugnaciously forward, replied that Jose and Manoel were talking —— (censored), and that if Haile Selassie was a coward, what about Mussulooni? Hadn't Mussulooni bombed and gassed hundreds of thousands of innocent women and children? If that wasn't cowardice what was cowardice?

Manoel said that war was war and that whatever the methods employed, Mussulooni had every right to civilise those barbarous Abyssinian —— (she-dogs)!

At this point the crescendo became too *assai* for words, and words failing, fists followed.

★

CREOLE CHIP NO. 12

The Editor
THE CHRONIC ARGONAUT

Sir,

I trust you will permit me a column of your most valuable space in order to point out to the public some of the scandalous happenings in the matters of our village-council. In the first place, why is it that Mr. Hawker, the village-overseer, cannot make a clear statement in regard to the financial status of our Council's Finance? Why is it that Mr Hawker can never tell us straight out what rates we owe instead of telling us that he has not yet worked out his estimates and cannot say directly what sum we are indebted to pay for our rates? Is this Efficiency? Is this Proficiency? Why cannot our Administration Department instal proper Overseers who can do their jobs efficiently and sift matters to a satisfactory close in our Financial Debts to Government?

In conclusion, sir, I would respectfully suggest as our Overseer a worthy and efficient gentleman in the person of Mr. Rupert Emmanuel St. Saviour Squair who has for a long while been proven to possess Sterling Qualities in all matters sociological and appertaining to our village affairs.

Thanking you in anticipation for your most valuable space,
I am respectfully,
Jacob Blunt

FIERY HALL VILLAGE,
CORENTYNE.

★

CREOLE CHIP NO. 13

J. Wordsworth Nowall, Esquire, headmaster of St. Jeeves's Government School, E.C. Demerara, had condescended to take the Third Standard in English Grammar. Cane in hand, thumb in waistcoat pocket, the gentleman paced to and fro before the class.

"And you, boy, I want you to give me an example of the Present Continuous."

The boy rose and said, "The man goes."

"What? What's that? I said the Present Continuous, boy! Come! Hold out your hand!"

Ply! Went the cane. *Ply*!

"That is an example of the Present Continuous. 'My teacher is caning me'." *Ply*! "'John is holding out his hand'." *Ply*! "*That* is an example of the Present Continuous. Sit down. That will make you remember in future. And you there, boy! Why are you fidgeting? What are you playing with? Teacher James, I've been observing this boy before. He is always frittering away his time with marbles. Boy! Get up and give me an example of the Pluperfect."

The boy rose and was speechless.

"I am waitING! An example of the Pluperfect."

The boy remained speechless as though he had had a stroke.

"Boy! I am waiting! An example of the Pluperfect!"

"I – I – the man –"

"Yes. The man what?"

Silence.

"I am waiting, boy! Proceed!"

"Teacher, me ain' know."

"ME AIN' KNOW!...... ME AIN' KNOW!......"

★

Death, the coroner's jury decided, was due to an apoplectic fit while in the execution of scholastic duties.

★

CREOLE CHIP NO. 14

Susan, the housemaid of Mrs. Jones-Jones of Main Street came one day to her mistress and said that she was sorry but that she would have to give notice at once. Mrs. Jones-Jones asked Susan what was wrong and Susan said that she couldn't go on working in the same house as the new cook. Mrs. Jones-Jones told her not to be a silly girl, that if anything was wrong with the new cook, Susan must tell her.

But Susan would say nothing.

Mrs. Jones-Jones naturally felt somewhat intrigued at this sudden mystery. She had no intention of losing Susan who was a good housemaid. Accordingly the lady decided that one or two discreet investigations in the culinary quarter might not be amiss.

But at the end of two days, discreet investigations proved barren of any satisfactory result. She could find nothing against the new cook who seemed perfectly efficient and (if a little silent and gloomy) in no way impertinent.

On the third day the mystery deepened. Bill the chauffeur approached her and said that he had come to give notice. His reason was that he couldn't go on working in the same premises as the new cook. Now, this was puzzling, because Bill of all people had always got on well with the new cooks – indeed too well, as three former cooks had told the magistrate. Why was it then that he should find this particular cook so unbearable as to cause him to give notice?

When questioned, he refused, like Susan, to explain.

The solution to the mystery came a day later when Mary, the chambermaid, came indignantly to Mrs. Jones-Jones and said that she was leaving the house instantly if the mistress didn't sack the cook.

Why? Mrs. Jones-Jones wanted to know.

Why? Because the cook was a bad woman, that was why, Mary explained. She cooked the servants food without a grain of salt, said that pumpkin was her "kinna" and took home the head of every fowl she killed. These were sure signs that the cook danced wind. No servant was going to work along with a woman who danced wind.

Mrs. Jones-Jones had no other expedient but to get rid of the cook.

★

CREOLE CHIP NO. 15

James, the nine-year-old son of Mrs. Forest, the washerwoman, had been absent for over an hour one evening, and on his return home he found that his mother was in a decidedly nasty temper. She demanded of him where he had been "all dis time", and James confessed that he had encountered a few of his companions who had led him into the irresistible temptation of a game of marbles.

Mrs. Forest raised her arms to the sky and asked the sky in a loud voice what she was going to do "wid a chile like dis". She grabbed James with the intention of biting his ear (a favourite form of chastisement), but Cousin Jane, who happened to be present, intervened and "begged" for James. An argument ensued. Mrs. Forest claiming that "dis chile too bad", and that she was determined to learn him a lesson. Cousin Jane said that she knew he was bad, but that Mrs. Forest must "spare 'e dis time", just to please her (Cousin Jane).

Pending this verdict, Mrs. Forest still clutched James's shoulder. She gave it a sharp twinge every now and then so that James squealed "Ow mudder", whereupon Mrs. Forest gave a sharper twinge and said "Ow mudder, eh? Ah going teach you 'ow mudder'!"

Cousin Jane, quite undaunted, continued to intercede for James, employing many supplicating "ows!" until, at length, Mrs. Foster decided to let James off, doing so with a great display of aggrievement and condescension and mentioning (to the accompaniment of one last excruciating twinge of James's shoulder) that the next time he went and played marbles when she sent him out she would burn his hand in the coal-pot.

James, happy at his escape, swore to be a good boy and went to bed. But an hour later (after Cousin Jane had departed) his mother roused him and said: "James, since yesterday morning Ah did promise to bite you' ears fo' breaking dat soup-plate. Ah got to learn you a lesson. You going t'ank me in years to come."

So James's ear was bitten that evening, after all.

CREOLE CHIP NO. 16

James, the nine-year-old son of Mrs. Forest, the washerwoman, came home at a trot and informed his mother that Dear Aunt had just died and that Sister Jane asked mother to go round at once.

Mother gave a cry of alarmed incredulity (Dear Aunt was only ninety-seven), immediately left off her washing and wrung her hands in distraction, uttering quick panting grunts. She rushed out forthwith and moved in an agitated trot up the street, wringing her hands all the while and saying in jerks: "Oh, gaad! Oh, gaad! Oh, gaad!" Mrs. Tryer, the Smithson's cook, asked what had happened and Mrs. Forest replied that Dear Aunt "jus' dead". Mrs. Tryer offered her sympathy and Mrs. Forest, as though taking heart, broke into louder pants, wrung her hands more distractedly than ever and whimpered.

Arrived at the cottage of death, Mrs. Forest found Sister Jane prostrate on the floor beside the corpse. Sister Jane not only sobbed and hammered on the floor with her fists, but at odd intervals she uttered a piercing crescendic yell. "A-ah-ah-ah-ow!" – something like that.

Mrs. Forest, thinking this a good idea and observing that a small crowd was gathering outside the cottage, decided to join in these yells. She went to the door occasionally, lifted her arms and her eyes to heaven and shrieked: "*Wha'* we going to do widdout Dear Aunt now! *Ow! Ow!*"

That same night the corpse of Dear Aunt was laid out in the small parlour. Sister Jane, Mrs. Forest, Cousin John and several other relatives and friends gathered in the parlour and passed the night singing hymns and eating plantain and salt-fish. Cousin John provided a big bottle of rum, too, and Sister Jane and Mrs. Forest cracked jokes, wept and related some of the happy incidents of the past in which Dear Aunt had participated.

★

CREOLE CHIP NO. 17

"Brethren," preached the Reverend Stillson of St. Moonshyne's church, Ithaca, "brethren, the Lord hateth all wrong-doers, therefore see that ye walk into no vile traps that men may set for ye. Be circumspect in all your actions lest the rigid men of the Law wreak evil upon ye in your honest travail. Yea, brethren, the Lord hateth a coward, but I exhort ye to observe care in your movements by day and by night, but most chiefly by night, as the Devil walketh in the Dark, and the Dark hath eyes.

"A still tongue maketh a safe still, and hard labour awaiteth the imprudent drunkard who displayeth his liquor that all may see. In your recreations be loquacious but circumspectly liquorous. Behold, Brethren! The eye of the law is keen, and the wrath of the Lord falleth on him who faileth to keep vigil in the darkness of the stilly night!

"Ears have they and hear not, saith the Holy Book, but I say unto ye, brethren, the ear of the Law is keen. Let no man hear ye speaking indiscreetly of thy neighbour. Fine is the eye of the needle! Fine, I say! But hearken unto me what I tell you this morning! 'Tis easier for a camel to pass through the eye of a needle than for ye to get past the fine which the Law imposeth. The Lord is gracious unto him who battleth with the devil, but wrathful unto him who bottleth without caution.

"The collection to-day, brethren, will be dedicated to the defence of Brother James who had fortuitously and through no serious fault of his own, fallen by the wayside into the evil hands of the Devil who, as ye all know, had lain in ambush for him last Thursday night. Give with an open heart, brethren."

★

CREOLE CHIP NO. 18

Mr. Borde, the carpenter, had been paying "honourable" court to Miss Bent, the superannuated spinster, for fifteen years without any definite sign as yet of matrimonial climax.

Miss Bent, not unnaturally, had now come to fear that if no climax were soon forthcoming, Mr. Borde's "honourable" intentions would probably continue to the end of her life's span and this, without doubt, would be a terrible anticlimax after so many years of honourable courtship. Hence, deciding to adopt the most extreme measure (musk, love-philtres and various boiled bush stay-at-homes having already failed), the lady took herself to Mr. Thomas Bone, the well-known obeah-man, and put the matter before him.

Mr. Bone, after listening solemnly and displaying impressively several turkey feathers, a black bottle, two rat skulls and a rooster's head, told the lady that he would be glad to take on the case if she would deposit with him the fee of two dollars, the balance of three dollars to be paid on the day after Mr. Borde and Miss Bent were joined in wedlock. The lady agreed and paid two dollars to Mr. Bone, who promptly made a pass with his hand over the black bottle and handed to Miss Bent one of the turkey feathers, instructing her strictly never to let it leave her person.

Three months passed and still Mr. Borde would make no move to precipitate a climax, so Miss Bent again approached Mr. Bone. Mr. Bone said that an evil spirit had broken one of his special "goobies" (meaning a scooped-out calabash with a hole in the top) and that was why the prospective bridegroom had not yet made any move in the direction of the altar. If Miss Bent cared to give him a further two dollars, however, he would try and secure another goobie. Miss Bent handed over the two dollars, and then the ambushed police appeared on the scene – and that as it proved, was the only notable climax Miss Bent ever witnessed in her life-time.

CREOLE CHIP NO. 19

Mr. R. Oswald Benfield, assistant master at St. Breese's Government School, New Amsterdam, was leading the motion in a debate at the Z.Q.C.A. Hall (Excelsior League *versus* Z.Q.C.A.) The question which worried the crowded hall was "Is it better to die happy or live miserably?" Mr. R. Oswald Benfield (Excelsior League) was arguing that it was better to die happy. Following is an excerpt from his remarks:

"......we are not concerned with the exigencies of the circumstances, ladies and gentlemen. What we have to occupy our reflections with this evening" (a glance at his notes) "is whether it is more FELICITOUS for a man to die pondering happy thoughts than for a man to live on throughout his complete span of existence in a condition of abject misery and despondency!

(Pause for dramatic effect, arm raised in Fascist salute. Murmurs of approbation from the audience.)

"Now, ladies and gentlemen, this appears to me an extremely simple matter for solution. We do not require to delve profoundly into the realms of human experience in order to arrive at a logical conclusion!"

(Murmur from the rear: "God, man! Dah fellow proper know English.")

"I shall in the first place sketch briefly, ladies and gentlemen, my chief arguments appertaining to this momentous question!"

Voice of irresponsible junior Z member: "Man, take care you break you' tongue!"

The General Secretary and the President of the Literary Committee rose as two men and called for order in a severe tone.

★

CREOLE CHIP NO. 20

Ramjan, the beggar, stood at the foot of Mrs. Green's backstairs and asked for alms. Ramjan was attired in a grey suit composed of about five hundred little sections of cloth, none of which, for a certainty, had been to Ah Wash, the launderer, for three or four years. Ramjan also carried a large bundle of which the Chief Sanitary Inspector would not readily have approved. He carried something else too – a strong smell.

Ramjan gazed supplicatingly up at the back door and, holding out a withered hand, wagged his unkempt head and said in weak *pianissimo*: "Missy!" Pause. *Poco a poco crescendo, e con espressione*: "Gi' poor beggah-man somet'ing!"

Catherine, Mrs. Green's cook, suddenly appeared at the door and told Ramjan (in *fortissimo*) to get out of the yard "Na-a-asty coolie," she added in *diminuendo* and swept back into the kitchen.

But Ramjan was in no way daunted. He continued to gaze up at the back door. Very softly: "Missy!" Pause. Gradual rise in tone and with expression: "Gi' poor beggah-man somet'ing!" (*Da capo...... Da capo.*)

At length, after several repetitions, Mrs. Green herself happened to pass the back door on her way from the pantry to the kitchen. She saw Ramjan, heard his supplication and, being a kind lady, sent down a penny for him. As Ramjan took it he lifted his face to the zenith. His dark brown teeth appeared in a grin of gratitude. "*Ga-a-d* sah bless, missy! *Ga-a-d* sah bless!" he groaned with wagging head and shaking spindles.

A fortnight later a policeman found him dead on the pavement of a spirit-shop. His bundle contained one thousand, two hundred dollars.

★

CREOLE CHIP NO. 21

Bella, on being taken on as cook by Mrs. Smith of 999, Robb Street, had not been aware that Mrs. Smith was the granddaughter of a gentleman called Isaac Meinstein and the daughter of Andrew MacStingie. Hence when Bella came from the market on the first morning of her employment, the following dialogue took place: —

MRS. SMITH: You've spent thirty-eight cents, Bella!
BELLA: Yes, mum.
MRS. SMITH: But how do you make that out? Thirty-three cents is what the other cooks spent in the market every morning. If anything, less. Let me hear how you spent it, please.
BELLA: Penny salt-fish. Penny butter –
MRS. SMITH: A cent butter would have been enough, girl! Do you think I'm a millionaire?
BELLA: Cent lard. Penny tomato paste. Three cents potatoes –
MRS. SMITH: THREE cents potatoes! No child this won't do. You're far too extravagant for me!
BELLA: Penny eddoes. Penny margarine. Cent black-pepper –
MRS. SMITH: Black-pepper! I NEVER use black-pepper! You'll ruin me at this rate, Bella.
BELLA: Penny cassava. Penny yam. Cent bird-pepper. A tin o' sardines, eight cents –
MRS. SMITH: EIGHT.......!

Sarah Bernhardt could not have done the swoon better than Mrs. Smith. On her recovery she dismissed Bella on the spot. She had met with extravagant cooks, but, really, this girl took the cake with a vengeance.

CREOLE CHIP NO. 22*

Mr. Jacob Jones, bush rum-distiller of Ithaca, was annoyed with Mr. Thomas Brown, bush-rum distiller of Rosignol, because information had come to the ears of Mr. Jones that Mr. Brown was nightly to be seen arriving at the cottage of Miss Susan Lashley and matutinally to be seen departing. Mr. Jones had always considered himself to be the only gentleman in the world who had the right to be seen at the cottage of Miss Lashley. This right he had exerted for many weeks until a row with the lady had caused him (in his own words) to "apply sanctions 'pon she". It was during the period of these "sanctions" that Mr. Brown had stepped in and furnished the lady (in his own words) "wid de key supplies".

Mr. Jones's first action was to hasten to the cottage and inform the lady that he was ready to lift sanctions and resume diplomatic relations (at least his words were to this effect) but the lady treated him with much scorn and told him in words which meant the same thing that the goods now supplied by Mr. Thomas Brown were of a superior quality to the goods formerly supplied by Mr. Jacob Jones, hence Mr. Jones could transfer his negotiations elsewhere.

The vanity of Mr. Jones was, naturally, much hurt and the gentleman swore he would wreak vengeance on Miss Lashley and her new partner in commerce.

Accordingly, a few hours following the dispute, Mr. Jones called "the boys" together and held a conference, with the result that one night a week later, Miss Lashley's cottage was raided by the police. Mr. Brown and the lady were arrested and taken to the station along with a bush-rum still and a dozen bottles of spirit discovered on the premises.

Mr. Brown and Miss Lashley are at present spending a six-months' honeymoon at one of the pleasure resorts maintained by His Majesty.

★

CREOLE CHIP NO. 23

Mrs. James-James of Main Street was interviewing applicants for the post of housemaid. The first applicant had failed. The second was now in process of cross-examination.

"Have you any references, my girl?"

"One, ma'am. From Mrs. Jones-Jones. Here it is."

"H'm. Yes, this is good. I think you'll do. I'll give you a trial. You may turn on to-day."

A short distance off, Mrs. Waspe of Robb Street was also interviewing applicants for the post of housemaid. The first twenty-two applicants had failed. The twenty-third was now in process of cross-examination.

"H'm-ff! Don't stand so near to me, child. Where you been working before?"

"At Mrs. Fryer, mum."

"P'ff! Mrs. Fryer! Who is she at all? Why you' foot tie up so? I hope you ain' got filaria?"

"No, mum. Is a cut ah had."

"A cut? What sorta cut? H'm-ff! Don't stand so near to me, girl. Where else you work?"

"At Mrs. Byler, mum."

"And why you had to leave there?"

"Mum, Ah couldn' stan' she airs. An' de life she used to lead – Ah couldn' stan' it."

"The life she used to lead?" Mrs Waspe leant forward eagerly. "How do you mean?"

"Mum, you know de men she used to –"

"Oh! Oh! I see. It's all right, Kathleen. You can turn on to-day, my child. I'll try you and see how we get along."

*

CREOLE CHIP NO. 24

Discussion in the Flying Camoodie Spirit Shop, Mahaicony, was progressing serenely.

Jose Rumeiro was in command of the Big Bottle of Flying Camoodie Special Fruit-Cured. Jose was the proprietor, and in his rum-shop he preferred propriety to sobriety, though he never insisted too strenuously even on the former. "You shee me here," he told Ramgollal, the East Indian pan-boiler, and Emmanuel Plow, the negro farmer. "You shee me here, me na tr-rouble nabady. But when dem two-chentsh man come up from Joshtown and break down here wid deh car, deh know quick to come in an' ashk me fo' assishtance. Eh-heh. Deh know quick. But me na fool. When deh come ashk me fo gasholene, me tell dem me gat. But wha' price you t'ink me charge dem? Eh-heh-h-h-h! Dah wheh de catch come in, boysh. Me charge dem DOUBLE de price! Y-e-sh. Eh-heh. DOUBLE wha' deh gat fo' pay in Joshtown. You t'ink me stupid, na?"

Ramgollal and Emmanuel gave vent to leisurely guffaws – in keeping with the spirit of propriety which Jose always took care to sponsor. Emmanuel's eyes strayed suggestively toward this spirit, and Jose raised his brow and enquired: "Annoder roun'?"

Emmanuel made a doubtful sound.

Ramgollal nodded decisively. "Put it down to me, Jose."

"Eh-heh," said Jose and poured out three rounds of Flying Camoodie Special Fruit-Cured (prunes, raisins, citron, spice and old boots guaranteed). "Watch de colour, boysh," smiled Jose, with the air of a poet. He wagged his head. "Ish who shay deh gat bettah rum dan de Flying Camoodie? You caan' beat de Flying Camoodie. Eh, boysh?"

Ramgollal and Emmanuel concurred automatically.

THE FINAL CHIP

"You run, you run. WHY-Y-Y-Y you run…?! Foo-foo. Foo, foo, FOO! said the euphonium. Too-tooroot-too-TOO-OO! trumpeted the trumpet of the trumpeter. "Oh me gaad! Ow me laad!"… "Ow, boy! Ow!"

"If 'ooman sweetah dan me Ah will t'row meself in de sea…" Foo, foo, foo! Foo, FOO!

"Way-y! Hay-hay-hay-y-y-Hay! wailed the saxophone of Jokey the Jazzy Jouster. Jokey was on his feet. His body swayed to and fro. Everybody's body swayed to and fro. And the Billy Goat was loose. Smell how he smelled!

"Ow, gal! Ow! Show me a motion!"

"Ah-ow! Ah-ow! Have you heard de CAR-I-OCA…"

Brang-brang said the piano. Thrum, thrum, answered the banjo. "Oh, gaad! Hol' me! Hol' me tight, baay!"

Susan uttered a streak of laughter and Ralph Magnate the son of the Hon. James Magnate, M.L.C., held her tighter than ever, while P-c Batton, in mufti, gyrated cork-screw-wise down to the floor and up again.

"Yeah-h-h-h! Have you seen Anacona…?"

"YES SIR!"

"Dancing de rumba?"

"YES SIR!"

Foo foo FOO! Too-tooroot-too-too-TOO! Brang, brang! "Ow, baay!" … "Ow, gal!" Thrum, thrum….

On with the bram!

THE ADDING MACHINE

A FABLE FOR CAPITALISTS AND

COMMERCIALISTS

FOREWORD

The British Caribbean has in the past produced good writers, here and there, now and then. Today for the first time, the region has become the source of a general flowering of talent. There can be no doubt about it. All the larger units and some of the small ones are represented by successful titles. Critics in London and *New York* refer to "the current West Indian school." Leading publishers recognise a trend and are disposed take a chance on a new Caribbean author for the main reason that he is Caribbean.

The names that spring to my mind are those of the novelists Victor S. Reid, Lucille Iremonger and Roger Mais, of Jamaica, Edgar Mittelholzer, of British Guiana and Samuel Selvon of Trinidad; the raconteur George Lamming, of Barbados; and the poet Derek Walcott, of St. Lucia.

Decidedly Edgar Mittelholzer is one of the strongest of the group. He is also among the earliest, a statement that takes us back only five or six years. His initial popular success was made with *A Morning at the Office* in 1950. It was a subtle, quiet study of envious race relations in Port of Spain, where he once lived. I imagine most readers thought then that Mittelholzer's scope was limited. If so, they were wrong. He is a child of ferment and one of its most telling voices, an astonishingly versatile and prolific writer.

Without respite, following *A Morning at the Office* he has poured out novels dealing with British Guiana, and one bizarre mystery story, the scene of which is laid in an English village. The violent *Children Kaywana* has perhaps been the most discussed. It is Part 1 of an historical epic seething with the carnage of slave-revolts on the plantations carved out of the jungle by the Dutch. I prefer *Shadows Move Among Them*, strange fantasy of sex and religion in a forest Arcadia that it is. In *The Life and Death of Sylvia,* his latest, the cards are inexorably stacked against the heroine, resulting in so mordant an exposure of social problems, that the news-magazine, *TIME* praised the book as unique.

The Adding Machine, a brilliant modern fable, was written for the Pioneer Press, which is proud to issue this first edition of one of Edgar Mittelholzer's works.

W. ADOLPHE ROBERTS. General Editor.

One day a thin grey man came to see Mr. Hedge.

Mr. Hedge was sitting on the veranda of his bungalow feeling depressed. Caterpillars were eating fronds of his coconut palms and the coconut crop, as a result, was going to be poor this half-year-end. Mr. Hedge was in debt and his plantation was only a small one. All his efforts to check the caterpillars had failed.

"What have you come to bother me about?" said Mr. Hedge to the thin grey man. "Can't you see I'm worried?"

"Perhaps I've come to relieve your worry," said the thin grey man. He carried a bulky parcel. "May I sit?"

"Very well. Sit down. What's your name?"

The thin grey man sat down. "You can call me Lesort. Just call me Lesort."

Mr. Hedge frowned suspiciously. "You sound as if you aren't certain. Is that an assumed name?"

"No, that's my name. Lesort."

"Are you French?"

"Yes. But sometimes I can be English, too. Even German or American. I'm not at all patriotic."

Mr. Hedge shifted his feet about, not liking this reply.

"Where are you from?"

"Me? Oh, I'm a nomad. I wander around. I've been everywhere. I come from everywhere."

"Are you a globe-trotter?"

"Ah! There's a neat way of putting it. Yes, I'm a globe-trotter."

"And what do you want here on my coconut plantation? If you're selling something I may as well tell you I have no money."

"This little adding-machine I have here is a useful thing."

"Adding-machine! What do you think I would want an adding-machine for? An adding-machine on a coconut plantation?"

"Don't you want to make money with your coconuts? Surely you'll want a machine to add up your money as it accumulates from day to day."

"I went to school. I can add without a machine."

"That may be so, but nowadays machines can save a lot of trouble and time. When I was in a certain country I tried to sell them a certain line of machines, but they shrugged and wouldn't buy. For years and years I tried, but they still shrugged and wouldn't buy. Only a certain other country would buy. They bought thousands and thousands from me. And what happened? This country that bought my machines took over the country that wouldn't buy. Using my machines they just blitzed in and took over. How do you like that?"

"All that," said Mr. Hedge, "is pure sales talk."

"Then you won't buy this, little adding-machine of mine?"

Mr. Hedge fidgeted and said: "What's the price of it?"

"Only twenty-five cents."

"Twenty-five cents!" Mr. Hedge laughed. "Oh, you can't catch me so easily, Mr. Lesort. I'm too wily for that. You mean I pay twenty-five cents now and another twenty-five cents next week, and I go on paying twenty-five cents every week for the next hundred or more weeks. I was once a vacuum-cleaner salesman. I know all the works."

The thin grey man smiled and shook his head. "I mean," he said, "you pay twenty-five cents now and you keep the machine for good. You don't pay a single cent more."

"Is this a joke? An adding-machine for twenty-five cents!"

"Yes. But this is a special adding-machine. Only you can use it. It would be no use my trying to sell it to anyone else, because it will only add for you."

"Look here, you seem to take me for a simpleton. Let me tell you, Mr. Lesort, I've had a very varied career. I've even worked on the Stock Exchange. I've met all sorts of tricksters."

"Have you ever met yourself, Mr. Hedge?"

"Very well. Don't try to be clever now. I'm worried, I tell you. I'm in no mood for jokes about adding-machines that will only add for me."

"It's not a joke. I'm serious. It's a special machine. I had it made specially for you – and it will add only your money."

"It will add only my money?"

"That's what I said. It will add only your money – not coconuts or sheep or pigs or buttons. Only your money – your dollars and cents. If you make ten dollars today, touch the keys and record ten dollars. If you make fifteen dollars tomorrow, touch the keys and record twenty-five dollars. If you spend or lose five dollars tomorrow touch the keys, touch the subtracting key and record twenty dollars. Very simple. Only you must be honest with this machine. It's a very sensitive machine."

Mr. Hedge laughed. "Anyway, I don't want it, so it doesn't matter whether its a sensitive machine or not."

"But it will bring you, luck, Mr. Hedge. The caterpillars will die, your trees will flourish and your crop this half-year-end will be good."

Mr. Hedge laughed again. "A magic-machine, eh?"

"Call it a good-luck machine. A mascot machine."

"A mascot-machine. I see. But I still don't want it. I don't believe in mascots. I'm not superstitious, Mr. Lesort. I'm a realist."

"Is that final? You won't buy it – not even for twenty-five cents?"

"Not even for a cent. That's final."

"Very well, Mr. Hedge. In that case I'll let you have the machine for nothing. I thought I could have persuaded you to pay for it; but as I have failed to talk you out of your meanness I must leave it with you."

"You could take it away, of course. I wouldn't stop you."

"I couldn't. It's too essentially yours now. I could no more take away this machine than I could your heart."

Mr. Hedge tried to laugh again, but the laughter that came from him sounded uneasy. "Oh, well," he said, 'if that's the way you feel about it, leave it by all means. I never object to getting something for nothing."

So the thin grey man undid his parcel and brought out the adding-machine. "You'll find it in good working order," he said, placing it on a small bamboo table. "Ah! But there's one thing I'm forgetting."

"Aha! I was waiting for the catch."

"It's not a catch. In fact, I wouldn't need to do it if you gave me that twenty-five cents I asked for."

"Well, you're not getting it."

"It's your last chance, Mr. Hedge. Only twenty-five cents."

"I'm not paying it. That's final."

"Very well. Then I must attend to a little matter."

"What's that?"

"I must debit you with twenty-five cents."

"Debit me with twenty-five cents! What do you mean debit me with twenty-five cents! Didn't you just say you were giving me the machine for nothing. Look here, I won't be tricked. I'm not paying a cent for this machine. Not a single cent. Not today nor tomorrow, nor next month. Have you got that clear?"

"Just a moment, Mr. Hedge. Don't misunderstand me. When I say debit you with twenty-five cents I mean *on the machine*. It's a very sensitive machine, as I've mentioned before, and this is a matter of book-keeping. It might take offence, if I don't keep my books straight. Now look. See this little group of keys all by itself here? This is the debit group. You don't have it on all adding machines. Only on this one as it's a special one made for you. Now, watch."

Mr. Lesort pressed "2" and "5" and pulled the handle and "25" registered in red in the separate glass-cased oblong above the debit group of keys. "That's all. The deal is over. The machine is yours, Mr. Hedge. Essentially yours. For better for worse. For richer for poorer."

Mr. Hedge laughed, but it was an uncomfortable laugh. "You're full of monkey tricks, aren't you."

"Full of tricks, Mr. Hedge. I've never lost a rubber nor bid a slam and never made it. I've never backed a dictator who didn't dictate, nor a beggar who didn't beg himself to death. Oh, by the way, before I go, just a hint or two. Be honest with this machine if you want good results. And be kind to the men who pick your coconuts. Give them enough to support their homes and lead a comfortable life. Give liberally to deserving charities, and help your fellowmen when they are in difficulties. Don't encroach on your neighbour's lands or try to oust your fellow-landowners. Be content with your living-room. And above all, don't let your money at any time exceed twenty-five thousand dollars. With twenty-five thousand dollars you can be happy and you can make others happy. This machine, I may mention, Mr. Hedge, considers any sum in excess of twenty-five thousand dollars an immoral total. An odd little machine. Brings stupendous luck, but can be spiteful when it gets ready. Good day, Mr. Hedge."

Then Mr. Hedge woke up, for it had been only a dream, of course. A very vivid dream, though, he told himself, as he got out of bed. He remembered every detail of it.

It was morning, and the sun was shining in at the window. He looked out at the coconut palms and wagged his head. Pity, he thought, that the caterpillars hadn't been a dream, too. But unfortunately they were only too real. All the fronds would soon be completely bare. And then the caterpillars would attack the heart of the trees: the young stalks and the young fronds. He would be ruined. The crop this half-year-end would be negligible. The young nuts would fall before they reached maturity. Some would survive, but not ten per cent of the whole lot.

When he had finished his toilet and had had his breakfast, he went out on to the veranda to wait for Miguel, the foreman of the labourers, who would be coming at half past seven to report to him before resuming work on the campaign against the caterpillars.

He lit a cigarette and was about to seat himself in the one wicker chair when his gaze fell on something.

On the little bamboo table (which with the wicker chair and two wooden-seated chairs, constituted the only furniture on the veranda) there stood an object. An adding-machine.

Mr. Hedge took a pace toward the table and stood staring down at the thing. Where had it come from? Whose was it? What was it doing on the table here?

He remembered his dream, and his heart beat as he noticed that the machine was divided into two sections of keys. Above one section, in the glass-cased oblong where the amounts were recorded, the numbers read: "000000025". The numbers were red.

In the other section the numbers were black and all were noughts. Nine black noughts.

Mr. Hedge put out his hand hesitantly and touched the machine. It was solid. Real. Nothing dreamlike about it.

He looked round him, feeling his flesh crawling and hot along his limbs. He did not like uncanny happenings.

"Sammy!" he shouted, and Sammy, the Indian factotum, answered: "Yes boss!" from inside, and when he appeared on the veranda said: "Yes, boss?" again, this time in enquiry.

"Where did this thing come from, Sammy? This machine?"

Sammy looked at the machine and shook his head. "I don't know, boss, I didn't see it there before." He spoke in a low, frightened voice, waiting for his master to kick or clout him for negligence.

"You didn't see it here before!" barked Mr. Hedge. "Don't be a blithering fool! How did it get here? Someone must have put it here. Haven't you been out here for the morning?"

"No, boss. I was busy making your breakfast, boss."

"Didn't you hear anyone knock before I woke up?"

"No, boss. No one knock."

"Well, that's damned funny. How did this machine get here? Human hands must have put it here."

"I don't know, boss. I didn't see no one put it there. This is the first time I see it."

"Didn't you see anyone hanging about the house?"

"No, boss. I didn't see nobody."

Hedge stared at the machine, then frowned at Sammy who was trembling in expectation of a kick. "All this is just a lot of tomfoolery. It's your business to see that no strangers enter this house."

Mr. Hedge was about to clout Sammy and order him to take the machine and hurl it into the river when Miguel, the foreman of the labourers, appeared. He came at a run and seemed very excited.

"What's the matter, Miguel?"

"Boss, you see what happen?"

"What? Nothing pleasant, I can bet my last boot."

"Boss, come. Come with me and see, boss."

"What's happened, man? What's all the excitement about?"

Miguel began to go down the stairs again. "You come, boss," he said. "Come with me and see."

Mr. Hedge was so impressed by his urgency that he followed him, fearing that some disaster had occurred.

Miguel came to a halt under the nearest coconut palm.

"Look, boss! Look!" He pointed at the ground. "Look what happen!"

Mr. Hedge looked and saw that the ground was covered with caterpillars. There was a thick carpet of them on the grass. They were still and lifeless.

"They all dead, boss," said Miguel.

"All dead! But how? That stuff we use yesterday didn't seem much good. No good at all, in fact."

"Same thing I say to myself, boss. But they all dead. All the other trees same way. All worms dead."

"But this is strange," said Mr. Hedge, joyful within, but frowning in a puzzled manner. For an instant he felt a dart of fear go through his joy. He remembered his dream and the thin grey man. The thin grey man had offered him an adding machine which, he had said, would bring him luck. The caterpillars would die, he had said, and the trees would flourish. The crop this half-year-end would be good.

But that had been only a dream.

Yet there was that machine on the table on the veranda. How had it got there? Who could have put it there? It was the very same machine he had seen in his dream. Not a single detail of that dream had faded from his memory. Very odd, because it was seldom that he had dreams. Even on the rare occasions when he did dream he could never on awakening recall clearly anything of what he had dreamt.

A shiver went through him.

"Very well, Miguel. Get the men to clear away these dead worms. We mustn't take any chances. Make a heap of them, get some twigs and dry leaves and burn them."

"Yes, boss. I will do that right away."

Mr. Hedge returned to the house and stared at the machine. He did not like mysteries, and he had no belief in magic. He was, as he had told Mr. Lesort, a realist. All his life he had been a realist. Money, so far as be was concerned, was the only real thing worth bothering about. Everything else was so much irrelevant frippery. Books, pictures, music, God, politics, idle fancies and superstitions – and even love – interested Mr. Hedge not in the slightest.

However, he took the machine into his room, deciding that he would, at least, have a good look at it before giving it to Sammy to throw into the river.

He placed it on the rough untidy table on which he kept his daybook, bills, receipts and other papers relating to his coconut business. He cleared away a spot for it, and then sat down and had a long look at it.

Apart from the fact that it had two sets of keys and that the number "25" was recorded on the red numbers, it might have been just an ordinary adding-machine like those in the office he had worked in two or three years ago when he had been a mere cashier: the office from which he had purloined over ten thousand dollars, in small instalments and then resigned his job and come out to this tropical island before the fraud could be discovered.

He looked for the name of the makers but could find none. Nor was there even a patent number or the name of the country in which it had been made. That was another really odd circumstance, though certainly nothing to get alarmed over. By some chance slip, the makers might have omitted to have their name and the patent number embossed on the thing.

He tried it out and found that it worked perfectly, though search as he would, he failed to find any handle or gadget that would alter the red section – the debit section, as Mr. Lesort had called it. No matter how he manipulated the handle, no matter how he slapped and tapped the back and the bottom of the machine, the "25" would not budge.

At length, he gave up trying, and turning his attention to the other section, he struck three numbers at random. "4", "8" and "6". He worked the handle forward and backwards and "4.86" recorded. He pressed the key marked "Clear", worked the handle and "4.86" disappeared and left the original line of nine noughts.

Gaining courage, he struck four numbers, "6", "2", "8" and "0", manipulated the handle and saw "62.80" record. He added "2", "7", "1" and "65.51" recorded. He added "4", "9" , "0" and "70.41" recorded. He touched "2", "4", "6", touched the subtracting key, and working the handle, saw "67.95" appear.

He cleared, and touched seven numbers: "2", "7", "4", "8", "2", "0", "9", and "27,482.09" recorded.

He sprang up and started back, knocking over his chair.

The machine had begun to make a low groaning sound. The sound came from deep within it and grew louder and more intense as the seconds passed.

Mr. Hedge slapped the back of the machine, but the groaning continued to get louder. Even began to assume the nature of a rasping snarl.

Mr. Hedge again and again slapped and struck the thing, but to no avail. The snarling grew louder, fierce, and menacing.

In a flick of memory Mr. Hedge recalled his dream. "This machine," Mr. Lesort had said, "Considers any sum in excess of twenty-five thousand dollars an immoral total."

Mr. Hedge pressed the key marked "Clear" and worked the handle, bringing back the line of nine noughts. The machine grew silent.

Mr. Hedge was pale. This thing was uncanny. What sort of machine could this be? That snarling had had a human sound. How could a machine make human sounds? It was opposed to reason. Unless there was some clever gramophone apparatus inside it? But a gramophone could not have such a fearful, intelligent sound. There had been real menace in it. A threatening ugly note.

He didn't like it one bit.

He stood frowning at the machine, shivers passing up and down his back. Should he throw it away and be rid of it? Have it hurled into the river – or into the sea.

He thought, however, of the dead caterpillars under his coconut trees. If the presence of this machine in the house here had, in some miraculous way, been responsible for the death of those caterpillars, then its absence might cause the caterpillars to return. Of course, it was ridiculous to assume such a thing – ridiculous and superstitious. On the other hand, that dream last night had been unusually vivid.

He could remember everything, could remember every word Mr. Lesort had uttered. And this machine was the very one he had seen him place on the bamboo table on the veranda.

On final thought, Mr. Hedge decided that he would not throw it away. He would keep it. He would put it away and forget it. If it brought him good fortune, all well and good, but as for using it to add on – nothing doing. It was far too uncanny for his liking.

Hauling an empty soapbox from under his bed, he put the machine into it and pushed the box back under his bed.

During the next two or three months Mr. Hedge's plantation flourished. Fresh fronds came out and the trees bore abundant fruit. The nuts were unusually large and the crop promised to be a record one.

On the four neighbouring plantations, however, the caterpillars continued to destroy the trees. The fronds were stripped bare and the once greenly waving plumes of the palms looked like grey spiders against the sky.

Mr. Robinson, who owned one of these neighbouring plantations, came to see Mr. Hedge. He was very worried, "What's it you're using against these caterpillars, Hedge?" he asked. "It's most peculiar. Your trees are absolutely untouched and yet look at mine. Every one stripped bare."

Mr. Hedge smiled. "I haven't the remotest idea what could be responsible, Robinson," he lied. "I've been using the same old, stuff we've all been using. I just haven't the faintest idea why my trees should be flourishing and holding out against the worms and yours are as they are."

"There's some tale that you woke one morning and found all the worms dead under your trees. Is there any truth in that?"

"None whatever," laughed Mr. Hedge. "A silly exaggeration. The worms died off within the course of a week or so. They died in great numbers, I admit, but, well, I suppose that sometimes happens, Why, I'm not a magician!" laughed Mr. Hedge – very loudly.

After Robinson had gone, Mr. Hedge chuckled to himself and rubbed his hands together. "The sons of guns! I knew they'd be puzzled. Ha! Before long I shall gobble them all up. One by one. And then I shall be in sole control of the whole coconut industry in the island. I alone!"

He went to the window and looked out at his green laden trees. "I shall oust," he chortled, "every one of them. Then I'll have the whip-hand. I'll be master. A power in the land."

He rubbed his hands together.

Turning after a moment, he went inside, went into his room and pulled out the soapbox with the machine. He smiled and dusted it with his hands, though it did not need dusting. He patted it, murmuring: "Never believed in the occult before, by jove, but there's something funny about you. A good-luck mascot all right."

He was about to put it away when he noticed something.

On the bottom edge there was a small red spot – a sort of scab of dried paint, it seemed to be. He could not remember having seen it before, and only this morning he had taken the machine out to dust it.

He held the machine upside down in the bright glare from the nearby window.

He moistened the tip of his finger and rubbed at the little red spot. But to no avail. The spot would not be rubbed off. He took up his penknife and began to scrape at it, but with no success.

He continued to dig away, then paused. A deep snarling sound began to emanate from within the machine.

Scared, Mr. Hedges desisted and put the machine hastily back into the soapbox, and the snarling ceased at once. He remembered what the thin grey man had said. "It's a very sensitive machine."

"Oh, all right," muttered Mr. Hedge. "Since you're so touchy I won't trouble you any more. I was only trying to keep you clean. This red spot doesn't look tidy, that's why I wanted to scrape it off."

Henceforth Mr. Hedge ceased to take out the machine to dust it. He left it entirely to it self.

The machine did not *seem* to mind this neglect, for it made no sounds whatever. Often when lying in bed at night Mr. Hedge would listen to see whether it would groan or snarl. But no sound came, so he decided that perhaps that was what it preferred – just to be left alone under the bed. Very well. He would leave it alone.

At the end of the half-year Mr. Hedge reaped such a large crop that he was able to clear all his debts. He went to town and deposited in the bank the sum of two thousand, six hundred and seventy-two dollars and forty-six cents. $2,672.46. Going through his books, he found that this sum represented nearly a thousand dollars more than the last half-year's yield.

That night Mr. Hedge celebrated with a large hunk of roast mutton and a bottle of wine. He ate the meal by himself and drank the wine in two or three great gulps, then smacked his lips and patted his stomach and muttered: "That's good. And there'll be more like this soon. More and better. I shall be the most prosperous man in this land. I shall make a million or bust."

That night something odd happened.

Mr. Hedge had just got into bed and was settling himself with a comfortable sigh under the mosquito net when he heard a soft thump.

The sound came from under the bed, and his first thought was that that mangy mongrel dog of Sammy's must have crept into his room and had decided to spend the night under his bed. He got out of bed determined to haul the dirty brute out by its tail and kick it flying through the door.

He took up his electric torch and flashed it under the bed.

But there was nothing there. All he could see was the soapbox with the machine – and his chamber-pot.

Telling himself that he must have imagined the sound, he switched off the torch and got back into bed. "Too much wine," he chuckled. "Wine can play some odd tricks with a man sometimes."

He had hardly, however, rested his head on the pillow when there came a soft thump under the bed. He lay still and listened.

The thump came again. And then again – louder.

"What the devil!" exclaimed Mr. Hedge. "Must be a rat in that confounded box. Wonder what it wants in there. Nothing edible in there."

He got out of bed once more, and this time he hauled out the soapbox and flashed the light into it.

Except, however, for the adding-machine – very dusty now from neglect – there was nothing in the box that could have caused those thumps. No rat, no mouse. No living thing. Not even an insect. To make sure, Mr. Hedge lifted out the machine and looked. He saw nothing but dust and a few rags of thin cobweb. Puzzled, he put back the machine and shoved the box back under the bed. He searched all over the room but could find no rats or mice. No living creature – except two cockroaches.

He got back into bed.

The thump began at once under the bed.

Quickly swooping out of bed, Mr. Hedge flashed the light underneath.

The thumps ceased at once, but there was no rat or mouse.

A shiver passed down his back. What could this mean? Could it be the adding-machine? But how? How could a machine thump around?

He remembered the groaning and snarling it had indulged in on its first day when he had made it record over 25,000.00 – and the snarling when he had tried to scrape the spot of red paint off. If it could groan and snarl perhaps it could thump about, too. A most ludicrous thing to think, but there it was. He had searched all over the room and could discover nothing that might have caused that thumping.

It was frightening. What could suddenly have got into the thing's head that it should want to thump around tonight? It had never behaved like this before. On the one or two occasions on which it had groaned and snarled it had had some sort of excuse, but he could think of no reason why it should want to misbehave itself tonight. And the strange thing was that it didn't start thumping about until he got into bed and rested his head on the pillow. It was almost as though it was out to keep him awake out of wanton spite.

Mr. Lesort had said that it could be spiteful when it got ready. Could this be an instance when it had decided be spiteful?

As a try-out Mr. Hedge got into bed and lay down.

The thump-thump began under his head.

He continued to lie down.

The thump-thump continued – grew louder.

Shivering with fear, he set his jaws and continued to lie down. And the thumping grew louder and louder and more frenzied. It soon became a stamping.

Mr. Hedge sat up.

The noise stopped.

Yes, the thing was being spiteful – wantonly spiteful. It was determined that he should not sleep tonight.

For several minutes he sat in bed frowning in the dark and wondering what to do. He was sleepy. The wine was taking effect. His whole system demanded that he should sleep. It occurred to him suddenly that perhaps he could lean up against the back of the bed and sleep in a sitting posture. He tried this, but no sooner did his head sag forward on his chest in a doze when the thumping began and roused him.

He got out of bed and began to pace in the dark, muttering curses on the machine. And at the same time shuddering with fear.

He thought of taking the thing out of the room and putting it in the pantry larder. Or taking it to the small outhouse where the implements and tools were kept. But he rejected this plan. It might go and kick up a racket in there and bring out Sammy or Miguel. He didn't want the story to get around that he was keeping any magic-machine on the plantation. It might scare off the labourers. These Indians were a very superstitious lot and were ready to be scared at the slightest tale.

Another idea occurred to him. Mr. Lesort had said that this machine had been specially made for him and that it would only add for him, and that it would add only his money. His dollars and cents. He had also emphasized that it was a sensitive machine. Could it be that it was put out because he had banked some money today and had omitted to register the amount. Could it be that it felt slighted and so was making a noise in order to spite him?

Mr. Hedge pulled out the soapbox, took out the machine and dusted it. Placed it on the table. It looked the same as before: an ordinary, harmless-looking black adding-machine. There were the nine black noughts in the one section and the seven red noughts and "25" in the other. There was the small red spot on the bottom rim – the red scab he had tried in vain to scrape off some weeks ago.

Deciding to try out his idea, he pressed the keys, worked the handle and recorded 2,672.46, the sum he had deposited in the bank that day. He put the machine back in the soapbox, put the box back under the bed, lay down and rested his head on the pillow.

There was silence.

He lay listening for a long while. But the silence continued. The cheep of crickets and the chirrup of frogs outside were the only sounds in the night.

Mr. Hedge smiled and told himself that he had got the hang of the thing now. Since it was merely a matter of recording the sum he put into the bank, then there was no trouble. He would record it. In fact, he would record everything in the future. When he drew any sum from the bank he would record it. Anything to keep the silly thing quiet.

He woke the following morning feeling fit and refreshed and contented. Life was good. Everything was fine.

In shaving he noticed that there was a boil on his neck – a boil that must have appeared overnight, for he could not remember having seen it the day before.

Nothing to bother about, he decided. He rubbed a little ointment on it.

By afternoon, however, the boil had grown larger and was very painful. He examined it in the mirror of his shaving-set and stroked it gently, wondering what could have caused it. He was not in the habit of getting boils. Daresay he must have eaten something that disagreed with him. He would take a dose of fruit salts on going to bed and apply some more ointment. Nothing to bother about.

Despite the fruit-salts and the ointment, he woke the following morning to find that the boil had developed into an extremely painful abscess. He had a temperature and could not get out of bed. And as he lay tossing and holding his swollen neck he could have sworn he heard a soft dry chuckle. The sound seemed to come from under the bed.

He lay still and listened, but heard nothing more of it.

He sent Sammy off for the doctor, and the doctor came and lanced the abscess. Soon after he had gone, Mr. Hedge's temperature dropped and the pain subsided. The following morning Mr. Hedge felt quite normal, and there was hardly any pain. The abscess was healing rapidly. But as he lay in bed staring at the rafters and thinking about the money he would make with the next crop, he heard a soft dry chuckle under the bed. His skin went rough and hot.

He got up and pulled out the soapbox. He looked at the machine and saw that the black section still registered 2,672.46. But – he bent his head suddenly, frowning – the red section had altered.

Instead of "25" the number now read "24".

Very strange, thought Mr. Hedge. What could have caused the alteration. He had not tampered with the thing. Then something else occurred to him. Mr. Lesort had "debited" him with twenty-five cents. Could it be that the "debt" had been reduced to twenty-four cents? If so, why?'

Oh, the whole thing was most absurd and perplexing. The best thing he could do would be to forget it. He couldn't be bothered. His life would be a misery if he would always have to be puzzling over the whims and idiosyncrasies of the adding machine.

So he put it away and forgot it.

Not a fortnight later he exclaimed aloud, with joy, for he read in the newspaper that one of the neighbouring plantations was up for sale. Robinson's plantation. Aha! The caterpillars had ruined Robinson. Robinson was deep in debt. Now, thought Mr. Hedge, is my chance. I'll buy out Robinson's plantation. I can get it cheap. Robinson, in his present plight, will be forced to sell out for next to nothing, because there won't be many people ready to make an offer. People aren't eager to buy coconut plantations devastated by caterpillars. As for me, I don't have to fear caterpillars. Caterpillars won't trouble the palms if I become the owner of the plantation. This machine of mine will see to that.

So Mr. Hedge went to see Robinson.

"I notice you've put up your place for sale, Robinson," said Mr. Hedge. "I'm terribly sorry, old man. I can well understand how you must feel. These worms are dreadful things, Really can't understand how it is I've been so lucky in escaping their depredations."

"Yes, I'm ruined," said Robinson. "Done."

"Poor chap. And what are you asking for the place?"

"I'd take seven hundred. What's the use of asking more? Nobody's going to give me more. And, mind, I bought this place for a thousand when it was in a worse condition than at the end of the month before last."

"Yes, I understand, old fellow. Hard luck. In fact I came over because I thought I ought to help you out. But at the moment I don't think I could manage as much as seven hundred."

"How much would you give?"

"Perhaps four!"

"Four hundred wouldn't clear my debts," said Robinson. "I couldn't sell at four hundred."

"Sorry, old man," said Mr. Hedge. "That's really about all I could manage, and even that would be strain. As it is, it would be just to help you out. Those worms have got your trees in a pretty bad way. They might prove a hopeless burden on me."

"You couldn't even consider five hundred?"

Mr. Hedge made a doubtful sound, shaking his head slowly. He had planned on paying six hundred and that would have been cheap. "Five hundred?" he said. He shook his head again. "Don't think I could, old chap." Abruptly he rubbed his chin and said: "Of course I'd like to give you a helping hand, old boy. I hate having to let down a fellow-struggler. I know how hard it must be for you to have to sell out." He squirmed in his chair and pretended to go through a great mental struggle. After a long silence he said: "Very well, Robinson. I'll do it. I can't see you go down like this without trying to do my best to help brace you up. I'll pay you five hundred for it, old fellow."

After the deal had been settled and all the details of the transaction finally attended to, Mr. Hedge pulled out the machine and recorded the five-hundred-dollar deduction from his bank-account total. The total on the machine now read 2,172.46.

As he was about to put the machine back into the soapbox something caught his eyes. On the bottom rim of the machine another little red spot had appeared, not half-an-inch from the other one. A red scab.

Mr. Hedge frowned at it and touched it with his finger, wondering what could be responsible for its appearance. The previous one had appeared on the same morning that Robinson had come over to see him. On the morning he had lied to Robinson about the caterpillars, pretending that he had no idea how they had died. Now another one had appeared just when he had completed this deal. Very strange.

But why bother? If it chose to break out in red spots, that was no concern of his. Let it go ahead.

He put away the machine and forgot about the matter.

A fortnight had hardly passed when the palms on the newly-acquired plantation began to throw out young fronds. (On the first morning after the sale, heaps of dead caterpillars lay under the trees and were burnt and swept away by the labourers). Within two months the trees were a bright green, with thickly blossoming stalks. By mid-year there were large, heavy bunches of nuts.

"Ha, I knew it," said Mr. Hedge. "I'm going to prosper. I'm going to make big money. I'm going to gobble them all up. Robinson has gone. Smith will go next. I hear he's in bad water already. Then Brown. Then Harris. One by one I shall gobble them up. I shall control the whole industry in this island."

Late in June, Mr. Hedge's working expenses had brought the total on the machine down to 1,567.62. But after the half year's crop had been reaped and sold, he went to town and deposited in the bank the sum of five thousand, two hundred and seventy-six dollars and fourteen cents. $5,276.14. On his return home he recorded the amount on the machine, making a total of 6,843.76.

He gave the machine a pat. "Good fellow. Good fellow. You're doing fine. You're making me rich. I'll smash those other chaps. Ha, ha. I'm going to be millionaire. Wait and see."

On his table Mr. Hedge found a letter. It had come by post. He opened it and discovered that it was from a hospital. They were soliciting a donation.

"Donations my big toe!" sneered Mr. Hedge, and crumpled the letter up, tossing it through the window. "What am I going to give them a donation for? I want my money for myself. I made it and I'm going to keep it. Let the hospitals take care of themselves."

He was lifting the machine to put it back into the soapbox when he noticed something.

A third scab had appeared on the bottom rim. A red scab.

Most odd, thought Mr. Hedge, because not a moment ago there had been only two. Where had this third one come from all of a sudden like this? What tricks was the silly thing up to?

He shrugged. Why worry? Let it continue to break out in red spots if it wanted to. What did *he* care!

That night he celebrated with a large hunk of roast mutton, two bottles of wine and a cake. He ate the meal by himself, devouring every scrap and crumb and draining the two bottles to their dregs. He went to bed happy and exceedingly contented.

On the following morning, while shaving, he noticed that two boils had appeared on his face – one on either cheek. He frowned, wondering what could be going wrong with his blood. It was most peculiar. He had never suffered from boils before.

Remembering the abscess not many months ago, he applied ointment at once and stuck a piece of plaster on each boil for safety. He took a large dose of fruit salts.

By afternoon, however, the boils had grown larger and very painful. He was obliged to sleep flat on his back that night, because even resting his cheeks on the pillow caused him almost unbearable pain.

The next morning the two boils had developed into abscesses, and Mr. Hedge lay in bed with fever. The abscesses felt like red-hot spots of fire in his cheeks. Every now and then a dagger would jab through each abscess, and he would cry out in agony. His body blazed with the fever.

He sent Sammy for the doctor, and the doctor came and lanced the abscesses. Only then did Mr. Hedge get relief. The pain eased, and the temperature dropped.

The following morning he felt normal again and there was hardly any pain. The abscesses were healing rapidly. But as he lay on his back staring at the rafters and thinking about the money he would make with his next crop, he heard a soft dry chuckle. It came from under the bed. Springing up, he pulled out the soapbox. He looked at the machine to see what could be wrong with it.

The black section still registered 6,843.76. But Mr. Hedge noticed that the red section had altered. Instead of "24" the number now read "22".

"What the devil!" he exclaimed.

From "24" to "22"? Why? What had caused the reduction? What confounded absurdity was this?

Then in one flick of revelation Mr. Hedge saw it.

For every cent deducted from the debit total he would have to suffer the agony of one abscess.

"Tut, tut! If only I'd known I would have paid the fellow his miserable twenty-five cents!"

Twenty-five abscesses seemed a most painful price to have to pay to clear off a mere twenty-five cents. Tut! tut! A great pity he had been so mean in his dream. Anyway, it was too late now to think of that. He would have to make up his mind to bear the pain and inconvenience of another twenty-two abscesses. He mustn't grumble, for, after all, things were getting really prosperous for him. This machine might be odd in its habits, but by Jove, it was certainly serving him well. At the rate he was doing, he would soon be wealthy beyond all his hopes. He would be a millionaire. A billionaire. He would be a colossus of finance. He would control world markets. He would be a world power.

What were twenty-two abscesses! Pah!

He paused in these perfervid cogitations. As though an invisible hand had laid hold of his thoughts. The words of the thin grey man came back to him: "Above all, don't let your money at any time exceed twenty-five thousand dollars... This machine considers any sum in excess of twenty-five thousand dollars an immoral total."

It was not the first time that this warning had arrested Mr. Hedge's excited dreams and ambitions. But now, as on the other occasions, he uttered a sound of contempt. To the devil with that! He would find some way of circumventing the stupid warning. If he had to bury the machine to smother its snarling and thumping, nothing would hinder him in making his millions. In fact, once let him get hold of twenty-five thousand dollars, and this coconut business could go hang. He would sell out and go in for gambling on the Stock Exchange. He would double and treble his capital in a fortnight. To hell with the snarling of any silly adding-machine! He would have it flung into the sea if it persisted in making too much of a din. It could snarl and thump around at the bottom of the sea if it liked!

Exactly as Mr. Hedge had surmised, Smith was the next to go down. Smith put up his plantation for sale, and Mr. Hedge immediately offered to buy. Smith asked for eight hundred – he had a wife and family – but Mr. Hedge shook his head. "My dear fellow," he said, "I'm awfully sorry. You don't know how it grieves me to see you in this plight, but eight hundred is quite beyond my means. I have an old invalid mother who is a steady drain on my resources. Only yesterday I had to remit two hundred dollars for her – and a fortnight ago she had to undergo an operation for gallstones which cost three hundred."

"You won't even give seven?"

"My dear chap, working expenses are going to be exceptionally heavy this half-year, and your trees are in such bad condition. No, really, much as I would like to assist you in your misfortune, old man, I simply couldn't give you seven."

"Six?"

'To tell you the truth, old chap, I don't think I could see my way to give you as much as six..."

So, at length, Mr. Hedge brought Smith right down to four hundred and fifty dollars, even though Smith wept.

When all the details of the sale had been settled and Mr. Hedge had paid over the four hundred and fifty, he pulled out the adding-machine, dusted it and muttered: "One more in my hands. One more. Now, just you kill off those caterpillars for me, there's a good fellow." He stroked the machine, noting the three red scabs on the bottom rim and wondering idly why they had appeared.

He started back.

Even as he watched, another red scab appeared. Right before his eyes it appeared. He touched it with his finger to make sure that it was real. He turned the machine upside down and held it to the light.

Yes. There it was. A fourth red scab. Like a speck of paint or – dried blood. Yes, like dried blood.

A shiver passed down Mr. Hedge's back. Then he told himself not to be an imaginative fool. Why should he think it was like dried blood? Absurd. Let him not trouble his head about these red spots. If the damn thing wanted to throw out red spots, let it do so, damn and blast it!

Yet it did give him an uneasy feeling in the background of his consciousness. The last three had appeared after Robinson's visit (that was the first); after the closing of the deal with Robinson (that was the second); and after the receipt and crumpling up of that begging letter from the hospital – the third. Now the fourth had come out after the purchase of Smith's plantation. What could be the significance of these scabs?

Oh, why bother? Why bother? They didn't hurt him. They didn't cause him any inconvenience. Forget them. Simply forget them.

Mr. Hedge recorded the four hundred and fifty dollar deduction and put away the machine.

The new plantation flourished. The caterpillars died and the trees bloomed and bore abundant fruit.

By the end of the half-year, working expenses had reduced the total on the machine to 6003.19. But when Mr. Hedge went to town he deposited in the bank the sum of six thousand, two hundred and fourteen dollars and fifty-nine cents. $6,214.59. On his return home he went into his room and pulled out the machine preparatory to recording the amount. He was dusting it when a knock sounded on the outer door, a brief sharp "tat-tat-tat!"

It was on the door that opened from the veranda into the sitting-room.

Mr. Hedge stood still, his skin going hot and rough. Who could it be that wanted him at this time of day? It was most unusual for anyone to visit him at all – let alone at this time.

"Yes! Who's that?" he called out, his fingertips cold.

"Me, boss! Miguel!" came the answer.

Mr. Hedge swore. He stamped out on to the veranda to Miguel. "What is it, Miguel? What is it? What have you come to bother me about at this time of the evening?"

Miguel smiled sheepishly. "Boss, I come to ask you if you can give me a little more pay, boss."

"A little more pay!"

"Yes, boss."

"Aren't you getting enough?"

'Boss, my wife get another child, and times hard."

"Indeed! The nerve! The impudence!"

"Times very hard, boss. We got to feed the children."

"Oh so! And what have I got to do with that! That's your fault for having children. You should learn to practise birth-control. It's no affair of mine if you go spawning children like rabbits. I'm paying you too much as it is. If you aren't satisfied with what you're getting, you can leave and I'll get a new foreman. There are a dozen others who would be only too eager to fall into your shoes."

"Boss, times very hard. New baby take more money."

"Very well. You're sacked. Go and look for a better job where you can make more money. Come tomorrow and I'll pay you off."

"No, boss. No. I beg you. I will stay. Don't sack me, boss."

"Are you satisfied to continue working for what you're getting now, or are you going to come again wailing to me for more?"

"No, boss. I won't come again."

"Very well. But as there is a sky above, if you come to me again with any tale about wanting more money, I'll sack you on the spot – and I won't have you back again if you flatten yourself on your stomach before me and eat the dust under my boots. Is that clear?"

"Yes, boss."

Mr. Hedge returned to his room and chortled. "Knew that would scare him. More pay. New baby. Ho, ho! What does it matter to me how many babies he gets? I've got to keep my working expenses as low as I can. New babies! To the devil with new babies! New babies aren't more important than my profits."

Mr. Hedge gave a gasp, craning his head forward.

A new red scab had appeared on the lower rim of the machine, making five in all now. When he had left the room a few minutes ago there had been four.

What ruddy nonsense was this! Where could these scabs be coming from!

Oh, forget it! Forget it! He laughed. Though, there was an uneasy note in the laugh. "Red scabs won't frighten me. Not even blue or green. All damned ruddy nonsense! Just ruddy nonsense!"

Assuring himself that everything was well, he recorded the new amount on the machine, bringing the total to 12, 217.78.

That night he celebrated with a roast chicken, two bottles of wine, a cherry cake and a mug of ice-cream. He ate the meal by himself, devouring every scrap and crumb and drop and draining the bottles to their dregs. He went to bed happy and dreamily contented.

The following morning he woke with the full expectation of finding that two or three boils had appeared on his face or neck. Such, however, was not the case. He searched his whole body but could find not the slightest trace of any boil or skin eruption.

"Well, well. That's odd. What about the debt? Surely I'm not going to be let off this time."

Out of curiosity he brought out the machine and looked at it. It still registered "22". He guffawed briefly, and put it away, though deep within him he felt puzzled and not entirely at ease.

Throughout the morning he kept looking at his face in a small pocket-mirror to see whether any boils had appeared. He would come to a sudden halt on the pathway and look around to see that no-one was observing, then bring out his mirror and gaze anxiously at his face and neck. He would pass his hands over his body and even open his shirt and look at his chest. But there were no boils.

Nine o'clock. Ten o'clock. Eleven. Still no boils. No eruptions of the skin or any other afflictions.

Mr. Hedge felt nervy and apprehensive. He would have preferred if the boils had appeared first thing this morning as they had done on the previous occasions. This waiting for them was annoying. Made him jumpy.

At noon, when he was returning to the bungalow after his usual tour of inspection round the plantation, he became aware of a burning sensation in two or three of the toes of his right foot. He thought this odd, as he had never suffered from corns.

On getting home, he took off his right boot and saw that two painful corns had begun to form on the third and fourth toes, respectively, and on the side of the great toe there was a redness which seemed to indicate that a bunion was developing.

Mr. Hedge applied ointment, padded his boot with cotton-wool, and decided not to make a fuss. Then it occurred to him that perhaps this was the form the payment of the debt was taking on this occasion. Instead of abscesses, bunions and corns! He laughed. The thing was becoming decidedly farcical. Two corns and one bunion – three cents. Ho, ho, ho. What a scream of a joke!

By evening, however, Mr. Hedge had ceased to see the humour of the situation. By evening he was compelled to keep to the house. He could not wear his right boot. The corns became livid and fierce. They felt like hot needles continually stabbing into the bones of his toes. And the bunion was like a live coal stuck to the side of his great toe.

Many times during the next week Mr. Hedge found himself blubbering like a schoolgirl. Often he howled and danced around the room. He tried all sorts of ointments and liniments, healing oils and bath salts, but to no avail. The hot needles stabbed into the bones of his toes. The live coal seared the side of his great toe.

After eight days of this torture, the corns and bunions began to subside. The corns dried up and eventually dropped off and the bunion grew less inflamed until the pain it caused ceased altogether.

When Mr. Hedge examined the adding-machine he saw that the red section had altered from "22" to "'19". Two corns and one bunion from "22" left "19".

Mr. Hedge gave a weak smile, trying to feel amused and contemptuous of the whole thing, though his system felt a bit shaky from the ordeal through which he had just passed.

Putting away the machine, he sighed and told himself that those two corns and that bunion had been far too painful to be valued at only three cents. However, he must not grumble. He had had his chance to pay the twenty-five cents Mr. Lesort had asked for the machine, and he had been too mean to pay it, so he must suffer. And, in any case, he was well prepared to suffer the pain of nineteen more corns and bunions – or abscesses – if it meant increasing his wealth at the rate it was increasing. He would suffer any torture so long as it meant money. Money. Dollars. Thousands of dollars. Hundreds of thousands. Millions. Billions. Yes, any torture, no matter how terrible and excruciating, no matter how many tears of pain he had to shed, no matter if he had to writhe and twist himself into a tree-root-like knot of agony. Pah! Nineteen more corns and bunions! What were nineteen more corns and bunions! Or abscesses!

During the next half year the caterpillars did not worry Mr. Hedge's two remaining rivals, Brown and Harris, and neither of these two gentlemen put up their plantations for sale. On the contrary, it seemed as though a period of prosperity were about to set in for Messrs. Brown and Harris, for their trees began to bloom and bear even as plentifully as Mr. Hedge's. Their crop at the end of this half-year promised to be exceptionally abundant.

Mr. Hedge was disturbed. This did not suit him. He had hoped to oust both Brown and Harris during the course of this half-year. Things had gone badly with them during the past year and a half and he had expected them to put up their plantations for sale. Now it seemed as though their luck had changed. They were going to do well, which meant, of course, that their creditors would not press them this half-year, and in another year's time they would have paid off their debts and recovered to such an extent that they would not want to sell out. No, that would not do. Some action, decided Mr. Hedge, would have to be taken in the matter.

Mr. Hedge sat down to think, and after thinking for some time, conceived a plan. The wages paid to coconut pickers on all the plantations were by mutual agreement, stable. That is to say, Brown and Harris paid the same as Mr. Hedge, even though they were not half as prosperous. Ordinary labourers were paid eight cents per hour, gang-foremen ten cents and head foreman (like Miguel) twelve cents. Now, suppose, thought Mr. Hedge, he announced two or three weeks before reaping time that he was prepared to pay ten cents to ordinary labourers, twelve cents to gang foremen and fourteen cents to his head foreman, and, further, that he required double the amount of labourers than of yore. It would mean that Brown and Harris would not be able to get any labour. The labour would flock to Mr. Hedge in entirety. Brown and Harris would be unable to compete with the prices paid by Mr. Hedge. It would mean that their crops would remain unreaped. Their creditors would begin to press them, and if their crops were reaped late they would miss the market and get such poor prices that they would be ruined – utterly ruined.

Mr. Hedge carried out this plan – and it worked. Brown and Harris came to him and pleaded with him not to take such a step; that it would ruin them. They couldn't afford to pay such high rates. Even the old rates would have strained their resources considerably. In the name of compassion and out of consideration for their families would Hedge refrain from doing this thing?

Mr. Hedge told them that business was business. "I need all the labour I can get this half-year-end, old chaps, and I'm prepared to pay for it. And think of these poor fellows! They're badly off, old men. It's only fair that I should pay them well. They've been appealing to me for a long time for a rise in their wages. Their families are ill-fed and ill-clad. They're in misery. I've got to think of their welfare, old boys," said Mr. Hedge, moisture in his eyes. "My heart," he finished, "bleeds for them, old chaps."

Within two days Brown and Harris were ready to sell out. Mr. Hedge bought Brown's plantation for four hundred and Harris's for five.

No sooner had he closed the deal and acquired the two new plantations when Mr. Hedge announced that the scale of wages would have to remain as before. "I've spent nine hundred on those two new plantations, Miguel," said Mr. Hedge. "I can't afford to raise wages now. It would ruin me. Go and tell them that. I can't help if they're disappointed. I've got to consider myself."

Alone in his room, Mr. Hedge rubbed his hands together. He threw back his head and laughed. "I've outwitted them! They didn't think I was so clever. By Jove! I've ousted them all now. I'm sole master of the whole coconut industry in this island. Sole master! The labourers are in my hands now. I – and I alone – can dictate the price of wages. From now on they'll take what *I* give them – or starve. Ha-ha-ha-ha!"

He pulled out the machine to record the nine-hundred-dollar deduction. As he placed it on the table something caught his eye. He recoiled and paled.

On the bottom rim of the machine a red blotch had appeared. The sixth. But this was no mere spot like the others. The five others were tiny things varying between the size of a pinhead and the head of a small nail. But this new one was about the size of a shilling. An ugly thing, like a spatter of freshly dried blood. It had a scaly, sinister look, and watching it, Mr. Hedge felt a clammy hand closing around his heart.

For a long while he stood staring at the repulsive thing. Then gradually he thought he could see the significance of it.

For every mean or corrupt act he committed, one red spot appeared. On the first occasion he had told Robinson a deliberate lie when Robinson had come to ask him what was responsible for the healthy condition of his trees. Just a tiny pinhead spot had come out as a result of that lie. The second spot had come after the deal with Robinson – that deal in which he had taken advantage of Robinson's hopeless plight to gobble up his plantation for a sum far below the value of the property. That second spot had been a trifle larger. The third spot had resulted from his crumpling up and contemptuously ignoring the begging letter from the hospital: a spot no larger than the second. The fourth or fifth had been the size of nail-heads: the purchase of Smith's plantation and the refusal to raise Miguel's wages. And now the sixth… a blotch.

Mr. Hedge stroked his cheek uneasily.

"I don't like this," he murmured.

After a moment, however, he grunted and recorded the nine-hundred-dollar deduction. To the devil with the damn spots! Let a dozen of them appear! Let the whole machine become splashed with them. What did he care! So long as they didn't hinder him in his career. So long as the dollars piled up, the whole machine could turn red. Green if it wanted. Blue. Yellow or pink. *He* didn't care.

At the end of the reaping, the machine registered 10,926.17. But Mr. Hedge went to town and deposited in the bank the sum of nine thousand, four hundred and twenty-seven dollars and eighty-one cents. $9,427.81. On his return home, he pulled out the machine and recorded the amount, which brought the total to 20,353.98.

That night he celebrated with a roast turkey, two bottles of wine, a cherry cake, a prune cake and a mug of ice-cream. He ate the meal by himself, devouring every scrap and crumb and drop and draining the bottles to their dregs. He patted his stomach and nodded and sighed, telling himself that this was the life. He went to bed happy and glutted with contentment.

The following morning he sent to town and bought a pair of felt slippers in readiness for the corns and bunions. The slippers arrived shortly before noon. But at noon no signs of corns and bunions had appeared. He took off his boots and examined his toes. No redness. No burning. He took off his clothes and examined ever inch of his body, but could find no boils or eruptions.

During the afternoon he was in an agony of suspense, wondering what form the afflictions would take this time. He strode up and down, frowning and glancing about the room as though fearful of some invisible plague waiting to pounce on him from out of a corner.

One o'clock. No boils or corns or bunions. Nothing. Two o'clock. Still nothing.

Sweat oozed from his face. His fingertips felt cold, and were purple. Once, he found himself trembling. Once, he pulled out the machine to make sure that the debt still stood at "19", hoping that by some odd chance it might have reduced of its own volition and so let him off on this occasion.

As in the back of his mind he had dreaded, the hope was a vain one. The debt still stood at "19".

Three o'clock. No boils, no corns, no bunions. Four o'clock. Nothing. The sweat continued to pour out of Mr. Hedge. He used up three handkerchiefs.

Shortly after four, a low thump sounded in the sitting room.

Mr. Hedge nearly cried out with terror. He pulled open the door and looked out. It was only Sammy laying the table for tea.

Mr. Hedge rushed out and grasped him by the hair. "What the bloody hell do you mean by padding around the place like a confounded tiger-cat! In future see that you walk like a human being. Let that teach you!" Mr. Hedge clouted Sammy. Kicked him on his shin.

Returning into his room, Mr. Hedge sat down on his bed and stared out at the fronds of his coconut trees glittering in the hot sunshine. He felt miserable. A hopeless sack of nerves. Why couldn't the damned corns come out and be done with! Or if not corns, well what else it was that was going plague him. What was the idea of this suspense? He hated suspense.

Five o' clock. Still nothing. Six. Nothing. Darkness closed down and then it was seven. Mr. Hedge had eaten nothing since lunchtime. He did not feel hungry. His whole body felt chilly with fear.

When he got into bed at nine o'clock he felt so chilly that despite the warmth of the night he found it necessary to cover with a blanket. He could not sleep. He stared round at the darkness and listened to the cheep of the crickets and the chirrup of the tree-frogs. He tossed. Once he sat up, lit the lamp and tried to read but found reading impossible.

A coffin-bird made a dull "coop-coop-coop" outside and he gasped with fear. Began to tremble.

It must have been eleven o'clock when he felt a slight itching on his calf. He scratched the place, assuming that a flea must have bitten him.

Five minutes or so later, he felt another itching – this time on his chest – and he scratched the spot. Probably another flea he assured himself. Then there was an itching on his rump. Then on his elbow. This made him suspicious, and getting out of bed, he lit the lamp again and took off his pyjamas.

Examining himself, he found that round red patches had appeared, one on his right calf, one on his chest, one on his right elbow, one on his rump, one on the heel of his left foot, one on his neck and one on the sole of his right foot. Seven in all. Red patches that looked like incipient ringworms. Yes, he was sure they were ringworms.

Breathing in relief that the suspense was, at last, at an end, he rubbed ointment on the ringworms and settled himself down to sleep as he was tired from the nervous suspense of the day.

But there was to be no sleep for him. Every five minutes or so he was obliged to scratch. Now it would be the heel of his left foot. Now his neck. Now his elbow. Now his calf. Now the heel of his left foot again. Now his chest. One spot would no sooner stop itching when another would begin. It was most annoying. On occasion there would be a lull of say, two minutes, and just as he would be falling into a peaceful doze, a sharp urgent itching would begin on the sole of his right foot compelling him to reach right down to scratch.

By morning the ringworms had grown livid and raw from his scratching them, and now he not only had to endure an itching but a burning as well. They all burnt him at the same time.

He sent to town and bought all sorts of ointments and lotions and plasters, but none of these, on application, made any difference. On the other hand, the ringworms grew worse. All seven of them began to itch at the same time. This simultaneous itching would last for say two minutes during which time Mr. Hedge would writhe and pant, his hands darting from spot to spot. Each ringworm seemed to have its own individual kind of itching and demanded individual attention. Had they all itched in the same way it might not have been so bad. When the itching ceased the burning followed – a sharp glowing burning – not a cutting as had been the case with the corns and abscesses, but a glowing like the bunions. As though a live coal were stuck on to each of the seven spots.

For a fiery, itching week Mr. Hedge suffered. A week that seemed to him a year, especially as during this time he scarcely slept at all. If he slept two hours out of those one hundred and sixty-eight he slept a lot.

The ordeal left him weak and hollow-cheeked. On the eighth day he slept. Slept for sixteen hours without stirring. On awakening he felt as though he had slept only an hour. A sense of heaviness and depression settled on him.

Getting slowly out of bed, he pulled out the machine and saw that it now registered "12".

Seven terrifying ring worms – seven cents.

He groaned. Oh, no, he thought. Those seven ring worms had been far, far too savagely agonizing to be valued at only seven cents. It was not just. It was not equitable. That thin grey man, whoever he was, has no sense of fair-play. He was a monster to have devised a system of payment like this.

It took Mr. Hedge another week to be himself again. The ringworms vanished and he grew quite fit once more. So fit, indeed, that he told himself that, after all, life was full of worse things than ringworms, and that to make a fortune and become a financial magnate it was only meet that one should go through many hardships and ordeals. Worthwhile objects, Mr. Hedge consoled himself, were only attained through pain and struggle. He would set his jaw and bear the agony of whatever else was to come.

Mr. Hedge was hardly well and about when he informed Miguel that from now on the scale of wages would be as follows: Head-foreman, thirteen cents per hour; gang-foreman, nine cents; labourers, seven.

Miguel, even though pleased at the raise in his own rate, was dismayed. "Boss, the men going to grumble," he said. "Times hard, boss. Men can't live on seven cents an hour."

"Oh, so! So you're taking up their cudgels, are you? What are you? A labour leader? Look here, do you know what will happen to you if you try to take their part? I'll sack you – on the spot. Now, what's the position? Are you their leader or not?"

Miguel, hardly understanding what Mr. Hedge meant, said, "No, boss, I'm not a leader."

"Oh, you're not a leader. I'm very glad to hear it."

"Yes, boss."

"All right. Get away. Get away and go and tell them what I have said about the new wages. Tell them they'll either take what I offer or starve. Do you hear me? Tell them

I have money and can sell or destroy these plantations if I please. And by God, if they get me annoyed, I'll hire some tractors and bulldozers and have every one of these trees knocked down. Then I'll set fire to them and leave this island. Then *see* who will give them work. You go and tell them that."

"Yes, boss."

Back in his room, Mr. Hedge chortled and rubbed his hands together. "Hee, hee. See if that doesn't scare them out of their wits. Grumble, eh? I'll teach them to grumble. I'll teach them who is their master. I'll show them who is a power in the land."

The labourers did grumble. But they were helpless to do anything but grumble. They belonged to no union, hardly understood what a union was. They had to take what Mr. Hedge gave them.

One day, about a fortnight later, when Mr. Hedge had occasion to take out the machine to make a deduction, he saw that another blotch had appeared, the size of a florin. A very ugly thing. Not only was it red and scaly, but in parts it even had a slight greenish tinge, as though it might be gangrenous.

Mr. Hedge hastily recorded the deduction and put away the machine.

During the course of this half-year Mr. Hedge received a great many begging letters – letters, from people and institutions really in need of financial help. He tore them all up – and for every one he tore up, a red spot the size of a nail's head appeared on the bottom rim of the machine. The red spots could hardly be counted now. They formed a chain right round the lower rim of the machine, the two ugly blotches standing out like pendants in some evil necklace.

Mr. Hedge pretended not to care. He laughed – though his laughter was shaky.

At the end of the half-year he found himself faced with a problem. The total on the machine, through the usual working expenses, had been reduced to $18,782.18. But the profits now on hand amounted to ten thousand, four hundred and sixty-two dollars and eight cents. $10,462.08. This amount if added to the total now on the machine would bring the total to $29,244.26.

Mr. Lesort had particularly warned him that the machine considered any total above twenty-five thousand dollars an immoral total. On that first day when Mr. Hedge had tried out the machine he had recorded an amount over twenty-five thousand dollars and the machine had snarled. Was it not likely that it would behave the same now if he recorded $29,244.26?

Mr. Hedge frowned and scratched his head. What was he to do? He couldn't very well throw away four thousand dollars. Or give it away. Out of the question. He was determined to get stupendously wealthy. What was twenty-five thousand dollars. He wanted millions. Billions. He wanted to control the markets of the world. He wanted to be known as the Coconut King.

Mr. Hedge stood at the table and picked up the bank-notes and cheques that went to make up the half-year's profits. Money. Just look at it. The stuff that could make or smash a continent. Bank-notes. Blue, crisp cheques. The stuff that could build skyscrapers – and tanks and warplanes. Atom bombs.

Why should he not have piles and piles of it? Why should he not build skyscrapers? And loan money to governments to make tanks and warplanes? And atom bombs? Why should he let a silly machine stop him? Let it snarl if it wanted to. He would bury it if it made too much noise. He would go downstairs this evening after dark and dig a hole six foot deep. He would dig it just under the bedroom window, and he would bring up a large box full of earth and keep it under his bed. If when he recorded the amount in excess of twenty-five thousand the machine began to create a din, he would snatch it up, take it to the window and drop it into the hole. Then he would empty the box of earth after it, rush out of the house and fill in the hole thoroughly, ramming the earth well down. See if that didn't settle it effectively!

After considering this plan for a while, however, Mr. Hedge decided that it was rather a desperate thing to do. Perhaps he should find some other way out for the present. He would resort to the burial plan only if the situation became absolutely hopeless.

At last, he thought of another plan. Suppose he took to town and banked $6,217.82. That would bring the total on the machine to $25,000. Good. Then suppose he stored away the balance of $4,244.26 in the iron safe in the corner there. Would that satisfy the machine? He wondered. Anyway, it would be worth trying.

Yes, he would try it.

All the same, for safety, Mr. Hedge had Sammy dig the hole under his bedroom window. A hole six feet deep. At first, he had wanted to dig it himself in secrecy, but, on second thoughts, decided that this might create too much curiosity on the part of Sammy or Miguel who might happen upon him digging and go and spread the tale that he was digging his own grave or some such foolish tale. He must not do anything to get a rumour like that started; he must do everything he could to avoid it being said that he was indulging in eccentric or mysterious practices.

He explained to Sammy that the hole was for experimental purposes. He wanted to make a scientific test of the soil at a six-foot depth to see whether it was good for coconut palms to grow in. Sammy, who had worked long enough on modern plantations to have heard of soil-testing experiments, readily accepted this explanation, even considering it quite in order when Mr. Hedge made him carry a large box of earth upstairs into his bedroom.

That evening, however, on his return from the bank, Mr. Hedge felt decidedly nervous. His fingertips were cold and purple when he entered his room, and there was a hollow feeling in his stomach. A tremulous, breathless tenseness.

He paused just within the threshold and looked round the room. Somehow he had expected to find that something horrible had taken place in his absence. What he could not define; just something horrible.

Everything, however, seemed the same as he had left it. He strode over to the window and looked down into the six-foot-deep pit Sammy had dug, then turned and looked round the room again. The box with the earth stood nearby, against the wall.

The air in the room had a dank, earthy smell. It reminded him of a graveyard. Memories of his mother's funeral came back to him. Will anyone, he wondered be present at my funeral?

He shuddered.

Ugh. Why must I be thinking such things? So foolish. Let me, he thought, be sane and realistic. Only money is real. Realistic men are men who think in terms of money.

He pulled out the box with the machine. Pulled it out slowly, as though fearful that the machine might snarl at him.

But not a sound came from it.

He lifted it out of the box and placed it on the table where he kept his books and papers. It looked the same as when he had last seen it. The red scabs and the two red blotches still formed a sinister necklace around the lower rim. The total on the debit section was still "12", and the total on the black section 18,782.18.

Mr. Hedge looked at the machine. Squeezed his cold fingers together and glanced round the room. His eyes stopped at the small iron safe in which was stored the $4,244.26 balance. Would the thing detect the fraud he was about to perpetrate on it?

Oh, hang it! Go ahead. Take the chance and see. He could always hurl it down into the pit under the window if it made a noise and wouldn't stop. And there would be no difficulty in lifting the box with the earth and tilting the contents over the window-sill.

Mr. Hedge put out his hand and then drew it back. Should he? He pressed his palms together. Think of the millions to come. Billions, perhaps. Who knew? Billions and billions. If he could only conquer this machine. If he could only discover some way of side-tracking its vengeance!

Oh, risk it. Come on. Risk it.

Mr. Hedge swallowed. Set his jaw and struck "6", "2", "1". Gulped and took a deep breath. Struck "7", "8" and "2". He worked the handle forward and backward and the machine registered 25,000.00.

Mr. Hedge retreated a step.

But no change took place. The machine made no sound.

He kept watching it, his hands clasped tight around the back of the chair, his nails cold and purple,

Still nothing happened. He even looked to see if a new red spot or blotch would appear. None appeared.

Mr. Hedge uttered a whispering, nervous whimper. Then laughed. His laughter came in spasms. "I've beaten it! Beaten it! Oh, I've beaten it I'm going to be rich! Rich! Rich! I'm going to be a millionaire. I'm going to be a Tycoon! I shall hold countries in my hands! Break or make them at my will! Hee-hee-hee! Ha-ha!"

With trembling hands, he put away the machine – hands that trembled now with joy and excitement. He was going to be a power. The financial monarch of all times.

That night he celebrated with a roast turkey, a chicken, three bottles of wine, a cherry cake, a prune cake and two mugs of ice-cream. And he had a pretty Indian girl in to spend the night with him. He ate the meal by himself, devouring, every scrap and crumb and drop, and drained the bottles to their dregs while the Indian girl looked on. Then it was her turn to be enjoyed. Mr. Hedge enjoyed her all night. Fiercely and unrelentingly. He sent her away the next morning effete and tottering and in tears. He was happy and dizzily contented.

That day he told himself that he would not be nervy and apprehensive about the form the payment of his debt would take. He had got the hang of the thing now. On the first occasion, that boil had appeared the very next morning on his awakening. On the second occasion of the two boils it had been the same. But on the third with the corns and bunions he had had to wait until noon. On the fourth occasion not until night before those ringworms had appeared. Good. That meant that on this occasion he need expect nothing until tomorrow morning. Very well. He would not trouble about it until then. If that silly machine thought he was going to be a victim of suspense every time it was mistaken. Nothing doing. He was up to all its tricks now.

On the following morning, however, nothing had happened. He examined his body. No ringworms. No abscesses. No corns or bunions. Nothing the matter.

He shrugged. "Oh, well, suppose it'll be later in the day, I am certainly not going to worry."

He went about his toilet as usual, had his breakfast and then set out on his tour of inspection round the plantation.

Despite his resolve not to worry, however, he would every now and then come to a halt and examine his arms and legs and chest to see if any ringworms or boils had come out. Once an insect bit him on his neck and he gasped and took out his pocket-mirror hastily to see whether it might not be some kind of skin eruption beginning to show itself. Seeing that it was only an insect bite, he clicked his tongue and told himself not to be a fool. Not a few minutes later he clenched his hands and to his annoyance discovered that his fingertips were cold.

"All damned nonsense," he muttered, scowling.

Nine o'clock. Ten. Nothing.

Eleven. Still nothing.

At noon Mr. Hedge found that he was not hungry. He sweated and paced from his sitting-room to his veranda. He felt as though he were at the dentists, waiting to have a very bad tooth pulled out. A tooth he knew for certain would cause him terrifying pain.

Abruptly he halted. He began to touch his teeth one by one. Perhaps it would be his teeth this time. A violent and wracking toothache affecting five or six of his molars. Ugh. He detested toothaches.

One o'clock. Still nothing.

Mr. Hedge almost wept from nervous suspense. He wrung his hands and sighed, wagged his head and even whimpered, holding his face between the palms of his hands. Sweating, clammy hands.

At shortly after two o'clock he noticed that a dull purplish spot had appeared on each of the fingers of his left hand. Five purplish spots. He stopped pacing and looked at them. What could these be now? They didn't look like ringworms.

He sat on his bed and for nearly an hour watched his fingers.

But the spots remained purplish spots.

No pain of any sort. Not even a tenderness. No itching or irritation.

Four o'clock. Five. Six. No change. No pain, No tenderness. No itching. The spots just remained purplish spots.

What new subtle horror could this be?

Mr. Hedge groaned with dread and anxiety. This thing was devilish. Devilish. Why couldn't he contract some straightforward affliction and be done? The last time it had been ringworms. Very well. Well, why not ringworms again and have it over? Why a new and mysterious affliction to keep him guessing? Good God! All this nervous waiting, all this mental torture, and presently, no doubt, fearful agony of body – all for the settlement of a debt of a few contemptible cents. The desperate irony of it! Why, he could pay twenty-five cents a thousand times over and not even know he had spent any money, and yet here he was, suffering acute and refined torture for a few dirty cents! If only he had paid that thin grey fool his stupid twenty-five cents! A mere quarter of a dollar. Think of it! And he possessed over twenty-nine thousand dollars.

That night he sat up staring at the five fingers of his left hand.

But the spots just remained purplish spots.

Nothing worse. No pain, no itching.

Ten o'clock. The crickets cheeped outside, and the tree-frogs chirruped. Eleven. Midnight.

The spots just remained purplish spots.

Mr. Hedge examined the back of his hand, the palms, his nails. He massaged the fingers, splayed them out near the lamp. But he could see no difference. There was no alteration. He could feel no aches, no itching. Nothing whatever.

At two o'clock, from sheer nervous exhaustion, he fell into a troubled sleep. Burglars were at his safe. Thin grey men with blow-lamps that hissed jets of purplish flame. The door of the safe fell away, melting into a red lava like thick clots of blood. The thin grey men simpered and sniggered and fought silently over his money. They hit each other, but the blows were soundless. There was no jingle of money. No rustle of notes and cheques. Money in coins, money made of paper began to sail all over the room. Silently. Ghosts in a ghost room. They settled on the bed. Settled on Mr. Hedge. Piled up. And up and up. What a glorious mountain they made. But the mountain was smothering him It was covering his face. Pushing the breath back into him. Money. Money...

He woke with a gasp and sat up, his skin clammy. The light of dawn, grey like the grey men, was coming in at the window. He looked at his left hand and saw that the spots on his fingers had grown a deeper purple and had spread. They were patches now. Patches the size of a florin. Yet there was no pain. No pain. No itching.

Getting out of bed, Mr. Hedge bathed the fingers with lotion and bandaged his whole hand.

By noon, however, the purple patches had spread, and now his fingers were almost entirely covered. They looked puffy and ached a little. Only a little. Mr. Hedge again, bathed them in lotion, then applied mercury ointment and bismuth formic iodide and bandaged them carefully. He felt worried and was undecided whether he should send for the doctor or not. On former occasions the doctor had not been able to help him – except, of course, in lancing those abscesses. But as for curing him or arresting the trouble the doctor had proved useless.

By the following day, however, Mr. Hedge found that medical aid would have to be sought, for the fingers had grown puffed to double their normal size, and were a bluish-black in colour. They even smelt a little offensive. So Mr. Hedge sent for the doctor.

When the doctor came and saw the fingers he looked grave. "Why didn't you send for me before?"

"Is it very serious, doctor?"

"Serious? Why, man, you've picked up a dangerous infection. Your fingers are septic. How did this happen? What have you been doing to yourself?"

"Nothing. Nothing at all. Can you do anything to help?"

"Yes I can, but I'm afraid I'm going to give you a nasty shock." The doctor shook his head. "A very nasty shock," he said.

"What's that? Shock? What shock? Tell me. Go on."

"Well," said the doctor, "there's only one thing for it. Those fingers have got to come off."

"Come off! My fingers! All my five fingers!"

"All your five fingers. It's your fingers or your life. If they aren't taken off – and taken off within the next twelve hours – you'll be a dead man, Mr. Hedge."

So that was it. Mr. Hedge's five fingers were amputated. The fingers of his left hand.
    Five fingers – five cents.
    When he returned home after three weeks in hospital and looked at the machine he saw that it registered "7". Five fingers from "12" equalled "7".
    Mr. Hedge wept. For the first time he wondered whether this striving after wealth were worth the agonies he had to suffer. Of what use was his left hand to him now without fingers? Oh, it was unjust. Five fingers – five cents. Why, the thing was getting worse and worse. What would happen on the next occasion? Suppose he lost the other five? Why, he would be of no use to himself. A quake of despair went through him. He cursed Mr. Lesort. Perhaps it would have been better if Mr. Lesort had never brought the horrible machine. The coconuts would eventually have been rid of those caterpillars, and in the normal course of things he might have prospered. He might not have done it in this spectacular fashion, it was true, but he might still have done it and without these terrifying ordeals.
    Anyway, what was the sense in bothering? He had lost the fingers already. He could only hope for the best now. There was only seven cents left to be paid off. If he lost five toes next time, well, that was that. Grin and bear it. Nothing else to do. For he was determined that come what might, he would be a millionaire. Nothing would hinder him in his determination to amass a stupendous pile of money. No matter what he had to suffer, no matter what agony he had to go through, physical and mental, he would go on piling up the dollars. Up, up, up. Millions. Hundreds of millions. Thousands of millions. Billions.

★

One night two or three days later, as Mr. Hedge lay in bed, he found that he could not sleep. He kept tossing. The air in the room seemed strangely oppressive tonight. He got up and looked out of the window, noting the bright moonlight. The fronds of the palms glittered. The crickets and frogs cheeped and chirruped in endless monotony, and in the deep shade under the trees he could see the tiny flashing of candle-flies.
    Under the window gaped the hole he had had Sammy dig. Gazing down into the darkness of it, he chuckled, remembering how he had cheated the machine. Mr. Lesort had warned him to be honest with the machine. Honest. Who was honest in this frantic world! Hypocrites. Hypocrites everywhere. Cheaters, liars. Well, and why not, thought Mr. Hedge. If cheating and lying were means to acquiring more and more money why not?
    Yet for an instant a cold breeze seemed to blow through his heart. A breeze of denial. For one instant he saw himself as a boy of nine building a snowman and unaware of the importance of money. Dreamingly pure like the white, wintry slopes of the hills. Unburdened by the dross of greedy schemes. From where, and when, had the first pips of poison dropped into his soul?"
    But what was this? What utter nonsense was he allowing himself to think? Phew! It was oppressive tonight. No wind at all. Look at those palms. Absolutely still. Weird.
    What was that?
    He turned. He could have sworn he had heard a grunt. A warning gob of sound. His skin went rough and hot. Frightened, he lit the lamp and sat staring around the

room. It was so oppressive that even breathing seemed difficult. He had a feeling that something was going to happen. Most odd that tonight he didn't want to sleep. He had never known himself to suffer from insomnia.

He swallowed three aspirins. But sleep still would not come.

The lamp bothered him, so he put it out. Still he could not sleep. For no reason whatever he found himself listening. Every two or three minutes he would cock his head and listen. Listen for what? he asked himself irritably.

He sat up and looked around. Was it his imagination or had the room gone darker?

He got up and looked out of the window. It had got darker outside, too. Oh, quite simple. The moon had gone under a cloud. Most ordinary and natural explanation. See how easy it was to go imagining horror? Let him lie down again and stop this fanciful nonsense.

He lay down again. But sleep still would not come. He tried counting coconuts. One coconut. Two coconuts. Three coconuts...

Still no sleep.

He tried counting dollars. One dollar, two dollars, three dollars... Oh, this was tomfoolery! Let him get up and do a little reading.

That, too, proved fruitless. In the middle of reading he would look up. Reading always bored him, anyway.

The night was black. Sooty black. Strange. What could have gone wrong? What had happened to the moonlight?

Mr. Hedge felt a shiver pass through his body. He looked slowly round the room. It was as though the furniture were staring at him with ominous eyes, as though aware of something of which he knew nothing. And there was such a silence. Only the crickets and frogs – and even they betrayed a twittering in the timbre of their insistent refrain.

Sitting where he was, Mr. Hedge heard a sound. At first he was not certain what it was – whether it were just a creak of the bed caused by his shifting his position slightly – then he told himself the sound had come from outside. He looked around the room again. Waiting.

He heard it again. He had no doubt now. It had come from outside the house. Perhaps from out of that hole under the window. A moaning.

He sat rigid, his fingertips – the five fingertips of his right hand – cold. Automatically he brought them across to the other hand with the intention of squeezing them with the fingers of the other hand, then with a shock remembered that there were no fingers on his left hand. He uttered a whimper.

The moaning. It grew louder as the seconds passed. A doleful sound. To Mr. Hedge there were menace and vengeance in it. It was coming from out of that hole under the window. He knew it. Louder and louder. It began to assume the nature of a whining snarl. In his fancy he could see it as a huge black wing of evil whirring toward him.

The leaves of the book in his hand began to rustle. The snarling grew into a shriek. A prattling roar descended upon the roof of the house followed by a white dazzle of fire.

A hurricane had struck the island.

The whole night the hurricane raged, and the whole night Mr. Hedge crouched on the floor trembling and whimpering. At every flash of lightning he thought the house would go up in a roar of flame. The sound of the wind and the thunder threatened to burst his ear drums even when he pressed the palms of his hands against his ears. The wind would shriek now and the shriek would whirl round him like a live, intelligent thing out to wrap him round in a fierce tentacle. Now it would moan and snarl past the house, and the house would shake as though in an earthquake. It had a searching, savage sound, and made him think that it was intent on hounding him out and tearing him to pieces. And now the lightning and the thunder would come avalanching down from the sky and the noise of the thunder and the wind combined penetrated into the very marrow of his being and seemed about to smash his whole system into vibrating fragments so that the wind could whisk them away into the waiting waves.

The following morning the bungalow was still standing, but the roof had been lifted off and there was nothing but open sky above Mr. Hedge.

Weak in spirit and in body, soaked to the skin from the tons of rain that had descended upon him, Mr. Hedge got slowly to his feet and looked through the window.

He gave a cry and tottered.

As far as he could see there was nothing but a waste of gaunt grey stumps. The green, fruit-laden plumes of his coconut palms had been snapped off and blown away as though deliberately plucked by some gargantuan hand and dashed far into the invisibility of space.

And as he stood there gazing upon the scene, there came from under his sodden bed a soft, dry chuckle.

On a tour of inspection, Mr. Hedge discovered that two-thirds of all his trees had been completely destroyed. The trees that had survived had survived only because they happened to be situated in a deep sheltered valley.

Mr. Hedge wept.

During the next two or three weeks he had to spend the money he had hoarded in his iron safe at home and over six thousand of what he had in the bank to get things cleared up and put in order on his plantation. When the half-year came to an end he found that the profits amounted to a bare one thousand, three hundred and four dollars and seventy-three cents. $1,304.73. When he returned from the bank he added this total to the 18,878.59 now registered on the machine, making a new total of 20,183.31.

That night he celebrated with a small hunk of roast beef. He ate the meal by himself and drank a glass of water with it, then groaned and smote his breast and gnashed his teeth.

He went to bed unhappy and discontented.

On the following morning he sat gloomily wondering what form the affliction would take this time. No doubt it would be toes. Five toes. Purplish spots would appear upon them, turn septic and necessitate an operation. The five toes would be amputated.

A cold flame of despair curled itself around his heart.

Several begging letters arrived that day. But with an angry exclamation he tore them up and hurled them away.

By nightfall no purple spots had come out on his fingers or toes. Nor when midnight came had any sort of affliction come upon him. He sat all night in his room waiting. It was useless his attempting to sleep, so he sat in a chair by his bed gazing nervously round the lamp-lit room. At intervals he would raise his feet to the lamp and examine his toes or splay out the fingers of his right hand to see whether any purple spots had begun to show up.

But there were no purple spots.

Two o' clock came. Three. Four. Five. Still no purple spots.

Dawn. The sun came up and spilled a red mildness over the expanse of unkempt vegetation and grey stumps that had once been tall, gay-rustling coconut-palms.

Still there were no purple spots.

The day grew hot and dazzling. Noon. Mr. Hedge made no attempt to leave his room. When Sammy came to announce breakfast, and then lunch, Mr. Hedge gave him a thunderous shout and told him to be off.

Night set in and still there were no purple spots. Mr. Hedge felt weak from hunger and nervous exhaustion. Was this to be another night of dreadful anticipation? More sweating by lamplight? More anxious lifting of his feet to the light?

At about eleven o'clock when, from utter exhaustion, Mr. Hedge was about to fall asleep, something woke him.

He sat up straight and looked around the room. What had awakened him in this abrupt manner from the doze he had fallen into he could not say. Perhaps it had been a tap on his left arm. But there was no other living thing in the room. What could have tapped him on the arm?

Very cautiously he bent and pulled out the soapbox with the adding-machine. As his gaze fell upon it a shudder went through him.

The whole thing was covered with red spots and blotches. Like ugly spatters of blood. They were too numerous to be counted now.

He put it away hastily, grimacing. To think that each one of those spots and blotches represented an act of meanness or despicability committed by himself!

He clutched the upper part of his arm. He felt a tingling in it. Tearing off his pyjama, he examined the arm. Examined it inch by inch. There was nothing, however, the matter with it. No purple spots. No spots at all. No eruptions or marks of any sort.

What, then, could have caused that sharp tingling? Could this be the first symptom of the new horror?

For a quarter of an hour he sat waiting for a repetition of the tingling. He was about to lie down when it happened again. A sharp tingle in his left arm. As though a vein had been electrocuted and had wriggled protestingly within his flesh. There was no pain. No itching. No after-sensation.

Mr. Hedge sat trembling. He wanted to scream. From sheer nervous suspense and terror. During the next few minutes he examined his arm so often that he got tired of doing it. He squeezed the arm, nudged it, stroked it, massaged it. For an instant be wondered whether it could be simply bad circulation. Was he making an unnecessary fuss?

Nursing his arm, he paced from his room into the sitting-room and on to the veranda, until utterly weary and heavy with sleep, he lay down on his bed and fell into a troubled doze.

Tall thin grey men crowded round the bed, leered at him and dropped bank-notes on his stomach. But the bank-notes sent sharp tinglings through his body and left red blotches on his chest. They were diseased notes. He could see the micrococci crawling on them. Tiny green and yellow dots with antennae.

He awoke and brushed at his chest, whimpering in fear.

When morning came the sharp tinglings in his left arm had become more frequent. By noon they were almost continuous. He paced the house, from room to room, nursing the arm, in a staring-eyed frenzy. He groaned.

"What can this be? My God! What can this be?" he kept muttering. "This is unjust. This is fiendish. Fiendish."

He sent for the doctor. But when the doctor came he confessed that the symptoms baffled him. "Tinglings? What sort of tinglings? Pins and needles?"

"No, no," said Mr. Hedge. "Tinglings. As if a thousand little wires are wriggling through my flesh."

The doctor shook his head. After long consideration, he decided that bad circulation must be responsible. He suggested electrical treatment if the condition persisted, and said he would call again in a day or two.

On the following day Mr. Hedge's arm had grown puffy, and pink bumps had appeared. The tinglings grew worse. Suddenly, to Mr. Hedge's horror and disgust, one of the bumps burst with a "plup!" and out wriggled a number of little green worms accompanied by pus and a most offensive smell.

Mr. Hedge leant out of the window and was sick. When the doctor came he expressed dismay. "Good heavens, man! Your arm is a mass of putrefaction!"

Mr. Hedge groaned.

"I don't like to have to say it, Mr. Hedge, but I'm very much afraid you'll have to lose this arm."

"Lose the arm!"

"Afraid so. There's nothing I can do to help you. This is the first case of its kind I've encountered in my career. Most puzzling."

"An arm is a valuable thing to lose, doctor."

"I know, Mr. Hedge. But it can't be helped. Look at it! The flesh is rotting off. I can't imagine how you could have picked up such a terrible trouble. It's quite beyond me."

Four weeks later Mr. Hedge returned from the hospital with an empty left sleeve, his face drawn and dull with misery. With his one remaining hand he pulled out the machine and looked at it. The total in the red section read "6".

One arm – one cent.

Mr. Hedge became a terror to Miguel and the labourers. He shouted and bawled at them. Cursed and threatened them. He made a further cut in their wages and told them that it was a matter of indifference whether they and their families starved. As for Sammy, Sammy went about in perpetual dread. Mr. Hedge hardly spoke to him once without clouting or kicking him. On occasions he would deliberately search for him and pick a row, clouting and kicking Sammy at every two sentences.

Once, when getting into bed, Mr. Hedge shook his one fist down at the machine under the bed and snarled: "If I have to lose all my limbs, you demon, you won't stop me from making my millions. Wait and see. Millions and millions. Billions! I'll be the greatest financier of modern times! Just you wait and see!"

By the end of the half-year things had improved somewhat. The young trees planted after the hurricane were doing well. The grey stumps had been destroyed and the wild vegetation cut down. The trees in the valley that had survived the hurricane bore plentifully. Mr. Hedge went to town with two thousand, seven hundred and eighty-six dollars and forty-nine cents – $2,786.49 and on his return home from the bank added this total to the total on the machine, bringing the final total to 21,792.76.

That night he celebrated with a hunk of roast beef and a bottle of wine. He ate the meal by himself and gulped the wine down – but not too heartily. He left the dregs.

He went to bed not too happy – nor too contented.

On the following day he was in no suspense concerning the new payment of his debt because he knew nothing would happen then. He went to bed with a heavy heart, wondering whether his other arm or a leg would be next to go. In the middle of the night he found himself awake and staring round into the darkness.

Something had awakened him, he was certain.

Oh, but why bother? Why bother? Uncanny happenings had become part of his life nowadays. What was the use of his sweating and worrying himself into a fever of dread? It wouldn't stop the weird happenings. It wouldn't stop the affliction which was about to come upon him.

In this moment of anguish he shut his eyes and asked himself, as he had done once before, whether this ordeal were worth it. Money. Why was it that money should seem so overpoweringly marvellous a possession? Was it the power that it gave one? But why should power be sweet when one was lonely; without friends and without an intimate companion? Did he enjoy the knowledge that he was bringing misery to the lives of his labourers? Was it a soothing memory the memory of his having put Smith, Robinson and the other fellows out of business?

Only a blue-black wall seemed to face Mr. Hedge behind his tightly shut lids. Only the thin singing of his taut nerves answered his tortured questions. "I should not have been born," he muttered. "It's not right that a man should have to suffer like this because of his yearning for wealth. I may be greedy, I may be evil – but I didn't make myself. If we are to believe what the church people say, God made me. Why did he make me greedy and evil? He must have had a purpose. And I'm fulfilling his purpose. So why should I have to suffer like this?"

"Oh, poppy-cock! Poppy-cock!" shouted Mr. Hedge. It's all poppy-cock! Do you hear me, God?"

Trembling, he tried to control his hysteria. Tried to compose himself for sleep. But he had no sooner fallen into a doze when he was awakened by a light touch on his right thigh.

He sprang up, lit the lamp and examined the spot. But there was nothing the matter. No purple red spot or bump. No boil. Nothing.

Sighing, Mr. Hedge put out the lamp and settled himself once again for sleep. He slept and was not disturbed for the rest of the night.

When he woke at six and was getting out of bed, however, he felt a strange stiffness in his right leg. Strange because it was the sort of stiffness that did not restrict the bending of his leg. It was not a muscular stiffness but just a tenseness of the very skin and flesh of which his leg was composed. Could this, he asked himself, be a symptom of the new affliction? Would his leg become septic and have to be amputated? Oh, what a miserable business! A whole leg for one cent! One dirty cent!

But no signs of septicaemia appeared. No tinglings. No itching. No purple spots or pink bumps. Only this tautness of the skin and flesh.

Mr. Hedge went to bed that night in a spirit of wretched resignation. He slept badly, dreaming of thin, hungry adding-machines that thumped restlessly round his sitting-room, searching for bank-notes to eat.

When he got out of bed in the morning something gave him a start.

The skin and flesh of his right leg had reduced. The leg was a trifle shorter and looked thin and bony like the leg of a person who was suffering from some wasting disease. When he tried to bend the leg it bent perfectly. He tried to wriggle his toes and they wriggled – perfectly. There was not the slightest sign of numbness. Nor of tingling or itching. Nor of red humps or purple spots. Everything about the leg was healthy except for this mysterious thinness that had come upon it.

His right boot would not fit. He was obliged to strap it to his foot to prevent it from flopping about when he walked. He walked with an up-and-down motion.

By noon the leg had grown thinner and more bony. But when he tried to bend it it bent – perfectly. When he tried to wriggle his toes they wriggled – perfectly. No numbness. No itching. No spots or bumps. No tinglings.

By nightfall the leg had grown so thin that the bones were visible almost as clearly as the bones in the leg of a skeleton. The sight of it gave Mr. Hedge a fright. It somehow brought back to his mind the phrase "one foot in the grave", especially as under his window that six foot hole still gaped. Ugh. Why did things conspire to be so weird?

Hastily he put the bony foot back into the boot which surrounded it like a useless box, despite the paper he stuffed into it to pad it.

For a long while he sat gazing out into the gathering twilight. No wind blew and the young palms were still in the cool, scented air.

A slight twitching began in the withered leg, and he had just begun to massage it gently when a sound came to his hearing. It came from the sitting-room. A slow, uneven clacking. Clack... Pause. Clack.

Springing up, he moved as quickly as he could in his up-and-down manner to the door. He pulled it open and looked out.

No one there. The clacking had stopped. And so, strangely enough, had the slight twitching in his leg.

Mr. Hedge shut the door and returned to the bed where he seated himself and lit the lamp.

It was not long before he again heard that sound in the sitting room. Very leisurely. Clack... Pause. Clack... Clack. Someone walking in there. Someone walking slowly on one padded foot and one booted foot. And simultaneously Mr. Hedge felt that twitching in his right leg.

He rose and rushed awkwardly to the door. Wrenched it open.

Not a single living thing in sight.

The clack-clack had ceased. The twitching in his leg had ceased.

What devilry, Mr. Hedge asked himself, is this?

He felt afraid to shut the door. Something desperately uncanny was happening in the sitting-room. The air in there held a brittleness. A dusty silence.

He shut the door. Seating himself again on the bed, he waited for what next was to happen.

Almost at once there came a thump-thump in the sitting room. He started up, then realized that it was only Sammy's footsteps. For the first time he could recall, he found himself grateful for Sammy's presence in the house.

In a moment, however, Sammy had gone back to the kitchen and all was silent again in the sitting-room.

Mr. Hedge waited. The minutes went by. The evening was quite dark now. Insistently, monotonously, the crickets and frogs cheeped and chirruped. The candle-flies flashed in the dark.

It began again. His leg twitched. And from the sitting-room came the clack-clack. Someone walking. Someone limping slowly on one padded foot and one booted foot. Booted foot? Or bony foot. A bony foot like his own here that kept twitching. Twitching in sympathy with the one in the sitting-room. To whom did the one out there belong?

Mr. Hedge sat and trembled. And listened.

The twitching in his right leg ceased. The sounds in the sitting-room ceased.

There followed a silence that, to Mr. Hedge was hollow and deathly. It was as though the owner of those leisurely, bony foot-treads had halted outside the bedroom door.

The minutes went by. The crickets and frogs. The candle-flies.

Then – he had been dreading it far back in his consciousness – it happened. The doorknob turned with a slow gradual creak.

Mr. Hedge covered his face and collapsed in a faint.

When he recovered a few minutes later, the door was still shut. He shouted for Sammy. Heard Sammy's footsteps coming. Heard them pause outside the door. "Yes, boss," said Sammy.

"Come in! Come in, you blithering fool! I called you!"

Sammy came in, trembling. "Yes, boss?"

"Were you outside the door a short while ago?"

"Yes, boss. I was polishing the door-brass as you tell me to do. It shine and bright, boss. I do it good."

Mr. Hedge felt so relieved that he could not bring himself to bawl admonishments at Sammy. "All right, all right," he growled. "I don't want to hear about the door-brass. What I want you to do is this. You must remain in the sitting-room for the rest of the night. Go to the kitchen and bring in my dinner, then make up your bed outside the door and sleep there. If I open that door at any time during the night and find you not there I'll twist your head off your body when I see you again. Do you hear me?"

"Yes, boss."

After eating, Mr. Hedge got into bed and settled down for the night. He left the lamp burning. From outside the door he could hear the soft snoring of Sammy, and the sound gave him some assurance.

At first he could not sleep. He lay listening. Frightening thoughts darted through his head. The withering of his leg. What could have caused it? It wasn't natural. It was fantastic. On the other occasions the afflictions had been of a rational sort: abscesses, corns and bunions, ringworms, septicaemia, worms in his arm. But this was out of all reason. This was grotesque. And those clacking footsteps. To whom or to what had they belonged? Why did he hear them only when his right leg began to twitch?

He fell into a dismal sleep plagued by skeletons that clacked slowly about the house searching for him. Skeletons playing paper-chase with bank-notes. Everywhere they went they left a trail of bank-notes behind them. Mr. Hedge forgot terror and stared with fascination at the oblong notes, crisp and ready to be crunched in the hand. He stretched out and gathered a few of them eagerly. A warm shiver of delight went through him as he heard them rustle in his grasp. He hid himself under the dining-table and greedily watched the skeletons scattering other notes about the floor. One fluttered down and came to rest near his knee, and he saw it was a thousand dollar note. Furtively he put out his hand to grasp it. But in the same moment he lifted his gaze and saw that one of the skeleton figures had paused and was staring at him out of its tomb-dark sockets. He had been discovered.

With slow clacking treads the skeletons all began to advance toward the table under which he crouched, their bony arms outstretched in macabre welcome… Clack… Clack…

Mr. Hedge awoke with a half-stifled yell, his right leg twitching.

The room was in darkness. The lamp had gone out.

He sat shivering with terror. The sound was in the room here with him; only a few yards from the bed some gaunt creature from an unknown world was pacing. Perhaps watching him with amber orbs that his own eyes could not see. Clack… Clack…

"Sammy! Sammy! Where are you? Come in here quickly!"

Sammy snored on outside the door.

Clack… Clack…

"Sammy! Wake up, you fool! Wake up and come in here!"

Clack… In the corner near the safe. Clack…

It stopped – and Mr. Hedge's right leg stopped twitching.

With a whine of terror, Mr. Hedge got out of bed and relit the lamp. But there was nothing out of the ordinary to be seen in the room. Outside the door the snoring of Sammy continued, and the crickets and tree-frogs cheeped and chirruped in the warm night outside the bungalow.

Mr. Hedge's gaze moved down to his right leg. He exclaimed.

The leg was no more a leg. It was a length of bones. Pulling up his pyjama trousers leg, he saw a thin, skeleton thing, bloodless, fleshless and without any visible fibres of muscle. Just dry bones with a dry, wrinkled parchment stretched tightly over the whole. He might have been gazing upon the leg of a mummy two thousand years old.

He tried to bend it. It bent – but with a dry, crackling noise. The noise of bones. He tried to wriggle the toes. They wriggled but with dry, crackling noises. The noises of small bones.

He tried to walk. He walked – but with an uneven, clacking sound.

He paused, a terrible thought within him.

The sound he made when he walked was precisely the same as the sound he had been hearing in the sitting-room – and in this room a few minutes ago.

He walked again.

Clack… Pause. Clack… Clack…

It began to come upon him. He saw what it was now. Whoever or whatever had made those foot-treads had done so in anticipation of this grotesque metamorphosis of his leg. A deliberate, devilish mockery.

Henceforth, night after night, Mr. Hedge would wake to hear those mocking foot-treads. Limping in the sitting-room. Limping in the room with him. Sometimes remotely on the veranda or in the pantry. He began to grow desperate with fear. His appetite fell off. He was losing weight.

At length, it occurred to him that perhaps if he had the dried up leg amputated the invisible mocker would desist in his mockery as there would be no mummified leg to mimic. The sacrifice of his leg, even desiccated as it was, was a terrible one. But he could see no other way out. And besides, the sight of the thing was beginning to sap his morale. It terrified him. It reminded him of the leg of an Egyptian mummy he had seen stripped of its wrappings. It made him think of himself as partly mummified – partly dead. The fear kept nagging at him that this withering might spread. Suppose he woke one morning to find that his buttocks and the lower part of his body had withered to the bones, or that the other leg had grown mummified, too! No, he would have to make the sacrifice. The leg must go.

So the leg was amputated. It created a sensation among the hospital staff. The doctors were perplexed. They had never experienced such a case before. They questioned Mr. Hedge persistently, but Mr. Hedge simply shook his head miserably and said that he had no idea what could have been responsible for the withering of his leg.

When, after several weeks, he returned home, he was a very low-spirited man. The ordeal had turned the hair at his temples silvery grey, and he looked nearly fifteen years older than he really was. His cheeks were hollow and his skin sallow and unhealthy. His shoulders drooped, and his chest had a sunken look.

Laying down his crutch, he bent with a groan and pulled the machine from under the bed. The debit section, as he had expected, read: "5". One leg – one cent.

Meanwhile the plantations flourished. The young trees in the replanted areas had begun to bear. At the end of the half-year when he assessed his profits he found that they amounted to five thousand, six hundred and, eighty dollars and twenty-two cents. $5,680.22. The present total on the machine read 20,781.69, hence with 5,680.22 added to this the final total would be 26,461.91.

Now, it happened that just at this time Mr. Hedge received one of the usual begging letters. This one was from a mechanic who said that he had lost a leg in an accident and was in desperate circumstances. Would Mr. Hedge have mercy on him and loan him a hundred dollars? His wife had to have an urgent operation and he had no money. Whatever interest Mr. Hedge charged he would be prepared to pay.

For some reason – it might have been the fact that the man had lost his leg – the letter touched Mr. Hedge a great deal. After some thought, he said to himself: "Oh, well, why not? To begin with, the total on the machine can't read more than twenty-five thousand. If I try to trick it again it'll only mean more trouble. Another hurricane perhaps. I'll send the poor devil the excess, and good luck to him!"

So Mr. Hedge wrote out a cheque for $1,461.91, enclosed a brief note to the man telling him he could have the money free of interest, and, in fact, forget about paying it back. It was a gift "And," added Mr. Hedge, "as for the oddness of the amount don't take any notice of that. Simply a whim of mine."

After posting it, Mr. Hedge went to town, as usual, and banked $4,218.31. On his return home, he pulled out the machine and recorded the amount, bringing the new total to 25,000.00

That night he did not celebrate.

The following day passed, and the next day. Mr. Hedge began to look out for the new affliction. But it did not come. He felt gloomily resigned, and told himself that he would not worry. Let whatever was to come upon him come. He was tired. He was almost indifferent whether he died or not. His left arm gone. His right leg gone. What next would go? Perhaps his other leg or arm. Oh, well, what could he do about it?

The second day, however, passed. The third. The fourth. Still nothing had happened. No boils, ringworms, purple spots, tinglings. No twitchings or deathly footsteps.

A week passed. Mr. Hedge continued to wait, telling himself that something exceptionally horrible must be brewing this time. The longer the delay, the worse the affliction.

A fortnight passed. Still nothing.

At this stage Mr. Hedge began to be puzzled in real earnest. Why this delay? A fortnight and still nothing? Most odd.

Then it occurred to him to have a look a the machine. He pulled it out and placed it on his table.

His mouth sagged open.

The total registered on the debit section read "4".

But how? How? After losing that leg the total had read "5". He had not suffered any affliction since then, so how was it that the total had reduced to "4"?

Mr. Hedge frowned and scratched his head. What could this mean? Could it be that he was going to escape on this occasion? But if so why? Why should the debt be reduced by a cent in this painless fashion?

Of a sudden a tremendous thought struck through him. He clutched the edge of the table, feeling breathless. Could it be that his giving that money to the mechanic fellow who had written him had been reckoned to his credit to the extent of one cent and so reduced the debt?

For a long while Mr. Hedge sat staring into space. Abruptly, in a trembling, panicky hurry, he put away the machine, brought out his chequebook and began to write in it. He wrote out a cheque for $500.00 to the hospital which had so often written to him soliciting a donation. He wrote out another for $800.00 to another hospital, another for $100.00 to the Injured Seamen's Home, and another for $100.00 to the Institute for the Blind. Four cheques.

He posted these cheques off, enclosing brief notes. And then with shaking hand he pulled out the machine and looked at it.

The debit section registered nine red noughts.

Mr. Hedge wept and wept and wept.

And after weeping, he cursed himself and beat his one fist against his temple. Great God! What a roaring colossal fool he had been! Those abscesses. Those corns and bunions. Those ringworms. His five fingers. His arm. His leg. All the pain and torture he had gone through, the physical and mental suffering – the nights of sweating and sleepless misery – all that he could have avoided had it only occurred to him to be less selfish and give to other people! Why, he could have cleared the debt painlessly in less than a month. A week!

The whole of that day Mr. Hedge moaned and groaned and wagged his head. Gnashed his teeth.

As the days and weeks went by, however, his spirits revived. That debt was now settled. It was one great burden off his mind. He had nothing to fear now. There would be no more afflictions. No more nights of sweating and sleeplessness, of nervous suspense and waiting for unknown horrors. That was over. And what was more, his plantations were flourishing. The young trees were already yielding plentifully, and the old trees in the valley were laden to breaking with heavy bunches of nuts. What did it matter that he lacked an arm and a leg? It might even increase his fame in the years to come. He would be know as the one-armed, one-legged financial giant. The Two-limbed Money Magnate. That was it! Ha, ha! Two-limbed Hedge – Wall Street King. His photograph would be published in the leading financial papers. *Time* Magazine would feature him on their cover. A colour portrait. He would be an international figure.

Yes, he would be a world figure in finance. To hell with the machine! It couldn't harm him now. The debt was paid off. The worst it could do would be to make a noise – and if it tried on such tricks down it would go into that hole under his window. With six feet of earth on top of it it would be effectively smothered. Not all the snarling in the world could penetrate thick heavy clay rammed tight to a depth of six feet. Oh, he would settle it, no fear. On the occasion when he had tried to play a trick on it to deceive it by recording 25,000.00 on it and hoarding the rest in his safe it had taken its revenge in that hurricane. Very well. This time he would be frank with it. He would record *all* his profits on it and exceed the 25,000.00 mark and let it snarl and stamp.

During the next two or three weeks several begging letters arrived. He laughed and destroyed them all. "Oh, no, my friends! No more of my money for you. I've paid off my little secret debt. I have no more need to give to charity. Hee, hee. Take me for a mug, eh? Hee, hee, hee."

★

When the half-year came to a close and Mr. Hedge assessed his profits he found that they amounted to seven thousand, four hundred and two dollars and nine cents. $7,402.09. Working expenses and the thousand dollars he had given to charity to clear the four-cents balance on his debt had brought the total on the machine down to 22,609.71. The new total would have to read 30,011.80. Very well. That was what it would read, decided Mr. Hedge.

He went to town, as usual, banked his money and then returned home. Despite his outward air of defiance, he felt a trifle nervous. He went to the window and looked down into the hole. There was soft mud at the bottom. Good. Just, he assured himself, the thing.

He examined the box with the earth and nodded. He pushed it a few inches nearer to the window.

He pulled out the machine and placed it on the window sill. If it snarled or uttered any threatening sounds, he would simply have to tilt it over down into the hole. No trouble. No trouble whatever.

He could not repress a shudder of loathing as he stood there with his crutch watching the machine. In the bright daylight on the window sill the red spots and blotches showed up like ugly sores on the black surface. Ugh. It was only left for them to suppurate, they looked so real. It was dreadful to think that each spot and blotch represented a low, dirty act committed by himself.

Oh, to hell with it! Forget that! Let him record the amount and be done. After all, it was only a machine. Why should he be scared of a little adding-machine! He was a man. He was Mr. Hedge. Two-limbed Hedge. The man who would hold the markets of the world in his one right hand. The Money Monarch. The Money God! Just wait and see how he would be venerated. He would be in a position to starve millions if he so desired. Whole populations. He would be empowered to bring war and pestilence on nations.

Taking a step forward toward the window, Mr. Hedge pressed the keys. "7", "4", "0", "2", "0", "9".

He worked the handle forward and backward and the total of 30,011.80 recorded in the machine.

Leaning there on his crutch, Mr. Hedge watched and waited.

Perhaps five seconds elapsed and nothing happened. No sound came from the machine.

But what Mr. Hedge saw was this. The red spots and blotches had begun to change in colour. From red they became greenish. And then they began to bubble and give off a yellowish vapour.

Mr. Hedge stared at them, unable to move.

To his nostrils came a foul and utterly disgusting odour. An odour like that of all the carrion and all the filth in the world clotted together and throwing off every conceivable kind of rotten and diseased miasma. Mr. Hedge leaned against the window-sill to retch, and in this moment the machine gave a rasping, fiendish howl and leapt upon his chest.

Mr. Hedge shrieked. He stumbled and dropped his crutch.

"Help! Oh, Christ! Sammy, help! Help!" Leaning on the window-sill, he grasped the machine with his one hand and tried to tear it off. But to no avail. From each spot and blotch there emerged a greenish bony tentacle. A tentacle with a sharp claw. From the two large blotches came two thick, scaly, powerful tentacles. From the smaller spots came correspondingly smaller tentacles. Each tentacle burrowed, with an easy and knowing familiarity, into Mr. Hedge's chest.

"Sammy! Sammy! Help! Come quickly!" yelled Mr. Hedge, struggling with the foul cankerous thing, his face purple, his breath coming in gasps.

Sammy appeared, saying; "Yes, boss?" from habit. At the terrible sight he recoiled.

"Don't stand there gaping, you fool ! Bring, an axe or a hatchet and hack it off. Oh, Christ! I'm choking!"

Sammy dashed off and returned with an axe.

"Go on! Hit it!" yelled Mr. Hedge, almost black in the face. One tentacle had burrowed into his left eye and the eyeball bulged and seemed on the point of pulping out.

"Hit it, Sammy! It's strangling me. It's killing me. Quick!"

Sammy lifted the axe, took aim and brought down the blade in one great accurate blow on the machine.

There was a tearing, grinding, snarling sound, and the machine fell away from Mr. Hedge's chest.

But its tentacles had gone deep. As they came away they brought Mr. Hedge's heart entangled in their writhing midst. A heart black like the machine and as spotted and blotched and putrescent.

It jumped about on the floor with a cold, dull, metallic clank-thump, then lay still amid the tangle of slowly writhing tentacles. Mr. Hedge's lifeless body sagged and slumped over the window-sill. It gave a low, wheezing moan and dropped with a muddy squelch into the six-foot deep hole that he himself had had dug.

Then as though governed by some evil magnetic influence, the machine, its numerous horny tentacles waving in the air, leapt through the window and down into the hole, carrying the black, diseased heart with it.

In less than two minutes, machine and corpse had merged and become transformed into a writhing, turgid mass of worms and slime.

The stench that came up was so horrible that Sammy hastily lifted the box of earth and emptied its contents down into the hole, covering up the green, seething broth.

SHORT STORIES

MISS CLARKE IS DYING

ASK anyone at Oistins and they'll tell you. Miss Clarke? Yes, poor lady, she's dying. And if you enquire from what, they'll tell you it's from an excess of white corpuscles.

Miss Clarke lives in a well-kept, not-too-shabby-looking grey shingled cottage that stands isolated in an extensive plot of land overgrown with brownish, drought-afflicted grass. Three straggly casuarina trees grow near the front door, relics of the days when a whole line of casuarina trees stood elegant guard along the driveway that leads to the cottage from the road.

Miss Clarke is fifty-two, and up to five months ago had thought herself in perfect health. So had her nephew, Basil, who works in a drug-store in Bridgetown. So had her sister, Mabel, who keeps a small guesthouse at Maxwell (and does embroidery work as a sideline). In fact, it is likely that nobody would have known that Miss Clarke is dying from an excess of white corpuscles had not Basil tactfully suggested to his aunt one Sunday, when on a visit, that it would not be a bad idea if she were to have her life insured.

Miss Clarke was well accustomed to acting upon the tactful suggestions of her nephew, Basil, for Basil is a qualified chemist and druggist, and, to Miss Clarke, anybody who could be so clever as to learn enough about chemicals and drugs, so that even the Government took notice and gave him permission to compound mixtures, was a person to be looked upon with respect and confidence. Suggestions coming from such a person, Miss Clarke felt, could not be spurned or treated lightly. Indeed, one person only can claim predominance over Basil in Miss Clarke's scale of esteem, and that person is Doctor Corbin. For, naturally, a doctor is a man not only clever with chemicals and drugs, but versed also in the secret workings of the human machine. It goes without saying, therefore, that Miss Clarke, when it came to the point of choosing a wise mentor, unhesitatingly accepted Doctor Corbin in preference to Basil.

When Basil suggested to Miss Clarke that she should have her life insured Miss Clarke had replied: "Insure my life? But, Basil! Whatever for, boy? I'm in the best of health. Why should you suggest such a thing to me all of a sudden like this, boy?"

Basil wriggled a little. He cleared his throat and said:

"Well, you see, aunty, it's like this. It's because you're in such perfect health that I'm making the suggestion."

"You see, aunty," he went on, wriggling again and fidgeting in his chair and trying to show how concerned he was about her welfare, "I'm going tell you something. I'm the kind of man who is known in educated circles as a psycho-pathologist." He paused in order to let the sound of this word reverberate impressively throughout her senses. Then when he thought that the desired effect had been achieved he said: "Yes, aunty, I'm a psycho-pathologist, and I can tell you this. I *know* from my extensive knowledge that when a person gets his life insured it always has a good effect both on his body and on his mind. A person who gets his or *her* life insured never dies in a hurry. And you see me here? I don't want you to die in a hurry, aunty. You're my only friend in this whole Barbados, aunty, and if you was to die, life wouldn't hold anything for me no more. Nothing more no more."

Miss Clarke, in her guilelessness, was touched. She said: "You really that fond of your old aunty, Basil?"

Basil went off into more phrases expressive of deep devotion, and the upshot of the matter was that Miss Clarke decided that she would take immediate steps to have her life insured for two thousand dollars (Basil suggested the amount). And that Basil should be named sole beneficiary in the event of her death was also another decision she came to (again, with the help of another tactful suggestion by Basil).

She planned to go to town on Wednesday to see the insurance people, but as things fell out, on Monday evening Doctor Corbin, her good friend, dropped in to see her, and in the course of conversation she mentioned the matter to him, telling him of Basil's visit the day before.

Doctor Corbin expressed dismay and astonishment – almost alarm and annoyance. "Insure your life, Susan! But whatever for, child!" He leaned forward earnestly. "Look here, don't you go listening to that boy. Huh! To tell you the truth, Susan, I don't like that nephew of yours at-all, at-all. I well believe he has an ulterior motive in this thing."

"Ulterior motive?" Miss Clarke was shocked. Imagine her good friend Dennis saying such calumnious things of poor Basil! "But, Dennis, I'm surprised at you. How can you say such a thing! Basil is very fond of me. I'm sure he has my welfare deep, deep at heart. He said it would help me in mind *and* body if I got insured – and that boy is no fool, Dennis. He has his good learning, you see him there. He knows Latin, and he's a patho-something-or-the-other, besides. Everybody can't be patho-whatever-it-is."

But Doctor Corbin wagged his finger at her. "I tell you, Susan, you listen to me. That boy may be clever in some things, but remember that I'm an older man and what's more I'm an L.R.C.P. and an L.R.C.S. You know what those letters mean? Huh! All right. You see Basil? He's only a druggist, you know. And I can tell you this, Susan, from my knowledge of the workings of the human body and the human mind, especially of psycho-therapeutics" – he paused for effect – "yes, especially of psycho-therapeutics, I can tell you this. That boy has an ulterior motive behind this thing. You listen to me, Susan. Listen to me as an old and wise friend, a Licentiate of the Royal College of Physicians and a Licentiate of the Royal College of Surgeons. You heed my words, Susan. I know what I talking about."

"But, Dennis, I've already promised him to do as he suggested. I can't back down now. It would hurt his feelings."

Doctor Corbin grunted pensively (remembering that as Miss Clarke's old and respected friend he was down for quite a substantial sum in her will). "All I know, Susan," he said in a tone of grave solicitude, "is that this thing doesn't smell good. That boy wants you to throw away your money on keeping up this policy so that he can benefit when you're gone along. But," he added quickly, noting her rising agitation and annoyance, "I can tell you what, Susan. I going make a little suggestion on my own, now, and as a dear friend I can only hope you will grant it."

"Certainly, Dennis. I'm always willing to listen to anything you suggest."

"Very well. Well, Susan, before you go to Bridgetown, let me give you a run-over first to see that your system is in good order. These insurance people are going to make you undergo an examination by their doctor, and since you look as if you're set on taking out this policy, well, it's no harm if I just give you a look over first to see that you're in sound health."

"But I am in sound health, Dennis. You know that very well. You examined me only last month and you said so yourself."

Doctor Corbin wagged his finger at her. "Look here, Susan child, you see me here? I'm an L.R.C.P. you know. *And* an L.R.C.S. Bear in mind my qualifications, Susan, when I tell you this. You see this thing the human body? It's a funny, funny thing, child. Today you can be in the best health – everything sound – and tomorrow? Huh; tomorrow everything turn topsy-turvy, and when you catch yourself you treading straight on the highroad to your Lord and Saviour!"

Miss Clarke nodded, deeply impressed. "Yes, Dennis, you're right. You quite right. I should have borne that in mind. Yes, you're a wise man, Dennis. Life can be very uncertain."

"I *know* I'm right, Susan. I know I'm right. And that's why I insist as your good friend who has your welfare at heart that I should put you through an examination before you go to town. Those Bridgetown doctors? Hoi! Susan, you don't know how wicked and scoundrelous those men can be. They turn up their noses at us old retired country doctors, but they! More scoundrelous men you couldn't wish for, child! It would be just like one of them to tell you that something wrong with you and that the insurance company can't see their way to give you a policy. I know them good!"

So Miss Clarke agreed to have Doctor Corbin give her an examination before her trip to town.

The doctor came on the following day, Tuesday, and he was in a jovial mood. "Of course, Susan," he said casually, "I know perfectly well that not a thing is the matter with you. You're a strong girl. You can't die just now. You have at least forty more years before you."

"Me, Dennis! Forty more years! Look, don't make fun at me! I ever tell you I want to live to ninety-two?"

"We can't decide these things for ourselves, Susan. If we got to live to ninety or a hundred we got to live to that. And if we got to live forty-three all the wild horses in the whole world couldn't make any difference."

"That's true, Dennis. You're a wise man. A wise man."

As the examination progressed Doctor Corbin nodded and muttered in satisfaction, carrying on, so to speak, a running commentary on his findings.

"Heart sound – perfect." And later: "Yes… Lungs – perfect. No dullness. No rhonchi." And again: "Nerve reflexes excellent." … "Spleen – splendid! No signs of enlargement." But toward the end of the examination he suddenly stiffened and frowned and said: "Mm". He put his hand to his chin reflectively and after a silence said slowly: "Now, what's this? What's this at all?"

"What's what, Dennis?" asked Miss Clarke.

Doctor Corbin did not reply. He pursed his lips, looking grave. He uttered another ominous "Mm."

"Dennis, don't you hear me addressing a question to you? What's wrong? Why you looking so serious?"

Doctor Corbin' nodded with gravity and stroked his chin slowly. He said: "Mm" and shook his head. He sighed and muttered: "What is life? What is life?" At length, he told Miss Clarke: "Susan, I have something extremely grave to impart to you. I have made a grave discovery."

"A grave discovery?" Miss Clarke went pale. "What's that, Dennis? Something wrong with me?"

Doctor Corbin nodded slowly, wagged his head and sighed. "Susan, I wish it were not incumbent upon me to have to break forth this piece of news upon your respected and dear self. But I have to inform you that you are in a most critical condition, Susan."

"A critical condition, Dennis?"

"Yes, Susan." Doctor Corbin averted his face and brushed hastily at his eyes. "It grieves me to have to tell you, Susan, but it is now useless for you to go to Bridgetown to try and take out that policy on your life. The doctors wouldn't pass you."

Miss Clarke paled again – this time in great alarm. The policy didn't matter now. What mattered was her health. "But Dennis, what you mean? What has gone wrong with me sudden like this?"

"To all appearances, Susan, you are in good health. In fact, I'm sure that even as you lie there you feel quite fit. But to a medical man, Susan – to an L.R.C.P., things are not always that they seem to ordinary people. I have made a serious diagnosis, and I can tell you now with certainty that you are in a low state. You are suffering from a rare disease. You have an excess of white corpuscles."

"An excess of white what, Dennis?"

"White corpuscles. Phagocytes. But you won't know what I mean. You won't understand all these medical designations."

Miss Clarke, trembling now, asked: "But, Dennis, is it very serious? How serious?"

Doctor Corbin was silent for a moment, then looked at her and said quietly: "Susan, I'm in a difficult position. What I mean, as your dear friend, it gives me great grief to have to tell you that it is now only a matter of time for you before the Lord calls you." Doctor Corbin's eyes were moist. He dabbed at them hastily, averting his face and heaving a sigh.

After a silence of profound dismay Miss Clarke looked at him and asked: "And how much longer I got to live, Dennis?"

Doctor Corbin, seemingly too moved to reply at once, shook his head, fumbling for his handkerchief, his face drawn. At length, his face still averted, he said quietly: "It might be a year, Susan. Or it might be eight months. Or only six. You're a dying woman, Susan." His voice broke and he walked over to the window. "There's no cure, Susan," he said in a voice barely audible in the room.

"No cure?"

"No cure. Leucocythemia is beyond medical aid, Susan."

And that is why Miss Clarke never went to Bridgetown to see the insurance people about the policy. Her nephew, Basil, came to Oistins on the day after the examination to enquire what was the matter, and when he heard the facts he scowled and said: "Look, aunty! You don't worry with that man! That man Corbin! He only throwing dust in your eyes because he knows that you got him down for a big sum of money in your will –"

"But, Basil! How dare you say such a thing of my old and treasured friend, Doctor Corbin! I won't have it!"

Basil, trying with difficulty to restrain his fury, said: "I know, aunty! I tell you, I know! That man Corbin! He no good! And you listen to me and come to town and let another doctor examine you, and see if you don't hear a different, different story about what wrong with you!"

"Then what you mean is that Dennis don't know his job! That's what you mean to tell me, Basil? Look here, boy, I've always respected you because I know you have studied your books and passed your examinations, but I'm not going to stand here, Basil, and hear you say all those calumnious things about a dear trusted friend of mine. I won't have it, Basil!"

Basil returned to Oistins on at least three other occasions to try to persuade his aunt to get another doctor to examine her, but on each occasion she proved firm and decided in her intention not to heed him. Furthermore, Doctor Corbin came every day to attend upon her, and he never failed to express what he felt about Basil.

"Hoi! That boy, Susan! He certainly hasn't taken after you. He's an evil-minded boy. You don't listen to him, Susan. Heed your old and wise friend. With me, Susan, you have naught to fear. I shall attend upon you to the last. Never a day shall I desert you, my dear friend. Here I have brought you a bottle of medicine which will relieve your condition, my dear. Take it three times a day after meals. It will make your end more easy when the hour strikes. I shall bring a bottle every week for you, Susan, free of all charge. It is the least I can do for my old and dear friend."

And so Basil's visits ceased entirely, and the situation is exactly the same today, five months after the examination. Miss Clarke is dying – from an excess of white corpuscles. If you ask her she will tell you that every day she gets paler and paler and thinner. When a neighbour enquires after her health she says: "My dear. Just the same. The little white devils have got me looking paler than ever this morning."

And she sniggers and sighs philosophically!

SOMETHING FISHY

THE Rector was staring out into the churchyard and contemplating the movements of the Curate.

There may be something fishy about his past, thought the Rector. You never can tell. Or, of course, on the other hand it may be nothing worse than just a touch of homesickness. After all, he hasn't been here more than a week, and Devonshire is a long way from British Guiana. Then he's only a young chap. Twenty-four at the most. Quite likely he's just pining for some girl he's left behind in the Old Country. That may be all the matter... And yet he told me he liked Georgetown. "I've always wanted to come to the tropics," he said at lunch a few days ago. "Sunshine and palms and all the rest of it. This place is even more lovely than I'd imagined it to be."

Now I come to think of it, a fellow who is homesick or who's pining for a girl he's left behind doesn't talk that way. No. I really believe there's something else behind it all. Just have a look at him out there now, for instance, mooning about in the churchyard and staring up into the cabbage-palms and the silk-cotton trees. Not natural, that, you know. And he's got a decided air of brooding. See! He's paused now by the stone steps that lead up to the vestry door. He's staring down at the steps: staring at them as though there may be something written on them that he's trying to read. Ah! He's glanced round quickly now – in a furtive sort of way as if he fears he's being watched. There's a look on his face now... Well, it isn't the kind of look you'd expect a young curate to have on his face. It's a conscience-stricken look, I'll warrant. He's got a worried air. Something dark is weighing on his mind, I feel sure of it. I've noticed it for some days now – ever since he arrived, in fact. I wonder if it's something he's done back home in Devonshire of which he's ashamed or something the consequences of which he dreads may fall upon him even far out here in British Guiana. He certainly has a haunted air. And look how he fidgeted when, to test him out, I told him at breakfast this morning about the murder of a girl in the churchyard that occurred some weeks ago. Just a little psychological test, but it worked in such a significant way. A man whose conscience is free doesn't react in the way he reacted this morning.

Aha! He's coming toward the Rectory now. Watch the way he walks: slowly and with his hands thrust deep in his trousers pockets, his eyes on the ground.

He's gone out of view around the angle of the building now. Perhaps he intends coming up into the study here. Had better not let him find me standing at the window here or he may guess I've been watching him. Don't want the poor fellow to feel in any way uncomfortable. Better to sit by the bookcase over there and pretend to be engrossed in that book I was looking through – the one he lent me yesterday.

Ah! Just as I thought. He's coming here to the study. Hear his steps along the corridor.

"Oh! I'm sorry! Didn't know you were in here, Rector! Thought you were upstairs resting as usual."

"Come in, my boy! Come in! It's perfectly all right. I decided in favour of that book you lent me yesterday. It's interested me sufficiently to make me forego my siesta today."

"Oh, I see. Glad you like it. Thought I'd do a bit of reading myself – that is, if I won't be disturbing you in here."

"Not at all! Not at all! Go ahead – by all means. Make yourself comfortable, my boy. Don't mind me at all."

Only an excuse, that, of course. He hasn't come in here to do any "bit of reading". He's come in to sit at the desk and gaze blankly at the wall as I caught him doing the day before yesterday. He wants to be alone in here so that he can continue his brooding. So odd in his habits, poor fellow. Perhaps he isn't all right up here.

See how hesitantly he's coming over to the bookcase? Seems to be suffering from an overdose of inferiority complex. Always afraid of causing me annoyance when, on the other hand, I'd welcome his presence more often. Don't suppose he realizes how lonely I am.

He's taking down a volume… What's it? *Tales of Mystery and Imagination*. Poe. H'm. A bit peculiar he should choose that. Only yesterday he was telling me he didn't care for mystery stories. He prefers the heavy-weight type of literature: biography, belle-letters; Virginia Woolf and the Russian novelists… "I don't know why," he said, "but these murder thrillers and mystery tales never appeal to me. I don't mind seeing a good thriller on the screen, especially the kind with gangsters, but to sit down in cold blood and read it – nothing doing." And now he's chosen Edgar Allan Poe, of all writers! See! Something is wrong. It's a little fishy, this. Distinctly so. Shows, if nothing else, that he wasn't speaking the truth yesterday.

"Think I'll have a go at this, Rector. Not too fond of mystery, as I mentioned, but I've heard a lot of Poe's prose style."

"Yes, yes. That's so. His style is very dignified and elevated. Poe is certainly good. You should try his poems, too."

H'm. Now I wonder if that's just a clever piece of bluff. I suppose it may be a bit far-fetched to think such a thing, but isn't it possible that, in reality, he's deeply interested in things morbid, but (because of that dark something he's done back in the Old Country) is anxious to conceal this interest from other people?

Not impossible, of course – yet, as I say, a bit far-fetched. Anyway, I think it would be worthwhile keeping an eye on the fellow and observing his reactions on various occasions. Perhaps he may be one of these cases of homicidal insanity that have remained undiscovered. Far-fetched again, and yet… well, I've heard of queerer things proving to be fact in the long run. Only the other day I was reading of a case of homicidal mania. The writer said that the majority of cases that had come his way seemed in ordinary life the most harmless-looking fellows imaginable. You would never have dreamt for an instant that they could hurt a fly, and their behaviour would appear perfectly normal. It's only when they're alone and think no one is observing them that they may betray any signs of furtiveness or deep brooding. Sort of schizophrenia. Double personality business… And they generally did their best to conceal, at all costs, their interest in things morbid.

Listen to him fidgeting about in the chair over there by the window. He must be uncomfortable because there's a human presence other than his own in here. A homicidal maniac, however sociable he may appear to be, is, in reality, fond of solitude. Solitude is conducive to brooding.

He's lighting a cigarette. Ah! He's just shot a rather furtive glance this way. Barely managed to lower my eyes in time to avoid that glance. Mustn't make him realize that he's being watched. That would discomfit the poor chap. Don't want to upset him in any way.

Listen to him fidgeting again. Why can't he keep still? Definitely nervy. A sign that he isn't at ease in his mind. And see that? His brows have just puckered heavily. Why, his eyes aren't fixed on the book at all. They're looking into space – and so intently.

Why, good Lord! What makes the fellow start forward so? "Hallo! Anything wrong, my boy?"

"I could have sworn I saw something dark dart along there."

"Something dark?"

"Yes. Just there!"

Aha! He's having delusions now.

"Where did you see it, my boy? Are you sure?"

"Yes, Rector. Just there – oh! There it is! It's some sort of lizard, isn't it? Look!"

"Oh, that? Yes. You'll come across them occasionally around the house. They live behind pictures and in crevices. Perfectly harmless, really. They're called geckoes."

"Gave me quite a start."

"Oh, you'll get accustomed to them in time. Very friendly little creatures, I can assure you. They were my only companions in this place before you came along."

That makes him fidget afresh. I said it purposely to see what effect it would have on him.

Perhaps he's excited at the sudden reminder that the two of us live alone in the Rectory here. If he's a homicidal maniac that ought to suggest possibilities to his warped mind. Ugh! But this thing is getting a bit creepy. In future it may be safer if I keep the door of my bedroom locked when I retire at night and when I take my siesta. And it will be no harm observing some caution when I go round corners in the corridor or when I enter the vestry alone after dark.

There he goes again. Fidgeting, fidgeting all the time. Poor fellow. It's pitiable when you come to think of it. Perhaps he was repressed during childhood? Many cases of homicidal mania are due to repressions in childhood or to excessive pampering on the part of the mother, or to an anchoretic existence. I wonder what sort of life he led in Devon. He's spoken very little of the Home Country, now I come to think of it. Strangely reserved. All he's told me is that he held an appointment as curate in some town not far from Exeter. Forget the name of the place now.

Hallo! He's getting up. Better be careful. These fellows make sudden rushes sometimes. It won't be surprising if he has some kind of weapon concealed on his person – a revolver or a knife. More likely a knife. Most homicidal maniacs, I understand, glory in the sight of blood when they commit any act of violence. Oh, but this is getting a bit absurd. I'm letting my imagination get the better of me. For all I know, the poor fellow may be as normal and harmless as the verger...

Just look at him now. He's standing at the window staring out at the hot day. Something is certainly on his mind, that's quite plain. He stands so rigidly now as though deep in thought.

He's left the book on the chair. His back is to the room... Seems far, far away in some reverie of his own... His back is to the room. Yes, his back is to the room, and he's so far, far gone in reverie that even if anyone spoke to him in a loud voice, I doubt if he'd hear...

And his back is to the room...

His back is to the room... Yes, his back...

The Rector slid a hand into an inner pocket, and rising, made a dash toward the Curate's back. But the Curate turned just in time.

The younger man succeeded eventually in knocking him out, though in the struggle he received a deep gash on his right shoulder.

"I couldn't understand why he kept watching me so closely on the sly," he told the police later. "It wasn't until this morning at breakfast when he told me about a girl who had been found stabbed to death in the churchyard here that I began to feel definitely suspicious and put two and two together. I just couldn't make up my mind what was the best thing to do under the circumstances."

"Yes, it was a pretty narrow shave for you," the District-Superintendent smiled. "If he had succeeded you would have been his fourth victim."

BREAKDOWN

YOU who have lived for any time in British Guiana will know what I mean. If
you have travelled from Rosignol to Georgetown by car in December you will
remember the lonely section of road between Cotton Trees and Bath. Burnt
earth churned into a pap of mud by the prolonged rains and deep gutters into
which your tyres sink down with a sudden sloshing jolt and then jolt out again
with a sound of swishing water. And all around you bush and more bush – and
the monotonous drip of rain: not very heavy, but just dripping, dripping with
an air of being settled for all time. Plip-plip! Plip-plip! Steady and persistent,
dismal and wetly gloomy, from a sky grey all over. The sound of hurrying water
in the swollen trenches: water swirling under culverts and wooden bridges and
then disappearing under overhanging shrubs and rain-sagging black-sage bush
and bowing arrow-leafed *mucca-mucca*. And perhaps a donkey-cart appears ahead
and you have to veer precariously to the side of the road almost on to the drenched
grass parapet.

A depressing scene, you'll admit – especially when the time is six o'clock on the
afternoon before Christmas Eve and you want to get into town in time for a dance at
nine o'clock.

Reggie said: "And I got the first dance booked, mind you."

I told him: "To hell with the first dance, man! We ought to be glad if we get into
town at all. You see these roads? And you forget that jet I've been telling you about?"

"Jet? What about the jet?"

"It was giving trouble again this morning, but I hadn't time to bother with it. We
got to take our chance."

He looked at me in dismay. "And suppose it goes bad?"

"Eh-eh, well what? Get out and clean it. What else we going to do about it?"

"But you cool, eh?"

"What's the use of getting in a flurry, boy?"

And, of course, Fate must have overheard us, because five minutes had not gone
when we heard a splutter and the engine stalled.

"Mm-h'm. That's all. Hear that? The jet."

"What you mean, then? We stuck here till we can get it repaired?"

"You're getting clever. That's just what I mean."

He looked at me. "But you're a hell of a fellow, Charlie!"

"All right! All right! Don't jump out of your skin. I'll get it going in a couple
minutes. You just keep cool."

"The rain will do that for me, no fear."

Yes, the rain just dripped and dripped, and water gurgled and swirled in the
trenches, and you could smell the rank vegetation all around. Darkness was coming
down rapidly, helped on by the thick blanket of grey clouds. A dray overtook us, and
the East Indian driver hailed out to us: "Breakdown, na, boss?" And I nodded and

returned: "Yes, boy! Breakdown!" Another fellow was approaching up the road – that is to say from the direction of Bath Estate. It was another East Indian – a youngish man. About my age – twenty-four or twenty-five. He carried a silver-handled stick and his khaki trousers and yellow shirt were soaked, the shirt sticking to his skin. He seemed to be seeing Christmas already, for he walked with a rather uncertain gait, and he must have been spreeing, spreeing in *pagwah* fashion, for he was liberally splashed with red. He stopped for a moment and chuckled.

"Car break down, chief?"

I nodded. "Yes, I've got a lil' trouble here, man."

"Bad road to break down, chief. No gas nowhere about dis part."

"It's not gas. We have plenty of that. It's the jet. Choked. I say, Reggie! Start up lemme see, boy!"

Reggie pressed on the starter. The engine whirred, then spluttered and stalled.

"Cold morning, boss. Cold morning."

Yes, the fellow was certainly well corned. I grinned and said: "You right, boy. I can see you happy. You don't even know morning from evening. I know the stage."

He chuckled and passed on, muttering: "Cold morning, boss. Rain fall all night. Morning cold."

He made off toward a lonely-looking little wooden cottage some way off amid mango trees and coconut palms on the northern side of the road. He crossed the wooden bridge which was almost covered with water and disappeared up a muddy pathway.

"Lucky fellow, anyway," Reggie said. "He home already – no matter if the house a lil' rickety and right behind God's back in this Berbice."

"You telling me! Start up again lemme see!"

He started up again, but again the engine whirred and then stalled.

"Oh, Lord! Look, hand me that torchlight. Look in the side-pocket there you'll see it!"

A donkey-cart came squelching up in the mud and went past, but the occupant, a small black boy, with a pile of plantains in bunches and two baskets covered with rice-bags, took no notice of us except to give us a curious stare. We couldn't blame him. The poor fellow looked drenched. His skin gleamed, and you could see the trickles of water running down his temples.

"Eh-eh! But wait! Charlie, it don't look as if we going to this dance tonight. Eh?"

"Man, you shut your mouth in there! Forget the dances. You didn't hear what I tell you just now? We ought to be lucky if we can get to town at all."

"But you're a man! If you knew the car wasn't in good condition for the trip, why you didn't do something before we left New Amsterdam?"

"Because if the heavens collapsed I wasn't staying in New Amsterdam tonight. Don't know why the hell the Government had to transfer me to a hole like New Amsterdam!"

"Boy, you let the Berbicians hear you! We haven't passed the Abary yet, you know! Mind your mouth!"

"Give another start there, boy!"

The engine whirred and whirred.

"You mother's son of a – yes, I think we got it, the son of a gun!"

"Think she all right now?"

"Think so. Anyway, we can only try."

But I hadn't engaged the gears when there was a splutter – and there we were, still stuck up in the mud by the parapet. "Oh, well!"

Reggie laughed. "Boy, it looking too much to me like we going got to go and spend the night with our friend Balgobin."

"Balgobin? Which Balgobin is that?"

"The fellow who passed us just now."

"His name is Balgobin?"

"I don't know. It might be Ramsarran. Anything you like."

"If he got a nice bettay with him I won't mind spending the night."

"If he cut off your head with a cutlass will be another matter."

And all the time it got darker and darker and the rain dripped down in a steady, slow, monotonous hissing. A more dreary scene it would have been hard to picture. Once a bird uttered a cawing note far off in the bush, and the sound came dismally through the watery air, and there must have been a koker not too far, for we could hear a deep rushing sound of water somewhere on the southern side of the road.

Reggie looked around and said: "Boy, this place looks very creepy to me. I won't like to get held up here all night. I don't like Berbice jumbie, you know."

The koker kept rushing with a subdued menace.

"Start up again let's see what's happening here."

Nothing doing.

Reggie hugged himself, looking around slowly.

We could hear that bird again. There was nothing in sight on the road in either direction. We seemed to be the only human beings in the open, and the dusk was coming down like a dense shroud – something almost tangible that was bent on wrapping itself about us with a steady insidiousness and then perhaps pressing us down into the mud. I clicked my tongue at these silly fancies, but I found myself inclined to shiver for no reason at all, and it was not from the chill of the rain, for I was in perfect condition. A wetting never worries me.

"I wonder what bird that is, Charlie."

"I don't know."

It got darker. It was so dark now that the bush on either hand loomed up in black silhouette against the heavy December sky. Frogs had begun to croak now and then – bullfrogs in the swampy lands to our left. Once a cricket cheeped sharply and stopped, cheeped and stopped – and I thought of the engine behaving the same way – starting and stopping in such an irritating manner.

Reggie chuckled and said: "I don't like the look of this thing."

"Start up again lemme see!"

This time we seemed to have got her going in earnest. We tested over and over before I engaged the gears.

Then it stopped.

Reggie sighed and looked back through the bush in the direction of the East Indian fellow's cottage. There was a weak light burning in a window. I had to chuckle as I followed his gaze. I nodded and said: "Yes, boy, I understand."

"You understand? You don't understand one thing. Boy, I got a good mind to go and beg Baburam for some curry and roti. Baburam must be eating his Christmas dinner."

"I brought sandwiches, you know."

"All right. All right. All in good time. I'm not perishing yet."

The koker or whatever it was kept on rushing with a hollow sound over yonder. Somehow, it got on my nerves. Water everywhere. Water dripping from the sky. Water rushing through a koker, water in the trenches swirling and gurgling past. Water dripping from the thick bush all about us. Even a dead place like New Amsterdam was better than this.

"Flood her again! Give her a flood, boy, lemme see what happening this time. I think I got her now!"

It whirred and whirred – steadily, hopefully. I straightened up and stared down at the messy thing.

A donkey-cart came jogging slushily on its way toward Bath. When it was abreast of us it stopped, and the old black fellow inside grunted and said: "You break down, skipper?"

I nodded. "Yes, but it looks as if we'll soon get fixed up. She's going pretty steadily now."

"Wedder bad for breakdown, boss. Going to Georgetown?'"

"Yes, man. But from the way this car is going on we're wondering if we won't have to sleep with Balgobin tonight. Car behaving so bad."

"Who is Balgobin, chief?"

Reggie grinned. "The Indian fellow who lives in the cottage over yonder there. I don't know if his name is Balgobin. I only call him so because I don't know his name."

The old fellow grunted. "No, boss. He name Pemwarree."

"Pemwarree, eh? But wait! His light seems to have gone out. I don't see it anymore. He must have gone to bed. I almost wish I was in bed myself."

"No, boss. Nobody not in dat house now."

"Eh? Nobody in there now? But Pemwarree passed us only a minute or two ago. He said he lived there. He went up the path to the house."

"Pemwarree, boss?"

"Yes – if you say Pemwarree is his name. Short fellow carrying a silver-handled stick."

"Wearing khaki trousers and yellow shirt?"

"Yes, that's right."

He looked at us. "Boss? Your engine working all right now?"

"It looks so. Why?"

"Well, get in and try go 'way from dis spot quick, quick. Early dis morning when Pemwarree was coming home from work at Bath Estate t'rough de rain somebody knock him down and cut him up – right near dis same spot. 'E corpse and de silver-handle stick lying in de morgue at Fort Wellington Police Station now – dis very minute."

SAMLAL

I KNOW SAMLAL personally, and have always thought him somebody I should one day write about; that is why I have decided to present this cross-section of his life in order that you who have never met him might be able to understand why it is that everybody in Georgetown finds him such an irresistible fellow.

We can begin with the Saturday morning late last year when he stood at the back gate of Miss Rawle's cottage hesitating to go in because of the dogs. The dogs were barking, but presently Miss Rawle appeared and silenced them, and after she had done so she told him to come round to the back steps. She gave him a sixpence and said that if he came back the following Saturday morning she would give him something again. It was on his second visit that she got into conversation with him. She asked him how he had managed to lose his leg, and so, seating himself on the third treader from the top, he rested his crutch on the lower treader and told her the tale of his life up to the present.

He came from Berbice, he said. At fourteen, on leaving school, he had gone to work as a gardener's assistant in the Public Garden in New Amsterdam. He kept this job for over two years, then had a fight with the nephew of the caretaker of Colony House and was dismissed. It was after this that he came to Georgetown where he found work at a big Main Street residence as yard-boy and messenger. He learned to drive a car in his spare time, and, eventually, found himself promoted from yard-boy to chauffeur. He wore livery and everybody used to tell him how smart he looked. But anyway, he told Miss Rawle, he lost this job after a few months because the daughter of the house took a liking to him and always wanted to drive about in the car with him alone. People began to talk, and her father, who was a big-firm attorney, decided that that kind of thing could not go on and that Samlal would have to leave, but he was a good gentleman and he worked things so that a bus-company employed Samlal as a driver.

It was a hard blow, and the bus-people did not treat him well. Think of it! He who used to wear chauffeur's clothes driving a bus now in an ordinary shirt-and-trousers! And having to stand about in the Stabroek Market Square jostling with the crowds and bawling and trying to encourage would-be passengers to come into his bus. No! That kind of life did not suit him at all. So he left the job and after a while brought about a little arrangement with some diamond prospectors and pork-knockers and went up the Mazaruni. But malaria struck him down and he had to return to the city. He got thin as a stick and nearly died. When he was better he worked for a time in a rum-shop in Bourda, then a Portuguese gentleman who was an insurance canvasser and who had some influence with big people in the city got him a better position as assistant barman in one of the Main Street hotels. This was at the time when tourists used to come down every fortnight on the Lady boats. One night, he said, an American lady sent down to the bar and asked for a bedroom-steward, but nobody was around at the time to pass on the message, so he, Samlal himself, went upstairs to see what she wanted. The lady took a liking to him right away. Yes, right away she took a liking to him, and she talked to him nice and made him rub her back with liniment.

"How Ah could help it, ma'am?" said Samlal, looking up at Miss Rawle as though asking her to judge the matter. "De lady lay down in bed on her stomach and ask me to rub her back wid liniment. How Ah could refuse her, ma'am? Ah had to do it. If Ah didn't do it Ah mighta loss me job. You t'ink it was me fault, ma'am?"

Miss Rawle, very pink in the face – she was a spinster of thirty-four who earned her living as a dressmaker – nodded as gravely as she could, and agreed with him that it was certainly not his fault.

Anyway, continued Samlal, he soon lost this job, too. He quarrelled with the head barman over a matter of wrong change, and the manager sent him off, saying that he was not suited for the job. After this he worked as a porter and a stevedore on the wharves and, for a month, as an office-boy, but ill luck followed him – a fortune-teller once told him that he was born under a bad planet – and one morning at two o'clock he was knocked down by a car on the Sea Wall road. The driver did not stop, and the car was never traced. It was this accident which had caused him to lose his leg.

"Yes, ma'am," he ended up, "you watch me here, Ah'm a proud man. Is only dis leg what bring me to begging today, ma'am. They ain' got no other man in dis Georgetown who see more of big life dan me. All dem tourists at de hotel – you know what stories I can tell you about dem, ma'am? And de family Ah work wid in Main Street? I can tell you plenty, plenty about dese big people, ma'am – but I is not a talk-man. I always keep my tongue quiet. It pay to keep you tongue quiet, ma'am."

Yes, Samlal is certainly an attractive fellow. Apart from being a fascinating raconteur, he is handsome. He has dark, thick eyebrows and deep-set brown eyes, and his teeth are perfect; white and even. It is true that he uses a crutch which could be two or three inches longer, and as a result walks with an up-and-down motion, but he keeps his head erect and, at a sidewise tilt, and this posture – a posture more defiant than proud – contributes a great deal to his striking appearance.

The district he frequents is Queenstown, that quiet semi-rural suburb of George-town, and the residents give him money and sometimes food, and do this always without ever considering him a nuisance. His anecdotes concerning his past life are famous in the district, and people are inclined to welcome him rather than turn him away.

At the time of this narrative Miss Rawle not only gave him a shilling every Saturday morning but listened to him for nearly an hour sometimes on the back stairs. Then shortly after he began to visit Miss Rawle, Mrs. Hurst, her neighbour, a widow who lived with an old aunt Mrs. Hicks, called him in and gave him a sixpence.

Samlal's response contained both humility and gallantry.

"Ma'am," he said to Mrs. Hurst, "Ah can look at you and see it ain' only you' face wha' good-looking. Yes, ma'am, you got good looks outside – and you' heart inside good, too. Ah can always tell a good lady when Ah see she. Ah wasn' always like dis, you know, ma'am. Ah used to be a butler wid a big family in Main Street, and Ah work at de hotels in Main Street as a desk-clerk, and Ah meet plenty big people. Oh, yes, ma'am, if Ah didn' loss me foot Ah woulda been in a high position today because de manager of de Park Hotel tek a liking to me and say: 'Samlal, you is only a coolie, but you going get far in dis world, hear what I say.' Yes, ma'am, dat's what de manager tell me…"

For the next half an hour he gave Mrs. Hurst a brief and very racy sketch of his past

– a new and completely revised version, incidentally – and she listened with interest, a smile on her face. He spoke so convincingly and had such an attractive way of nodding and letting his hair fall over his forehead that she did not attempt to challenge him on any point. Before he left she told him that he must come every Saturday afternoon and she would give him something.

"Come at about two o'clock. I'm not always at home on Saturday mornings. I work at an office in Water Street. It's only a touch of 'flu that kept me in this morning."

"Awright, ma'am. Ah will come. But, Mrs. Hurst, ma'am!" He paused in going down the steps and looked back, and in his eyes there was an earnest, almost concerned look. "You mustn' t'ink Ah coming jest for what you can gimme, ma'am. Ah coming because Ah want to look at you' face. Ma'am. I meet plenty people in my day, but sometimes when I stand up and look at you Ah say to meself: 'Samlal, boy, you meet plenty handsome ladies in you' life, but dis lady Mrs. Hurst, she hard to beat.' Morning, Ma'am!"

One Saturday after this Miss Rawle smiled at him and said: "I hear you go next door, too, Samlal – to Mrs. Hurst's place."

"Yes, ma'am," he said. "De missy, she call me in one Saturday afternoon. She's a kind-hearted lady, too, ma'am – jest like you."

"Is she?" Samlal missed the slightly chilly note. "Anyway, I'm very glad for your sake, Samlal. It means you'll have a little more to see you through the week."

"Dat's so, ma'am. Every lit' bit add up. Money is a funny t'ing, Miss Rawle ma'am. Sometimes you look at a shilling and you feel you got plenty in you' hand. Ha! But when you in de bush is a different story, ma'am. In de bush all de money wha' you got don't count for nutting. Food is what you prize most above everyt'ing in de bush. Ah never tell you how de Potagee boy and me nearly loss all de food we had in de falls, ma'am?" So he went on to relate the adventure. He sat there on the third treader and gesticulated graphically, lurched this way and that way to show how the boat rocked, cried out in a dramatic voice when he came to the part where the boat nearly capsized.

That morning Miss Rawle gave him a half-crown instead of the usual shilling. And that afternoon, when he told Mrs. Hurst about the tourist gentleman and his aunt from Montreal who lost a live snake which they kept in a cage no bigger than a soda-cracker tin and eventually found it coiled up in a lady's shoe in another guest's room, Mrs. Hurst said that he deserved two shillings – and gave him two shillings.

In thanking her he said: "Ma'am, sometimes when Ah look at you' hand, how it shape so nice, and Ah remember it was dis hand wha' give me dis coin, Ah don't feel like spending it. Ah feel like if Ah can keep it in a box wid velvet and put it away as if it's somet'ing valuable mek out of gold."

Mrs. Hurst pinkened a trifle and told him he was making fun. "I bet you, you tell every lady that, Samlal," she twinkled.

He shook his head gravely. "No, ma'am – not every lady I can tell dat to. Only a lady like you who mek me feel happy inside I can tell dat to. From de minute I see you, ma'am, dat first Saturday I come here, Ah say to meself: 'Samlal! Oh, gawd, boy! You born wrong. If you did born in good class you coulda ask dis lady to marry you.' Yes, dat's what Ah say to meself plenty times, ma'am."

Mrs. Hurst went a deeper pink and turned aside her face, shaking with laughter which she tried hard to suppress, for it would not have sounded well for the neighbours to hear her laughing and joking with a beggar.

The following Saturday Miss Rawle said to him as she handed him a dollar-note: "Samlal, I heard that Mrs. Hurst next-door won't be at home this afternoon. She's gone into the country, and I thought it might shorten your cash for the coming week if you don't get anything from her today, that's why I thought I'd give you a dollar."

Miss Rawle made this speech in a self-conscious voice, and did not meet his gaze as she spoke, but Samlal saw no reason why he should doubt her word, so that afternoon he did not call on Mrs. Hurst.

Next Saturday, Miss Rawle handed him a dollar again, and when he asked her whether the lady next door had come back from the country, she became shifty-eyed and replied: "What's that? Oh, I don't know. I have no idea at all." Her tone was so definitely stiff that Samlal had to wonder whether he had done or said something to offend her. In a deeply concerned voice he asked: "Miss Rawle ma'am, you ain' vexed wid me dis morning, Ah hope, ma'am?"

"Vexed with you? Most certainly not, Samlal! Why should you think so?" She spoke so emphatically and smiled so reassuringly that his fears vanished. He grunted and said: "Why Ah ask, ma'am, is because so much time in me life people get vexed wid me for nutting at all. Ah have bad luck, you know, Miss Rawle ma'am. Very bad luck. Ah never tell what Professor Zimbar tell me when Ah was working at de Hotel Tower, ma'am? One day Ah was walking through de dining-room serving as a waiter, and Professor Zimbar was sitting at a table talking to a rich lady who live in Kingston. Ah won't call names, ma'am, but Ah can tell you dat she used to go for drives to Scandal Point wid a gentleman who working at de Treasury. Well, ma'am, Professor Zimbar tell me dat day Ah born under a funny planet..."

Before he left Miss Rawle was chuckling and twinkling in her old way, and she told him not to forget to come again next Saturday.

But as he was about to go past the cottage next door he heard a voice call his name. He stopped and looked up. It was Mrs. Hicks, Mrs. Hurst's old aunt. She leant out of a gallery window and smiled: "Samlal, why didn't you come last Saturday afternoon? The missy looked out for you."

Samlal hobbled closer to the parapet. "Ma'am, Ah hear de lady was in de country, dat's why Ah didn't come."

"In the country? Who could have told you such a thing? That's not true. She went nowhere at all. She looked out for you and wondered why you didn't come."

His face went blank. He stammered out: "Oh! No, no, ma'am. Ah did t'ink – somebody tell me she was in de country. Awright, ma'am. Ah will come dis afternoon."

That afternoon Mrs. Hurst's manner was inclined to be chilly. She said: "I thought you had decided not to come back, Samlal."

Samlal wagged his head and assumed an expression of deep grief. "Ow, ma'am! Ow, Mrs. Hurst ma'am!" he exclaimed. "You say a t'ing like dat, ma'am! How you can say dat to me, Mrs. Hurst ma'am! Every day, every night Ah have you in me mind, and yet you can say such a t'ing, ma'am! Ma'am, de lady next door tell me last Saturday dat you gone in de country, dat's why Ah ain' see me. Otherwise, you know Ah woulda come, ma'am!"

"Oh, the lady next door told you I was in the country? Miss Rawle?"

"Yes, ma'am. Miss Rawle tell me so, dat's why Ah ain' come."

"Oh, I see. Well, in future I'd advise you not to pay attention to everything you hear. I never go anywhere on Saturday afternoons. You can always find me here between one o'clock and five. I can't imagine why Miss Rawle should have told you such a thing. Or perhaps I do know," she added in a mumble, grunting significantly.

"Perhaps she hear wrong, ma'am. But dat's what she tell me. She even give me a dollar to mek up for what you would give me dat day."

"She did, eh?" A cryptic smile passed over her face. "All right, Samlal. Anyway," she went on, in a voice falsely cheerful, "I asked a gentleman friend of mine for a few old shirts, and I had them here since last Saturday to give you. You can have them now if you care."

Samlal went off into a gushing speech of gratitude. "Ma'am," he ended up, "they shoulda have more ladies like you in dis world, true! True, Mrs. Hurst ma'am! Ah used to say dat same t'ing when Ah was working as butler wid some big people in Brickdam a few years back. Ah say to de mistress one day: 'Ma'am, you ain't got a heart or you woulda give me dis old jacket wha' belong to de master.' And she turn to me and say: 'You not having a single t'ing dat belong to my husband, you nasty coolie!' Yes, ma'am, dat's what she say. And, Mrs. Hurst ma'am, Ah know you won't talk, tell dis to nobody, ma'am, but dat lady – Ah won't call her name – but she had over twelve gentlemen friends, and she husband, he was a invalid…"

Before he left Mrs. Hurst gave him a two-dollar note, and, laughing, told him: "All right, Samlal, come back next Saturday. Believe me, you're a cure! I know who is the lady you mean, but don't repeat what you've told me to everybody, or it might get you in trouble."

The following Saturday he appeared at Miss Rawle's place in one of the shirts given to him by Mrs. Hurst, and Miss Rawle opened her eyes and said: "Why Samlal ! You've got a new shirt!" But when he explained how he had come into possession of it, Miss Rawle raised her brows and exclaimed: "Oh ! So *she* gave it to you! I see."

"Yes, ma'am. Is a nice shirt. Ah like it. Mrs. Hurst is a very good lady. She got good looks, and she got a good heart –"

"Oh, I've heard you say that before. You needn't repeat it. Look! Here you are!" She suddenly fumbled in her skirt pocket, handed him a sixpence, then turned abruptly and went inside.

The cook, at the kitchen window, sniggered, and Samlal stared at her and uttered a faint: "Eh-eh!"

Later that day he told Mrs. Hurst: "Ma'am, well, it look like dis shirt you gimme bringing me trouble. De missy next door speak to me short dis morning." When he related what had happened, Mrs. Hurst frowned and said: "You mean, you told her that it was I who gave you this shirt?"

"Yes, ma'am. She ask me where Ah get it and Ah say you give me. Ah tell she how you so kind and how you ask you' gentleman friend for some clothes for me –"

"What! But, Samlal! How could you have told her such a thing! Didn't I mention to you that you weren't to say anything about it?"

Samlal looked dismayed. He shook his head weakly. "No, ma'am. You didn' tell me that."

She clicked her tongue. "But you ought to have known better than to go discussing my business with her. Samlal. I suppose she'll go telling everybody now that I'm cadging clothes from my gentlemen friends to give to you, and I'll be the laughing-stock in the city!"

"But, Mrs. Hurst ma'am, why she should want to talk you' name –"

"Oh, shut up! It's the worst when anyone tries to be kind to your class of people!"

She moved inside, slamming the door in his face, and all he could do was to stare at the weather-mottled surface of the closed door and exclaim: "Eh-eh?" in a stupefied murmur. When he was going down the steps he added: "Well, I really did feel I did know how dese big people behave, but dis best all – true! Eh-eh!"

As he was on his way along the street, he heard a voice call his name, and looking up, saw a lady's face at the window of a gallery. She smiled and said: "Samlal, come round to the back. I have something for you."

He stared at her uncertainly, hesitated, then mumbled: "Awright, ma'am," and a few minutes later she handed him a threepenny bit and said: "Samlal, I hear you're famous for your stories. Sit down and tell me one."

He shook his head. "No, ma'am. Ah don't know no stories."

"You don't know any stories! You're making fun, man. Tell me one."

"No, ma'am. Ah never got no more stories to tell nobody again."

"But why? What's happened to change you so suddenly?"

When he told her what had just occurred she gave him a sympathetic nod and said: "Yes, I understand, Samlal. Some people are very narrow-minded. You mustn't trouble."

"Anyway, ma'am, I cure from today. Ah not talking one more story to nobody in me life again. Ah keeping a quiet tongue in future. Oh, yes, ma'am. It don't pay to talk too much. Ah remember once Ah meet a gentleman from New York when Ah was working at de Park Hotel, and he tell me dat same t'ing. He stop me one day in de lounge and he say: 'Samlal, tek a advice from me. You mustn' talk so much. It going to get you in trouble one day'."

"He told you that, eh? And what did you say?"

"Ah agree with him, ma'am. Ah shoulda follow his advice, because he was a fine gentleman, ma'am." He seated himself on one of the steps and rested his crutch. "Oh, yes, he was a fine gentleman. Ah meet him one day again in de bar and he talk nice wid me. He say he used to work in a big skyscraper in New York, and his wife, she was a lady who had a sister who was a film-star – Ah won't call no names, but you see she often at pictures, ma'am – and de gentleman tell me dat once he and his wife, they go to Hollywood and they see some funny sights wha' everybody don't see. Oh, Lawd! Ma'am! De t'ings dat gentleman say he see! He say one day he was walking along de street and he happen to glance aside into a swimming-pool…"

"All right, Samlal. You must come again, see? Here's something else to go along with what I gave you just now. Come again…"

THE CRUEL FATE OF KARL AND PIERRE

I could tell this tale in a spirit of levity, but there are too many tears in it; too much of that indiscriminate cruelty which is so often a blind feature of our human destiny. I have been able to piece it together through three people who must remain anonymous. One is an acquaintance who was in the Trinidad navy with me; the two others are ladies, who like my naval acquaintance, were in close touch with the family about which our story is concerned.

This family, the de la Framlins, is of French Creole stock, and, therefore, considerably well up in Trinidad society. "De la Framlin" is, of course, a fictitious name, for convenience (and good taste), I intend to use; though, in any event, I think the name sounds rather well for such a family.

The grey stone house of Norman-Gothic style situated on the outskirts of Port-of-Spain has, for more than seventy years, been the residence of the de la Framlins who have intermarried a great deal, and, as a result – I have been informed – are today not quite in a eugenically satisfactory condition. However true or not this may be, it is well-known that Karl, the second son of the present generation, is never allowed to leave the house, "the health of his nerves being not very good," and Pierre, the youngest son, "now presumed dead," was of somewhat undeveloped mental capacity.

As what I am about to relate is chiefly concerned with these two members of the family, I think it would be fitting to paint a brief picture of each before proceeding to the events which culminated so ruefully – and I say "ruefully" because I am still undecided whether "tragically" would be the *mot juste*. However, later you will judge for yourself.

Karl, according to one of my lady acquaintances, is very pale, with sunken cheeks, and his blue-grey eyes contain always an unnatural, fanatic stare. He wears his light-brown hair long, but is "generally well-groomed about the chin and lips."

It was not until after leaving school at the age of nineteen that he showed the first signs of "serious nervous unrest." He was a runner-up for an Island Scholarship, and his disappointment at not being a winner affected him profoundly. His family could easily have afforded to send him to Oxford without the aid of a government scholarship – and, indeed, had had every intention of doing so – but Karl was not satisfied with this; his vanity had received an irreparable wound, and he accused the examiners and the Scholarship Board of unfair treatment. He refused to be consoled, and within a fortnight of the announcement of the Scholarship results had worked himself into a frenzy against both his family and the government. Everyone was opposed to him, he said. His parents and his brothers and sisters and the Director of Education were plotting to disgrace him, to "cast him into outer darkness", to quote his precise words.

He took to pacing in the front garden and reading aloud passages from Isaiah and the Psalms and calling down vengeance upon his persecutors.

This was Karl's "first major nervous breakdown" (for reasons agreed upon between my informants and myself, we must satisfy ourselves with descriptive phrases of this nature, which I quote faithfully as they were told to me; perhaps it would be unnecessary for me to mention that this story delves into the affairs of a well-known family whose connections are of the very best). He did recover to some extent, but, upon a medical advice, his people decided that it would be best to keep him at home under continuous surveillance, and, as it proved, this was no unwise decision, for he suffered a relapse within a few months of "the first breakdown" and from that time to the present day "has not been well"; so much so, indeed, that it was found compulsory to employ an extra male domestic to attend upon him unremittingly (my naval acquaintance, before joining the navy, happened to have been the domestic thus employed).

We must now turn to Pierre.

From babyhood, Pierre had "betrayed signs of lacking mental brilliance", and as he grew older the rest of the family were compelled to resign themselves to his unfortunate condition, realizing that there was no remedy. Ironically, he was a handsome and well-formed young man, blue-eyed and fair-haired, and always of a pleasant disposition, though, due to "his misfortune", possessed only a limited vocabulary and was much given to sucking his thumb and going through somewhat unorthodox choreographic motions on awkward occasions – especially when visitors were present in the "spacious and very tastefully decorated drawing-room." But save for these embarrassing habits, he gave no trouble whatever and even indulged in afternoon walks on the Savannah, unaccompanied, returning without misadventure.

He was the only member of the family whom Karl, "during his illness", could tolerate in his room which was situated in the north-eastern section of the house. In their odd way, Karl and Pierre got on very well together, the bond that linked them being one of "higher philosophy of an eschatological trend" (Karl's exact words overheard by my naval acquaintance). For many days, or even weeks, Karl would become Spinoza (or sometimes Comte) and murmur to himself of "the final phases of the human soul in relation to the idealistic conception of cosmic matter" (Karl's exact words overheard by Miss —).

Our story really centres around the events of a certain day in July, 1941, but to allow you to appreciate fully what occurred on this day I must first dwell with some detail on the relationship that existed between Karl and Pierre during the two years preceding this day.

Pierre was a soft-hearted fellow, but his world (for ostensible reasons) being of limited scope, he found very little upon which to bestow his affection. Moreover, before Karl's "indisposition", Pierre had found himself an object of complete disinterest. Indeed, he was spurned and jeered at by the rest of the family, and sometimes even physically mishandled, for, because of his "mental inadequacy," he was a great nuisance who often had to be apologized for to visitors and kept out of the way as much as possible in order that the family's name and prestige might not suffer too great a humiliation. From early boyhood his one object of affection had been a tree – a distant tree that stood out prominently on the summit of one of the jungled hills which form a semicircle around Port-of-Spain.

Many a time Pierre could be observed standing at the window of his room, in the north-western section of the house, smiling up at the hills and wagging his head. And if you were within earshot (as my three acquaintances often were) you could hear him murmuring endearments addressed to the tree. It had become a minor legend in the family. "Pierre's tree on the hills"… "Pierre is in love with a tree"…"I believe it's a saman"… "Looks like rain this afternoon. There's a cloud over Pierre's tree"… "An aeroplane is passing over Pierre's tree"…

Then when Karl "fell ill", he, too, began to share his younger brother's interest in the tree. Sometimes he would call Pierre into his room and tell him that it was time to "lift up our eyes to the hills and contemplate upon the infinity of yon tree" (exact words overheard on several occasions by Mrs— and my naval acquaintance), and the two of them would stand at the window for an hour or more watching the tree, Pierre rubbing his hands together and wagging his head beatifically and crooning softly, "My tree. My lovely tree," and Karl, his face grave and vacant and transfigured with a baffled reverence, staring up in a tranced silence.

Presently, Pierre would show signs of boredom and say that he was going, but his brother would pay no heed to him – and so Pierre, with a soft cooing simper, would indulge in a caper and leave the room, sucking his thumb happily as he went downstairs or made his way to his own room.

Karl's solemn vigil might continue for a long time after Pierre's departure, and, finally, he would whisper something inaudible, raise his hand to his forehead in a leisurely salute and then begin to pace agitatedly, arguing with an unseen debater on problems of an eschatological nature. The tree figured in many of these discussions. Indeed, it appeared to be the focal point of all differences and doubts, and once Karl was overheard to remark passionately: "But I tell thee, Pilate, such a tree by its very remoteness suggests ethereal sacrifices."

A pause while it must be assumed that he was listening to "Pilate's" reply. Then: "I see thy point, but whence can one obtain an animal to offer in crucifixion?"

Pause. Pilate's turn…

"Him, sayest thou? Mine own brother, Pilate? What would Caesar say? To Caesar must we answer for our acts, remember! Thy governorship over Judea will surely be imperilled by such rashness, man!"

Pause…

"Perhaps thou art right, after all. Pontius. Very well. The axe in the stable. An afternoon of dense blue mist. I shall remember and obey. *Ave, Caesar! Morituri e salutant*! 'And then and then came Spring, and Rose-in-hand – My threadbare Penitence apieces tore.'" Karl sat down on his bed and burst into tears.

This incident (witnessed by two of my informants) occurred in April, 1941, and might, in many ways, be considered the prelude to what followed between April and July and on the particular day itself in the latter month.

Daily after this Karl would demand that his younger brother should come to his room for "communion with yon ethereal tree." Once (says my naval acquaintance) Pierre happened to be out on one of his Savannah promenades when Karl's shrieking voice flared through the house demanding the presence of his younger brother, and even though both the Master of the House and my naval acquaintance tried to quiet him it was to no avail. He gibbered and capered and indulged in "unmentionable profanities both of word and deed."

At this point I deem it essential to interpose a word of caution. Like any sincere recorder, I am doing my best to tell this tale in a spirit of truth. This, of necessity, involves, at times, a certain lapse of delicacy, despite efforts to the contrary, and I am sure that my readers will pardon any obvious *faux pas* I may commit if they bear in mind that errors of taste perpetrated in the cause of truth cannot always be considered opprobrious.

Karl, I must record, then, on this notable afternoon, cursed not only his parents and sisters and brothers but "the priest of the Holy Church" and the respective governments of Trinidad and Great Britain. He raved about "the effeteness of degenerate French creole families" and elaborated on this topic, referring to the airs that "this aristocratic riff-raff of the tropics" assumed. He indicted the country Club where (he said) "the corrupt backwash of the Island's population" besported itself with "simpering artificiality that passes for high social distinction." He bawled the details of past scandals and recounted the "insidious manipulations" of certain highly placed government officials, going on to say that because of the "invulnerable loftiness of those exploiting stooges of a decadent imperialism" their deeds were "hushed up and condoned."

At this point in his absurd and fatuous ravings, he was overpowered and gagged, the gardener and yard-boy having come to the assistance of my naval acquaintance and the Master of the House. The family doctor was summoned, and after an injection of morphine had been administered, "the indisposed young man" fell into a troubled slumber.

Between this day and that critical day in July he was fairly quiet, and except for the usual "dialogues" in his room and the tree-gazing ritual at the window in the company of Pierre, he indulged in no outbursts. For this the rest of the family was thankful, for the marriage of the eldest daughter, Avril, was approaching, and though it was not planned to hold a very grand wedding reception (for reasons which I shall presently state), it would not be pleasant if Karl became violent when the function was in progress. His shrieks were always audible in every section of the house and grounds – and even on the street – and an outburst could no more be concealed than the rolling of thunder.

Avril, the eldest daughter, is a high-spirited, self-willed, and attractive girl (even today, after five years of marriage, she is unchanged), but it is these very qualities which brought down upon her the disfavour of her parents. Refusing to conform with the family custom of "mixing within her own class," she had fallen in love with a sergeant-major – an Englishman, brought out to Trinidad for the duration of the war, and, if not nationally and religiously, at least, racially, eligible. But nevertheless, a sergeant-major. As her father had pointed out to her, "such an attachment, is both ecclesiastically indelicate and socially undesirable." But Avril, firm of will and fashioned not precisely after the orthodox de la Framlin pattern, held out that not only would she continue to be in love with the sergeant-major but that she would "most assuredly" marry whomsoever she wished to marry. Discerning her determination and fearing that were she thwarted, "the consequences for her nervous state" might be as grave as they had proven in the case of her brother Karl, her parents gave in but in doing so, informed her that the wedding would have to be "a very quiet one."

"Had he even been a subaltern," said her father, "we might have considered a proper wedding. However…"

However, the point remains that Avril's quiet wedding was fixed for a certain Saturday in July (the exact date must remain undisclosed). Only a few relatives and close friends were invited and the guests, therefore, were not expected to number more than two hundred and fifty.

The day broke with a drizzle, and the hills could be seen through tissue curtains of mist so that the dark-green jungled slopes had an unreal and elfin look. Pierre's tree, far away on high, stood like a frayed spectre against the chilly sky. As the morning wore on, however, the mist and clouds dispersed, and soon you could watch the dense verdure emerging in detailed clumps deeply shadowed where the valleys made elongated dents in the whole humped pattern. Shale escarpments stood out bright-red, like abrupt wounds inflicted by some wanton giant on the looming landscape.

Preparations for the wedding had thrown the household into a state of bustling agitation. Servants hurried here and there, and the telephone rang at frequent intervals. Delivery vans from groceries kept arriving and departing. Voices and the clatter of crockery and cutlery and the lisp of garments combined to send an animated breath of urgency throughout the old house.

At around ten o'clock a painful and unhappy, though by no means untypical, incident occurred. I would rather not, but find that I must, record it; it is an illustration without which our overall picture would be robbed of much significance.

Pierre, discovered in the pantry eating meat pâtés intended for the afternoon's function, was being severely scolded by the housekeeper, Mrs.— (my lady acquaintance) when the Eldest Son happened to pass by.

"That's all he's fit for?" blazed the Eldest Son. "To eat and fool about the house! He's a damned curse on our family! Happy the day when we're rid of him! Happy the day! Get out of here! Get out!" Grasping Pierre by the collar of his shirt, he hurled him along the corridor toward the kitchen.

Pierre squealed and besought his brother not to hurt him, saying that he would not do it again. Please! Please!

But the Eldest Son, as though further infuriated by these childlike entreaties, rushed at him and kicked him several times.

Pierre collapsed in a cringing heap near the latticed wall, and his brother caught him by an ankle and dragged him toward the kitchen door.

"Outside, you pest! Get out, you filthy, unwanted fool! Outside!" With a hefty kick, he sent his younger brother tumbling down the stairs into the yard, and even though the cook and a kitchen-maid cried out in rebuke, the Eldest Son was in no way cowed or shamed. He told the servants to shut their blasted mouths and mind their own business if they valued their jobs.

In the yard, Pierre, bruised and in pain, moaned pitifully. Getting slowly to his feet, he trotted off toward the kitchen-garden which was a favourite resort of his when he was chastised, for it was on a sloping plot of terrain and from here he could squat amid the shade of pumpkin and cucumber arbours and gaze up at his tree for consolation.

In the general fever of activity, the incident was forgotten, and when Pierre, an hour or so later, came into the house sucking his thumb, no one paid the slightest attention to him, or even thought of sympathizing with him or enquiring whether he had been badly hurt or not.

Pierre went upstairs and asked permission of my naval acquaintance to go into Karl's room.

As it happened, Karl, only a few minutes before, had, in the course of a soliloquy, expressed a desire to see his younger brother, so my naval acquaintance did not hesitate to unlock the door and let Pierre in.

Pierre spent the rest of that day in the room with his brother.

My naval acquaintance, after taking in the midday meal, and seeing that it was eaten (Karl shared it with his younger brother), locked the two young men in and went down to the kitchen, for his services for the rest of the day had been demanded by the housekeeper who said that she needed all the help it was possible to obtain for the function. Both the Master and the Mistress of the House agreed that they would have to "take the chance of leaving those two boys upstairs in the room there without surveillance."

"It can't be helped," said the Mistress, "and Karl has been rather quiet of late. I don't suppose there will be much risk."

At around noon, the unstable July weather produced a violent cloudburst, with rumblings of thunder and fierce brassy flashes of lightning. Heads were wagged and qualms were experienced for the success of the function, and the Old Aunt mumbled superstitiously that unlucky would be the bride upon whom the rain fell.

But the rain was gone within an hour, and the sun shone brilliantly again. Faces brightened and activity continued to rise. The telephone trilled almost continuously. Garments lisped. The names of servants were called upstairs and downstairs, and footsteps made a drumming shuffle along corridors and up and down stairs.

At three o'clock cars tooted and blared in the driveway, and the drone of their engines impregnated the air with an exigence and a sanctimonious fervour, so that even though you were struck by the importance of the occasion, you could not but smile at the way men can magnify their simple doings into elaborate perambulations.

At four o'clock the crescendo was at its peak, for the ecclesiastical part of the ceremony had been accomplished, and cars once again hummed and blared in the driveway, gleaming like polished insects in the hot sunshine. The guests were arriving from the church in couples and trios.

When the bride and groom arrived, the house dissolved in a cacophony of agitated gaiety.

"My dear! Have you seen Angela? Isn't she *sweet*!"

"And Joyce's hat – oh, my God! How *awful*"…

"… as usual, the Control Board won't allow it. Man, I'm fed-up"…

"Graves, what's the c.i.f. cost of those saucepans you brought down a few weeks ago by the *Advisor*?"…

"In *green* chiffon, I said! *Green*! And where's the photographer? The picture must appear in tomorrow's paper, don't you know that? Oh, my God! You newspaper men exasperate me!"

"Yes, my dear, Peter rigged up a party and took us to the Country Club… John? No, John wasn't there. Well, you know – of course, well, you see, he doesn't move in our set nowadays…"

"When I look upon this couple here this afternoon I'm reminded of my own happy day years and years ago…"

"Hear, hear!" Chuckles. Champagne glasses poised.

"And I say this, of course, well bearing in mind that times have changed. Today I'm looked upon as just an old fogey –." He breaks off to smile about him whimsically. Chuckles and pleasant murmurs, shuffle of feet. Champagne glasses still poised…

"That's the trouble, man. All these new war restrictions…"

"We haven't been able to import any fabrics this year…"

"And since these Americans have come here the city hot…"

The clapping of hands and laughter. And the infinite rustle of chiffon and tulle. The perfume from female bodies twined in incessant delight through the multitude of jostling human figures so that only the hills were untainted.

There was mist again on the hills, for the noon rain had cooled the jungle, and now that the sun was sinking behind slate-grey anvils of stratus the moisture from the green slopes rose in clustered blebs that spun a ghostly veil of blue along the whole undulating range: a spirit-web that hovered over the mysterious valleys whose gloomed depths were saturated with the purest lapis-lazuli.

The afternoon air smelt of leaves and earth. The sky had a mild, mauve look, and wisps of cirrus, like moist feathers, hung arrested in the east and south.

Then evening, in violet and indigo swathes, came down upon the hills, and the city's lights appeared in dotted spangles, scattered desultory in the gloom.

A soft wind from the east hummed around Framlin House, its earthy fragrance lost amid the scent of human sweat and the myriad musks of many pomades that swirled within the noisy drawing-room. The petrol fumes of lines of gleaming cars destroyed its sweet wet simplicity. Only in the dark north-easterly wing of the house did something respond in tune.

A flimsy white wraith that trailed down from an upper window to the ground swayed in gentle appreciation.

Shortly before midnight, when all but two or three of the guests had departed, my naval acquaintance discovered that which you have probably long suspected: Karl and Pierre were missing. The bedsheet, torn into strips and knotted together, was tied to the bed-rail.

The Mistress pronounced it as downright carelessness. "You should never have left him alone up there," she said.

"But, madam, you said it would be all right."

"I don't need to be reminded of what I said. Don't be impertinent! And why was no dinner taken up to them? Wasn't it your business to have seen that Mr. Karl was fed at seven o'clock?"

"Madam, at seven o'clock, I told you I was going up to take dinner for dem, but you tell me not to bother. You say de gentlemen in de drawing room had to have drinks and dat was more important dan teking up dinner to Mr. Karl!"

"Oh, indeed! So you're going to *argue* with me! Of all the confounded impudence! Daring to argue with me? You're dismissed! Do you understand? Dismissed! Get out of here! Outside!"

By nine o'clock the following morning search-parties were on their way up the hills, and the family was in a state of great anxiety. "Poor Karl!"… "Poor Pierre!"… "And Pierre was such a good, quiet boy!"… "He never troubled a soul," murmured the Eldest Son.

"And think of the scandal if they're never found," moaned the Old Aunt.

"Be quiet, Aunty," snapped the Mistress.

At noon, as on the day before, there was a violent rain – and thunderstorm, for, in Trinidad, the weather can be strangely repetitive at certain seasons. The lightning was exceptionally dangerous, and the Turf Club paddock was struck and a donkey in Belmont killed. The rain deluged down in large, savage drops, and the air became hazed and dismal with clouds of spray which the wind sent hurtling in gauzy billows across the landscape. The hills vanished in a grey spume of wetness, and water rushed in tumbling torrents along the streets, disappearing into the underground sewers with a hollow gurgle of menace.

And, also, as on the day before, within an hour it was all over, and the sun was shining again.

At around five that afternoon, Karl came staggering down the hillside to the north of the house, and made his way into the kitchen garden. He was a terrible figure, his clothes hanging in soiled and bloodstained rags about his thin form, his face and body scratched and bruised and bloody, his long hair matted and wild, his eyes in a blank, desperate glare.

The servants saw him and gave the alarm.

He was led toward the house by the Master of the House and the Eldest Son. They tried to question him, concerning the whereabouts of Pierre who had not yet been found (and who, indeed, has, to this day, not been found), but, as always since "his illness", Karl seemed not to hear them. He stared dully at them, lost among the rainbows of his own peculiar world. More than once, however, he would murmur to himself, smiling with a happy, tranced satisfaction: "The axe. It was the axe that did it. He is at peace now with yon ethereal tree. And it was the axe that did it. I thank thee, Pilate. Thou wert right."

"What axe can he mean?" muttered the Master of the House, glancing at the Eldest Son. But the Eldest Son could only shrug and shake his head. "I'm just as much in the dark as you, Papa."

"Wasn't there an axe in the stable?"

"Yes, I think so. You don't mean..."

"He said something about a tree, too."

Karl was wagging his head as they ascended the kitchen stair. Again he smiled and murmured to himself: "The axe. It was the axe that did it. He is happy now with yon ethereal tree. Safe from the brutalities of a bitter world, poor nitwit! And it was the axe that did it.   I thank thee, Pontius... 'And then and then came Spring and Rose-in-hand...'"

"What tree is this he's talking about?" the Master of the House began – and then, as they were on the point of entering the kitchen door, he turned his head and lifted up his eyes to the hills. His body stiffened; he paled a trifle and exclaimed softly: "But that's odd!"

"What's odd, Papa?" asked the Eldest Son.

"It's not there!"

"Not there?" The Eldest Son also lifted up his eyes to the hills – and he saw that his father was right. The tree was not there. Pierre's tree.

"Yes, but that's odd."

"It must have been the lightning today. Perhaps it was struck. It must have been struck down."

"Yes. Yes, of course. The lightning."

"Poor Pierre. I wonder..."

"The axe." Karl was murmuring again to himself, lost among the singing spirals of his bubble-world. "It was the axe that did it..."

Evening, in violet and indigo swathes, was coming down upon the hills. The air smelt of leaves and earth, and the sky had a mild, mauve look. The mysterious valleys were saturated with the purest lapis-lazuli.

JASMINE AND THE ANGELS

MOST of my acquaintances seem to imagine that because I am a prison doctor my life consists of one round of romantic encounters with criminals who are only dying to narrate to me their personal histories and adventures. This is not so, of course. In actuality, the convicts with whom I come in contact are generally shy fellows, or if not shy, morose. Most of those I attend upon, in fact, are grumblers or cynics or just plain and simple bores. The interesting ones – that is to say, those who seem to have a spark of genuine imagination and a kind of pathological genius for bawdy wit – I encounter only at a distance, so to speak, for these fellows, as a rule, keep perfect health and never need my ministrations.

It was not until last week that something really interesting happened to turn up – something, that is to say, which I suppose can be called romantic, though, to me, it had far more of the real and the pathetic than of romance.

In the women's section of the prison in this island there is an aloof middle-aged negress called Jasmine Latouche (middle-aged in looks for later I learnt that her age is thirty-eight). Previous to last week I had seen her only once, and that was about two months ago when the wardress who was accompanying me on my rounds pointed and murmured: "That's the one who came in for that terrible murder, Doctor Brame. Life sentence."

"What terrible murder ?" I asked her.

"Don't you remember reading about it? She's Jasmine Latouche, the woman who snatched up a cutlass and cut off the head of her little two-year-old son."

"Yes, I did read something of it. Is that she?"

The woman she indicated was lanky and thin, and had a sad, quiet, rather aloof mien.

She sat on a bench not far from the laundry shed picking coconut fibre, her dark-blue prison uniform, if anything, augmenting the sad aloofness of her long face with its high cheekbones.

The wardress seemed to divine my thoughts, after she grunted and remarked: "To look at her you wouldn't think she could have done it."

I agreed. "What defence did she put up?"

"None at all. She hasn't said a word to this day to anybody why she did it. You didn't read the case in the papers?"

"I'm afraid I seldom read the reports on murder cases."

"Well she kept silent all through the trial. Even when the police arrested her and questioned her she wouldn't say a word. But of course, she couldn't deny it, because two neighbours witnessed it. A queer woman. The Crown provided defence counsel for her, but she wouldn't tell the lawyer a word – not a single word. They even thought her out of her mind, but after the doctors observed her for a few weeks they certified her sane. Since she came out here she won't say a word to a soul, either. Just moves around quiet, quiet, all the time."

"You say she wantonly lopped off the head of her child?"

"Yes, Doctor. The witnesses say she was sitting on the step with her head bowed in prayer – she's very religious; always reading her Bible and praying. And a pigeon flew past over her and lighted on the roof just above the steps. The little child was playing in the yard, and seeing the bird, he just pointed up at it and called out Hi! Hi! and that must have disturbed her at her prayers, because she jumped up and snatched a cutlass and rushed down and cut his head right off. I really believe she ain' right in her head, even though the doctors certify her sane."

"You mean just because the little fellow called out hi at the pigeon she did a thing like that? It doesn't sound feasible to me."

"Well, Doctor, that's what both the witnesses say at the trial."

I did not argue.

Last week it was the same wardress who informed me that Jasmine Latouche was in need of medical attention. "She refused to work this morning, Doctor Brame. She say she has pains in her hands, but I believe it's nothing but just pretence. She ain' feel like working today, that's the whole matter."

We found her on the cot in her cell – lying on her back gazing up at the ceiling. She turned her head slightly at our entrance, but, on the whole, did not seem interested in us. The sad, aloof look was still on her face. When the wardress ordered her to sit up she obeyed but took her time about it, and somehow, I could not help being impressed by a certain dignity in her poise as she sat there, hands on her knees, her gaze on the floor, but not ashamed or humble – just unperturbed and detached.

"What's the matter with your hands, Jasmine?" I asked her.

"They hurting me, Doctor," she replied without looking up. It was a simple statement. There was hardly any emotion in her voice.

"Let's have a look at them."

Without a word, she raised them, palms upward, and I saw that there were water-boils on her thumbs and a slight puffiness about the tips of three other fingers. I called the attention of the wardress to this, but she clicked her tongue and said it was all pretence. "She can very well work, Doctor. I offer to put a piece of plaster on her thumb, but she won't let me." I nodded and asked her to leave the cell, for somehow, I sensed something unusual. I felt particularly drawn to this lanky creature sitting on the cot here. Murderess or no murderess, she had a nobility of her own, and my curiosity was whetted. I decided to learn what was behind these aloof eyes – behind this calm, sad face.

After the wardress had gone I looked at Jasmine and twinkled: "I can see you don't get on well with her, eh?"

She just smiled quietly and noncommittally murmured: "T'ank you, Doctor."

I seated myself on the cot beside her. She betrayed no surprise – just kept her head slightly bent, her hands on her knees, her eyes still fixed composedly on the floor. We might have been on a settee in a drawing-room about to begin a casual intimate conversation.

I told her that I believed something was on her mind. "It isn't only your hands that are sick. Jasmine. Am I right?"

She said nothing, but I heard her emit a soft grunt, and her lips seemed to twist slightly, though I could not be sure. I had the feeling that she was appraising me, silently sounding me out.

"What's the trouble? Care to tell me about it?"

The grunt she gave this time was more definite. It was as though she had arrived at some conclusion concerning my intentions. She nodded slightly, and the sad light in her eyes seemed to intensify. "Doctor, you talk like if you is a parson. You touch me soul."

I fidgeted. "The Government wouldn't like to hear that. They'd think I was exceeding my duties. I hear you're in prison on a lifetime sentence."

She nodded, but her face revealed nothing.

"You don't look the kind who could have done what I heard you did."

"Ah don't look so, na, Doctor?"

"What made you do it?"

She moved her head slightly and gave me a sidewise glance, seemed to consider something, staring past me, then she grunted deeply and said: "Ah didn' mean to talk about it to nobody, Doctor, but Ah jest mek up me mind."

I found myself fidgeting again. "Well, I'm very glad you trust me, Jasmine." I smiled.

"I always know who to trust, Doctor. Doctor, you see me here, I is funny woman. Ah doesn' carry on converse wid everybody. Me spirit must go out to a body before Ah can talk to dem. Ah don't mind if you repeat what Ah going to tell you dis morning. You can tell anybody you like – but as for me meself, no, Doctor – Ah wasn' going to converse wid one person except de Almighty God. Only He can understand what I do, dat's why I keep silent. But as you touch me soul dis morning, Doctor, Ah will tell you.

"Doctor, de Scripture say: 'Judge not lest ye be judged.' People look at me and they call me a murderess. Awright, Doctor. They say Ah brutal because of what Ah do four months back. But it matters not nutting to me what people t'ink, sir. So long as de loving God on high can see into my heart and know I is a righteous woman – dat's all dat matter to me. God know, Doctor, dat what Ah do dat day Ah do it because it was a righteous act. Yes, it was a act what Him above ordered – and so Ah do it."

She fell silent, and I saw that her eyes were moist. A tear swelled and glistened, hovered then ran down the dark brown cheek. For a while she almost seemed to forget my presence. She sat wagging her head slightly, her hands clasped together in her lap, her gaze fixed on the closed door.

I heard a sound that might have been a sigh or simply a deep breath taken as though to steel herself to go on.

"Ah know you must fancy Ah off me head for saying such a t'ing, Sir. It sound funny that a woman like me shoulda kill her son – and he was me only child, Doctor, and Ah did always pray to God to give me a child. When Alfred born it was in answer to a prayer – a earnest prayer. A year after he born me husband tek sick in de bush with blackwater fever and dead. He was up in de Mazaruni doing diamond work. During de year afterwards Ah do washing and mek souse and black-pudding – Ah work hard, Doctor, because one day me son woulda grow into a good man and serve de Lawd. Ah always say to meself: Jasmine you' boy must follow in de footsteps of de Saviour. He must tek holy orders. He must preach de gospel to sinners all over de world. He must save souls from damnation everlasting.' Yes, sir, Ah used to pray night and day to God to give me strength to work and save to send Alfred to school so dat he can grow up and serve de Lord Jesus.

"Ah watch that baby grow up day by day, Doctor. Mih spend me time caring him. Plenty nights he cry wid gripes, and Ah set up all night giving him bush-water to drink till de gripes pass. Once he get spasms and ah rush out de yard wild, calling 'pon Janie who live in de next cottage. Janie is a good friend, and she run and call Mr. Gobin, de dispenser, and Mr. Gobin come and put hot fomentation on de child, and save 'e life. Yes, Doctor, ah didn't spare no effort to care Alfred. Ah had all a mother's love for dat child, and nutting woulda break me heart more dan to see him stretch out in a coffin.

"But, Doctor, God is a wise and good God. He know all – all. Man can't know more dan God, Doctor. Man presumptious. Man build aeroplane to flyin' and God wrath! Yes, and man build submarine to sail under de water. Man defy de law of God in every way he can – *every* way! Dat's why war come and mek mankind suffer. God punish mankind for his presumptiousness. Ay, Doctor! when Ah sit down and study what going on in de world today Ah shed bitter tears. Ah bow down wid sorrow for mankind. I am not without sin, Doctor. I am a humble woman, and when Ah hear de voice of God speaking to me, I tremble. From childhood Dear-aunt train we-all up to read de Scripture and Worship de Almighty in His wisdom on high, and now in me thirty-ninth year Ah can't afford to let Satan use me. No, Doctor!"

She was silent again, sighing deeply and wagging her head, and watching her, I knew I was in the presence of a great and simple honesty. There was no hypocrisy here. She believed in herself, believed in her way of thinking, believed that the world about her was false while she herself was true – she Jasmine Latouche who had been put in prison for life for murdering her two-year-old son. She was a child of God, and no argument would alter her outlook; she said her prayers morning and night, read her Bible, and walked in the path of righteousness – and a whole army would not change her views. To have interrupted and told her that she was talking to a confirmed atheist who believed that religion was the most retarding influence in the civilized world would have been not only irrelevant but even irreverent. So I simply kept silent, too, and waited.

"On de night before Ah kill Alfred, Doctor," she continued, "Ah had a dream, and in dat dream de Lord God of Hosts send a angel to speak to me. Yes, Doctor, Ah can tell you because me soul go out to you, and Ah know you won't laugh at me. De police woulda laugh at me. De judge and de jurymen woulda all laugh at me, so Ah keep quiet in de courthouse and won't say not a word to defend myself. But Ah say it again, Doctor, de night before Ah kill Alfred Ah had a dream – and, Doctor, you listen to dis dream and see if you, as a God-fearing man, wouldn'ta do jest what I do.

"Doctor, de angel of de Lord appear to me in me sleep, and de angel say: 'Jasmine, de Lord God hath send me to speak to you, woman.'

"Ah fall down before de radiance, Doctor, and cry out: 'Your humble servant listening, angel.' And de angel blow a trumpet and other angels appear and bear me up to heaven like Elijah.

"And de first angel say to me: 'Jasmine, you now in de presence of your Almighty God. Hearken to me and hear what I have to say to you.'

"Ah crouch down, Doctor, and Ah shut me eyes tight to keep out de shining light of Eternity from above, and de angel speak: 'Jasmine, you have a son – dat not true?'

"And Ah say: 'Yes, angel dat true. Ah have a son who God give me two years gone, praise be to His name!'

"Den de angel blew his trumpet and a loud voice sound from above me, and God speak to me, Doctor. God: say 'Jasmine, you is a unhappy woman. You have done no fault in my sight, my child. But to you fall de lot of bearing a son who when he grow into a man will bring death and destruction to millions of people. Yes, Jasmine, I say unto you, you have give birth to such a man as Hitler or Mussolini. Woman, what will you do? Will you let dis child grow to manhood and cause misery to de world?'

"Ow, Doctor! Ow! De Almighty, talk and tell me dis. What I must answer and say, Doctor? What to say? Doctor, I tremble. I tremble and tremble, and den I feel de sweat a running down me face, and Ah don't know yet what to answer. Den de Lord God speak again. He say: 'Jasmine, you have done no wrong in my sight, but dis great evil hath befallen you. Go, woman, and do as thy conscience direct you.'

"Sudden me voice come up, Doctor, and Ah reply. Ah say: 'Ow, heavenly God! Alfred is me only child and I care him well all dese days. Ah want him to grow into a man and serve you, God. Ah promise to bring him in de Light. God, spare his life to grow up and serve you, Ah beseech you!'

"Ah wait trembling, Doctor, trembling and sweating. Ah feel sick and don't know what to t'ink. Den de Lord God speak again. He say: 'My child, man must go his way. Your son was born under a evil planet, and he must grow into what the evil direct him to grow into. I say he will bring misery upon millions of innocent women and children. He will rule the big countries and cause wars and death and pestilence. Go thy way and do as thou think fit, woman. Pray to me, and I will give you a sign dat my words are not in vain. Pray to me, woman, and I will direct you.'

"And den Ah wake up, Doctor, and Ah was sweating all over and trembling, because Ah know Ah jest come from de presence of de Almighty. All dat morning Ah couldn' do no work. All de washing pile up and leave in de tub. Me mind upset so much, Doctor, ow! Me only son, Doctor – de boy who Ah put me hopes in to grow into a man of God! And now de Almighty Himself appear in a dream and tell me dat Alfred going to grow into an evil man like Hitler. Doctor, Ah walk all over de yard dat day, watching de child play. Ah shed tears, and people see me and ask me what Ah crying for, but Ah jest keep all in me chest here. Ah so worried Ah ain' know how to sit down or stand up, Doctor. Den Ah fall asleep after one o'clock, and sudden a angel appear in a dream, and de angel smile and say: 'Jasmine, if you don't want to kill you' son, don't do it. Let him grow into a man. Everyt'ing will be well with you.' Ah wake up wid a start, Doctor, and me head turn all round confused. But Ah *feel* glad. Ah feel happy Ah didn' know what to do. Ah walk around shaking me head and giving thanks to God for letting me see de Light. Ah begin to do me washing, Doctor, but sudden a voice begin to whisper dat suppose the second angel what Ah see in me daytime dream was Satan disguised. Suppose it was Satan appear to me to sow evil in my mind! Ah begin to get worried again, and Ah stop washing and walk about. But after a while Ah decide dat Ah must obey the words of de second angel. It was God speaking to me telling me how to act. Ah must have faith and not doubt. So Ah decide dat me worries all pass and Ah must go on working and bringing up Alfred to a man who can serve de Lord.

"Toward late afternoon Ah feel good in me mind, and Ah kneel down on de steps to pray to God to give Him thanks for his goodness during de day. Alfred was playing about nearby in de yard, Doctor, and Ah had no thoughts of evil whatsoever in me mind. Ah jest kneel dere praying.

"Sudden, Doctor, what happen? As Ah had me head bowed down dere praying, Ah hear a fluttering above me, and a voice inside me tell me dat it was de angel of de Lord. A true angel, Doctor. De voice say to me: 'Jasmine, dat other angel what you dream today was Satan' angel. It speak to you in evil and misdirect you. Dis is de true angel of God over you now.'

"And den, Doctor, all of a sudden, a light shine in me soul, and de angel speak to me.

"It say: 'Jasmine, raise your eyes a minute and see what sign God has brought before you!'

"Ah lift me eyes, Doctor, and what Ah behold?

"Dere before me at de bottom of de steps, Doctor, me son Alfred was standing, and as Ah see you here, Doctor, dat lil two-year-old child raise 'e hand and cry out: 'Heil! HEIL!'

"In dat minute, Doctor, Ah see dat de Lord God speak true. My son was a evil man. Dat lil' child raise 'e hand again and cry out: HEIL! HEIL!' Just like Hitler, Doctor! 'HEIL! HEIL!' Alfred cry out. And, Doctor, Ah jest rush downstairs and Ah pick up a cutlass and ah cut-off 'e head. And Ah would do it again, Doctor. I have saved de world from misery! I have saved women and children in de future, Doctor! I have killed a dictator! De Lord's name be praised!"

WEST INDIAN RIGHTS

We are gathered to welcome him home – the demobilized airman from England. The ship was expected to dock at about seven o'clock that evening, and the airman, Rupert, should be with us by eight o'clock – perhaps earlier. So we were at his parents' home waiting. As soon as he came we would have dinner.

It was a fairly large cottage, and the sitting-room was spacious. The furniture was not luxurious – if anything, antiquated and shabby – but it was comfortable.

Mr. Albert Borman, Rupert's father, sat opposite me on the Chesterfield with his daughter, Pearl, and a very good friend of Pearl's, Yvonne. Mrs. Telfer, Mr. Borman's sister-in-law and an aunt of mine, had taken a Morris chair by the radio which stood on a low mahogany table with carved legs in the north-western corner, and not far from her Mrs. James sat in a bent-wood rocker, her four-year-old daughter Pamela in her lap. Mrs. James is Mr. Borman's second cousin.

Raymond, a good friend of Rupert's – Rupert and Raymond grew up together and were school-chums – half leant, half sat on a windowsill smoking and addressing occasional comments to the room in general. He has a droll, chaffing manner which females find attractive; males think it entertaining, as a rule.

As for me, it may be well to mention that I am Horace, a nephew of Mrs. Borman's – her sister Edith's son.

Mrs. Borman you will have noticed, was not with us. It had been agreed that she should be on the wharf to meet Rupert. Her husband had wanted to go with her, but she had told him no, how could he go and leave us all in the house like this! It would not be the correct thing.   My aunt has a strong sense of propriety.

From where I sat I could see into the dining-room. There was a clock on a shelf – a black clock with polished nickel ornamentations and ornamental hands. It said twenty-five past seven.

Perhaps Mr. Borman discerned that I was noting the time, for he suddenly called to Raymond: "Well, he should be here any moment, Ray!" As he spoke his hand darted a little nervously into an inner coat pocket, but then he has always been a fidgety man. Some people say he suffers from St. Vitus' dance, but I doubt that this is really so; it is simply in his nature to fidget. Something like his smile. He is never without a smile, even in moments when he should be serious. Being a Christian Scientist probably accounts for this, however. A Christian Scientist, I understand, must never look gloomy.

Raymond said that he thought he had heard the ship's siren. Raymond is of middle height, thickset, twenty-five, and very dark in complexion, with close-cut kinky hair. His features are European.

Pearl laughed and said that he was imagining things.

"You always think I imagining something! I hear the siren, I tell you! You think I telling a dry lie straight so, man?"

"Well, I didn't hear it," said Pearl.

Yvonne giggled.

Pearl is a deep olive, not very pretty, twenty-two, and with black, kinky hair artificially straightened. Yvonne is sallow, twenty-four, with reddish, kinky hair, also artificially straightened. Her features are more negroid than Pearl's, but her eyes are grey-green while Pearl's are dark-brown. Pearl has personality, is witty and gay, but Yvonne is quietish, retiring, and has a habit of giggling at the slightest provocation.

In the dining-room the table was laid for dinner, and now and then the clink of cutlery or the clatter of crockery could be heard as the servants fiddle about with things. These sounds filtered through the dance-music the radio was emitting.

Pearl asked me if I could see the clock from where I sat. I said yes and told her the time.

Pamela, Mrs. James's little girl, ran across the room to Raymond.

"Why you sitting on the window?" she asked, smiling up at him. She is a pretty thing with a perky face, bright eyes, sallow complexion, and resembles her mother very much. Her mother is an extremely attractive woman – twenty-eight and slim and shapely, and with hair like an Indian's and a pale olive complexion. She has been married six years, but Pamela is her only child.

Raymond laughed. "But child, you rude, yes! Eh-eh!" He glanced at her mother. "Kathleen! You hear what this child come and asked me? She want to know why I sitting on the windowsill!"

"I don't see how that's a rude question!" Pearl called him. "The child perfectly right! We have chairs to sit on, you know!"

"I didn't ask your opinion!" Raymond called back. "I talking to Kathleen! Why you don't mind you' own business, na?"

"Boy, you properly conceited!"

Kathleen smiled round at him and called out a brief pleasantry in an absentminded tone, for she was relating to Mrs. Telfer how easy it was to get cloth in Trinidad nowadays. "Anything you want. They begging you to buy the cloth. And a year or two ago! Oh, Lord! You had to scheme to get a half-yard…"

Eight o'clock came, but Rupert had not yet turned up.

"Perhaps the boat was delayed at the *boca*," Yvonne murmured.

"What could delay it at the *boca?*" I said.

Raymond had just joined Kathleen and Pamela and Mr. Telfer. He had pulled up the piano stool and had seated himself beside Kathleen to whom he was talking, his tone and his eyes making it obvious that he was not averse to a little flirtation. Kathleen seemed flattered by his attempts but her manner toward him was one of amusement rather than of response.

The radio was playing a tinkling tune. Something Spanish. Tinkle, tinkle – and then a flute opened an animated melody; the tinkle-tinkle continuing as an accompaniment.

Mr. Borman, who had been relating anecdotes concerning the lighter side of his occupation as a Chief Clerk in the Civil Service, rose in his abrupt fashion and went to the front door. He looked out at the street which this evening was not lighted, for the moon was nearly full. Gazing past him, I saw the young fan palm at the gate glittering in the bright moonlight.

Mr. Borman's hand plunged into his inner coat pocket. I saw him take out a few papers, glance at them and then put them away. He stroked his chin, pulled a bunch of keys from a hip-pocket, jingled them and then returned them to the pocket from which he had taken them. He turned and came toward us, his smile suddenly widening as Pamela rushed up to him and clasped him about the legs. He bent and ran his fingers through her tresses, then lifted her up and threatened playfully to heave her out of the door. She squealed and said no, no! to put her down!

"Heave-ho! Heave-ho!" cried Mr. Borman, swinging her perilously toward the open door. And the child shrieked half in pleasure, half in fear.

I lit a cigarette and glanced at the clock in the dining-room.

Seven past eight.

Pearl uncrossed her legs and smoothed down her dress. "Look, Rupert better hurry up and come," she said. "I getting hungry."

Yvonne giggled behind her hand, and leaning toward Pearl, murmured something into Pearl's ear which made Pearl throw back her head and laugh.

"Child, you right! I believe you!"

I heard Mrs. Telfer chuckling deeply, and watched her plump body shaking. Something Raymond had said seemed to have called forth her mirth. Kathleen, too, was laughing – though there was a scandalized expression on her face. She kept staring at Raymond, exclaiming once: "But, boy, you fresh, you know!"

Mr. Borman, Pamela still in his arms – but snugly now – moved over to them and asked what was the joke. He is partially bald, and I could see the bald patches gleaming like bronze under the frosted glass shade which enclosed the light immediately about him on the ceiling. He is a trifle lighter in complexion than I; and his eyebrows are set high above his eyes – not unlike mine. This, in conjunction with his perpetual smile, makes him appear sometimes (to me, at least) almost frightening. Regarding him now, the child in his arms, I felt a slight shudder go through me. It was as though I somehow expected to see his arms tighten about the child's body until all the breath departed and left it a limp corpse.

The telephone rang in the dining-room, and Pearl sprang up, but her father put down the child and hurried in ahead of her. Pearl returned to her seat saying: "I'm sure that must be Mother. How much you want to bet the ship hasn't come in yet!"

But a few minutes later when her father reappeared he replied on an enquiry from Pearl: "Yes, yes. It was Mother who called. The ship has come in, she says. He'll be home at any moment now."

"Why did she ring?" Pearl asked – but he had hurried off and was making faces at Pamela. He began to frolic around the room with the child, Pamela squealing in mock fear and he uttering deep baying sounds and making menacing lunges at her. Finally, he caught her near the piano and swung her aloft. She shrieked and gurgled, and he asked her whether she wanted him to throw her through the window to the jumbies outside.

Pearl kept shaking her head as she watched him. "Daddy behave like a real child himself sometimes."

I proffered my cigarette case to Yvonne (Pearl, I already knew, was not a smoker), but she smiled shyly and shook her head, mumbling: "No thank you, Horace. I don't smoke."

At twenty to nine we were still waiting. Somebody – Pearl, I think – had switched off the radio. Raymond had been trying to entertain us with boogie-woogie. Kathleen broke off saying something to Mrs. Telfer to glance at Mr. Borman who stood chatting with Raymond, still seated before the piano. Kathleen called: "But, Bertie, what happening, man? Rupert not coming? Pam getting hungry. It's long past her meal-time."

"Oh, he'll be here any second now," Mr. Borman told her. Don't trouble your head. But look! Give her some milk in the meantime, na? Let me go and get a glass of milk. Ray boy, excuse me a moment, lemme go and get this milk for Pam." He spoke rapidly – almost in a chatter. I saw his face twitching. His smile looked rigid.

Raymond was gazing after him with a puzzled expression. Mr. Borman moved toward the dining-room door in such agitated hurry that he appeared to dance.

Pearl and Yvonne were murmuring confidences. Pearl's face had a subdued look, but Yvonne continued to giggle spasmodically.

I strolled over to a window to watch the moonlit garden. Mrs. Borman is very fond of her garden. At the time of these events there were beds of zinnias and coreopsis and a few tubs with rose-plants. Besides the fan palm at the gate there were three others of the feathery variety spaced at equal distances along the border wall, their fronds overhanging the sidewalk. Regular paths were cut between the miniature lawn, which was green and smooth. The moonlight converted the garden into a place of cool and magic. No wind was blowing, however, and I thought that the zinnias and coreopsis seemed unnaturally still. The fan palm generally rustled at the faintest breeze, but now it struck me as having a hushed air. It, too, might have been waiting for Rupert.

I turned as a loud peal of laughter came from the dining-room. It was Mr. Borman. I noticed that Yvonne was wincing. She looked pale.

Pearl sat staring toward the dining-room door.

Mr. Borman appeared holding Pamela's hand.

"Mummy! Mummy!" he cried to Kathleen. "She drank every drop of it! Every single drop! She is a good girl! Oh, she's a good, *good* girl!" He began to laugh again. Toward the end of his laughter a cracked, panicked note was evident. The sound of his voice trailed away like the fraying of a thin cable as he shouted more words in praise of Pamela.

He was hopping about now, throwing the child up and catching her. "Up! *Down!* Up! *Down!*" he cried, while the child shrieked more in terror, it struck me, than from the fun of it. Once I caught a glimpse of her eyes, and they seemed to contain a bright, staring glitter. She had the air of a creature fascinated – hopelessly lost in fascination.

It was now five to nine.

When it was twenty past, Mrs. Telfer rose and said that she was going. "Na, child, I can't wait any longer. I promised Dulcie to be home by half past nine at the latest."

Mr. Borman, who was at the piano playing *The Blue Danube* (not very well, though; he struck several wrong notes and his rhythm was not always perfect) must have become aware of the fact that Mrs. Telfer had risen to go, for he stopped playing and hastened across the room. "What's this? What's this? Running out on us, Beryl! Eh-eh! Oh, no, no, no! Sit down! You can't go like this, man. You don't want to wait to welcome Rupert?"

"But look at the time, Bertie! It's long after nine. Why isn't he here yet? Ent you say the boat land up already? Man, Dulcie's mother is sick, and I promise to get home by half past nine to give Dulcie a lil' help in caring her."

"Oh, nonsense, Bee! Don't tell me that you *must* be home by half past nine to help Dulcie care her mother. Come, man, come! You ought to know better than that? If you want Dulcie's mother to get well, what better way than praying? Sit down where you are and pray. Direct your thoughts to good, and good will come. Don't let evil overpower you! Come along, child! Have faith!"

"It's all well and good for you to talk like that, Bertie –"

"And I have a right to talk like that way! Come, Bee! Sit down and have faith. There's no death! You know there's no death. Why trouble about an ill woman?" His voice, like his whole frame, was trembling. His eyes were shifty and bright.

Mrs. Telfer sat down, though her air was one of bewilderment and uneasiness. She seemed about to say something, for her brows knitted and her lips parted – but she was silent. She settled back in her chair with a soft sigh of resignation, glancing at Kathleen who smiled in response, her brows lifted, her face, on the whole, strained looking.

Pamela stood by her, a small hand grasped tightly over one handle of the rocker.

Mr. Borman moved back toward the piano. In his agitated haste he tripped against a Klim tin which Pamela had brought from the pantry a while ago and left lying carelessly on the floor. He laughed and, stooping, picked up the tin and hurled it at the nearest window. But his aim was faulty and it crashed through a pane of glass, the fragments falling with a soft tinkle into the garden. Mr. Borman clapped his hands together, exclaiming: "Just you look at that!" He made clicking sounds with his tongue and murmured that he would have to get a carpenter tomorrow to fix the pane. Not for an instant did his smile desert him. It was so fixed now that it seemed stuck on to his lips as though it might have been part of a Carnival disguise. He had hardly settled himself on the piano stool when he rose and snapped his fingers.

"Tell you what! I'll go and get you-all a lil' something to eat. How about a few sandwiches, eh? Help to occupy your mouths until Rupert shows up."

"But Daddy!"

"Eh, Pearl?"

"What's happened?"

"What's happened? How you mean what's happened?"

"Where's Mother? What did she tell you when she 'phoned?"

"Tell me?"

A green bush-bug made a buzzing arc around one of the lights on the ceiling. Pamela recoiled against her mother, and Mr. Borman took a swift glance upward as though disturbed by the sound.

"Daddy, I asked you a question."

Mr. Borman began to laugh. His body shook in rigid spasms. He might have been a wooden figure manipulated by a string.

"You see what an inquisitive daughter I have, Ray! Your mother spoke from Artie's house, child!"

"Artie's house? But didn't she go down to the wharf to meet Rupert?"

"Of course, of course! What you hurting you' head for, Pearl? Everything is all right. All's well with the world! Rupert will be here in a minute or two. Any second now. *Any* second!"

He went scurrying off (I can think of no better way of describing it) into the dining-room, leaving Pearl to sigh and shake her head.

We were glad for the sandwiches he brought. He told us that he had prepared them himself, as the servants had gone home. "They are so damned independent nowadays, these servants," he remarked as he passed round the dish.

He himself ate nothing. He returned to the piano after resting the empty dish on the table. He announced that he would play a few tunes for us. He began to render *"Tea for two"* in a jerky rhythm and an uneven tempo.

I heard Kathleen murmuring in a worried voice that Pamela was getting sleepy. This must have been a cooked-up excuse, though, preliminary to announcing her intention to go, for I glanced across and saw that Pamela was wide-eyed and alert. She was staring at Mr. Borman.

Presently, I noticed that the child was straying across in the direction of the piano, though she moved with hesitancy and caution.

Perhaps Mr. Borman saw her approaching out of the corner of his eye, for suddenly he stopped playing, twirled on the stool and shouted: "Ah! Caught her! *Caught* her! Creeping up on me, eh?" He made a spring at her, but the child gasped and ran back to her mother. She was trembling.

"But, Bertie! What's the matter with you?" Kathleen protested. You're frightening the child!"

Standing in the middle of the room, Mr. Borman broke into loud guffaws. Hollow, hacking sounds in which there was the suggestion of a sob.

I saw Yvonne clenching her hands tightly.

Then Mr. Borman took off his coat and flung it toward my chair asking me to keep it for him. "The night too hot, man. I going play some really good music for you-all. Some grand old-fashioned waltzes."

Mrs. Telfer said: "But, Bertie, we don't want music. Where Rupert and your wife? The ship hasn't come in yet? What happening?"

"Don't be impatient. Beryl."

"But look at the time!"

"Sit down and wait, Bee."

Sit down and wait. Wait and pray."

"Wait and pray?"

"There is nothing but good in this world," he said, as though she might not have spoken. "Evil is a myth. Eradicate evil from your soul."

"Man, you contradicting yourself. How I can eradicate evil from my soul if evil is a myth?"

He bellowed with laughter. "Ah! Ah! You got me there! You got me there!"

"Look, Bertie, this is no time for fun. I got to go home."

"Again I say it, Bee. Don't let evil invade you."

"But who talking about evil at all?"

He held up his hand. He was perspiring. His face looked grey. I watched his throat move as though he was swallowing. "You're not talking about it, but you're implying it. There is no death, Bee. You hear me? There is no *death!*"

He swayed slightly. I expected him to collapse, but somehow he kept his balance and staggered over to the piano.

It was as he began to pound out an old waltz tune that I noticed his coat lying beside my chair. I picked it up automatically, and as I did so two or three papers slipped from the inner pocket and settled on the floor. I retrieved them.

One was a letter bearing a local stamp and addressed to Mr. Borman; another appeared to be an old receipt.

I was shuffling them all together to replace them in the pocket from which they had come when my attention became fixed to a battered looking envelope – one of the kind that the Cable Office uses. It bore our host's name and address in blue carbon. The cablegram form it contained projected nearly three parts way out as a result of the envelope's journey from the coat pocket to the floor, and hardly realizing what I was doing – the evening had grown so unreal and incredible – I unfolded the form and read the message. It told me that Rupert had been killed in a car accident in Brighton while on a few days' leave. The message bore a date nearly two months old.

When I look across at the piano I saw that Mr. Borman's eyes were tightly shut. His head swayed stiffly from side to side as he played "Early in the morning".

THE PAWPAW TREE

It happened a few years ago. A kindly old negro called Ralph whom Rachel and I had known since childhood gave us a great deal of help when we were moving into our new cottage in the Queenstown district of New Amsterdam, and the first piece of advice he gave us was that we should have the pawpaw tree in the backyard cut down. Rachel asked him why, and he replied: "Dat ain' a good tree to keep near de house ma'am."

"He's probably thinking of the old superstition concerning pawpaw trees, Rachel," I put in. "Isn't that what you mean, Ralph?" I asked him. But our old friend shook his head. "No, sir. Ah ain' mean dat," he said gravely.

Rachel laughed and said that she hoped I was not one of those who believed in the superstition. I assured her that I was not, but added: "All the same, I think I am in a position to sympathise with Ralph's views. My grandmother always took a most serious view of pawpaw trees. She would have preferred to permit a boa-constrictor to roam around the yard rather than have a pawpaw tree grow near the backstairs. She said it brought sickness, if I remember rightly."

Ralph grunted ominously and said, "Sir, it ain' dat I mean. I know about dat superstition, but it's something else about dis tree I mean. Dis ain't a good tree, sir. Dis is a evil tree. You better tek me advice and cut it down."

"But why? I can't see anything the matter with it. It seems the same as any other pawpaw tree to me. It's got some lovely fruit, too."

Ralph smiled mysteriously and said, "Yes, sir, its fruit taste good, but di tree plant over a grave – a ole Dutchman' grave. And he wasn't a good man when he was alive, sir."

"Where did you hear such a tale?"

"De ole people tell me, sir. Ever since I was a child I know a pawpaw tree to grow up on dis same spot. Every time you cut it down, another one spring up. Widdout no seeds fall on dis spot a pawpaw tree does grow up on dis spot. It's not a natural tree, sir. Evil make it grow up, and it got evil in it. Cut it down, sir. Tek my advice. Don't leave it there."

After he had gone, Rachel and I discussed the matter, and discussed it at some length, for Ralph might be a simple old fellow, but he was no fool. From our childhood days we knew him to be a level-headed fellow whose advice it always paid to heed. However, his tale intrigued Rachel and myself so much that we decided that if there was any sort of haunting attached to this tree, then why should we not leave it and see for ourselves what the ghost looked like. We both regarded the matter in a flippant spirit. I told her, "My dear, I've never seen a ghost in my life, but nothing would give me greater pleasure than to witness a nice little chunk of ectoplasm materializing in our backyard one night. I mean, New Amsterdam is not a town noted for its startling or diverting events, and, if anything, we ought to do everything in our power to encourage this old Dutchman to pay us a call if he so desires."

"I agree with you," she giggled. "We'll leave it to see what happens."

And we did not have to wait very long for something to happen.

One afternoon during the following week it fell out that I was not in the mood for tennis. I should have been, of course, because the weather was at its best – blue sky streaked with cirrus feathers, a soft north-easterly trade and the smell of grass and flowers in the air. But the fact was that I had that afternoon received a booklet of poems from a very good friend of mine in Georgetown, and I was eager to get down to sample its contents.

Rachel was disappointed, for she was playing in a challenge game and there was a bet on it, and, naturally, she had wanted me to witness it. But once I have made up my mind I have made it up – and she knew this, so we did not argue very much.

Having seen her off, I took a Berbice chair into the backyard and settled down to what I assured myself would be two hours of quiet enjoyment (I had a great deal of confidence in the ability of my friend as a poet).

I had the place entirely to myself. We only kept one servant as the cottage was very small, and she had gone home a short while ago and would not be returning until seven o'clock.

The sun was low in the west, and slanted mildly into the backyard. Shadows lay long and shapeless everywhere, and the trade wind made a soft peaceful sizzling in the fronds of the coconut palms in the next yard.

I had perhaps been reading for about half an hour when, for some reason, I found myself with the inclination to glance down beside my chair.

I did so but there was nothing of particular interest to see.

It was not until I had been gripped by the same inclination that I looked and became aware that the shadow of the pawpaw tree had crept up to the handle of my chair. Chuckling at my silly fancies, I adjusted myself more comfortably in the chair and turned my attention once again to the book.

But try as I might I could not keep still.

Somehow, the air seemed to have grown a little oppressive. I looked up at the sky, but it was cloudless; even the cirrus feathers had melted away. There was no sign of a thunderstorm.

I glanced toward the cottage, and it suddenly struck me that the place seemed unusually silent and empty – especially empty: empty in a way that did not seem right.

Again I chuckled and told myself not to be an instinctive fool.

And then I sat forward. I could have sworn I had heard my chuckle echoed somewhere close by. Was it – could it have been from beyond the trunk of the pawpaw tree?

I let my gaze move slowly up the gnarled trunk, thinking that for a pawpaw tree it should have had a trunk far smoother. I knew that it was simply a case of letting my subconscious mind get the better of me. I was letting that stupid tale Ralph had told me last week play upon my fancies.

So once again I settled down to read.

Perhaps I must have fallen into a slight doze, because I was suddenly conscious of sitting up with a jerk and staring straight before me. There had been a sound behind me – a soft whirring cheep, like the movement of a furry wing. Then I turned and looked down.

I grunted and wagged my head. It was just a pawpaw leaf that had fallen. I stretched back and picked it up, examining it idly. The long stalk was yellowish and shrivelled, and the leaf at the end had a brown and crumpled look. Somehow, it had an impelling quality about it. I had to keep staring at it.

Abruptly, to my horror, I found myself seeing not a withered leaf but a human hand – a dead, wrinkled hand. I shuddered and exclaimed and flung it off. But when it reached the ground I saw that it was only a withered leaf, after all, and I had to click my tongue and scold myself for my childishly vivid imagination.

To my relief, I heard footsteps in the house and saw Rachel appear at the kitchen door. She came out into the yard, and I expressed surprise. "You're back rather early, aren't you," I said. "Bet you lost?"

"Oh, I'm furious, furious!" she exclaimed. "Madge played an awful game. Spoilt every shot that came our way. Bungled everything."

"Such is life – and tennis."

"Oh, I know you don't care a jot!" she flared. "Sometimes I can kill you, Hilary! Kill you!"

"My dear, please! Why such a violent tone!"

She stood there staring at me, and there was something in her eyes that alarmed me. Something cold and unnatural and most unlike herself. It was as though I were gazing upon an entirely new person – a new evil Rachel. Her lips were pursed together in a thin, cruel line, and, on the whole, her fury seemed perfectly unwarranted. I half-sat up and said: "But what's the matter with you? You don't seem yourself. And why did you come home without Madge? Did you have a row because you didn't win? You said you'd bring her here for a cocktail."

"Yes, we had a row," she snapped. "I won't argue with you."

I sighed. "A pity you should have quarrelled with Madge. I rather like Madge. Always have had a soft spot for her."

"Oh, you don't need to tell me that! I've known, too. Don't think you've been clever in concealing it from me. Really, sometimes I could kill you, Hilary! Kill you, I tell you! Kill you!"

She rushed at me, and I saw her racquet descending…

Then there was a deep buzzing and humming and a sensation of confusion in my brain. It seemed as though I could smell a rank vegetable odour that penetrated the mist of my bewilderment. A smell of green pawpaws, perhaps. Or was it a dank, earthy miasma? The emanation from an old tomb? I felt as though I was slowly suffocating but could do nothing to help myself. I seemed to realise now that I must have fallen into a doze and dreamt all that had passed. Rachel had not yet come home. I had imagined it all – dreamt it. But why had the whole yard grown so dark? I could not make out a single object. Not even a star in the sky. Perhaps I had slept on until late. But no. Rachel would have roused me, surely.

Then I heard a shrill scream from the house and the sound of footsteps. I felt a violent shiver go through me, and I shook myself and sat up gasping. I had the sensation of having just emerged from water. The afternoon had darkened, but there was still enough light left to make out the scene around me clearly.

I saw Rachel and Madge rush out of the kitchen and come toward me.

"Hilary! What was it? Did you strike it off?"

"Strike what off?" I asked. "Are you just back from tennis?"

"Just this minute back. I've brought Madge for a cocktail as I said I would. But what was it, Hilary? That thing on your face?"

"What thing on my face? What on earth are you talking about?"

"But there was something on your face. You seemed to be asleep, and there was something resting over your face. I saw it from the dining-room window. That's why I screamed."

I chuckled, shaking my head. "I'm afraid I haven't the faintest idea what you mean. What could you have seen on my face?"

"It – it was like a great wrinkled brown hand. It was pressing down on your face as if it wanted to smother you. Madge saw it, too. Didn't you, Madge?"

"I should think I did," Madge nodded.

"Well that's funny," I murmured. "Surely you couldn't both have been seeing things that weren't there. All I know is that I had a most peculiar dream. I didn't like it at all. I seemed to have fallen into a doze or something. The only thing I can think of that might have resembled a brown hand was that pawpaw leaf that fell just before I dropped off into a doze."

"What pawpaw leaf was that?"

"It fell to the ground just behind my chair here, and I picked it up and examined it – hullo! Well, that's odd!"

"What's the matter?"

"It's not there anymore."

She nodded grimly. "Exactly. And so far as I can see there isn't a single dead leaf under this tree or anywhere in the yard here."

Madge gave a slight shudder and reminded us about the cocktail.

And, as you may well guess, the very next day the pawpaw tree came down. We had Ralph in to cut it down – and I told him that on future occasions we would know better than to scoff at his advice.

THE BURGLAR

I told him to stop or I would have to shoot. He continued to run down the stairs, so I called again and told him that I meant what I said. I would shoot if he didn't stop. And this time he stopped. He stopped and turned and looked up at me – looked up into the little revolver I was levelling at him, his face shiny-black, wide-eyed with uncertain fear, as though he had not yet quite made up his mind whether I were serious about shooting him. And the truth is, I wasn't serious. I was bluffing. The revolver I held was a toy. I have never used a revolver in my life. But living as I did high up on Chancellor Hill, far from the populous sections of Port of Spain, I had always thought it would be wise to have a revolver on my bedside table in case of burglars, even if it *was* only a toy. Some toy revolvers look very businesslike. This one did; it belonged to my little son who, with his mother, was at present on holiday in Grenada.

I went down the stairs, and told him to do the same.

"Go on," I said. "Right down into the living room."

He gave nervous grunt. I heard his breath coming in gasps. His face registered fear, defiance, desperation in swift succession.

"Chief, don't shoot," he implored me. "Ah beg you! Please don't shoot!"

Yes, fear had won. He was trembling visibly.

I laughed. A hard laugh. I would have shot him, if it had been a real revolver. There is one thing I can't tolerate… a stranger trespassing on my domain. It makes me savage. I shiver and feel like a wild beast. My strength doubles, trebles; I lose my sanity.

We were in the dining room now. I had switched on the lights, of course. There are switches at the top of the stairs that control the lights in the corridor as well as in the dining-room downstairs.

I watched him silhouetted against the square of light at the window near the sideboard. He was still trembling. He wore a sweat-stained singlet and dirty khaki trousers. He was barefooted. I saw him, I repeat, silhouetted against the square of light at the window. There is an excellent view of the city from that window. Often I have stood there of an afternoon and watched the trees and housetops, with the harbour beyond, the water turning red in the sun, in the far distance the mountains of Venezuela purple and misty.

I saw him glance out of the window, but I laughed and told him: "I don't think you'll want to make your exit through that window. If you go through it you'll find yourself with a drop of a hundred feet down the cliff."

He looked at me… and again there was that about him that was uncertain; he seemed to be sizing me up; assessing my strength, physical and moral, in comparison with his own. He was trying to gauge my determination. Perhaps he was wondering whether he could play on my soft side and beg off. He reminded me of a sugar-ant I once cornered in a saucer. I kept frustrating its efforts to climb over the edge until, at length, it paused, irresolute, waving its minute feelers about, and almost seemed to be asking me, Well, what's it all about? What are your intentions? Are you going to kill me, or let me go? Are you really the big strong giant you appear to me, or can I possibly outwit you with one last clever move?... In the end I let it go. But this fellow was different. He was no sugar-ant. He was a human intruder come into my house to take what did not belong to him. Very well. I know it sounds a little priggish, but, as I said before, it makes me furious when anyone invades my domain. I lose all human compassion.

"Did you succeed in getting anything?" I asked him, very calm, very matter-of-fact. When my voice is matter-of-fact, I'm most dangerous, as all my friends know.

"No, sir," he replied. "Ah ain' tek nutting. As soon as ah reach de top o' de stairs you switch on de lights, and ah see you standing in you' bedroom door pointing de revolver at me. Don't shoot me, sir. I beg you! Lemme go!"

"But you came here to rob me," I said.

He hung his head. "Sir, ah ain' eat nutting for de day."

"You didn't? Then why didn't you go to the kitchen if you were hungry? Did you expect to find food upstairs in, the bedrooms? You're lying!"

He couldn't answer this. He began to fidget and squeeze his hands together. Miserable-looking creature. In a way, he did look hungry. I almost wanted to believe he was telling the truth.

"Where do you live"? I asked him.

"Duncan Street, chief."

"In the slums, eh? I suppose." I added, "You must look upon me as one of the terrible people who oppress you and your kind. You think I'm a fit person to rob."

"No, sir," he mumbled. My sarcasm had not registered. He was too afraid of the revolver in my hand... and my manner must have seemed grim and forbidding. I have often been told that my eyes gleem like a beast's when I am in moods like this... a mood of calm fury.

I kept watching him. He rested a hand on the window sill, clutched the sill hard and stared at me. He appeared puzzled now as well as afraid. He was probably wondering why I should engage him in this conversation instead of telephoning for the police.

I laughed and told him: "The police won't have a hand in this. You've come into my house to rob me... and I'm going to settle the matter with you myself. Are you hearing me?"

He nodded and murmured: "Yes, sir." He made a ducking motion and whimpered, as though to avoid the bullet that never left my revolver. I feigned that I was going to pull the trigger.

I could hear his breath wheezing in terror. His head kept obscuring the lights of the city. It was most fascinating. To myself, I wondered what anyone, any in the savannah, would think if by chance they happened to train a pair of binoculars onto that window, and saw this fellow standing rigidly before it, staring into the room. What would they conjecture was happening in this house? Would they guess he was a burglar and that the master of the house was standing a few yards away levelling a toy revolver at him?

I began to advance towards him. I would teach him that he could not break into my house as he pleased... not even if he lived in the slums of Duncan Street and was hungry. I would give him a sound beating... with my fists... and send him away. My compassion began to rise up, but I suppressed it. I didn't believe he was really hungry. He was lying. He was just another common lout who thought he could help himself to other people's property. He hated me because I was well-to-do and lived in this big house. He knew I held a big position in the community... that I was a power in the land... and automatically he thought he had a right to break into my house.

I could feel myself trembling. The room seemed to sympathise with my fury. It circled around me in spirals... spirals that rose out of the floor and then came down again from the ceiling. The lights of the city at the window made a crown of jewels around the fellow's head. A tiara of rubies, I thought.

I listened to his breathing. Getting faster. He stood there poised, awaiting my attack, He must have sensed in a kind of animal way what was in store for him, must have known that the rage which possessed me transcended anything normal, anything human.

I was within three feet of him now. The lights of the city made a wheeling rainbow behind his head. Did he suspect what had just entered my mind? I meant not to thrash him as I had formerly intended, but to give him a sudden push and send him hurtling through the window... down to his death a hundred feet below.

I paused. I wanted to tell him what I was going to do, but the fury in me made me speechless. I could only gnash my teeth and glare at him.

I knew now what it meant by the saying "to see red". In this instant I saw him surrounded by an aura of pure scarlet.

He began to plead again, began to implore me not to shoot him, to let him go.

I said nothing, prepared myself to spring at him. That rainbow of lights round his head intensified in brilliance.

And then I heard Maxwell's voice from the stairs. He asked me what I was doing downstairs here. "Dis is de second time for de week you do dis t'ing, sir," he said. "De next time you leave you' room an come down here I will write de madam and tell her you not getting better, and you'll have to go back to de St Ann's Hospital."

I began to explain about the burglar, but, as usual, he cut me short. Maxwell never believes me when I tell him about these burglars. He says it's just because I'm not well. He won't even believe me about the rainbow of lights and the spirals rising from the floor.

TACAMA

DON'T look for a village or any kind of settlement. You won't find it. It isn't a neat huddle of cottages or huts amid the trees awaiting immortality through the agency of a traveller's camera. All you'll see is a gap in the jungle on the left bank of the river. Quiet, undramatic sand undulates whitely, like a ruffled counterpane, up as far as the grey wooden rails and barriers of the corrals. In these corrals cattle are penned when they arrive after a perilous trek from the Rupununi Savannah – the survivors of three weeks' and three hundred miles' of thirst, fatigue and lack of good grass.

This is how I knew it fifteen years ago. It may have changed since – though I doubt it. On the upper reaches of the Berbice River, the changes wrought by mankind take place with a speed that makes the natural forces of evolution look like a Macdonald Bailey.

The jungle appeared not to like Tacama. The jungle must deem it pretentious that a mere break in its verdure – a rendezvous for cattle – should be given a name. Or it might be that the jungle is like a Tory snob. Perhaps it remembers the eighteenth century when Dutch plantations spread such a tide of cultivation along the banks of this river that the jungle was intensely aware of its serfdom and knew its place. But now that it is supreme again, it must feel scornful of this barren, plebeian patch of territory which has taken to itself so romantic-sounding a name, and this, no doubt, is why the vegetation immediately surrounding Tacama is straggly and of a desultory nature.

When the corial drew up by the bank that February day, I stepped ashore and told Charles that I wanted to do a bit of exploring.

"This spot rather takes my fancy," I said.

He waved me off.

"Not coming with me then?"

"No, thanks. I'll stay just here and laze. A holiday was made for lazing – not to go tramping about in the hot sun asking for sunstroke."

"I won't be five minutes," I told him.

He covered his head with a towel against the eye-flies and stretched out under a wild cacao tree by the water's edge.

"See and keep to the track, Peter!" he called after me, lifting the towel an instant.

"My sense of direction is excellent," I assured him, as I began to plod up the sand. "I won't get lost, if that's what you mean."

The track that leads past the corrals is clearly defined. Out of curiosity, I followed it until it came to a point where I could see it snaking without interruption into the mirage-distance of the vast savannah that opens out to the west and south. I had no inclination to go any further along it. It was the jungle that interested me. I like jungles.

Imprinted indistinctly, but unmistakably, everywhere on the sand were the marks of beasts and men; no rain had fallen for weeks to wash them out.

A crooked tree to the left of the track attracted my attention. It was bare of leaves except at the very top, and appeared to be slowly dying from the drought. It looked like a young mora. It seemed to grin greyly at me in its death-thirst, seemed, as I watched it, to wilt visibly in the heat that rose from the sand.

I stood and observed the heat for a minute. It swirled around me like swathes of molten silk.

The tree caught my attention again. As I have said, a crooked tree. A tree, I thought, fatally enmeshed.

This thought gave me a mental pause. In this instant, it was as though an arresting tick had sounded in my brain... Why fatally enmeshed? Enmeshed in what? Surf... The wind makes a noise like surf in the tops of the trees. You listen and hear it coming. You mistake it for rain. But it is only wind...

I shook myself and walked toward the tree. I felt the sun on my bare head. It might have been a brassy ghost sinisterly subjecting me to an unpleasant barbering.

Ants kept crawling up the thin, sap-dry trunk of the tree – a long cavalcade of large black ants. One of them paused and regarded me with enquiry – mayhap with warning. It seemed to make signals. Infinitesimal semaphore... The others left it behind for a moment. Then it went on abruptly, no doubt considering that it had given me far more attention than a mere specimen of homo sapiens deserved.

I watched them for a while. Hundreds, thousands, of black jungle ants. There are no ants like these on the coast.

I wondered about them. Ants were supposed to be intelligent creatures. Science has even hinted that they may communicate with each other by means of a definite language. Who could tell if these black ants did not keep a history of their race written on particles of leaves and stored underground in vaults known only to themselves? Could it not be that their ancestors had smiled cynically at some hapless Dutch planter of 1763 pursued and hacked to death by a party of slaves? Perhaps these ants possessed, in pinpoint catacombs, lost beneath this white sand, more valuable records of the great slave insurrection than Rodway's *History of British Guiana*. One never knew about ants.

The whim took me to discover where they were coming from. I noticed that they were moving from the sand up on to the trunk of the tree. Without disturbing the line, I edged away and traced it into a copse of swizzle-stick trees. I entered the copse. It was not dense, and there was ample room for movement. I was now in the jungle proper, but no lianas stretched across my path, as Hollywood might have depicted it. No crocodiles slithered out of a swamp and opened toothy jaws at me, nor did any evil, spotted snakes uncoil themselves in readiness to strike. In fact, the silence seemed to be the only threatening presence. It lived. It swirled and groped at me, insinuated itself into my senses with deliberate purpose. It allied itself to the sun and smothered me with unwelcome caresses. It watched me and smiled secretly to itself.

I glanced back to make sure that I could still see the crooked tree, deciding to keep it always in view, as a landmark, just in case, by chance, I did feel uncertain of my bearings.

I followed the line of black ants further into the copse. I trod on a dry leaf, and the sound rose like the cracking of glass, and seemed to evoke from the silence a snarl as at a sacrilege committed. It gave me a guilty feeling. I nearly apologized. In future, I vowed, I would tread on no more dry leaves.

I moved on.

The vegetation was low and still sparse; it afforded no protection for my head. The ants led me to a clump of wild-pines. The line turned off toward another copse of swizzle-stick trees, but at this point I decided that the game was too pointless and puerile. The sun was too hot; I must get out of it and return to Charles. I could feel a dizziness which I knew was not good. I rested my hand on my head; my head felt baked.

Before I could turn off, however, I caught sight of something white down the centre of the wild-pine clump. A wild-pine sends up long, pointed, tapering leaves – leaves hard and saw-edged. To fall into or against a clump of wild-pines can result in serious injury – ugly gashes and scratches. So I had to be careful how I leaned over and peered down into the core of this cluster.

I saw a milky-white web spun across the young leaves far down within the hollow of the cluster. There was a hole in this web, jumbie-dark and mysterious. But there was no jumbie in this hole. Out of it protruded two hairy, blue-black legs, tipped with crimson.

I stood entranced – dizzy and entranced.

All spiders are my enemies – and here was a bush one. A large, hairy blue-black one.

A shudder crawled down my back – a shudder which my brain translated into blue-black hairy legs scurrying on my bare skin. I wriggled and slapped at my back. I laughed a low perverse laugh.

A new situation faced me now. I had to do something about it.

I stooped and picked up a twig. I smiled and trembled, but stretched out and dropped the twig deliberately down into the web.

It was a light twig, and when it landed on the web it stuck and hung.

Four blue-black, hairy legs sprang horribly out of the hole, and two fangs waited, poised and savagely expectant.

This was good – terrifying but good.

The scientists say that there is none of us without a streak of masochism. Well, this was the form mine took. I stood there for how long I don't know, dropping twigs down and teasing that spider and at the same time frightening myself to death. Suddenly it occurred to me to glance up to make sure that the crooked tree was still in view.

It was not – and a hollow ache moved inside me. I stiffened and lost interest in the spider.

Something crackled behind me.

I started round.

Not a twig moved. Not a leaf. So I had to conclude it must have been the silence chuckling at me.

I turned round and round, thinking to catch it off-guard. But it was too clever.

A black lizard darted across the sand from one twig to another.

I heard the surf… far away, dying almost as it began. I must look for the line of ants, I thought. It would be a simple matter to follow the line back to the crooked tree. I looked – but there were no ants.

I turned round and round again, and smiled. I wanted to chuckle, as the silence had chuckled, but my chuckle would have sounded like thunder, and I wasn't in the mood to hear thunder.

I moved around a bit, then came back to the wild-pine cluster. I looked down into the web, but could not see the spider. It must have retreated deep down into the hole.

My twigs should have been there caught in the web. They weren't there.

This, I knew, was laughable. The spider wouldn't have pulled my twigs down into its web. A twig wasn't a fly. A spider couldn't say to a twig: "Come into my parlour…"

It must be a different wild-pine cluster. I must have wandered off from the original one. This was a new one.

It began to shake inside me – a brown sponge. My mouth felt dry.

I clasped my hands together and rested them on my head. My head felt like a hotplate with the current not too long ago switched off. When I pressed on it I found that I wanted to stagger. For a moment I did stagger. And the wild-pine leaves reached at me. I had to dodge to evade them. They were blue-black and hairy, and tipped with crimson.

I nearly whimpered, but knew that it would be fatal to show fright in sound as well as in mime. I always had to reckon with the silence.

Somehow, I managed to steady myself. I sat down and felt something solid come up to meet me. I looked down and saw that it was the trunk of a fallen palm. I had no idea where the trunk of a fallen palm could have appeared from, but I wouldn't let this new topic corrode my morale. It was job enough dealing with the heat and the silence.

I sat very still and tried to concentrate, tried to stop the heat from wrapping me round with too much molten silk. There were yards and yards of it all round me. An endless winding-sheet.

Not a good thought, that last one… Winding sheet…

I made no move, would not answer. I looked down and thought I would have seen white sand, but there was a carpet of leaves – soft and damp. Leaves that must have been piling up since the time of Governor van Hoogenheim… I noticed that the shadows had a strange shape. They oughtn't to have been so long as they were. When I had left Charles it was noon. That was a few minutes ago, so why did the shadows look so elongated? At noon shadows are short: dwarves that move under you so that you can stamp on them and keep them in subjection. It's only when they grow tall behind you in the afternoon that they get out of control and follow you round with evil intent.

I looked up.

The sun was more than halfway down to the horizon in the west…

I heard the voice calling me again. It sounded so much like Charles's voice that I rose and moved toward where I fancied it came from.

I went on moving toward it, and it called louder.

Then I saw the crooked tree, moved round a cluster of wild-pines, round a clump of swizzle-stick trees – and there I was back on the track. And there was Charles coming toward me, shouting my name.

He said that he had fallen into a doze and awakened at half-past three, and had seen no sign of me. "You gave me a fright, man. Did you get lost or what?"

I told him not to be an ass. Of course I hadn't got lost.

I laughed. "See that crooked tree there? I kept it as my landmark. How could I get lost with a tree like that for landmark?"

I laughed again. "It was just the heat that delayed me a bit, Charles. And the silence. Wicked. Tried to wrap me in a winding-sheet."

He gave me a funny look, caught my arm and hurried me to the water's edge, began to bathe my head.

WE KNOW NOT WHOM TO MOURN

It was an afternoon of grey clouds like old rice-bags, and the wind smelt of cow-dung and stagnant water and the iodine of the sea, for the savannah surrounded the house on all sides, and on the dry parts small island-cakes of cow-dung lay spotted – still, piteous islands amid the larger islands that moved, for these were the cows and sheep and the goats. Now and then the wind brought a lowing or a bleating, or the voice of a herdsman, for this was the hour when the animals were coming home to their pens, and it was the hour, too, when Hoolcharran, who owned them all and the house, was dying.

Only Harry, the third son, sat on the back veranda, long-headed, hands clasped in his lap, not smoking. Just watching the animals come home to pen, his eyes not sad but with a haunted calm, as though he were a man to whom death was not a thing for grief or fear but for thought. He seemed a lonely, brooding man, Harry.

In the sitting-room and dining-room – only a large archway separated the two rooms – were gathered Toolwa, an old aunt of Hoolcharran's wife, Dookie, and Tommy, the eldest son, who, at thirty-four, was one of the richest rice-millers on the Corentyne Coast, and Gobin, the dispenser from Kildonan, who was sixty-seven and an old friend of Hoolcharran's. Hoolcharran and Gobin, as boys, had run in shirt-tails on the Public Road, and, naked, had caught sherrigas and hassars in the canals; had fought and quarrelled at school, and laughed and climbed mango trees. Gobin in his little drug-store in Kildonan had made up all the medicine Hoolcharran and his family had ever used. Also in the sitting-room and dining-room sat Doris and John and Edward, Tommy's children; Doris was fifteen (she was at High School in New Amsterdam), and John thirteen and Edward eleven. John and Edward were quiet boys, and today the awe of death made them quieter. But Doris, who could never keep back her giggles, was giggling now at a joke about two goats that Bella had just told her. Bella was present, too; she was the black cook, and had worked for the Hoolcharrans from the age of nineteen; she was forty-two now, and no other cook, it was said, on the whole Corentyne Coast, could make a coconut curry like Bella. She was fond of telling jokes, especially smutty ones about Burroo Goat and Burroo Tiger.

Toolwa, the old aunt, gave Bella scolding glances, but did not try to scold her with words, because Bella was like a second mistress in the house. Bella's mother and Dookie (Mrs. Hoolcharran) had planted rice together as girls, and Dookie had always treated Bella as the daughter of her good friend rather than as a menial. Bella called Dookie Aunt Dookie, not ma'am. Hoolcharran's wealth had not turned Dookie's head, and Dookie, though she liked her big house and the car and all the things that money could buy, had never forgotten the old days of want. Bella had always been fat and plain – she had a cast in her right eye – and no man had ever asked her to marry him. Not that this made her any the less cheerful.

In this hour of death, Dookie was upstairs in the room with the dying man. She sat on a large old trunk near a window, Phyllis Rambarry with her. Phyllis was the fourth child and only daughter; she was the wife of Deane Rambarry, a barrister who practised in New Amsterdam; she was educated and dressed well.

The doctor – his name was Ribeiro – and the nurse – a short black girl called Turpin – stood by the bedside doing what they could to save Hoolcharran. The doctor was a tall, slim Portuguese of thirty-five or so, and he was supposed to be the best doctor in Berbice. He had told Dookie that he would do all he could, but that from what he could see the chances were slim. He spoke with a sneer, for he was that kind of man. He did not like coloured people, especially East Indians. It was only because he was supposed to be the best doctor in Berbice that Dookie had sent for him when Hoolcharran got the stroke at around ten o'clock that morning. Only a few minutes before ten o'clock Hoolcharran had been laughing and talking in his jovial way, his fat paunch trembling, his silver hair glinting in a shaft of weak sunshine from the slightly overcast sky. Nobody in the big house, painted a bright yellow and blue, had guessed that death was so near Hoolcharran.

Doctor Ribeiro had ruled that no more than two members of the family could be allowed in the sick-room at a time. He wouldn't have a crowd, he had said – and had said it in a curt voice. Dookie had tried to persuade him to let her call in three more doctors, for she was so grieved and upset she felt that she must do everything she possibly could, with the aid of money, to save Hoolcharran. Doctor Ribeiro had given her a cold look, but, after an hour or so, he had agreed to have Doctor Bembridge from Skeldon, higher up the coast. Doctor Bembridge was an English doctor who had been practising for two or three years on the Corentyne Coast.

Maurice, the second son, was on his way from Georgetown, nearly a hundred miles off. Maurice had a big grocery shop in Georgetown. His wife was an invalid and could not travel. They had no children. Dookie was praying that Maurice would arrive before Hoolcharran died, because Maurice had been his father's pet son. Hoolcharran was not conscious, it was true, but, still, felt Dookie, his spirit might sense Maurice's presence if Maurice came in time. Dookie and Hoolcharran were Presbyterians. Hoolcharran never cared too much about the church, but Dookie was a staunch believer in Jesus Christ and the Christian faith as taught by the Presbyterians. She went to church every other Sunday, and whenever anyone in the house was sick, she always prayed for their recovery. Hoolcharran had often laughed at her, but he was always very generous in his gifts of money to the church, and would sometimes even humour Dookie by going to church with her.

Jim Rambarry, Phyllis's husband, had gone off in the car to get Doctor Bembridge.

And now the wind moaned, and Harry, the third son, watched the twilight deepen. Toolwa got up and crossed over to where Gobin sat in a rocking chair near the big cabinet radio set. She bent and whispered something. She asked him about the will. Did Gobin know if Hoolcharran had made a will? Her manner was furtive and scheming; she cast quick glances round at the others, as though feeling that she was doing something wrong. Her grey-edged, dark-brown eyes were shiny with greed. The wrinkles of her seventy-odd years looked like shadowed gutters of evil, perhaps dug in the night by the jumbies strayed from the faraway courida bush. Toolwa lived in a lonely wooden cottage three miles away, and the wind and the rain, and perhaps the jumbies, were tearing it down shingle by shingle. Toolwa would have liked some money to build a big house, though if she had got the money she would not have built the house, but would have put the money in the bank. She had over three thousand dollars in Barclay's Bank, for she was thrifty and saved as much as she could out of the allowance Dookie made her. Her son, Palwan, had died at the age of nineteen, and it was said that, at that time, Toolwa had had a lot of money, for her husband had owned two rice fields and had saved his money carefully in the mattress of his bed. But Toolwa had been so stingy and had denied Palwan good food for so long a time that he got tuberculosis.

Gobin shook his head and said he didn't know if Hoolcharran had made a will, but he supposed so. He looked a little impatient with her, and only because he was polite he checked himself from telling her to move away from him. Gobin was grieved. As soon as the news had reached him that his good friend had taken ill, he had shut his drug-store and taken the bus and come.

The telephone began to ring. It was in the dining-room: a wall-'phone.

Doris sprang up and went and answered it. She said yes several times, then no, then told the person at the other end that yes, the doctor said there was little hope. Yes, grandma was upstairs in the room with him and the doctor…

Toolwa asked Gobin if he thought Hoolcharran would leave anything for Harry.

"Harry, disappoint 'e bad," said Toolwa.

"Me can't tell you, Toolwa," said Gobin, shaking his head patiently. "Only 'e lawyer can tell you wha' 'e leff and wha' 'e ain' leff."

Toolwa glanced round again, and then asked: "Why 'e didn't tek Rambarry for 'e lawyer? Ent Rambarry 'e son-in-law?"

"Me can't tell you, Toolwa," said Gobin, fidgeting and frowning now.

"It funny," said Toolwa. "Ah believe 'e didn't too like Rambarry for Phyllis. Ah hear 'e did want Phyllis marry white overseer."

"Dat's a lie, Toolwa."

"So me hear. Me only tell you wha' me hear, Gobin."

Gobin made a puffing grunt of anger, and his lips moved soundlessly.

Toolwa tittered and moved off, went back to her chair by the upright piano.

And the wind moaned around the house, and Harry saw a weak light glowing in the distance where the gloom was dense. Harry smiled slightly, as though he could hear a voice in the wind that spoke only for him. Since he was a boy, Harry had listened to the wind. No one knew what went on in his mind. He was not married. He was a schoolteacher and taught in the village school. He lived home here, and had many books, and when he came home, he went to his room. He sat some evenings alone on the back veranda, as he was sitting now. A strange, brooding man, Harry. As distant as the sea beyond the line of *courida* bush. Only the wind and the savannah knew him.

The drone of a car sounded. It was Rambarry, Phyllis's husband, coming back from Skeldon with Doctor Bembridge. The headlights could be seen by John from the front door. John had gone to the front door to catch a lizard which had streaked past his chair into the gallery and out under the door. John had a special piece of wire with a noose at the end for catching lizards. He liked to see a lizard squirm in the noose by its neck, and sometimes he would hold it over a fire, if he was near a fire. Edward, who did not like to see any creature suffer, often scolded him for his cruelty, but John still went on catching lizards. Flies, too, and bees and pond-flies. One day in New Amsterdam, John had gone hunting with a Daisy air-gun, and had shot four kiskadees and three blue sackies. He was a deadly shot with an air-gun. One of the blue sackies fell from a telephone wire only maimed in the wing, so John spread it out on the grass parapet and pinned it down with two stones. He brought out a box of matches and burnt every feather off it, and then stuck it with pins till it died.

The car bumped its way toward the house along the uneven grass and gravel track. And presently Rambarry came up the stairs with Dr. Bembridge, a thin, short, red-faced Englishman with a small brown moustache and a quick, nervous way of glancing this way and that way and smiling. He said "Evening, Evening!" to everybody in the sitting-room and dining-room as he passed on his way to the stairs that led to the upper storey. Tommy rose and said: "Good night, Doctor," his manner respectful and awed. For Tommy, in spite of the education Hoolcharran had given him, was still, at heart, a shy and salaaming coolie. Tommy, though he was one of the richest rice-millers on the Corentyne Coast, had never learnt how to be self-assured. He was timid in his relations with people. Only in business he knew how to be shrewd and bold. He never made a false move in business. But people, especially white people, frightened him. As a boy, he had often watched the white overseers on their mules aback of the nearby sugar-estate and trembled. Overseers, he had heard, kicked and shouted. They kicked the coolies who cut canes, and shouted curses at them, and threatened to shoot. One day he had seen an overseer kick a thin old coolie who was in charge of the oxen pulling the cane-laden punts along the canal.

Rambarry accompanied the doctor upstairs. And Tommy sat down.

Bella was telling Doris a story about Bill, Burroo Rabbit and Burroo Monkey. Doris giggled, and Edward asked her if she didn't know that Grandpa was ill upstairs.

Bella looked at him and said: "Boy, death can only come once to everybody. What you hurting you head for? Let de girl laugh!"

"You're too callous," said Edward.

Bella laughed softly and told him that it was what was inside your heart that mattered. "Not what you' face show. Dis is a life, boy, we never know who to mourn over. Sometimes it's de people who alive who we should cry for – not de dead ones, or de ones we t'ink dying. Run off and play wid you' marbles boy." Her fat bulk shivered with fresh mirth, and Edward turned off and went sulkily toward the gallery.

And so the wind went on moaning round the house, and the clouds moved faster in the sky. Inky cloaks they looked like now, for night had come, and Toolwa was calling to Bijoolie to bring in the gas-lamps. Bijoolie was the man-of-all-work. He was an illegitimate son of Hoolcharran's, for Hoolcharran had been a gay young man in his youth. He had drunk his rum and had his women. The son of a cane-cutter, Hoolcharran had begun as a provision farmer, and lived in a mudhouse. All the land he possessed was an acre of swampy savannah. But he had mingled industry and thrift with his love for pleasure. The first cow he owned had strayed on to his land, and he could have had it impounded, but he saw a way of making it his own. It belonged to the widow of Poolram who lived a mile up the Public Road. Hoolcharran took the cow to Poolram's widow, and Beekwa – that was her name – was very grateful, and invited Hoolcharran to some curry and roti, as Hoolcharran knew she would have done. Beekwa was still young and pretty, and Hoolcharran was a handsome young man. Hoolcharran did not go home until the next morning. Six weeks later Beekwa made a present of the cow to Hoolcharran. The cow was with calf. Hoolcharran's career as a cattle-rancher had begun.

The moaning of the wind never stopped. It was still moaning past Harry's chair on the back veranda when (it was after nine o'clock) Phyllis brought the news from upstairs. Phyllis was breathless with excitement which she tried to suppress, for she moved with good-class coloured people in New Amsterdam and had to be careful not to show any vulgar feelings. Phyllis told them that Hoolcharran would live. Yes, the doctors said he had tided over the worst. It had been touch and go, she said, but he would recover. He might be laid up for several weeks, even months, but he would live. Oh, she was so glad – for Mother's sake... A sigh of relief and joy went through the house, as though the wind had pushed a bright tributary out of its dark moaning in upon them.

But...

And then Edward's cry rose. Edward came in from the back veranda, pale and frightened-looking, and his cry rose. A cry of horror. Perhaps he was remembering, too, what Bella had told him an hour or two ago... "Dis is a life, boy, we never know who to mourn over" ... And they all went out on to the back veranda and looked at Harry who still sat in the bright-blue wicker chair. His head was slightly thrown back, and he was staring at the clouds in the wind. But his eyes were so steady. And beside his chair, on the floor, lay the bottle, not bright-blue like the wicker chair, but a dark blue, and with a red label bearing a skull and crossbones. A lonely, brooding man, Harry. About him was a smell of bitter almonds. About him the wind still moaned.

SORROW DAM AND MR MILLBANK

There is a road that leads out of the south-eastern end of the town of New Amsterdam toward the Canje creek, and it is one of the dreariest roads in British Guiana. The first stretch of it is known to the townspeople as Sorrow Dam. On either hand the terrain is flat and swampy, with a profusion of wild vegetation, mostly, courida and black-sage shrubs. In the rain season it is nothing unusual to see the snout of an alligator protruding out of the swamp, only a few yards from the grass parapet that borders the road. It is a road built up of burnt earth, and is often full of the ruts which become muddy pools in the wet season. Further east – that is to say beyond Sorrow Dam – a few isolated dwellings begin to appear: thatch-roofed huts, mud-houses and very tiny shingled cottages, all occupied by poor peasants, people who depend upon their provision-patches and one or two cows and sheep for a livelihood.

It was along this road every evening, around five, that Mr Millbank came for a walk – his "daily constitutional", his fellow townsmen called it, though he himself did not like the description; he hated trite, conventional tags, and, besides, he did not consider his walk beneficial only from a point of physical health; he looked upon it really as a means of escaping from the dull urbanity of the town. To him there was nothing dreary about this road with its red uneven surface and the bush and swamp through which it runs. The smutty tales people told of it as a popular trysting place at night and of the motor excavators that dumped their sewage – their "sorrows" in "graves" on the southern side of the road had no effect on Mr Millbank for whom this road had become a place where he could be at peace with himself, where he could forget the ledgers and journals in the office where he worked, and be his natural self. And his natural self was a very simple, retiring and contented self.

He was forty-three, a bachelor with hardly any friends, and had not ambitions to be anything but what he was – the third accountant in the large office on the Strand where he had started out as a ledger clerk and been promoted automatically during the past twenty-four years. Besides this walk every evening, his recreations were reading and listening-in on the radio. An elderly uncle and aunt in Georgetown and a cousin in Barbados were the only relatives he possessed, and these might have well not have existed, for he neither visited them or corresponded with them. For the past fifteen years he had lived as a lodger and boarder in the home of a well-known family. His room was next door to the dining room – the only bedroom on the first storey – and the family treated him with an indulgent fondness as though he were a very well-behaved pet dog. Mr Milly, they called him.

They were fond of him at the office, too, and often teased him about his bachelor state and about his evening walks – and his deep religiousness. For it must be explained that Sunday was the only day on which Mr Millbank did not go for a walk. He was an active member of the Church of England, and not only attended morning mass and evensong, but was also a Sunday-school teacher and turned out every Sunday afternoon at three to take his class.

He had a sense of humour, and did not mind the teasing of his colleagues – even when they teased him about his churchiness; sometimes he would agree that going to church did not necessarily make people good, and he never took up a self-righteous attitude. Indeed, it was his sense of humour that saved him from much more ragging.

To the peasants along the road where he walked he was as familiar as though he was part of the landscape. Some of them even looked out for his tallish, slim figure clad in shorts and shirt of khaki drill, and black stockings. They always had a smile and a word for him – and sometimes he stopped to talk to them, asking them about their families and their work: how the cows and sheep were getting on, how was the weather affecting the crops, had young Balgobin got over his malaria?

It was not unusual for him to take a parcel of mangoes or jamoons or sapodillas, a gift from Ramjohn or Benji or Mary; and the Lamports – that was the name of the family who boarded him – would rag him about it.

"We're going to have to watch Mr Milly. I believe he has a girlfriend on Sorrow Dam." Or – "Mr Milly, when is the wedding coming off! She must be a rich widow with a lot of land if she can give you all these fruits!"

To which Mr Millbank might reply with a smile and a blush: "I'm keeping it a secret for the present. I'll let you know all about it in good time."

Rain did not prevent him from taking his walks. Indeed, he preferred rainy evenings. In his mackintosh and rubber overshoes and old sun-helmet, he stood by the grass parapet one evening and told Ramjohn: "I like walking through rain like this – and yet it saddens me, because I always think of you poor people and what you have to go through when the swamps overflow and come right over your doors. What about your yam beds? You think this water will trouble them?"

"Ah don't t'ink it, chief," said Ramjohn, passing a hand over his hair which the heavy drizzle had pasted flat to his skull. "De drains ah dig round dem working good. De water running off quick."

"Oh fine! The drains are a success, eh? Last rain season they let you down, remember?" Mr Millbank's gaze moved across the swollen trench to the distant provision-patches beyond Ramjohn's thatch-roofed hut, and there was a yearning light in his eyes, as though were it not that it would mean wading through ankle-deep, or even knee-deep water, he would have gone with Ramjohn to inspect the beds. Last Christmas he had made Ramjohn a gift of a shovel and a rake.

A half a mile further along, he stopped to smile at Benji who had just driven in the cows for the night. "It's a wonder they didn't get drowned," he said to him, after he had listened to Benji's tale of hardships on the flooded pastureland.

Benji, dripping wet, his black face shiny and cheerful despite his troubles, laughed. "Sah, de way you say dat it almost make me feel you woulda like to come an help me fetch dem in from de pasture."

Mr Millbank gave him a quick look, then as though catching himself, smiled and said, "Yes, yes, Benji, sometimes I do feel I'd like to."

When he moved on eventually, his face took on a thoughtful look, and now and then he smiled secretly to himself as he gazed around at the wild, drab scene overburdened with wetness. The rain hissed around him, steadily and with an insistence that made it seem as if it would go on for weeks and months without cessation. Water hurried along in the trenches with a bubble and gurgle, and kept the weeds that grew in them at a perpetual slant and in perpetual waving animation. The huts and mud-houses and the tiny cottages stood each on their spacious patch of land looking drenched and lonely but somehow suggestive of warmth and cosiness within. Whenever Mr Millbank's gaze rested on one of them his eyes would narrow wistfully and he would shake his head slightly.

On his way back – he never went further than the Water works – he saw two of Mary's four children wading in a pond which the rain had made before their shapeless mud-walled home. One wore a dirty, ragged shirt, one nothing at all, but they were both shrieking and happy, splashing water on each other, churning the pool into a muddy slush. Mr Millbank shouted and waved, and their activities ceased as suddenly as if someone had pressed a button. They stared and grinned sheepishly and called: "Howdy, sah!"

Their mother heard the voices and appeared at the door, drawing aside the rice-bag which served as a curtain. Her broad black face turned broader in a smile as she waved and called: "Howdy, Mr Millbank! Ow, sah! In all dis rain! Tek care you ketch cold!"

"No chance of it, Mary! I'm too accustomed to the rain now!"

In his voice were mingled both bravado and camaraderie – and slight regret; it was as if he felt guilty because he knew that in half-an-hour he would be safe and dry and reading a book by electric light in his room, while she would still be close to the damp earth and the wild, rank vegetation, struggling to prevent rain-laden gusts of wind from putting out her kerosene lamp, listening to the gurgle of water and wondering when it would invade her home.

"See and get home safe, sah!" she called.

"I will, Mary! I will! How is the new lamb?"

"It getting on good! If de wedder fair tomorrow when you pass you can come in and ah will show you it!"

It might well have been this evening that proved the deciding spark that brought into flame Mr Millbank's long-smouldering yearnings. It might have been. No one can be sure. But during the next few months he became a very active man; so much so that he was the subject of much speculative gossip and the object of renewed and persistent ragging.

"I hear you're spending your evenings in some queer places, Mr Milly," Mrs Lamport teased. "And keeping funny company. I always said Sorrow Dam would spoil you."

"Sometimes it's good to be spoilt," smiled Mr Millbank – but in his manner there was no vague weariness. Had the Lamports been more perceptive they would have realised that he was only being good-humouredly polite, that their ragging and their unoriginal banter had long ago ceased to amuse him.

At the office it was the same.

"I hear a rumour that you are spending all your savings on a widow, Mr Milly. Is it true?"

"Yes," nodded Mr Millbank, switching on his sense of humour as usual, though nobody seemed to detect that he did so with a sighing effort. "She lives in a cottage a little past Sorrow Dam."

Only the peasants beyond Sorrow Dam did not have to wonder and speculate about Mr Millbank's activities.

Ramjohn said one evening, "Your friends going t'ink it very funny, chief. They going say you gone mad. But I understand how you feel."

Mary told him: "Don't mind what people talk, Mr Millbank. Dem townpeople ain' know what living is yet. From what ah see of you all dese evenings since you passing here ah know is a good step you taking."

Benji, too, was certain it was a sound move. "Ah don't t'ink you will regret it, sah. It's a few years very well since you been taking walk on dis road. You must know you' mind by now."

Several others said they thought he was doing right, and wished him well.

When, at last, he handed in his resignation at the office and told the Lamports that he was leaving them it was just as the peasants had predicted. Everybody said he was mad – and they said it as though they meant it. This time there was no ragging. No conventional jokes.

"But why," they wanted to know, "why did you have to spend your money buying land and building a cottage in that awful part of the country?"

"How," they demanded, "how could you possibly exist farming and keeping cows? Do you know what a hard life it is?"

And now Mr Millbank did not have to be careful about hiding the weariness. He sighed and told them: "Yes, I do know what a hard life it is, that's why I'm going away from you all to live such a life. And believe me, I am going to live."

And Mr Millbank, despite all that was said, despite all that everyone did to dissuade him, went and lived in the little cottage he had built. And he still lives there and works hard and wades barefooted through the rain to bring in his cows. Like any of the peasants. Himself a peasant. The silly madman!

MR. JONES OF PORT-OF-SPAIN

For the sake of discretion, I'll call them the Joneses. Well, the Joneses moved in to the cottage next door to us, on the west; a cottage which had been vacant for as long as two weeks in spite of the acute house shortage in Port of Spain. The Smiths – I'll call them that – our eastern neighbours, had told us that the Joneses were expected, and had hinted that they were not much of a family, socially speaking, though they were very well off. Mrs. Smith said to my wife and myself one evening, during one of our cross-portico chats, that she had heard that Jones used to be a chauffeur.

"Just an ordinary chauffeur," she said. "But he started up some sort of mechanic shop – that's how he made his money. It's a big concern now."

Besides this, she mentioned something about his complexion and the quality of his hair which made it quite plain that she, at least, did not intend to cultivate him and his family as acquaintances. Her snobbery always amused us, but, at heart, she is not a bad sort, so we've never chided her for it.

Anyway, the Joneses moved in, as I've said, and we found them a very pleasant and friendly family, though it was some time before we really got to know them well. For the first few weeks, we could only observe them as neighbours and speculate.

Mr. Jones was a shortish, strong-looking man of about forty-eight, dark of complexion, with kinky hair. He always had a smile and a tentative wave for us when we encountered him, and it was obvious that had he not considered it unconventional he would have called out some cheerful remark. Once, when he was on the point of getting into his car, a light-blue Buick which was always parked by the side of the road, like many others, for lack of a garage, he did call out to me: "A lot of rain today, eh?", though his voice sounded self-conscious.

"Yes. Awful, wasn't it?" I smiled back, not feeling at ease myself.

His wife, fair-complexioned and of a faded prettiness, seemed shyer; if our eyes happened to meet she would smile and nod and immediately avert her gaze. There were a daughter and son, too, the daughter about twenty-two and the son eighteen or nineteen, both of whom appeared far too preoccupied with their activities and pleasures to notice the neighbours. The son was a footballer, and often came home on an evening muddy and perspiring and full of laughter and banter. The daughter seemed to have a lot of acquaintances, and there was a continuous coming and going of them with shrieks and shrill chatter between five in the afternoon and nine or ten at night. She played the piano, but, oddly enough, it was always serious music we heard. Never jive.

One evening, an unexpected shower caught me on the Pitch Walk, the promenade that borders the Savannah, and as I was hurrying along, making for the shelter of Queen's Royal College, a car drew up by the kerb – a light-blue car – and a voice called: "Come in, let me give you a drop home!"

It was Mr. Jones.

I thanked him as I got in beside him. "Never dreamt it would have rained," I said. "The sky was absolutely clear when I left home."

"Yes, very funny weather we're having," he said, and gave an ingratiating little laugh. After a brief silence, he fidgeted and said that he hoped it would be fair next week for the Municipal Elections.

Was I interested in them?

"Not very," I told him, and did not think it necessary to go into details, because I could see that he was merely trying to make conversation.

His round, dark face took on a whimsical look, as though my reply, though brief, had intrigued him. He smiled and said he couldn't blame me.

"The kind of men they put up as candidates, how you can put any confidence in them? They've asked me to do some canvassing, but I'm not keen myself. But I suppose I've got to show my face, for the sake of policy." He laughed self-consciously, and fidgeted again. Asked me abruptly: "In a hurry to get home? What about taking a spin round the Savannah?"

I told him it was all right. I was in no particular hurry. There was something about him I liked. He had none of the airs one would expect of the *nouveaux riches*. And he exuded a spirit of friendliness.

So, instead of turning off from Queen's Park West, we continued around the Savannah, one of the endless line of cars that travelled round and round. Every car owner in Port of Spain considers it his duty to drive round the Savannah in the early evening; it is a ritual that distinguishes the financially successful: it signifies beyond all doubt that you have arrived.

We must have encircled the Savannah three times before Mr. Jones decided to turn off into Cipriani Boulevard and make for home. By this time he had lost much of his initial diffidence and was entertaining me with various little anecdotes relating to the men who worked for him in his motor-repair shop. He seemed fond of talking, but I could detect that he was of the rare kind who knew how to make his conversation genuinely interesting and lively; not once did I have the inclination to yawn.

When we were getting near home, however, I noticed that he began to get fidgety again, and his conversation died away. Died away with a suddenness that he himself must have realized was very conspicuous. He did not seem so much diffident now as worried. It was as though his cheerfulness had been a screen for something that was on his mind. After a silence, he glanced at me in a half-preoccupied way and remarked: "By the way, how about your laundry? Do you have any trouble in getting your things washed?"

"No. No, I can't say I do," I replied. "Why do you ask?"

"Oh, well, everything is so difficult nowadays, you know," he said, shifting about and frowning. Then he tried to smile as though to cover up the frown and said in a too offhand tone: "You like crossword puzzles?"

"I'm afraid not," I said. "Never been particularly keen on them."

I did my best to make my voice sound as casual as possible, for I didn't want to increase his discomfort, but inwardly I felt very curious. Why should he have asked me two such irrelevant questions in quick succession?

He laughed and said his wife was very enthusiastic about crossword puzzles. "That's all she takes the *Evening News* for," he said. "Not for the news – just for the crossword puzzles." Half to himself he murmured: "I'm always pulling her leg about it. Got to humour these wives, you know. Must humour them if you want a little peace." He gave a slight start as though he had said more than he had intended, glanced at me and asked, "You play bridge?"

"Well, now you've put your finger on something," I smiled. "I'm a positive fiend. Do you play?"

"Always been a keen player. Well, look, you must come over one evening and make a four. Bring the wife, too, if she plays."

I told him by all means, and he said what about Friday night.

"Yes, we have nothing particular to do Friday. Nine-ish, say?"

He hesitated, then said: "Better make it half-past eight, if it won't put you out." He gave a little uneasy chuckle and added: "The truth is, the wife doesn't like to play too late. She likes to retire at half past eleven at the latest. Got to humour these wives."

He seemed on the point of saying something else, but evidently thought better of it. I saw the worried frown on his face again.

Friday night was a success. Mrs. Jones was a good player, even better than her husband. In fact, once or twice she had reason to chide him gently for little slips, even though she was my partner and did not suffer any loss.

"You could have made that hand," she said, on one occasion, "if you hadn't discarded that three of spades."

She was right, but from his hesitation I could see that he was not sure on the point. However, he agreed. "Yes, I think I see what you mean," he smiled, his manner indulgent, as though she were a child. "That three of spades, eh? Yes, I ought to have kept it. Sorry, partner," he said, smiling at my wife who was his partner. "My mind plays little tricks now and then."

Mrs. Jones laughed and asked him if he intended that as a pun, and he fidgeted and laughed, too. But awkwardly, his face going darker as he flushed under his deep tan. He looked in this moment like a schoolboy in class embarrassed by something the schoolmistress had said.

We were playing on the back-veranda, which, apart from being very cool, was separated from the sitting-room by the dining-room; Jacqueline – that was the daughter's name – was entertaining some of her friends in the sitting-room, and it would have been impossible to concentrate on any sort of game in there. In fact, Mr. Jones quite frequently made clucking apologetic sounds and murmured about the noise "those young people" were making. Once he smiled and made a few sententious remarks about youth and tender hearts, and then glanced at me and said: "Jacqueline is engaged, you know."

"Is she? When is the wedding?"

"Oh, some time soon." He began to fidget, and I could see the worried look coming to his face. He forced a laugh and said: "You'll soon see it listed in the *Sunday Guardian*. You know the column in the *Sunday Guardian* where they give the names of couples who have registered – I mean who have applied for licences," he hurried on. He reached back to a small bamboo table and took from a brass jardiniere on it a copy of the *Sunday Guardian*. He pushed it toward me, and I saw that it was folded into a narrow pad, as though purposely to mark and show up the column headed Forthcoming Marriages.

I told him I knew the column, but to be polite took the paper and pretended to be interested.

"Not a bad idea, eh?" said Mr. Jones, and there was an eagerness in his manner that puzzled me. "I mean publishing a list of the couples every week. Mr. Brown, tailor, to Miss Smith, seamstress."

He laughed.

Mrs. Jones was looking at him very intently, I noticed. Suddenly she smiled and said: "It's your turn to deal, Charlie."

"Is it? Oh, sorry! Cut already?"

"Yes, cut and mounted," said his wife, and he took up the pack of cards with such confused haste that he dropped two of them. After this, I had no doubt whatever that something was definitely wrong. He wanted to confide whatever was worrying him in me, but hadn't the courage. Could it be that he needed advice in some matter and thought that I was qualified to give it? Was it something that concerned his daughter's engagement? But why would he consider me as qualified to advise him on this subject?

On Sunday morning, when I opened the *Guardian*, I found myself, for the first time, interested in the Forthcoming Marriages column. "Barrister to marry City Stenographer" was the headline this Sunday, and my eyes travelled down the list. Mr. So-and-so, clerk, to Miss So-and-so, typist, and Mr. So-and-so, chauffeur, to Miss So-and-so, domestic servant. It was a regular social document, in its way. Yet, I couldn't see why it should seem so intriguing to Mr. Jones.

We had him and Mrs. Jones over on the Wednesday night to bridge with us, and on this occasion he played so well that we had to congratulate him on several instances. At shortly after eleven, when they were about to leave, I noticed that his manner became a little detached. He did not seem inclined to join in the usual postmortem, but instead kept looking slowly around the sitting-room.

Suddenly he said to my wife, ignoring the fact that we were supposed to be listening to a detailed exposition by his wife as to how she had made her contract of five spades redoubled in the last hand – he said: "I like your window curtains. Do you have them washed at home, or do you send them to a laundry?"

"To a laundry," my wife told him.

Mrs. Jones broke off and glanced at him, and it was no ordinary glance. In it was surprise, admonition and a touch of derision. She smiled slightly, and went on discussing the last hand, her husband hastily apologizing for having interrupted her.

"Couldn't help remarking on the curtains, though," he murmured. He seemed so uncomfortable that he evoked my compassion. He began to drum with his fingers on the table, listening – or pretending to listen to the wife – a faint, fixed smile on his face. Observing him unobtrusively, I could detect a frustration and impotence that seemed both puzzling and pathetic.

The following afternoon, at about five, I set out on my usual stroll. I generally went along the Pitch Walk as far as the tram-terminus, and then either sat on a bench and smoked a cigarette or wandered down into the Rock Garden to look at the fishes in the ponds. This afternoon I decided on the Rock Garden.

Seated on a rock beside the easterly of the two ponds was Mr Jones. He was smoking a pipe and gazing reflectively into the water.

He glanced up and smiled, in no way surprised at seeing me. He said, holding out his hand: "I felt you were going to come here this afternoon. I wanted to have a little chat with you. Something I've been wanting to ask you for a little time."

I told him to go ahead. "I knew you were worrying over something. Why didn't you ask me before?"

He laughed briefly – awkwardly – and crossed his legs and then uncrossed them. "I should have, I know," he said hesitantly, "but I couldn't bring myself to, somehow. It might seem to you so stupid. That was what I was afraid."

He gave me a swift, shy glance and rose. Laughed and said that perhaps he had better not bother. It was really such a trifling matter – and so stupid.

"Never mind. Let's hear what it's all about." I urged. "Get it off your chest, and it mightn't worry you any more."

"Yes, I know, but…"

He laughed again, and knocked out his pipe. I could see he was going through a struggle with himself. At length, as though the torture of indecision was too much for him, he said: "Well, look, I'll tell you. It's just a little word that's bothering me. I know you know plenty about words. I'm not an educated man, if you understand what I mean. And it's not something I can talk to the children about. You see, the wife is a little particular about some things, and it's really because I want to please her. It's hard to explain."

He stopped speaking, almost breathless. He kept smiling and flushing and tapping his pipe against his hand.

He gave me a glance and asked me if I thought him foolish.

"Not at all," I said, feeling uncomfortable but doing my best to appear at ease. "You just go right ahead and say what you want to say. What word is this that's troubling you?"

He looked down at his shoes and said: "Well, it's – well, to tell the truth, it might be more than one word." He glanced up suddenly and asked: "What you'd call a man who washes clothes?"

"Why, a laundryman, of course," I said.

He nodded. "Yes, I know. But I mean, suppose you didn't want people to know right out that he was a laundryman, what you'd call him? You can't think of a good word or – or a good phrase you can describe him by?"

I rubbed my chin for a bit and then said: "I suppose you mean a sort of euphemistic term, eh?"

He grinned and said: "Don't forget. I warned you. I don't know any big words."

"Sorry," I said. "I didn't mean to sound highbrow. Well, look here, suppose we say 'clothes machine operator' or something like that. I take it this fellow you mean works at a modern steam laundry?"

"Yes. Yes, it's a modern steam laundry." There was a note of hope in his voice. His eyes sparkled. " 'Clothes machine operator', eh?" He repeated the phrase over and over, as though abruptly forgetful of my presence, his eyes fixed on the distance. Then his face registered disappointment. He shook his head. "No, I don't think that will do. The wife won't like that. We mustn't mention the word 'clothes', you see. That's what we've got to avoid."

I thought again, and then said: "Well, what about this: 'Raiment renovator'?"

I said it, I admit, more or less with my tongue in my cheek, though with the sincere wish to be helpful, for I was sorry for him in his obvious plight of distress and discomfort.

He gave a start and snapped his fingers. His face was like a lamp that had flashed alight. He gripped my arm and said: "That's it! Yes, that's it! 'Raiment renovator'. Good Lord! Why we couldn't have thought of that all along! 'Raiment renovator'. It has just the right sound."

"Of course, it's a bit far-fetched," I said.

"Far-fetched? No. Oh, no! Not at all! It's just right. 'Raiment renovator'." He repeated it again and again, as though it were a magic password he had just learnt. He gripped my hand and wrung it.

"I don't know how to thank you," he said. "You've done me a great favour. You see, the wife was so upset, and I don't like to see her like that. I like to humour her. You know what these wives are like. You've got to humour them."

He asked me if I'd like to go for a drive round the Savannah. I said I didn't mind, and we moved off toward the roadway. I thought that the matter was ended and that he would leave my curiosity unsatisfied. But I was wrong. As we walked he explained that his daughter Jacqueline had gone and got herself engaged to be married to a young man beneath her socially – a laundryman, to be exact – and her mother was so worried. "It's not that we're really snobs," he said, "but, you see, my wife has her little whims. She said how it would look to see it appear in the *Sunday Guardian*! Mr. Jack Green, laundryman, to Miss Jacqueline Jones, stenographer. It wouldn't have sounded nice, you see. We puzzled our brains until we were tired and we couldn't think of another word or phrase to use instead of 'laundryman'. But now you've solved the whole problem. 'Raiment renovator'. That's just the thing! Sounds proper and respectable and kind of high-class, even. Really, I can't thank you enough…"

AMIABLE MR. BRITTEN

I'm writing this in the hot sun, sitting on a bench without a back in Mr. Britten's yard. Roughly made bench, one end higher than the other, and I'm not in a comfortable position, but I don't feel uncomfortable. I have a lap-board for the paper I'm writing on. Mr. Britten lent it to me. It's like an oversize slate but without a frame and made of thin purple-heart wood. Not as even a surface as I could have wanted; now and then my pencil-point sinks through the paper into sudden little pits and nearly breaks – but I don't mind. It doesn't discourage me. I just go on writing. It's about Mr. Britten I'm writing, and I'm enjoying doing it. Whole thing moves so smoothly I feel as if my brain is oiled. Nothing sensational, nothing exciting. No plot, no love-interest. Not even, a story, strictly speaking. I haven't got to stop to think or anything. No trouble about construction or punctuation. Yet it's coming out perfectly. Not a flaw. And easily. Like magic – or electricity. It must be because Mr. Britten is such a pleasant man. Being with him makes you feel at ease, and I suppose that's why it's easy to write about him.

Old black man. Short. And he has white hair like lamb's wool. It grows round his head, leaving the top bald. Sometimes it seems like snow on the slopes of a mountain – but warm, cosy snow that wouldn't make you shiver if you sat on it. He's old – about seventy-five – but he doesn't behave like it. His manner isn't old, and he does carpentry work and cabinet-making. And washes his black-and-white dog. When I dropped in at his place today he was washing his dog. He's doing it now. The dog is standing in a large white enamel basin with black patches where the enamel has flaked off. I can see them from where I'm sitting here.

He's sitting on a chair – one of the chairs he himself made. It's crude-looking but strong, and seems as if it can bear any weight. The usual pleasant look is on his face. Not an old-man look. Nothing dreamy or drooling about him. He's as alert as you or I – as any of the chaps who come here to see him. His complexion is dark brown – so dark it almost seems to have a touch of red in it. Rich, seasoned tint. His head could easily have been carved out of some hard wood and carefully stained and polished. His body is upright. Not in any way decrepit. You never hear him groaning, either, or puffing or muttering to himself as many old men do. No slouching. And he doesn't walk with a stick. He might be a young man, though the big reason why he couldn't be is because his face always looks so composed and wise and agreeable. I don't care what you say, no young man's face could look like this, no matter how he tried.

He never talks a lot. No reminiscing about the good old days and that kind of thing. Man of very few words – reassuring words.

When he says anything to you you feel he just couldn't be wrong. And not only that; he makes you feel that if you remain in his vicinity you'll be safe from any danger – even from atom bombs. The other chaps who come here think so, too. They haven't told me so, but I know they feel this way.

He lives in the Belmont part of Port of Spain, Trinidad. His house stands on the higher of two terraces of land. More a hut than a house, really. It's just an oblong thing with a corrugated iron roof – rusty – and walls made of more rusty corrugated iron and some old boards nailed together anyhow. The front part consists of a kind of veranda with a rail but no balusters. There are two doors. Always closed. Not one of us has ever been inside his hut; he never asks anybody in, and nobody asks him to let them go in. He does his entertaining – if it can be called that – in the yard.

On the lower terrace of land there's an old open shed, and it's under this that he does his carpentry work and cabinet making. It stands near two mango trees, and when you come into the yard and look around you you have the feeling that the mango trees, Mr. Britten's work-shed and his hut and Mr. Britten himself want you to be there. You never feel uncertain whether you should come into the yard. You never feel you might be in the way or prove a nuisance to anybody.

Mr. Britten will most likely be at work in his shed, though sometimes he will be sitting on his verandah smoking a pipe – a black pipe with a gnarled bowl, and very bad-smelling – that's assuming you don't like the smell of strong pipe-tobacco. He's always in black serge trousers and a white shirt. The trousers look dusty and oil-stained in patches. If it's Sunday he'll be in his good black serge suit. Clean. Waistcoat, too. Not a speck on his clothes, and his trousers well-creased. He doesn't go anywhere on Sundays – or at any time; he just sits on his verandah on a backless stool or bench and smiles round at the yard, his face composed and pleasant. And don't think he looks ridiculous doing this. A man of dignity. You can't help respecting him.

As you come into the yard he'll give you a slight smile and a nod and make a gesture with his hand – very casual – to indicate that you must make yourself at home the best way you can. "Sit down," he might murmur. He speaks perfect English. Reminds me I should have mentioned he's supposed to be a retired civil servant living on a pension. Not a Trinidadian. He came from British Guiana nineteen years ago. He likes Trinidad but doesn't like the Trinidadians. That's what he tells you, but there's generally a good natured smile on his face as he says it. You can sense he means it, though – yet, curiously, his manner doesn't show any dislike. And the chaps who drop in to see him are Trinidadians – Belmont chaps – and he welcomes them all with his smile and nod and the casual make-yourself-at-home gesture. There's this about him, too, I ought to tell you. He never does anything to entertain us in the way a host should. No asking you to be seated or offering you a cigarette or a drink. It's as though he considers his presence enough. His presence and his yard-room. If you expect more than that, his manner seems to imply, you can go to the devil for all he cares.

The chaps who come to see him come mostly, it appears, to study or to discuss books and bookish topic. Studious. Grave-faced. They never laugh. They seem not to have any sense of humour. You can generally see two or three of them squatting or lying on their stomachs near the hut or the shed – anywhere at all in the yard – talking with frowns or reading. You would think the place belongs to them. They don't take any notice of Mr. Britten, and Mr. Britten doesn't take any notice of them. Though sometimes just abruptly one of them will get up and go to him and ask him a question. Ask him to settle some argument, and right away he'll stop what he's doing and smile and chat with them. Then they'll wander off again, and that's that. No fuss, no formality.

I wish you could see him now. He's drying the dog with a pink and white towel, his face quietly absorbed. His bald head gleaming in the sun. The shadows of the mango trees have got past where he's sitting. The dog looks indifferent. One of the most emotionless dogs I've ever seen. Has a sort of nonchalant, bored-aristocrat air, too.

I must tell you, before I forget, about Mr. Britten's hobby. Apart from his carpentry and cabinet-making, he has a special hobby. His most important. You'd hardly believe it, but he writes stories – very short things about fifty or sixty words and very simple. No involved plots. No clever dialogue. No sting in the tail and all that kind of thing. He showed me one a few minutes ago – just before I started writing mine here. It was about two young men who came into his yard to read and talk bookish things. A woman looked over the fence and saw them and began to giggle. Then she went off and began to talk a lot of stupid gossip about the two young men. The End. That was all the story. And guess how he does these stories: He never pens them or types them. He carves the letters of the words out of little bits of wood, and glues them together on a square slab of harder wood like a draughts board. The finished product looks like some quaint miniature mosaic. I told him once that it must call for a lot of patience and skill to do this, but he only nodded and said: "Yes. But no hurry. I have plenty of time on my hands."

He's just strolled up and is watching me. "Writing?" he smiles. He's filling his pipe.

"Yes," I answer. "About you and this place here."

I feel him looking down at me with a kind of quiet indulgence and passivity. No patronage in his manner, though. It just strikes me that he doesn't seem very real. It's as though his presence beside me is some queer mistake in time. I'm not in the least worried, all the same.

The words keep oozing off my pencil. That's all I care about. Such neat writing. I've never written so neatly before. Really amazing the way I can't do anything wrong today.

"Want my lap-board," says Mr. Britten.

"Oh, good," I say, and give it to him at once. He moves away but I still go on writing. I have the paper laid out flat on the bench now, and the seat is very rough, but my handwriting just can't help being neat. The sun is shining through blue-grey clouds. Thunderclouds. This makes the sunshine seem hotter, but I don't mind; I feel no discomfort. I like it. Its pleasant warmth. Welcome – like Mr. Britten's yard. I'm comfortable here, and feel good inside. Easy and at peace. I have an idea. I'm going to ask Mr. Britten to set up my story in wood as he does his own.

This didn't happen, though, because I may as well tell you – if YOU haven't guessed already – that I dreamt all this about Mr. Britten on a winter night in Bagshot, Surrey. Temperature thirty-eight degrees Fahrenheit by my room-thermometer. I got out of bed at ten past one and jotted down the essentials. If I hadn't done this it would have faded out of my memory by the time I got up at seven. I shut my eyes now and the details swim back easily into my mind. And the mood. The mood was not easy to retain. It's all right now. I've got it down, but I know that in a few hours it will go tailing off like thin smoke, and I'll never recapture it.

It seems, I know, as if I've tried to pull a fast one on you, but believe me, I really did dream this. No frillings. Nothing added. Anyway, to console you a little more, I'll tell you this: I did know Mr. Britten. In Berbice, British Guiana, as a boy in my early teens. I'd forgotten him utterly and completely until I dreamt about him on this winter night. Died about ten or fifteen years ago. He was a retired schoolteacher and a churchwarden. A sidesman, too. He took up the collection at choral Eucharist and at evensong, and helped the rector to count it after the service in the vestry. Amiable old gentleman.

A PLAGUE OF KINDNESSES

She was an elderly lady, plump but rather tall, in a faded purple dress, and she smiled all the time when she was showing us over the large double room. She said she was sure my wife and I would be comfortable here. See? There were two gas-rings; we could do all the cooking we wanted. And we mustn't be afraid about the current; she herself retired very early every night and hardly used any. Another thing, too, was that we could have in all the friends we wanted at any time; they wouldn't disturb her. We must make ourselves *quite* at home... Oh, and she mustn't forget about the bath! It went, without saying, that we could share the bath with her; she bathed on Friday nights only, so we could have it to ourselves on the other nights. And she wouldn't need it in the morning before ten, by which time, of course, we would be at work.

Her smile widened, and we could almost see the good nature vibrating out of her as she clasped her fat pink hands together on her full, though shapeless bosom and regarded us. Tiny wrinkles gathered around her twinkling blue eyes as she said, "There's always hot water. I keep the boiler going all day and night."

Something else occurred to her, and she moved with an easy thump and swish to the window nearest, and pointed. Struck the tip of her forefinger against the glass and said: "Just around the corner there is the tube station. You travel by bus, you said; we're near to the tube, too. Three minutes' walk. I've done it in two when I was in a hurry."

She added a few remarks about the park, and I agreed with her that the view was not at all bad. I asked her about the rent, and she replied: "Three guineas. For both of you."

She looked at us with an air of drama.

"Yes, three guineas for both of you. I purposely wouldn't state it on the card I put in the news agent's window because it might have left the wrong impression." She laughed, revealing a denture that seemed too large for her mouth.

"You see, people would have been sure to think there must be a snag somewhere. Not many good double rooms can be got nowadays for such a price."

She grew suddenly grave and sighed. "No", she said. "No, it's simply that I realise there isn't much money about now. People can't afford to pay the high rents that are being demanded. Oh, I really think it's shameful the profiteering being practised. I can't understand why people should want to take advantage of the housing shortage. This world is getting more terrible every day. Everyone is growing so hardhearted. There's no kindness. No kindness at all."

She looked slowly round the room, her wide, much-veined face earnestly sad and regretful. But gradually the smile returned, and she asked us if there was anything more we could think of that might have slipped her.

"Oh! I was to have mentioned this!' she said quickly.

"There are two blankets on each bed, but if it gets colder and you require any more, just let me know. And about the laundry, I'll see after all the bed linen myself. And any towels you may need washed – I'll have them done at my expense. I've calculated for that so don't let that bother you."

She pointed to the rug before the fireplace and asked us how we liked it. "Don't you think it rather quaint? My husband brought it from India years and years ago. He was in the Army. I'm a widow."

We agreed that we liked it.

"I thought you would. Everyone who sees it likes it." She clasped her hands together again with an air of childish satisfaction.

"Must I expect you on Saturday, then?" she asked, after a pause. "I'd have to do a little cleaning up, of course. Oh, that's something else I ought to have mentioned. You won't have to worry about cleaning up.   I do that myself. I like doing things about the house, so it won't be any trouble. And if you have to be out at work, you won't have time to make the beds, naturally, so you can leave that to me, too. Oh, no it won't be too much work for me. You mustn't feel so. I like work. Often I think it's all that keeps me alive. I so detest being idle."

On Saturday, she took our ration books and said that she would attend to them for us, have our addresses changed and get us registered with the various trades people. No, it was no trouble. She enjoyed doing these things.

"I know what it's like for you working people," she said. "You have so little time to attend to your personal affairs. If you don't mind, I could help you so at times with your shopping. You can leave a list of what you want and I'll take your ration books and do my best for you. No, no! Please don't look on it as a bother for me. I have to do my own shopping every morning, and it won't be any trouble."

She was so sincere about it that it would have been both ungracious and ungrateful for us to protest any more than we did, so we fell in with this arrangement, and after a week or two found it so convenient that we let her keep our ration books altogether and buy our groceries. We had no oven, so at weekends she did our joint for us; she said that it would be a shame to let our meat ration lapse week after week when she had the means of cooking it. We offered to let her have it as we were not so keen on meat and could very well do without it, but she said no, our health would suffer if we didn't eat meat.

'I had a cousin who took up with this vegetarian fad," she told us, "and in no time her health broke down. She came out in a scaly rash. Oh, she was a terrible sight for weeks! Really, you mustn't consider doing without your meat. I do my own joint every Saturday, and it won't be any extra work doing yours at the same time."

Soon we came to look forward to Saturday evenings, for she certainly knew how to cook a joint and she had a knack of judging exactly when we had come to the end of a meal, and just at the right moment there would be a tap on the door and in she would come with something on a tray for our dessert: stewed apples with cream, or pudding, or some homemade ice-cream.

On Monday mornings she took away our bath-towels and dishcloths to have them laundered, and there was the Sunday morning when we went for a stroll in the park to take advantage of the brilliant sunshine – my wife generally did her washing on Sunday morning – and returned at noon to find that the contents of our laundry-bag were missing. On investigation, we discovered that everything had been washed and was hanging on a line in the backyard.

"It was such beautiful sunshine. I can so well understand your wanting to go out and enjoy it," smiled our landlady, her sleeves rolled high above her elbows, her whole robust person smelling of soapsuds. "I simply couldn't resist the temptation of doing them for you. In less than an hour they ought to be dry. The weather seems to have taken a turn for the better, at last. We did need some sunshine, didn't we?" she sighed.

It was fine the following Sunday, too, and she came in and said: "Now, you two just go out into the fresh air and sunshine and take as much of it as you can. Cooped up the whole week long in an office! I think I'm going to do a little washing, and I'll take your soiled things and see after them as I did last Sunday. Now, now! Please! I won't hear of any objections!"

We did try to make a few more, insisting that we thought it would be imposing on her to expect her to do it again, but realising that she was determined and in earnest, we thanked her and went out.

It was rainy the next Sunday, but she came in and took charge of our washing just the same. "I can dry them before the fire," she explained. "I do it whenever I wash my own things. It's nothing new to me."

My wife mentioned that she had two pairs of socks of mine she wanted to darn before they were put in the wash, and our landlady interrupted her and agreed that certainly it was always best to darn socks before washing them. "Which reminds me," she hurried on, "I have some darning to do. Perhaps I could make one job of it while I'm about it. I've always been fond of darning. It was a regular joke with my husband when he was alive. He used to say that if I did neglect him in some ways, I'd never let him go with undarned socks. I have an idea he meant it as some sort of wicked little pun," she tittered, "but I could never see the point. Ah, well, he's gone now and I don't like *saying* it, but I'm afraid he wasn't always appreciative of everything I did for him." She looked a trifle sad and wistful and shook her head slightly. But in an instant her smile and twinkle had come back and she hurried off with our washing – and socks to be darned.

On the Thursday of the same week I had to take to bed with the 'flu.

"What! Aren't you at work?" She stared at me in dismay.

And no ordinary dismay; she really seemed taken aback and shocked.

When I explained about the 'flu, her brows creased up with annoyance. "But a little flu to keep you at home! My husband went out with worse than that. It's incredible that you should let such a trifling ailment keep you in bed! How do you expect me to tidy the room with you lying here all day! Oh, this in really most upsetting! I never, never bargained for this!"

She bumped out of the room, grumbling and clicking her tongue.

"Perhaps it's my fault for not explaining to you," she said, later that day when she swept in upon me suddenly after a brief knock.

"I simply can't tolerate illness of any kind. You can put it down to a little oddness on my part," she went on, looking everywhere but at me and taking up things from the dressing-table and putting them down. "A little quirk, if you like, but there it is! I've never been laid up in bed in my memory. I don't say I mightn't suffer from a cold like anyone else, but I never make a fuss over it – and I just can't stand people who pamper themselves. Really I can't! Oh, it annoys me terribly. Would you like a cup of hot Oxo and a biscuit? Or a pot of strong tea?"

I had to ask her again what she had said. When she repeated her offer, I mumbled thanks – yes, I wouldn't mind. If it wouldn't be any trouble, I added, too ill and too astounded at her abrupt change of front to protest or argue.

But I found I was mistaken. She had not changed front. The frown was still on her face. "It would be no trouble at all," she snapped. "I keep telling you that so often. It's a habit of mine being kind to people. I like being kind. Well, what is it to be? Oxo or tea? I think it had better be Oxo. It's more nourishing."

Later, when I was sipping it, she asked me if I'd like a mustard bath.

"My husband never could develop a sniffle but he had to have one. And he a soldier! Oh, he was a terrible disappointment to me. A most exasperating man, I can assure you."

I told her I did not wish a mustard bath, and she did not insist.

"Very well," she said, "but don't blame me if you get any worse. You men always think it beneath you to listen to the advice of women. Do you wish another blanket" she asked, as she was on the point of going out.

I told her I didn't think so.

She grunted and went out. But the following morning she apologised. "I'm afraid I've been overworking a bit. My nerves are on edge. You mustn't take me too seriously when I lose my temper! She was all smiles and affectionate purrings. She moved about the room with quick whisks and thuds, dusting and putting things right, dressed in deep red, her hair done up in elaborate coils on her head.

That day she brought me chicken broth.

"My spiv brought me a chicken this morning," she said. "Whatever would we do without these spivs! Ah, well! I suppose the worst of us have our uses. I was never tired of trying to impress that on my husband – not that it made any impression on him, for he was such a bitter man. Even common gratitude I never succeeded in getting from him. Would you like a custard at tea time? I have an egg or two to spare. All right! Shush! Don't say a word. I'll go right ahead and make it."

About three weeks later when I told her that I had been lucky in securing an unfurnished flat she stared at me for fully five seconds without saying a word – then she smiled and exclaimed: "How nice! How nice! How glad you must be! Oh, you're fortunate, indeed! I shall miss you dreadfully, of course, but you deserve a home of your own. I know so many poor couples who have to live with relatives under the most terrible conditions."

She hurried out of the room, sighing and blinking rapidly.

Later, she said, "If I can assist you in any packing you want to do, don't fail to let me know. How soon will you be going?"

I told her at the end of the following week. We had intended giving her notice on Saturday coming.

"Oh, I'm so glad for your sake. I am sincerely."

For the rest of our time with her she said very little, and seemed unusually pensive and inclined to sighing, and on the day before our departure she said: "I do hope I'll get another couple like you. You've been so good in letting me do kindnesses for you. It's been my trouble all my life, you see. I can't be happy unless I'm doing kind acts and I get people's backs up against me before long. People get so tired of having too much kindness done to them. That's what soured my husband and embittered him against me. But you two! Oh, you two have been so patient and understanding in accepting my plague of kindnesses. That's why I shall miss you dreadfully. Dreadfully!"

She brushed at her eyes and hurried out.

THE SIBILANT AND LOST

Don't try to hurry me, and, above all, don't interrupt. I can't tolerate people who cut in when I'm narrating anything. I get annoyed, and I feel puny and flattened out – no, more like a balloon, if you know what I mean. I like being a balloon. I want to be big. Tall and inflated. In reality, I tower far above heaven, but your friend, the other doctor, wouldn't agree with me. He wouldn't co-operate with me at all. I nearly went mad when he came in the room here earlier today. Every word he uttered wounded me. But you're different. I behold love trembling around you like a pale-blue aura. Oh, I can be a Yogi when I want to be. You mightn't believe it, but quite often I float away and dwell on a Higher Plane.

I like the way you react toward me. I thought you might have been tempted to interrupt. I'm beginning to wonder if your heart and my head have not combined into one great political poem. No, no! Don't frown like that. *They* won't like it. We've got to be careful with *Them*, for I've made a pact with *Them*. Better for you to look bland and bright. Pretend the world and everybody in it are happy and never baleful. Pretend we have no Bomb to dread… Ah. Fine! Now I feel more comfortable and confident. Now I can begin to tell you how it happened. I know you're eager to learn the truth about the affair. I *mean* the truth – not propaganda.

No, no! Go on writing. I don't mind. In fact, I want you to take down my account of the happening. The event *ought* to be chronicled. Don't forget how important I am. I'm a pylon… Looming… Far up beyond the nebulae.

Well, we were holidaying on a little island off the mainland. We remained there for the better part of a month, and by "we" I don't mean *They* but my wife, Myrna, and my little boy and I. I'd hired a comfortable bungalow high up on a cliff overlooking a wide bay. Delightful view. The water looked green and clear. Green and pure. Like the plane of thought where I frequently retire to perfect my unworldly outlook.

We could hear the water lapping in the bay. Delicately plucking, lulling; foretelling tale upon tale in Delphic vein. All day we heard it, but only I could read the purport; only I knew what tale it foretold. I remarked to my wife that I didn't think it boded any good. I warned her that I had an idea my head might betray me even while my heart remained true. But that made her laugh and reply that if I wanted to be funny, who could prevent me? Her tone and manner dribbled ridicule, and a deep fury fermented in me, but I kept it in abatement. "Control," I muttered. "Learn to be controlled. No man may get to Nirvana without control. Oh, Gautama, hear my prayer!"

Her mother never wanted her to marry me. A grave woman, her mother. A carrion-bird, well-balconied – meaning embonpoint. From the beginning her mother detected the oddity in me – the bent bone. A leaning, probing woman, curved of beak, her mother beheld in me the phantom that moved in the Further Field and knew that a day would come when *They* would call me and demand that the pact with them be kept – or broken. But love hung in a great web, tarantula-hairy, before the yearning eye of my wife, then a mere girl of eighteen, erratic and, I fear, erotic; love curtained from her the other me that belonged to *Them*.

We were wedded quietly one day in April; no organ or oboe played our party down the aisle, but on coming out of the cathedralled fog into the kingdom of heavenly flower-cool air, a drifting leaf alighted upon her head, and everyone proclaimed it a happy omen. Only I – prophetic I – noted the tear on her ringed finger. Oh Fate! Murderer of the mellow moment when memory ought not to dwell on the dark tomb waiting!

For a year, and then another year, all went without turgid or untoward event. The flame of love wore well; no warped fork warned of what lay ahead. Even her mother, falcon-woman, deemed our mating to have panned out fair.

But at midday on the third day of our holiday on the island I remarked to Myrna that the wind gave me an odd feeling. It hummed too dankly, I told her, and with too great a dolour over my right temple.

"Don't bother about it," I heard her reply. Heard her a long way off, for I had drifted infinity-ward. From afar I probed her manner for mockery but found none. I looked at her reclining on the veranda, her hair waving in the wind. A beautiful woman – and forever ready to give in to any whim of mine. Too perfect a wife, I often felt. Too yielding to me. Not enough of the Teutonic battle-light in her eye… Many a night I dream of Brunnhilde doing love-combat with me. Binding me with her girdle. I break the girdle and then overpower her. I hear the foiled laughter of Gunther clanging through the gloom…

"The wind," I told Myrna. "I don't like it."

"Forget the wind. Get a book and read. It'll take your mind off the wind."

I wagged my head in doubt. "I don't think it will, my dear," I murmured. "Can't you detect the violet portent coming from the north?"

That alarmed her a bit, made her lean forward and frown at me. "Look here, you're letting your mind wander again. Remember what the doctor told you. Read a book or a paper whenever you feel it coming on. Go on. Get a book."

I obeyed, but within me I tittered, knowing my mind to be unaffected. But only I and *They* could know that. No matter how mad people thought me, my pact with *Them* held firm; no matter how cruel the mumbling crowd, I – I drifted above the world. I knew the radio-activated realm that none on earth could even in a dream preview.

I got the book and tried to read. I bided my time, and fooled her that I had forgotten the forlorn wailing in the wind. At about five o'clock that afternoon I looked at our little boy who, from early morning, had been banging an empty Ovaltine tin on the floor, beating time, all unaware, to the new rhythm that had come alive in me. I got up, went over and patted him on the head, and murmured: "Play on, dear young man. Play on. Time, not rhythm, will make our world revolve. For you and me – and for *Them* beyond the Barrier – twilight and decline are already mingled in that ulterior dream your mother will neither admit nor admire. If we could only make her know how real we are – we the phantom band! If only we could twine the thread of frightened Ariadne through the labyrinth of her mind and let her learn with what anger the brume will lower when *They* leap in arrival at our depleted door!"

He gave me a blank look, but didn't laugh. In the green quiet of that infant brain he knew. He fathomed the murk: the pall in the orient. He heard the hammer-blow falling in the not-far dawn. A red, red dawn.

"You and I," I told him, "in our blind valley, *we* are not mad, my boy. We know that the weak are doomed. We know the rule of Reality that men have forgotten."

"Ta," he replied. "Pa."

"How I agree with you, my lad," I nodded. "*Tel père…*"

"Ra," he told me. "Ra. Bah. Ra."

"Yo," I parried. "Yo-ho-ho! And a bottle of… Ah. Remarkable, my young friend, how we do agree upon everything!"

No, don't interrupt, Doctor. I beg you. One word from you and you'll break my contact with *Them* humped behind the curtain. I think I know what you want to find out. You want to know whether my wife and her family fathomed the gloom that threatened me. They did. My wife knew – and her mother and father.

Everyone knew. Yet they made no attempt to have me put away. Weak. They were all weak. A drooling, pampering crowd. They coddled me. Me waiting to puff them all into infinite dark, and they let me grow bigger and blacker and more looming.

A terrible thing, Doctor, when people grow too liberal-minded. Too over-mellow with humanity. The criminal and the mentally unfit ought to be liquidated quietly and without pain – for their own good and for the good of the community. Cruel? Not really. To build up a healthy, virile community you have to do many an act that might appear cruel. Today people think it kind – oh, what a fine thing! – to be lenient with a criminal. No death penalty. Not even a little flogging. But in reality they're not being kind; they're being weak. And the weak go under. Why deny the truth? Turn your mouth to a cruel man and you get a blow in the teeth – and another and another. The mad man and the criminal are never kind. Offer them power for power and they'll cower and retreat. If only our country could learn that! But hark!… A drum.

One evening, toward the end of the month, at about eight, we were dining on the verandah, when I heard a drum. In the bay. Muffled… No, not the wind. The wind had died down during the afternoon. Evening had come with bright yellow and red, and now the bay lay wrapped in a deepening mauve. The water held an indigo hue, faked here and there with emerald and purple. Oh, you could feel the venom in the air – if you were tactile in the temple. The temple about to be rent in twain… "Father, forgive them, for they know not. . ." Ah. But *They* know what They do. *They* never forgive me.

Our infant boy had already been put to bed. No danger from the night could penetrate him in the dark room. But I and *They* were here. We were the danger… Again I heard the thumping of that drum. It travelled like an angered ghoul over the gloomed abdomen of the bay.

"Do you hear it, Myrna?" I murmured, looking at her.

"Hear what?"

"The dampened thunder in the bay."

"You'd better keep your mind off that kind of thing."

"I can't. I have no ordinary mind. The doctor told you, didn't he?"

"Don't begin to pretend anything now. The doctor told you to forget about your mind, or you won't get well."

I laughed. "A great number of people today adopt your outlook, my dear. Forget the mud in the pool; only think of the blue reflected. Do all you can to prevent the truth from triumphing. That way, Myrna, can only lie defeat. We may ignore the Ugly Fact, but the Ugly Fact won't return the compliment. It will overtake you."

"Go on eating and don't talk rot."

"But I'm mad. I have the right to talk rot, haven't I?"

That made her wriggle.

"I greatly fear," I told her, after an interval, "that *They* have come. *They* are here."

"What do you mean?"

"What I'm telling you. Have you forgotten my pact with *Them*?"

"All right, I don't want to hear about it."

I toyed with my knife. I cut a potato. I thought within me: How dull people can be. They have known no earthquake, no hurricane, therefore they think it cannot happen to them; no building can tumble down upon them, no high wind can waft them into a dithering death. Life, they feel, will forever be filled with everyday routine, everyday traffic-rumbling. Only we few of the mercury mind can behold the phantom in the mire: the fell demon murder-burdened.

Even when I looked toward the room where our boy lay, my eye bright with intent to do bodily harm, Myrna could divine no threat.

"You know, my dear," I murmured, "I really ought to have been liquidated."

"Liquidated?"

I nodded. "Quietly – with a hypodermic needle." A thoughtful, troubled air came upon her.

"Too late now, though," I went on. "*They* leap eagerly at our portal."

Again the drum rumbled in the bay.

"Our boy," I told her.

"What about him?"

"Any day now he might utter the Forbidden Thing. Already he can tell me Pa and Ta and Ra. At any moment we can look forward to hearing him employ the tongue of the adder – and then what? *They* would be infuriated. Before that can happen I'll have to liquidate him. Tonight I mean to do it."

"Why don't you go on eating? You know you couldn't harm a fly. We'd have had you put away a long time ago if we'd thought you might prove –what are you getting up for?"

I made no reply, continuing to finger the blade of the knife. I wiped the food from it with my napkin. Even now, Doctor, Myrna didn't believe I meant to do anything. What a woman! Beautiful but incapable of looking beyond her mouth. Very good at protecting me from the prying world, very good at directing the doling out of my wealth. But her mind? Dull. Pewter dull.

"You're very typical of the time we live in," I told her.

"Put down that knife!"

"You fear me – yet you have let me undermine your kingdom, in the belief that you were being liberal in your outlook. But you were wrong. You were only being weak. I? I am mad and cruel. I am grand and powerful. I am blind and inhuman. And you? You with your belief in freedom of thought and in individuality – you and your bubbly kingdom of God and your anaemic morality – you are in a corner. We the grand and the powerful are bound to triumph, my dear, over people like you."

Myrna got up, white and alarmed.

"Too late," I told her, wagging my head. "You can't muddle through now. Not every time. Now you go under, you weak fool."

I hit her hard on the mouth. Knocked her out at one blow. Then I turned, and, with the knife, went into the room to deal with the boy.

Now you might want to know, Doctor, why I killed the boy and not Myrna. Well, the boy contained my own blood and bone; Myrna did not. I couldn't have the little fellow develop until he came to a point where he would give tongue like the adder, could I? I had my pact with *Them* to keep. I had to do the right thing and get rid of him.

No, no. Be quiet. Don't tell me anything. Let me do all the talking – to the brave, bitter end. You detect how I'm panting now? I'm near the end. In a moment I'll be gone… Up… Beyond the nebulae to Gautama in Never-never Nirvana… All in a big umbrella-puff.

No, don't pity me. I want no pity. I ought to have been killed off a long time ago. You have all been incredibly weak. Weak, weak, weak…

Really good of you to have heard me through, Doctor – and without interrupting. I think there could be no better way of rewarding you than by telling you about my pact with *Them*. I made it at eighteen when the prime cloud appeared above my right temple. I'm twenty-four now, and I haven't yet broken it… God, how I'm panting!… I behold the red light. *They* have come for me, Doctor. But no pity. I want none, I tell you. I merit none. I'm cold and cruel; blind and baleful.

I hear my heart beating… in the vale of unveiled vanity. Now it can be told. Now I can break my pact. I'm lost, Doctor! Sibilant and lost!

WEDDING DAY

"The car come yet, Ann?"

"No, Miss Edith, but it will soon be here."

"What about the flowers for the church?"

"The flowers all right. Jamsie gone to see after them."

"You sure Jamsie can choose the right flowers?"

"Yes, Miss Edith. Jamsie can get the right ones. He know about flowers. Look what a nice morning, Miss."

"Yes, it's a nice morning."

"Bright sun and everything fresh and green. Nothing to worry over, Miss Edith. You mustn't worry."

"You think nothing will go wrong, Ann?"

"No, nothing will go wrong. You mustn't afraid."

"That the car coming now? I think I heard a sound."

"No, it's not the car. It's only the pig grunting. I don't know why Jamsie didn't shut it up in the pen. I tell him to do it, but he must be forget."

"When he come back tell him to shut it up safe. It wouldn't do for the guests to come and find it roaming about."

"The guests won't mind, Miss. They know they coming to a country cottage. They must expect to find pigs running about."

"Still, we should have it lock up in the pen. It won't look proper. Mr. Graham have plenty good-class town friends who he invite to the wedding. It might make him feel shame to see the pig running about."

"Mr. Graham not a stupid man. If his friends same like him they won't think it funny to see a pig running round. This not a farm, Miss? A farm must got pigs and chickens on it. Don't worry your head over the pig, Miss Edith."

"I had a queer dream last night, Ann. I dream Mr. Graham and me had a row and he tell me he don't want to marry me anymore."

"Dreams don't mean nothing."

"With me they mean something. I have very bad luck, Ann."

"Bad luck don't last for always, Miss."

"With me it last for years and years, though. I don't know once things go straight with me. Since ten years ago, when I was twenty-three, I should have got married – and look what happen!"

"That was a accident, Miss Edith. It could have happen to anybody."

"No, Ann, that was plain bad luck. How many other men don't get their finger cut with a rusty knife and nothing go wrong with them! Why Robert had to get blood-poison and die off just four days before our wedding-day! It was my bad luck, Ann. Since I was a baby, bad luck follow my steps. Nothing ever go right for me. At the very last moment something always turn up to disappoint me."

"You mustn't think so, Miss Edith. Everything will go right this time. Mr. Graham going to make you a fine husband and you going to be happy with him. You will never have no regrets."

"You mean if the wedding take place?"

"What can stop it from taking place?"

"What can stop it, eh? All right, wait and see, Ann. I tell you, I have bad, bad luck, don't fool yourself. How much you want to bet at the very last minute today we get some terrible news and the whole wedding got to postpone? Perhaps postpone for ever!"

"You only fancy so, Miss Edith. You mustn't take up such a attitude, Miss. You must look on the bright side. Your luck turn. Not a single thing can go wrong no more. Look what a nice, handsome man Mr. Graham is – and such nice ways!"

"Nine o'clock striking, Ann. Better run in the kitchen and ask Janey how the chicken getting on. Tell her to keep basting it. I don't want it to get too brown."

"I going now, Miss. I must see about the sorrel drink, too."

"Janey!"

"Yes, Miss Edith?"

"The tarts finish baking?"

"Yes, Miss! I just take out the last one!"

"Ann in the kitchen there with you?"

"Yes, Miss Edith, I in here. You want something?"

"I think I hear the car coming. It's nearly eleven o'clock. I don't know how the man so late. Go down and see if he bring the right amount of ice. We'd be in a fix without enough ice!"

"All right, Miss!"

"What's it, Janey? Oh, the flowers, na? Where you get them?"

"Miss Chalmers send them, Miss. The boy just bring them. You like them, Miss Edith?"

"Yes, they nice. Very good of Betsy. Tell the boy say to tell Miss Betsy many, many thanks."

"Jamsie, where you going to now, boy? Don't get in me way."

"Miss Edith, I going to the church now."

"All right, Jamsie. Give Mary a hand to decorate. Come back as soon as you finish. I got several little jobs here for you to do."

"Yes, Miss. I going come back right away. Soon as I done."

"You lock up the pig in the pen, Jamsie?"

"Yes, Miss. Ann tell me, and I lock it up."

"All right, well, run off quick and go and help Mary in the church."

"Miss Edith!"

"Oh, heavens! Yes, Ann! What's it? What happen now?"

"Just come a minute, Miss!"

"Yes, Ann? What wrong? What wrong? What happen?"

"Miss, why you look so pale? Nothing happen, Miss. I just call you to see the ice. We get a nice big block. It will more than be enough. And look what a sweet present you get from Mr. Graham' mother!"

"Lord, my heart beating at a rate! You call me so sudden I could swear something had happen."

"Look on the bright side, Miss Edith. Nothing can go wrong now, Miss. I tell you that so much times. Look at the clock. In four hours from this minute you safe in the church getting married. What can happen between now and then?"

"Ha, ha! You don't know, Ann! You don't listen to me. Something *always* go wrong with my affairs. At the very last minute some disaster can happen. It's my fate. I born under a bad star. Look what happen last year. Mother was to go with me on a six months holiday to England, and a week before we due to sail she didn't take ill and die off? What you call that? Not bad luck? Everything I set out to do – anything I plan to do – it must fail at the last minute."

"But look how good you running this farm, Miss. You can't say the farm not prospering."

"The farm all right, Ann. I won't deny that. But I talking about me – me Edith Harker, child. Nothing ever go right with me. Yes, Janey! What you want, girl?"

"The champagne and the rum just come, Miss. Where I must tell the man to put it?"

"Bring it in here, Janey. Help the man bring it in and put the bottles in the corner there near the sideboard. I hope he bring the right number I order. I order six bottles of champagne and a dozen bottles of rum. It will be real trouble if they short. They right, Janey?"

"Yes, Miss. They right. I count them. Six champagne. Dozen rum:"

"Who that shouting outside? What wrong?"

"It sound like Albert."

"Yes, it's Albert. Eh-eh! Come to the window here, Miss Edith. I see smoke over the trees there. I wonder if a house on fire."

"Albert! Boy, what you shouting like that for? What happen?"

"Fire, Miss! I hear the church on fire!"

"What! The church on fire! Oh God! Ann, what I tell you? I didn't say something bad must happen to prevent me from getting married? You see that now? Where Jamsie? He gone to help Mary with the flowers. I wonder if he was smoking in the church."

"Peter! Hi, there, boy! What fire is that? Where you going?"

"I hear the church on fire, Ann! I going to see!"

"Oh, heavens! Look! Look at the thick black smoke!"

"It's brownish-blue smoke. Perhaps it ain't the church!"

"It's the church, Ann. Don't try to comfort me, child. It's the church. It's my bad luck. The wedding got to postpone! How I going to get married today if the church on fire? You see you don't hear me when I talk? I born with a weight on me head, child! No use! Everything I turn my hand to must fail. Hurry to the post-office and send a telegram to Mr. Graham, Janey. Tell him the church on fire –"

"Don't get excited, Miss Edith. They might put out the fire! I hear them dashing water on it!"

"Where you going to, Ann? Don't leave me alone in the house here. Please! For God's sake. I can feel disaster hanging over my head. Don't leave me alone. Let Janey go to the post-office."

"Miss Edith, not better to wait before sending a telegram to Mr. Graham? Suppose it's nothing serious and they manage to put out the fire. You might alarm the gentleman for nothing."

"All right, Janey, wait, then. Don't send the telegram yet. But it's no use. The wedding got to put off. I can feel it in my bones. It never going to take place. I doomed to be disappointed."

"No, Miss Edith. You must be cheerful. Hope for the best. Everything will go good. Your luck change now, Miss."

"It ain't change, Ann. You don't see what happen? Who would have dreamt that the church would have catch fire today of all days! Just when Jamsie was going to help decorate it. It's a curse on me. I won't be surprise if I hear Mr. Graham meet with a accident and dead. Oh, God! What is this on me? What is this?"

"Calm yourself, Miss Edith. Wait, look I see Peter coming back. Let me ask him if the fire serious. Peter! They put out the fire? What happening over yonder, boy?"

"No, the fire still burning, Miss. They trying to dash water on it."

"What part of the church catch fire?"

"It's not the church, Ann. It's only some rubbish and dry leaves in a corner of the churchyard. The flames was getting out of hand and the Sexton sound an alarm. They got it under control now, Ann!"

"Thank you Peter! You see that, Miss? No fire in the church. You mustn't despair so quick. Everything all right. You letting yourself think too much dark thoughts, Miss Edith."

"The church not on fire in truth? You sure? Peter say so?"

"Yes, Peter say so. Only some rubbish and dry leaves in the churchyard. You didn't hear him say so himself? Cheer up, Miss Edith. Cheer up. Another three and a half hours and you will be Mrs. Graham and a happy woman. Forget about the past, Miss."

"How I can forget about the past, Ann? After all the big disappointments I suffer? Look what happen when I was fifteen! My father decide to send me to school in town. Everything arranged. All my school clothes bought – and what! Suddenly he take ill and die of jaundice. Two days – just two days – before I was to go to the boarding school he died. After I look forward so much to going. After I tell all the village children goodbye and they hold a farewell party for me in Sunday school. After all that I couldn't go, because when my father died we weren't so well off. It was a squeeze trying to send me to this boarding-school and my mother had to go careful with money. No more salary was going to come in from my father's job as a accountant on the estate. We had to depend on the farm alone. Ann, you don't know half, child. You don't know the number of times I get let down. Always at the very last minute something must happen to disappointment me."

"I know you had a hard time, Miss Edith, but this time it different. This time you going to beat your bad luck for once and all. Wait and see."

"I hope you right, but I won't believe it until I hear Mr. Graham arrive safe in the church and I dress and ready to leave the house. Not till then, Ann."

"Mary?"

"Yes, Edith?"

"What the time there, girl?"

"Ten to three, Edith. Don't turn round, man. Stand still and let me see if your petticoat showing. No, it's all right. Edith, why you trembling so much? Don't be so nervous, child."

"Same thing I been telling her all the morning, Miss Mary."

"Ann, you remember to tell Jamsie to get the sawdust for the ice? We don't want the ice to melt away before evening, you know."

"No, Miss Edith. Jamsie get the sawdust. I see him myself putting it over the ice. Stay quiet, let Miss Mary hook up your dress. Look how nice you looking!"

"Yes, stand still, Edith. But look how you trembling! Eh-eh!"

"You hear if Mr. Graham arrive at the church yet, Ann?"

"No, Miss, but Peter gone to find out. As soon as Mr. Graham arrive Peter will come and tell us."

"That mean he hasn't arrived yet, or Peter would have come already. Something must be gone wrong. He should have arrive at the church at a quarter to three. That's the time he agree upon with the parson."

"The car must be delay on the way from town. It will soon be here. Don't trouble your poor head, Miss. Look how sweet you looking in your bridal dress! Everything going good. Even the weather so nice today. Bright sun shining since early morning – and yesterday we had so much rain and thunder."

"Same thing I was telling Violet this morning. You lucky you had such a nice day, Edith. Why you got to upset yourself like this, man?"

"Mary, you don't know what bad luck I got, child, or you wouldn't talk so calm."

"Turn round let me pin up this flounce. Wait. Stand still a minute."

'Oh, Lord! Mary, I hear a bicycle bell."

"And what about that?"

"You don't hear it?"

"Ow, Edith! Look you make the pin fall out my hand. Stand still, na!"

"Ann, you didn't hear a bicycle bell?"

"It must be Mr. Harvey' bicycle, Miss. Oh, no. Wait, it's somebody coming here. It look like it's the postman."

"Oh, God! I bet you it's some bad news. It's a letter with bad news he bringing."

"Who can write you a letter with bad news, Miss Edith? Stay quiet."

"Edith! Heavens! Where you going to child?"

"Wait, Mary. I just want to look out the window and see who it is. Oh, Lord, yes, it's the postman. No. It's not the postman. It's the postboy. It must be an express letter. They always send the postboy when it's an express letter."

"And what of it, Edith? Look, you going damage your good dress if you don't careful!"

"The postboy must be bringing a parcel, Miss. Somebody must be send you a present. What it making you upset for?"

"No, Ann. No, Ann. No parcel in his hand. It's a letter. I can see it from here. I'm sure it's a express letter with bad news."

"Come from the window, Edith."

"Let me go down and see what he bring. Don't upset yourself, Miss."

"Postboy! Postboy! Come! Come under the window here! What's it you got there? It's a express letter for me?"

"No, Miss! Not a letter. It's a telegram."

"Oh, God!"

"Edith!"

"Quick, Miss Mary! Quick! She fainting. She fainting. Hold she! Let me get some water!"

"No, wait; fan her. Lower her on the bed. Quick."

"Let me go and get some water."

"No, don't sprinkle water on her. It will damage her dress. Get the door-key. Get some ice."

"Let me go and get some rum, Miss."

"Who that? Janey? Yes, come in, Janey. What's it?"

"What happen, Ann? Oh, heavens! The mistress faint away?"

"Yes, but she coming round. Keep fanning her, Miss Mary. Janey, go and get a glass of water."

"No, wait, Janey. Don't go."

"The postboy bring this telegram, Miss Mary. I just take it from him at the kitchen door. It's for Miss Edith."

"All right, Janey. Put it aside. Edith?"

"She coming round, Miss Mary. She opening her eyes."

"Mary?"

"Yes, Edith. Lie quiet. Everything all right."

"Where the telegram? What it say?"

"Don't mind the telegram. You feel all right?"

"Where the telegram? You open it? See what it say. Maurice dead, na? He meet with a accident this morning? Tell me! Tell me! Let me know. I resign to it. Don't afraid to tell me. I know me fate, child."

"Edith, you too stupid. Look. Look what the telegram say. Read it for yourself. 'All good wishes and prosperity. Aunt Kate'. It's your old Aunt Kate in town. She too old to travel, so she send you a telegram. And you behaving as if the world come to an end."

"Who's that calling?"

"It's Peter. Peter what's it, boy?"

"Eh-eh! He must be was running fast. The boy breathless."

"Peter! What's it, boy?"

"I was running to come and tell you, Ann! Tell Miss Edith Mr. Graham just arrive at the church!"

"Thank you, Peter. You hear, Miss Edith! Mr. Graham just arrive at the church. You satisfy now everything all right? You satisfy now, Miss?"

"Oh, Lord. Yes, Ann. Yes."

PORTRAIT WITH A BACKGROUND

Rain coming. High up in the air, carrion-crows followed each other round and round in a black circle, and the foliage of the mango trees near the house had a glazed stillness. Far away, the canefields looked already trapped in a bluish gauze of moisture. The rattle of a punt-chain jolted through the afternoon like a jet splotch and the regular chugging rumble of the factory thickened the pall of tension. Added to the weight of the lowering thundery clouds.

The scene, to Eva Weekes' fancy, seemed building up to a shriek. A bellow of cataclysmal flame and a convulsion of the earth. Wind came, and the mango trees rustled with a noise of busy interior flames; the rumble of the factory died away as though erased. Then the wind passed, and the trees fell still again; the factory rumble came back, more pronounced now; it could have been the throbbing of an artery buried in the flat landscape. Rain pattered in sparse drops on the corrugated iron roof. The carrion-crows rocked frenziedly as though aerial tennis champions were slamming them about. The stillness had a padded quality now, stifling, and the clouds darkened into a deeper gun-metal. Indeterminate frayed clumps of grey moved against the more remote, rigid slate-grey masses.

It seemed imperative to shut the window, but she made no move. She felt caught in a fascination, and was afraid. At any second an unknown hoarse terror would wipe out her consciousness. Smiling, she moved away from the window, the tension leaving her manner. She often indulged in such extravagant fears. Deliberately. It was her love of the dramatic combined with a desire to convince herself that though her life was a sheltered one there were elements of danger on all sides. She liked stimulating herself with the thought that she might be on the verge of a great adventure. Some upheaval that would give her the opportunity to show how fearless she was. Yet at the same time, she loved security. A threatening sky gave her a deeper sense of safety within the walls of this house. No matter how it rained and thundered, she would think, her happiness was dry and protected. Lightning could strike the house, set fire to it, but that was a chance one must take; the knowledge of this danger tended to quicken her interest in things rather than depress her; it added to the situation an exciting uncertainty.

Before leaving the room to have her cold shower, she stood naked before the wardrobe mirror to appraise herself, a habit of hers every day at bath-time. She pondered on her age – twenty-eight – and decided that she looked twenty-five. She had a round face, low cheekbones, and pale brown eyes set far apart. Her complexion was very fair, and her hair dark brown and long nearly to her waist; no one could possibly have told that her great-great-grandmother was a negress. She was five feet seven barefooted, and her body strongly built and big-boned but of a pleasing shape; her stomach could have been flatter, but after two children there had to be, she assured herself, a surplus of not-wanted fat, However, her breasts were full and only slightly drooping, and this counteracted the effect of the just too protuberant stomach. Her waist curved inward and then sharply outward to her hips – wide hips with no ungainly thickness – and her legs were long and tapered gradually down to smallish ankles and feet. Last week at the estate office she had weighed nine stone, five pounds.

Wind rushed into the room in a warm gust, bringing large drops of rain and the smell of earth and grass and cane-juice. She moved to the window again and looked at the sky, shook her head and thought: a sham. She had known it from the beginning. Whenever the sky looked over-terrifying nothing happened. It would clear up in less than an hour. If it were going to rain, the clouds would have come up stealthily, with less ostentation. The sun might even have been shining in the west. A light drizzle would have begun and gradually thickened, and the clouds would have looked whitish-grey – not grey-blue. She experienced slight disappointment. She had to be in New Amsterdam by five for a rehearsal of *The Mikado*, and it would have been exciting to drive the car through pouring rain and thunder and lightning. She would have felt like a heroine opposed to the wrath of evil forces. Brunnhilde. Or Boadicea.

Footsteps sounded in the corridor, and the black nurse appeared in the open doorway. "Mistress," she said, "rain coming. Ah better not take out de children."

"I don't think it will fall, Rachel, but let them play about a bit under the house for the time being, just to be on the safe side. When it clears up you can take them for their walk as usual."

"Yes, mistress." The girl sniggered. "Mistress, you ain' fraid people see you naked? They can spy at you from de overseers' quarters."

"If they take the trouble to focus a pair of binoculars on me it means they must think me worthwhile looking at. And I have no reason to be ashamed of my body. Have I? Tell me."

Rachel sniggered again.

Eva gave her a wide grin with her large, white, but not too even teeth. "You must hear a lot of gossip about me, eh, Rachel?"

"Yes, mum, people talk all kind o' thing about you, but I'se shut dem up soon as they come to me. I know you ain' a bad woman because I live here and see for meself."

"I like being gossiped about, though. Honestly I do. It stimulates me tremendously. People only gossip about you when you're different from them and refuse to conform with the ways of the herd. If they stopped gossiping about me I'd begin to think I was getting stodgy and stereotyped like the rest of them."

Rachel laughed. The sound went round the room like a spatter of ripe pumpkin. "You too full o' big words, mum. Me ain' understand half wha' you saying."

"I know you don't. I'm too damned bookish. That's my trouble. Put me in my place whenever I sound too highbrow, there's a good girl."

"Ah ain' care how you highbrow. You'se de best mistress they got on dis whole sugar estate. Even de whole o' British Guiana – and I can tell anybody dat. I work plenty places, so I know. They got some white people, they treat you as if you is dirt. You is de first white lady I meet who talk to me as if I'se a human being. And look who your family is! Sir Hilary MacNairnon your father. You' grandfadder was manager on dis estate. It's you who should be conceited and put on airs –"

"Run off and see about those young devils. You can be a sentimental bitch when you get ready."

"What Ah talk is de truth, mum. Nobody can say Ah lie. Oh, gawd! You see de lightning!"

"Was that lightning? I wasn't sure. Nothing will come of it, though."

It fell out as she predicted. By the time she had had her bath and dressed, the clouds had broken up into elongated ranks and were moving toward the north-west. A chilly land-breeze blew in gusts. In the south and east there were two clear patches of sky. In a matter of minutes the sun would be shining. Because her judgment had proved sound she felt an elation of pride burn softly within her. Her reflection in the mirror satisfied her the more now because once again she had confirmed her belief that behind her pleasing exterior lay a balanced mind and a strong character. She smiled at her egotism, but told herself that she saw nothing wrong in people being egotistic. What was wrong was to let your egotism take on the form of vain, superior airs.

The telephone was ringing downstairs. The black housemaid appeared at the door, her manner breathless and sensational. She said it was Mr. Thorndon, the Chief Engineer. He said that the master had met with an accident. He had fallen down from a landing in the factory.

"From a landing?"

"Yes, mistress. So 'e say. 'E say they take him to hospital and you better hurry over quick."

In her fancy she saw the carrion-crows circling in the sky. Wheeling and tilting in the upper currents of the air, black and foreboding.

"Was it – did he say if it was serious?"

"'E didn't say, mum."

Hermine waited, staring. She seemed to expect an outburst of hysterics.

"Very well, Hermine. I'll go right away."

"Ah sorry, mistress. Ah hope it's nutting bad."

"Thanks. I hope not."

Hermine went. The room swayed a little, and space contracted. She must steady herself. Thorndon was an excitable man. It might be a trivial accident. On the other hand, it might be serious. She saw herself a widow. The room swayed again. The illusion came upon her that she had become squashed in and elongated like a woman in a Modigliani picture. Laughter began to tremble inside her, and her hand powdering her cheek shook.

Going down the stairs, she thought: Funny how the world can, in a flash, seem twisted and unreal when you receive a piece of disturbing news. The amber furniture and the plain buff rug in the sitting-room, reassuring symbols of security when she had last seen them at lunch time, now had a threatening air – like the sky a short while ago, and the crows that she could still, in her imagination, see circling against the grey. The walls, cream-painted and hung with small oils and watercolours, held the sheen of an unknown dimension. Her hearing seemed sharpened to new vibrations. The shrieks of the children under the house came to her like splotches of scarlet emitted by unseen trombones.

Going down the outer stairs, she listened to her footsteps, and thought that they sounded remote; she might have been hearing the echo of them in a rocky valley where there was no life except the life of a stupendous silence.

The salmon-painted pillars on which the house was raised – ten foot brick pillars – glimmered in the background of her vision like sunset cirrus clouds. She had to turn her head to stare at them directly – to be sure that they were solid and on the earth.

The children came running toward her. She patted their cheeks and bent and kissed them, scolded them affectionately... "You've been playing in dust, Jim. I've told you that's naughty... Valerie, spit out that seed!" She called to Rachel who sat on a stool doing crochet work: "I think you can risk taking them for their walk, Rachel. The rain has passed off."

"Awright, mum."

Obvious that Rachel had heard nothing yet.

Hold an open mind. Keep a cool head. It was solely in her fancy that reality looked distorted. This was an afternoon in September, 1927, and the sugar factory on Plantation Vreedvoort, East Canje, was grinding; the grinding season had commenced a little over a fortnight ago. Commonplace facts. Let her see them as such. An accident to the Deputy Engineer could not alter them. Even if it were a fatal accident, the factory would continue to make its chugging rumble, as sugar-factories on every estate in British Guiana were doing at the moment; the punts would continue to arrive along the canals, pulled by the oxen from the canefields; the overseers would go on being boisterously gay when they returned from aback on their mules and settled down to an evening's drinking in the quarters. Chilly actualities. Let her see them as such and not colour them with her own individual tints.

The hospital was situated about a quarter of a mile east of the overseers' quarters and just before you came to the "ranges" that housed the labourers. The scene about her was pleasant. Sandbox and saman trees, green swards – though the grass was brownish-green now because of the long dry weather. Red burnt-earth lanes that wound between the trees, connecting one residence with another, and all with the main highway. The highway ran east-west; the factory and its outbuildings lay to the south of it, and the residences to the north. West of her own home, she could glimpse the red-roofed three-storied house that was the manager's, situated in about four acres of well-kept grounds. More to the north, the outbuildings of the deputy mManager's house were barely visible between the smooth trunks of two young cabbage palms – elongated, barn-like structures with shingled roofs; twenty years ago they had been stables for a carriage-and-four; today they accommodated Manfred's Studebaker and his chauffeur, and the gardener. The homes of the chief engineer, the chemist and the doctor were screened from view by the trees, though when she had passed the overseers' quarters she would be able to see the south-western portion of the doctor's house.

The sun came out, its heat kindly on her back: soft, late-afternoon sunshine. The shadows of the trees slanted along the grassy swards. She smiled, letting the loveliness of the sight seep into her; trying to let it swamp the tension spread out in her inner vision like sinisterly glittering strands of hair.

A car appeared ahead, and she recognized it as Malcolm Rawle's. Malcolm Rawle was the chemist. He himself was driving, a man in his early forties, thickset and with a round, double-chinned face, red-veined. He stopped as she knew he would and smiled: "Of all the surprises! Where are you off to?"

"The hospital. I'm in a hurry. I can't stop."

"Let me drop you there. Jump in."

"No, I prefer to walk, thanks. I could have used our own car if I'd wanted to go by car."

"I insist. Just to please me."

She gave a short laugh. "Very well. I haven't time to argue – and I won't hurt your feelings." She got in.

As he manoeuvred the car to turn it in the opposite direction he asked: "Who's the patient? Arthur taken ill?"

"He's met with an accident," she murmured. She explained about the telephone call from Thorndon, and the gaiety drained from his manner. His face grew concerned; it was concern for her she knew – not for Arthur.

"And you were walking so calmly."

"Why should I walk excitedly?"

"You're an odd little soul," he said, shaking his head and frowning. "I can't make you out at all."

She smiled a trifle but made no comment.

They were passing the overseers' quarters, an elongated red two-storied building that could have been a military barracks. She caught a glimpse of Teelacksingh, the East Indian butler, at a window. Malcolm saw him, too. He remarked: "In another hour it'll be all over the place that I drove you to the hospital."

"I daresay. Albertina, if no one else, will be furious."

His face took on a troubled look – troubled and shifty. He had close-set, rather ferrety eyes and heavy eyebrows. He mumbled without glancing at her: "I'd risk anything to be near you even for two minutes."

"I know you would." She patted his hand gently. "But I'm still not encouraging you."

He nodded, his manner a trifle aggrieved. He was pitying himself.

She listened to the humming of the car; to her fancy it was like an umber dust blowing through the twilight of a nightmare land, bearing her with it. She wondered at her calm.

They came to a stop at the foot of the long wooden stairway that led up to the main entrance of the hospital. The hospital was a one-storied building about a hundred yards long, raised on ten-foot wooden pillars, and painted pink, with brown facings. The grounds were planted with fan-palms and crotons of all varieties and cannas and zinnias.

She got out and thanked him, and he asked – in a very humble voice – if she would like him to wait for her. He wouldn't mind waiting, he said.

"No, please don't."

"You look pale," he said, smiling uncertainly. He gave a furtive glance up at the hospital windows.

"I feel pale," she said.

She went up the steps one at a time. No one could have said that she was in a hurry. In the portico there were hanging ferns. A mason marabunta was buzzing indeterminately around them. Looking for those tiny green worms, she thought, Her heart was beating a mile away, contained in a dusty room into which a shaft of white sunlight shone. A black nurse met her on the threshold of the open doorway – a varnished screen was visible; it obscured a view of the interior – smiled ingratiatingly and said: "I saw you getting out of the car, Mrs. Weekes. Come right in and I'll take you to him. He's in the Special Ward."

"Nurse?"

"Yes, Mrs. Weekes?"

"What – I mean, it isn't anything serious, then is it?"

"No. Oh, no. Only his ankle – and a bad bruise on his forehead."

"I see. Oh." The shaking that began in her nearly translated itself into unrestrained laughter, but by an effort she kept silent. She took deep breaths of the disinfectant smell as she walked with the nurse along the corridor. She liked it. And the walls painted pale green.

The Special Ward was on the northern side of the building. It contained only six beds, for it was intended for the use of the white estate executives exclusively. The walls were painted a light blue, and from the windows you could see beds of red and bright yellow cannas and two very tall cabbage palms; they were believed to have been planted since Dutch days.

Arthur was the only patient at the moment.

She sat by him and he told her how it had happened. His shoe had got caught in a rag of waste, and before he could say knife he went slithering down the steps. At the next landing he had tried to check himself, but he hit his head against a boiler pipe and dropped to the concrete floor twelve feet below. "Didn't know a thing until I found myself in Thorndon's office. Thorndon kept shouting at everybody at once. You'd have thought the place was on fire."

"That gave me hope. I knew about his excitability."

"Did you come in the car?"

"No. It seems foolish, but I preferred to walk. I didn't want to get here too quickly. I was afraid of hearing that – that it was serious." She put out her hand and touched him.

He laughed when she mentioned, a moment later, that Rawle had brought her part of the way. "Poor son of a bitch. He's going to get it from his Albertina."

"I told him. Do you want to be brought home?"

"No, I think I'd better remain where I am here," he said. "The ankle will have to be dressed every morning. Have the children gone for their walk?"

"I told Rachel to take them. The rain has passed off."

He grinned, watching her. "You look 'pale and shaken'."

"I am. For an instant I imagined my universe had collapsed."

She got up. "I'm going. I've got to go to that rehearsal in New Amsterdam. I'll come back to see you about eight or half past. Or do you prefer me to ring and say I can't come?"

"No. Go. I'll look out for you at eight."

In the corridor, making her way toward the entrance-way, she heard feminine voices raised in argument. Beyond the screen at the end of the corridor… "You can't see Mr. Weekes now. His wife is with him. You had no right to come here, in the first place. You too brazen…" The voices stopped abruptly. A black nurse glanced round the screen. Her face showed dismay, embarrassment, was quickly withdrawn. Eva heard a fierce whispering, and footsteps. When she got round the screen she saw an East Indian girl going. Well dressed, attractive. The nurse, self-conscious and smiling, said: "Good afternoon, Mrs. Weekes."

"Good afternoon," smiled Eva. She moved on, turned a corner, went past the screen that stood before the entrance-way and began to descend the stairs. The East Indian girl was going down ahead of her.

Eva caught up with her, and moved past, giving her a casual but interested glance. So this was one of them!

The girl returned the look – with intensity, with almost open challenge. Eva smiled and began to move on toward the roadway, then stopped and turned. "Did you come to see Mr. Weekes?" The girl gave a gasp. Only stared at her.

"It's all right. I'm not going to eat you because you go to bed with him occasionally. Go back and see him. Tell the nurse I've given you permission to see him."

As though by intuition, they both glanced up at the window. They saw the nurse, again dismayed, embarrassed. Before she could withdraw, however, Eva cried: "Nurse! Here is a visitor for Mr. Weekes! Show her in!"

The nurse began to speak, then stopped. She seemed to gulp. She smiled foolishly and said: "Very well, Mrs. Weekes!"

Eva went on toward the roadway.

ONLY A GHOST WE'LL NEED

Elizabeth came in and said they were doing their best. She had kept very well. The tropics had not aged her as might have been expected. At fifty-six she looked forty-five.

"I know you are, my dear. You generally do. Did you succeed in getting the imitation holly?"

"Yes. And some mistletoe. Rebecca is busy with it all in the sitting-room. It's looking quite Christmassy in there."

"Sssh! No details. Remember what I said. I want it to be a surprise – a nostalgic surprise."

"You and your perpetual nostalgia for England."

"Exiles with bad hearts have a right to feel nostalgia for their homelands, my dear. Ah, well! If only I could have died in Dorset! No, no, please, Elizabeth! Don't sneer at my sentiments. It affects my heart. Where are you planning to hang the mistletoe? Over the settee?"

"Rebecca thinks it would be better to have it over the piano."

"Excellent. Rebecca has ideas. I believe she's taken after me. Elizabeth!"

"Yes, Richard?"

"I won't go near the sitting-room until nine o'clock on Christmas Eve when the full company is gathered. On the dot of nine I shall enter, and when I do so I must feel I'm entering our old parlour in Dorset. Do you remember the old cottage?"

"Yes. Yes, of course."

"Don't sound so indulgent. I really believe you've forgotten our Dorset days. You're a British Guianese, Elizabeth."

"Don't be silly." She patted his cheek, and adjusted the cushion at his head.

"You think it will look like the real thing? An English parlour? Think it will take me back to the old days in Dorset? Mm. Imitation holly and mistletoe. And a log fire in a mock fireplace. Good. For Christmas Eve night I'll forget I'm in British Guiana."

"I'm certain you will." She laughed. "We're even screening off the lattice-work at the top of the wall. We'll have the whole room as perfectly English as we can. Only a ghost we'll need to give things the final traditional touch."

Richard shifted in the easy chair. "What a pity," he said, "we couldn't arrange for a ghost. Isn't there a story that a Dutchman once haunted this house, Elizabeth?"

"Is there any old house in this colony that isn't supposed to be haunted by a Dutchman?"

"Yes, Dutch ghosts are popular. The Dutch held this colony before we English came along and ousted them. Anyway; if we're striving after English effects at this party we can't very well have a Dutch ghost. It would be a distinctly upsetting note."

"I think you've chattered quite enough for the afternoon. The doctor said you must be perfectly quiet for the next day or two – or else no Christmas party."

"The doctor may know about bad hearts, but he doesn't know the English temperament. Have you ever heard of an Englishman who died of conversation, Elizabeth?"

"Oh, don't be tiresome. If only you wouldn't keep harping so much on England and the English. There! I'm sure I hear Rebecca calling me. I must be off."

"We'll have to do something about that ghost, my dear. Would you prefer a moaning one, or one that merely appears?"

But she had already left the bedroom.

The brief tropical twilight was fading. In fifteen minutes it would be night. Here night always fell at six o'clock, June or December. He looked out of the window at the panorama of housetops interspersed with coconut palms, corrugated iron roofs and palm fronds. No tiles or slates; no chimneys. No smell of coal smoke in the air. How difficult it is, he thought, to conjure up the illusion of an English Christmas in such a setting! If I take a look at the thermometer hanging near the dressing-table I'll see that the temperature is seventy-six. Good God! That's a heat-wave in Dorset.

"Stop it! Stop harking back!" It was the jumbie in the coconut fronds shouting at him. During the past few months of his illness his fancy had created a jumbie. It lived in the gloomed spaces within the fronds of the coconut palm in the next yard. In the instants when he had thought he was dying he had carried on conversations with it, his gaze fixed on the fronds. Often it scolded him when he indulged in boring thoughts. It was scolding him now.

"Elizabeth is right. You're a tiresome old twerp. Anyone would imagine you've been living in this colony a mere three or fours months instead of twenty-three years."

"Disgusting of me, I admit. Yes, it is twenty-three years. I left the Old Country in August, 1928. Arrived in Georgetown early in September. Think of it! The newly appointed civil engineer bound for Purl & Reifer's sugar plantation on the west bank of the Demerara River."

"That's it. Recount it all. Tell us now about Plantation Schoonflucht."

A soft wind was causing the fronds to rustle. He could smell wet leaves and canal water. He could hear the cooing of pigeons. The people next door kept pigeons.

"Plantation Schoonflucht. I'm glad they let those old plantations retain their Dutch names, I envisaged for Elizabeth and myself an idyll-like existence on Schoonflucht. We would live in thatched bungalow-hut in the middle of a jungle-clearing, with a few vague canefields visible between breaks in the jungle foliage. That was the Schoonflucht of my fancy."

A carrion-crow flapped softly, like a jet skirt magicked out of space, and alighted on one of the fronds. The frond swayed gently in the rainy breeze. Somewhere in the neighbourhood there was the irritable gobble-gobble of turkeys.

"You haven't finished," said the jumbie. "Tell us about the actuality."

"Ah, yes. The actuality. The actuality was different. A two-storeyed house with electric light and a shower-bath and up-to-date lavatory, four bedrooms, sitting-room, dining room and veranda. Well-laid-out grounds with tennis courts adjoining. Other staff-residences visible everywhere you looked. Instead of jungle, a vista of canefields as far as the eye could see, with the big brick chimney rising importantly above the factory buildings. At night the factory buildings a cluster of lights. Lighted lanes, motor traffic and the chug of machinery, tennis and bridge parties had not been my idea of life in the wilds…"

"Schoonflucht… Beterverwagting… Meten-Meer-Zorg… Vreed-en-Hoop…"

"Yes, such music in these Dutch names. When Elizabeth arrived a month later at Schoonflucht and we set up house with a cook and housemaid and gardener, it didn't take me long to adjust myself to a life of luxury in the civilized manner. Queer how one can always adjust oneself to conditions of luxury. It's poverty that perpetually seems incongruous and uncomfortable. After our small cottage in Dorset, Schoonflucht was indeed luxury. In Dorset, Elizabeth had had to cook and wash, and clean."

"Yes, and now here you are at sixty-one, a retired Deputy Manager living in greater luxury on the outskirts of Georgetown with a still-devoted wife, and a daughter engaged to be married, and a son in the Colonial Civil Service. What have you got to grumble about! How far would you have got as a road engineer in Dorset! Haven't you heard it said before that life in the colonies is a paradise for English people?"

"Yet… "

A piano in the neighbourhood was tinkling "Hark the Herald Angels Sing", and he could hear the peep-peep of chickens settling down in a backyard coop. Was there another city like Georgetown where piano music and traffic-rumbling went together with poultry noises?

"Yet I have never ceased to long for Dorset. Elizabeth and I might have lived there permanently after my retirement, but what with my heart and my malaria, the doctors have advised against a cold climate. The exertion of travelling would be disastrous for my heart, they said. And the damp climate of England wouldn't help my malaria. So there it is, I must end my days in this colony."

"You petrified old bore!"

"Oh, but I'll have a good Christmas. No illness will stop me from enjoying that Christmas Eve party. If only we could have arranged for a jolly old ghost…"

"You miserable old spook!"

"No need to get nasty with me. And don't call me a spook. It unnerves me. Reminds me how near I am to the grave – me with my bad heart. Perhaps I'll join you and the carrion-crows out there in the coconut fronds when I'm dead. The doctors don't give me more than six months. This is my last Christmas. You know that, don't you?"

"How relieved Elizabeth should be to be rid of you and your sentimental whining!"

"Yes, I've become a filthy companion for her. She often scolds me about it. 'It's only', she says to me, 'your quaint sense of humour that saves you from being unutterably abominable.'"

"No fear, I'll know how to deal with you when you join me in the fronds here."

"I don't doubt it. I'm fearfully curious about death. Tell me, does one really wander about corridors scaring living people out of their wits?"

"Oh, shut up and have a nap."

"Yes, I think I'd better have my nap. I'll see if I can dream up some idea for faking a really convincing ghost for our party. 'Only a ghost we'll need', Elizabeth said…"

"Richard refuses," said Elizabeth, on Christmas Eve night, "to make his entrance before nine o'clock. I left him a short while ago just getting into his bath."

Madge Jameson glanced at her wrist watch. "It's just on nine," she said. Madge's husband was the Managing Director of Wheeler Brothers, Ltd.

The room seethed with people. Ronald and Mary Wilkinson, of Plantation Great Hoosten, sat with Pamela Purley, only daughter of the Deputy Subsidiary Colonial

Treasurer, before the blazing fire. They were entranced. A log fire in a fireplace in Georgetown, British Guiana! *How English!* Made one sigh for the Old Country. What matter that the temperature outdoors was in the seventies and in the room here in the nineties! What matter that next week the workmen would have to return to restore the square portion cut out of the wall and remove the temporary metal chimney installed outside the house?

"Oh, isn't it sweet!" cried Jasmine Dickinson, daughter of the Commissioner of Rivers and Creeks. She stood behind the Wilkinsons staring at the mantelpiece on which stood two Toby jugs. And Ann Robinson, beside her, turned and pointed at the mistletoe that hung over the piano. "Oooh," squealed Ann. "I wonder if Susan and Tommy know they're sitting under the mistletoe!" Ann was eighteen and the niece of Jimmy Freeman, Chief Factory Engineer of Plantation Straatslust. And the Susan she meant was Susan Pemberton, elder daughter of John and Daisy Pemberton who, at that moment, were gazing in admiration at the Christmas tree. John Pemberton was Managing Director of Purl & Reifer's. Susan was trying to strum *Carol sweetly carol*, and Tommy Barron was trying to sing the words. Tommy was a bit soft on Susan. He was twenty-three and a police superintendent.

Yes, the room seethed with people. People talking, eating drinking, exclaiming and admiring … "The holly looks so *real! So English!*" … Under every picture a sprig of imitation holly had been tacked… "And what a wonderful tree!"… Apple and apricots and blue and green and orange tinsel ornaments dangled from the limbs of the Christmas tree. Also toy-filled net stockings and crackers of all sizes and shapes. Fairy lights. And at the very top – the glimmering tinsel star. "Oh, star of Bethlehem!' bayed Malcolm McBrodie, who had already had more White Horse than was good for him. He lurched against Madge Beavers, and Madge exclaimed: "Oh, Malcolm!" Madge was a Puisne Judge's wife.

"Where's Richard? I haven't seen Richard."

Elizabeth was asking the same question – of herself. He ought to be down by now, she thought. It's after nine.

At that instant there was a shriek from Susan Pemberton. "Oh Tommy! How could you? You know I hate being kissed on the back of my neck!"

"I never did!" Tommy denied, very red.

The room was lit only by the glare of the fire and the soft radiance of the fairy lights. How the room seethed!

Another shriek. This time from Maisie Kelly who was drinking sherry with Millicent Buyers near an open window. "Now, who could have done that!"

"Done what?" asked Millicent, sister of George Buyers, Deputy Chief Accountant of Income Tax. "Why did you *shriek* like that?"

"Someone pinched me," said Maisie. She was the widow of Jack Kelly, late Chief Secretary to the Sub-Comptroller of Customs.

Across the room, Elizabeth whispered to Rebecca: "Have you seen your father? Has he come in yet, do you know, Rebecca? There are so many people here it's difficult to tell –"

"I haven't seen him, Mother. Lord! Isn't it hot!"

A hoarse gasp.

"What's that?"

"Oh, but this is *shocking*! Really!"

"What's the matter, Flora?" asked Elizabeth. Flora Denham was Ralph Denham's wife, and Ralph was a director of Willows & Hawkes, the shipping agents.

"Didn't you see, Elizabeth?"

"See what, Flora?"

"Someone seems to have no sense of propriety, my dear."

"What do you mean, Flora?"

"I distinctly saw a man dodge round the Christmas tree there, and – and he hadn't... he wasn't... oh, it's shocking!"

"He wasn't what, Flora?"

"He wasn't wearing any trousers, Elizabeth. Not a thing on but his shirt. I know it's Christmas, my dear, but I do think that's carrying a joke too far."

"Who could it have been? I don't see anyone near the Christmas tree improperly clad."

"Oooh! Oh!"

"What's that? Daphne! What's wrong, dear?"

"Someone tickled me."

"Tickled you?"

"Yes. And – and in such a place."

"Who could it have been? Oh, but this is silly. There must be some practical joker amidst us."

"Mother, where's Dad? Do you think I should go up and tell him to hurry? Everyone is asking after him."

"Yes, dear, please go up and see what's keeping him so long."

Rebecca had hardly left the room when there was a loud thump. It was poor old Mr. Leafer. He was sitting on the floor, nursing his left hip.

"Someone pushed me over," he complained. "I've been assaulted."

"Eeee!" That was Pamela Purley. Someone, she protested, had touched her. Indecently... From the other side of the room Diana Minckley squealed. "Oh, I've been insulted; insulted!" She was the wife of Donald Minckley, Deputy Chief Auditor to the Department of Roads and Canals.

"What on earth is happening!" said Elizabeth.

"Oooh!"... "How dare you?"... "This is intolerable..."   .

From every corner, from every side of the room came protests, male and female. Someone had been touched, pinched, pricked, knocked over, indecently fondled.

Suddenly Rebecca returned and hurried up to her mother.

"Mother! Come quickly. Come upstairs with me."

"What's it, Rebecca?"

"Daddy. It's – it's happened. I found him lying on the floor. He must have just come out of his bath."

"You mean... You mean he's – he's – passed away?"

"Yes. Poor chap. And he was looking forward so much to this party."

"My God! Then it must be *he*..."

"He? What's it, Mother? What do you mean?"

"Oooh-hoo!" screamed Ann Robinson. "Who did that?"

Elizabeth shut her eyes. "Oh, Richard," she whispered. "Such behaviour, dear! It's not *English*, rest your poor soul!"

HURRICANE SEASON

Since early morning the air had been calm, oppressive, and the wind, whenever it did blow, seemed to come from all directions at once. It came in hot, brief gusts, as though afraid to commit itself, or as though it were the breath of some monster whose throat were being pressed upon at jerky intervals by a giant thumb. The sea, under the overcast sky, pounded continuously on the pebbly beach, hoarse and angry, one breaker curling high and crested after the other in quick succession. The white pebbles of coral that strewed the beach clicked and rattled as the hissing foam rushed furiously over them.

Old Jacob Everett had lit a fire so that he could watch the smoke and tell how the wind was blowing. The smoke kept whisking this way and that, a purposeless ghost that often would insinuate itself into the rickety, two-roomed hut and cause Mother Everett to cough. Whenever it did this, Mother Everett would put her head out the tiny window of the back room and scold her husband – scold him in a voice that lacked confidence, for she had long resigned herself to the fact that he was a self-willed man upon whom scoldings had no effect.

"Why you don't come insoide, ole man? Is what you tink you doing? You can't stop God's works…"

"Ole fisherman loike you so 'fraid de wedder. Shame 'pon you, Jacob! You doting too bad in you' ole age! Ef hurricane come to-noight it's de will of Jehovah. Put out de fire. De smoke choking up me pore lungs."

Everett, as usual, took no notice. He kept the fire going with odd pieces of anything he collected along the seashore. Coconut branches the sea had washed up and half-buried in the sand, seaweed dried crisp by the sun, twigs and dead leaves from under the sea-grape trees and the manchineels and tall casuarinas that lined the shore, coconut shells and even an old boot.

As he watched the smoke, which sometimes would be grey-blue and sometimes dark-brown, the tint of his troubled face, he shook his head and mumbled to himself, "Dis look very bad."

Every hurricane season – from the beginning of July to the end of September – for the past three years, he had suffered from this fear, and Mother Everett blamed it on two things – "ole age doting" and Francis.

Francis, their youngest son, was a brilliant boy, and with the help of his sister Doris, who had married a schoolteacher, he had got a secondary education, and was now a teacher himself. He came often to the fishing village to see his parents, but Mother Everett said half-jokingly that it was an evil day when he had brought "dat big black book some few years back."

The big black book she meant was one of a pile Francis had been taking home with him; he lived with Doris and her husband further along the coast. He had just come from the Public Library in Bridgetown, six miles away, and his father had said proudly: "Well, look dis! Boy, you mean tell we you studying all dem big books? Heh!"

And Mother Everett had grunted and said between sucks at her clay pipe: "Dis island o' Barbados na able hold Francis when he done study all dem books, you hear what Oi says, Jacob." And then Francis, embarrassed and trying to be modest, had changed the subject by remarking: "Something in this one moight interest you, Papa. Remember we used to talk about hurricanes and how Barbados never had one for more than a hundred years? Well, this book is a history of Barbados. A man called Schomburgk wrote it, and it describe the two biggest hurricanes we ever had here. Long, long time ago. One happen in 1780 and the other in 1831."

Francis had read aloud for them the vivid accounts of the two great hurricanes, and old Everett had nodded and groaned and grunted, absorbed and deeply impressed… "Red sky. Yes. Oh, yes. Oi always did hear say red sky mean trouble in de heavens. My fadder tell me so plenty toime." But Mother Everett had laughed. "All-you fishermen, you always says dat! Red sky mean rain and t'under-lightning. How much red sky me ain' see since I was a girl and no rain and t'under-lightning come – much less hurricane!"

But Everett never forgot what Francis had read from the history book.

"See how de wind blow," he muttered to himself, watching the smoke this day in August. "Dis way now, dat way now. Variable de word mean, and it was the very word de book use. Variable. Same as de big book Francis read from say. Francis tell me what wind blow variable in 1831, de day before de big hurricane break. And it was a August day loike today wid de sea rough and de sky overcast. Yes, dis look bad. Dis look very bad."

His gaze shifted over to the hut, and took note, perhaps for the fifth or sixth time that day, of its condition. The shingles he had nailed to the walls more than thirty years ago were grey and ragged at the edges; some of them were askew, some falling out. On the roof the corrugated iron was a red-brown hue – the colour of the shingles when they had been new. But this red-brown was the red-brown of rust. At night, before he fell asleep, he would listen to sections of the corrugated iron flapping screechily in the wind. It leaked in two or three places. He had stopped leaks more times than he could count during the past ten years.

In his fancy he could see the whole flimsy structure toppling off its foundation of coralline limestone blocks, could see the waves – waves twenty feet high – smashing down upon the rotten walls from which cockroaches and centipedes scurried. The history book from which Francis had read had said that during a hurricane the sea rose and pounded the beach with huge waves. What hope would there be for this hut if the sea rose and the wind turned into a hundred-mile-an-hour gale!

Somehow, he did not fear death. It was the loss of the hut that worried him. It was the one thing that had always meant security in his life. He and Mother Everett had built it with their own labour and their own tools over thirty years ago when his own parents had been alive. To lose this hut would be to feel as exposed as a snail would without its shell.

That was what Mother Everett did not understand. She thought he was afraid for his life. Why should he be when he and his fishing-boat had battled through so many murderous seas and merciless squalls! It was true that now, at seventy-one, his fishing-days were over; Doris and Francis helped him along with an allowance every month, and James and Harry helped, too, when they could; James and Harry, not having clever brains like Francis, had done like their father and become fishermen.

Yes, his fishing days were over, but that didn't mean that he had turned into a coward. Why, he was even convinced there was no storm that could kill him.

No, it was the hut. "Dis hut," he muttered, turning his gaze out upon the sea. The waves had a purplish-grey tint under the dull sky. Yesterday, in the sunshine, they had looked such a bright, cheerful blue. . . "What we will do if dis hut get smash up!…"

As the afternoon progressed the sky became blacker, and in the south and south-east thunder muttered frequently. Hurricanes always approached from the south or south-east and travelled north-east or north-west.

The wind, after four o'clock, increased in strength and came definitely from a south-easterly direction. Sometimes it veered to the south, but at no time did it come from the north-east. Another bad sign, Everett noted. When the north-east trades were blowing there was little chance of a hurricane. The trades brought fine weather.

At five o'clock rain began to fall in large, coarse drops, and Everett's fire hissed and went out. He retired into the hut for the meal Mother Everett had been calling him since three o'clock to come and eat. Two three-cent loaves of bread and a cup of hot water mixed with a teaspoonful of sweetened condensed milk. The third and last meal of the day. This morning at seven it had been exactly the same: two three-cent loaves and a cup of hot water with condensed milk.

As Everett ate he remembered something Mr. Franklin, the village grocer, had said a few months ago. Mr. Franklin had told a customer he had read in the newspaper that people all over the island were advised to put in a big stock of foodstuffs in July in the event of a hurricane. Old Everett had shaken his head and uttered a moan to himself. Poor people like him could barely find rice and potato and bread and milk from day to day. How could the newspaper advise them to put in a big stock of foodstuffs? That advice was for the rich people: the big sugar planters and the merchants and their families in Bridgetown – and the Civil Servants and the holiday people who came to Barbados. Another piece of advice Mr. Franklin said the newspaper gave was that when a hurricane warning was sounded, people should board up their windows and doors with good lumber – not just any kind of lumber but good lumber. Old Everett had groaned on hearing this. People like him didn't even have bad lumber, much less good lumber. If he had had lumber of any kind at all he would have used it to repair the hut, not board up windows and doors.

The rain grew fiercer, and drummed loud on the corrugated iron roof. Mother Everett brought an enamel basin from the back roam to set down on the floor near the old bamboo table, and the basin at once began to give out sharp ping-ping sounds as the rain leaked into it in slow, big drops.

Everett listened, but he could hear only rain. The wind seemed to have died down.

Mother Everett sat in the rocking-chair, her ragged Bible in her lap. Her lips kept moving as she read. Her sight was perfect. Every afternoon at this time, bad weather or good, she read her Bible. This afternoon she had lit a stump of candle and stood it on the table beside her chair, for with the wooden shutters closed against the rain, the hut was as dark as though it were after sundown.

Everett finished his meal, and remained seated on the box that served him as chair – the rocker was the only authentic chair in the hut – staring at the floor and pondering still on the weather. He waved his hand before his face. This heat was another very bad sign. Since early morning – long before the sun had come up – the heat had begun.

Suddenly he glanced up. The rain had stopped – abruptly and ominously. There was still no wind. Why had the wind died away like that?

The sea continued its riotous crashing roar on the beach, and far away he heard a prattling roll of thunder. Rising, he opened the door, and Mother Everett glanced up and said: "You going outside mek more smoke, Jacob? Why you don't stan' insoide, ole man?"

"Going watch de wedder, Susan. It looking bad, girl. Very bad."

"You say dat two weeks back, and nutting happen."

"It wasn't so bad as dis. Today Oi see all de soigns, Susan. Jest as Francis read from dat big book. Hurricane coming for sure to-noight."

Groaning, he went outside.

The sea-grape trees dripped solemnly, and the huge manchineel trees, further along the beach, looked frowning and threatening, as though thunder were concealed in their dense foliage. They bore poisonous berries. Berries you even had to be careful not to tread on with bare feet, for the juice in them caused blisters. As a boy his parents had often warned him to be careful of them... As a boy... Such a long time ago that was. In 1898 he went on a trip in a schooner as a deck-hand. They touched Dominica, St. Lucia, Antigua. And when he came back his father, he remembered, told him that a big storm had struck Barbados while he was away. Not a hurricane, but nearly a hurricane. The wind had uprooted a few trees and knocked down some huts here and there. He had been so disappointed that he had been out of the island and had missed the experience. Stupid fool that he was then...

He came to a halt.

The sky in the west and the south was slowly turning a deep crimson. The blue-grey thunderclouds moving slowly toward the north-west stood out dramatically against this background of crimson. Large fans of crimson that splayed out upward to the zenith and that gradually, as he watched, began to infect the thunderclouds whose edges grew pink and then mauve, and this mauve spread and spread until the very depths of the clouds were aglow with a sombre, regal, purplish red.

A gust of wind came puffing from the south-east, hot and making a drone in his ears. But now it was not the wind that troubled him. It was the sky. A red sky.

He sank down on the damp earth and held his head in his hands. Now it was only a matter of waiting. Now he must resign himself and take what was coming. God's works... "You can't stop God's works," Susan had said.

So he waited.

Darkness fell, the crimson fading from the sky. He could hear thunder rumbling in the distance again. From the south-east. Some large drops of rain fell, but only sparsely, and not for long.

The wind died away entirely. The heat increased – and the oppressiveness. The heat seemed like a mesh around him. Mother Everett called twice, but he took no heed. Would not even answer. The heat had him trapped, so that whether he had wanted to or not he could not have moved.

He must sit here and wait... God's works...

The sea darkened, and the waves seemed to gather a new agitation, a new fury, as they thundered down on the beach. He listened to the swishing prattle of the pebbles at each onslaught.

The sky shut down upon the land and the sea, hanging heavier and heavier like a black furry carcase laden with moist death.

He sat without moving. Sleep, after a while, made him nod. And Mother Everett called again and again. But he did not move. He could feel the salty, sticky spray from the sea damp against his face and arms as it billowed across the short stretch of grassy land that separated him from the beach.

He continued to wait, nodding off and on as sleep bore down like the clouds upon him. And after one of these nodding spells – it seemed a long one – he woke and shook his head, and saw that the sea had taken on a phosphorescent look. Each wave came clear and crested through the darkness, glittering blue-green. It was weird. Terrible and weird. At least, it was so until he looked up and saw a half-moon in the sky, inclined to the west. It was the moon, then, that made the waves look phosphorescent.

Funny, he thought, that the moon should be shining. He looked around and saw stars. Scorpio was sinking in the west – not far from the moon. Everywhere he looked there were stars. In the north and in the south and in the east as well as in the west. And the air was very cool.

Behind him the hut was in darkness. Mother Everett must have gone to bed.

He rose and looked around again to make quite sure.

Not a cloud in the sky, except a few wisps low down on the horizon. And the wind seemed to have shifted back to the north-east. The good, kindly, cooling trade winds. Portent of fine weather.

TOWARDS MARTIN'S BAY
Excerpt from An Unpublished Novel

On the path to Martin's Bay goat-dung and sheep-dung lay in frequent pellets in the baking-hot sun. Ghouls' eyeballs lost. Parched pure of evil peering. Many sea-pebbles and chunks of white coral strewed the way, baking in the baking-hot sun. And now and then they saw a sheep or goat grazing on the stunted grass that grew on the slopes, and it would stammer a detached greeting before they passed it. A forlorn, daytime sound through the droning strands of the trade-wind and the commotion of the sea down below on their left.

After they had passed the inlet where the fishing-boats moored in the afternoon and where the Atlantis Hotel, a rather shoddy-looking building, stood, they saw not a human on the path – nor on the sun-scorched rocks and the swards that rose undulatingly on their right. The solitude sat upon their heads like a hot phantom intending more good than ill. A more benevolent than neutral thing, it drifted down from the warped landscape above; rose from the gullies and chasms between the gnarled rocks on their left, out of the pebbly coves that dispassionately received the passionate assaults of the persistent breakers.

Neither of them spoke, each trudging with his own thoughts. And the lonely sea-weed scents saturated their awareness in a pall, soothing yet at the same time stimulating: throwing a lightning of vigilance through their beings, so that their contemplation consisted of a questing amid the labyrinths of their dreams and despairs.

His parents, Ronald remembered, had spent their honeymoon in a small cottage not far from the hotel. Ronald had overheard his mother saying so to a friend one weekend when the family had come here on holiday. Bathsheba was a favourite honeymoon district. For a certainty, thought Ronald, his parents must have wandered on this path – though in those days a railway line ran here. Metre-gauge tracks. Then there had been order. Measured sleepers upon which to step. Now there were pebbles and bleached cow's teeth. And goat dung. The railway had failed. The motor car and the motor bus had proved too powerful as competitors.

I wonder, thought Ronald, if my father ever experienced this wild and scattered discontentment I feel. This not knowing where to reach out for true fulfilment. Probably not, he decided. No, his father had not been that kind of man. A respectable merchant whose father before him had been a respectable merchant, Mr. Eversley Barkley must have permitted himself no unstable extravagances of emotion. The dry goods shop in Swan Street must have encompassed him about with ramparts too secure for him to feel world-weary and discontented. And later, the commission agency with its office in Broad Street. Yes, the commission agency must have seemed to him an even more impregnable fortress. Who could be discontented as the part-owner and managing-director of Barkley & Bros., especially when one's own ingenuity had gone into establishing this handsome business! Other commission agencies there were in Bridgetown, but could any of them hope to rival Barkley & Bros. for sheer respectability, for the reliability and solidity of the firms in the Old Country that Barkley & Bros. represented!

Yet for me…

The rest of the thought was wafted away to the wilderness of trembling heat that grew out of the humped terrain that hoisted itself hundreds of feet above them. A distant goat munched distant grass invisible from here, and was this not a dog's skull he was about to step on? Did animals come here deliberately to die, or were their carcases dumped here to disintegrate in the sun and throw their stink into the soothing solitude? Solitude and sea-scents. Solitude and death-scents. What baffling essences must the wind, as it wound its way round these hard rumps of rock, not distil with the smells of sea, sea-weed and flesh going to dust!

Yet, for me, respectability has lost its savour.

In the champing teeth of the wind, salty and fishy, the thought insisted on completing itself.

For me, Barkley & Bros. is no fortress safe against besieging evils.

Even against the shattering swirl of spray and green water calamitously gurgling in collision with the jagged rocks far down the cliff-edge that crumbled away a mere few inches on their left, the thought would not be denied, surviving both sea-noise and super-ego's prohibiting voice.

With the death of his father, less than two years ago, he had become managing director – as his father and uncle had planned – but there was no glory in it. Yet the old firm must be kept going – the old firm must be kept in the family. In his way, he loved the firm no less than his father had. So much did he love the firm, indeed, that he had seen nothing outrageous in his uncle's suggestion that he should marry Sybil, his widowed cousin-in-law. Apart from inheriting a large share in the business on the death of her husband two months after their wedding, Sybil possessed other valuable property in her own right. Not four months ago, on the afternoon his uncle lay dying, Ronald had assured him: "You have nothing to worry about, sir. I've asked Sybil to marry me."

Fish skeletons one could understand, for the fishermen often dumped their flying-fish when the catch was too big. These had not been dumped so long, for the stench that rose about the spot was strong and penetrating. It triumphed above the iodine from beyond the rocks on the left. He and Albert held their noses, and for the first time the silence between them was disrupted. Albert said: "Not so romantic a smell, this."

Silence returned between them, insistent like several stringed ghosts oozing from the claws of crabs' skeletons that strewed the track. Groping up, up, crawling, growing tight in crusty strands about their sun-hot bodies. They puffed and sweated. The rocks leaned down upon them, and the solitude settled about their spirits like a phantom sponge, cousin of crabs' claws, that would rather absorb their troubles than plague them, rather protect them from the bile and buffoonery of the world beyond these rocks than oppress them.

Here, thought Ronald, I feel less discontented. *Weltschmerz* cannot harrow me. These rocks are above respectability. Aloof. Barkley & Bros. mean nothing to them. They would grunt disdainfully in their aged cores should you dare to discuss such trifles as the virtues and sins of mankind. To them, only the briny wind and the brave breakers down there connote the greatness of the earth.

These rocks, he was certain, would have sympathised with him when, as a boy at Harrison College, he had sniffed at cricket and played it only under protest. What could be more respectable, in Barbados, than cricket! And there was he, audacious young whippersnapper of fourteen, telling his schoolfellows that cricket bored him. Oh, horrible heresy! To utter such words in Little England where, as in Mother England, cricket was an institution. No wonder he had always been looked upon as being "not all there". Had he not been the son of Mr. Eversley Barkley and the nephew of Mr. Darnell Barkley and Lieutenant Malcolm Barkley, men of supreme worth in the society of the island, he would probably have been ostracized. Perhaps even sent into exile.

Another thing was that he was irreligious. He never went to church on Sundays, and even openly admitted that he did not believe in God. In Barbados where the very politicians quoted from God's Holy Scriptures before passing an iniquitous bill, where bus-drivers speculated on the smooth running of their engines, "Our Saviour permitting"! Was it any wonder that his father and uncle had felt anxious about him? … "He is the kind of boy," Uncle Darnell had once been overheard to say, "who might easily marry one of the housemaids. You're going to have to watch him carefully, Eversley."

The wind never failed to make its presence known. Nor did the sea cease to foam and thunder on the invisible beaches beyond the hanging cliffs of rock, rattling the pebbles and shells on the sand, crashing like cruel bat's wings against the crags down there. Down there where they could see but could only guess at what was going on. The mystery of green water swirling into hidden alcoves, into crab-infested caves, into dungeons, perchance, where tentacled monsters unseen by human eye held horrid sway; where, who knew, there were jellyfishes red as blood and whirling swift as flying-saucers of the deep.

I have fallen in love with this island, Albert kept saying to himself. A simple fellow, Albert, he had no problems of world-weariness, discontentment nor futility to bother him. Yet he had his plaguing fancies and his fears. He was dreading the day his father would recall him to Montreal. He had come to Barbados four years ago to introduce Crabbe's Crackers –"Crisp and Crunchy" – and had been so successful that his father had instructed him to stay on and work in conjunction with Barkley & Bros. in handling and advertising the product. Crabbe's Crackers had become so popular during the past few years that they threatened to become an institution. No high tea in Barbados was complete without Crabbe's Crisp Cream Crackers. As someone had remarked at a cocktail party (and Albert had been swift to use it in an advertisement in *The Barbados Advocate*): "Crabbe's Crackers, like cricket, will never die." What made the situation, for the island, more satisfying still was that Crabbe's Crackers, though originally of Canadian manufacture, were imported from England where a branch of the firm had been established. Not only were currency difficulties circumvented but the crackers were clearly marked *Made in England*, a legend that in Barbados carried magical significance. God save our Gracious Queen!

Albert felt – and it was as though a tiny egg within his intuition were getting ready to hatch out – that before long his father would issue the command: "Come back to Montreal." The product, his father would argue, and not unreasonably, was now well on its feet. There was no longer any necessity for him to remain in the island. Barkley & Bros. could carry on the advertisement campaign.

Albert detested Montreal. He had never been happy there. Had his father suggested his going to England he would not have minded so much, for he liked England: its lovely, undulating landscape, the mellowness of its country people, the peace of its hedged lanes, plum and apple blossoms in spring. But Montreal – he had never been able to cultivate any affection for that city. That humped excrescence pretentiously called a mountain, with its lighted cross vulgarising the night, had never impressed him. The loud crudity of his schoolfellows, at high school as well as at McGill's, had never ceased to cause him shudders of intolerance. The stupid provincialism of its people intensified by a sulphurous fog of Roman Catholicism had oppressed him. He could never be in love with a city where the car you owned and the fur coat your wife wore were set up as the standard of values affecting one's social and, verily, moral and spiritual aspirations. A city where the cultivated few were so few that one almost needed a Geiger counter to discover the radiations of their influence.

The freshness of this island stimulated him. Its landscape was the landscape of England with tropical vegetation; for poplars and elms there were the tall, feathery, sighing casuarinas; the complicated network of roads was there, and the many country lanes; except for chimneys, the cottages and houses were built in the style of England. The climate was equable: warm yet always windy and rather dry for the tropics. The peasants were unspoilt; kindly and charming people. The cultivated groups were really cultivated: to find them it was not necessary to search, for the island was small – a hundred and sixty-six square miles – and once entrenched among these groups one could laugh at the antics of the very socially conscious white upper-class and the simperings of the too, too English and refined coloured middle-class.

In this island one had an identity; in Montreal one was lost in a cauldron of gross philistinism, with the Holy Fur Coat and the Holy Cadillac as one's only hope of salvation. A salvation that was dust. Only the lost could derive happiness from a million dollars: the happiness of agitation, anxiety and unctuous ambition. In this island there was work but no frenzy.

A booming and a moist clack, loud and clear, as of a gargantuan hand slapping a gargantuan cheek – such was the sound that rushed up from beneath the jutting ledge of limestone they were passing. It startled them both out of their contemplation, though neither exclaimed or spoke. They turned their heads to glimpse the fierce spray that rose only to vanish at once, a thousand glistering crystalline jewels churned back into the frothing green whirlpools gnashing and twisting amidst the coral chunks they could see more than fifty feet down.

Ahead of them they saw the grey shingled shacks and hovels of Martin's Bay. The wind assaulted them with renewed fury, bringing richer odours of fish; the tang of flotsam, foetid and from more faraway corners of the ocean; a new note of thunder upon reef and sand. A fresh invigorating rankness laced with a whiff of sea-eggs and the gasped breath of some small octopus.

GERALD

It was in the days when I was living in digs in Bayswater that I met Gerald – a likeable chap, tallish, lanky, blue-eyed and cheerful, but of the type I knew intuitively would involve me before long in some desperately embarrassing situation. Yet I didn't hesitate to cultivate his acquaintance, because apart from liking him, I discovered that he and I had similar tastes in a large number of things, and it isn't every day, nor haphazardly, I can find people like that.

Gerald read the kind of books I read, and, like me, he preferred slightly plump red-haired girls. He sniffed at ballet ("stuff for aging spinsters and the la-dee-dah," we both heartily agreed), but he liked Wagner – and at that time, in 1948, there were few people who failed to tell me outright that Wagner was not their cup of tea, and, moreover, looked at me with a sort of nasty suspicion because I'd dared to mention such a name. Again, Gerald, I discovered, was a methodical fellow, and meticulously tidy in the flat he shared with his aunt. Tidiness is one of my major vices; I was getting sick of hearing my landlady praise me on the neatness of my room. Finally, as though all this were not enough, Gerald was keen on photography, which has always been my pet hobby.

In fact, we met at the Round Pond in Kensington Gardens one exceptionally fine Sunday morning in May, he busy with his movie-camera taking shots of the little motorboats snarling across the water, I with my Rolleiflex doing stills of the swans and other groups I thought striking enough to merit using up some film.

I've never experimented with a movie-camera.

"I can't develop movie-films myself at home," I said, after we had got chatting. We sat on a bench under the chestnuts in the Broadwalk. "And somehow I insist on doing my own developing. I'd hate having to send my stuff to Kodak or some other place like that."

He nodded. "Sort of feel they were stealing some of your thunder. I know. It's a kind of jealous feeling. A picture isn't really all yours unless you presided over every phase of the process – from the first click of the camera to the last little satisfied pat when you've mounted it. I used to feel that way myself, but I outgrew it. You will, too, take it from me."

There was patronage in his voice, yet it was not offensive, because as he spoke he kept smiling and nodding, and his eyes twinkled in a humorous, disarming way. I judged him to be about twenty-eight or twenty-nine – at least five years younger than I – which made patronage on his part appear to me too absurd to be noticed.

Added to which, just at that moment, as he was fumbling out a packet of Weights from his coat pocket, a small, flat tin fell with a clatter to the bench, hopping off on to the pathway right in front of us.

I uttered a discreet "Oh," and he uttered a hoot of laughter as he bent to recover it. He flushed slightly but did not seem extraordinarily abashed.

"No ladies present," he grinned, "so no cause for alarm."

"You seem a good Boy Scout, if nothing else," I said solemnly. "Believe in being prepared."

He scowled at the drabness of my cliché, and told me what I ought to have remarked in the circumstances if I wanted to sound bright and original (it is unprintable, of course), and then nodded and went on: "I'm a methodical old tramp – always been like that. Look here, you must drop in soon," he said, rising with an abruptness almost startling. "This afternoon if you like. How about tea?"

"But I don't know your aunt."

"Aunt Rita loves meeting strangers, especially the camera breed. You come along. We'll look out for you. Four-thirty-ish."

The flat was a first-floor one in one of these red-brick Victorian houses in Palace Court, and Gerald's aunt greeted me as though she might have known me for years. A small elderly person with white hair cut short and with a lilac streak running through it. Her green eyes twinkled not unlike Gerald's – in the same humorous, disarming manner. I liked her on the spot.

Another lady was present – a Miss Bailey. She was a regular Sunday afternoon visitor, I gathered, and belonged to the committee of some social welfare organisation of which Gerald's aunt was also a member.

A film projector and a screen were set up as though in readiness for a show, and Miss Ladbroke (Gerald's aunt) said to me: "Take no notice of that. We're having a little show this evening for our committee members. Gerald had everything ready for it since lunchtime."

"That's how my methodicalness shows up," grinned Gerald. "I believe in having things fixed up and ready hours before the event."

"A splendid trait, a splendid trait," tittered Miss Bailey. "I wish many of us were like that. It would be a better world."

"How angelic that makes me feel!" sighed Gerald. "I ought to think up some naughty things to do – just to disillusion you and Aunt Rita."

"You couldn't be naughty if you tried," tittered Miss Bailey. She looked at me. "I don't know what we'd do without Gerald. He takes pictures for our organisation. If you stay for the show you'll see what I mean."

I did stay, as it happens, but the show bored me to rigidity. The films were chiefly about slum children in the Portobello Road and the shoddier parts of Bayswater and Maida Vale. Really drab, uninspired stuff. And when I met Gerald two days later on the Underground – he was on his way to Oxford Street where he worked at an advertising agency – I tackled him about the films, and he nodded.

"You haven't got to tell me. I know they're deadly, But I do it to please Aunt Rita and her committee members. Come in one evening, and I'll show you the kind of thing I like. Devon and the Lake District and Hyde Park. You won't think those so dull."

I saw nothing of him again until one evening about a week later when, with my redhead, I dropped in at a pub in Westbourne Grove. We entered the saloon bar to find Gerald already installed at a table with his own redhead, and we joined them.

Myra, Gerald's girl, was having a bit of trouble with him this evening, but she seemed accustomed to it and was not unduly perturbed. "He's got a weak head. Can't hold it," she told me.

"Some of us are like that," I nodded.

"Look at him now," she chuckled. "He's at the Latin stage – but that's not so bad. It's when he starts spouting philosophy I've got to see him home."

"Myra knows all the phases," grinned Gerald. "She's – hic! – she's an intelligible – I mean, an intelligent creature – hoc!"

"See that?" said Myra. "Listen for the *sir*!"

And the words were hardly out of her mouth when Gerald uttered a hiccuping "Sir!" and drained his glass. "Time for another," he said. "On me – hoc!"

In less than half-an-hour he was waving his hands before his face and talking about "the film of unreality that shurrounds us on all shides."

"Come on, we've got to go, Gerald," said Myra, rising.

"Oh, behave yourself," frowned Gerald, brushing off her hand. He was very solemn and pensive now. "Nothing ish real. Why worry? Everything in the world – a muddle. Mixed up. We're all pawnsh in a magnifishent game." He looked at me for confirmation. But I glanced at Myra and asked: "What's the next stage?"

"That's the trouble," she sighed. "There's no next stage. The rest is silence."

"Then we've got to help you see him home."

He went without trouble, and Sybil, my own redhead, took it in good part, and did not mind going with us to help in the operation of piloting him safely to the flat in Palace Court.

"Not often I reach that stage," he told me a few days later when we were having tea in a little Greek café in Queensway.

"Sometimes it's good to let oneself go."

"I agree," I said. "I do it myself sometimes."

'Of course," he told me a trifle worriedly, "I've got to cover up so far as Aunt Rita is concerned. I tell her I'm ill. Suffer with my stomach."

"And does she believe you?"

"Mm. She's awfully gullible – especially where I'm involved. Good sort. Shouldn't like to let her down, you know. I like keeping her illusions intact," he added, winking slyly. "She's not a bad old bird."

"I like her a lot."

"Come and see those films I told you about," he said abruptly. "I've got several you won't find as dull as the social welfare things. The Lake District one especially." But I did think them dull when I saw them, though wouldn't tell him,

That summer I got to know his aunt and her social welfare friends very well. I helped with the projector at their film shows, and they began to look upon me as a second Gerald – a dear, good, helpful boy who couldn't be naughty if he tried. When Gerald went off to Paris for a fortnight's holiday in August, I took his place as cinema operator. Sybil sometimes accompanied me round to the Palace Court flat, and that helped to relieve the drabness of the shows for me. What on earth these spinsters could find in those deadly dull scenes of slum children playing street games or running in and out of dismal-looking terrace houses in depressing streets really floored both Sybil and me, but we endured it because we had grown fond of Miss Ladbroke and the atmosphere of her cosy flat.

Myra, Gerald's girl, incidentally, never went there. For some reason, Gerald felt that his aunt would not have approved of her. Myra told me in confidence one evening: "They think he's a plaster saint – his aunt and her cronies. And he likes to make them feel it's true. That's why he can't even let them know he's got a girl friend."

"Strange chap in many ways," I nodded. "Don't always understand him myself."

She chuckled and said: "One day I'm going to surprise him and walk right into that flat when they're all gathered for their show."

"He'd never forgive you. Don't try it."

On Gerald's return from Paris, he told us enthusiastically about his film adventures.

"It was a regular feast, I can tell you. The Luxembourg Gardens. Versailles: The Place de l'Opera. The Boul' Mich. Montmartre –"

"Not the Folies Bergère, too?"

"Sssh! I don't go in for that kind of thing," he grinned.

"Aunty's little prude," teased Myra.

He arrived back on a Wednesday, and on the Friday following he rang me and asked me to drop round that evening. He was giving a show for his aunt and the committee members.

"What! Have you had the Paris films developed already?"

"No, no. Those won't be ready for a week or two. It's some new ones about conditions in Rouen and Bordeaux I managed to purchase for Aunt Rita over there. Usual line. Bad housing and all the rest of it. Dull as mud. But we've got to endure it, old lad. We're altruists, don't forget."

I dropped in at five, as he asked, to find everything, of course, ready for the show, the projector in position, and the screen set up.

"I've promised to meet Myra at the Gryphon," he murmured. "Come with me?"

"Well, we don't want to be late, you know. Your aunt's friends are going to be here by six, didn't you say?"

"We'll be back in good time. I promised to meet Myra. Can't let her down."

"What are you two murmuring about?" asked Miss Ladbroke, suddenly entering the sitting-room. "Was that a girl's name I heard you mention, Gerald?"

"A girl's name?" Gerald gave me a look of shocked innocence. "Good Lord, no! I – we were talking about the show, weren't we?"

"Of course, of course," I confirmed hastily.

"Is everything ready, Gerald dear?" asked Miss Ladbroke. "All set, as usual?"

"All set, as usual, Aunt Rita. Just running out for a minute. We'll be back by six."

"Very well, dear. I know I can depend upon you."

So off we went to the Gryphon.

Halfway there, Gerald came to an abrupt halt, and made a snapping sound with thumb and forefinger. "Just remembered something," he frowned. "Oh, damn!"

"What's the trouble?"

He shook his head a little worriedly, then broke into a grin. "It's all right. When we get back to the flat I'll make sure."

"What's the mystery, Gerald ?"

"No mystery," he said. "Oh, it'll be all right. Tell you about it another time."

I didn't press the point. He had probably left a hairbrush in the sitting-room in a moment of rare carelessness. It had happened to me, too.

Myra was waiting for us in the saloon bar. "Thought Aunty's boy might not have turned up," she jibed. "I bet it was you who had to haul him out," she added, looking at me.

"You've lost your bet, then."

"Myra has a low opinion of me," said Gerald. "Not like Aunty and her friends. I wish I could get Myra to see me wearing a halo."

"It wouldn't be round your head, though, sweetheart," said Myra.

"Tch, tch, tch! What conversation!" I deprecated.

By a quarter to six Gerald was at the Latin stage, so I mooted leaving. But he refused to budge. "No bother, old man. Everything's set and ready. Hic! That's where we methodical chaps come out on top. Hoc!"

In the middle of his next ale, however, he began to frown worriedly. "Jusht remembered something," he muttered, staring down into his tumbler.

"What something?" Myra asked him.

"Nothing, nothing," he grinned. "I'll see about it when I get back home."

"Forgot to flick a speck of dust off the bedsheet before going out, I suppose." She looked at me. "That's the kind of thing that can worry him like mad."

"Me, too," I said. "I can sympathise with him there."

"You're a pair," sniffed Myra. "Your tidiness will be your downfall."

Gerald rapidly entered the philosophic stage. "The film of unreality gathers about ush," he was telling us presently, waving his hands graphically. "What ish thish life we work ourshelves into a frenzy about?"

I rose. "Come, Gerald. Time to go. It's five to six."

Myra rose, too. "Yes, Gerald dear. Aunty won't like you to be late."

"Oh, sit down, and don't be shpoil-shports. All a muddle, so what'sh the use? Whole world. Let the old crones wait."

"You've created a reputation and you've got to keep it up," I told him.

"They won't see a halo round your head tonight," giggled Myra.

By the time we persuaded him to leave he was virtually incoherent. It was nearly half past six when I helped him up to the flat in Palace Court. Fortunately we did not have to pass through the sitting-room. I slipped him into his room which opened directly into the hallway.

"Better take it easy and not try to show your face," I warned him.

He shook his head as he slumped down on to the bed. "Musht go out to shee – after projector... Mixed up... Musht check up... Film of unreality–"

I heard Miss Ladbroke calling: "Gerald! Gerald dear: We're waiting! You're late, dear!"

"I'll tell her you're unwell. The usual thing. Stomach."

"No, no," he protested, trying to struggle up. Waving his hands about feebly. "Musht go out there. Shee everything in order... Important."

"You take it easy. I can handle it as efficiently as you, old man. You're in no condition –"

"Yesh. Important. I – all mixed up... Film..."

"Look, you're about to pass out. Lie just where you are."

"Gerald! Gerald dear! We're waiting..."

I hurried out to the ladies gathered in the sitting-room.

"I'm afraid Gerald is not up to officiating this evening, ladies," I said. "A bit of stomach trouble. The old thing. It takes him suddenly sometimes."

There were exclamations of "Oh!" and "Poor boy!" and "Dear Gerald!"

"I keep telling Gerald about that stomach of his," said Miss Ladbroke. "I can't get him to see a doctor."

"Has he tried Phillip's Milk of Magnesia?"

"He ought to go on a diet."

There were about ten of them present, seated about the room on divans and settees – and all flutteringly concerned about poor dear Gerald.

"Anyway, you won't be disappointed about the show," I assured them. "He had everything set up before he went out. I'll get it going for him."

"Such a methodical boy."

"A rare trait in young people nowadays."

I heard Gerald utter a retching wail, so I pressed the necessary switch and got the projector going. The titles appeared – in French – and were in focus, so I hurried off back into the patient's room to see what I could do for him and his stomach trouble. At all costs I had to prevent him from making a scene and perhaps rushing out into the sitting-room to collapse and pass out. I was not too soon, either, for he was crawling on the floor towards the doorway and seemed intent on getting out of the room. I was yanking him upright to get him back to bed when the pandemonium of shrieks broke out in the sitting-room.

He struggled violently, pointing urgently toward the door.

"Hear that? Quick! Lemme go out! Lemme go!… Mishtake!… Sushpected it… Washn't sure…"

"You fool, what's the matter with you? You want to go out there and let them see you're drunk? Quiet!"

"Lemme go!"

I pushed him hurriedly on to the bed, and dashed for the door, wondering what could be the cause of the commotion in the sitting-room. I thought of fire. The projector must have caught fire.

"Gerald! Gerald!" shrieked Miss Ladbroke. "Oh, dear! Gerald!"

"Oh, dear! Oh, dear!"

I found them in a terrible state, cowering against each other, hands to their faces, as though to shut out some horrible sight.

"What's the matter?" I began. "What's…?"

Then I took a glance at the screen. I gasped and nearly collapsed.

I made a dash for the machine and switched it off, muttering obscenities.

It's just as I said in the beginning. My intuition had not played me wrong. I had known it. Had always known inside me the damned fool would eventually have involved me in something like this! And a *French* film, at that!

HEAT IN THE JUNGLE

Charlie Musson felt angry with himself – then tried to put the blame on the heat. The heat and the silence and his loneliness. Every day it happened. Nothing to be upset about, really. Every day the heat shut down upon him like a butterfly-net wielded by some unseen monster hand – and then the hatching began. The hatching of this and that fear, this and that thought of omen. This and that foolish irrational fantasy.

As soon as Parry came it would be all right. Parry would be here at any moment now. Company made a big difference in this jungle. Alone, even for ten minutes, you began to hear the silence murmuring at you, hollow and vast and oppressive, bubbling like the bubbles in the river, hissing and wheezing like the insects in the thick ferns and the dragon's blood chirruping threats like the occasional tree-frogs hidden amidst the wild cacao and the swizzle-stick trees, breathing humid secrets down your neck that you know could not be good for you to hear.

Alone, as he was alone here now, you were inclined to glance askance at the webs of the black hairy spiders and wonder if they could be ghostly projections of the silence that had come stealthily into being along the fronds of the cookerit palms when you happened not to be looking. The cookerit palms – and the awara and paraipee palms – all prickly-trunked and foaming and glittering dark-green in the hot sun, had conspired with the silence and the spiders. And the ugly black spaces that burrowed deep into their dense fronds were frowns that you knew, for certain, had been shaded in by the silence and the heat to heighten the effect of the menace quivering around you and hazing the white sand. The shiny black lizards that darted from spot to spot on the sand were all bits of the general lightning of illusion that the silence and the heat employed to dazzle your senses and bring out the sordid and the morbid in you.

He looked across the river at the glitter of the varying shades of green on the opposite bank, and felt that nothing would have been more delightful than to take a swim across to the bush there. But… Ah, yes. But you couldn't do that because the perai were waiting for you in swarms – the savage little swordfish that infested the rivers and creeks of British Guiana. Yet the urge was so great that he could have defied even the perai.

He gasped and pressed his hands to his cheeks.

The detonation that came on the air rent the silence into nervous wisps of web – web no spiders could have woven, for it dissolved too quickly, leaving too grey a dust of shock.

It must be Parry. Parry had shot something up at the bungalow. Or it might have been Greta, his wife. Greta, too, could use the rifle. Both she and Parry were excellent shots.

There had been talk of jaguars worrying the cattle and poultry in the Indian village. Perhaps one of them had strayed near the bungalow…

"Bringing her to live with us here was a mistake…"

The thought issued from a fissure of his mind, and he uttered a snarling exclamation and tried to flick it away by sawing his hand through the air. Once again he felt angry with himself… A mistake Why a mistake? She was Parry's wife, wasn't she? Why shouldn't Parry have decided not to leave her in Georgetown but to bring her here in the jungle? She hadn't minded coming and roughing things with the two of them in the bungalow…

Yet… Yet what? Two's company, but three's… Oh, damn!

That old nonsense?… Look here, get it straight, Charlie, it's only the heat that's bringing out all these morbid thoughts. Only the heat. No, no. Get it quite right. The heat and the silence and the jungle and your imagination…

"This is madness," he murmured – and stood up and chuckled. Tried to tell himself that everything was all right. He must contain himself until Parry came. He brushed at the eye-flies, whistled at the heat, wagged his head, thought of the perai in the river. He began to write a letter to his sister in his head. Susan in Hampstead where the temperature at this minute must be fifty-five… "Dear Susan – The eyeflies are weaving round my face like tiny black full-stops…" How should he continue?… "It's the heat, Susan. The heat and the silence and my own imagination. I'm not really anticipating any trouble over Parry's wife, though in my bones I know there's going to be trouble. She's making a pass at me, Susan, and Parry knows what she's doing. I try to pretend I don't notice anything, but it's hard, because she has so little discretion. I doubt she's really in love with Parry. And Parry is such an odd fellow. You simply can't guess what's going on in his mind. Outwardly he's the same towards me. Treats me just as he did before Greta arrived – yet I can sense that underneath he is beginning to resent my presence here. Why can't Greta leave me alone? I like her – but my feelings don't go any deeper than that. I tell you, I knew from the outset it was a mistake bringing her to live with us here…"

"Oh, shut up! Shut up!" he began to shout at himself. He put his fingers into his ears. Then suddenly removed them and looked around.

But he was wrong. It was not the splash of paddles. Only one of the bubble-sounds in the water. It was too early for the bleeders to return – though yesterday they had arrived before two o'clock. But that had come about because of the accident at Mappa Lake when one of the canoes had been damaged by a falling battery-box. Today they would probably not turn up before four o'clock, and he must be here to meet them, to see that they accounted for every item in their paraphernalia, to check the amount of latex collected. It was his job. The company paid him to do it, and he believed in being conscientious.

He turned with a start. Footsteps. Ah, what a relief! Parry.

Thickset and balding at the temples, with the distinct bulge of a paunch, wearing his ten-gallon hat slung over his shoulder, Parry was smiling his usual indulgent smile as he approached. In his hand was a sharp-bladed machete. It was not often that he bothered to carry a machete.

"You look frantic," said Parry. "What's up? What's biting you now?"

"It's this heat, Parry. What did you shoot?"

"Young tapir. It got away. Get back to the bungalow. Greta will give you some tea. She asked me to tell you she was getting tea ready."

"Thanks. Decent of her. Decent of you. I – I…"

"Run off! Run along." Parry laughed, slapping his leg with the machete.

As he made his way towards the path-opening in the bush, Musson began to mutter to himself, "I have a filthy mind. I might even be wrong about Greta's trying to make a pass at me. Just my conceit. Parry doesn't feel anything against me. I'm cooking it all up. I'm not myself. I should be back in London travelling between Hampstead and Bond Street, thinking up advertising slogans for toothpaste and lipstick. That's the job I'm suited to – not jungle life in British Guiana…"

He stopped muttering and came to a halt.

Unless it was his fancy, he could have sworn he had heard a swishing sound in the ferns on his right. Sunshine did not penetrate here, and in the sepia half-light one could never be certain about anything.

He moved on. The path was ascending now. The bungalow was situated on top a low hill whose base was at the river bank.

Again he heard it. A swishing. It stopped the instant he stopped.

It could be a snake. What kind of snake, though? Then he remembered. The bushmaster. Parry had told him about it. In these jungles it was the equivalent of the cobra. A six-foot monster, ruthless, vicious. It attacked without provocation. It had been known to track down unwary men, lie in wait and suddenly strike. Sometimes it gave chase, and it was incredibly swift. His Wellingtons would avail nothing against such a brute, for it could get you anywhere from shoulders downwards.

His imagination got to work again. Why had Parry suggested that he should go back to the bungalow for tea? Could Parry have known that a bushmaster was on the prowl? Had he sent him deliberately…?

Oh, God! Stop it! Stop distorting things!

He moved on, and for a while heard nothing, though he kept his head at a tilted, listening angle. Suddenly, however, the swishing came again. On his left this time. Ahead, the path took a turn round the trunks of two tall mora trees. There was a spring there. He could hear the trickle of water.

He was about to move on when he saw it. Not ten paces off. The diamond markings gave it away. It was lying along a rotting palm trunk that lay diagonally across the path. It would have struck out just as he was about to step over the palm trunk.

He stood absolutely still. If he turned now and ran back it would give chase. He would not stand a chance. It would hurtle after him like lightning.

A slight dizziness came upon him. He felt the inclination to laugh and assure himself that it was all illusion. He was being melodramatic. It was only the heat that had produced this hallucination. There was no snake lying there waiting to strike at him. It was nothing but pure heat-fantasy.

He decided to test the matter, and stooping, picked up a crumbly piece of dead branch that lay in the sand. He tensed himself and then threw it at the thing with the diamond markings.

And the thing moved. It reared up. It came plunging towards him.

He backed away with a gasp. And at that instant an explosion shook the silence so that the heat seemed to quiver before his gaze like a mist in an impalpable gust of wind.

A thud sounded in the sand, and he stumbled back another pace or two and watched the brown coils twisting erratically about, lashing the twigs and dry leaves right and left, tossing up little tufts of sand.

"Run to the left, Charlie!"

It was Greta's voice, and he obeyed automatically, and in the same instant saw the muzzle of the double-barrelled rifle raised beside the trunk of one of the mora trees at the bend in the path ahead. Another explosion rent the twilight, and when he looked at the writhing coils he saw that the head was missing. The whole mass began to subside and grow still.

Seconds later, she was gripping his arm, and they were both trembling.

"Didn't he tell you, Charlie?" she gasped.

"Tell me what? I don't understand. How did you arrive just at the right moment to kill... I – I don't..." He had to break off, for he had begun to babble incoherently, hysterically.

She was still gripping his arm. "He meant that snake to get you," she said quietly. "They travel in pairs."

"In pairs? It's a bushmaster, isn't it, Greta? I – I thought I was imagining it all. The heat. The heat has been getting me down."

"He's discovered what I feel about you," she said. "I tell you, he meant that snake to get you. They travel in pairs. He shot one of them not fifty yards from here. The mate got away. Or perhaps he didn't see it at all – I don't know."

"But he said it was a tapir he shot. A young tapir. It got away, he said, Greta."

She led him round the bend in the path and pointed, and he saw the other one. The mate. Coiled up in death at the foot of a palm.

He began to tremble afresh. He whimpered. Began to babble hysterically.

She slapped his cheek, and that brought him to himself. The hysteria passed. He stopped wanting to blubber. He let her coax him, let her lead him off towards the bungalow. She made him feel that she was the he-man and he the damsel in distress. It was humiliating, but her coaxing voice was like cool water in this heat. It soothed him, and he felt himself relaxing.

HERR PFANGLE

I was so furious that I approached two American M.P.'s and asked them if they knew how I could get in touch with the British consul. They were immediately sympathetic when I told them about Herr Pfangle. They took me into the office in the Hauptbahnhof reserved exclusively for the use of the American forces, and got on the phone. They spoke to their headquarters, and eventually succeeded in putting me in touch with a British liaison officer who dealt with civilian problems. There is no British consulate in Heidelberg, it appears. I repeated the story to this officer, who took down the essentials and promised to report the matter to the British consul in Stuttgart.

I felt better after that. In fact, less than three hours later, on my way to Boppard on the Rhine, the seeds of forgiveness had already begun to germinate in me. And long before I took train for Cologne, the following day, on the first leg of my journey back to London, I was remembering Herr Pfangle not with bitterness or anger but with amusement and compassion and even a little affection.

I had met him for the first time on the Friday before. I got into Heidelberg from Mainz at shortly after midday. Determined not to endure any more nights of traffic-troubled sleep, as I had done in Cologne and Koblenz and, worst of all, in Wiesbaden-Biebrich, I approached a taxi the instant I emerged from the Hauptbahnhof, and asked the man in my just-workable German if he could take me to a quiet little guest-house (*ein ruhiger Gasthof*).

He looked hesitant, then nodded and murmured: "Rohr-bach."

This meant nothing to me, but I decided to put my trust in him, so off we went, I beside him and my holdall and haversack in the back. I was doing a wandering tour of the Rhine, so was travelling very light.

The car shot across the wide square – a square I disliked at a glance. It had the look of a desert, especially as people and traffic were sparse and the day was scorchingly hot. The nearest buildings from the Hauptbahnhof seemed a mile away when in actuality I don't suppose they were more than three hundred yards. I felt a distinct disappointment in this first impression of Heidelberg. I'd expected to find a town like an overgrown village that simply dripped antiquity. Instead I was greeted by a slick, modernistic railway-station, complete with shopping arcade. And now the buildings I saw across the square were hardly less modern in appearance. I just couldn't reconcile them with the picture of an ancient university town I had always carried in my fancy.

As the taxi turned into a wide street with tram lines – Rohrbacher Strasse, I noted – I looked round and continued to feel disappointed – and disapproving. A distinct Montreal touch, I decided. The buildings had that brand-new look of those in the recently built-up area on the outskirts of Outremont, and the tram lines, if anything, heightened the Montreal effect.

The taximan drew up before a small hotel, but I told him no, this wouldn't do. Too much traffic. Try somewhere else down a side-street. It must be a quiet place off the main street.

He nodded with a look of patience, and turned into what seemed the right kind of street. About two corners from the traffic-infested thoroughfare we had just left we stopped at a spreading two-storied house with a sign at the entrance that said: PENSION ILSENRUH. It looked a quiet, cosy place, so I said, "Yes, this might do. Let's try it."

The door was shut. The taximan pressed a white button and a bell rang inside. Almost at once the door opened to reveal a shortish man of about forty with a potbelly in shirt and shorts. He had a large, round head with greying yellow hair, thinnish on top, and his blue eyes glittered inquiringly, even anxiously, at us through horn-rimmed spectacles, a smile widening a wide mouth and displaying a fierce array of teeth. At the corners of his mouth his overlong eye-teeth hung out in canine fashion.

"*Ich mochte ein Einzelzimmer,*" I told him.

"*Einzelzimmer!*" His shoulders jerked nervously. He shook his head, waved his hands before his face. "*Nein, nein! Keine Einzelzimmer! Besetzt!*"

Only once before, at a tiny one-horse town on the Rhine called Eltville, had I heard this dismal word. I groaned and asked him if he was sure there was nothing at all.

He shook his head again. "*Nein, nein! Besetzt!*" Then abruptly: "*Amerikaner oder Englander?*"

"*Englander,*" I told him.

He laughed as though just remembering a good joke. Last night, he said, he had accommodated twenty-seven Englishmen. "*Ja, ja! Siebenundzwanzig Englander!*"

This didn't seem much of a joke to me, however, so I asked him if he didn't know of anywhere else quiet where there might be single rooms available.

He gave his nervous start, clasped his hands together and said: "*Wollen Sie ein Doppelzimmer? Ich habe ein Doppelzimmer!*"

Light broke through. He wanted me to take a double room and pay the price of a double room.

I thought quickly. Heidelberg was only a diversion. I hadn't planned to spend more than forty-eight hours here, and already I was disappointed in the little I'd seen of the town. I said good, let's see the double room. He had one upstairs I could have, he said, but he took me into a similar one on the ground floor so that I could have an idea of what the one upstairs was like. It was well furnished, looked clean and cosy, so I said: "Yes, this seems all right. How much?" Nineteen marks, he said, including breakfast. (The hotel in Cologne had charged me seventeen-ten for a single room, with seven marks extra for the use of a bathroom, and three marks for breakfast). I said: "Agreed. I'll take the one upstairs like this."

"*Ja?* Agreed?" (He seemed disappointed that I hadn't tried to argue the matter). And I nodded. "Yes. Agreed. I'll pay nineteen marks."

"*Gut, gut! Zwei Tage?*"

"*Ja,*" I said. "*Zwei Tage.*"

He nodded briskly, smiling so widely that his eye-teeth really looked the authentic Dracula thing. But it was, somehow, not an evil smile. It had a nervousness and uncertainty about it, an ingratiating and cunning quality, too – yet behind it lay good-nature: a cringing, hesitant good-nature, perhaps, but good-nature all the same.

Suddenly he began to explain that it would be better (*wir arbeiten besser*) if I could pay in advance for the two days.

"Why?" I asked, at once on my guard, and rather inclined to give him a bad mark in grace of the good one I'd just awarded him. "At every hotel along the Rhine I've paid on leaving."

"*Ja, ja*," he nodded, clasping his hands together tight and smiling lavishly. I mustn't think he mistrusted me, but it was just that it would be better if paid in advance. "*Wir arbeiten besser so.*"

I didn't like it, and gave him the bad mark, but I told him very well, I'd pay in advance.

He sat down at once and wrote out a receipt and handed it to me, and I paid him his thirty-eight marks. He asked me to wait at a table in the back parlour and he would go and get the usual form for me to fill in. I knew all about this, so sat and waited, pen in hand. He bustled off into the next room – and then silence followed. I sat waiting. As the silence lengthened I thought it a bit odd, so got up and went into the next room which was a dining-room of sorts.

He was seated at the table eating.

I said in surprise: "*Ich warte noch immer!*"

He started violently and rose. "*Verzeihung! Verzeihung! Ich vergass.*"

He darted into a corner, took up a pad of the pink forms all hotels and guest-houses give you to fill in, handed it to me, laughed and apologized again, then sat down and went on eating.

I went back into the next room and filled in the form, and had just finished when he came in in his scuttling, nervous manner and bent over me. "*Ach! Ja, ja! Gut!*" Then he noticed something. "*Bitte!*" He pointed. I'd put down the number of my passport but not the date of issue nor the place of issue. He tugged my Parker 50 away from me before I knew what he was about, took my passport and flicked through a few leaves, then wrote down on the form the necessary information, remarking as he did so: "*Englische Feder, nicht? Schreibt so eben!*" To myself I was swearing, because he pressed so heavily on the nib that I expected to see it break. Moreover, his fingers were greasy with food.

He took me upstairs and showed me the room I was to have, and I liked it instantly. It was well furnished, and commanded a striking view of the Heiligenberg and Konigstuhl. And it was a cool room, which meant a lot to me, for the heat of the past few days had been inclined to get me down.

It was only after I had unpacked my toilet things that I noticed there was only one towel on the rail near the washbasin – a plain white linen towel. Could this be stinginess on the part of Herr Pfangle, I wondered? Or was it simply an accidental omission? I thought of going down and asking him for another, for in all the other places I'd been supplied with two. Eventually, I decided not to bother. I had brought one of my own – and a much larger one – which I hadn't yet had cause to use; I could easily bring it into action if this one proved inadequate.

Remembering I must go to the bank to cash a traveller's cheque (my stock of marks was getting low), I went downstairs with the intention of going out but found the front door locked. There was no key in the lock. Puzzled, I made my way into the back parlour where I found Frau Pfangle, a youngish (thirty-fiveish) woman with a gold-toothed smile. I told her that the door was locked. How was I to get out?

"*Ja, ja. Ein Augenblick!*" She called to her husband who, it seemed, was pottering about in the courtyard at the back.

He came in, smiled and hurried past me into the hallway. He opened the front door, and said that it was the custom to keep it locked. Any time I wanted to go out I could ask him to open it for me. And when I returned I must ring the bell and he would come and let me in. Did I have my room-key? I'd better leave it with him for safety. I said I preferred to keep it. It was only a small latchkey.

Shaking my head at this extraordinary arrangement, I went out, almost with the feeling that I was under arrest and was now being given an hour's freedom as a special concession. At no other place I'd stayed at had things been like this.

When I returned, half an hour later, I had to ring. And when I went out to do some preliminary sightseeing an hour later, I had to look for Herr Pfangle so that he could open the door for me with his longish chromium-plated key. And when I returned at about half-past ten I had to ring to be let in. Ah, well, I brooded, I must endure it. Only thirty-eight hours. On Sunday midday I'd be off to the Rhine again. I began to look forward with pleasure to my "freedom".

Before getting into bed, I was smoking a cigarette at the window when I heard feminine giggles. Putting my head out, I noticed that two girls were leaning out of their window in an adjoining room. They were peering downward in a curious, amused manner, and suddenly I became aware that someone was snoring loudly and steadily in a room on the ground floor. It was this snoring that seemed to be amusing the girls.

A few minutes later in bed, with my window wide open, I continued to hear the snoring. It didn't disturb me really, but I thought that I certainly shouldn't like to have to try to sleep in the same room with anyone who could make sounds like that.

The telephone began to ring in the hallway.

The snoring stopped as though switched off. There was a patter of footsteps, then Herr Pfangle's voice was bellowing into the phone. I'd heard him once or twice before at the phone. He always bellowed.

The conversation lasted about five minutes. I heard references to *Einzelzimmer* and *Doppelzimmer* and *Fruhstuck* and "*Ja, ja! Zehn Uhr!*' and assumed he must be arranging to receive a party of guests – perhaps twenty- seven Danes or Japanese, who could tell? His phone call at an end, footsteps pattered again – and almost like magic the snoring downstairs was resumed.

Twice again within the next two or three hours the phone rang, footsteps pattered, and Herr Pfangle's voice could be heard bellowing. I lay there in bed and sighed, telling myself that there was no traffic here to disturb my rest – but could this truly be called *ein ruhiger Gasthof*?

Dawn light had hardly begun to filter through my window curtains when activity of a noisy kind broke out in the courtyard. I peeped out and saw Herr Pfangle, in shirt and shorts as though he had never got into pyjamas for the night, pushing tables and chairs about. Evidently, because of the dry, warm weather, breakfast was going to be served in the open. When he had finished arranging everything to his satisfaction he turned his attention to a motor-bicycle whose engine began to splutter. I heard his voice in mid-day loud conversation with one of his guests. The engine was switched off, and he bawled something at Frau Pfangle. Frau Pfangle bawled back. Footsteps shuffled and lisped in the yard. No more sleep was possible.

After breakfast, I called him to open the door for me. He smiled and asked if I was going sightseeing again. I said yes – I'd probably be back in the late afternoon.

"*Ach, ach! Warten! Eine Karte! Sei mussen eine Karte haben!*"

He bustled off into a tiny room under the stairway and reappeared with a folder-map of Heidelberg that incorporated a list of the hotels and guest-houses in the town: I must take this, he said. It would help me to find my way about. He showed me with a fat finger what route to take to get to the Tiergarten, and what route to take to get to the Kurpfalzisches Museum. Was I going to the Schloss? Well, this was how to get there… Finally, he smiled his widest and fiercest, held out his hand and shook mine, nodded briskly and wished me *eine gute Reise*. I might have been setting out for somewhere in Siberia.

Thanking him for his kindness – I was really grateful for the map, for I hadn't got one yet and hadn't intended getting one – I set out on my sightseeing.

When I returned in the evening, I found the door wide open. But the occasion was a special one. A motor-coach stood outside the house, and a crowd of people was milling about the entrance-way. A party of Dutch guests, Frau Pfangle explained to me. They were staying for the night. Thirty-three of them.

An hour later, from my window I looked down and saw Herr Pfangle moving continuously here and there, in and out of the house, and always with something bulky in his arms – a suitcase, a stack of blankets, a sleeping-bag, once a small table – and always calling out instructions to somebody, Frau Pfangle or a guest. And several of the guests were still not yet settled in. For an instant the anxious thought came to me that at any moment my host might knock on my door and ask me if I'd help out by sharing my room with one of the party.

Two hours later when I was about to get into bed, I glanced out and could still see a young couple leaning disconsolately against the bonnet of a car parked in the courtyard. It was quite evident no bed had yet been found for them. The house buzzed and thudded with voices and footsteps. Herr Pfangle continued to shout and move about with bulky objects. The telephone kept ringing.

It must have been two o'clock before some sort of quiet was established. But at shortly after three I was awakened by a violent row between two of the male guests. I'm sure everyone else in the house was awakened, because Herr Pfangle's voice almost at once joined in, no doubt in an attempt to make peace.

A good half-hour must have elapsed before things grew quiet again. So far as sleep was concerned it was one of the worst nights I spent since my holiday in the country had begun ten days before.

At breakfast I was blunt and emphatic about it. On Herr Pfangle's inquiry as to if I'd had *einen guten Schlaf*, I said "*Nein! Ich schlief nicht gut.*" And catching the local habit of repetition for emphasis, I added "*Larm! Zuviel Larm! Ganze Nacht, ganze Nacht!*"

He apologised profusely, but it was the weekend. At the weekend there were many guests to deal with this weekend – thirty-three of them. "*Ja, ja! Dreiunddreissig!*" He himself had hardly slept. His manner disarmed me completely. He was genuinely sorry. I thought he was going to pat me on the back to console me, but abruptly he laughed, shrugged and hurried off to attend to something for another guest. He never glanced at me again. It was Frau Pfangle who came up smiling her gold-toothed smile to ask me if I wanted tea or coffee.

I was about to go upstairs after breakfast when footsteps sounded behind me, and

Herr Pfangle touched me lightly on the shoulder. In a confidential voice he murmured: "*Eine Mark*."

I scowled. "What's this now? *Eine Mark*?"

He nodded, smiling, and reminded me that I'd had an egg at breakfast the previous morning and another this morning.

An egg was extra. "*Funfzig Pfennig. Zwei Eier – eine Mark. Verstehen?*'

"Yes, I understand," I said stiffly. "You needn't be afraid. You'll get your mark before I leave."

He hesitated, and I could sense that he wanted to press for it now – this instant – but something in my manner must have put him off, for he gave a nodding, fluttery laugh, gestured nervously and turned and hurried away.

I went up and packed, a cool relief spreading through me. I had not been happy in Pension Ilsenruh. Apart from the noise at night, the strong element of distrust in my host had created an uncomfortable atmosphere, and I am very sensitive to atmosphere. And this locking and opening of doors had irritated me more than I had even wanted to admit to myself. Packing now, I felt as though I were about to escape from a suffocating enclosure, a place of claustrophobic discomfort where a potbellied jailor-host had kept me in a state of perpetual emotional uncertainty.

At five past ten I came downstairs with holdall and haversack and looked for Herr Pfangle. He was in the courtyard. Frau Pfangle called him.

"*Eine Mark*," I said, holding out the coin.

He thanked me and shook my hand. I must come again. Where was I off to now? The Rhine? Boppard? "*Ja, ja. Wunderschön wunderschön an dem Rhein!*" What train was I catching? Didn't I want a taxi to take me to the station? No, I told him. My train didn't leave until after one. Plenty of time. I'd just stroll quietly towards Rohrbacher Strasse and catch a tram for the Haupbahnhof. Then I'd do a little shopping in the arcade and kill time generally until one o'clock.

"*Gut, gut! Gute Reise! Wiedersehen!*"

The long eye-teeth lapped over the corners of the wide mouth, the fat hands gestured nervously, the blue eyes glittered behind the thickish lenses of the spectacles.

Frau Pfangle added her quota of farewells, and I was off.

I began to stroll slowly towards Rohrbacher Strasse, a free man in the Sunday morning sunshine. How lovely to be moving away from Pension Ilsenruh – and moving away for good. No more pressing of a white button marked *Klingeln*. No more scuttling footsteps and pot-belly and fluttering fat hands.

I got to the corner, crossed the tram lines and began to make my way very slowly towards the tram-stop. It was another scorching day, and I had loads and loads of time, I reminded myself. No need to hurry and start perspiring. My watch said twenty past ten. My train left at 13:14.

A light-grey car came to a stop by the kerb. I glanced casually sidewise and saw the door open. Herr Pfangle was smiling at me.

I started in surprise and smiled back, thinking: Well, look at that! See how bad it was to form hasty judgments of people! The man had actually come to give me a lift to the station.

He kept on smiling. And then he pointed. Pointed at my holdall. He said something, and I caught the word "*Handtuch*." German for towel.

"What's that?" I asked.

He repeated what he had said, and now I got his meaning. He was saying that he believed I'd taken one of the towels from the room. Could I open my holdall and get it out and let him have it back?

I couldn't believe it. I told him I was sure he couldn't be serious. One of the towels from the room? But there had been only one towel in the room.

"*Nein, nein! Zwei Handtucher!*" he said. And he pointed again at my holdall. I must open my *Gepack* and search for the towel. He knew it was in my *Gepack*. Yes, actually. He wanted me right there on the pavement to open my holdall and go through its contents so that he could show me up for the thief I was. How I wished I knew the language well enough to be able to crash out a broadside of really colourful swear-words at him!

To the best of my ability I told him to go to hell, and whether he understood me or not, my tone of voice and manner must have sufficed, for he gave up the struggle, nodded in a frustrated way, slammed the car door shut and drove off.

I moved on towards the tram-stop with feelings of fury, incredulity and awakening amusement. The irony of the thing: I'd deliberately decided not to bother them for another towel, and now here it was– the man had had the nerve to follow me and accuse me of running off with a nonexistent towel!

I was chuckling to myself when the tram came up. My fury began to subside. Poor Herr Pfangle. Something was seriously the matter with him. Not normal for anyone to be so distrustful of his fellow men. Perhaps he lived too much on his nerves. Didn't sleep enough. At heart he was all right, I felt convinced.

In the Hauptbahnhof I wandered along the arcade buying one or two knickknacks to take back for my family. I remember I had just paid the girl for a little liqueur glass with the arms of Heidelberg embossed on it and was tucking it into my haversack when I felt a touch on my shoulder.

Out of the corner of my eye I saw a uniformed figure, and thought, as I continued tucking the glass in, an American serviceman. Probably discovered from my accent that I'm English-speaking and wants to ask me something.

Casually I turned, smiling. "Yes?" I said.

The uniformed man spoke – but the language was German. Very quietly he asked if I'd been staying at the Pension Ilsenruh in Rohrbach.

I said yes – and then in one incredulous flash the situation froze into focus. This was a station policeman. He had been informed about the towel by Herr Pfangle.

My manner stiffened, my voice turned icy, as I asked him what was the matter. What did he want?

Still quiet-mannered but grim of face, he beckoned me to accompany him. And I accompanied him into a small room in which I found another policeman waiting. Also quiet-mannered but grim, this second man asked me if I knew anything about a towel that was missing from the room in which I had stayed at Pension Ilsenruh.

I said no. There had only been one towel in the room. And I related how Herr Pfangle had followed me and stopped me on the street and wanted to search my holdall. And I spoke in the voice of a man prepared to do battle to the death. It impressed them, I could tell. They still looked grim, but they blinked and avoided my gaze for an instant.

At this point a door opened softly, and out of an inner room popped Herr Pfangle, a glassy, triumphant smile on his face. Thought I'd given him the slip, had I? his manner implied *Nein*, *nein*! He was too swift and clever for me. Now it was he and the Authorities versus me.

I glared at him, glared at the policemen, and told them loftily and in my halting German what I thought about the whole business. *Ein billiges Handtuch*! What would I want to steal a cheap linen towel for!

They all three listened, silent, then one of the policemen stiffly beckoned at my holdall. Open it, he said.

"Very well," I snapped. "Why not? I'm not afraid to open it."

I opened it and took out my things, laying them one by one on a table.

Poor Herr Pfangle! His head kept jerking forward, his eyes glittering in hungry anticipation.

A policeman shook out my green corduroy trousers – and then my maroon. No *Handtuch* fell out.

Getting near the bottom, something white showed up. Herr Pfangle started nervously, eagerly, and pointed.

It was only a vest.

The pile on the table grew. The holdall began to sag at the sides. The policemen shook their heads. Then suddenly only the brown khaki canvas bottom of the holdall lay revealed.

One of the policemen, in desperation, pointed at my haversack. I opened that, too – but no *Handtuch* showed up.

It was pathetic to see Herr Pfangle's disappointment. Even through the mist of my fury I could sense with a sort of low-gear pity the frustrated dejection on his face as he turned away and began to talk to the policemen.

I packed my things back with deliberate care and in a leisurely manner, half-waiting, half-alert to hear Herr Pfangle offer an apology.

But I finished and pulled the zip shut, and no one had apologised. Herr Pfangle still stood talking to the policemen. He spoke in a lowered voice – so unusual for him – but I caught a word that gave me a clue to what he was suggesting... *Draussen* was the word. I heard it more than once.

He was trying to make out that I must have disposed of the towel somewhere outside. Perhaps on the tram I had passed it on to an accomplice, anticipating that my bags might be searched in the station!

I gave the three of them one last icy, arrogant look, and walked out.

CHILDREN'S FICTION

POOLWANA'S ORCHID

A TALE FOR JUVENILES

PART 1

Far away in a country that no child in England has heard of – in fact, not even grownup people in England would know in what part of the world it is if I said its name was Guiana – there lived a tiny creature called Poolwana. I have to say "creature" because Poolwana was not a boy or girl nor exactly a fairy. Poolwana was only partly a boy; partly an animal, too, and quite likely partly a flower as well because Poolwana lived in an orchid in the jungle. From now on I think it would be much better if I spoke of Poolwana as "he"; I'm sure your schoolteacher must have told you that there are such things as pronouns and that pronouns are made to be used. I know I ought to call Poolwana "it" as he was only a creature, but sometimes it's good to break rules, and, anyway, perhaps we can look upon him as a creature-boy and that might excuse me a bit.

Now, first of all, you'll want to hear what Poolwana looked like. Well, he had three tiny blue legs, each with a very tiny blue foot. Instead of two arms he had four, each with a very tiny hand, and these arms and hands were green. His body was green, too, but of a lighter green, and it looked like a very, very small pea, though this was only when Poolwana was hungry; after he had had a meal his body didn't look so very, very small, and it was pale brown in colour. Poolwana, you see, fed only on honey – there was plenty of honey in the orchid; I'll tell you more about this in a minute — and so after a meal his body not only became very slightly larger but also took on the colour of the honey he had eaten.

The orchid in which Poolwana lived was a rare orchid – so rare that it didn't even have a long Latin name as most orchids have; nobody had found it yet to give it a name. It was shaped like an old man's head – and looked like an old man's head, but an old man without a face. It hung all by itself on a long grey stem – a stem covered with shiny yellow bumps which were the eggs of some fine red-and-black ants. On each side of this orchid jutted what looked like a withered-up ear, and from the top part, right down the back to the bottom part where the stem joined it, the orchid was covered with a silvery down something like an old man's hair. Where the face of the old man should have been there was a cave, and the walls of this cave were blue. Thin, strong bright red prongs like teeth formed a sort of barricade before the inner part of the cave so that Poolwana, who lived in the inner part, could never at any time get out. The truth is Poolwana was a prisoner in the orchid.

Poolwana, however, didn't grumble because he was a prisoner. He had never known what it was like to be outside of his cave, so did not worry about what he had not seen, and, in any case, he was not a curious or adventurous creature. He was quite content to remain in his cave and watch other creatures going past. Apart from this, it was always very pleasant in the cave. Rain never fell, and when Poolwana looked around him he saw nothing but bright blue. At night he went to sleep without having to count sheep, because the sides of the cave gave off a wonderful perfume which not only smelt sweet but sent Poolwana to sleep in a few seconds. Another thing, too, was that the floor of the cave held many pools of honey – pools that never ran dry, no matter what the weather – so Poolwana was never without food. And not being a boy but only a creature-boy, he needed only calories – ask your schoolteacher what are calories; honey has lots of calories – to keep him alive. If the honey was poor in vitamins – ask teacher about vitamins, too – as most days it was, it never troubled Poolwana, because Poolwana didn't need vitamins.

Sometimes the sun sent shafts of light through the prongs like teeth that guarded the inner part of the cave, and the pools of honey would gleam like bright new pennies, for they were round pools. Other creatures were often attracted by these pools, and stopped to look enviously at Poolwana. Some of them shook their heads and said that it was not right that one creature alone should have so much honey. Some of them shook their fists at Poolwana and threatened to hurt him if he didn't give them some honey, but Poolwana only laughed, because he knew that he was safe from them in his cave; in fact, that was one of the reasons why he didn't mind being locked in as he was.

One day a creature called a jee happened to stop at the orchid to hide from a larger jee that was chasing it. It was a little pink jee with black legs – six legs – and two green arms, and had a body shaped like a banana, though the banana part was pink and not yellow as a banana should be.

"You don't mind me hiding here, do you, Poolwana?" asked the little pink jee whose name, I ought to mention, was Joomeel. Joomeel and Poolwana were friends, and sometimes when the day was very hot and Joomeel was not too busy looking for honey – that was Joomeel's work; to look for honey and take it home – Joomeel would drop in at the orchid to have a chat with Poolwana.

"Not at all, Joomeel," Poolwana replied. "Hide if you want to, but what are you hiding from?"

"A big red jee caught me stealing his pollen jam and he's after me. He says he's going to strip me and eat me if he catches me."

Poolwana laughed. "I can hardly blame him for saying that. I've always told you you look very eatable-ish, Joomeel."

"Don't poke fun at me, Poolwana. I'm in danger. It isn't good taste to poke fun at creatures in danger. If you weren't my friend I'd be annoyed."

Poolwana laughed again, and waved his four arms about. He tried to dance in his glee, but one of his three legs tripped him up and he nearly fell back into a pool of honey.

"I'm sure pink bananas must taste nice," said Poolwana, not laughing so loudly but still laughing.

Joomeel laughed, too. "And what about you and your pea-body filled with honey?" he said. "I've heard many a creature say they'd like to eat you. Honey is scarce outside your cave. Do you know that we creatures out here have had our ration cut since the rains began? We only get one drop a week now."

"That's too bad," said Poolwana. "I wish I could give you some of what I have in here, but I simply can't."

"You always say that," said Joomeel. "Why can't you? It's yours, isn't it? All yours."

"No, it isn't," said Poolwana. "It belongs to the pools."

"That's a silly thing to say," said Joomeel. "Don't the pools belong to you?"

Poolwana shook his head, and said earnestly: "No, they belong to the orchid. I've told you that before, and it's true. You must, believe me, Joomeel."

"And doesn't the orchid belong to you?" said Joomeel.

"Of course it doesn't," replied Poolwana. "I only live in it. If anything, I belong to it. You really must believe me, Joomeel."

"Who told you you belong to it?"

"I grew up feeling so, and a lizard once told me I must always believe what I feel. Lolopo is the name of the lizard, and he's a very wise lizard. He drops in sometimes to give me good advice."

Joomeel grunted. "Anyway," he said, "all the creatures I've met out here say you're a selfish creature to keep all that honey to yourself. They say that one day some bad creatures might raid you and capture your orchid, and then they'll kill you and take all your honey."

"I never listen to such talk. Lolopo said I must never listen to talk." Poolwana looked sad, and after he was silent a moment he said: "And, in any case, how can I help being selfish if I'm a prisoner in this cave? You other creatures ought to be sorry for me instead of talking about raiding me and capturing my orchid."

"Ssh! Wait!" cried Joomeel, in a soft voice. "I think I hear the red jee coming."

"Huddle up close against the bars and don't breathe!"

Joomeel huddled up close against the bars and didn't breathe, and the big red jee, after a while, went past with a loud jeeing sound. It did not even glance in at Poolwana's cave. Poolwana and Joomeel could hear him muttering to himself in a deep drone.

"If only I catch that little pink jee," said the red jee "how I'll strip the skin off him and eat him up!"

When he had gone, Poolwana laughed and said: "Did you hear what he said, Joomeel? Oh, I can just see him smacking his lips over you,"

Joomeel snorted. "He's a big silly fat apple of a jee – and over-ripe, too! I hate apples – especially red, over ripe apples."

"Oh, is that so!" cried a deep jeeing voice.

Poolwana and Joomeel gasped in surprise and alarm, for there at the entrance of the cave stood the big red jee.

"Thought I wouldn't catch you, eh?" said the big red jee whose body was shaped like a cherry – not like an apple as Joomeel had said; Joomeel had only said that to be spiteful. The big red jee's body was the size of a cherry, too, and he had two strong small legs and five strong small arms, all black and shiny (every morning he had to have them polished; he was a rich jee and had servants to do this for him).

"Thought you were being clever by hiding in here, eh?" said the big red jee whose name was Bumbleboom. "I have sharp ears, my little pink friend. I heard Poolwana laughing soon after I passed, and Poolwana never laughs unless he has visitors. But for Poolwana I might never have caught you."

Joomeel shivered in all his limbs, and his body grew speckled with fear. Bumbleboom stepped quickly forward and seized him by two of his legs.

Joomeel cried out and struggled, but Bumbleboom was strong and merely laughed.

"You little thieving pink jee!" said Bumbleboom. "I've always wanted to strip you of your skin and eat you, and now I'm going to do it!"

"Please, Mr. Red Jee, I won't steal your pollen jam again," said Joomeel, frightened to death and growing limp all of a sudden, and a paler pink.

"My name is Bumbleboom," said Bumbleboom. "Don't call me Mr. Red Jee. I'm a very important jee, don't you know that? For calling me Mr. Red Jee I'm going to strip you very slowly so that it hurts you more than if I'd given you a quick stripping."

"Please, Mr. Bumbleboom! Please let me go!"

Poolwana, very grieved to see his friend in such a plight, decided to do something to save Joomeel's life. "Mr. Bumbleboom, I'm sure Joomeel didn't mean to steal your pollen jam when he left home. He must have seen it through a window and felt tempted. Won't you spare his life if I ask you very nicely?"

"Oh! So! So that's it, eh? You're pleading for his life, eh? Why don't you come out of that cave of yours, Poolwana, and give other creatures a chance to get at all those pools of honey you have in there?" Then a sudden gleam of cunning came into his eyes. Still gripping Joomeel's two legs firmly and sitting on the four other legs, Bumbleboom said: "Well, now, I've just thought of something. What about striking a bargain since you're so concerned about my sparing the life of your friend? Suppose I say I'll spare his life will you agree to give me three pools of honey?"

"Oh," said Poolwana, his eyes very wide.

"Oh, eh?" said Bumbleboom. "Is that all you can say in reply?" Bumbleboom began to laugh, his eyes twinkling in such a way that there could be no doubt that he was a big bad jee – and a greedy one, too.

"But, Mr. Bumbleboom, the honey in the pools is not mine to give you."

"No ? Then to whom does it belong?"

Poolwana sighed. So many times before he had had to answer this question! It was really tiresome. Anyway, Joomeel's life was in danger, so for the several thousandth time Poolwana said: "All the honey in here belongs to the pools and all the pools belong to the orchid, and the orchid doesn't belong to me. I belong to the orchid."

"That's how you explain it, eh?" laughed Bumbleboom, sitting more firmly still on Joomeel's four legs and gripping the other two legs so tightly that Joomeel squealed with pain. "A very nice way to explain your sly selfishness, Poolwana. Yes, it's a sly selfishness. I believe you have more sense than we creatures out here imagine. But I won't change my mind. Unless you give me three pools of honey I'm going to strip this little friend of yours and eat him. And I'll do it right here before your eyes."

"Ha! A crisis!"

This voice came from the entrance of the cave, and glancing round, they saw that it was Lolopo, the lizard. He was a very wise lizard, as Poolwana had said, and was well-known among the creatures for his comments. Making comments was his hobby, and he never charged for it. He liked using big words.

"What's a crisis, Mr. Lizard Lolopo?" asked Bumbleboom, and his voice was mocking, for he did not like Lolopo. Lolopo had once advised him to get rid of his servants and do his own work, that it was not right to let some creatures do dirty work while other creatures lazed around and did nothing, not even clean work.

"Don't you know what is a… crisis, Bumbleboom?" said the lizard.

"I don't," said Bumbleboom. "When I was young I was too busy getting rich to go to school. You tell me what is a crisis."

"Well," said Lolopo, the lizard, "as I was more lucky when I was young and learnt a lot of lessons, I'll tell you what a crisis is. It's when something happens and you're not sure what's going to happen after."

"Oh, is that what a crisis is ?" said Bumbleboom. "Well, you're wrong in thinking that this is a crisis, because I'm sure what's going to happen after what's happened already. I'm going to strip and eat this little thieving pink jee if Poolwana doesn't give me three pools of honey. That's exactly what's going to happen – and you're not so wise as I'd thought you were."

Lolopo smiled and said: "Perhaps I'm wiser than you think, Bumbleboom. How can you be sure of what will happen when you don't know whether Poolwana will give you the honey or not? If Poolwana gives you the honey you won't strip and eat little Joomeel, and if Poolwana doesn't give you the honey you will. So don't you see I'm right, after all? None of us here really knows what's going to happen – not even Poolwana, for I can see he is in two minds whether to give you the honey and save Joomeel's life or not give you and let Joomeel die."

"But, Lolopo" said Poolwana, in a very worried voice, "I've told everybody so often. It isn't my honey to give. Who knows what might happen if I give away the honey in these pools? The orchid might get offended and close up and crush me to death. Would you like to see that happen ?"

"I wouldn't," said Lolopo.

"Poolwana is a stupid creature," said Bumbleboom. "How could the orchid get offended and close up and crush him to death? The orchid is not a living creature. It's only an orchid."

"Ah," said Lolopo, "but you don't understand, Bumbleboom that Poolwana believes in his orchid as though it were a living thing, and if he believes it would be offended it might be offended."

Suddenly, a wind began to blow, and the orchid swayed and shook.

Poolwana cried out in fear. "Did you see that ? Did you see that? The orchid can hear what we're saying. It's just given us a sign that it can. I believe it's a sort of creature, and even though it doesn't talk it can hear what we say. And perhaps it can kill us all if it wants to."

"I've always thought you were a stupid creature, Poolwana," said Bumbleboom, sitting more comfortably on Joomeel's four legs, and tucking Joomeel's two other legs more securely under his arms.

"Is it stupid to believe in something?" asked Poolwana.

"It's stupid to believe in an orchid," said Bumbleboom. "Why don't you believe instead in lots of rich honey as I do? When you have lots of honey as I have in my great palace-nest you can keep lots of servants and lots of wives, and other creatures say yes to everything you say. That's something to believe in. Not a silly orchid."

Poolwana shivered, and looked up at the bright blue walls of the cave, expecting them to collapse upon them because Bumbleboom had called the orchid silly. But nothing happened. The orchid didn't even shake and sway as it had done a moment ago.

Poolwana was about to scold Bumbleboom for calling the orchid silly when a squeaky voice at the entrance said; "Poolwana, what's happening today in your cave? You seem to have a lot of visitors."

They looked and saw that it was a blue mosquito. Her name was Memba, and almost all the creatures had heard of and heard her, because she was a famous singer, and gave concerts regularly, especially during the long rain season. She had the best voice in the jungle, and no other creature could take a note as high as she could.

"I'm worried, Memba," said Poolwana. "Very worried."

"It's a crisis," said Lolopo.

"Don't say that word, please," said Memba. "I don't like it."

"Why don't you like it?" asked Lolopo.

"It makes me remember what I used to be called before I became famous."

"What were you called then?"

"They used to call me a cry-sister. A cry-sister is a singer who can't sing well. In fact a cry-sister is an awful singer."

"I'm quite sure you're not an awful singer, Miss Memba," said Bumbleboom who had been staring with shining eyes at Memba from the instant she had come into the cave. "I think you're a very fine singer – and a very beautiful creature. For a long time I've been wanting to ask you up to my palace-nest."

"Oh, indeed!" said Memba stiffly.

"Please don't misunderstand me!" cried Bumbleboom hastily, wriggling so much that Joomeel squealed in pain. "I meant to sing for me and my family and – and my household. Only that I meant."

"I'm glad you only meant that, Mr. Bumbleboom. Anyway, nobody has explained to me what's happening here. Why are you sitting on that little pink jee, Mr. Bumbleboom? Has he done anything?"

"It's a crisis," said Lolopo, then caught himself and gasped: "Oh, I'm so sorry! I was forgetting your little idiosyncrasy!"

"What's that ?" cried Poolwana and Bumbleboom in chorus, staring.

"Yes what's that ?" asked Memba. "I've never heard such a long word in all my life. Are you cursing me, Mr. Lolopo?"

Lolopo smiled. "If you'd gone to school as I've done," he said, "no long word would puzzle you, because you'd know that all you have to do when you hear a long word is to take it in slowly one syllable at a time."

"Never mind about going to school," said Bumbleboom a little irritably, because he never liked to be reminded that he had never gone to school. "Just tell us what the word means."

"It means," said Lolopo, "something queer that belongs only to you."

"Your tail is an idiosyncrasy, then. Is that what you mean?" asked Bumbleboom.

Before Lolopo could reply Poolwana cried out anxiously: "But look here, what's wrong with poor Joomeel? He hasn't uttered a word for such a long time! Have you squeezed him to death, Bumbleboom?"

"I haven't – yet. But how can you expect him to speak when Lolopo's tail is in his mouth ?"

"Oh, I'm so sorry. Is my tail in his mouth? I had no idea it had worked its way round as far as his mouth."

Lolopo withdrew his tail from Joomeel's mouth and Joomeel cried: "Oh, I thought I'd never be able to utter a word again. And I've never tasted such a horrible tail in all my life!"

"That couldn't be so," said Lolopo. "I carried out my morning ablutions most punctiliously."

"More big words!" sighed Bumbleboom. "I do believe he's cursing us all and we don't even know it!"

"Oh, but please! *Please!*" pleaded Memba. "Won't somebody explain what's happening in this orchid this morning? I'm so curious and no one will tell me a single word."

"I'll tell you all about it, Miss Memba," smiled Bumbleboom. "And I shall be charmed to do so, believe me. This little pink jee I'm sitting on stole some of my best pollen jam, and I'm going to strip him and eat him if Poolwana doesn't give me three pools of honey. That's all. It's very simply explained."

"I'm surprised at you to be so cruel," frowned Memba.

"You think it is cruel, Miss Memba?" said Bumbleboom. "Well, if you think so I'll let Joomeel go this instant." Then a gleam of cunning came into his eyes, and he said: "If I let him go will you promise to come up to my palace-nest with me and have a cup of honey-brew?"

"Aha," said Lolopo. "The plot thickens."

"If you're hinting at my honey-brew, Lolopo," said Bumbleboom stiffly, "I'd like to inform you that my honey-brew is the thinnest and best in all the jungle. There isn't any as thin and mellow anywhere in this country."

Before anybody could say anything else there came a swift tinkling sound outside the cave, and several red dots went hurtling past.

"The firefly brigade!" exclaimed Poolwana. "There's a fire somewhere!"

The words were hardly out of his mouth when a breathless little black jee arrived and gasped: "Oh, lord and masters! Oh, dear Lord Bumbleboom! There's terrible news for you! Your best and oldest honey-brew vat is on fire!"

PART 2

"What!" roared Bumbleboom, springing up but still keeping a tight hold on Joomeel's two legs. Joomeel struggled and kicked out with his other free legs and cried: "Oh, please let go, Mr. Bumbleboom! Please let go! My legs are quite numb from your sitting on them!"

But Bumbleboom did not even hear Joomeel. Bumbleboom glared at his servant – for the little black jee was his servant – and bellowed: "How could such a thing have happened! I turn my back for five minutes and fire breaks out in my best and oldest honey brew vat! What have you servants been up to?"

"It's sabotage," said Lolopo.

"Who is he?" asked Bumbleboom red as a cherry – redder than a cherry, I mean – with rage. "Tell me where to find him and I'll have his legs and arms cut off one by one."

"It's the name of a something not of a someone," said Lolopo.

"Oh, please don't quarrel," pleaded Poolwana. "In the meantime poor Joomeel is suffering."

"Who wants to quarrel ?" said Bumbleboom. "Tell this silly lizard to stop talking in riddles. He said a creature called Sabotage set the fire to my honey-brew vat, and when I ask him where to find Sabotage he says Sabotage is a something and not, a someone. Who wouldn't get impatient at an answer like that, I ask you!"

"Please, Mr. Bumbleboom, please let go," moaned poor Joomeel, "My legs feel like ice they're so numb."

"They won't feel like anything at all in a minute," said Bumbleboom angrily. "This decides me finally. If Poolwana doesn't give me enough honey to put back what I've lost in my honey-brew vat I'm going to strip you and eat you as I said I would."

"No one would be surprised at your doing such a dreadful thing," said Memba in a cold voice.

Suddenly two black-and-red ants came into the cave with frowns on their faces. They paused and stared around at the company gathered and then looked at Poolwana, and one of them said: "Poolwana, you never mentioned that you were having a party. Have you forgotten we black-and-red ants have our eggs on the stem of your orchid? They've just hatched out and we can't keep the children from crying because of the noise in here. I'm surprised at you, Poolwana, for asking these noisy creatures into your cave."

"The cheek!" roared Bumbleboom. "Are you calling me a noisy creature! I won't be insulted by a silly black ant! Do you know who I am, madam?"

"You," said the black-and-red ant, "are a foolish, conceited black-and-red jee, and I can excuse you for calling me a silly *black* ant!"

Bumbleboom went so red the little black jee, his servant, began to tremble in dread, thinking that his master would burst.

"Do you know, madam," said Bumbleboom, in a rage that made him sway from side to side so that poor little Joomeel nearly got squashed to death on the floor of the cave, "do you know, madam, that if I wanted I could have my palace-guards come here and smash all your eggs to bits so that you would be childless? How dare you speak to a powerful jee like me in such a manner?"

"Oh, please! Please! Don't quarrel in my cave!" pleaded Poolwana. "The orchid might be offended and close up and crush us all to death."

But the black-and-red ant, who did not believe in the orchid as a thing that possessed any magic powers, replied to Bumbleboom: "I'll say just what I like to you. I know you hate all of us black-and-red ants, but I don't care."

"It's the colour question," said Lolopo.

"You shut up, you foolish lizard!" bawled Bumbleboom.

"Mr. Lolopo is right," said the black-and-red ant. "You're prejudiced against us black-and-red arts because you know we have your colours. You hate to know that there are black-and-red ants in the world because you happen to be a black-and-red jee."

"She's an educated ant," said Memba in a whisper to Poolwana. "Did you hear the big word she used? She said 'prejudiced'."

"I heard it," whispered back Poolwana. "Aggie went to school."

"Is that her name? Aggie?"

"Yes. And the other black-and-red ant with her is called Baggie."

"What pretty names!" said Memba.

"Aggie lays the eggs," said Poolwana, "and Baggie bags them."

"How strange!" said Memba. "But, Poolwana, why don't you give Bumbleboom the honey he wants and let him release poor Joomeel? I hate to see a sweet little pink jee like that have to suffer so much."

Poolwana sighed and looked up at the blue in the orchid's ceiling. "It isn't my honey to give, Memba," said Poolwana wearily. "And if even if it were I have no large spoon or jars to put it in so as to give it to anyone."

"But that's where I could be of help if you like," said Memba. "I could push in my probo – I mean my long sucker, and suck up as much as any jar could hold. And I could take it to the palace-nest"

"What!" exclaimed Poolwana, "You mean you'd go to Bumbleboom's place!"

"If it's an errand of mercy I would. That's what it's called, I've heard. My uncle was well educated, and he used to call it that when he sent me to get a drink for him. He was too old to go himself."

Poolwana now became very worried, indeed. He said to Memba: "Thanks for the offer, Memba, but I'll have to think it over for a few minutes. I really must think it over first. I'm so scared of doing anything that the orchid mightn't like. This is a magic-orchid. You other creatures don't believe it, but I believe it."

"It's faith," said Lolopo who had been listening to Poolwana and Memba's little chat and not to the quarrel that was still going on between Bumbleboom and Aggie. Every time Bumbleboom shouted at Aggie he gave Joomeel's legs a quick angry squeeze, and Joomeel was in tears.

"We'll really have to do something and do it quickly, Poolwana," said. Memba. "He'll soon kill the poor little fellow at this rate. Can't you give the matter a very quick think and decide to let me take the honey? My probo – I mean my sucker can reach the pools easily. These bars won't trouble me."

Bumbleboom stopped shouting at Aggie in the middle of a long sentence, because another of his servants had just arrived – another little black jee.

"Oh, lord and master!" cried the little black jee. "Oh, Lord Bumbleboom! The fire has spread to two more of your honey-brew vats! The firefly brigade is doing its best but the fire still spreads and spreads!"

"What! It isn't true! It isn't true!" roared Bumbleboom, so put out that he nearly let go of Joomeel's legs. Joomeel groaned in disappointment, and began to cry. "If that didn't make him let me go," he murmured, "nothing ever will. I may as well prepare myself to be stripped and eaten."

"What are we paying the firefly brigade for!" shouted Bumbleboom, fiery-red with rage. "A silly little fire in one honey-brew vat and they can't put it out! What are they fit for!"

"It's inefficiency," said Lolopo.

"It's what? You shut up, Lolopo! I'm tired of your big words!" Bumbleboom turned suddenly toward Poolwana. "Poolwana," he said, "this makes it more certain than ever. If you don't give me enough honey to make up for all I've lost in my three honey-brew vats I'm going to strip and eat this thief of a pink jee – and I'm going to strip him an inch a second to make it more painful for him. So you'd better hurry up and decide."

"But even if I could give it to you," said Poolwana miserably, "how will you be able to fetch it away? I have no large spoons nor – nor anything that honey can be fetched away in." Poolwana gave Memba a quick glance as if to say: "Please, Memba, don't offer to do it for him. I know you want to help Joomeel but I haven't made up my mind yet whether I ought to give him."

Bumbleboom snorted. "What a silly excuse!" he shouted. "Don't you know I have hundreds of servants at my command, you idiotic little creatures! I can send twenty of them at a time with pots, and in less than six trips I'll have got all the honey I want from your pools!"

"Transportation," said Lolopo.

Bumbleboom took no notice of Lolopo, however. He said to Poolwana: "This is your last chance to save this young thief of a pink jee. My patience is at an end. I've remained in this cave long enough. I want some fresh air. Unless you give me your answer in half-a-minute I'm going to start stripping the skin off your little friend here."

Bumbleboom began to count. Everyone listened to him in silence. Joomeel groaned softly and perspired. Memba looked sad, and Poolwana began to pace up and down, shaking his head with worry and anxiety. Lolopo was calm, and seemed not to care what happened one way or the other. Aggie and Baggie, the red and black ants, glared sulkily at Bumbleboom. The two black jees trembled with fear.

"…twenty-eight, twenty-nine, thirty!" counted Bumbleboom and stopped.

"Time is up," he said, his hold on Joomeel's legs tightening. "What's your answer, Poolwana? Speak!"

Poolwana stopped pacing and looked at Bumbleboom.

Bumbleboom looked back at Poolwana.

"It's drama," said Lolopo.

But no one bothered with Lolopo.

Poolwana cleared his throat, took one last fearful glance at the bright blue above, and then nodded and said in a low, husky voice: "Very well, Bumbleboom. I can't do anything else but say yes."

"You'll give me the honey to replace what I've lost in my three honey-brew vats?" asked Bumbleboom.

"Yes, I'll give you."

"You promise? On your sacred word as a creature in this orchid?"

"On my sacred word as a creature in this orchid," said Poolwana.

"Very well," said Bumbleboom, and released Joomeel's two legs.

Joomeel chirped with jeeful joy. "Oh, Poolwana!" he cried. "I'll never forget this! You've saved my life. Oh, you've saved my life!"

"It's nothing, Joomeel," said Poolwana, glancing up at the bright blue and expecting something dreadful to happen at any instant.

Joomeel began to do a dance round the cave while Bumbleboom grunted and frowned. "Don't you crow too soon," he said to Joomeel, "I haven't got the honey yet. If Poolwana doesn't keep his word when my servants come to take the honey I'll have my palace-guardsmen hunt you down and strip you into threads."

Joomeel stopped dancing and looked anxiously at Poolwana, "Poolwana, you'll keep your word, won't you?"

"Of course I will."

"We'll test him out right, away," said Bumbleboom, and turning to the two black jees, his servants, said to them: "Sons of dirt and black wax! Up you get and off to the palaces! Tell my housekeeper to send twenty kitchen slaves with twenty pots for honey from these pools."

"Yes, lord and master!" said the two black jees in chorus, as though they had rehearsed it several times. They turned and left in breathless haste.

Poolwana kept sighing to himself, and every now and then he glanced round at the pools of honey. Once or twice he looked up at the bright blue overhead as if expecting to see a white light appear and hear a loud rushing noise. The wind caused the orchid to sway slightly, and Poolwana started and cried out: "Oh, did you see that! The orchid shook!"

"And what of that?" snorted Bumbleboom. "It's only a gust of wind. Are you afraid of the winds too! I never thought you were such a coward."

"It wasn't the wind," said Poolwana, moaning. "It was the orchid. It's angry with me for agreeing to give you the honey in the pools."

"Poolwana, you were silly to let this big bumptious jee trick you," said Aggie, the black-and-red ant.

"What word is that you used?" asked Bumbleboom, moving a step toward Aggie. "Bumptious. What is bumptious? Lolopo, what does that word mean? If it's an insulting word I'm going to have my palace-guardsmen attack those eggs outside on the stem of this orchid. And I mean it."

"What's the difference between your palace-guardsmen and your palace-guards?" asked Aggie, not in the least afraid of Bumbleboom.

But Bumbleboom ignored her. "Lolopo," said Bumbleboom, "please tell me the meaning of 'bumptious'."

" 'Bumptious'," said Lolopo, "means so rich that you can bump us all and we dare not bump you back."

Bumbleboom grunted, not certain whether to be pleased or angry. After a moment he said: "Well, if that's all it means I won't do anything about it. But I'm not going to be insulted by a tiny *black* ant who is not even good enough to walk on my jee tracks."

At this point, the two black jees appeared at the entrance of the cave.

They trembled so much that they nearly toppled backward. Their tiny eyes looked white in their tiny black heads – white and wide with fear. In chorus, they gasped: "Oh, lord and masters! Oh, Lord Bumbleboom! A dreadful, dreadful thing has happened! All your honey-brew vats are on fire. The fire has spread. And not only that, oh, lord and master! Oh, not only that, Lord Bumbleboom! The fire has crossed over to your big storehouses with your best and richest pollen, jam. Nothing can save your storehouses now. Not even the firefly brigade."

Bumbleboom was so shocked by this news that he could not speak. He stood swaying from side to side and getting lighter red and lighter red. At long last, he gasped: "But this could not be! If my pollen-jam storehouses are on fire and all my honey brew vats are on fire, too, then my riches are going from me. I'm becoming a poor man."

"It's a crash," said Lolopo.

Memba whispered to Poolwana: "Why, he's getting lighter red and lighter red every minute, Poolwana. Do you notice? He'll soon be as pink as Joomeel at this rate. Oh, I'm so thrilled! I wouldn't have missed this for anything."

"Where are the servants I sent you for?" wailed Bumbleboom. "Why aren't they here yet with the pots to fetch away the honey from the pools in this orchid? Have my orders been disobeyed?" asked Bumbleboom getting less lighter red and lighter red, and moving threateningly toward the two black jees.

"Oh, lord and master! Oh, Lord Bumbleboom! All the servants are helping to fight the fire. They won't listen to any orders from anybody," said the two black jees, trembling so much that they looked like four black jees trying to dodge each other.

"Not even *my* orders they won't obey?" shouted Bumbleboom, quite red again. The two black jees now looked like one hazy black jee they trembled so much.

"Oh, l-l-lord and m-m-master!" they stammered. "Oh, L-l-lord Bumbleboom! The servants are all grumbling and s-s-saying things against you."

"Saying things against me?" roared Bumbleboom. "What's that you're saying, you sons of dirt and black wax!"

"It's insubordination," said Lolopo.

The two black jees were so scared now that they trembled backwards out of the cave and fell over the edge. And they were so weak from fright that they could not fly. They just dropped straight down into the leaves below the orchid and died – and a black spider grabbed them and pulled them into its nest.

Bumbleboom began to stagger about the cave in his rage.

"What ill luck is this that has come upon me!" he groaned. "My riches are going from me, and my servants are saying things against me. They won't even obey my orders. Oh, why should this have happened to me? Why?"

He began to grow lighter red and lighter red again, and Memba said to Poolwana in a whisper: "I'm a little sorry for him, Poolwana. Look how he's getting lighter red and lighter red again. If he gets any lighter he might die, don't you think so?"

"Would you be sorry if he died?" whispered back Poolwana.

"Of course I would. I hate to see anything die." There were tears in Memba's eyes. She sniffled.

"You're a funny creature," said Poolwana. "I thought you hated Bumbleboom. Didn't you say he was cruel for the way he treated Joomeel?"

"That was when he was rich and powerful and red," said Memba. "Now he's getting poorer every minute and less powerful – and he's losing his red. Won't you offer him some honey? Perhaps if he ate some honey he might get back some of his colour, at least."

"I think he deserves to be unhappy," said Poolwana. "He's a bad jee."

"I don't care if he's a bad jee," said Memba, "I'm still sorry for him. Hear how he's groaning and shaking himself. Don't be so hardhearted, Poolwana. Offer him some honey."

"If even I did offer him some honey, how would he get it? He has no spoon to reach through the bars to get it – and I have no spoons."

"That's no trouble. I could easily push in my probo – my sucker – through the bars and reach any of the pools, and I'd take up a good sackful and give it to him."

"What! Do you mean you'd do that for him! You'd put your probo into his ugly jee mouth and feed him with honey?"

"And why not?" said Memba. "If it's an errand of mercy why not?"

"But he's a big bad jee, Memba," said Poolwana, amazed. "Why should you have mercy on bad creatures?"

"I don't care," said Memba wiping the tears that flowed down her cheeks. "I still want to do it."

"You're the queerest creature I've ever heard of!" Poolwana exclaimed, staring at her.

"I don't care how queer I am," said Memba. "Are you going to let me get the honey for him, or not? Oh! Just look at him! Poor fellow! He's getting lighter red and lighter red every second. I believe he's dying." Memba sniffled.

Aggie and Baggie and Lolopo and Joomeel crowded curiously round Bumbleboom who was lying on his back groaning, his eyes shut, his body barely pink.

"He's going," said Aggie.

"He's going fast," said Lolopo.

At the entrance of the cave a black jee suddenly appeared – a small servant jee from Bumbleboom's palace. "Oh, lord and master! Oh, dear Lord Bumbleboom! Is anything the matter? Are you ill, lord and master?"

On hearing the voice of one of his servants, Bumbleboom sat up, some of his red coming back. "What is it?" he asked, a light of hope in his eyes. "Is the fire out? Was anything saved?"

"Oh, lord and master! Oh, dear Lord Bumbleboom, I'm your only servant left, who is still faithful to you. All the others have decided to search for you and kill you. The butler is leading them – that green jee who always secretly envied you your riches and power."

"Indeed!" said Bumbleboom, rising slowly, his red coming back very slowly but very steadily. "So that's it, is it? That upstart has turned against me, has he? Where is he? I'll break him in two when I meet him."

"He's looking everywhere for you, Lord Bumbleboom, and I don't believe he's very far off. He's burnt down your palace and killed all your wives and all your children and aunts and uncles. He says he was tired of being butler for so many creatures. He says he hated the palace and all your honey-brew vats and all your pollen-jam. I believe he's a little mad, oh, lord and master!"

Bumbleboom swayed on his feet. "My palace! Oh, my great palace-nest! My palace-nest burnt down! My wives and my children and my uncles and aunts all dead! I have nothing to live for anymore! Nothing at all!"

"It's the end," said Lolopo.

"Yes, the end," said Bumbleboom, with a low moan, and sat down slowly, shaking from side to side. "The end. The end for poor Bumbleboom."

"I could take you to a safe hiding-place, lord and master," said the little servant-jee. "Come quickly before that bad green jee butler and the other servants find you. We have no time to waste. They may be here any minute."

Aggie glanced outside and said: "They're coming. I can see them. They're at the purple blossoms only a little way off. They're looking toward the orchid here, too. I believe they know he's here."

"I don't care," moaned Bumbleboom, "I have nothing more to live for. Let me lie down and die."

"Won't you even live for me, Bumbleboom?" said Memba, moving a step toward him. She was trembling a little.

Bumbleboom turned and stared at her.

"You?" he said. "Memba? You want me to live for you? Oh, I'm not hearing right. I must be dying, that's why it sounds like that to me."

"No, you heard right, Bumbleboom," said Memba in a soft voice. "I want you to live. Live for me."

Bumbleboom tried to sit up and managed. "How sweet of you to say that, Memba.

I wish I could live for you. But it's too late. I've lost too much red, and there's no more honey. If I could get a drink of honey perhaps I'd be able to get back some of my red and live. But it's too late now. Too late."

"It isn't. I'll get you some honey."

Memba turned, and without waiting for Poolwana to say yes, pushed her probo – her sucker – through the bars and into a pond of honey. She sucked up a full sackful and hurrying up to Bumbleboom, put her probo – her sucker – into Bumbleboom's mouth and began to feed him with the honey.

"Oh, look! Look!" cried Aggie in alarm, and Baggie gave a squeal.

Lolopo looked, and what he saw made him hurry out of the cave and out on to the stem of the orchid. Aggie and Baggie followed him, and the little servant-jee, with a frightened cry, darted out, too, and flew off, Joomeel after him.

Poolwana looked and began to dance up and down and shout warnings to Bumbleboom and Memba.

"Look, Memba! Look, Bumbleboom! Look what's happening! Hurry! Get out of the orchid!"

But Bumbleboom was too busy drinking in the honey that Memba was giving him to bother about any warnings, and Memba was too happy at the sight of Bumbleboom getting red again to care what was going on around her.

When, at last, Bumbleboom had drunk all the honey Memba had sucked up from the pond for him, he sat up and smiled at Memba.

"I've never been treated so kindly in all my life," he said. "If only I had my palace nest still! I'd give it to you and all my honey-brew vats, Memba – all for your own self. I mean it."

"What a nice thing to say!" smiled back Memba. "Are you feeling quite well and alive again, Mr. Bumbleboom?"

"I feel in the pinkest – I mean the reddest, thank you, Memba. You've saved my life."

"Yes, she's saved your life," said Poolwana, "but look what's happened to you in the meantime. You're both prisoners like myself."

"What do you mean?" asked Bumbleboom. And then he looked toward the entrance of the cave and saw what had happened.

A network of fine silvery down – like the hair on an old man's head – had formed over the entrance, making the whole orchid a trap from which nothing could escape.

Memba, too, looked, and Memba said in a soft, voice: "We're prisoners. We can never get out of here again. We're like Poolwana now."

"It's because you took the honey from the pool," said Poolwana. "I told you this was a magic-orchid but you wouldn't listen. See! You all laughed at me because I believed in my orchid!"

Suddenly Bumbleboom began to laugh. Bumbleboom got up and began to dance about. "But I'm glad! I'm glad! In here I'll have no one to bother me. No wives or uncles or aunts or servants to pester me. I'm happy. Oh, I'm happy!"

"But you're a prisoner," said Poolwana. "Don't you understand?"

"I don't care," said Bumbleboom. "I have Memba with me as a prisoner. Memba, do you mind being a prisoner with me in Poolwana's orchid?"

Memba smiled – a little coyly – and said: "Well, now you mention it, Bumbleboom, I don't think I mind at all."

Bumbleboom danced about again. "Poolwana, did you hear that? She called me Bumbleboom – not Mr. Bumbleboom!"

"I heard," said Poolwana. "I do believe she likes you. She's a queer creature. I've never seen such a queer creature as Memba in all my life."

"I'm not at all queer," said Memba. "It's only that I sort of felt that Bumbleboom wasn't so black – I mean so red – I mean so bad as he was painted. I – I – anyway, you know what I mean," said Memba confusedly, growing a little pink around her probo – her sucker.

Well, that is the way everything ended. Bumbleboom and Memba lived happily ever after in the orchid with Poolwana. Whenever it was feeding time Memba would push her probo – her sucker – through the bars of Poolwana's cage and suck up enough honey for herself and Bumbleboom – and Bumbleboom's happiest moment was when Memba was feeding him. After a meal, he would always say: "I'm sure I'm the happiest jee in all Jeeland – I mean in Poolwana's orchid."

DRAMA

THE SUB-COMMITTEE
A SKETCH

CAST

Mr. LOPING: Chairman
Miss BREEN: Secretary
Mr. GROOM: Member of Sub-committee
Mr. SEARLE
Mr. TAME
Miss BARKE

A very bare room in any Government office-building. And a longish table around which are seated the six members of the Sub-committee, four men and two women. The men are dressed alike – staidly and sombrely – and each has, besides a small trimmed moustache, an air of solemn sobriety, giving the impression that matters of great moment are about to be discussed. The Chairman differs only in that he wears pince-nez. His secretary, who sits next to him on his left, is thirty-ish, with an air of extreme alertness and efficiency. Before her on the table is a stack of papers, notebooks and office directories. The other woman member, Miss Barke, is younger, nervous and evidently very eager to please – and to submit to Higher Authority. As the curtain rises, Miss Breen, the Secretary, has just finished reading the minutes of the last meeting.

MR. LOPING: (rubbing his hands lightly together) Yes. Y-e-s. H'm. Well – ah – you have heard the minutes of the last meeting read (*adjusts his pince-nez suddenly, hesitantly, and consults a slip of paper before him.*) Y-e-s. M'm. Ah – yes. I see here that the next item on our agenda reads: Confirmation of minutes (*looking around the table with an air of frowning enquiry*). Could someone – does anyone –or perhaps I should say, would someone move the confirmation of the minutes if – ah – if it is considered that there are no discrepancies.

Silence. There is a soft shuffling of feet and a gazing around and clearing of throats. One or two gentlemen even produce handkerchiefs and dab delicately at temples and foreheads.

MR. GROOM: (*very cautiously*) As a matter of fact, Mr. Chairman – ah – if you don't mind my pointing it out, I think I – of course, I don't want to seem too critical, but I did seem to notice just a slight discrepancy – at least, what appeared to me to be a slight discrepancy. I don't want the Secretary to feel –

There is a knock on the door, very loud and urgent.

MR. LOPING: (*clicking his tongue and glancing frowningly at the door*) Now, who on earth... This is really too annoying. Really, I...

Miss Breen rises, but Miss Barke springs up and moves toward the door.

MISS BARKE: It's all right, Miss Breen. Don't bother. I'll see who it is.

(*She opens the door an inch or so and carries on a whispered conversation with someone in the corridor. Meanwhile, however, ignoring the interruption, Mr. Loping, after his exclamation of annoyance, continues with the business of the meeting*).

MR. LOPING: You were saying, Mr. Groom. A slight discrepancy.

MR. GROOM: Oh, yes, yes! Well, the fact is (*wriggling in his chair*) – the fact is – well, I don't want to seem hypercritical, but I did think I ought to point it out, Mr. Chairman.

MISS BARKE: (*her manner breathless*) Oh, Mr. Loping! Please! Could I say something, if you don't mind? (*Shutting the door and approaching*).

MR. LOPING: (*frowning and holding up his hand*) Miss Barke, really, I... Do you think it is quite proper to interrupt us in this way? I mean ... well, really... Mr. Groom has discovered a discrepancy in the minutes.

MISS BARKE: I'm sorry, Mr. Loping, but I just wanted to say –

MR. LOPING: (*interrupting*) Just a moment! Just a moment, Miss Barke. Before you go any further, tell me. Is it something relevant to the item under discussion?

MISS BARKE: Well, not – not exactly, but –

MR. LOPING (*interrupting*): Then I certainly must insist on your reserving your statement for a more fitting moment. Item four on our agenda reads: Any other business. (*Smiling with extreme blandness and also with veiled reproach*). When we come to that stage of our meeting, Miss Barke, we should be only too pleased to hear whatever it is you wish to communicate to us.

MISS BARKE: (*crushed*) Very well, Mr. Loping, but I just thought... I didn't... (*Lapses into murmuring silence*).

MR. LOPING: (*rubbing his hands together in a relieved and self-satisfied manner*) Now, Mr. Groom, as you were telling us. This slight discrepancy...

MR. GROOM: (*squirming*) Yes. Of course, Mr. Chairman, I don't for a moment want to appear niggling, if you know what I mean, but – ah – well, the fact is, I did seem to notice that in the course of reading the minutes Miss Breen referred to Mr. Robinson as Mr. P. A. Robinson.

MR. LOPING: Mr. Robinson of our Rooms and Cellars Department or Mr. Robinson, of the Rooms and Shelves Sub-Division? If you could make it clear...

MR. GROOM: (*wriggling more animatedly*) Oh, I apologize! Yes, I should really... Mr. Robinson of our Rooms and Cellars Department. Yes, I really ought to have made that clear. I. Yes.

Miss Barke keeps fidgeting and glancing toward the door, very upset.

MR. LOPING: Proceed, please, Mr. Groom. Mr. P. A. Robinson of Rooms and Cellars Department. (*He scribbles rapidly*).

MR. GROOM: Yes, I did notice, as I was saying, Mr. Chairman, that Miss Breen referred to Mr. Robinson as Mr. P. A. Robinson (*squirming and clearing his throat*). Now, actually – of course, I – well, I could be wrong – but I rather think the gentleman's initials are A.P. – not P.A.

Grunting sounds of great concern. Deep frowns.

MR. LOPING: (*in tone of gravity*) Is that so, Miss Breen? Are Mr. Robinson's initials A.P. and not P.A.?

MISS BREEN: I had always thought they were P.A. (*Quickly, efficiently, worriedly she consults one of a pile of booklets before her*). Yes. Here it is in the Staff Directory. P.A. Robinson.

MR. GROOM: (*wiping his face hurriedly with his handkerchief*) Of course, I did mention that I might be wrong, Mr. Chairman (*titters self-consciously*). But – ah – well, I'm sure I distinctly saw it as A.P. in the Telephone Directory.

MISS BARKE: Mr. Chairman, could – could you permit me to say –

MR. LOPING: Yes, Miss Barke? Something to tell us concerning Mr. Robinson's initials?

MISS BARKE: No, not quite about that, but –

MR. LOPING: (*smiling in a fatherly but firmly reproachful manner and raising an admonitory finger*) Then you must be patient and wait, Miss Barke. It is essential that we should observe some order at these meetings. You were saying, Mr. Groom. The Telephone Directory. Miss Breen, shall we consult the Telephone Directory?

MISS BREEN: (*busily flicking through the Office Telephone Directory*) I'm doing that now, Mr. Loping (*pausing*) Oh. (*She is dismayed*).

MR. LOPING: Yes, Miss Breen?

MISS BREEN: That's funny.

MR. LOPING: (*clearing his throat*) Funny?

MISS BREEN: It's down here as Robinson, A.P. I can't understand...

MR. LOPING: (*adjusting his pince-nez*) Robinson, A.P. H'm. Peculiar.

MR. SEARLE: (*with a slight squirm*) Seems to create a ticklish situation.

MR. TAME: (*also with a slight wriggle*) It's certainly irregular. An irregularity somewhere.

MR. LOPING: (*gravely*) We shall have to do something about it, ladies and gentlemen. I mean – ah – it's undoubtedly an irregularity.

MR. SEARLE: (*leaning forward, as though with a sudden brainwave*) What would you say, Mr. Chairman, about the advisability of discussing the expediency of sending a minute to the Director of Official Publications? I think the Staff Directory comes under his supervision. I may be wrong, but... Miss Breen, could you perhaps...

MISS BREEN: (*with brisk efficiency*) That's right, Mr. Searle. The Staff Directory does come under the Director of Official Publications.

MR. TAME: But – ah – if I may venture to say so, Mr. Chairman – subject to correction, of course –. I have an idea that the Telephone Directory comes under the supervision of the Director of Deeds and Dockets, and if this is so I think it would necessitate sending a separate minute...

MR. LOPING: (*clicking his tongue*) I hadn't thought of that. Is it really so, Miss Breen? Does the Telephone Directory come under Deeds and Dockets Department? Somehow I was under the impression it came under Official Pamphlets and Propaganda.

MISS BREEN: (*after a swift, expert flicking through the papers*) Yes. Yes, that's quite correct, Mr. Chairman. It does come under Deeds and Dockets. You're probably thinking of Office Circulars. Office Circulars come under Official Pamphlets and Propaganda.

MR. LOPING: (*stroking his chin*) H'm. I'm afraid that seems to complicate matters considerably.

At this point there comes offstage the sound of loud bumpings. Everyone starts and glances towards the door.

MR. LOPING: Oh, but this is shocking. I shall have to make a complaint about these disturbances. There's far too much noise in these offices. The traffic in the street is bad enough, but –

MISS BARKE: Really, Mr. Chairman, I do feel I must tell you –

MR. LOPING: Yes, Miss Barke? You have a suggestion to make? Is it about the noises or about the Telephone Directory?

MISS BARKE: Well, it's about neither, really, Mr. Loping –

MR. LOPING: You mean what you want to say has no direct bearing on anything we are discussing in here?

MISS BARKE: Well, no, I must admit it hasn't—

MR. LOPING: Then, please, Miss Barke, I must ask you not to speak. It would be entirely out of order. (*Smiling paternally at her, then clearing his throat in a businesslike manner.*) Now, to go back to what we were saying, ladies and gentlemen. I am afraid what has just been revealed somewhat complicates the situation.

MR. SEARLE: A further complication.

MR. LOPING: You said something, Mr. Searle?

MR. SEARLE: (*wriggling and smiling self-consciously*) Oh – ah – nothing. No, nothing at all. I just thought I'd correct you on the point. What I mean is – ah – the matter is further complicated. Not merely complicated.

MR. LOPING: (*enlightened*) Oh, I see what you mean. Oh, quite. A further complication. (*Smiling benevolently*) Quite right, Mr. Searle. Just as well to have these little points clear.

MR. TAME: (*earnestly*) Of course, the real trouble as I seem to see it is the question of sending a minute. I mean – ah – we couldn't very well send a minute to the Director of Official Publications pointing out an error in the Staff Directory when, in actuality, the error may be in the Telephone Directory.

MR. GROOM: (*gloomily*) Just what struck me, too. And we couldn't –ah – we couldn't very well send a minute to the Director of Deeds and Dockets pointing out an error in the Telephone Directory when the error may actually be in the Staff Directory.

MR. LOPING: Precisely! Precisely! In fact, an even more serious aspect has just occurred to me. Really, this thing is getting most difficult and involved. I just can't see how we're going to cope with it… Now, the point is this: if we can't verify at this meeting that Robinson's initials are A.P. or P.A. it means that we're placed in the awkward position of being unable to move the confirmation of the minutes.

Murmured grunts of consternation.

MR. LOPING: (*leaning forward and clasping his hands earnestly*) I hope everyone sees what I'm driving at. We can't be certain that this isn't a discrepancy in the minutes. And, naturally – all – well, it goes without saying that it would be irregular to confirm the minutes if they contain a discrepancy –

MR. TAME: (*interrupting*) A possible discrepancy.

MR. LOPING: Eh? Oh, granted! Granted! I stand corrected, Mr. Tame. A possible discrepancy.

More bumping noises offstage. Miss Barke rises with an air of alarm.

MISS BARKE: Mr. Loping, please, could I be excused?

MR. LOPING: (*taken aback*) Excused?

MISS BARKE: Yes. Could I leave the room at once?

MR. LOPING: (*vaguely shocked*) Oh, but, Miss Barke, surely! I mean, really... (*He mops his forehead*) Is that all you have been trying to tell us? Surely if you wanted to be excused you could have said so all along without so much ah – hemming and hawing!

MISS BARKE: (*stammering*) I'm – I'm afraid you misunderstand me, Mr. Loping.

MR. LOPING: Do I?

MISS BARKE: That isn't what I've been trying to tell you all along (*she is a trifle indignant now*).

MR. LOPING: Then may I ask what it is you wanted to tell us?

MISS BARKE: I wanted to tell you what the messenger who knocked at the door a few minutes ago said.

MR. LOPING: Yes, and what did he say? (*Very indulgently*).

MISS BARKE: He said that a large package delivered by some person unknown and discovered down in the cellars has begun to give out ticking noises – and it's smoking, too. It's suspected to be almost certainly a bomb, and we've been ordered to evacuate the building without delay. And if you'd like to know, he did mention that the package was addressed to Mr. P. A. Robinson, Department of Rooms and Cellars! (*She runs to door and opens it, and smoke billows in*).

Quick Curtain

BEFORE THE CURTAIN ROSE

The scene is the auditorium of a West End theatre. We see only a section of two rows of seats – perhaps four or six seats. The size of the stage must dictate this.

Three members of the audience enter – they are KENNETH, SHEILA *and* RALPH. *They are youngish people – early thirties. They proceed to take their seats in the following manner – in the row nearer the edge of the stage. An unobstructed view of them must be had by the real audience.*

RALPH: (*glancing at ticket butts*) K 21... 22... 23... Here they are!

KENNETH: How do we arrange ourselves?

SHEILA: Oh, I'll sit in the middle, of course.

RALPH: Of course. Of course. Goes without saying.

SHEILA: Why that tone, Ralph? What's the matter?

RALPH: What tone? What have I said?

SHEILA: All right. Never mind. (*She seats herself between them*).

RALPH: (*with a dry laugh*) Kenneth probably knows what I mean.

KENNETH: (*uncomfortably*) I'm afraid I don't.

RALPH: Oh, but surely, my dear fellow, you wouldn't want me to sit next to you in preference to Sheila. Would you?

KENNETH: Oh.

SHEILA: I do wish you'd stop all these silly insinuations, Ralph.

RALPH: Are they insinuations? I wasn't aware they were. Perhaps it's a guilty mind that makes you think so, my dear.

SHEILA: Guilty? What have I done to be guilty about?

RALPH: Ssssh! This is not the place to discuss it.

KENNETH: What sort of play is it, by the way? Comedy or something serious?

SHEILA: Serious. Didn't you see the reviews?

KENNETH: No. I'm afraid I haven't read anything about it. First time I heard about it was when you people asked me to come along with you.

RALPH: "You people?" Are you sure that's accurate, Kenneth?

KENNETH: What's wrong with it?

RALPH: Nothing – except from what I can remember, it's Sheila who asked you to come along with us. I didn't know you were coming with us until she announced it about an hour ago.

KENNETH: Oh, I see. I... Look here, we haven't got programmes. (*Rising*) Let me go and get two at once.

RALPH: One would do! We're sharing and sharing alike, old man, don't forget!

Kenneth stares at him, hesitates, clenches his hands – then goes out.

SHEILA: (*staring at Ralph*) My God! My God!

RALPH: (*with feigned surprise*) Well? Why the dramatics?

SHEILA: Aren't you ashamed of yourself?

RALPH: Why? What have I got to be ashamed of?

SHEILA: Must you always be a boor? Always?

RALPH: Have I been behaving boorishly?

SHEILA: I'm sick of you – sick to the teeth!

RALPH: Tell me something new, for a change.

SHEILA: Not tell you. The time has come for me to act. And it's going to be soon – very soon, Ralph.

RALPH: You seem to thrive on being emotional.

SHEILA: And you! You thrive on being utterly callous and unemotional!

As Ralph laughs, Kenneth returns with two programmes.

KENNETH: (*holding out a programme to Sheila*) Here's a programme, Sheila. (*He resumes his seat*).

SHEILA: Thanks, Kenneth.

KENNETH: (*glancing round*) Not a very full house this evening.

SHEILA: No. Not yet, at any rate. There's still about ten minutes to go.

KENNETH: Nine, to be exact.

RALPH: How nice to be precise!

KENNETH: Look, as we've got time, what about a drink and a cigarette in the bar?

RALPH: Excellent idea! Take her along, old man.

KENNETH: I meant all three of us, Ralph.

RALPH: Did you? That's considerate of you.

KENNETH: (*uncertainly*) Sheila, do you... Shall we go and have a drink?

SHEILA: No, Kenneth. I don't think I'll bother. During the first interval if you like.

RALPH: I'll go to the Gents and leave the coast absolutely clear for you.

KENNETH: Look here, Ralph...

RALPH: Yes, Kenneth?

KENNETH: I don't like this at all.

RALPH: What don't you like?

KENNETH: I mean, if you think me in the way you've only got to say so outright.

RALPH: And what would you do?

KENNETH: I'd go, of course! You don't think I'm going to remain if you don't want my company.

RALPH: Oh, you wouldn't do that, Kenneth! What! I simply couldn't see you walking off and leaving my dear wife to the mercy of her cruel husband. You're far too gallant for that – and you care for her too deeply.

SHEILA: Kenneth, take no notice of him, please!

Ralph begins to laugh irritatingly.

SHEILA: (*in exasperation*) What's the joke now? What's the joke?

RALPH: Is there a joke?

SHEILA: Sometimes you make me want to scream. Scream!

RALPH: You're almost doing it now. Take care! I can see a programme-girl staring
    at you.

SHEILA: What a monster of an egotist you are! It's incredible!

RALPH: Do be original, my dear. I've been hearing that every day for the past
    five years of our married life.

SHEILA: And you weren't hearing a lie, were you?

RALPH: Why haven't you done something about it yet?

SHEILA: When I do it will be final – utterly and desperately final.

Ralph laughs again. A pause.

KENNETH: (*looking through programme*) Can't say I know any of the cast.

SHEILA: They're all new to me, too.

KENNETH: This thing has been running for a month now, hasn't it?

SHEILA: Yes. Why don't you try writing a play, Kenneth?

KENNETH: I'm sure I'd never bring it off. Not in my street. Advertising slogans
    and play-writing don't go together.

SHEILA: Don't be modest. You've written some marvellous short stories.

RALPH: Rich material for a play in our flat, old man. Why don't you ask Sheila
    to give you the gen on it? Or has she already?

SHEILA: I don't think I need to.

RALPH: Ah. That's interesting. Is he so often round at our flat that he knows
    about our happy life? Or do you meet him outside and have pleasant little
    heartwarming conferences?

KENNETH: Ralph, I object to this, you know!

RALPH: Do you? What exactly do you object to? My nasty attitude – or my nasty
    insinuations? Make yourself clear, old man.

KENNETH: My God! Now I'm beginning to see you for what you really are. I
    thought Sheila was exaggerating.

RALPH: Ah: So you're admitting you discuss me behind my back!

KENNETH: Is it surprising that we do?

RALPH: Not at all, Kenneth. I'm sure it must console you both to take me to
    pieces. You must feel much less guilty when she tells you what a rotten
    fellow I am. You must feel you have every right to supply the affection
    which I deny her. Oh dear, oh dear! How fortunate for your conscience
    that I'm the dirty dog she makes me out to be!

SHEILA: If you only knew how stupid and affected you sound!

The programme-girl suddenly enters.

PROGRAMME-GIRL: Coffee for you?

SHEILA: No, thank you,

KENNETH: No, no, thank you.

RALPH: (*with a laugh*) We're having a row, my girl. No time to think of anything
    so trivial as coffee between acts.

The girl gives him a surprised stare, then withdraws and goes out.

KENNETH: (*rising*) Sheila, I don't think I can stay.

SHEILA: (*catching his hand*) Kenneth, please! Try to stick it out – just for tonight.

RALPH: But, of course, my dear fellow. You must try to stick it out. Treat me as insane. Ignore my barbed comments. It's for her sake, you know. Can't let her down.

KENNETH: You're perfectly incredible, Ralph! I almost want to take you at your word. You do sound insane.

RALPH: Well, there we are! You're taking my advice. Sit down and stop being melodramatic, for God's sake. We'll be seeing enough melodramatics on the stage before the evening is out, I'm sure. No reason why we should indulge in that sort of thing ourselves.

KENNETH: (*seating himself again*) I think you ought to see a psychiatrist.

SHEILA: It's I who ought to see one, Kenneth. I don't know how I've kept sane these past few months.

RALPH: I can tell you how you have, my dear. Kenneth! It's he who has saved you from complete mental disintegration. Don't be ashamed to admit it. What's shameful in having a lover if your husband is an impossible boor – and a callous egotist into the bargain!

SHEILA: See what a coward you are!

RALPH: A coward! In what way?

SHEILA: Kenneth knows what I mean. You wouldn't have dared say what you just have if we weren't here in the theatre.

RALPH: Wouldn't I?

KENNETH: No, you wouldn't have. I'd have knocked your teeth down your throat. That's what she means.

RALPH: Tch, tch, tch! How uncivilised! And you an artist, my dear Kenneth! A short-story writer of promise! I didn't think you were in the habit of indulging in fisticuffs. I'm learning a lot about you this evening I didn't know before!

Three other members of the audience come in and take their seats behind.

RALPH: (*glancing round*) Filling up. They're trickling in from the bar. (*Looking at his watch*) Another three or four minutes for curtain-up, then we'll be able to sit in silence and hate at ease.

SHEILA: Don't flatter yourself. It's only in your own eyes you see yourself as important enough to be hated.

RALPH: That sounds like a line Kenneth may one day put into that play you keep urging him to write. When are you going to write that play of yours, Kenneth? Don't you feel you've gathered enough material from what's happened so far between you and Sheila?

KENNETH: Look here, tell me, Ralph! What do you feel has happened between Sheila and me? Stop beating about the bush in this pitiable fashion and spill it out.

RALPH: So you think I've been beating about the bush! Good Lord! I'd have thought I'd made it only too clear what I meant. Surely you aren't such a

simpleton that you need me to tell you in schoolbook English what I think
has been happening between you and Sheila these past few months?

SHEILA: Oh, I'm sure he knows what you think about that. No one can be in
the slightest doubt about your filthy insinuations. But he asked you to tell
him what you feel has been happening. There's a difference – unless you
perhaps are too insensitive to discern that there is.

RALPH: I was no good at metaphysics. I'm only a grubby stockbroker. And I
admit quite unashamedly that I fail to discern the difference, my dear. I'm
insensitive to everything but money and stocks and shares. Explain it all for
me. Unravel it. Reduce it to vulgar language so that even a boor like me can
understand.

KENNETH: It'll be useless trying to explain to you. Because your trouble is that
you can't feel. You think you know what has been going on between Sheila
and me – but your dismal tragedy is that you lack the ability to sense the
true situation that has been building up between the three of us. Your gross,
limited mind can only grasp it in terms of two dimensions. She's either my
mistress or she's not. For you there's nothing else to it than that!

RALPH: (laughing) I'm afraid I'm no good at literature, Kenneth. When you stop
quoting from the masterpiece you're working on at the moment and you
think you can tell me in plain down-to-earth English what you mean, then
I'll listen. Mind lending me your programme, Sheila?

Sheila rises and throws the programme into his lap.

RALPH: Hallo! Where are you off to?

SHEILA: In down-to-earth language, I'm going to the ladies' room.

RALPH: You'll have to hurry. Only about two or three minutes to curtain-up.

SHEILA: Don't let that upset you! (*She goes out. A pause while Ralph looks through
the programme. Kenneth stares tensely before him*).

RALPH: (*glancing at Kenneth suddenly*) Of course, you're mistaken!

KENNETH: Mistaken about what?

RALPH: In imagining that I haven't sensed the subtleties of the situation between
the three of us. Don't fool yourself, my dear fellow. I'm not quite as insensitive
as you probably think.

KENNETH: If you do really sense what has been happening, then you're even
more despicable than you appear.

RALPH: Meaning that I should have retired gracefully from the scene and not
made myself a nuisance? Just allowed you to have a clear field, eh?

KENNETH: No, I don't mean that. I mean you could have spared her more than
you have. I mean you could have refrained from humiliating her – especially
on occasions like this. Don't you realise what it's been doing to her? She's
getting pretty near the edge, you know, Ralph.

RALPH: But she'll never fall off. (*Laughing*) Too well balanced, Sheila. If you
knew her as I do you wouldn't be afraid for her.

KENNETH: I wonder how well you do know her.

RALPH: Oh, I know her through and through. She's tougher than you think!
Tougher than either of us.

KENNETH: That's where you're very much mistaken. She isn't tough. She appears
to be tough – but it's only a pose. A pose she adopts as a means of self-
defence. You've been driving her so hard that she's been forced to build up
a kind of illusory hardness to keep YOU at bay. That's all it is… It isn't a
real hardness, Ralph. It's thinner than an eggshell – and it's going to crack
soon. Didn't she warn you when we first came in? Didn't you hear what
she said? She meant it. She's desperate – and she's going to act. She's going
to act… (*He breaks off distractedly*)

RALPH: Act, you say? Of course. Sheila's always acting. She's an excellent actress.
That's why she's always advising you to write a play, my dear fellow.

KENNETH: God, I wish you'd be serious – just for once!

RALPH: Under my banter I'm dead serious, believe me. I wouldn't be making
myself so objectionable if I weren't serious.

KENNETH: But why can't you leave her alone? Why must you keep on deliberately
harrowing her spirit? What pleasure do you get out of punishing her?

RALPH: My punishment creates a contrast, Kenneth – it gives a keener edge to
the pleasure she derives from your company. So in a manner of speaking,
she should look upon me as a benefactor.

KENNETH: I give up. You're impossible! I wish it were in my power to take her
off somewhere – somewhere well out of your reach. That's the frustrating
part of the whole damned business. I just can't do a thing to help her.

RALPH: But you do help her, Kenneth. You give her spiritual aid of the highest
order. Tch, tch, tch! Don't underrate yourself. Why, she virtually sleeps with
that book of your short stories. She keeps it on her bedside table as if it
were the family Bible. (*Laughing*) The only trouble is that she's so confoundedly
fond of her physical comforts that she'd never dream of leaving me for you.
Oh, no! Not Sheila, my boy! Sheila may like her spiritual champagne – the
kind of champagne you serve up for her when you take her to concerts and
discuss your highbrow topics – but she can't do without my kind, either.
The fizzy kind that comes out of a solid bottle with a pop and a hiss. You
know it? That's where she's a realist, Kenneth. That's where she parts company
with you. That's why she tolerates me and my alleged cruelty. It's nasty
stockbrokers like me who can provide her with a fifteen guinea flat and all
that goes with it. But you… Ho, ho! Advertising slogans and short stories!
No money in that, my boy! And Sheila likes money. She loves money…

KENNETH: That's enough. I don't want to hear any more.

RALPH: Oh, she loves money. You wrote a short story about a woman who loved
money, didn't you? It's in that book of yours. She's always talking about it.
The woman who sold her soul for what money could provide even though
it was the spirit she hankered after. The spirit! Ah, you people and your talk
of the spirit! Sometimes I wonder if you really know what you're getting at!

KENNETH: Just a moment! Did you say something about a story of mine? Has
she been talking about the story of the woman who… who… (*He breaks off*).

RALPH: Yes. Your story. Woman who sold her soul for money. Perhaps she saw
herself in the heroine.

KENNETH: My God! My God!

RALPH: What's it? What's the matter now?

KENNETH: Do you know how that story ended?

RALPH: I'm afraid not. I didn't read it. But I think it was rather tragic, from what I remember her saying.

KENNETH: Ralph, go and see where she is. Go at once.

RALPH: But she's gone to the ladies' room. Didn't you hear her say she was going there? Surely you don't expect me to go there...

KENNETH: Go on. No matter where she is, go, I tell you...

RALPH: What's come over you all of a sudden? Why the alarmed manner? What do you think has happened to her?

KENNETH: I suppose I must sound like a damned idiot – but I'm almost certain... That story you say she read – do you know what it was called? I called it BEFORE THE CURTAIN ROSE.

RALPH: Ah! Quite right! I remember the title. That was it. She mentioned it once or twice. But what has that got to do with her going off to the ladies' room? Why the panic?

KENNETH: If you'd read the story – and if you knew Sheila as I know her – you wouldn't have to ask. (*Rising*) If you don't go, I have to go myself. I mean it, Ralph. I've got a suspicion... I'm certain she's... she's... oh, my God! Why didn't it occur to me before?

RALPH: Look here, what the devil are you blabbering about? What suspicion is this you've got? What has occurred to you? Explain yourself. I can't make head or tail of what you're saying.

KENNETH: Are you going or aren't you going, you dull fool! (*He holds Ralph's shoulder and shakes it*).

RALPH: Are you mad? Going where? Where do you want me to go? Why don't you sit down? Look here, you'll have the management throwing us out if you're not careful. You can't make a scene in public like this...

KENNETH: I don't care what scene I make. If you don't go and ask them to see about her I'll go...

RALPH: Kenneth, control yourself, for God's sake. Look! There! The lights are dimming. In a few seconds the curtain will be going up. Why don't you sit down?

The lights begin to dim. And as they dim, the programme-girl suddenly hurries in. She pauses and looks from Ralph to Kenneth.

PROGRAMME-GIRL: I'm sorry to trouble you, but which of you is the husband of the lady who left her seat here a few moments ago?

RALPH: I am. What's the matter?

PROGRAMME-GIRL: Could you come at once, please sir?

RALPH: But the curtain is going up. What is the matter?

PROGRAMME-GIRL: I'm sorry – but the manager would like you to come at once. It's about your wife. It's very serious, sir. You must come right away.

Curtain

VILLAGE IN GUIANA
A Radio Sketch

CAST

NARRATOR
His Friend JOHN
JACKSON PETERS — a negro farmer
HARRY GRANT — another negro farmer
NANCY PETERS —wife of Jackson Peters
GEORGIE — a village carpenter

The scene is Sandvoort, a village on the lower reaches of the Canje Creek, British Guiana.

NARRATOR: It was my interest in the history of the place that precipitated the whole thing. I won't call it an adventure. That would be too pretentious a word – but it was certainly an experience that my friend John and I had never bargained for.

Sandvoort – the name is Dutch – is a little village on the lower reaches of the Canje Creek. The Canje Creek is a tributary of the Berbice River, one of the three big rivers of British Guiana. In the eighteenth century the banks of both the Berbice River and the Canje Creek were cultivated from the mouths of these two streams right up to a distance of more than a hundred miles. But the land had deteriorated, and the planters – they were Dutch in those days – had gradually moved down to the coast where the alluvial soil proved much more fertile and not so easily exhaustible. Today all those brave old plantations have reverted to dense jungle. Where sugar-mills and slave-huts and the residences of Dutch planters once stood, hairy black spiders, boa-constrictors, peccaries and tapirs, and all the wild creatures of tropical South America roam amidst towering vine-tangled mora and courida and greenheart trees and innumerable varieties of palms.

Sandvoort, now a village of peasant huts, and three miles from New Amsterdam, a little town at the mouth of the Berbice, was once a flourishing Dutch plantation, and it was I who asked John to drive me there in his car one afternoon in June of 1938. At that time, I was obsessed with the idea of discovering relics of the old Dutch days. I even had in mind that afternoon, a forage into the bush – and there is a lot of bush at Sandvoort – in the hope of happening upon the ruins of some sugar-mill or plantation house, or – who knows? – that fabulous jar of buried jewels or money. During the slave insurrection of 1763 many a Dutch family is said to have buried their valuables in earthenware jars, and there is hardly anyone who has grown up in or near

New Amsterdam who has not cherished the hope of one day finding buried treasure in his back-yard.

June is a rainy month, but, not every day during the rainy season is a rainy day; many days are quite hot and cloudless. And on this particular afternoon that John and I set out for Sandvoort it was positively scorching, though every now and then we could hear distant thunder in the south. But from June to September there is always distant thunder somewhere in the south over the jungle. It never comes to anything, as a rule. On the coast, thunderstorms and rainstorms approach from the northeast, blown in on the general trade-wind drift.

This afternoon, however, something went wrong with the routine, for as we were nearing Sandvoort, the afternoon darkened, and rain came down in a swishing deluge. Really fierce, spiteful rain. John looked at me and wagged his head.

JOHN: Oh, well! See what you've put me in for! You and your Dutch relics.

NARRATOR: It's probably only a passing shower. It came from the south.

JOHN: Whether it's passing, or whether it came from the south, it's certainly turning the road into a nice little morass.

NARRATOR: Personally, I like these burnt-earth roads. I should hate the day when the government decides to have them asphalted.

JOHN: That's because you're not a motorist. This isn't a road. It's a bridle path putting on airs. Whoa! There was a lovely little rut for you (*Sound of squelching water and a bump*).

NARRATOR: He was quite right, of course. The road was disgracefully kept. It was hardly wide enough to accommodate one car, though the grass borders were wide, and two cars could generally squeeze past each other, making use of the grass borders. Beyond these areas of grass there were muddy ditches on either side, and beyond these ditches the land stretched away, on either hand, flat as a playing-field, swampy and bushy, with the huts and two-roomed shingled cottages of the peasants each in their little isolated clearings, and water gurgling and streaming past the short wooden blocks on which many of them were raised off the black, clayey ground. Here and there you could see breaks in the bush, and vistas of savannah land were visible. Odd cows and sheep, looking lonely and lost, in the savage curtain of rain, nibbled at the blades of grass pushing, up through the rising flood of water.

The district we were passing through is called Lochaber, and it was still, in 1938, more or less, a functioning sugar-plantation. About a mile away on our left, beyond the huts and the bush, there were canefields that extended to the bank of the Canje Creek, and a punt-canal where we used to go swimming in the days when we were Boy Scouts.

Suddenly we went over a flimsy wooden bridge, and John brought my attention to the fact that we were now in Sandvoort.

JOHN: That bridge we've just gone over puts Lochaber behind us. Here's your wonderful Sandvoort.

NARRATOR (*sighing*): I can't see us trying to search for Dutch ruins in this downpour.

Though we did bring our Wellingtons to cope with the swampy bits we expected to come upon.

JOHN: Our Wellingtons are remaining right where they are in the back of the car there. What I'm trying to search for now is a wide enough turn spot, where I can manoeuvre and turn the car to go back to town. Whoa! There again! Another nasty big rut (*Sound of squelching water and bump*).

NARRATOR: These ruts are really the end. I wonder when last they thought of putting some fresh burnt-earth on this road.

JOHN: And the soil is so clayey and sticky. It never seems to enter their heads to put down a good foundation of rocks and road metal.

NARRATOR: See about getting yourself elected to the Legislative Council, then you can institute a proper road-building scheme.

(*Sound of car's wheels whirring and swishing.*)

NARRATOR: Hallo: What's up now?

JOHN: We're in a rut – that's what's up.

NARRATOR: You don't mean to say we're stuck?

JOHN: I won't be surprised. (*Sound of engine racing and wheels whirring and swishing*) Aha! Hear that? I have an idea both our back wheels are involved. (*Racing engine again.*)

NARRATOR: What a nuisance!

JOHN: Look at the road! It's a bog. (*Racing the engine again*) No, it's no go, I'm afraid. We're stuck just where we are.

NARRATOR: This is silly. I never anticipated anything like getting bogged down on the road.

JOHN: Next time you come to Sandvoort you'll walk the three miles.

NARRATOR: Nothing new. I've done it before. Look here, we'll have to get out and do some pushing.

JOHN: I suppose that's the only thing for it. Nice little soaking in store for us, too, while we're about it.

NARRATOR: Hallo, wait! Before we plunge into the deluge… There's a chap coming along the road. Halloo-oo there! (*Hailing out*).

(*There is an answering hail.*)

JACKSON PETERS: Hey, chief: Wha' happen? You stick fast?

NARRATOR: Just one minute if you don't mind! (*In hailing voice*) I know a chap called Harry who lives about here. He's a farmer. If we could get in touch with him he might be able to help us. (*Sound of squelching footsteps.*)

JACKSON PETERS (*a shortish negro wearing only shorts, and with tarpaulin over his head*): Hey! You stick fast in de mud, boss? Dis is a bad spot for cars.

JOHN: You haven't got to tell us, old fellow.

NARRATOR: I say, do you know a farmer called Harry Grant who lives about here?

JACKSON PETERS: Harry Grant? Eh-eh! But yes, sah. I must know Harry Grant. He live furder up de road on de leff side. Harry is me god-brother. You know Harry, chief?

NARRATOR: Since I was seven or eight. He used to be our gardener in New Amsterdam.

JACKSON PETERS: I name Peters. Jackson Peters.

NARRATOR: And you're his god-brother, you say?

JACKSON PETERS: Yes, sah. Harry and me got de same godmother. Miss Sarah Batenburg is we godmother. She stand for we both at our christening.

JOHN: Batenburg! That name seems to ring a bell, somehow. Wasn't there a governor of Berbice in the late eighteenth century called Batenburg?

NARRATOR: Van Batenburg. He is rumoured to have had over eighty children. (*Coughing*) Not many of them with benefit of clergy.

JACKSON PETERS: My godmother' great-grandmother used to work for van Batenburg at Colony House. In Slavery days.

JOHN: And I suppose she adopted the name?

JACKSON PETERS: All slaves in longtime days used to take their masters' names, sah. And when Slavery abolish, they keep dem same names and pass dem down to their sons.

NARRATOR: My God! But you're getting wet, Peters. This tarpaulin thing you've got over your head is a farce.

JACKSON PETERS (*laughing*): You call dis rain, chief! You ain' see rain yet. Hay, hay! Me accustomed to rain. You want me to give you a lil' push and see if I can get you out dis rut, chief?

JOHN: We'd be glad. Save us getting a wetting.

JACKSON PETERS: Awright. Race your engine, and let we see.

(*Sound of car's engine racing. Swishing and whirring of wheels.*)

NARRATOR: Anything doing?

JOHN: No luck. She simply won't budge.

JACKSON PETERS: Chief, dis look serious. De tyres gone down deep in de putta-putta. De more you work de engine de deeper they sinking. Only thing now is for me to go and get some lengths of wood – one or two old boards might help if we put dem crossways in de mud.

NARRATOR: The devil! Where are you going to get old boards from, Peters?

JACKSON PETERS: Look, chief, I tell you what. We better wait till dis rain done fall. We can't do nutting till dis road stop running wid water.

JOHN: What! You don't mean you expect us to sit here and wait until this storm chooses to work itself out, Peters. Why, that might not be until after midnight.

JACKSON PETERS (*laughing*): Ah, na, na! I know dis weather, chief. Dis rain can't last more dan a hour. It come up from de land-side. Look, why you don't tek dis tarpaulin and run come in at my lil' house. You can sit down and keep you'selves comfortable until de rain stop. I got some ginger-beer setting in a old Dutch jar. It must be just right now for drinking.

NARRATOR: What's this? An old Dutch jar?

JACKSON PETERS: Yes, chief. You know de kind o' jar I mean. Dem big two-foot-high earthenware jars wha' de Dutchmen used to use in de old days. I find it one day when I was digging in de fields across de way dere.

NARRATOR: A relic! That settles it. Come on, John. We must take a peep into Peters' little house.

JOHN: You and your confounded relics. Very well, come along. And I do hope Peters is right about this rain. I'm in no mood to be stranded here for the rest of the night. I can't stand Dutch ghosts.

JACKSON PETERS: Hay, hay! You believe in ghosts, chief! We got plenty Dutchman ghost in Sandvoort! But we know how to handle dem. They don't frighten us no more. Hay, hay, hay! Here de tarpaulin. Come on across!

NARRATOR: Perhaps we'd better put on our Wellingtons, John. That ditch seems to be getting the better of Peters' little log bridge.

JOHN: Left to me, I'd take off our shoes and go barefooted. I hate fussing about with those Wellingtons.

NARRATOR: Quite all right with me. Come along, then. We'll do it barefooted.

JACKSON PETERS: Look Harry up de road coming now, chief!

NARRATOR: Is that Harry? By George, you're right. It does look like him. Just in good time to join our ginger-beer party, Peters.

JOHN: All right. Come on. I'm opening the door. Let's make a dash for it.

NARRATOR: The next minute we were sloshing our way across the grass border in the rain. Using the tarpaulin Peters lent us, we managed to keep off most of the rain from our clothes. It was not far to go. After we had crossed the small wooden bridge that spanned the ditch, it was only a distance of twenty or thirty yards to the small two-roomed shingled cottage that was Peters' home. A tall, rather thin negress was standing in the open doorway to welcome us, and we assumed she must be Peters' wife. Though, for some reason – we didn't discover why until sometime later – she did not have a very welcoming expression on her face. She seemed suspicious of us and even a little afraid. She backed off inside to let us enter the tiny room that seemed to serve the dual purpose of sitting and dining-room. It was very sparsely furnished, and the furniture was of the most rudimentary kind – a small table on which there was an oil-lamp and a flower-pot and two enamel plates and a large enamel cup, and an upright, unpainted wooden chair. Then near this table stood an old-fashioned dinner-waggon laden with an assortment of glassware, though it didn't seem as if there were two tumblers that matched each other. Afterwards, I learnt that it was Peters himself who had constructed this dinner-waggon – not that it was such a bad job. It looked quite sturdy, though it lacked varnish or any kind of polish. The rest of the furniture consisted of two soap-boxes which were evidently used for sitting on. A doorway opened into the other room, and we could see what looked like quite a respectable double bed. I had a glimpse of a red blanket and dungaree-blue pillows. The place was clean and tidy despite its appearance of poverty. It smelt of paraffin and old clothes which the moths had got at.

Anyway, let me get back to Mrs. Peters. She backed away, as I said, for us to enter, then standing with her hand resting nervously on the dinner-waggon, asked us who we were.

MRS. PETERS: You friends wid Jackson? He tell you to come in here?

NARRATOR: Yes, we got stuck in the mud, See our car out there! You're Mrs Peters, aren't you?

MRS. PETERS: Yes, I'm Jackson' wife, Eh-eh! But where Jackson?

JOHN: He's talking with Harry out there, I think.

NARRATOR: I've known Harry Grant since I was a small fellow, Mrs. Peters. I asked your husband if he knew where he lived, and just before we dashed in here I saw Harry coming.

JOHN: Here they are now.
Sound of footsteps and voices of Harry and Peters.
JACKSON PETERS: Look dem here, Harry boy! I tell dem to come in and try
    some of me ginger-beer until de rain stop.
HARRY (*heartily*): Eh-eh! Well to me God! How you do, sah! But you grow big now!
    Eh-eh! You wasn't more dan fourteen when last I know you.
NARRATOR: How are you, Harry? You don't seem to have got one year older.
    Look at that, John! Not a single grey hair, and he's nearly sixty, I'm sure.
HARRY (*laughing*): You giving me sweet-mouth, chief! If you look close you see
    plenty grey hair. Look! All at de back here.
NARRATOR: Well, it doesn't show at a glance. So you're a prosperous farmer
    now, Harry. What do you plant?
HARRY: Anything dat good to eat, chief. Cassava, eddoes, yams, plantains, bananas.
    And Ah got one-two sheep and cows Ah struggling wid. What work you
    doing, sah? Keeping plenty big books in a office?
NARRATOR: Worse than that, Harry. I'm in the government service. John here
    is a book-keeper, but he doesn't like it, either. We envy you fellows who
    plant and keep your cows and sheep. Eh, John?
JOHN: Only too right. One day I'm going to turn up suddenly in Sandvoort
    and ask you and Peters to take me into partnership, Harry. Don't you need
    somebody to assist you mind your cows and sheep?
JACKSON PETERS: Hay, hay! Farming is hard work, chiefs. You got to get up
    early in de morning and walk in rain and mud. But look, all-you siddown.
    Ah ain' got a lot of furniture, chief. You got to make-shift wid dis one chair
    and dese boxes.
NARRATOR: I'm always comfortable on a box. Remember when we used to go
    camping, John! Near the punt-canal at Lochaber? We used to draw lots among
    our patrol to see who would get the soap-box to sit on at the camp-fire.
JOHN: Yes, and I remember the evening when you sat on it so hard it broke,
    and you found yourself mixed up with some cooking-butter.
There is general laughter.
HARRY: All-you boy scouts was more worry dan anything else. Always raiding
    somebody coconut or mango tree. Nancy child, where dis ginger-beer Jackson
    say you got? You not going to offer de young gentlemen some?
JACKSON PETERS: Yes, Nancy, come on quick. Get de ginger-beer.
MRS. PETERS: How you know de gentlemen like ginger-beer? You ask dem?
JACKSON PETERS: Who don't like ginger-beer! Dat's a drink everybody like.
    Eh-eh!
NARRATOR: Oh, but look here, Peters, you haven't got to put yourself out over
    this ginger-beer, you know. After all, we've only come in to shelter from
    the rain –
PETERS: Eh-eh! But it's manners to offer you something to drink, sah! Look,
    sah, you don't mind Nancy. Nancy is a woman, she got she moods. Who
    trouble you dis af'noon, woman? Eh? Dese is gentlemen who Harry know
    good since they was lil' boys so high.
MRS. PETERS: Awright, Jackson. Awright. Don't let's mek no quarrel.
JACKSON PETERS: Who meking quarrel? You ain' hear what Ah say? Dese gentlemen

is Harry' friends. Harry is me god-brother. Anybody who welcome in Harry' home welcome in my home.

NARRATOR: The situation began to look so awkward that I felt like rushing back out to the car, rain or no rain, but I was sure Harry and Peters would have felt let down – Harry would have been very hurt – so I looked at John, and he looked back at me, and we silently decided to wait a bit longer to see if things could be straightened out. It seemed so strange that Nancy should take up this attitude towards us, because these village people are always so friendly and warm-hearted, especially when you happen to be in any difficulty on the road through the weather or any other cause. Anyway, in the long run I came to understand why Nancy behaved as she did. In fact, even at that awkward moment of our visit, she began to thaw out and look apologetic. She turned to me and said:

MRS. PETERS: Young gentleman, Ah don't doubt you is anybody who shouldn't be in dis house, but my husband is a man who does do some funny things sometimes, so I got to act accordingly.

NARRATOR: But you needn't bother about the ginger-beer, Mrs, Peters. Really, it doesn't matter –

MRS. PETERS: De ginger-beer no trouble, sir. Ah got odder matters in me mind – and Jackson know what Ah mean. Anyway, don't let's mek no unpleasantness. Ah will go in de room now and get de ginger-beer.

JACKSON PETERS: So much talk, talk, talk! Oh, gawd! Women eh? Why they like talk so much!

MRS. PETERS: Look, while I getting de ginger-beer you see and get some glasses ready off de dinner-waggon. Dat's what you can do. You better dust dem off, too. (*She gives a grumbling sound and goes into the bedroom. We hear the door slam after her.*)

JACKSON PETERS: Oh, me gad! See dat! She gone in de room, and she slam de door on de company. You see manners! Women, Jackson boy! Women! You got to put up wid their lil' funny ways. Chief, you ain marry yet?

NARRATOR: Me? No, not yet, Harry.

PETERS: Well, tek good note, sah, and see what you got to put up wid before you mek de plunge. Serious business, getting married, chief. More serious even dan farming, Ah can tell you straight.

JOHN: Are you married, Harry?

HARRY: Twice. Me fust wife dead soon after Ah come to Sandvoort – and Ah ain' learn me lesson. Ah had to go and do it a second time. But Ah can't complain. De second time work out better even dan de first. Kate is a good woman. She mind me good.

NARRATOR: I remember your first wife, Harry. Wasn't she named Elvira or something like that? There was something the matter with her right eye, if I remember –

HARRY: You' memory good, chief. Yes, she injure her right eye since she was a child. She used to work as a cook at de Lutheran manse–

NARRATOR: That's right. I used to see her there sometimes when I happened to drop in. What did she die of?

HARRY: She was a hard-ears woman, chief. Never like to listen to advice. One night me godmother had us in to a lil' feed-up, and Elvira eat crab-back. Ah warn her not to eat it, because crab was her kinna. But she eat it, and dat same night she get sick, and two days later she was a dead woman.

JACKSON PETERS: Don't bother wid Harry, sah. Elvira dead from sugar in her blood. For years she suffer from it, and de doctor say dat's what she dead from.

HARRY: Ah don't doubt she had sugar in her blood, but she shouldn't have eat dat crab-back. She know crab was her kinna.

NARRATOR: Her kinna! I'm interested in these creole words. John, where do you think that word kinna could have come from? African?

JOHN: Don't ask me. Like all of us here I've just grown up hearing it, and all I know about it is that it means something you're allergic to. Harry, can you tell us where kinna came from?

HARRY: Can't tell you, chief. Like Mr. John say, I just grow up hearing it.

NARRATOR: There's another word, too. Ah, yes! Suppose I threw a tumbler at you there, Harry, and I missed, what would you say?

HARRY: Eh-eh! What I'll say? You aim bad. What else, sah?

NARRATOR: Peters, you tell me. What would you say if I threw something at you and missed.

JACKSON PETERS (*laughing*): Me? Hay, hay! What Ah going say, chief! Ah'll say your hand kanta.

NARRATOR: Ah! There you are! That's the word! Kanta.

There is general laughter. Then Nancy comes in.

JACKSON PETERS: Here Nancy wid de ginger-beer! Nancy know plenty creole words from Slavery days. Nancy' grandmother could speak African from long-long time back. She was a hundred when she dead. Na true, Nancy?

MRS. PETERS: Where de glasses? You ain' dust de glasses yet?

JACKSON PETERS: Eh-eh! Look trouble! It's me business to dust glasses! Dat's woman work. Hay, hay! Awright, awright. Lemme dust out some glasses. (*We hear the clink of the glasses as he takes them from dinner-waggon*).

NARRATOR: Hallo! But wait. You've got the ginger-beer in bottles there, Mrs. Peters. I thought your husband said you had it setting in a Dutch jar.

NARRATOR: I'd no sooner uttered the words when I realised I'd made a *faux pas*. Mrs. Peters gave me a startled look, then turned her gaze on her husband. I'm sure that under her dark-brown pigment she had paled. For an instant I thought she would drop the bottle of ginger-beer she held in her right hand. Suddenly she looked at me again and said:

MRS. PETERS: What you say me husband tell you, sir? What jar is dis he tell you about?

JACKSON PETERS: What you look so serious, Nancy! Eh-eh! Don't bother wid Nancy, chief. Come on, come on. Gimme de ginger-beer, woman. You behave like dis, you mek de young gentlemen feel funny in de house.

MRS. PETERS: Jackson, I got a right to talk. You got too much mouth, man. Ah warning you every day. You' mouth going get you in serious, serious trouble,

NARRATOR: But I say! What's the trouble now? Did I say something I oughtn't to have said? I only asked about the jar you said you had the ginger-beer setting in, Peters. You said you found it when you were digging in a field one day.

JACKSON PETERS: It's awright, chief. It's awright. Don't upset you'self. Lemme pour out dis ginger-beer, den I can tell you about de jar. (*We hear the gurgle of the ginger-beer being poured out.*)

JOHN: You don't mean to say there's some mystery about it. Some kind of ghost story?

NARRATOR: Aha! See that, John! Always laughing at me for my interest in Dutch relics, and you with your nose for ghost stories!

HARRY: (*laughing*): No, chief! No ghost story mix' up wid Jackson' Dutch jar. Jackson, Nancy right, you know, boy! You got too much mouth.

JACKSON PETERS: My mouth awright. I know when I can talk and when Ah can't talk. Dese gentlemen not you' friends? You ain' know dem since they boys? Well, what you mean? What if I tell dem about de jar? Come on, you want some ginger-beer, Harry? (*Pouring ginger-beer*)

HARRY: Awright, gimme some. But on a rainy af'noon like dis I could do wid something to heat up me inside. Nancy child, you ain' got lil' rum hide away in a corner you can spare your friend Harry?

MRS. PETERS: No, Ah ain' got no rum.

Sound of footsteps squelching outside.

JACKSON PETERS: Eh-eh! Who is dis coming: now? Oh, it's Georgie.

HARRY: Wha' Georgie want now, I wonder.

Footsteps on the stairs. The voice of another peasant, Georgie.

GEORGIE: Jackson? Eh-eh! You got friends?

JACKSON PETERS: Yes, boy. Dese young gentlemen sheltering from de rain. Harry know dem good.

GEORGIE: Harry know dem? Oh. Ah see de car in de road and come to tell you.

JACKSON PETERS: Yes, it's awright, Georgie. It belong to dose young gentlemen. They get stick fast in de putta-putta.

NARRATOR: Georgie gave John and myself searching looks. In fact, his manner was not unlike Mrs. Peters'. He seemed to suspect us of something fishy, and despite the assurance Peters gave him he still looked uncertain. Peters asked him to join us with a glass of ginger-beer, but he refused, and after a moment he said he was going.

GEORGIE: Awright. Ah running back home. See you tomorrow morning, Jackson.

JACKSON PETERS: Take care of you'self, Georgie boy. You bring in you' cows yet?

GEORGIE: Not yet, but Ah going just now. It gone five o' clock.

HARRY: When you passing, tell Kate to see if de water reaching near me fowl-coops, Georgie. Don't forget.

GEORGIE: Awright Harry. I will tell she. (*We hear his footsteps squelching again as he goes off*).

NARRATOR: Is Georgie a farmer, too?

HARRY: No, he is a carpenter, chief. But he got his lil' provision plot like everybody in dis neighbourhood. And one or two cows.

JOHN (*chuckling*): He gave us some very suspicious looks, if you ask me. Almost made me feel as if I'd done him something.

NARRATOR: Yes, I noticed that. And why did he have to come here to tell you he had seen our car, Peters?

JACKSON PETERS: Just for so, chief. He must be wonder how de car come to stop dere by de roadside.

NARRATOR: But what about this Dutch jar, Peters? I'm beginning to feel there must be something funny about it. You haven't shown it to me yet, and you haven't explained why Nancy scolded you for mentioning it.

This time I knew I was being indiscreet, but I didn't care. I was determined to get to the bottom of this odd atmosphere of suspicion and secrecy Nancy had built up. And then there was this carpenter fellow, Georgie, turning up to tell Peters about the presence of our car. What was it all about? I gave Peters a keen look as I asked him about the jar, and he began to fidget about and chuckle in an uncomfortable manner. He gave Harry a quick glance, and said:

JACKSON PETERS: Harry, you think Ah should tell him about de jar? What you say, man? Nancy going bite off me head, Ah know, but I got a good instinct about people. I can see dese is gentlemen we can trust.

HARRY: Its awright, man. I tek responsibility. Bring de jar, show de gentlemen.

MRS. PETERS: Ay! Ay me God! You see all-you men, na? You see all-you men! You don't listen to advice. Awright, when you go to gaol you going alone, you hear me? I ain' going wid you. I wash me hands of dis! (*We hear her hands clapping together*) I ain' got *nutting* to do wid dis!

JACKSON PETERS: Woman, you like to get hot about everything. Don't trouble you'self. I tek blame. Dis is my responsibility. Wait a minute, chief. De jar in de bedroom under de bed. Lemme go in and get it.

MRS. PETERS: Go on! Go on! Ah wash me hands of dis Ah tell you, You didn' hear me?

NARRATOR: Mrs. Peters, I'm sorry if I've started a quarrel, but look, you can take it from me, I'm only interested in this jar because it's Dutch. I'm interested in all old Dutch jars and everything belonging to the old days in Berbice. If there's anything you want kept private about this jar, you can depend upon me and my friend John here. We won't whisper a word beyond this door here. What do you say, John?

JOHN: This ginger-beer is the only thing I'll talk about when I leave your cottage, Mrs. Peters. It's really first-class stuff.

MRS. PETERS: Young gentlemen, Ah ain' got nutting 'gainst you, Please don't get me wrong. But dere is a right way and a wrong way to act in everyt'ing we do. And Jackson know he act wrong in talking about dat jar.

NARRATOR: Anyway, here he is with it now. (*Sound of a bump as Peters puts down the jar on the floor*)

JACKSON PETERS: See, chief! Just a ordinary old Dutch jar.

NARRATOR: Mm-h'm. I know the kind. We've got two like it at home. One not so big, and another just about as big. So it's in this you set your ginger-beer, Mrs. Peters?

Silence. We hear the rain on the roof.

NARRATOR (*clearing his throat*): Ah-ah! Have I slipped up again? Shouldn't I have asked that?

HARRY (*with a sudden laugh*): Look, let we end all dis stupidness. It gone too far now. Chief – (*in a lowered voice*) – chief, it ain' ginger-beer. We can trust you. It's bushy!

NARRATOR: Bushy! What! (*with a sudden laugh*) Oh, no Bushy? Bush-rum!

MRS. PETERS: Ay me God! Ay me God!

JOHN: Good Lord! (*laughing too*) Well, I wouldn't have guessed that in a years. You mean that's a whole jar full of bush-rum?

JACKSON PETERS: You want a lil' shot, chief? To warm you up?

NARRATOR: Certainly. No objections. I've never tasted bush-rum.

JOHN: No wonder Mrs. Peters wanted to bite off your head, Peters. You're a hell of a fellow, you know.

HARRY: Nancy is a woman, she will suspect even her grandmother, chief. She trust no one. Everybody she feel connect wid de police.

NARRATOR: It was certainly a shock to me. The distilling or storing of bush-rum is a serious offence, and it was the last thing I would have connected with Peters or Harry, even though I knew that a lot of it went on in Sandvoort and the district around there. Almost every two or three weeks the newspapers would report some case of a police raid on Sandvoort or on Ithaca, another village on the West Bank of the Berbice, and the seizing of a bush-rum still. It was not often, though, that an arrest was made, because the *esprit-de-corps* between these bush-rum people is solid. John and I couldn't stop chuckling, as we looked at Harry and Peters and Nancy.

NARRATOR: Nancy has every right to be cautious. And, Peters, how did you know you could trust us enough to bring us in your house here? We could have been police spies, you know.

JACKSON PETERS:I got a instinct wid people, sah. Hay, hay! And besides, when you tell me you know Harry, well, what mek Ah must suspect you? Come on, chief. Hold out you' glass, lemme give you a taste.

We hear the gurgle of the bush-rum as he pours it from jar.

NARRATOR: But look at that. It's absolutely clear. It's like gin.

JOHN: I've never imagined bush-rum like this. I thought it was brownish like the usual fruit-cured rum we get in the rum-shops.

HARRY: Not bushy, sah. Not bushy. Bushy clear like water. See it! Good rum, dis, chief. Don't let nobody fool you, Bushy better dan any rum you can buy in de rum-shop.

MRS. PETERS: Ay me God: Ay me God; You see dis t'ing, na? Now, what will happen if a police officer walk in here now!

JOHN (*laughing*): Well, I daresay it'll be nine months in gaol for each of us. Come along, Peters. Pass me a nip. This will be my first taste of bushy, too.

NARRATOR: Well – and that's how our trip to Sandvoort that afternoon ended up. Sampling the bush-rum in Peters' old Dutch jar. And it was good rum, too. Nothing fiery or stomach-scalding, as I'd always been told bush-rum was. It had just the same mellow, high-wine flavour of good rum, though it lacked the fruity quality, I admit.

We remained chatting with Harry and Peters until the rain stopped – Peters, predicted right; it did not last very long – but I'm afraid we never succeeded in putting Nancy in a good mood. She continued to sulk on us to the very end. When Harry and Peters, with the aid of some lengths of coconut branches, managed to get the car out of the rut and we were on the point of getting in, I said to Peters:

NARRATOR: Well, now that you know you can trust us, Peters, the next time we come up here you must take us into the bush and show us your still. I've never seen a bush-rum still.

JACKSON PETERS: Oh, God! Well, sah, look what you want to put me in for! If Nancy behave like she behave just because Ah tek you in de house dere, what will happen if I carry you and show you de still! Not only Nancy, chief, de whole village will rise up 'gainst we if we give away de hiding place where we does keep de still.

   You didn't see how Georgie come quick to warn us when he see your car standing up here? Every car dat stop on de road in Sandvoort we got to watch, sah. De Police always spying 'pon we.

NARRATOR: Well, if you'll take my advice, you'll fill up all these ruts in the vicinity of your cottage so as to make sure no other cars get stuck when it rains. Come on, John. Let's get going. And thanks for getting us out of the mud, Peters, Thanks, Harry.

JOHN: And thanks for the bushy. Sorry I can't recommend your brand to my friends, Peters. (*Sound of the car's engine starting up*)

JACKSON PETERS (*laughing*): Dat's one t'ing we don't like in dis village, chief. Advertisement. Not in Sandvoort. Hay, hay, hay!

NARRATOR: All right, we'll remember that. Cheerio, Harry! Cheerio, Peters!

JACKSON PETERS: Good night, Chief! Sleep warm.

HARRY: Good night, chief! Look we up again soon. Na mind Nancy!

Sound of their laughter as the car's engine rises in tone and moves off.

END

BORDERLINE BUSINESS
A play in three acts

CAST

HENRY STRADDICK
EILEEN STRADDICK
MARY TRIPPETT
NORA TRIPPETT
ROSEMARY SWAYNE
OLIVER GREATCAKE
ERNST GANTER

The action takes place in the living room of Borderline Farm house
Time – The present

ACT ONE
An evening in summer

ACT TWO
Scene One – The following morning
Scene Two – Evening of the same day

ACT THREE
Later the same evening

ACT ONE

The scene is the living room of Borderline Farm. It is on the Surrey side of the Surrey-Hampshire border.

The house is a half-timbered one, very large and spreading. Many black oak beams are in evidence, crude and roughly hewn. The living room is a very spacious room. Two doors open on to a corridor, and the large fireplace for log-fire is on the extreme right. On the extreme left a window opens on to a landscape of fields that is only partially visible to the audience. Pictures, very large, hang on the wall space between doors, and between doors and window and fireplaces respectively. Pictures in black heavy ornate frames representing cows and deer and still-life (fruit and vegetables and fish very realistically executed). Two shotguns, double-barrelled, sixteen-bore, are leant up one on either side of the fireplace.

The furniture is old-fashioned, solid and Victorian. Dominating the scene, in the space between the two doors, is the massive mahogany sideboard on which is arranged an array of glassware and crockery (Willow pattern china chiefly). There is a large centre table mid-stage on which stands alone a vase about twelve inches tall; rather Chinese looking and possibly of some value. Also in evidence are three occasional tables and two leather-lined armchairs. And a sofa. The sofa is not far from the fireplace, and an occasional table stands right beside it, and on this we see a wireless set and the telephone. Travelling left through this jungle of furniture, we encounter an armchair, then another armchair, then another occasional table, and right near to the window the third occasional table.

It is at this third occasional table that MARY TRIPPETT *is seated. The table is heaped with wild flowers of various kinds, and there is an open book – the Penguin book of wild flowers in colour – and Mary is very busy trying to identify the flowers. She is a wiry spinster of 67, dressed rather eccentrically in khaki shirt and shorts and boy-scout stockings and brogue shoes with thick soles. Her manner is serious and intent – though now and then she nods and smiles to herself in a somewhat loony way – and she takes absolutely no notice of the presence of the two other people in the room. These are* HENRY STRADDICK *and his wife,* EILEEN.

Henry is a shortish man, sandy-haired, thickset and with a small reddish-sandy moustache. He has a round practical-looking face, intelligent, ordinary and mildly good-natured. Eileen, about an inch taller, is slim and with a straight erect carriage, a distinctly attractive woman, dark and with an alert, intense, if somewhat restless air. He is 47, she is 44.

Henry is sitting at the occasional table in the left half of the stage. Before him are several account books and piles of bills and receipts and an adding machine. He is jotting down things in an account book and working the adding machine.

Eileen sits in the armchair in the right half of the stage. She is at work on an elaborate patchwork bedspread. Cloth, in various colours and patterns, forms a heap beside her chair and the bedspread is draped over her lap and the arms of the chair as she works.

EILEEN: I can't say I like it at all, Henry.

HENRY (*in an abstracted voice to himself*): Nine pounds, twelve and six. (*Writing in the account-book*).

EILEEN: Henry, I spoke.

HENRY: Did you?

EILEEN: I say I don't like it at all.

HENRY: What's that?

EILEEN: This business between Rosemary and her boyfriend.

He makes no reply. Touches various keys on the machine and pulls the handle. Jots down something.

EILEEN: Did you hear what I said?

HENRY: Vaguely. I'm rather busy with these accounts, Eileen.

EILEEN: You're accustomed to discussing things while you do the accounts. Don't pretend.

HENRY: I'm not pretending. What business is this about Rosemary?

EILEEN: Surely you've noticed what's happening!

HENRY: You mean the way she and this fellow keep messing around?

EILEEN: Yes, I do mean that. I don't like it.

HENRY: It's agreed she isn't normal, I think.

EILEEN: She's normal enough to know something she oughtn't to do.

HENRY (*writing busily after another go at the adding machine*): Forty-seven, eight and six.

EILEEN: What's that?

HENRY: What's what?

EILEEN: That number...

HENRY: Oh. Forty-seven, eight and six. Repairs to the tractor last month. That's what Loveday's carelessness has cost us.

EILEEN: Well, you've got rid of him, haven't you?

HENRY: Sometimes I wonder if it really was his fault. People do stray on to our land and make themselves a nuisance.

EILEEN: You needn't bring that topic up again.

HENRY: I'll never forgive that blasted Council for running their footpath across my fields.

EILEEN: You protested against it without any result. No point in harking back to it now.

HENRY: Gets me hot whenever I think of it.

EILEEN: Then don't think of it. I was talking about Rosemary, in case you've forgotten.

HENRY: No. I remember.

EILEEN: I'm serious.

HENRY: Look here, we've got to give her a chance, you know.

EILEEN: What sort of chance?

HENRY: A chance to... to... what's the word? (*Graphic gestures with his hand*) Untangle herself. Sort herself out.

EILEEN: Why should she need to sort herself out? She led a perfectly normal life until her parents died two years ago.

HENRY: Yes, but how did they die? Gassed themselves in their flat.

EILEEN: They did it as a fine gesture. A protest against the H-Bomb.
HENRY: We won't go into their motives.
EILEEN: Motives are important.
HENRY: Anyway, put yourself in her place. Imagine yourself a girl of seventeen
    at boarding-school and suddenly hearing of a thing like that.
EILEEN: I never went to boarding-school. I was convent educated. A day girl.
HENRY: I know that. But still try to imagine it.
EILEEN: I can understand it upsetting her terribly, but not unbalancing her to
    the extent that she had to get mixed up with this Soho crowd.
HENRY: It wasn't her fault. It was the fault of those cousins in Kilburn she went
    to stay with. They're studying crime in Soho for some documentary film
    they want to make.
EILEEN: Was it they who made Rosemary get herself arrested for being implicated
    in various unmentionably dirty offences?
HENRY: You make it sound so desperately unsavoury!
EILEEN: It's as well to stare it straight in the face. After all, we've taken the risk
    of harbouring her in this house.
HENRY: Harbouring?
EILEEN: A harsh word, perhaps. I withdraw it.
HENRY: And substitute?
EILEEN: We've taken her under our wing, then, since you prefer a cliché.
HENRY: It sounds better.
EILEEN: The point is we've got to be realistic about the problem.
HENRY: She's my niece. Let me do most of the worrying.
EILEEN: I have to live with her as well as you, so I've got to worry just as much.
HENRY (*after working the machine*): Twenty-nine, three and four (*Writing. Brief
    silence while they continue with what they are doing.*)
MARY: (*calling out*): Nora! Nora dear!
NORA (*off*): Present, Mary! What can I do, love?
MARY: Methinks I've found a Bloody Crane's Bill.
NORA: (*off*): Hast thou? Exceeding exciting!
MARY: It's either that or Shining Crane's Bill. But I'm strongly inclined to think
    it must be Bloody Crane's Bill.
NORA: (*off*): Yours truly be along to see it in a jiff! Yours truly just putting the
    finishing touches to Operation Fish-net!
Henry chuckles.
EILEEN: Do they still amuse you?
HENRY: Still. I mean, well… oh, but I shouldn't say it, I suppose.
EILEEN: Why not say it? It won't hurt me. They're soft in the head.
HENRY: How true!
EILEEN: My batty twin aunts. We all know it. I've resigned myself to their battiness,
    so you haven't got to be hypocritical.
HENRY: In a way, we're lucky we didn't have any children.
EILEEN: Why?
HENRY: Obvious.
EILEEN: Not to me.
HENRY: Well, think of it! What with your two potty aunts and my delinquent

niece, it does look as if we've got some tricky blood in both our families, doesn't it? No knowing what sort of monstrosity we ourselves might have produced.

EILEEN: You haven't got to be so cold-blooded about it.

HENRY: I'm staring it straight in the face – just as you suggested a moment ago I should do about Rosemary.

EILEEN: Anyway, Aunt Mary and Aunt Nora are harmless. They don't trouble anyone. They live in their own fantasy world.

HENRY: So does Rosemary, I suppose, in her own fashion.

EILEEN: Yes, but in her case, there may soon be unpleasant complications.

HENRY: Baby?

EILEEN: Yes, I do mean that.

HENRY: We can only hope they know what they're about.

EILEEN: I don't trust that boy. I don't like him.

HENRY: Have we got to go on talking about this?

EILEEN: It's highly necessary.

HENRY: Well, if you want me to be frank, I don't dislike Oliver. In fact, I rather like him.

EILEEN: I can be equally frank and say I don't believe he's up to any good with his highbrow sculpture. All those wires and bits of rusty metal he strings together seem to indicate as much mental instability as Rosemary's.

HENRY: He's fitting in very well on the land. I've had no complaints so far.

EILEEN: I still feel it was a mistake letting him come here to be with Rosemary.

HENRY: Why?

EILEEN: He's a Londoner.

HENRY: Just that?

EILEEN: He's the big-city type. He wasn't cut out for work on a farm. And the conversation I've overheard between him and Rosemary is simply appalling.

HENRY: But we had to have him here. Rosemary wouldn't agree to stay unless he lived here, too.

EILEEN: That's what I call pampering. We ought to have tried her out alone here first. I was never in favour of the boy staying here. You know that. I said so.

HENRY: I know you did, but she would have run away if we hadn't taken Oliver in. If she goes back to Soho and gets arrested again for anything it will mean prison for certain. She's on a bond, remember.

EILEEN: Nevertheless I'm going to speak to Oliver. The first time I can get him alone.

HENRY: I don't think it'll do any good. Better to let things ride for the time being.

EILEEN: I don't believe in that policy. Chamberlain tried it out in the 'thirties and look what happened!

HENRY: Twenty-two, nine and ten... Seven, thirteen and six... (*Writing*)

NORA *enters, She is dressed exactly the same as her twin sister but carries a pair of binoculars slung over her shoulder by a strap.*

NORA: So you've found a Bloody Crane's Bill, dear?

MARY: Yes. And look, Nora! I'm sure this is Silver Weed. Look at the illustration and see if you don't agree with me.

NORA (*looking*): H'm … Hm … Oh, no no, no! It's Creeping Cinquefoil. Here! This one here. See?

MARY (*dismayed*): But the description at the back of the book tallies exactly with Silver Weed. (*Flicking over leaves of book*) Look. See what they say. "Perennial giving off procumbent runners." Wouldn't you call this a procumbent runner?

NORA: But doesn't "procumbent" mean "creeping"? Let's see what they say about Creeping Cinquefoil. Here! "Perennial herb with creeping stems."

MARY: Are you sure "procumbent" and "creeping" mean exactly the same thing?

NORA: I wouldn't swear to it, but the leaves don't look the same to me. Cinquefoil should have five leaves on each stalk, and these stalks do have five leaves each.

MARY: Good gracious! So they have. I hadn't noticed that. How really upsetting!

NORA (*wagging an admonitory finger*): Ah! Be more alert, centurion! Thou canst not afford to fall asleep.

MARY: It's the description that led me astray.

NORA: But "cinque" in French means five. Cinquefoil – five-leafed. See how simple? (*She smiles, then goes to window and raises her binoculars to her eyes scanning the countryside keenly*).

MARY: Is Operation Fish-net shaping up according to our expectations, Nora?

NORA: Sssssh! Not so loud, dear. There may be enemy agents under the window. We can't be too careful.

MARY: (*stage whisper*): How goeth the Major Plan?

NORA (*in stage whisper*): Tomorrow at dawn we strike.

MARY (*in ordinary voice*): Anything interesting in sight yet?

NORA: Not yet, but I've got everything ready outside.

MARY: When I was gathering these specimens I thought I observed some patrol activity across the border.

NORA: I won't be surprised. Something big is brewing. But we are prepared. Our forces are ready for any eventuality. (*Still scanning the landscape with binoculars*)

MARY: That's the spirit, centurion! Vigilance! Vigilance! Always vigilance!

HENRY (*chuckling*): Poor creatures. I wonder if they're really happy living out that sort of fantasy.

EILEEN: Don't they seem happy?

HENRY: It has its dangers, though.

EILEEN: In all the three months they've been here they haven't caused us any trouble, you must admit.

HENRY: Except for the few times they stopped cars on the road to inquire after "enemy agents".

EILEEN: I spoke to them about that and they haven't done it since.

HENRY: To the best of your knowledge, you mean. They wander all over the countryside. Who knows if they don't stop cars on the by-pass?

EILEEN: They never go as far as the by-pass.

HENRY: Oh, of course not! I was forgetting the by-pass is supposed to be in enemy territory. I wonder why they should have got it into their heads that Hampshire is enemy territory… Eleven, nine and a penny. (*Working the adding machine*).

NORA (*lowering her binoculars abruptly, alertly*): I must be off for a minute, Mary. Keep vigilant.

MARY: Seen anything? Troop movements?

NORA: There's a suspicious looking plane circling over Sector Forty-six.

MARY: A spy plane? Shoot it down!

NORA: I'll send a signal to HQ. (*She hurries out*)

HENRY (*chuckling*): Seventeen, eight and six. (*Writing*)

ROSEMARY SWAYNE enters. She is a girl of nineteen, attractive, red-haired (her hair is in two plaits, schoolgirl fashion behind her back and tied with ribbon as if she were only 14). She is dressed in yellow shirt and green jeans. She is playing with a small rubber ball. Throwing it up and catching it. She pauses abruptly and smiles round at them all, then strikes a dramatic attitude, arms outstretched rigidly, ball clutched in one hand.

ROSEMARY: I feel... Do you know how I feel, Uncle Henry?

HENRY: Did you go for a walk, Rosemary?

ROSEMARY: I feel... Guess how I feel.

HENRY: I won't try.

ROSEMARY: I feel just like this. (*She makes a sudden lunge forward and utters a grunting, snarling sound, and stands with arms drawn back rigidly, bust prominently thrust out. She grimaces and shakes her head*) Just like that!

HENRY: Interesting.

ROSEMARY (*laughing and relaxing, beginning to throw the ball up again*): I feel like killing something.

EILEEN: You'd better suppress the feeling.

ROSEMARY: Stamping on it. Smashing it. Killing it.

HENRY: You'd be spanked if you did that.

ROSEMARY (*with a lunge at Eileen*): I might kill you. Yes, you! You! You with your sniffy-snuffy, nose-in-the-air manner.

HENRY: Curb your high spirits, Rosemary. You're nineteen – not fourteen.

ROSEMARY (*relaxing with a gay laugh*) Guess what I've just been reading.

HENRY: Have you been reading? I thought you went for a walk.

ROSEMARY: No, I've been reading. A book on sex. It's Oliver's. It tells you all about the different positions.

Henry and Eileen are silent. Eileen merely breathing a little hard.

ROSEMARY: Well? No reactions? Nobody horribly shocked?

EILEEN (*falling for the bait*): It certainly doesn't seem a nice book.

HENRY (half-jocularly): Is that the kind of book Oliver reads?

ROSEMARY: He's a wide reader. I asked him to lend me a book on sex – something really stinkingly hot. And this book *is* hot, no fooling! It was printed in Paris.

EILEEN: You see what I mean, Henry?

HENRY: Look, Rosemary, go easy. The idea of your being here is to lead a clean life. This isn't London.

ROSEMARY: I know it isn't. It's the country. It's clean, clean, clean. (*She takes a deep breath, tiptoeing*) Clean air smelling of good strong manure. Phew! I smelt some yesterday that nearly knocked me over. (*With a yelp of laughter and a skip*). (*She suddenly runs towards Mary and peers inquisitively at the wild flowers.*) Wild flowers. And a book with coloured drawings of them, too.

Mary ignores her. Behaves as if entirely unaware of her presence.

ROSEMARY (*gazing at her curiously, and then laughing*): Isn't she funny? Just sits here as if nobody else is around. (*Putting her face close to Mary's*) Hey, Aunt Mary sweetheart! Hey! See me? Hear me? I'm looking at you. I'm talking to you. I'm a living person.

Mary still behaves as if nothing has happened.

ROSEMARY: Hey ! Hey! (*Snapping her fingers right under Mary's nose*) Wake up, dope! Wake up! This is the world. You're alive. People are in the room with you.

Mary reacts to the extent of brushing her face as though a fly had bothered her. She goes on impassively studying her flowers and book. Rosemary pirouettes away, shrieking with laughter.

ROSEMARY: Oh, isn't she rich! English reserve gone crackers! I wish I were like her! I wish I could pretend nobody else existed around me.

HENRY: Don't you like people?

ROSEMARY: Do you?

HENRY: Yes, I'd say I do.

ROSEMARY: You're lucky. I can't stand people. (*Stiffening and looking grim*) Especially people who go and gas themselves.

HENRY: All right. That will do.

ROSEMARY: It won't do. Isn't it the truth? They did gas themselves. Your sister and her husband. Supposed to be my parents.

HENRY: Quiet, quiet!

ROSEMARY: No quiet. This is a moment for noise. Didn't they gas themselves in their posh Maida Vale flat? (*Sniffs*) And look at the silly letter they left. "We do this in despair. The world is no longer a place of beauty. Beauty and fiendish bombs don't go together."

EILEEN: You ought to see something fine in such a gesture.

ROSEMARY: Fine! What's fine in that! Taking your life because you're afraid of a stupid H-Bomb! A bomb nobody will ever probably use!

EILEEN: You must admit there's nothing beautiful in an H-Bomb.

HENRY: Eileen! *Eileen!* (*Making ineffectual signals to Eileen not to follow up the argument*)

ROSEMARY: That's where you're wrong. I've seen a picture of an H-Bomb exploding. It was a lovely sight. Lovely big mushroom thing, all purplish-reddish and white. Some people just don't know anything about beauty. Oh, I'm sick of people. Sick, sick, sick! People are all namby-pambies. They don't like facing anything that's real. A whole clutter of shuddering jellyfishes! Cringing and whining and running away – or marching. Aldermaston marching.

EILEEN: What would you call real? Sex, I suppose?

HENRY (*desperately*): Eileen! Eileen! Don't follow it up!

ROSEMARY: Of course sex is real. Sex and crime. Yes, crime, too. It's real because it's beastly. When anybody coshes you you know all about it. Coshing, raping, murdering – they're all damned real. Oh, God, I feel... I feel... How do I feel? (*She begins to pirouette wildly and whistle and sing by turn*)

Nora comes in, and passes her as though she were a chair. Nora goes up to the table where Mary is seated.

NORA: It was one of our planes. It sent me a signal.

MARY: That's a relief. Look. I think this is Field Scabious. See if you agree with me.

NORA (*looking*): H'm. Yes... No, no. Oh, no. Look, my sweet. It's this one here. Devil's Bit.

MARY: Oh, it couldn't possibly be, Nora. The leaves are all wrong for Devil's Bit. And look at the description for Field Scabious. "Perennial clothed with stiff downwardly directed bulbous-based hairs." That fits exactly.

ROSEMARY (*cackling shrilly*): "Stiff downwardly directed bulbous-based hairs!" Let me see that book again. Is it about sex? (*She runs to the table and peers down at the book, but both Mary and Nora ignore her.*)

NORA: I give in. I think you're right this time. It must be Field Scabious

ROSEMARY: No. Call it Devil's Bit. I prefer Devil's Bit. It sounds more exciting.

EILEEN: Rosemary, don't you think you should leave your aunts to themselves?

ROSEMARY: Why? Don't you want me to be chummy to people?

Nora goes to the window and focuses her binoculars on the landscape.

EILEEN: Not everyone cares for your kind of chumminess.

ROSEMARY: Too bad for them. And they're not even my aunts. I only call them Aunt because you're Uncle Henry's wife. They ought to be damned glad I take any notice of them. (*Turning to Mary and Nora again*) Did you hear that, you two loonies? You should feel yourselves lucky I talk to you.

HENRY: Put on the light, Rosemary. It's getting dark.

ROSEMARY: With pleasure. Time Oliver came in from the fields. (*She goes to door [R] and switches on ceiling light*) We've got a whole heap of things to talk over.

HENRY (*half-jocularly*): What do you talk about, by the way?

ROSEMARY: Don't you hear us talking sometimes? Mostly about sex. It's my favourite subject.

EILEEN: We've gathered that already. Don't insist on it so much.

ROSEMARY: See! She doesn't like it. Another namby-pamby. No honesty.

HENRY: Aren't you interested in anything else but sex?

ROSEMARY: I've told you. Crime. Coshing people and robbing them. And doing lewd dances in nightclubs. That's what they ran me in for, don't you remember? Oh, it was lovely dancing in my bare skin. (*She holds her skirt and dances*). Wish I could strip now and do it for you. A good red-hot can-can. How say?

HENRY: I don't think it would be advisable to try it here. (*Trying to repress a chuckle*)

ROSEMARY (*shrieking with laughter*): Look at his face! You're blushing, Uncle Henry! Oh, hell! That means you're pining to see me misconducting myself. How about a little hot misconduct, Uncle Henry?

Henry's chuckle now becomes audible and visible. He shakes.

ROSEMARY (*pointing derisively at him*): See! Oh, jumping hell beans! He'd like me to do it for him! He's an honest man. It's only she who's the wet blanket. Why do wives become wet-blankets as soon as they turn forty and can't be gay like teenagers and twenty-agers!

Henry continues to chuckle.

EILEEN (*with heavy sarcasm*): Extremely amusing!

ROSEMARY: Of course, it's amusing. He's got an honest sense of appreciation. If something is amusing he laughs. And why not? What's wrong with laughing?

EILEEN: And what could be more amusing than sex?

ROSEMARY: True thing. You should take a look at the book Ollie's lent me.

Glorious, glorious. Forty-six different positions described in detail. No illustrations, though. A pity.

EILEEN: And you feel that sort of thing is going to do you good?

HENRY (*making sign again at Eileen*): Eileen! Eileen, don't...

ROSEMARY: Let her needle me. I don't care. I can needle her back. Yes, it does me good. Don't you see how skipping-wild I am this evening? It's the... what's the word? It's the something in me. Help me out, Uncle Henry.

HENRY: Exuberance.

ROSEMARY: No. That's too commonplace a word. Never mind. Anyway, it's that book I've read that's got me hopped up like this. I feel like trying out all forty-six positions right now!

HENRY: Ssssh! Hold hard, Rosemary!

ROSEMARY: Wouldn't you like to try out a few with me? (*Approaching him and stroking his head*) Come on. Be a man and admit it.

HENRY (*trying to sound severe*): Oliver shouldn't have lent you that book.

ROSEMARY: Why not ? He's just as interested in sex. Did you think he was no good? He's bloody good, I can tell you.

Henry guffaws in spite of himself.

EILEEN: I really can't see much to laugh at in that, Henry!

ROSEMARY: You can't, but he can. That's why I love him so much. (*Crossing quickly again to her uncle and stroking his head briefly, then skipping away gaily. She pauses behind Nora who is still viewing the landscape through her binoculars*) Oh, cheers! There's Ollie coming now! My woopsie-wopsie he-man! He's driving the tractor. Doesn't he look like Victor Mature on the desert!

NORA (*turning abruptly to Mary*): I think we ought to go and inspect the newly prepared positions, Mary dear.

MARY: Yes. It is getting dark.

ROSEMARY: What positions? Are you interested in positions, too?

NORA (*addressing Mary*): The N.C.O's have been given instructions in case of a surprise raid tonight.

MARY (*rising*): Yes, we never know when or where they might decide to probe our lines. (*She and Nora go out while Rosemary screams with laughter.*)

ROSEMARY: Aren't they screams! Just sizzling screams! Uncle Henry, guess what they've got outside near the big hayrick! A sort of fish-net thing and pieces of rope. They've had it there for days. What do you think they're trying to do?

HENRY: They seem to have an idea we're going to be invaded by enemy troops from Hampshire. The net and ropes are in case an enemy agent should stray over the border.

ROSEMARY: That's to trap him, you mean?

HENRY: Something like that, yes. I keep overhearing scraps of their conversation, and that's the conclusion I've come to.

OLIVER GREATCAKE *comes in. He is in shirtsleeves, and bits of hay can be seen adhering to his clothes. He is a well-built young man of 24, with a mass of wavy fair hair and looks more country-like than citified. Nothing obviously arty about him.*
Rosemary rushes at him and throws her arms round him, kissing him uninhibitedly.

ROSEMARY: You big fuzzy-wuzzy farmer-man! We've just been talking about you. Isn't he sweet!, Sweet!... Sweet! (*On each "sweet" she kisses him with a loud smack*).

OLIVER: Hey! Hey! Give me a chance to respirate.

ROSEMARY: To what? Respirate? Is that a new sex word?

OLIVER (*to Henry*): We've got everything fixed up on the west field, Mr. Straddick.

HENRY: Oh, good. How is the tractor behaving? No breakdowns?

OLIVER: No. She's going like a dream. Stop mauling me about, Rosy-posy.

ROSEMARY: I love to maul and to be mauled. I've been reading your book, fuzzy-wuzzy. It's smish-smashing! Funderful! We've got to try out some of the positions.

OLIVER: Shut up, shut up.

HENRY: Oliver, why did you lend Rosemary this book she's been telling us about?

OLIVER: She wanted something instructive on sex. It's a good book.

HENRY: Would you call it healthy for her ?

OLIVER: It's good for her to know about sex. Sex is a natural function, you know.

Eileen utters a loud emphatic sniff, stirring in her chair.

OLIVER (*chuckling*) What are you sniffing at? You should agree with me. (*Holding out his cigarette case to Henry*). Have a cigarette, sir.

HENRY (*Hesitating*): Russian or Turkish?

OLIVER: Russian. Got them from a fellow in Camden Town.

HENRY: No, thank you. If they'd been Turkish I might have risked one.

ROSEMARY: I don't like cigarettes at all. Turkish, Russian or Virginia. Only one thing I like. (*Putting an arm round Oliver*) Fuzzy-wuzzy, we must try out Position Twenty-seven tonight. I've marked it off specially. How say?

OLIVER: Shut up, shut up. You talk too much, Rosy-posy.

ROSEMARY: It's good for my therapy. Didn't you hear what the psycho johnny said? "Talk," he said. "Talk as much as you want. It'll help you release your excess energy." I won't tell you what else he told me on the sly. (*With a shriek and a wave at her uncle and aunt*) Not in front of the children!

Henry and Oliver laugh, Eileen breathes hard.

HENRY: Seriously now, Oliver, I don't like this going in and out of each other's room, especially at night. I meant to speak to you about it.

OLIVER: I don't see any harm –

ROSEMARY (*interrupting him*): You mean Aunt Eileen doesn't like it. Come straight, Uncle Henry. Don't let me down. I've said you're honest. Tell us it's Aunt Eileen who's been prompting you to give me a telling off –

HENRY: Ssssssh! Rosemary, be quiet!

ROSEMARY: It's true she's jealous. It's nothing but jealousy.

EILEEN: What do you mean jealousy ?

ROSEMARY: It's in the Dictionary: J-double E-L-O-U-S-Y. You're jealous of me, you old, lump of sour porridge! You'd love to sneak into Ollie's room and let him put you through the works, but you know he wouldn't sniff on you. Confess it!

HENRY: Rosemary, cut that out, please.

EILEEN: I have to excuse you. You're not right in your mind.

ROSEMARY: Oh, cheers for me! I'm a certified psycho-case, so I can say and do what I like and get away with it. Fuzzy-wuzzy, isn't it a great life, the life of a psycho-case! Let's waltz. Come on. (*Trying to waltz with Oliver*)

OLIVER (*giving her a gentle spank on her bottom*): Pipe down, honey-love. Time for supper. I'm starving.

ROSEMARY: Are you going to work on your sculpture thing this evening?

OLIVER: After supper, yes. Did you leave any supper for me, Mrs. Strad?

EILEEN: My name is Straddick. I don't care for abbreviations.

OLIVER (*with a mock bow*): Apologies.

EILEEN: Go into the dining-room. Your supper has been waiting for you in there for the past half-hour.

OLIVER: Cold supper, eh?

EILEEN: I had cold supper, too. We all had it cold this evening.

ROSEMARY: Never mind, sweety-love. I'll make you some tea. Let's leave the children to their evil thoughts. Coo-ee-ooo! (*She grabs his arm and they go out. We hear another "Coo-ee-ooo!" offstage*).

Henry shakes his head in a resigned way.

EILEEN: You take it very casually, don't you?

HENRY: What do you want me to do ? I can't change her basic character, can I?

EILEEN: No. But you've elected yourself her guardian. At least, you could do something about this boy.

HENRY (*rising as he begins to put away his account books and papers*): How am I to stop him going to her room?

EILEEN: Send him away. Send him back to London.

HENRY: And have her run off after him?

EILEEN: I doubt if she'd run off after him.

HENRY: I think she would. I don't care to risk it.

EILEEN: But if she's really determined to go to the devil I don't see how keeping her on the farm here to get herself involved with this boy is going to stop her.

HENRY: She's under our eyes here.

EILEEN: That doesn't seem to prevent her making a nasty exhibition of herself. I'm quite disgusted now with her perpetual chatter about sex.

HENRY: Half her talk is just bravado. Can't you see she does it on purpose to try to shock us? That's why I treat it lightly. If you were sensible you'd do the same.

EILEEN: I'll never learn to take filth lightly.

HENRY: Sometimes it's hard to believe you're half Irish. You behave as if you're English through and through.

EILEEN: Do the Irish wink at prurience? From what I hear, they ban more than half the books published in this country.

HENRY (*with a guffaw*): That's no guarantee they're milk-white saints.

EILEEN: We're straying from the point.

HENRY: Give her a chance, Eileen. Leave them both alone. They've only been here ten days. Before long they may settle down.

EILEEN: Settle down to what she was reading about in that book.

HENRY: That's only a phase. It'll pass. I won't even be sure anything happens between them in their rooms.

EILEEN: What a naïve optimist you can be!

HENRY: It's a question of being tolerant.

EILEEN: That's all we hear nowadays. Tolerance. We're expected to tolerate everything from the criminals and delinquents who infest this country. That's why they're getting out of hand.

HENRY: Do you look on Oliver as a criminal?

EILEEN: We don't know anything about him. He may have a police record. He's got a lot of friends in Soho, he said. That doesn't sound very promising to me.

HENRY: I'm sure everybody in Soho isn't a criminal.

EILEEN: All the same, I wouldn't say it's the kind of neighbourhood where Sunday School teachers abound.

Nora and Mary come in. Without a word, they each take up a shotgun.

MARY: Are our stocks of ammunition ample, Nora?

NORA: Ample. I had HQ send up seven lorry-loads of shells and cartridges to our advanced positions along the whole line.

MARY (*examining the gun*): This weapon seems in beautiful order.

HENRY: I suppose they're going to take up sentry duty by the hayrick. Good thing we're having a fine summer.

EILEEN: Aunt Mary, I hope you won't stay out of doors too late.

MARY (*starting*): A message is coming through, Nora.

NORA: Take it

MARY (*approaching Eileen*): Have you something to communicate?

EILEEN: Yes. Don't stay out of doors too late.

MARY: I'll pass on your message. (*She moves back to Nora*) Signal just received from Agent 413926: "It's never too late to mend."

NORA: Good. I'll decode it later. I don't think it's important. Come now. Let's hurry. We've got to take up guard at the usual spot. Squad!... Squad! 'Shun! (*They come to attention*).

NORA (*in voice of sergeant-major*): Slope *arms*! (*They slope arms*) By the right – *march*! (*They go marching out, guns at the slope*)

HENRY (chuckling): There you are! Haven't we got to be tolerant towards people like that?

EILEEN: But they aren't doing any harm, Henry. There's a difference.

HENRY: And what harm are Rosemary and Oliver doing?

EILEEN: Oh, it's no use discussing it with you. It's quite obvious we'll never be able to see eye to eye on the question. (*She rises and goes to the sideboard to get some cotton*)

HENRY: Tolerance. Tolerance. (*Picks up a corner of her bedspread*) Pretty thing this. When do you think you'll be finished doing it?

EILEEN: In another week or two. I wish you could get Rosemary to occupy herself with something like this. It might help to take her mind off the disgusting things she seems obsessed with.

HENRY: Has it struck you, my dear, that you yourself are getting just a little bit obsessed with the subject?

EILEEN: What do you mean? I getting obsessed with sex!

HENRY: I mean obsessed with the question of Roesmary's being obsessed.

EILEEN: That's nonsense. I'm concerned, that's all. Any decent-minded woman would be if she found herself up against a situation like the one we've got to face here.

HENRY: Are you hinting that I'm not a decent-minded man because I'm not concerned?

EILEEN: You're not practical, that's what I know. (*She goes back to her chair and resumes her seat*)

HENRY: Not even about the affairs of the farm?

EILEEN: Oh, I don't say that. With the farm you go to the other extreme and worry over unnecessary trifles. It's people you're not practical about. People and human problems.

HENRY: I just haven't got that kind of outlook – that's probably the truth of it. (*Handling the bedspread again*) I believe you must have something in common with that fellow.

EILEEN (*starting and stiffening*): Who's that? What fellow?

HENRY (*uncomfortably*): Only pulling your leg.

EILEEN: I insist. What fellow?

HENRY: Don't be so touchy. Oliver, of course. Who else could I mean?

EILEEN: What are you trying to hint at, Henry?

HENRY: I didn't mean... forget it. I – I... oh, Lord!

EILEEN: I want an explanation.

HENRY: No need to get so heated... I just meant – well, he with his bits of wire and metal he calls sculpture, and you with your coloured bits of cloth. What I mean is... well, you ought to have taken a liking to him. You've both got the artistic streak.

EILEEN (*relaxing*): I don't look on what I'm doing here as art. It only calls for a little intelligence.

HENRY (*guffawing*): You lack romance, that's what it is. You see every thing in a prosaic light.

EILEEN: And don't you ?

HENRY: Yes, but it's expected of me. I'm only a dull, everyday cuss. At school, in the Army, in civilian life, I've never done anything to distinguish myself. Never even kissed a girl before I met you. And now at forty-seven I'm more mediocre than ever.

EILEEN: If nothing else, you certainly don't attempt to delude yourself about your qualities.

HENRY (*with a shrug and another guffaw*): But I'm quite content. I'm paying my way, and that's something, I daresay.

(*From outside comes a loud metallic "Bang". They both tilt their heads alertly. Then Henry laughs.*)

HENRY: Hear that? A bombardment. Artillery fire. Your aunts are bombarding the enemy across the border. (*Another "Bang" outside*).

EILEEN: What is it they strike to make that sound?

HENRY: It's that disused water-tank behind the small barn. They have a special sort of mallet wrapped in old rags. That's what they hit the side of the tank with. (*Another "Bang!"*)

EILEEN: Oh, dear! I hope they'll find some other occupation during the winter!

HENRY: Perhaps they'll keep indoors and confine themselves to discussing despatches.

EILEEN: They weren't always like that. And they were very good to me when I was a girl.

HENRY: What made them go that way? When did the change start?

EILEEN (*uncomfortably*): I don't know. They used to live with us off and on when we were in Limerick – and then Mother and Dad came to England, and we lost touch with them. I was only ten when we came to England. I believe they both had an unfortunate crush on some priest.

HENRY: That sounds bad.

EILEEN: Only hearsay, of course. They were supposed to have fought over him during a thunderstorm one morning early in December.

HENRY: A thunderstorm in December!

EILEEN: That makes it all the more remarkable. They were on their way to a Novena mass at half-past four in the morning.

HENRY: Good God!

EILEEN: A car knocked them down while they were fighting in the street. Not that *that* necessarily unbalanced them, but it might have contributed.

HENRY: It certainly might. (*Yawning*) Think I'm going to turn in now.

EILEEN: I'll be along in a few minutes. I want to finish this corner.

He goes out, and after a short interval Rosemary and Oliver enter. Oliver is eating a slice of bread, part of his supper and is carrying under one arm an object that looks like a huge metal spider. There are long, thin, clanking legs attached to a clattering central mass composed of rusty tin plates and empty tins, that once contained evaporated milk, luncheon meat, sardines, salmon, etc. Rosemary is carrying a large carton containing an ample supply of empty tins, rusty wire and other bits of metal. This is Oliver's "workbox".

ROSEMARY: You still in here? Ollie wants to do some work on his statue.

Eileen glances up but takes no notice of this remark.

OLIVER: Put my workbox there. Right there near the window. I like the smell of hay and manure when I'm working. (*Goes to the window and stands for an instant sniffing at the summer evening air. Suddenly turns and glances at Eileen and waves a hand at his "statue"*). How do you think it's coming on, Mrs. Strad? Sorry. Mrs. Straddick.

EILEEN: Are you addressing me?

OLIVER: Yes. How do you think it's coming on? My statue?

Rosemary meantime is busy rummaging among the tins and things in the workbox and whistling to herself as she does so.

EILEEN: It's intended to be a statue, is it?

OLIVER: It's the combined harvester that inspired me to do it. I'm going to call it... let's see. Yes! (*Slapping his thigh*) "Surrey Farm-hand on A Summer's Day."

EILEEN: Interesting.

OLIVER: How do you like the title?

EILEEN: There should be some mention of lightning, shouldn't there?

OLIVER: Lightning? Why?

EILEEN: To look as you have him there he must have been badly hit by lightning.

ROSEMARY (*cackling*): She's an old fossilised Philistine, Fuzzy-wuzzy. Can't appreciate elevated Art like you and me.

OLIVER (*laughing too*): Wait till the B.B.C. critics discuss an exhibition of my work one Sunday about a year from now. (*This is addressed to Eileen of course*) You'll take back everything you say.

EILEEN: Where did you learn your sculpture? Did you attend some art school?

OLIVER: Aha. It's coming now. I knew you were itching to get a squint at my dossier. No, I never attended any art school. After Grammar School I just knocked around and amused myself with my own experiments.

EILEEN: Knocked around Soho?

OLIVER: Seems you've got Soho on the brain. I've heard you running it down before.

ROSEMARY: Oh, she's always running down poor Soho. (*To Eileen*) One day they're going to find you lying dead in a Soho espresso, with a cup of steaming coffee balanced on your forehead.

Eileen smiles "disdainfully". She rises and goes to the sideboard to get more sewing cotton from the drawer there. Oliver throws the last of the bread out of the window and dusts his hands on the seat of his trousers.

OLIVER: Now for some work. Help me with the wire, Rosy-posy. For a start, I want six of the longest pieces you can find.

ROSEMARY: I've been searching, but I've only found two longish pieces, and they're rusty like mad.

OLIVER: I want them rusty. The rustier the better. Just right to express the vision that's building up in me at this minute.

ROSEMARY: I wish I could find a good vision. I'm always looking for one.

OLIVER (*pointing abruptly at Eileen his manner mock-dramatic*): There's a vision for you!

ROSEMARY: Where?

OLIVER: Don't see where I'm pointing? She's a beautiful woman.

ROSEMARY: That beautiful! With a face like a wet November afternoon?

OLIVER: You've got a lot to learn, Rosy. (*He makes a circling survey of Eileen, putting his hand to his eyes and monkeying about her generally, his manner playful*).

EILEEN (*trying to ignore this, but looking up abruptly*): Are your parents alive? Do they approve of your present way of life?

OLIVER: Yes, they're both alive. My father is a jeweller. His shop isn't farther east than Bloomsbury.

EILEEN: Why do you think it necessary to mention that?

OLIVER: In case you thought I came from the East End. Must get myself into social focus for you.

EILEEN: Do I seem as if I want to get you into social focus?

OLIVER: You can't fool me. I can tell you're panting to learn something about my background. My parents live in Golders Green, but they're not Jewish. Common or garden Church of England. Anything I've left out? Jog me.

ROSEMARY: Tell her about your sister.

OLIVER: Oh, yes. Only two of us. Me, and my sister. She works in Oxford Street. Either at John Lewis or Selfridges. Forget which. She's thinking of changing her name.

EILEEN: Why? (*She is trying to thread a needle*)

OLIVER: She wants to get into films. She's going for a film test next month. But can you see her on the screen with a name like Jennifer Greatcake ?

ROSEMARY (cackling): Tell her what you suggested she should change it into.

OLIVER: Yes, that's a good one. I said: "Sis sweet, how about calling yourself Jeannette Jellybubs? You've got the figure that goes with a name like that, and it sounds just as cheesy and eatable as Greatcake."

EILEEN: I notice we're back on the sex theme.

OLIVER: Let me thread that needle for you.

EILEEN: No thank you. I can manage.

(He snatches it from her, and she tries to retrieve it but he dodges away from her and makes an attempt to thread it.)

EILEEN: Give it back to me. Are you mad?

(Rosemary is shrieking with hysterical laughter)

OLIVER: Chase me if you want to get it back.

EILEEN *(trying to look dignified; standing her ground)*: Give it back to me, I say!

OLIVER *(surveying her admiringly)*: A real madonna. I should have been a painter instead of a sculptor.

EILEEN: Give that needle back to me!

OLIVER: Don't spoil it. When you use that tone you sound and look like the wife of an Indian Army colonel in a Victorian romance.

ROSEMARY: You see how widely read Ollie is!

EILEEN *(stamping)*: Give it back to me, you fool!

OLIVER: That's just how the colonel's wife would have stamped. *(He tries and succeeds in threading the needle. Suddenly takes a pace towards her and holds it with a smile and a bow)* There you are, Mrs. Dalrymple-Muggridge. I'm very good at threading needles.

She takes it without a word and returns to her chair to continue work on the bedspread.

OLIVER: You should have said thanks. Colonel Dalrymple-Muggridge's wife would have nodded stiffly and murmured: "I thenk you!" and swept off with a proud swish of voluminous skirts.

ROSEMARY: And in the next chapter the dashing young sculptor would have run off with her after she'd swooned into his arms.

OLIVER: And in the next chapter the colonel would have arrived at midnight after a hard ride from Chundrapore.

ROSEMARY: And he'd have rushed into the house calling: "Boy! Boy! Where's the Memsahib, Abdullah? By gad, there'll be the devil to pay if I don't find her."

OLIVER: All right. Enough, Rosy my sweet posy. Got to settle down to some serious work. What about the wire I asked you to search for?

ROSEMARY: I only found four pieces, and one piece looks as if it might crumble to bits. It's terribly rusty.

OLIVER: Never mind. It will fit into the general pattern of disintegration. I know my craft.

EILEEN: Mr. Greatcake!

OLIVER *(starting)*: Ooops! Is that me you're talking to?

EILEEN: I believe it's your name.

OLIVER: That's right. But my intimates call me Ollie.

EILEEN: I don't happen to be an intimate of yours.

OLIVER: A pity. Especially as we're living in the same house.

EILEEN: As a matter of fact, its something to do with that I want to talk to you about.

OLIVER: Something about our living together here?

EILEEN: Yes. I don't approve of your presence in my home.

OLIVER: Oh, no? Why?

ROSEMARY: See! What did I tell you, Ollie? She wants to make a showdown. I told you she was boiling up for a showdown.

EILEEN: I think the time has come for me to speak out. My husband has been too lax, but I intend to be firm. I don't like your goings-on generally, Mr. Greatcake, and I'd be glad if you would return to London as soon as possible.

OLIVER: Whoa! Hell of a speech Didn't think you had the guts – or the oratory.

EILEEN: Anyway, it means simply that I want you to get out.

ROSEMARY: Why don't you tell me to get out, too? Aren't you telling me?

EILEEN: I wish I could, but unfortunately you happen to be a relative so I've got to tolerate you.

OLIVER: I can get out of here any time you want me to. No bother to me.

ROSEMARY: And I'll get out with you. Did you hear that, dear Aunty? I'll go with him if he goes. I told Uncle Henry I'd only stay if Oliver stays. That's the condition I laid down, and I stick to it.

EILEEN: Who are you to lay down conditions!

ROSEMARY: Because I'm me, that's why. I'm a person. I'm not a parrot. I have the right to lay down conditions.

EILEEN: I don't give two hoots for your conditions.

ROSEMARY: You don't? Too bad. But Uncle Henry cares – and you'd better take that into reckoning.

EILEEN: That kind of blackmail isn't going to help you. I've already spoken to your uncle about it, and I mean to persist until I get both you and your friend out of here.

ROSEMARY (*uttering a long shrill whistle*): Did you hear that, Ollie? It's open war now. She's declared war on us.

OLIVER: It sounds like it. (*To Eileen*) Is this an ultimatum?

EILEEN: I don't care what you choose to call it but I'm determined to put a stop to what's going on between you and Rosemary.

OLIVER: You're changing your tune now.

EILEEN: What do you mean?

OLIVER: You're saying now you're determined to put a stop to what's going on between Rosy and me. Before that you said you wanted to get us out of here. Which is it you really want? Let's get it clear.

EILEEN: I'm not going to carry on any elaborate argument with you. You understand perfectly what I mean. Get out of here. Go back to where you came from. We don't want you on this farm.

ROSEMARY: You mean *you* don't want him! Uncle Henry likes him–

OLIVER: Leave this to me, Rosy. Look, Mrs. S., I suppose you know I'm paying my way here? I'm working on the farm. I'm not hanging round like an idle sucker.

ROSEMARY: And he's doing a damned good job of it, too.

OLIVER: And what's, more, I like it. I get a hell of a kick out of driving that tractor thing about the fields. After ten days of it I feel I can go on for six or sixty years, and now you want to drop down on me and mess up the whole works. Well, I don't like that, and I'm not getting out until Mr. S. tells me to go. Got it?

EILEEN: We'll see about that.

OLIVER (*chuckling*): You mean you're going to fight me?

EILEEN: I refuse to discuss the matter any further with you. (*She gathers up her bedspread and bits of cloth and makes an attempt to move towards the door, but Oliver dances in front of her arms raised, like a boxer. He is only doing it playfully*)

OLIVER: Stay and let's talk. I like talking with you. You've got fire. I admire people with fire.

EILEEN: Get out of my way, please!

ROSEMARY: We're going to fight you and win, you old acid-drop!

OLIVER: She's no acid-drop. She's a beauty. My madonna ideal. If I can get her in the right mood I'd do a bust of her. How about it, Mrs. S.? How'd you like to see yourself in old iron and rusty wire?

EILEEN: Get out of my way, I say!

OLIVER (*dancing about teasingly*): Suppose I don't.

ROSEMARY (*with a shriek of laughter*): Let's drop her down the well, Ollie. All's fair in war and love.

EILEEN: I think this has gone far enough.

OLIVER: Not yet. We can kidnap you and take you into the woods.

ROSEMARY: That's right. Take her across the border and lose her in Darkest Hampshire.

OLIVER: Yes, we can do that. I'm game for it.

EILEEN: Get out of my way! Do you hear me?

At this point we hear, offstage, the sound of voices and tramping steps. Aunt Nora shouts distinctly: "March on! March on! Hands above our head!" *Then in come the two of them, their guns levelled at a young man who precedes them, hands above his head and protesting in an accent that is recognisably German. His name is* ERNST GANTER *and he carries rucksack and rolled-up sleeping bag on his back, and is quite obviously a hitchhiker.*

ERNST: I do not understand. It is a great mistake. You must hear me...

NORA: March on! You dirty *spy!* We'll teach you to come nosing around our lines!

MARY: The impudence of it!

ERNST: You do not understand. I shall explain...

EILEEN: Aunt Mary! Aunt Nora! What's this ? Who's this you've brought in?

Her Aunts ignore her and urge Ernst into the room towards the table where Mary was sitting with her wild flowers.

NORA: Keep your hands well above your head, and none of your tricks!

Rosemary and Oliver can only stare in entranced dismay.

ERNST: This is very terrible. Very terrible. I do not understand...

MARY: You'll understand all right before we've finished with you.

NORA: We should have shot you on sight. You're lucky to be here at all.

EILEEN: Aunt Mary! Aunt Nora! Put down those guns. Oh, my God!

NORA: Mary, break off. A message is coming through. Take it.

Mary lowers her head and moves over to Eileen. She bends her head, ear cocked.

MARY: Is there a message for us, Agent 413926?

EILEEN: Who is this man you've brought in?

MARY: He's an enemy agent. We found him trying to establish himself near one of the haystacks. He was spying out our terrain.

ERNST: It is a great mistake. I am on holiday. I am making a hike of the country. Hitchhiking. It is a mistake to say that I am a spy –

NORA: Don't lower your hands.

EILEEN: Aunt Mary, you can't do this. The man is a harmless hitchhiker. You must let him go at once.

MARY: He came from across the border. He's on Surrey terrain now. He's an agent from the enemy entrenched in Hampshire.

ROSEMARY (*with a shriek, clapping her hands*): Now they've copped it! Oh, Ollie, isn't this funny!

EILEEN: Aunt Nora, put down that gun and let the man go. My man, you can lower your hands. The guns are not loaded.

ERNST (*lowering his hands*): I am not a spy. It is a supreme mistake…

NORA: Keep where you are, or I'll fire!

MARY (*running over to Nora*): Nora dear, we must desist until we receive orders from HQ.

NORA (*lowering the gun reluctantly*): It's an urgent matter, Mary. We were justified in dealing with it on our own.

OLIVER: This really beats everything!

ROSEMARY: Who says living on a farm is dull! They should come to *this* farm!

Henry, in pyjamas and dressing gown, appears at door (left).

HENRY: I say, what's the rumpus about? Who's this? What the devil!…

EILEEN: Henry, you'd better take charge. Aunt Mary and Aunt Nora seem to have caught this man on the land –

ERNST: I am hitchhiking. I walk over the country. It is a big tour. You understand? I am not a spy. It is a mistake.

NORA: You were settling down for a bout of spying near that haystack. Own up, you rogue!

HENRY: Oh, God! I could have guessed something like this would have happened eventually. Look young fellow, are you a foreigner? On holiday over here?

ERNST: *Ja.* I am from Germany. I am on holiday. I am making a walk of the entire country. A hike. I wish only to sleep on the field during the night. You understand?

HENRY: Yes, but this is private property. You really have no right to be on this land. Last year two hikers nearly set fire to a hundred tons of my best hay.

ERNST: You speak too quickly. I do not understand.

HENRY: Speak to him in German, Nora. Nora knows a little German. (*To Ernst*) *Sie sind ein grosses spy! Jawohl! Ein grosses*, spy! Go on. Tell him in good German, Nora dear.

ERNST: No, I am not a spy. (*To Nora*) *Können Sie deutsch?*

NORA (*stiffly*): *Ein bish. Ja.*

ERNST: *Ein bisschen?* (*Looking round at the others*) *Können Sie deutsch?*

ROSEMARY: *Nein, nein. Ich kann nicht.* I'm an ignorant delinquent. I only know about sex and crime.

HENRY: If it's just to spend the night, we'd better let him use the spare room, Eileen. What do you think?

EILEEN: Yes, that should be all right.

NORA: Mary, pass on a message to Agent 413926. Say it is impossible to have this person on the premises without proper safeguards. He is dangerous and may sabotage our whole war effort.

MARY (*to Eileen*): I've been asked to pass on a message from my C.O. He says it is dangerous to have this person –

EILEEN: All right, Aunt Mary. I heard. Could you please go to bed now? Both of you. Henry and I will take care of him.

NORA (*in a rage*): You need not transmit the message, Mary. I've picked it up already. Agent 413926 is becoming quite impossible. It's outrageous. After all our efforts to safeguard our troops this is the thanks we get from our Intelligence Department! (*She slams down her gun on the floor and storms out of the room*)

Rosemary and Oliver laugh, Rosemary dancing in merriment.

ROSEMARY: Oh, Jeezy-wheezy! I'm going to pass out!

ERNST (*bewildered*): Is it, at length, understood that I am on holiday? My English is not very excellent –

HENRY: It's all right. We're going to put you up for the night.

ERNST: You wish to put me…? *Bitte?*

HENRY: You can stay here for the night.

ERNST: *Ach! Gut! Danke!* I can stay during the night? *Sehr liebenswürdig!* I wish only to sleep. You understand?

EILEEN: Would you like a little cold supper?

ERNST: Supper? *Vielen Dank. Ja.* I thank you. It is kind of you.

MARY: You'll regret this, Eileen, I warn you. By morning this building will be lying around us, a smouldering heap of ashes.

ROSEMARY: We'll be ashes, too, so it won't matter.

Mary slams down her gun on the floor and storms out of the room.

HENRY: Wait in here, young fellow. My wife will fix you up.

ERNST: Yes, I wait. Thank you. (*Henry and Eileen go out*)

ROSEMARY: Take off your rucksack. Let me give you a hand, Jerry.

ERNST: I thank you. (*He lets her help him take off his rucksack and the rolled-up sleeping bag*) Today I have walked very much.

OLIVER: Where are you heading for now?

ERNST (*taking a dictionary from his pocket*): Heading? Let me find that word. I do not understand…

OLIVER: Where are you going to? What's your next stop?

ERNST: *Ach.* Now I understand. My next place to stop? That is Basingstoke (*he pronounces it Bazzingshtoke*). I have come from Aldershot. That was my last place to stop. I ate my lunch at Aldershot.

OLIVER: This farm is a potty outfit. You mustn't take any notice of those two old stinkers.

ERNST (*uncomprehending but polite*): Yes.

ROSEMARY: Ollie, don't speak to him in such specialised English. (*To Ernst*) He
    means the two old women are mad. (*She touches her forehead*) Understand? Mad.
ERNST (*laughing*): Yes. I understand. Mad. *Verrückt. Ja.* They called me a spy. I
    know that word. It is a great mistake, however.
ROSEMARY: What's your name?
ERNST: Ernst Ganter. I am from Mainz.
OLIVER: You came just in time to prevent us kidnapping the mistress of the house.
ERNST (*smiling in his incomprehension*): Yes?
ROSEMARY: Are you a good kidnapper?
ERNST: Kidnapper? I do not know that word. (*He pulls out his little dictionary again*)
    Spell it for me, please. I shall find it in my dictionary at once.
OLIVER: Never mind. Just make yourself comfortable.
ERNST: My English is not very good. Please excuse.
ROSEMARY: Our German is non-existent, so you've got one on us. (*Suddenly
    slapping her hip*) Whoo-eeee! Jeezy-beezy! I've got an idea!
OLIVER: Don't let it scorch your pants. (*He has begun to work on his statue*)
ROSEMARY: It's more than an idea. It the beginning of a vision.
OLIVER: Tell us about it.
ROSEMARY: I want to learn German.
OLIVER: Can't say I think much of that as a vision.
ROSEMARY: That's how I see it. It might even be good as a therapy.
OLIVER: Haven't you got me? What other therapy do you want?
ROSEMARY: I can never have too much. Whoops! This is something! Ernst, would
    you teach me German if I asked you nicely?
ERNST: I do not entirely... Teach German? Who shall teach German?
ROSEMARY: You. You teach me. How about it?
ERNST: It would be a great pleasure, but –
ROSEMARY: No buts. It's settled. I'm going to make it my new demand. That's
    it. Either Ernst stays and teaches me German or I run away back to Soho
    and commit beastly crimes.
OLIVER: Steady up now, Rosy. This fellow's doing a hike. How can he stay –
ROSEMARY: By asking him nicely. Ernst, I'm asking you officially. Won't you
    stay with us for a week or two and teach me German?
ERNST: *Bitte?*
ROSEMARY: *Bitte?* What's that? No, I've never bitten anyone in my life. I won't
    bite you, if that's what you mean.
ERNST (*bewildered*): I do not understand. If you will speak slowly...
OLIVER (*speaking slowly*): She says will you please stay here and teach her German.
ERNST: Stay here! *Ach*, but I am walking. I am making a hitchhike of the country.
    It would be a pleasure to teach her German, but... (*He shrugs expressively*)
ROSEMARY: Oh, please, Ernst. Are you in a hurry to go back to Germany? We'd
    feed you and treat you well if you stayed.
ERNST: I have one month to stay in this country, and I have stayed already four
    days. I have intention to reach Scotland by hiking, if it is possible.
ROSEMARY: Right up there! It isn't worth it. They're a wild lot, those Scotties.
    They'll lock you up in Glamis Castle with the Loch Ness monster, and that
    will be the end of you.

ERNST: Loch Ness? Yes, I have heard of Loch Ness. I wish to see it if it is possible. And the monster.

ROSEMARY: It's an awful thing. It'll swallow you slowly piece by piece. How would you like to languish in a dungeon in Glamis Castle and then be eaten up piece by piece by the Loch Ness monsters?

ERNST (*uncomprehending*): Yes.

ROSEMARY: Yes? You'd like that to happen to you? You must be a funny sort of fellow.

ERNST: Should you speak more slowly I shall perhaps understand.

ROSEMARY: Look, let's get it straight, I'll compromise and try to speak a little German for your sake. They did teach me some at school, though I could never get the hang of it. *Sie* prefer to *fahren* to Scotland and find yourself *gegessen* alive by a monster, or *Sie* prefer to *bleiben hier* and teach me *deutsch? Verstehen Sie?*

ERNST (*laughing*): *Nicht ganz.* No, no. I do not entirely understand.

Eileen comes in with a plate of cold ham and roast beef and slices of bread, also a glass of milk, all on a tray.

EILEEN: Here's your supper. Better sit at the table here. (*She puts tray on the centre table*)

ERNST: That is so kind of you. Thank you many times, indeed. (*Moving towards table and seating himself*)

ROSEMARY: Aunt Eileen! I've had a premonition.

Eileen makes no response. She goes to her bedspread draped over the chair.

ROSEMARY: You heard what I said? Something is beginning to crystallise in me. Oh, Lord: You hear the big words I'm using? Inspiration has found me, at last!

Eileen still ignores her.

ROSEMARY: You'd better listen to what I'm saying. I've asked Ernst to stay a fortnight and teach me German.

EILEEN: You've what? Asked whom to stay a fortnight?

ROSEMARY: Ernst. Ernst Ganter. That's his name.

Ernst rises at mention of his name and bows towards Eileen. Sits down.

ROSEMARY: See how polite he is? He's going to be a good influence on me.

OLIVER: Rosy, stop that. Don't take any notice of her, Mrs. Strad.

ROSEMARY: I'm serious. It's a demand. I want him to stay and teach me German, or I'm running off to Soho.

Henry comes in.

HENRY (*to Ernst*): Everything all right ? You can have a wash-up when ever you're ready.

ERNST: I thank you. Everything is all right. It is kind of you.

ROSEMARY: Uncle Henry, I've asked him to stay with us and teach me German.

HENRY: Who's that? What's this now?

ROSEMARY: I want to learn German. I think it'll be good for my psycho (*tapping her forehead*). I've asked Ernst to stay a fortnight and teach me.

HENRY (*chuckling*): Don't be absurd.

ROSEMARY: I'm serious. I've just informed your wife. Don't you see how she's looking at me all axes and daggers?

HENRY: All right, all right. I think you should go to bed now.

ROSEMARY (*to Eileen*): See! Uncle Henry doesn't raise any objections.

EILEEN: I haven't heard him say yes, all the same.

ROSEMARY: It's understood that he agrees.

HENRY: Agrees to what?

ROSEMARY: Are you deaf? Didn't you hear what I've been saying?

HENRY: Get to bed. Get to bed.

OLIVER: Yes, Rosy. Pack it up. You talk too much.

ROSEMARY: I've got to talk. It's my only hope of finding the vision I'm searching for. Uncle Henry, get it right. Ernst is staying a fortnight to teach me German.

HENRY: How can he stay? Isn't he hiking or something?

ROSEMARY: I've persuaded him that Scotland isn't a healthy place for him, and he's agreed to stay. I want him to stay. Is that good enough?

EILEEN: What's wrong is that you're thoroughly spoilt.

ROSEMARY: I've heard that before. I want an answer to my proposal. Is Ernst staying or isn't he? Tell me so I can know whether to pack my bags and get out of here.

HENRY: What's this nonsense about, Rosemary? What's suddenly got into your head?

ROSEMARY: It's no nonsense. I've spoken plain English. I want Ernst to stay and teach me German. For the hundredth time I'm saying it. Is it a go or isn't it ? I'm issuing an ultimatum.

EILEEN: Henry, why don't you send her back to London?

HENRY: Rosemary, you'd better go to bed. Tomorrow we'll discuss everything.

ROSEMARY: No. We're settling this right now. Your wife threatened Oliver and me with ejection. Now I'm hitting back. This is my chance.

HENRY: Eileen threatened you and Oliver... Eileen, is this true?

EILEEN: I won't discuss it now, Henry. Look, can you show this young man to the spare room when he's had his supper? I want to go to bed.

HENRY: Of course. But...

ROSEMARY: She's a coward, Uncle Henry! A squeezing, be-jeezing coward! She can't stand up and answer my charge.

HENRY: Rosemary, stop making yourself ridiculous. There's such a thing as going too far.

ROSEMARY: You haven't seen me go far yet. In a minute I'm going to scream. I want an answer. Now. Right now. Is it yes or no about Ernst?

EILEEN (*hesitating at door*): The answer is no. Just plain no.

ROSEMARY: You're going to stand purposely in the way of my vision?

EILEEN: I don't know what you mean by a vision, but I repeat that the answer is no.

ROSEMARY: O. K. That does it. (*She sits down abruptly on the floor and begins to utter a long, deliberate wailing scream*) Ah-ow-w-w-w! Ah-ow-w-w-w-w!

OLIVER: Rosy: Hey!

HENRY: Rosemary!

ERNST (*rising*): *Du lieber Himmel!*

ROSEMARY (*unheeding*): Ah-ow-w-w-w-w! Ah-ow-w-w-w-w!

CURTAIN ON ACT ONE

ACT TWO
Scene One

The following morning. Henry and Eileen are seated at the centre table having breakfast. Silence prevails. Then Mary and Nora enter, Nora carrying something that looks like a small suitcase. The two of them seat themselves at the table by the window reserved especially for them. It is already laid for them, teapot under a cosy. They silently pour   t e a . Then Nora opens the small suitcase and takes out a pair of earphones which she puts on. With the open suitcase held in her lap, she begins to make tapping sounds as though sending Morse code messages. She pauses and listens.

MARY (*breaking silence*): Any response?

NORA: Ssssh! (*She listens again, then taps out another "message"*) 999 calling Red Patrol. 999 calling Red Patrol. (*A pause while she listens*) 999 calling Green Patrol! 999 calling Green Patrol! Are you there, Green Patrol? (*She listens, then taps out a message*).

MARY (*anxiously*): What's the situation like?

NORA: The night was quiet.

MARY: Is that the official communiqué you wish me to issue?

NORA: Yes. Finish your breakfast, then phone it through to the B.B.C.

(*She shuts her suitcase and puts it on the floor, then starts to have her breakfast*).

A silence, then:

HENRY: Anyway, it won't do any harm asking him.

Eileen makes no response.

HENRY: Did you hear what I said, Eileen?

EILEEN: I heard.

HENRY: It's a case of humouring her, my dear. She's not well.

Eileen makes no response. A silence.

HENRY: You see my point, don't you?

EILEEN: I'm afraid I don't.

HENRY: He may refuse, and… well, that will probably settle the matter. She couldn't blame us then.

EILEEN: And what if he agrees to stay?

HENRY: Well, again, surely that should be no problem. We have two more spare rooms. It's a vast house this, you know.

EILEEN: That's not the trouble, Henry. The real point is that we have enough on our hands with Oliver. Are we going to add to our worries by being saddled with this German as well?

HENRY: How you do magnify things! I can't see why Oliver is such a worry. He works very hard all day outdoors, doesn't he?

EILEEN: Don't be so evasive. What happens when he's not working outdoors?

HENRY: He sculpts. Messes around with his bits of iron and wires.

Eileen makes no response.

HENRY: Well, isn't it true?

EILEEN: Is that what he does when he goes to Rosemary's room? Or when she goes into his room?

HENRY: You make too much of this bedroom business. You should write plays for the West End.

EILEEN: Go on! Be facetious!

HENRY: But… ah… how can you be sure that anything – ah – peculiar happens? Have you ever spied on them?

EILEEN: I don't need to do that. Any silly fool would know.

HENRY: You can't judge by the things they talk about. It's not fair.

EILEEN: I suppose you'd like me to produce evidence in the form of a film showing what they do in their rooms.

Mary, out of the blue, utters a shrill laugh. She shakes for a moment, then subsides into silence, for Nora is holding up a stern admonitory forefinger.

HENRY: See that? You're making even Aunt Mary forget her fantasies enough to laugh.

EILEEN: It's fortunate that at least one person in this house doesn't indulge in fantasies.

Ernst comes, smiling and bowing.

Mary and Nora immediately tense. Nora opens her suitcase and takes out the earphones. She puts them on.

ERNST: Good morning! Good morning!

HENRY: 'Morning, my boy. Spent a good night?

ERNST: I thank you. I slept very well.

EILEEN: Sit down here. (*Pointing to a space laid opposite*)

ERNST: Thank you. This is very kind of you, indeed. (*He sits*)

HENRY: Do you like it here, Ernst?

ERNST: Yes. It is very pleasant. Very pleasant. And such excellent weather we have. For England it is not usual.

EILEEN: Coffee or tea?

ERNST: Coffee, please. (*She pours him coffee and passes it*)

HENRY: You were quite comfortable last night?

ERNST: Yes. Very comfortable. An entirely comfortable room.

HENRY: Are you in a hurry to get on with this hike of yours ?

ERNST: My hike? Yes, I must hurry if I am reaching Scotland. I am spending only one month in this country.

HENRY: Don't you take a fancy to the south?

ERNST: South? No, no. Scotland is in the north. I go west first, then north to Scotland.

HENRY: You don't follow me. (*Speaking slowly*) I said, don't you like *southern* England? This countryside here?

ERNST: *Ja. Sehr schön!* Yes, I like this countryside. It is very beautiful. And the weather is so excellent. I like it very much.

HENRY: Won't you care to stay for a week or two with us?

ERNST: Stay? Here? For a week?

HENRY: Yes. I mean, if you're over here for a month, it won't matter very much if you spend the first two weeks in England. I'm sure you can get to Scotland before the rest of your stay is over.

ERNST: You speak too quickly. I have not understood everything.

EILEEN: Henry, why don't you forget this idea?

HENRY: It's for Rosemary's sake, Eileen. I must make some effort. Do you want
    a recurrence of that scene last night?

EILEEN: I certainly don't. But I'm convinced you're not going to help her by
    indulging her whims like this. It's going to make her worse if anything.

ERNST: Is something wrong? Can I help?

HENRY: Yes, Ernst. My niece, Rosemary. Remember last night?

ERNST: *Ach.* Yes. Last night. I could not understand why she screamed.

HENRY: She's not well, Ernst. You could help us if you stayed.

ERNST: I could help if I stayed? But I am not a doctor.

HENRY: She wants you to teach her German. Will you stay a week and teach
    her German? (*Growing enthusiastic*) You could charge a fee. Help you to get
    to Scotland more quickly. Or she could teach you English. Sort of *quid pro
    quo*. Wouldn't you like to improve your English?

EILEEN: Hffff! I can see *her* teaching him English!

Mary utters another out-of-the-blue laugh, shaking.

NORA: Ssssh! (*Mary stops suddenly and tries to look grave*)

ERNST (*bewildered*): I do not understand everything.

EILEEN (*with heavy sarcasm*): You can be pardoned for not understanding!

HENRY: Look, my boy, you asked if you could help, didn't you?

ERNST: Yes, yes. I would help if I could. Explain fully, please.

HENRY: Well, let's try again. You know who Rosemary is?

ERNST: Rosemary? Yes. She is the girl who screamed.

HENRY: Good. Well, she screamed because she is unhappy and unwell. Follow?

ERNST: She is unhappy and unwell. Yes, I understand that clearly.

HENRY: Right. But you can help her to get better if you stay.

ERNST: I can help if I stay? Help to make her better?

HENRY: Yes. That it. Will you stay for a week and do this for us?

ERNST: But my hike. How can I stay?

*Rosemary appears at the door. She comes in and then stops and stands rigidly still, staring
at her uncle and Ernst, her face, indeed, with the look of a psychopath.*

HENRY: Oh, here she is! Slept well, Rosemary?

She makes no reply. Just stares tensely, ominously.

HENRY: See, my boy? She's – ah– a little out of sorts.

ERNST (*rising and bowing*): Good morning! How are you this morning?

ROSEMARY (*in a sepulchral voice*): I'm very ill. Go on talking to Uncle Henry.
    I'm paying close attention.

ERNST (*sitting again*): Her voice is… unusual.

EILEEN: Very unusual.

ERNST (*to Henry*): You said I should stay to help?

HENRY: Yes. Just for a week.

ERNST: But how would I help? I know nothing of unhealthy matters.

HENRY: Just teach her German. That would do the trick.

ERNST: She wishes to learn German ?

ROSEMARY: Yes, I do. I'm dying to learn German. Just dying!

ERNST: You will die if you do not learn German? This is very serious.

HENRY: It is, my boy. Very serious.

Rosemary groans. She shuts her eyes and begins to sway on her feet.

ROSEMARY: Oh, Lord! I'm going to faint. Somebody hold me quickly!
Ernst rises and gives her his support.
ERNST: *Was ist denn los?* Are you very ill? This is terrible.
ROSEMARY: Speak to me again in German. Go on. Say something to me quickly.
ERNST: In German ? You wish…
ROSEMARY: Yes. Quickly. It's the only chance.
ERNST: What can I say… *Frühstück is fertig. Setzen Sie sich!*
ROSEMARY (*recovering with a sigh and a smile*): Oh, good! I feel better already. What was that you said? Translate.
ERNST: I said that breakfast is ready. Will you sit down?
ROSEMARY: With pleasure. Just next to you here. But you've got to promise to stay and save my life. Do you promise?
ERNST: Promise? What shall I promise?
ROSEMARY: To save my life.
ERNST (*laughing*): Yes. I wish I could save your life. Please sit.
ROSEMARY: You'll stay and teach me German? You'll stay for a week?
ERNST: My hike. I cannot say… I shall think of the matter.
ROSEMARY: O. K. Let's eat. (*She sits down next to him*) At least, I've managed to set you thinking!
HENRY (*with a significant glance at Eileen*): See that?
EILEEN: See what ?
HENRY: See the difference it's made to her?
EILEEN: I don't know what you're talking about.
ROSEMARY: Whenever it's plain what he means you never know what he's talking about.
EILEEN: What I do know is that you're making a fool of your uncle.
NORA (*abruptly*): Mary! Take a message to Agent 413926.
MARY: Yes, dear. What is it?
NORA: Answer me in official parlance, please!
MARY: Sorry. What is the message, C.O.?
NORA: Say that the exigencies of our war effort are such that it would be suicidal if a certain unnamed person were to be allowed to remain on these premises after dusk this evening.
MARY: Very well. (*She rises and salutes, then moves across the room to Eileen*) A message from my C.O. The exigencies of our war effort are such –
EILEEN: I heard it, Aunt Mary. The matter is out of my hands. I haven't invited anyone to stay here.
MARY (*going back to Nora*): Agent 413926 replies as follows: The matter is out of her hands. She has invited no one to stay here.
NORA: Go back and take this message: If the necessity arises we can employ a secret weapon to get our way.
MARY (*returning to Eileen*): Another message –
EILEEN: Aunt Mary, I've already said what I had to say. I can't add anything.
HENRY (*chuckling*): Aunt Mary, tell Aunt Nora we'll take all the necessary precautions to see that the war effort isn't sabotaged.
MARY (*stalking back to the other table without a glance at him*): Nothing can be added to previous message from Agent 413926.

NORA: Very well. (*She takes up suitcases and begins to send a Morse code message, after putting on earphones*)

ROSEMARY (*with a gurgle of laughter*): Ernst dear, do you savvy what's happening? Understand what they're palavering about?

ERNST: Has something happened? I do not understand.

ROSEMARY: Never mind. Wait until the two of us get set on our German. You can get your own back on them by saying the naughtiest things to me without their knowing.

HENRY: Now, Rosemary! Don't try to corrupt him. We're not asking him to stay for that.

ROSEMARY: He's a man, though, isn't he? If I take a fall for him and he takes a fall for me who's going to stop us from behaving as Nature meant us to!

HENRY (*indulgently*): What about Oliver? Oliver won't like it, will he?

ROSEMARY: Ollie's a two-faced son of a bastard. Every morning he runs off to work in the fields without even coming in to kiss me awake.

HENRY: Don't you admire him for working in the fields?

ROSEMARY: Why should I? I don't sleep in the fields. I sleep in my room. I thought he was supposed to look on *me* as his real job. Getting me better.

Eileen utters a sarcastic laugh.

HENRY: Yes, but he can't spend the whole day ministering unto you.

ROSEMARY: Can't he? Well, you see what Ernst is going to do. Ernst isn't going to work in the fields. He's going to sit in my room all day and talk German to me.

HENRY: Oh, no, no, no! If you're to do any sitting together you'll do it in this room and nowhere else.

ROSEMARY: You want me to scream again? Well, go on laying down the law.

EILEEN: I haven't yet heard the young man say he's remaining.

HENRY: He's said he'll think it over. I believe he'll stay.

NORA (*abruptly*): Is that General Staff? Intelligence Agent 999 calling General staff! Take a message. Enemy agent discovered last evening, but foolish asses – repeat, foolish asses – in this sector refuse to recognise danger. What shall we do in these circumstances?

MARY: Ask the Minister of War to see Churchill himself –

NORA: Sssssh! A message is coming through in code. (*She listens intently*) Yes… Yes… Very well, Field-marshal. Thanks. (*She takes of the earphones*)

MARY (*tensely*): What's it? What did they say?

NORA: They give us carte blanche to act according to our own discretion.

MARY: Good show. This will mean at least a D.S.O. each for us.

HENRY (shaking with laughter): What a bizarre pair!

ROSEMARY: Bizarre isn't the word!

EILEEN: Hmffff! Pot calling the kettle black.

ROSEMARY (*glaring at her*): I hope that wasn't intended for me!

EILEEN: If the cap fits…

HENRY: Eileen! Eileen!

EILEEN: What is it, Henry? Am I to muzzle myself now?

ROSEMARY: You'd better. I don't like to hear nasty things said about me. Let me hear one more nasty thing and I scream.

EILEEN: That's a new weapon you've found.

ROSEMARY: It takes a schizo mind to find new weapons. Ask any psychiatrist.

EILEEN: If I were the man of this house I'd know how to cure you of that.

ROSEMARY: Uncle Henry, she's hurting my sensibilities.

HENRY: Never mind, never mind.

ROSEMARY: If I hear just one more nasty thing from your wife – just one – I'm going to take action. I'm going to scream so loud they'll hear me in Germany.

ERNST: No, no. Please. It is not good to scream.

HENRY: Tell her for me, Ernst.

NORA: Ah-ow-w-w-w-w-w! (*It is a truly blood curdling scream*) Ah-ow-w-w-w!

HENRY: Oh, God!

EILEEN: Aunt Nora!

NORA: Ah-ow-w-w-w-w-w-w!

MARY (*imitating her*): Ah-ow-w-w-w-w-w-w!

ROSEMARY: The stinking copycats: Trust them to steal my patent!

EILEEN (*rising and moving towards them*): Aunt Nora! Aunt Mary! Stop that at once!

NORA & MARY: Ah-ow-w-w-w-w-w-w!

HENRY: Good God! What sort of madhouse have we got here?

ROSEMARY: The blasted thiefs! Take them away to a different madhouse!

ERNST: This is entirely astonishing.

NORA (*banging the table with her fist*): He's a dirty spy! He's a dirty spy!

MARY (*imitating*): He's a dirty spy! He's a dirty spy!

NORA: He must be shot at dawn! He must be shot at dawn!

MARY: He must be shot at dawn! He must be shot at dawn!

EILEEN: This is too much! Too much: Henry, tell them to stop, or I'll go mad.

HENRY: Stop, you wretches! Do you hear me? Stop it! Stop it!

EILEEN: Don't call them wretches. They're my aunts.

ROSEMARY: I'll call them bitches! You loony bitches! Shut your clappers!

NORA & MARY: Ah-ow-w-w-w-w-w!

EILEEN: Oh, Lord! I can't stand this. This is really too much. (*She bursts into tears and hurries from the room*)

HENRY (*approaching the aunts*): Hey! Hey! Aunt Mary! Aunt Nora! Be quiet! Stop that blasted racket or I'll wring your necks!

NORA: We will not have a spy in this house! We will not have a spy in this house!

MARY: We will not have a spy in this house! We will not have a spy in this house!

HENRY: Damn it all We've got to do something. This is... this is...

ROSEMARY: I know how to shut them up. I'll go and get a bucket of water and throw it on them. (*Beginning to move towards door*)

HENRY: Stay where you are, Rosemary. Don't be an idiot!

ERNST: This is greatly astonishing. I cannot truly understand...

NORA: No filthy spies! No filthy spies!

MARY: No filthy spies! No filthy spies!

ERNST: They are speaking of spies?

ROSEMARY: It's you they mean, honey-bunch.

NORA: We don't like filthy spies!

MARY: We don't like filthy spies!

ERNST: But they speak in the plural. I could not be many spies.

HENRY: Don't take any notice of them, my boy. They're nutty. Clean round the bend.

ERNST: It is entirely disturbing.

ROSEMARY: I'm going to fix them. Watch me do it. (*Pushing her face up to them and grimacing and snarling*) Shut up! Shut up, you two sillycoops! Do you hear? Shut your ugly mugs!

NORA & MARY: Ah-ow-w-w-w-w-w-w! Ah-ow-w-w-w-w-w-w!

ROSEMARY: Ah-ow-w-w-w-w-w-w! Hear that? I'll show you! That's the genuine patented article!

HENRY: Rosemary! Be quiet!

ERNST: Perhaps I should go. It would eliminate disturbance.

ROSEMARY: No. You stay, Ernst. You mustn't go. I'll murder them if you go.

NORA & MARY: Ah-owowoowowowow! (*A really special effort*)

ROSEMARY: Stinking bitches! Take that!... And that! (*She slaps their cheeks. Their howling stops at once. They spring up. Nora grabs her suitcase and attempts to hurl it at Rosemary, but Mary restrains her.*)

MARY: Don't, Nora! You'll damage our transmitting set! Leave her to heaven! Heaven will punish her.

NORA: I wish I could get my nails into you, you slut! I'd strip you from top to bottom.

MARY: She'll be punished in due course, never fear! Dirty accessory!

Rosemary shrieks with laughter, and Nora stamps out of the room.

MARY (*stamping and glaring at Rosemary*): Putrid accessory! (*She goes stamping out after her sister*)

ROSEMARY: Run off! Old crazy crocks! See, Uncle Henry! It's only two good hot slaps they wanted.

Ernst, meanwhile, has produced his pocket dictionary and is thumbing through its pages. Henry is groaning and shaking his head.

HENRY: Oh, my God! I'd have preferred to have T.B. in my family than *this*!

ROSEMARY: Ernst dear, what are you looking for in your dictionary?

ERNST: It is the word "accessory".

ROSEMARY: Want me to spell it for you? A-C-E-S –

HENRY: There are two C's. Oh, my God! Oh, my God!

ROSEMARY: That's right. Let me help you to find it, Fuzzy-wuzzy.

ERNST: Fuzzy-wuzzy? What word is that, please?

ROSEMARY: It's a word I use when I've got a crush on a boy. I used to call Ollie Fuzzy-wuzzy, but now it's you. Got me, honey?

ERNST (*uncomprehending*): Yes, that is so. Please. Let us find "accessory" and "fuzzy-wuzzy". I am greatly interested in words.

ROSEMARY: Fuzzy-wuzzy is my own word. You won't find it in here.

ERNST: *Ach*! Yes, I understand. It is of your manufacture. (*Laughing*) That is clever.

ROSEMARY (*putting an arm round him*): Let's go to my room and settle down to a good sizzling lesson in language. Come on.

HENRY: No. Not out of this room, Rosemary. I forbid it.

ROSEMARY: Are you going to start forbidding me things? Even you?

HENRY: I say not out of this room. I mean it.

ROSEMARY: O. K. You've been treating me good. I won't fight the issue. Come, Ernst sweet, let's sit here. (*Indicating the sofa*)

ERNST (*uncertain*): Why should we sit there? Should we not walk in the out-of-doors?

ROSEMARY: You mean you prefer us to roll in a haystack! See, Uncle Henry! Trust a German to turn up with he-man suggestions!

HENRY: I'm sure he doesn't mean that. Look, Rosemary, don't start up anything again.

Eileen enters. She is dressed to go out.

EILEEN: Henry! I'm going to London for the day.

HENRY: To London? What are you going to London for?

EILEEN: I must have a break. Too much has been going on in this house.

HENRY: Look, you haven't got to take it like this, Eileen. I mean...

EILEEN: I'm human, Henry. There's a limit to what I can stand.

HENRY: How is it going to help you – running off to London?

EILEEN: I'll go off my head if I don't get away from this place for a few hours.

ROSEMARY: Madness is everywhere. Not only on the Surrey border.

ERNST: I should better to go. It would eliminate displeasure.

EILEEN: I think you'd be wise if you did go, young man. Please go.

ROSEMARY (*clutching him*): Don't listen to her. (*To Eileen*) Why the scarlet hell don't you get out and go to London! Go and leave us. Perhaps you know why you're afraid of madness.

HENRY: Rosemary, quiet!

ROSEMARY: Oh, Christ! Say something original for a change, can't you?

ERNST: I must go. It is entirely compulsory. (*Trying to free himself from the clutching arms of Rosemary*)

ROSEMARY: Settled, then! If you go I go with you, Ernst. I mean it. I'll even go to Germany with you.

EILEEN: No one here would miss you, I'm quite positive.

ROSEMARY: Uncle Henry, did you hear that? Deny it. Deny it quickly.

HENRY: Deny what? Control yourself.

ERNST: Yes, please. Control yourself. It will help your health.

ROSEMARY (*stamping*): I'll die if you go, Fuzzy-wuzzy. You're my coming vision. I've got to hold on to you or I'll die.

ERNST: No. That is a mistake. You will not die.

ROSEMARY: You're right. I'll live. Live with you in Germany, and to stinking, crimson hell with the rest of them!

HENRY: Control your language –

EILEEN: I'm off. I'll be back by the last train, Henry. I'm taking the car to the station.

HENRY: But I may need it to run into Farnham.

EILEEN: You didn't say anything about going into Farnham today.

ROSEMARY: Don't let her go, Uncle Henry. Drop her down the well. That would solve all our problems.

Eileen goes.

HENRY (*holding his head*): Oh, God!

ERNST: I do not like this condition of affairs. I wish to go.

ROSEMARY: O. K., Fuzzy-wuzzy. I yield to your German will. Give me ten minutes to throw some things into a suitcase.

ERNST: Suitcase? No, no. I have my rucksack and sleeping-bag. I brought no suitcase.

ROSEMARY: My suitcase. *My* suitcase, booby!

ERNST: Your suitcase? What is the matter to your suitcase?

ROSEMARY: I'm going to stuff it with a few things, and I'm coming with you.

ERNST: No. How can you come with me? Are you a hitchhiker?

HENRY: Rosemary, stop being a child. For heaven's sake!

ROSEMARY: Ernst, you wait for me, sweetie. I'm going to pack. (*She goes*)

HENRY: My boy, you see what I've got to face?

ERNST: Rosemary is an unusual person. So it appears.

HENRY: I didn't know you Germans went in for understatement, too!

ERNST: You wish me to state it in German? Why is that?

HENRY: No, no! It's all right. Look, have you got to go, Ernst? Can't you remain even for a day or two?

ERNST: But it is not wise that I should remain. Have we not experienced displeasure from your wife? Your wife asked me to go.

HENRY: She didn't mean it. She was upset because of Rosemary. That's all.

ERNST: And the two old women screamed. They spoke of spies. It was of me that they spoke. I do not like that statement.

HENRY: They're potty. You haven't got to bother with what they say.

ERNST (*producing his dictionary*): Potty? Please to spell that word.

HENRY: Oh, good Lord! I wonder if you yourself aren't potty! Look, forget your dictionary for a moment. We're discussing the question of your staying. Just for a few days. What about it?

ERNST: *Ach*! We are returned to that question. It is difficult to say. I should not refuse to stay for two or three days if it would help Rosemary. But I wish to cause no disturbances –

HENRY: I'm master here, and I'm asking you to stay. Isn't that good enough?

ERNST: Yes. I appreciate your extreme kindness –

HENRY: I'll see you through. We'll muddle along somehow until Rosemary comes to her senses.

ERNST: Muddle? Yes, I am a little familiar with that word. I can spell it. Let me see if I can find it… (*Beginning to thumb through his dictionary*)

Henry sighs and walks off in exasperation.

ERNST (*finding the word*): Yes, yes. Here! *Verwirrung. Schmutz.*

HENRY: I don't know a word of German.

ERNST: No? I am very interested in the words of all languages. This is an excellent dictionary. I bought it in Koln.

HENRY: Anyway, what's your answer about staying?

ERNST: About staying? *Ach*! Once more we return to that affair. It is so difficult to decide –

HENRY: But you said you wanted to help.

ERNST: Yes, I wish certainly to help…

HENRY: Then stay. It's as simple as that.

ERNST: But you have yourself said that it would cause confusion. A muddle.

HENRY (*sighing heavily again*): I never said that. I said we'd muddle along.

ERNST: Precisely: You have said it again. Muddle along. Confuse matters. Make a mess.

HENRY: Look, get this straight. I'm pretty positive there's no German equivalent for the English phrase "muddle along" –

ERNST: No German equivalents! But my dictionary says that it means *Verwirrung*. *Schmutz*. Those are the German words for "confusion", "mess" as you say in English. Does not "muddle" mean the same as "confusion" and "mess"?

HENRY: It does, but not in the way you think.

ERNST: Please to explain, then. I am greatly interested –

He is interrupted by the entry of Rosemary. She brings a suitcase and also Ernst's rucksack and sleeping-bag. She dumps them all down.

ROSEMARY: Look, Ernie sweet! I got your things while I was about it. Let's be off.

HENRY: Rosemary, I'm trying to get Ernst to stay.

ROSEMARY: Still? Phew! You are persistent! It's too late, old bugger! I've made up my mind to go with him.

ERNST: Are you serious? Do you really make a plan to go with me?

ROSEMARY: It's made, honey-bunch. I'm ready. I've got everything I need for a desperate emergency in here. Toothbrush, comb, lipstick and essential undies. Even a nightie, though I shouldn't want that. I'll have you to keep me warm.

HENRY: Don't be a little goat. Take your things back into your room.

ROSEMARY: You know what's the matter with you, Uncle H.?

HENRY: All right, all right. Just take your things back into your room.

ROSEMARY: No, I must tell you this. I've been wanting to tell you a long time.

HENRY: What's it?

ROSEMARY (*with great deliberation, pushing her face close to his*): You're ineffectual.

HENRY: Very well, very well!

ROSEMARY (*dancing away and laughing*): Ernst, did you hear that? I tell him he's ineffectual – the worst insult a woman can fling at a man – and he just says: "Very well, very well!" You see what we English have come to! Take warning, you big bad Jerry!

ERNST (*smiling, polite uncomprehending*): Please. Do not scream again. It is inadvisable.

ROSEMARY (*tapping his cheek playfully*): No, lovey-dove. No screaming while I'm with you. When we roll together in the hay I'll just sigh. Oooooh-h-h-h-h! Like that! (*Snaps her fingers and strikes an attitude, pointing at their bags*) Now, off we go! How do you say that in German?

ERNST (*indulgently, smiling still*): *Geht es los!*

ROSEMARY: Come on, then. *Geht es los!* (*She assumes a striking pose of elegance and provocativeness one arm raised and pointing*)

ERNST (*to Henry*): Is she not...? There is a word I forget...

ROSEMARY: Irresistible!

ERNST: Yes! True! That is the word! Irresistible. I saw it in an English magazine for women.

ROSEMARY: Was it an advertisement?

ERNST: Yes. *Das ist richtig!* In an advertisement it was. There appeared a picture of a girl. She stood as you stand there now. (*He tries to mimic her attitude of elegance and provocativeness*) And there was the one word very big, in red letters. "Irresistible!"

HENRY: Well, now that you've both had your little play with words, just get unpacked and let's be sensible, shall we?

ERNST: Unpacked? No, no. I must go. My hitchhike is best for me. I'm so sorry, but I cannot stay.

ROSEMARY: Nor me, We're both off. (*She picks up her suitcase while Ernst begins to put on his rucksack*) Come on, Fuzzy-Fritz. By heck! That's an idea! Patented! Fuzzy-Fritz: That's my new name for you. My vision-man – Fuzzy-Fritz!

HENRY: Rosemary, I'm going to lose my temper now –

ROSEMARY: That's no tragedy. The real tragedy is that you've lost me.

HENRY: You're not really serious about this! Where can you go to with this young man? He can't take you to Germany.

ROSEMARY: Don't worry. I'll work my way there somehow.

HENRY: You have no passport, for one thing.

ROSEMARY: That's a detail. I never fuss over details.

ERNST: I think you should remain. Your uncle is correct. (*He is now ready to go*)

ROSEMARY: Come, sweetheart. Off we go! No argument. (*Taking his arm and urging him towards door*)

ERNST: I am serious. You should remain.

ROSEMARY: I'm more serious. Let's go. Let's walk into the land of my Vision!

ERNST (*shrugging and giving Henry a look of resignation*): There is nothing I can do. If she wishes irresistibly to come with me I cannot eliminate her wishes.

HENRY: She's off her head. Take no notice of her.

ERNST: But I cannot make her not to notice me. That is the very disturbing factor.

ROSEMARY: Good boy! Tell him. Your English is improving every minute.

HENRY: Rosemary, for the last time...

ROSEMARY (*urging Ernst towards the door*): Come on, Fuzz! Ignore him. Let's be off. *Geht es los! Geht es los!*

CURTAIN on Scene One Act Two

ACT TWO Scene Two

Evening of the same day.
The living room has an extraordinary appearance, for Nora and Mary have been "decorating'" it. Long streamers fashioned out of strips from old newspapers, twirled and pasted together, festoon the room, and around the light-shade bunches of wild flowers have been hung. Above the fireplace, on the mantelpiece, we see a crude black and white portrait of a girl (Rosemary?) by no means flattering to the subject, especially as there is an X scored across the face. Also prominently displayed is another portrait, this one of a man (Ernst?) with an X scored across the face. Under each portrait is the legend: DEFEATED!
When the curtain rises, we see Nora and Mary, attired as before but with coloured bits of ribbon

and cardboard medals decorating their chests. They are trying to decide where to place a large V-sign made out of two lengths of wood tied together and wrapped about with newspaper.

NORA (*pausing by centre table*): What about here, Mary? Couldn't we somehow manage to get it erected on this table?

MARY: It will be difficult, dear. What about our own table?

NORA: Won't it be just as difficult to get it on to that?

MARY: I see your point.

NORA: It must be in a prominent place. This is no mean victory we've scored today.

MARY: I should think not. Two big enemy formations smashed at one blow. We deserve to celebrate in a lavish way. (*She glances down at her chest*) Oh, dear! I've dropped one of my medals.

NORA: Careful with those medals. We've got to show them to our grandchildren in the years to come.

MARY: I should think we have. We'll have to tell them of our daring deeds in the service of the country. Those terrible Hampshire Huns!

NORA (*trying the V-sign on the sofa*): But this is only an interim celebration, remember! The war isn't won yet. There's still more to be done. Much more. How about here, do you think?

MARY: Yes. It looks quite heroic there. I'm sure, our dear Mr. Churchill would approve. Pity we can't have him in tonight for our little spree.

NORA: He's got his hands full planning the Second Front. I hadn't the heart to ask him. (*She stands back to survey the V-sign*)

MARY: Ah! Here's my medal. (*She stoops and peers at it, pausing before picking it up*) Nora!

NORA: What's it?

MARY: Look. It's lying plumb in the centre of a fleur-de-lys!

NORA: What fleur-de-lys?

MARY: In the carpet pattern. Look!

NORA (*looking*): So it is.

MARY: Do you think there could be any significance in that?

NORA: Well, I don't like to be superstitious, but it could mean that dear General de Gaulle may be calling on us this evening. The fleur-de-lys is a distinctly French symbol.

MARY: This evening? Or tomorrow? It's lying to the east of the fleur-de-lys. That could signify the rising sun of tomorrow.

NORA: It could – or the falling of a blockbuster somewhere to east of us.

MARY: I acknowledge that interpretation. But, let's look on the brighter side. (*Picking up her medal and pinning it to her chest with the others*) Have we any absinthe in case dear General de Gaulle calls?

NORA: I think so. Didn't we have a report yesterday that one of our patrols had captured a few bottles from an enemy position near that odious little town?

MARY: Odiham?

NORA: That's it.

MARY: I'm glad it was Odiham. I couldn't have tolerated any absinthe captured near Basingstoke.

NORA: Why?

MARY: I can't explain it. Just a sort of allergy.

NORA: I think we'll leave it on the sofa. (*Placing the V sign on the sofa*) It looks very dashing there.

MARY: I prefer heroic. Heroic is the word.

NORA: What's wrong with "dashing"? Have you an allergy for that, too?

MARY: Now, dear! Don't pick at me. You know I hate being picked at.

NORA: You said that once before in the past. On a grave occasion.

MARY: I remember. And it was true. You had picked at me.

NORA: I had cause to. You threatened to infringe my rights.

MARY: I didn't. It was you who threatened to infringe mine.

NORA: That's a foul lie!

MARY: It isn't. Father O'Maggarty asked *me* to attend mass that morning.

NORA: He asked us *all* to attend, but that was only his discreet way of telling me he hoped to see me there. And in any case, you had a heavy cold and should not have tried to go to mass.

MARY: What a cruel memory to resuscitate, Nora!

NORA: Don't use such long words in my hearing. They're bad for my figure.

MARY: You've never had a figure. Only a configuration.

NORA: Father O'Maggarty didn't think so.

MARY: Father O'Maggarty was far too saintly even to be aware of the existence of figures. You slander him grossly.

NORA: We're venturing into deep waters. You'd better shut up.

MARY: Oh, God! I'm tired of madness!

NORA: We can't afford to live a sane life, so hold your tongue and be sensible.

MARY: I'm tired of fantasy.

NORA: It helps us to tolerate this deadly bucolic place. You should be thankful we have the capacity to sustain our fantasies.

MARY: I'd be thankful if we had some money to live on our own. What fun is there in clowning from day to day to amuse that dull niece of ours!

NORA: It's Henry we amuse – never Eileen. Try to be perceptive.

MARY: Eileen loves it. It's only that she's such a chronic cold-blanket she never feels she should show it.

NORA: As for that slut, Rosemary, I could strangle her. She rouses the vilest of my Irish blood.

MARY: She is much what you were at her age. You oughtn't to complain.

NORA (*at the window*): Oh, God! There's that Oliver boy coming. Suppose he's finished for the day in the field.

MARY: He's a good lad. I like him. If he remains here long enough I'll fight you for him.

NORA: No need. You can have him for the taking. I swore everlasting devotion to Father O'Maggarty. My heart is still with him, God knows it. (*Brushing away a tear*)

MARY: Cease that pseudo sentiment. It never fools me.

NORA: It shouldn't. We've both got so accustomed to make-believe we never know what's real from what's pseudo, even in ourselves.

MARY: I know what's real in myself, no fear. My hatred for you.

NORA: Pouf! What do you know about hatred! A spineless puppy like you! It takes strong people to hate.

Oliver enters.

OLIVER: Whoa! (*Gazing round*) What's happening in here? Whose birthday?

Nora and Mary assume the old stiff, military manner, resuming fantasy.

NORA: Mary, I think we might still try to get Mr. Churchill to come. Could you phone the War Office and see if you can contact him?

MARY: Very well. In a few minutes.

OLIVER: Churchill? Is Churchill in this, too?

NORA (*ignoring him*): I'm sure the War Office can spare a helicopter.

MARY: Or a fast bomber. They could drop him by parachute in the hayfield out there.

OLIVER (*with a laugh*): Not in the field I've just put in order. Not even Churchill.

NORA: There's a nasty sound coming on the air, Mary. What do you think it could be?

OLIVER: It's my voice, Field-marshal. Look, you two, come out of it for once and explain what this is about.

MARY (*weakening*): It's to celebrate, you idiot!

NORA (*in rebuke*): Mary!

OLIVER: To celebrate what?

MARY: The riddance of Rosemary.

NORA (*in sterner tones*): Mary!

MARY (*exasperated*): Oh, go and choke yourself!

NORA: Well! (*Nora, shocked, glaring, stamps irately out of the room*)

Mary begins to sob and Oliver puts his arm round her shoulder.

OLIVER: Never mind. I understand. You're fed up.

MARY: I'm tired, tired, tired.

OLIVER: I know. It must be a strain keeping up that business.

MARY: Life is so pointless. I'd like to die.

OLIVER: Lots of us want to do that, old lady, but we've got to face up. Nothing for it. Just face up.

MARY: Face up to what? This? (*Throwing her arm out despairingly*)

OLIVER: But you've got your wild flowers. They, at least, are real.

MARY (*wiping her eyes*): I knew you were better than Eileen thinks you are. I'm convinced of it. I like you, Oliver.

OLIVER: Thanks. I like you, too. Where's Rosy, by the way? Hasn't she come back yet?

MARY: No. I've seen nothing of her since she went off this morning with that German boy.

OLIVER: She'll come back. Sure as hay is hay.

MARY: Tell me this. Do you think she's madder than Nora and myself?

OLIVER: She's just as mad as you and me and Nora. It's only that she's excitable and likes showing off her madness.

MARY: Are we all mad in here? What do you think?

OLIVER: If I think about it I might turn sane. Let's forget it.

MARY: It's important. We should pursue the subject.

OLIVER: Let's compromise, then, by saying we're all on the borderline. That's a geographical fact, if nothing else. Have a fag. (*Proffering his case*)

MARY (*hesitating*): I haven't smoked since... since I was thirty.

OLIVER: Time you started again.

MARY (*still hesitating*): At sixty-seven, it's too late. No, I mustn't.

OLIVER: Please yourself. Not for me to lead you into sin. (*He lights one*).

MARY (*with a bitter laugh*): Sin! I'd be a happy woman if I could learn how to sin.

OLIVER: Didn't they teach you how to at school?

MARY: At school I was only taught how to behave – and look what it's led to! (*With a wave of her hand at the decorations*)

OLIVER: Did you go to school in Ireland? You don't speak with an Irish accent.

MARY: No. I went to school in this country. Three years at a convent school in Lancashire and five years at Roedean. Isn't that enough to ruin any good Irish accent!

OLIVER: How come you've got to live here with your niece?

MARY: Our brother Patrick was our only means of support. He died four months ago after squandering all our money on racehorses.

OLIVER: One of these gambling johnnies?

MARY: He was not a gambler. He bought and sold racehorses. It was a serious, honest occupation, but he had no head for horse-deals. The Irish aren't good at horse-dealing. Only the English and the Arabs.

OLIVER: I don't know anything about horses.

MARY: Would you like to learn?

OLIVER: No. I'd like to learn about farming. I've fallen in love with farming.

MARY: I thought your first love was sculpture in scrap-metal.

OLIVER: I've started to lose heart for that since I've come to this farm.

MARY: What about that rotten girl? I wish you'd lose heart for her, too.

OLIVER: Rosy? She's a case. I'd like to help her, but it's difficult.

MARY: Have you really gone to bed with her?

OLIVER: Phew! What a question from a sixty-seven-year-old spinster educated at Roedean!

MARY: Remember the Irish in me. It's responsible for much that is unpredictable.

Nora comes in, stiff and stern. She glares at her sister.

NORA: Are you still infringing Army regulations, Mary?

MARY: You mean talking to this boy? Yes. I'm taking a holiday from all that. Go outside again and leave us alone.

OLIVER (*proffering his case*): Have a fag, Aunt Nora.

NORA (*ignoring him*): Are you coming outside to take up sentry duty, Mary?

MARY: No. I'm not moving from this room. Go to hell.

NORA: I shall have you court-martialled for this!

MARY: Go ahead. See how inflexible she is, Oliver! Who would think she and I are twins! Oh, God! Why didn't I run away with that piano-tuner when I was twenty!

NORA: For the last time, Mary, are you going on sentry duty?

MARY: For the last time, I say no. Go and fry your fantasy. (*Nora stalks out of the room*).

OLIVER (*laughing*): Did you really have the chance of running away with a piano-tuner when you were twenty?

MARY: Yes, yes. But that's a long story. Have you had your supper yet?

OLIVER: No. Have they left any for me in the dining-room?

MARY: I don't think so. Eileen went off to London this morning. She isn't back yet.

OLIVER: Yes, I heard. Her nerves couldn't stand the strain.

MARY: Would you like me to get you some supper?

OLIVER: Don't worry. I'll wait around a bit.

MARY: I'd like to. It's a long time since I prepared supper for a man. Not since Patrick was alive. I like preparing supper for men.

OLIVER: But not for women?

MARY: No. I've always been a man's woman. Irony, irony, irony, my boy! I deserve to be still a virgin.

OLIVER: Why didn't you do something about it when you had the chance?

MARY: No courage, that's why. And I was plain. A plain woman must have unusual courage if she's to achieve the glory of losing her virginity.

OLIVER: This is the first conversation I've really enjoyed since I came to live on this farm.

MARY: Let me go and get you something. What would you like ? An omelette?

OLIVER: A special kind of omelette?

MARY: If you like. I can do one invented by myself. I've dubbed it the Limerick Omelette. Five ingredients. As exciting as the dirtiest limerick ever composed. I'll go and get it done for you. (*She goes*)

She has hardly: been gone a few seconds when Henry comes in dabbing his neck with a handkerchief.

HENRY (*staring round*): What on earth! Is this a new conception of sculpture?

OLIVER: It isn't sculpture. Have you got your Italian rye-grass planted?

HENRY: Yes. All three fields. Phew! I'm perspiring like hell and leather.

OLIVER: I was, too – but I've cooled down.

HENRY: But what's all this for, Oliver? Is it your work?

OLIVER: Aunt Mary and Aunt Nora. It's to celebrate Rosy's going-away.

HENRY: That poor girl. I hope no harm comes to her.

OLIVER: She'll be back. Tomorrow at the latest – that's my bet.

HENRY: I hope that German fellow doesn't take advantage of her.

OLIVER: I was hoping she doesn't take advantage of him.

HENRY: Oliver, what do you think is going to happen to her eventually?

OLIVER: She'll end up either a star in Hollywood or a Cabinet Minister's mistress.

HENRY: I'm serious. I'm worried about her.

OLIVER: I'm serious, too – but I'm not worried.

HENRY: You wouldn't marry her?

OLIVER: If I had to, I suppose. Not otherwise.

HENRY: You're a funny sort of chap. I like you, but can't… I just can't fathom you.

OLIVER: What's there in me to fathom?

HENRY: Well, I mean, your outlook… your – ah – philosophy. I can't get at it, somehow.

OLIVER: That's simple. I take what's to hand, and enjoy it. I have no ambitions to be famous and rich.

HENRY: You're doing very well on the land. Everybody tells me that.

OLIVER: That's because I've taken a fancy to it.

HENRY: It would be ideal if you could get Rosemary to settle down here.

OLIVER: You mean marry her and let's be farmer and farmer's wife?

HENRY: And why not? Doesn't the idea appeal to you?

OLIVER: It's tempting all right – but I don't think it would appeal to Mrs. Strad.

HENRY: She doesn't really hate you. It's only... you know what. This business she feels is going on between you and Rosemary.

OLIVER: She's an anachronism, if you'll pardon me saying it.

HENRY: For that matter, so am I, I daresay.

OLIVER: But you're more fluid. It doesn't show up so much.

HENRY: If you married Rosemary I'm pretty sure Eileen would change her attitude towards you.

OLIVER: She might – but I mightn't change mine towards her.

HENRY: You dislike her?

OLIVER: No. I like her but I resent her.

HENRY: Why?

OLIVER: Can't explain it myself. Something stuffy about her. Something hypocritical. I keep wanting to knock it out of her.

HENRY (*uncomfortably*): She's all right really. (*Glancing at his watch*) Hope she won't come back too late from London,

OLIVER: She ought to have had some children. It might have softened her up and brought out something real in her.

HENRY: Oh. Yes. Children. (*Shifty-eyed with embarrassment*)

OLIVER: Don't you agree?

HENRY: Yes, yes. In a way. Suppose you're right.

OLIVER: Oho. I can see I've touched on a taboo subject.

HENRY: Well, it is a bit delicate, yes. I mean, I pull her leg about it myself sometimes, but I'm always careful.

OLIVER: Why have you got to be careful?

HENRY: You know. She's, at heart, disappointed she couldn't have a child.

OLIVER (*after a pause*): I'm sorry.

HENRY: About what?

OLIVER: I mean I'm sorry I said I resented her. Just in a flash my resentment has changed to pity.

HENRY: That's going to the other extreme. I don't think she's a person who should be pitied. She's... what shall I say? Big. Self-assured. Fine type. I admire her tremendously.

OLIVER: I can see that. That makes me even more... Well, it makes my pity deeper.

HENRY: Why should it?

OLIVER: Because it's so sad... so sad that you should only admire her. It would have been nicer – and more fitting – if you'd loved her as well.

HENRY: Oh, don't misunderstand me! I didn't say –

OLIVER: Look, let's stop. We shouldn't be talking about her like this.

An awkward pause during which a bang is heard outside. Oliver moves to the window. He chuckles. Another bang! sounds.

OLIVER: Aunt Nora bombarding the enemy. Doing it alone this time.

HENRY: Alone? Where's her sister?

OLIVER: In the kitchen preparing an omelette for me.

HENRY: Joking? (*Another bang outside*)

OLIVER: You'll see. She is bringing it for me. Any minute now.

HENRY: How did you work the miracle?

OLIVER (*still at the window, stiffens as he gazes out*): Wait...

HENRY: What's wrong?

(*From outside comes a wailing cry*)

OLIVER: She's running.

HENRY (*approaching*): Running? Who's running?

OLIVER: Aunt Nora. Towards the road.

HENRY (*joining him at the window*): Another prank. Some military exercise.

OLIVER: I don't like it. She's making damned peculiar noises.

The wailing comes again, more distant.

HENRY (*chuckling*): War cries.

OLIVER (*pointing*): There's a big lorry coming along the road... She'd better be careful... Christ: She's going to run across!

Sound of shrieking brakes heard distantly.

HENRY: Good God!

OLIVER: Come! (*He dashes for the door, Henry following him. They go out. They have hardly departed when Mary comes in. She is carrying a tray on which is a plate with the omelette she has made for Oliver. She looks round, wonderingly*)

MARY: Oliver! (*She begins to move aimlessly round the room, the tray still held out before her*) Where could he have got to?... Oliver! (*She pauses in the middle of the room and stares round, a look of panic coming to her face*) No! Oh, no! Was it only a dream, then? Did I or didn't I talk to him in here a few minutes ago? Oh, God! Am I suffering from aberrations? Is this the revenge on me for tampering with lunacy?... Oliver! Oliver! Come, please! Don't let me slip into the Dark! (*She continues to wander round the room tray still in hand*) Oh, God! I must have imagined it. It was only fantasy. I've dabbled too much in fantasy, and now I'm caught. I'm in a spell, a spell! (*She looks up at the ceiling, at the walls*) I've woven it myself, and now I'm going to be trapped in it forever. (*With one free hand she tries to clutch at the paper decorations*) Oh, my God! Oh, my God! What a retribution! To die is bad enough, but to die lost among newspaper streamers! Oliver! Oliver, why don't you come and save me! Don't let me die entangled. I'm afraid. (*She pauses by the sofa, and stares at the V sign*) See! The sign of V. Magic. That twin sister of mine is a bloody witch. She's after me. She and Father O'Maggarty. And the Devil. After my virginity. Oh, heavenly God! Who will save me from a witch? Who will save me from Father O'Maggarty? (*She places the plate with the omelette on the sofa before the V-sign*) Perhaps if I make an offering of this omelette... A sacrifice to Lucifer. Not a burnt offering. Only a fried one, Lucifer, but good. Five ingredients. Onion, parsley, ham, sultanas – and the fifth ? I must keep that a secret. My terrible, edible secret. Oh, Oliver, why don't you come and eat what I've prepared for you? Oliver! Oliver! (*She kneels before the sofa, buries her face in her hands and whimpers*)

Rosemary enters, blowing hard, and flings her suitcase down on the, floor. She sits down near it on the floor.

ROSEMARY: Oh, Lord! I'm blown.

Mary removes her hands from her face and turns and looks at her in silence.

ROSEMARY (*suddenly staring round, just become aware of the decorations*): For crying out loud! Who's been monkeying round in here?

MARY: Have you seen Oliver?

ROSEMARY: Oh, no! So you're talking to me, at last!

MARY: Have you seen Oliver?

ROSEMARY: I haven't seen a soul yet. I came across the fields by the public footpath. Oh, bees and Jeez! I've walked over eight miles since midday. Not a sucker would stop and give me a lift between Odiham and here. Would you believe it?

MARY: Yes, I can believe it. I can believe many things now.

ROSEMARY: I'm hungry. Ernst offered me German salami and rusks. Have you ever seen German salami ? Long, fat thing like this (*Illustrating it with her hands*) You cut it across, and it looks dark-red and funny. I wouldn't eat it. I only ate the rusks. We were sitting by the side of the road.

MARY: There's peace by the side of a country road.

ROSEMARY: Peace? With that traffic going past? We were on the by-pass. I was munching my rusks, and would you believe it? Some goat of a fellow shouted at me from a van. Know what he shouted? "Bitch-hiker!" Can you beat that? "Bitch-hiker." I couldn't stand that. It upset me. I mightn't look it but I'm sensitive. What that fellow called out went home. I told Ernst I couldn't go on with the trek. I couldn't stand hearing anyone shout at me again. How would you like anyone to call you a bitch-hiker, Aunt Mary?

MARY: I should resent it.

ROSEMARY: I should think you would. What have you got there? (*Sniffing*) It smells good.

MARY: It's an omelette. It's for Oliver.

ROSEMARY: For Ollie ? Where's Ollie? Hasn't he come in yet from the fields?

MARY: He had. But he has vanished.

ROSEMARY: And all this fiddle-faddle overhead. Who did it?

MARY: It's the cobweb of confusion woven by the spiders of disillusion.

ROSEMARY: I thought you'd come to your senses. Is your mind wandering again?

MARY: No. I'm dreadfully sane.

ROSEMARY: Better give me that omelette. I can use it. I'm hungry like mad.

MARY: No. It's for Oliver. I made it for Oliver.

ROSEMARY: How come this sudden chumminess with Ollie? You're on speaking terms with him, too?

MARY: Yes. We spoke, he and I – then he vanished.

ROSEMARY: You're still batty. (*Rising and reaching out for the plate on the sofa*) Ollie won't mind if I eat his omelette. You can do another for him.

MARY (*grabbing the plate and avoiding her*): No. Oh, no. It would be sacrilege if you touched it. It's for him exclusively.

ROSEMARY: Indulge me. Let me have it. Come on. (*Beginning to advance on her again*)

MARY (*backing away*): No. I won't indulge you. Keep off.

ROSEMARY (*advancing still; they begin to circle the centre table*): You know I'm a psycho case. Don't thwart me or there'll be trouble.

MARY: I'm a psycho case myself. Probably a worse one than you.

ROSEMARY: *Mary* and Rosemary. (*With a brief laugh as they still follow each other round the table*) We'll see who's going to win.

MARY: I'm bound to – in this particular instance.

ROSEMARY: Think you can put it past me, loony? (*She makes a grab, but Mary dodges her hand and quickens her pace, evading her*)

MARY (*as they pause and gaze at each other across the table*): I'll tell you why you can't win this time.

ROSEMARY: Look, I want that omelette. Give it to me. I must have it.

MARY: You know why you can't win? Because if I see myself about to lose I'll drop the plate and trample on what's in it. Very simple.

ROSEMARY: You're not so mad, after all.

MARY: Quite as mad as you. A case of Greek meets freak.

ROSEMARY: Don't try to be witty. It doesn't suit you.

MARY: Do you concede defeat?

ROSEMARY (*after a pause*): Yes.

MARY (*with a laugh*): Go and unpack your bag.

Rosemary doesn't move. Just stares at her.

MARY: Don't imagine you've disarmed me because you've said "Yes.". I'm still on my guard. I don't trust female serpents.

Rosemary still says nothing.

MARY: Get off. Take your bag and go to your room and stop trying so hard to look abnormal.

Rosemary is still silent. Staring at her.

MARY: Your staring at me won't intimidate me.

ROSEMARY: Where's your sister?

MARY: She went out. In a huff. We had a… let's call it a difference of feeling.

ROSEMARY: Isn't she bombarding the enemy this evening?

MARY: Who knows if she hasn't been killed in action!

ROSEMARY: I wish I had been.

MARY: Why?

ROSEMARY: I'm a deserter.

MARY: Whom have you deserted?

ROSEMARY: My husband.

MARY: You have one?

ROSEMARY: Ernst.

MARY: Did you marry him?

ROSEMARY: When I left with him this morning it was like marrying him.

MARY: You vowed to follow him to the ends of Germany?

ROSEMARY: The earth. He was the beginning of my vision.

MARY: Many of us make vows and have visions.

ROSEMARY: But I am different. I should have kept my vows *and* my vision.

MARY: Too late. Too too late!

ROSEMARY: Just suddenly I'm shivering with guilt. I feel guilt like a black winter-coat falling round my head. (*She begins to look up round her head*)

MARY: The black bat night.

ROSEMARY: Why are we alone in here? Why don't the others come?

MARY: Perhaps they're dead.

ROSEMARY: Dead?

MARY: And interred in some soot-dark catacomb.

ROSEMARY (*exploding*): Look, don't try to haul me after you into your loony world! I'm not going to follow you there, you old bitch!

MARY: Don't lose your temper.

ROSEMARY: I've lost it already – like everything else. Oh, Christ! I keep losing and losing and losing!

MARY: Your virginity, too ?

ROSEMARY: That was the first to go. I've forgotten that.

MARY: Happy woman!

ROSEMARY: As soon as I've eaten something I'm going off again after Ernst.

MARY: Don't. He was a nice young man.

ROSEMARY: That's why I want him.

MARY: Have pity on him. He must be relieved to be rid of you.

ROSEMARY: I believe he was. Oh, God! Not a soul loves me. Not a soul!

MARY: There's one I know of who does.

ROSEMARY: Who's that ?

MARY: You.

ROSEMARY (seizing *the vase on the centre table*): Shut up!

MARY: The truth hurts even the insane.

ROSEMARY: I'll throw this at your head if you don't shut up!

MARY: Throw it. Then you can eat the omelette over my corpse.

ROSEMARY: Where's everybody? Where's everybody?

MARY: Put down that vase. It seems to be of some value.

ROSEMARY: Where's Uncle Henry ? Where's Aunt Eileen? Why have I got to stand here hungry under all this… all this jungle of newspaper snakes! Who did this? (*Tearing down a few streamers*) Who did it?

MARY: It doesn't matter. It can't be undone.

ROSEMARY: I suppose it's you and Aunt Nora. (*Seeing the V sign*) And V sign. What's that for? V for virgin ?

MARY: Yes. (*Sighing*) Not for victory.

ROSEMARY: I wish I could kill something. I wish I could kill something. (*Marching about, the vase held precariously in one hand*)

MARY: That vase. It's valuable.

ROSEMARY: I wish I could smash something. But not a vase.

MARY: A skull?

ROSEMARY: Shut up! Shut up! Shut up! Shut up!

MARY (*sobbing and resting plate with omelette on sofa*): Poor vase, poor vase. And I've admired it so. Even loved it. (*She sinks down before sofa in an attitude of prayer*) Oh, let it not be broken, dear God. Let it be spared. It's such a beautiful vase. (*The back of her head is very vulnerable, and Rosemary has observed this. Rosemary, takes a stealthy pace towards her, hand with the vase slowly rising*) I've seen that vase with the sunlight on it, and it looked like a translucent pillar of pulchritude. Don't let her injure it, God. (*Rosemary's hand goes higher and higher, and her face takes on a fiendish expression*). I've seen it at night, a moonbeam making a tangent of silver past its connubial curves. It's too alive in its delicacy to be destroyed. Spare it, God... Spare it. (*Her voice falls very low. Then as it seems that Rosemary is about to strike, Mary, in a lightning move turns and grabs the girl's ankle. Rosemary falls forward on to the sofa, and the vase leaves her hand, tumbling harmlessly on the sofa*)

They are sitting in a tangle, breathing hard and staring in a bewildered manner at each other, when Eileen appears at door... (R) She stares at the decorations, then her gaze settles on Mary and Rosemary. She begins to laugh. A soft sound. Then it gets louder and shriller. Hysterical. She shakes and bends in two, screeching with maniacal laughter.

CURTAIN on Scene Two, Act Two

(End of Act Two)

ACT THREE

Later that same evening. The decorations have been cleared away. At the rise of the curtain the stage is empty. There is a flash of lightning and thunder is heard. Then Rosemary, in pyjamas with a dressing-gown over them, dashes in, pauses, looks round then moves quickly to the window and looks out. Lightning flashes again. Thunder rolls.

ROSEMARY: A storm coming up. The fine weather is breaking. If only they'd let me dance. The thunder could be my music. Oh, God! If only… (*She breaks off and begins to squeeze her hands together in a distracted manner.*)
Henry comes in. He is still in daytime clothes.
HENRY: What are you doing in here? Why aren't you in bed?
ROSEMARY: A storm is coming up. Don't you hear the thunder?
HENRY: All the more reason why you should be in bed.
ROSEMARY: I love thunder-music, Uncle Henry. Why don't you let me dance?
HENRY: Dance?
ROSEMARY: Yes. In the nude. It will cure me. I feel it will cure me. It will give me my vision and cure me.
HENRY: It's after ten. Get off to bed.
ROSEMARY: (*beginning to undo her dressing-gown*): Let me dance. Let me make one grand display of myself, naked – without a single thing on – oh, Lord! That will do it, I'm sure.
HENRY: Don't you dare take off that dressing-gown, Rosemary!
ROSEMARY: Can't you see it? Can't you see me dancing naked before you and Aunt Eileen and Ollie and Aunt Mary? Can't you see me spinning and hopping between the furniture and the lightning flashing and the thunder crashing out above us? Oh, Lord! I can taste it in my soul. Yes, right in my soul. Not on my tongue. Let me do it, Uncle Henry. Let me do it.
HENRY: I have no time for nonsense. I'm expecting the hospital to ring at any moment.
ROSEMARY: Is Aunt Nora really bad? Do you think she'll die?
HENRY: Her condition is very grave.
ROSEMARY: You're talking like a newspaper.
HENRY: That's what they said at the hospital.
ROSEMARY: Did the lorry run right over her? Was there a whole river of blood running across the road?
HENRY: I don't care to go into details.
ROSEMARY: What about Aunt Eileen?
HENRY: She's in her room. She needs quiet. Remember that.
ROSEMARY: I've never heard her laugh as she laughed when she came in and found Aunt Mary, and me near the sofa there. Gave me the beezy-wheezies!
HENRY: Her nerves were on edge. It – it was just a touch of hysteria.
ROSEMARY: A very big touch. What did she do in London? Did she say?
HENRY: She went to the cinema. Nothing more exciting.

ROSEMARY: It might cure her as well as me.

HENRY: What might cure her?

ROSEMARY: If she saw me dance in the nude. I can make it really exciting.

HENRY: She doesn't need that sort of excitement.

ROSEMARY: How do you know? She wants a little stimulation. It's lack of stimulation that's her trouble in this place.

HENRY: I didn't know you were a psychiatrist.

ROSEMARY: Oh, jeezy-wheezy: Nobody has any enterprise. I'm the only one with any kind of push. (*She goes out*)

Lightning and thunder.

HENRY (*glancing at his watch*): Why doesn't the blasted hospital phone and put us out of this suspense! (*He goes out*)

Mary comes in. She is still fully dressed. She is carrying a ragged collection of wild flowers. She seats herself at her table near the window and begins to look in the wild flower book to identify them.

MARY (*holding up a specimen critically*): St. John's Wort. Without a doubt.

She goes on examining the specimens. After a pause, Eileen, in nightgown, with dressing-gown over it appears. She looks round the room with an air of half-dreamy vagueness. Mary takes no notice of her. Eileen wanders over to the window and stands looking out at the growing dark.

EILEEN: No news from the hospital yet, Aunt Mary.

MARY: No?

EILEEN: I didn't know about the accident when I came in or... or I wouldn't have laughed like that. You – you do understand that?

MARY: Don't try to apologise. It was refreshing hearing you laugh.

EILEEN: It was cruel. Cruel.

MARY: But you've said you didn't know about the accident when you laughed.

EILEEN: Still, it seems so cruel. So terribly cruel. (*With a whimper*) *Lightning flashes but instead of thunder there is the sound of hoofbeats.*

MARY: What animal is that going past outside?

EILEEN: A heifer.

MARY: Not a rhinoceros?

EILEEN: No. A heifer. Not a rhinoceros. (*Eileen pushes her head out of the window as though to make sure*)

MARY: It's a relief.

EILEEN: What's a relief? (*She is still leaning out of the window*)

MARY: Knowing it's not a rhinoceros. (*After a pause*) What are you looking at so intently out there

EILEEN: Nothing.

MARY: Is there a hole under the window?

EILEEN: Why should there be a hole under the window?

MARY: I thought you were gazing into a hole.

EILEEN: Why should I want to gaze into a hole?

MARY: It might have been an interesting hole.

EILEEN: No, there's no hole.

MARY: Are you waiting for something or somebody?
EILEEN: The telephone.
MARY: I'm not waiting for anything – or anybody.
EILEEN: Oh, God! I hope they'll be able to save her.
MARY: Save whom?
EILEEN: Aunt Nora.
MARY: Is that what you're waiting for?
EILEEN: Aren't you anxious, too?
MARY: Yes, but I'm not *waiting*. I think waiting is idiotic.
EILEEN: Oh, God! Oh, God!
MARY: Is it the tinkle of the telephone you're waiting to hear?
EILEEN: You know I am. I've said so.
MARY: I hope it will tinkle soon.
EILEEN: Oh, God!
MARY: I hope it will be a really *resounding* tinkle.

*Eileen sighs heavily and goes out. Lightning and thunder. Almost at once Oliver comes in.
He is carrying his "statue" and his workbox. He sets up the statue and puts down the box.
He begins, without a word or a glance at Mary to twist wires and attach them to the statue.*

MARY (*after a pause*): I arrived but you were not there.
OLIVER: Me?
MARY: Yes. You. You had vanished when I arrived.
OLIVER: Oh. Get you now. That omelette you promised to make for me.
MARY: I made it and brought it, but you'd vanished.
OLIVER: Thanks. It was the accident. I had to give a hand.
MARY: It's gone very cold.
OLIVER: What has?
MARY: The omelette. (*Calmly she pulls out a drawer in the table and produces the
       plate with the omelette*)
OLIVER (*not seeing the omelette*): Pity. Why didn't you eat it yourself?
MARY: Look!
OLIVER (*looking*): So you kept it!
MARY: Here in my little drawer, yes. But it's cold. So terribly cold.
OLIVER: Perhaps before we go to bed I can heat it up. Never mind.
MARY: It was she who caused the diversion.
OLIVER: What diversion?
MARY: The accident on the road.
OLIVER: Nasty business.
MARY: Did it happen on this side of the border?
OLIVER: Almost right on the border. You know the sign saying HAMPSHIRE?
       Just there.
MARY: She timed it nicely, then. I didn't think her judgment was so good.
OLIVER: You believe she meant to get run over?
MARY: Without any doubt.
OLIVER: Stupid thing to do.
MARY: Did you go to the hospital with the damaged body?

OLIVER: No. I helped to lift her on to the lorry. Mr. Strad went with her. Has
    he come back yet, do you know?
MARY: I believe he has. Perhaps he is waiting, too.
OLIVER: Waiting for what?
MARY: The telephone.
OLIVER: Oh. I suppose the hospital's promised to ring up.
MARY: I gather they have.

*During a pause she rises and takes the plate to the window, empties the omelette outside,
then returns to her chair at the table and puts the plate back into the drawer. She goes on
with her wild flowers study. Lightning and thunder.*

OLIVER: Storm coming over.
MARY: I don't think it will come this way. It won't cross the border. It a Hampshire
    storm.
Rosemary enters, still attired as before.
ROSEMARY: You in here with your thing-me-gummy?
OLIVER: So you've come back, Rosy?
ROSEMARY: Yes. And you never came to my room.
OLIVER: Came for what?
ROSEMARY: Didn't you want to verify if I'd come back?
OLIVER: You're using big words nowadays.
ROSEMARY: I feel big this evening. But I could feel bigger – much, much bigger
    – if the rest of you would let me.
OLIVER: How are we stopping you?
ROSEMARY: By not letting me dance. I want to dance naked before you all so
    that I can have my vision, but nobody wants to see me dance.
OLIVER: I've seen you dance already.
ROSEMARY: In that Soho club – but not here.
OLIVER: This isn't a suitable place.
ROSEMARY: It's driving me mad. Ollie, can't you persuade Uncle Henry and
    Aunt Eileen to want to watch me dance?
OLIVER: It's bad enough to persuade them to *let* you do it, but I'd have to be
    God to persuade them to *want* to watch you do it.
ROSEMARY: Won't you enjoy seeing me dance in this room?
OLIVER: I suppose I might. You've got a good figure.
ROSEMARY: Of course I have. This isn't any dud figure. My figure is an A-1
    Top Drawer figure. Look at the umpteen women who try to fool you they've
    got good figures, but just let them take off their bras – and what a let down!
    In more than one sense.
Oliver is whistling as he works. He merely smiles.
ROSEMARY: Isn't it true ?
OLIVER: Of course it's true.
ROSEMARY: You might put a little more emotion in your voice!
OLIVER: I'm busy with this thing. Not in the mood to talk about brassieres and
    nude dancing.
ROSEMARY: See! No enthusiasm. Aunt Mary, how about you? Wouldn't you
    revel in the sight of me dancing nude?

MARY: I'd rebel at it.

ROSEMARY: See again! No enthusiasm. Oh, God, I'm lost, lost, lost! I'm a stinking creature. (She *throws herself down on the floor and bangs her head on the carpet distractedly, wailing, whimpering*) I'm a failure. A rotten, rotten failure.

Aunt Mary rises calmly, goes to the sideboard and takes up a little brass bell which she rings several times. She puts it down and returns to her table. Almost at once there is a thud of footsteps offstage, and Henry and Eileen appear at once, jostling each other to enter.

HENRY & EILEEN: Was that the phone?

OLIVER: No, it wasn't.

MARY: It was only a try-on.

HENRY: But there was a ring. A bell...

EILEEN: Yes, there was a ring. I'm sure there was.

MARY: There was.

HENRY: Well? Didn't one of you answer it?

ROSEMARY (*on the floor still moaning*): A crawling failure. (*She begins to crawl*) Oh, help! Help! I'm a failure!

EILEEN: Speak up, somebody! Did any of you answer the phone?

OLIVER: I didn't.

ROSEMARY: I wish I had, but I'm a *nasty* failure. Help! Help! (*Thumping the floor with her fists*)

EILEEN: This is intolerable, intolerable! Henry, I'm going to... oh, God! I wish I knew what to do.

MARY: Do anything but laugh.

ROSEMARY: Yes, don't laugh. It gives me the beezy-jeezies when you laugh.

HENRY: Oliver my boy, tell me. Did the phone ring?

OLIVER: I told you it wasn't the phone, sir.

HENRY: What was it, then?

OLIVER: The little brass bell on the sideboard.

EILEEN: Who rang it?

MARY: I did.

EILEEN: I should have known it! Why did you do that, Aunt Mary?

MARY: To help relieve your suspense. Weren't you waiting to hear a bell ring?

EILEEN: *Yes,* but the telephone bell – not the little brass bell on the sideboard.

MARY: Don't despise brass.

ROSEMARY: It's a base metal. And so am I. Base! Base! Base! (*Hammering the floor with her fist*)

MARY: What's the matter with you, Rosemary? Get up from there.

ROSEMARY: I'm down for good. I'm not a phoenix. I'll never rise again. I'm just ashes. Ashes! Eternal ashes! (*Hammering the floor again*) Lightning and a very loud peal of thunder.

HENRY: This fine spell is breaking. Blast! And I was hoping to reap that barley tomorrow.

MARY: It's only a passing storm. It will keep to enemy territory.

HENRY: For God's sake, don't start up that nonsense again!

MARY: I can risk it, because I'm sane this evening.

EILEEN: I'm going to my room. And Aunt Mary, please don't fiddle around with that bell again. I beseech you.

MARY: The next time you hear a bell it'll be the phone, I promise.

ROSEMARY: Unless I ring the one on the sideboard.

HENRY: I hope you won't.

ROSEMARY: I might do it for spite.

OLIVER: Rosy, get up from there and stop behaving like a fool.

ROSEMARY (*rising*): I may as well. I'm not impressing anybody.

EILEEN: Lord! I wonder when I'll find myself among sane people! (*She hurries out*)

MARY (*sighing*): That woman isn't right in the head.

HENRY: I'm going to my room, too. No fiddling about with that bell, please! (*He goes out*).

Rosemary begins to pace up and down.

ROSEMARY: I never thought frustration could be as frustrating as this.

Mary rises, and Oliver, suspecting another excursion to the sideboard, moves quickly towards her and grabs her arm.

OLIVER: Aunt Mary, please! Don't ring that bell again.

MARY: I wasn't going to.

OLIVER: Sorry. I thought you might have had it in mind.

MARY (*smiling*): Thanks for arresting me, all the same.

ROSEMARY: I wish he'd arrest you and put you in chokey. (*Pacing and moaning and wagging her head*)

MARY (ignoring her and regarding Oliver's statue): I got up because I wanted to have a closer look at this truly remarkable piece of work.

OLIVER: I'm not quite satisfied with it.

MARY: Understandable.

ROSEMARY: I wonder if I shouldn't try running into the path of a lorry, too.

OLIVER (*ignoring Rosemary*): It's hard to get it just the way you conceive it.

MARY: The image in the mind seldom coincides with the image in Space-Time. I follow.

Rosemary suddenly goes running out of the room. Her footsteps are heard thumping in the corridor. Lightning flashes and thunder rolls.

OLIVER: Hell of a girl.

MARY: Did you note her remark?

OLIVER: Don't worry. She won't run into the path of a lorry.

MARY: Pity.

OLIVER: Underneath she's all right. A question of digging to find the good in her.

MARY: You should know. You've probably done a lot of digging.

From outside comes a bang.

MARY: A bombardment.

OLIVER: Rosy trying to attract attention. No surprise.

MARY: It's intolerable that she should plagiarize Nora and myself.

OLIVER: She hasn't got an original mind, I admit.

MARY (*pacing*): It baffles me that anyone could have sympathy for that kind of person.

OLIVER: She has a good figure, though.

MARY: Do you fall for that kind of thing, too?

OLIVER: I'm human. And male.

MARY: How dreary. And I'd begun to feel you had more in you than mere mortal grossness.

OLIVER: Tell you what, I'm beginning to feel *grossly* hungry. Didn't have any supper. Go and heat up that omelette for me.

MARY: I've already disposed of it.

OLIVER: What have you done with it?

MARY: I threw it out into the storm. As an act of symbolism.

OLIVER: What did it symbolise?

MARY: Anything you care to think it does.

OLIVER: You're getting as bad as me and my sculpture.

MARY: It's the *avant-garde* fashion. In drama as well as sculpture.

OLIVER: Agree. Can you make me another omelette?

MARY: With pleasure. A Limerick omelette? With five ingredients?

OLIVER: Yes. Same as the last.

MARY: This time don't go. It would be the end of me if I returned and found that you had vanished.

OLIVER: I won't vanish. I promise.

MARY: I have the means of getting rid of myself.

OLIVER: What's that? Poison? Revolver? Rope?

MARY: None of those.

(*She moves towards the door while he resumes work on his statue. Suddenly at the door, before going out, she pauses, smiles and takes from her bosom a knife with a longish sharp blade. She looks at his back, looks at the knife, smiles again wags her head and then replaces the knife in her bosom and goes out.*)

Sound of rain is heard. A flash of lightning. Bark of thunder. Eileen comes in.

EILEEN: Did Aunt Mary go outside?

OLIVER: She's gone to the kitchen to make me an omelette.

EILEEN: I mean outside the house.

OLIVER: No. Not that I know of. Why do you ask?

EILEEN: I heard that banging noise.

OLIVER: That was Rosemary.

EILEEN: Was it Rosemary doing that?

OLIVER: Frustration. Didn't you see how she was behaving?

EILEEN: I did. (*Moving to the window*) It's raining.

OLIVER: We can't reap the barley tomorrow.

She gives him a long stare. He is busy with his statue. Does not see the stare. After a pause:

EILEEN: Thanks for helping with Aunt Nora.

OLIVER: Forget that. Tell me something I want to know.

EILEEN: What?

OLIVER: Why do you behave as if you're afraid of me?

EILEEN: I wasn't aware that I gave that impression.

OLIVER: You do. Fear of me hangs about you like a psychic musk.

EILEEN: I can't help it if you're imaginative.

OLIVER: It's not imagination. It's perception. Did you have a good day in London?

EILEEN: I went to the cinema.

OLIVER: That's all? Didn't you sit by the Round Pond and watch the boats?

EILEEN: I didn't feel inclined for that.

OLIVER: That's the setting for you. A large park with trees and a pond. You have the peace of trees under your restlessness.

EILEEN: Do I seem restless?

OLIVER: Restless and unfulfilled.

EILEEN: I hadn't realised I'd left such an impression on you.

OLIVER: That's only one of several impressions.

EILEEN: I wish the phone would ring.

OLIVER: Now about running away with me?

EILEEN: Doing what?

OLIVER: You heard me. I think we ought to do that. It would be the natural dramatic development of our destiny.

EILEEN (*agitated, fidgeting and beginning to pace*): You're talking utter nonsense.

OLIVER: I feel it in me we're going to do that eventually. Run right away into the night.

Eileen says nothing. Continues to pace. Lightning and thunder.

OLIVER: We've got the right dramatic weather for a runaway act.

EILEEN: I do wish to goodness that phone would ring.

OLIVER: It isn't only the phone you're waiting for now.

EILEEN: What do you mean?

OLIVER: You're waiting for me to make a move.

Eileen clicks her tongue and continues to pace. Oliver leaves his statue, approaches her casually and takes her in his arms. She gives him a stare but does not repulse him.

OLIVER: What did I tell you?

EILEEN: Aren't you being rather... peculiar?

OLIVER: No. It's expected of me to behave like this.

EILEEN: Who expects you to?

OLIVER: Anyone who might be looking on. And you yourself.

EILEEN: I think you'd better release me.

OLIVER: Not yet. It's expected that I should hold you like this for a minute or two.

EILEEN: You're being very odd.

OLIVER: You're being very co-operative.

EILEEN: Please release me.

OLIVER: That's right. You don't even try to repulse me. It would be disappointing if you pushed me off.

EILEEN: Disappointing for whom?

OLIVER: Our theoretical audience. And for you.

EILEEN: I repeat. Please release me.

Instead he kisses her.

EILEEN: Why have you done that?

OLIVER: It's the accepted thing to do. And I wanted to. Was dying to. (*He kisses her again*)

EILEEN: Aren't you being a trifle presumptuous?

OLIVER: A **trifle** – but not very. You're deliciously kissable. (*Kisses her again*)

EILEEN: I don't care for this sort of behaviour.

OLIVER: I know what you mean. (*He kisses her again. A prolonged kiss*)

EILEEN: I suppose you understand this is very upsetting for me.

OLIVER: I know. I can hear your heart. It keeps going buppity-buppity-bup!

EILEEN (*nestling closer to him*): My heart is in perfect condition.

OLIVER (*his eyes shut, dreamily*): Buppity-buppity-bup!

Rosemary appears silently at the door [L] and stares at them. Her hair looks wet from the rain. Her dressing-gown is decorated with bits of hay.

EILEEN: Are you really what you've told us you are?

OLIVER: I know what you're thinking, sweetheart.

EILEEN: This is becoming quite devastating. (*With a soft sigh*)

OLIVER: I wish I were a fairy prince in disguise, but it's just as I told you. I'm only a jeweller's son.

EILEEN: Sometimes I'm inclined to doubt you're real.

OLIVER: At heart, you're as much a romantic as I am.

ROSEMARY: Oh, sweet Maria!

Eileen breaks away from him, and they glance round at Rosemary.

OLIVER: You again?

EILEEN: And I was hoping you'd been hit by the lightning!

ROSEMARY: Caught! Fairly caught! Caught flagrante deliriums, or whatever the saying is!

OLIVER: Go to bed.

ROSEMARY: You stinking dog!

EILEEN: Get out of here, for heaven's sake!

ROSEMARY: Too late. I've caught you. Now it's just a matter of naked blackmail.

EILEEN: Let it be anything but naked you!

ROSEMARY (*snapping her fingers*): That's an idea! I can force your hand now. Either you let me dance naked before you, or else…

EILEEN: I've had enough of this. (*She moves towards the door*)

Rosemary runs quickly to the centre table and grabs the vase.

ROSEMARY: Stop! Don't go – or I'll smash this right in front of your eyes.

EILEEN (*pausing*): Put down that vase at once!

ROSEMARY: Well, don't run away. Stay where you are. I mean it. I'll smash it if you move another step towards that door.

EILEEN: What a pity you didn't go off with that German! Perhaps he would have known how to tame you.

ROSEMARY: Blistering hypocrite! You must have wanted him, too.

OLIVER: Rosy, put down that vase.

ROSEMARY: We've been to bed, Ollie. Have you told her that? (*To Eileen*) Has he told you? You guessed right. We've been to bed umpteen times. I knew you were after him you poker-faced Judas!

EILEEN: Be quiet! Be quiet!

ROSEMARY: Bloody brass-eyed sham! Staring us down like a statue of morality. Raising your hands in rebuke, and inside your rotten guts you were wriggling with desire for him. Why don't you confess it? I've found you out. Confess it! Confess it!

OLIVER (*clapping his hands*): Good speech! One night we're going to see you on the West End stage.

ROSEMARY: After all my dreams! After all my schemes! All those lovely positions
I read of in that book you lent me. We'll never be able to practise them now.
Just because this bitch has taken a tumble for you. You had your eye on her
from the start, hadn't you? Working in the fields like a good boy to fool
Uncle Henry. Oh, screaming jeezy-bees! What a ranting, tearing failure I
am! (*She flings herself on the sofa, the vase still intact*)

*Oliver runs quickly over to the sofa and rescues the vase and takes it back to the centre
table. Rosemary's wailing is interrupted by the thunder. Henry enters.*

HENRY: What's going on in here?

OLIVER: The usual. Rosemary being a failure for the hundredth time.

ROSEMARY: Nobody cares if I'm a failure for the thousandth time.

OLIVER (*crossing over and patting her head*): Come along. Up. Let me take you to
your room. Up you come!

HENRY: Yes, take her to her room like a good fellow, Oliver.

ROSEMARY: You'll really take me, Ollie? No fooling?

OLIVER: No fooling.

ROSEMARY (*chuckling and giving Eileen a triumphant glance*): He's still got a hankering
after me, see! (*She rises and moves towards door with Oliver*) It'll take more than
you to rob me of him. (*She thumbs her nose at her and goes out with Oliver*)

HENRY: I thought you'd gone to bed, dear.

EILEEN: Do you expect me to sleep before we hear from the hospital?

HENRY: That's true. (*Pausing at the window*): Tch, tch! Look at that rain pelting
down!

EILEEN: You won't be able to reap the barley tomorrow.

HENRY: That's right. Damned nuisance!

Eileen bursts into tears and hurries from the room.

HENRY (*starting; dismayed*): Now, what the devil did I say? (*He goes out*)

*Vivid flash of lightning and crash of thunder. Heavy rain. After a pause Mary enters tray
in hand omelette in plate as before. She pauses, stares round, a look of incredulity
coming to her face.*

MARY: He's not here... Again... Again he has vanished... Oliver! (*She moves
trance-like towards the centre table*) It's true. He's not here... Once again I am
left destitute of human companionship... Oliver! Oliver, wherever you are,
hear this. You've decided my fate. You have sentenced me to death. (*She
begins to move round and round the table, tray in hand*) This is the ultimate price
I must pay for a life of unsullied virtue. (*She pauses, puts the tray down on the
table*) But if I am to die I should make the most of my remaining minutes.
Why should I fade out like... like a badly developed photograph... Oh, no I
must be gay, effervescent. I should dance. Not in the nude, I grant – but
dance, nevertheless. (*She holds her skirt and does an awkward little jig*) Oh, dear!
It's not in good taste. After all, I was educated at Roedean. I must not let
down the old school... No, dancing is not for me. I know what! Destruction!
That's more in my line. (*She turns and takes up the vase*) A good smashing
spree. That's more fitting for an occasion such as this. Oh, Oliver! It's incredible
that you should have let me down in this fashion... Ah! An idea! (*She puts
down the vase, and turning, looks at the statue, smiles and nods*) I'll begin with
you. Yes, you, you metal demon! It's you who put a blight on my destiny.

(*She advances and lifts up the statue, takes it to the window. Lightning flashes, and she recoils. But determinedly she pushes it through the window. We hear it fall to the ground with a muffled tinkle and clatter. She dusts her hands and nods*) There! Wasn't that a satisfying sound!

Oliver enters.

OLIVER: What sound was that?

MARY: Your statue. I've thrown it outside.

OLIVER: Thanks. I meant to do it myself.

MARY: You're not angry then?

OLIVER: I'm delighted.

MARY: Oh, dear! It seems as though I am reprieved.

OLIVER: Reprieved?

MARY: I came in and found you not here. I was preparing to take my life.

OLIVER (*putting his arm round her*): Poor you. What a shame! I didn't mean to be away for long. I was seeing Rosy to bed.

MARY (*recoiling*): Oh!

OLIVER: Don't swoon. I just tucked her in and left.

MARY: I'm allergic to that girl.

OLIVER: I know. Come. Let me eat my omelette. (*He takes up the tray and goes to the sofa, seats himself*) Come and sit near me.

Mary goes and sits beside him.

MARY: You're an irresistible young man.

OLIVER: Thanks. (*Beginning to eat*) This is good.

MARY: I wonder if I'm being wise in getting so close to you.

OLIVER: It won't harm you.

MARY: You won't smother me with a cushion?

OLIVER: No. Why do you think I'd want to?

MARY: Well, night has fallen, hasn't it?

OLIVER: Naturally. Night must fall.

MARY: Precisely. Oh, dear, I'll try to be brave.

OLIVER (*tapping her knee*): There's a good sport.

MARY: I'm trying to be that, too. My mother wasn't mad, though.

OLIVER: Did I say she was?

MARY: I shouldn't like anyone to make sport of my mother, mad or otherwise

OLIVER: Goes for me, too.

MARY: Where have you left that abominable girl?

OLIVER: Rosy? In her room.

MARY: Not in a dustbin?

OLIVER: No. Why should I leave her in a dustbin?

MARY: I only wondered. I like exploiting every possible possibility.

OLIVER: This omelette is really good. What are the five ingredients?

MARY: Onion, parsley, ham, sultanas – the fifth is my secret.

OLIVER: Tell me. I won't whisper it to a soul. Solemn promise.

MARY: Can't you make a guess ?

OLIVER: Not in the mood to guess. Tell me. Go on.

MARY: Egg.

OLIVER: Of course. Stupid of me.

MARY: You're far from stupid. If you were younger I think I'd have proposed to you.

OLIVER: How old do you think I am?

MARY: Either twenty or eighty.

OLIVER: Good guess. I'm twenty-four.

MARY: When is your birthday?

OLIVER (*wagging his finger at her*): Wicked, wicked! I know what you're trying to trap me into revealing.

MARY: No, no. Just a harmless question. Really.

OLIVER: It's not the twenty-fifth of December.

MARY: How disappointing! I was so hoping it might have been.

OLIVER: I know you were. It's the thirtieth of April.

MARY: What an awkward day! In fact... (*She rises suddenly and stares at him with suspicion and alarm, then walks quickly to the window and frowns out at the storm*)

OLIVER, *smiling and whistling softly, regards her back in a sinister sort of way, meanwhile making a tinkling tattoo with his knife and fork on his plate.*

MARY (*turning abruptly*): Was it late at night you were born?

OLIVER: Ten minutes to midnight. So my mother told me. (*He stops the tinkling tattoo*)

MARY: Oh, God! Save me! What have I done?

Eileen appears at the door.

EILEEN: Was that the phone?

OLIVER: No. It was me. My knife and fork. (*He tinkles them by way of illustration*)

Henry appears.

HENRY: Was that the phone ?

OLIVER: No. My knife and fork. (*Tinkling again*)

HENRY: Oh, damn!

Rosemary appears.

ROSEMARY: Was that the phone?

OLIVER: No. I tinkled my knife and fork. Go back to bed, sweetie.

ROSEMARY (*sighing*): Poor me. I'm either being told to go to bed, or not to get into bed.

OLIVER: Quite right. The first is O.K., the second might be immoral.

MARY: May heaven have mercy on me! I've been dealing with the Devil. (*She has turned from the window and they see that she is holding a knife, the point of the blade pressed against her chest*)

EILEEN & HENRY: Aunt Mary! (*Two simultaneous shouts of alarm*)

HENRY: I say!

MARY: Don't come near or I'll do it this very second. I'll plunge it deep.

HENRY: Where did you get that knife from?

MARY: In a moment as melodramatic as this you really oughtn't to ask such a prosaic question.

HENRY: Drop that knife! Drop it!

ROSEMARY: No, don't drop it! Stab yourself! Please!

MARY: Who votes that I should stab myself? Show your thumbs!

Rosemary promptly gives the thumbs-down sign. Oliver gives the thumbs-up.
MARY: One for, one against. Eileen, your vote! Henry, your vote!
EILEEN: Aunt Mary, please! Please!
HENRY: Cut out this tomfoolery, can't you?
MARY: I'm waiting for your votes. I mean it. I'm going to stab myself. I'm in
    earnest.
HENRY: Oh, Lord! Humour her, Eileen. Humour her. (*He gives the thumbs-up*)
Eileen, sighing heavily, gives the thumbs-up.
MARY: Very well. The majority has it. Democracy wins. (*She drops the knife and begins
    to sway forward. Oliver rises and dashes to the rescue and she swoons into his arms*)
ROSEMARY: Oh, well done, sir! Good show! Neat work! (*Clapping vigorously*)
At that instant the phone begins to ring.
HENRY: Thank heavens! At last! (*He rushes towards the phone, and so does Eileen
    and so does Rosemary. Before any of them can reach it it stops ringing.*
HENRY: Damn and blast! (*All simultaneously*)
EILEEN: Oh, Lord! (*All simultaneously*)
ROSEMARY: Jumping Jeez! (*All simultaneously*)
MARY (*miraculously recovered from her faint*): It sometimes happens like that. I hate
    telephones.
HENRY: Perhaps I'd better give them a tinkle. This won't do. This suspense is
    driving me mad.
OLIVER: Better not, sir. These hospitals don't like being pestered. They promised
    to give you a ring, didn't they? Give them a chance.
HENRY: Surely by now they ought to know if she's out of danger.
MARY: Some people take a long time to decide on dying.
ROSEMARY: I wish *you* wouldn't.
HENRY: Rosemary, stop making remarks like that.
ROSEMARY: You're right. How right you are. The time has come for me to make
    some resolutions.
HENRY: Sssssh! Go to your bed.
ROSEMARY: *This* time you aren't suppressing me. I'm determined to make a
    change. The moment has come for me to develop.
OLIVER: You look developed enough to me.
ROSEMARY: It's not my figure I mean, you sucker! It's my character.
EILEEN: That, alas, will never change.
ROSEMARY: It's got to, if all's to end well. What would they say tomorrow?
HENRY: Who is "they"?
MARY: The critics, she means.
ROSEMARY: Of course. Anybody nasty enough to pass a frank opinion. They
    won't like it. (*Wringing her hands*) I've *got* to do something, and do it quickly.
EILEEN: Why don't you fall down dead:
ROSEMARY: That won't do. Too inartistic. You can't kill off a character
like me without a good reason. You think I'm Hamlet?
EILEEN: I wish that phone would ring.
ROSEMARY: You're saying that too often. That's called repetition.
MARY: Can't you gag yourself?
ROSEMARY: I can't. The situation is too urgent. You're all right. You've developed.

See how different you are from yesterday? Ollie, too. Ollie isn't the same. And Aunt Eileen, after being a wet-blanket and a prude, is now a sultry bitch panting to get into bed with Ollie.

HENRY: Be silent, Rosemary! Be silent!

ROSEMARY: Even you in your hangdog fashion have changed a bit, Uncle Henry. Yesterday evening you were complacent and dull as dish water. Tonight you're as fidgety as a tomcat on a cold tin roof, You've all changed. Only I am still the psycho girl, mad to jump about and smash things up and say outrageous things. Still trying to impress everybody.

EILEEN: How dismally true!

ROSEMARY: Of course it's true. I'm not afraid to face the truth. I want to face the truth. I'm a realist. I'm not a sentimental idealist. I don't want unilateral nuclear disarmament. I don't want nationalisation. I'm not a Liberal or a Socialist. I'm not even a Tory, even though I've never had things so good as I've had them now. But I've *got* to change. I want to be like the rest of you and develop into something I wasn't yesterday. I'm not fulfilling my destiny. (*She goes to the window, and immediately lightning flashes*) Jeez! Was that a dagger or a fork I saw?

Thunder rolls.

MARY: It was a rolling-pin.

ROSEMARY: You might be right. (*Staring out at the storm*) Anything can happen now. This is a moment of significance. (*Pointing tensely*) Look!

OLIVER: What's it? A fox struck by a thunderbolt?

ROSEMARY: No, not a fox.

MARY: An owl having triplets?

ROSEMARY: No, not that, either. This is something bigger. This is something beautiful. (*Sighing*) I feel transfigured. It's my vision. It's my vision! At last! At last!

Lightning flashes again. Thunder.

ROSEMARY: This is it, folks! Lightning has entered my veins. A thousand jewels of fire are thundering down the tunnels and runnels of my being, and my heart is bursting. It's a bursting sun of radioactive heat. Look! Oh, look yonder over the rim of the border!

OLIVER: What now? The Four Horsemen?

ROSEMARY: No. Only a man in a chariot. Oh, how exciting.

MARY: It's Ben Hur. (*Lightning. Thunder.*)

ROSEMARY: The storm is at its height, and the chariot rushes through the warring elements. Oh, what a spectacle! (*She claps*) Thanks! Thanks! Oh, thanks for the spectacle! Mr. Samuel Goldwyn couldn't have done it better. Mr. Cecil B. de Mille lies overshadowed. Soon, soon the music of the spheres will envelop me and transport me to realms unknown to Sir Edmund Hillary. High, high above Mount Everest… High, high above the stratosphere into the glorious expanse above the Steppes where all is harmony, harmony, cosmic rays and U-2 planes! Listen! Oh, God! Listen.

Music begins to sound. It is the Pilgrims Chorus from Tannhauser.

ROSEMARY (*swaying herself to the lilt of the music waving her hands*): Oh, divine music! Coming from outer space! Relayed from Jodrell Bank! Brought on the wake of who knows what wonderful flying saucer!

OLIVER: It's the Third Programme. I just switched it on.

ROSEMARY (*starting round as though stung*): You vandal! You evil, dirty twerp! You sizzling, stinking wrecker of beautiful dreams! Oh, I can tear your liver out! (*She collapses, sobbing wildly*)

The phone begins to ring. Oliver rushes to switch off the wireless. Eileen and Henry rush towards the instrument. Eileen gets there first.

EILEEN (*putting phone to her ear*): Yes? Borderline Farm. Is that the hospital? Yes... *They all grow silent and rigid and gaze at her, hanging on her every word.*

EILEEN: Yes... I see... Yes... (*Long, long pause*) Oh... Oh... I see... (*Long pause. They begin to fidget as they wait for her to go on*). Thanks. (*Quietly, limply, Eileen puts back the phone on its cradle. She stares round from one to the other of them*)

HENRY: Well?

ROSEMARY: What?

OLIVER: How?

MARY: What's happened? Has she crossed the Border?

EILEEN (*after a terrible pause*): They say she's turned the corner.

Pause. Then:

ROSEMARY: But we knew that all along.

HENRY: How?

ROSEMARY: She was always round the bend.

Brief pause – then Eileen begins to laugh – in jerks, then loud and hysterically. Henry joins in, in deep guffaws. Then Oliver and Rosemary. Then Mary utters a long, weird whinnying laugh. They are all convulsed with laughter when lightning flashes vividly and thunder crashes out. And –

THE CURTAIN FALLS

(*End*)

THE TWISTED MAN

A Play in three acts

The Cast
Timothy Cuttridge
Penny Harrow
Harry Leaver
Bill Harrow
Louise Harrow
Grace Benton-Mearns

Time: February 1958

The scene throughout is in the sitting-room of Timothy Cuttridge's Holland
Park flat

Act One
Thursday evening

Act Two
Scene One – Monday evening after supper
Scene Two – same evening – 11.30

Act Three
The following evening – 9.45

*The scene is the sitting room of a rather large flat in Holland Park. There are four doors,
three of which open into bedrooms, one into the hallway. It is nearly ten o'clock on a Thursday
evening in February 1958.*

*The room is tastefully, if austerely, furnished. The furniture is definitely modern, though
the pictures on the walls are a mixture of the old and the new schools of art. David's 'Madame
Recamier' is well featured with, on either side, two van Gogh landscapes. They are good
prints in suitable frames, the David in a heavy ornate frame of dark brown. There is also
Vermeer's 'Head of a Girl' and a Paul Nash battlefield scene.*

*The floor is close-fitted with a carpet of plain buff, and at extreme right there is a low
divan which can be used as a bed. Easy chairs and a drinks cabinet are other items of
furniture. At the extreme left are a writing table and an upright chair. There is a typewriter,
and beside it stacks of manuscripts and one or two books. At the extreme right is another
small table – and occasional table rather than a writing table – and near it an upright
chair like the one near the table at left.*

When the curtain rises, we see TIMOTHY CUTTRIDGE *at the writing table. He is clicking away at the typewriter – working on his novel. He is a man of medium height and build, dark, thirty-eight, rather handsome, but not by any means in a film-star way. A stern handsomeness that goes well with the tasteful austerity of the room.*

At the other side, HARRY LEAVER *is sitting before the other table. He is of medium height too, sandy-haired, and rather frail in build. He is thirty-two, but, mentally, is about four. He is a mental deficient. At curtain up, we see him with a slight smile, vacuous but good natured, as he patiently builds a tower with coloured children's blocks.*

Flat on her stomach on the carpet, heels in the air, wearing bright-blue jeans and a crimson shirt, Penelope Harrow – PENNY *– is engrossed in a comic paper. She is thirteen, with fair hair (she has a ponytail) and a precociously developed figure. She is on the short side.*

The only sound is the click-click of Tim Cuttridge's's typewriter. Then suddenly, Harry's absurdly tall tower of blocks wavers and comes crashing down. Harry chuckles and wags his head, philosophically, good-naturedly.

HARRY (*in piping tenor*): Too high, always too high. (*He starts to build again, in no way discouraged*)

Silence again, except the click-click of the typewriter. No one takes any notice of Harry or of what happened to the tower. Then Penny suddenly giggles.

TIM (*glancing round at her with a frown*): Those nasty comic papers again?
PENNY: They're not nasty. They're exciting.
Tim grunts and goes on typing. Silence again. Click-click of the typewriter. Harry builds.
    His tower crashes.
HARRY: Too high. Always too high. (*He begins to build again*)
TIM (*turning again*): Where's your sister? Where's Helen?
PENNY (*glancing up*): Helen? She's somewhere. Out.
TIM: Yes, but she shouldn't be out at this time. It's nearly ten.
PENNY: That's early.
TIM: Opinions differ, of course.
PENNY: She's sixteen. When I'm sixteen, I'm going to stay out until midnight.
TIM: I wouldn't be at all surprised.
Another silence. He resumes his typing. Then Penny giggles.
PENNY: He's going to rape her. I'm sure of it.
TIM: What? What's that?
PENNY: Badman Gringo. He's the villain.
Tim grunts deprecatingly, scowls and toys with a book.
PENNY: He has his eye on Flighty Kate. I'm sure he wants to rape her. In next
    week's instalment I'll know. (*She sits up slowly*)
TIM: How old are you, Penny?
PENNY: Thirteen. You've forgotten my age?
TIM: On the contrary.
PENNY (*pushing out her bosom and stretching to emphasise it*): But very developed
    for thirteen. Everybody says so. Helen envies me.
TIM: Where *is* Helen? Don't you know where she's gone to?
PENNY: I think she's at a skiffle party. She might be back by eleven.
TIM: One night she might never get back.
PENNY: Why?

TIM: If you'd read the newspapers instead of these silly comic things you'd know why.

PENNY: Every Sunday I read the *News of the World*.

TIM: Then you *should* know what I mean.

PENNY (*giggling*): Of course I know, stupid! You mean one night she might be indecently assaulted and strangled.

TIM: Where are your schoolbooks? Haven't you any homework?

PENNY: Oh, I polished that off before supper.

TIM: Why not have another go at it? This time you can polish it up.

PENNY (*flinging down the comic paper, rising and crossing to him*): Tim, you are sweet. (*Stroking his hair*) Sometimes you remind me of Badman Gringo. Dark and handsome. I believe one day you're going to try to rape me.

TIM: I can foresee where you are going to end up.

PENNY: Where?

TIM: An approved school. That's where precocious children of your particular mental slant generally end up.

PENNY (*giggling and stroking his hair*): I'm not worrying about it.

TIM: Nobody in this place seems to worry about anything. Not even your parents seem worried about you two girls.

PENNY: Are *you* worried about Helen and me?

TIM: If you were my daughters I'd be depressed – not merely worried.

PENNY: Oh, you are sweet! So cross – but not really cross. How is your novel getting on? Has the hero raped the heroine yet?

TIM: Is that all you think about? Rape?

PENNY: No. I think about love, too. That's why I'm stroking your hair like this. I think you're a thrilling man. I don't look upon you as an uncle at all.

TIM: You don't have to mention that. Leave my head alone. Get away and do something useful for a change.

PENNY: I love stroking your hair. I wish you'd stroke mine.

He sits still, staring at his typewriter and drumming nervously with his fingers on the table. There is a certain tension in his manner.
Harry's tower crashes.

HARRY: Too high. Always, always too high. (*He begins to build again*)

PENNY: I like oldish men like you. (*Pushing her face suddenly before his*) Now you look *exactly* like Badman Gringo. (*Giggling teasingly*)

TIM (*very serious*): I think I've told you before, Penny. I don't like this sort of thing.

PENNY: What sort of thing?

TIM (*gesturing nervously*): This – this mauling me about.

PENNY: Oh but you do. I know you do. I have instinct.

TIM: I believe you have. Too much – far too much, especially for your age.

PENNY: Anyway, you're not really my uncle. You're only Daddy's good friend. So that makes it all right between us.

He rises in sudden agitation and paces off.

PENNY: Poor dear! Now I've upset him!

TIM: Isn't there something on TV you'd like to see?

PENNY (*snapping her fingers*): Phew! Holy Gringo! Thanks for reminding me, Badman! Billy and his guitar are on the air! (*She dashes away and exits through a door at right into bedroom*)

TIM (*sighing*): Thank God that television set is kept in the bedroom. Hope it will always be kept in there.

Harry gets up and comes to him, smiles and puts out his hand.

HARRY: A little poison, Timmy? A little poison for me to drink?

Tim solemnly pretends to take a phial from his pocket, and as solemnly pretends to pour a few drops into a glass. He hands the mythical glass to Harry who takes it and quaffs off the "poison". It is a childish game that Harry loves to play, and Tim never refuses to indulge him.

HARRY (*smacking his lips and sighing ecstatically*): Ah-h-h-h! I love to drink poison! It does me good.

Tim begins to move back to his writing table. Harry goes to his table, opens a drawer and takes out a copy of the Evening News. He hurries across with it to Tim.

HARRY: Look, Tim, I was waiting for a chance to give this to you. (*Glancing about with elaborate furtiveness, as if fearful of being overheard*) The *Evening News*. Mrs. Newby on the ground floor said I could have it. I did her shopping for her this morning.

TIM: Thanks, Harry – but I've seen the evening paper already. I read it on the train on my way home.

HARRY: This one? This same one?

TIM: No, the *Standard*. I generally read the *Standard*.

HARRY: But Mrs. Newby said this was the *Evening News*. This may have something different in it. Couldn't you read it for me and see if it has anything about poisonings?

TIM (*taking the paper indulgently and opening it at front page*): All the news is the same. (*Glancing down the columns, then opening it and glancing at other pages briefly*) No. I don't see anything about poisonings, Harry. They seem to have taken a holiday from that sort of thing today.

HARRY: No poisoning today, eh? What about your things? The things you like to read about? Coshings and so on?

TIM: Oh, there's been a coshing all right. Hardly a day passes without a coshing or a strangling.

HARRY: Who is it this time?

TIM: Bank manager and two clerks ambushed by thugs. Hit on the head with crowbars, and then bound and gagged. (*Throwing paper aside in disgust*) What's the use? What's the use? Let them continue. (*He begins to pace about*)

HARRY: Very bad fellows. I know. Very bad. You'd kill them off, wouldn't you? The thugs and the cosh-boys and the stranglers?

TIM: Every one of them, Harry. Human vermin. They should all be treated like lice, bedbugs, cockroaches – and exterminated. But what's the use of telling anyone that? They think me a psychopath when I express such views.

HARRY: You write about that in your books, don't you?

TIM: Yes. That's why I can't get a publisher to publish one of them.

HARRY: Never mind, Timmy. You go on writing. One day a publisher will get
    coshed – and then he'll publish your books.
TIM: Who knows? Perhaps. All right. Go back to your blocks. I must see if I can
    get some more writing done.
HARRY: You don't find it hard? Working all day in an office and then coming
    home and writing your books?
TIM: No, I like it. Good relaxation. If you were a civil servant like me you'd
    know what a pleasant change it makes.
HARRY: Could you give me a little more poison, Timmy, before I go back to my
    blocks? (*They go through the mime again*)
HARRY (*smacking his lips, sighing*): Thanks, Timmy. You're very good to me. How
    I love to drink poison! (*He goes back to his blocks*)

*Tim is just settling down at his writing table again when the bedroom door opens and
Penny comes in.*

PENNY: Oh, Tim, come and hear Billy and his guitar. He's wonderful tonight.
    Really, really smashing.
TIM (*waving her off*): Go back. Go back into the room.
PENNY: Yes, but I want you to come with me. I like company when I'm listening
    to Billy and his guitar.
TIM: But I *don't* want to listen to Billy and his guitar.
PENNY (*giggling*): You know, I believe you are afraid to be alone with me in a
    room.

He says nothing. Begins to pick at his typewriter.

PENNY (*standing behind his chair and stroking his hair*): You find me too much of a
    temptation, don't you? Admit it.
TIM (*patiently*): Penny, will you go back into the room to your television programme?
PENNY (*undaunted, still stroking his hair*): You don't fool me one bit. You're dying
    to take me in your arms.
TIM (*losing his temper, rising*): Get out! Do you hear me! Get back into that room!

*Penny backs away slowly, smiling. At the bedroom door she pauses, wags her finger at
him.*

PENNY: One night you're going to follow me into this room. I know you will. My
    instinct tells me so. (*She goes into the room, shutting the door*)
HARRY (*glancing at Tim*): Penny is bothering you, eh, Timmy?

Tim says nothing. Taps away at his typewriter.

HARRY: She can be very naughty sometimes. (*After a pause*) Where are Bill and
    Louise tonight, Tim?
TIM: Maida Vale. A party. It's Bill's mother's birthday.
HARRY: Yes, I remember now. I did hear Louise say something about it. (*After a
    pause*) I wish my mother was still alive. I can remember her. A little. Just a
    little.

Tim says nothing. Types on.

HARRY: I can remember that black hat with the tiny purple berries she used to wear. I liked it.

TIM: She was wearing it that day in Aldwych when the doodlebug fell.

HARRY: Yes, yes. Louise told me that, I remember. And Dad was with her in the bus. They were both killed together.

TIM: Mercifully, yes. Would have been much more horrible if one had been killed and the other left alive.

HARRY: Louise has been good to me. A good sister. She didn't mind me living with her and Bill and Helen and Penny.

TIM: She oughtn't to. You earn your keep. Shopping for her and helping with the chores in the flat.

HARRY: You're very good, too, Tim. Good to me and good to Bill and Louise. This flat is yours, isn't it?

TIM: Yes, yes, it's mine alright. Another twelve years on the lease to go.

HARRY: It's good of you to let Bill and Louise and the rest of us share it with you.

Tim types on, pauses, types.

HARRY: You and Bill were in the war together, Tim, weren't you?

TIM: Mm. The RAF.

HARRY: You used to fly together in planes and drop bombs?

TIM: That's right. Until one night we had to drop ourselves and get put into a prisoner-of-war camp.

HARRY: That must have been exciting. Did they give you any lovely poison to drink in the camp?

TIM: Lots and lots of it.

They hear footsteps and voices.

HARRY: That must be Bill and Louise. (*He hurries to open the door*)

William Harrow – BILL – and his wife, LOUISE, appear, both in overcoats: Bill in a dirty grey macintosh, Louise in a dark-green coat of fairly good appearance. Bill is shortish, tough-looking, balding, ginger-haired, with a round, extravert type face. Louise, fair, tallish, good figure, good features of a somewhat distinguished cut, the introvert type. She is thirty-five to Bill's thirty-seven.

BILL: Thank you, Harry boy. Thank you. Brrrr! (*Slapping and shaking his macintosh*) Simply pelting down outside there!

HARRY: You mean it's raining, Bill?

BILL: That's it. You've got the idea first go. Rain and sleet – in big bucketfuls. (*With a glance at Tim*): How's literature this evening, Tschaikowsky?

LOUISE: Tschaikowsky?

BILL: Isn't that right?

LOUISE (*in a slightly superior voice*): Tschaikowsky was a musician.

BILL: Was he? Sorry, sorry. My mistake. Only an ignorant railway-clerk. Got to excuse me. What's the name of the big novelist johnny with the tongue-twister of a Russian name?

LOUISE: You probably mean Dostoievsky.

BILL: That's the bloke I was after!

TIM: I can see your mother must have been free with the beer.

BILL: Can't complain. Good for the weather. Ale for the plebs – sherry for the gentry. Meaning my wife, of course.

HARRY: Why do you always call Louise gentry, Bill?

BILL (*coughing ostentatiously*): Never mind, Harry lad! That'll strain your brain-works, if I try to explain it.

LOUISE: It might strain yours, too. Tim, where are the girls? Are they out?

TIM: Penny is at home – but Helen is out.

LOUISE: That skiffle party, I suppose. She ought to have been back by now.

TIM: I agree. I happened to remark the same thing myself not very long ago.

BILL: Helen's all right. Tough like her father. Can take care of herself.

LOUISE: All the same, I'm beginning to think it was a mistake giving her a latchkey.

BILL: Can't say I think so. But who am I to talk? I'm not a psychology expert like some people I know.

TIM: Go to bed, sergeant-pilot! Sleep off Mama's beer.

BILL: Right, squadron-leader! (*Coming to attention and saluting*) Send my wife into me when you've had your powwow on books and coming authors!

HARRY: Penny is in the room looking at the TV, Bill. You'll never be able to sleep. (*Harry is at his table with his blocks*)

BILL: I'll take a look myself until I fall off. (*He suddenly sees the comic paper Penny threw aside*) What's this? Penny's comic rag? (*He picks it up*) I've been following up something in here. There's a hot number called Flora the Flapper. She strips and gets into her bath every week. (*He begins to look through the paper*) Here she is! This is my cup of tea. (*He sinks down into an easy chair and grows absorbed in the paper*)

LOUISE (*who has lit a cigarette and given it to Tim, and lit one for herself. She is standing near his chair*): Well, how's it coming along now, Tim?

TIM: Perfectly – from *my* point of view.

LOUISE: But very imperfectly from *their* point of view?

TIM: Exactly. Sure rejection slip in it. I can feel it in my bones.

LOUISE: That last chapter has whang! I liked it.

HARRY (*turning*): What's whang, Louise? I don't know that word.

LOUISE: It's a word I've coined myself. It means guts.

HARRY: Mrs. Newby told me this morning I've got guts. She said: 'Harry, you can't read and write, but you've got guts.' Does that mean I've got whang, Louise?

Tim and Louise laugh.

TIM (*indulgently*): That's right, Harry. Lots and lots of whang in you.

HARRY: One day I'm going to build a high, high tower – and it won't fall. The whang in me will help me do it. (*He goes on building*)

BILL: (*with a hoot of laughter*): What a female! What a female! Why can't I run into something like this in our canteen! Blimey!

LOUISE: She's too strong a cup of tea, dear. They wouldn't brew her in any railway canteen, It would be against the rules.

BILL (*glancing at her*): Clever, clever. Put that in your novel, Tim.

Harry's tower crashes.

HARRY: Too high, always too high.

Penny appears at the bedroom door. She stands looking at Tim, a coquettish smile on her face, trying to look as sophisticated as possible. No one takes any notice of her for a moment.

LOUISE: I think you're just a bit *too* serious, though, you know, Tim. You should spice it here and there with some humour, dear. That might carry it off.
TIM: I'm no good at humour. My humour always sounds strained and heavy-handed.

A silence. Bill gives another hoot of laughter, slapping his thigh. Penny continues to stare at Tim. Then Louise notices her.

LOUISE: If you've finished looking at your TV, go to bed, Penny.
PENNY: I'm looking at something else, now. My big, bad boyfriend.
HARRY: Penny has been bothering Tim, Louise. She has been very naughty.
PENNY: Please, Uncle Harry! Don't exaggerate. Timmy liked it. I'm never a bother to him.
LOUISE: Has she been making herself a nuisance, Tim?
TIM (*shrugging*): Being precocious, as usual.
PENNY (*giggling*): I was making passionate love to him. He's such a sweet thing. Just like Badman Gringo.
LOUISE: Stop all that idiocy. Or at least keep it to yourself and your companions.
PENNY: The trouble is I don't like idiots like myself, Mummy. I like clever oldish men like Tim.
Louise laughs.
TIM (*snorting*): It's no laughing matter, Louise. You should take her seriously. I'm warning you and Bill about these two misses. You don't worry enough. This one is heading straight for an approved school...
PENNY (*interrupting quickly*): And the other one for a strangler's hands.
LOUISE (*with a frown at Penny*): What is *that* supposed to mean?
PENNY: Didn't you know? Tim is sure Helen is going to be raped and strangled one night.
BILL: What's this Sunday-paper conversation about now? Who did you say was going to be raped and strangled?
LOUISE: All right. Let's not take it any further. Penny, go to bed.
PENNY (*moving to Tim and running her fingers through his hair*): I invited Tim to look at telly with me, but he was afraid to be in the same room with me alone. He thinks me too tempting, Mummy.

Bill and Louise burst out into uproarious laughter.

TIM (*rising, furious*): That's it! Laugh. Wonderful joke. Instead of putting her across your knee and giving her the spanking of her life, you laugh. That's why there are so many delinquents cluttering up the streets. It's parental attitudes like this that do it!
BILL: Mr. Victorian Cuttridge on his soapbox in Hyde Park.
LOUISE (*getting serious*): No, Tim is quite right, Bill. We're too slack with Helen

and Penny. Penny, let this be the last time I hear you talking all this junk about Tim's being your boyfriend. You're too young for that kind of talk.

PENNY (*throwing out her bosom*): Not in figure.

BILL (*with a hoot of laughter*): She's got you there!

LOUISE (*still serious*): A figure doesn't make you an adult. It's your mind.

PENNY: Then Uncle Harry isn't an adult.

TIM (*furious, grips her shoulder and shakes her*): Stop that, stop that!

PENNY (*delighted*): See! He simply can't keep his hands off me.

Bill hides his face behind the paper, doubled up with laughter. Louise tries to frown at him.

LOUISE: Bill! Bill! I'm ashamed of you! (*Then she, too, succumbs to laughter*)

Harry rises and approaches the furiously pacing Tim.

HARRY: Never mind, Tim. Penny is very naughty. (*He pats Tim's shoulder*) You mustn't let her upset you. (*Tim ignores him and continues to pace*)

LOUISE (*approaching Tim and putting an arm about him*): Tim dear, you're quite right. We really shouldn't laugh it off like this.

TIM (*halting but not shaking her off*): It's alright, Louise. You needn't put on an act. I'm a damned fool – and I know I'm a damned fool. If I will keep putting my nose into your domestic affairs I deserve to be laughed at. Don't stop. Laugh your head off.

PENNY: See how angry he's getting, Daddy! It's the love in him for me.

LOUISE (*darting at her, slapping her head*): Stop that! Stop that!

BILL: Hey, hey! What's this wildcat display for, Louise! Why're you hitting her?

LOUISE (*really angry*): Because she deserves it. Go to bed, Penny.

HARRY (*wagging his finger in the face of the surprised Penny*): You're very naughty, Penny. Go to bed.

BILL (*serious now*): Blimey! But there's no need to cut up so rough. She was only pulling Tim's leg.

LOUISE: Well, that's no way for her to pull his leg. She's thirteen. Tim is thirty-eight – a year older than you, her father. She must have some respect for him.

BILL (*shrugging*): Go on, then. Lam into her. Hit her about – if that makes you feel better. (*He rises and throws down the paper, in a sulk*) Strikes me the big author is beginning to cast his influence over you in more ways than one.

LOUISE: And what is that remark supposed to signify?

BILL (*striking a pose and mimicking her*): "And what is that remark supposed to signify"? Grammar-school girl addresses Council school boy!

LOUISE (*sighing*): I don't know when you'll outgrow that inferiority chip.

TIM: Shrug it off, you mean. You don't outgrow a chip on the shoulder. Excuse my preciseness!

PENNY: Oh Lord! Another quarrel – and all over me!

LOUISE: Penny, I think I told you to go to bed.

PENNY: I heard you, Mother. (*She moves towards the bedroom door*)

HARRY (*moving after her, wagging his finger*): Naughty, naughty girl!

BILL: I'd better go to my bed, too, and leave the educated people to talk in peace.

Penny goes into bedroom.

LOUISE: Yes, go and sleep off your chip.

BILL (*piqued*): Look, if I've got a chip on my blinkin' shoulder, it's mine. Right? And it's bloody well going to stay there. Right?

LOUISE: You exasperate me sometimes, Bill – that's the truth. Life in this flat would be so much less complicated if you could only forget your father was a bus-driver and that you work in a railway goods office.

BILL: Why should I forget that?

LOUISE: Because there's nothing disgraceful in working at the railway and having a father who was a bus-driver. And when something isn't disgraceful it should be simple to forget it.

BILL: Have you forgotten that your old man was a grocer who piled up a nice little bit for himself? Have you forgotten that you lived in a comfortable home in the suburbs and had a good schooling? Has Tim forgotten he's a public school boy and that he works in Somerset House? Bet you not! Bet you he remembers the old solicitor father in Sunningdale. Why must I forget where I came from and where I work!

TIM: Go to bed, sergeant-pilot!

BILL (*coming to attention and saluting*): Right, Squadron-leader Dust-off-Piss-key! Teach the wife how to deal with vermin, then send her into bed to spray me with a strong solution of DDT! Goodnight, sir! (*He about-turns military fashion, and goes striding off and out through the door at left*)

LOUISE (*sighing*): That's done it! You've got him so red-hot mad now he won't even change into pyjamas. He's going to fling himself down and sleep in all his clothes.

TIM: Won't do him any harm.

LOUISE: The two of you are a pair. He with his social-inferiority chip – and you with your bigger chip –

TIM: Oh, mine is much bigger than a chip. It's a block. A blooming block.

HARRY: "Block"? Like my blocks, Timmy?

TIM (*with a hard bark of laughter*): Much bigger than yours, Harry. Much, much bigger. Ask Louise to tell you how big.

At this point they hear a metallic clattering noise outside, followed by uproarious laughter and then shrill screaming. A feminine sound. Fear and terror in it. They all spring to their feet.

HARRY: What's that outside, Tim?

LOUISE: My god! I wonder if it can be Helen and her lot. I'd better go down and see –

TIM (*gripping her arm*): You'll go nowhere. I'll go down.

Running footsteps and more uproarious laughter sound. Another scream. Tim moves towards the door that opens onto the hallway. Louise, as though just remembering something, darts after him, and taps his hip pocket, tries to hold him back.

LOUISE: Tim!

TIM: What is it? What is it?

LOUISE: You've got that – that thing in your hip pocket, haven't you?

TIM: My automatic pistol? Of course I have. What about it?

LOUISE: You're still going around with it? You shouldn't, you know. You haven't even got a licence for it.

TIM: Don't let that bother you.

LOUISE: But why must you keep it on you? What are you afraid of?

TIM: It's a precaution. Against human vermin. I'm not you or Bill, understand. I have no sentimentality about cockroaches and lice – insect or human.

LOUISE (*releasing his arm*): All right, all right. Go and see what's happening down there – but try not to shoot anyone, darling, for heaven's sake!

Tim goes. We hear his footsteps thumping down the stairs. Louise shuts the door, sighing.

LOUISE: Oh, dear! Sometimes Tim does frighten me.

HARRY: Not me. Tim never frightens me. He's too good. He could never frighten me.

LOUISE: He's got a warp in him, though. No doubt about it. Something twisted inside him.

HARRY: Tim likes me. He gives me poison when I ask him.

LOUISE (*chuckling*): You still play that silly game, do you? By the way, did you get through all the shopping this morning?

HARRY: Yes, I got it all done. But they had no Danish butter at the grocer's. They were out of stock, they said. I had to get English butter. And I got the salami from the Italian shop. I never forget anything.

LOUISE: Yes, you certainly have a remarkable memory for a shopping list.

HARRY: Did they work you very hard at the office today, Louise dear?

LOUISE: No, can't say so. The boss was in a very good mood. Things were a bit slack, for a change, too.

HARRY: I'm glad. You should ask your boss to let you bring home some of your letters and type them on Tim's typewriter.

LOUISE: Not so easy, Harry. (*Laughing indulgently*) They've got to be done on the spot and posted off the same day. (*Suddenly*) Did that woman on the ground floor ask you to do her shopping again today?

HARRY: Who? Mrs. Newby? Yes, I did her shopping. She gave me an *Evening News*. I brought it up for Tim. (*Suddenly*) Oh! but I shouldn't have told you that. (*Looking about him furtively*) It's all part of our secrets.

LOUISE: Secrets? What do you mean? What secrets?

HARRY: Sssh! Mrs. Newby and I have secrets. I can't say anything about them. It wouldn't be right.

LOUISE (*frowning at him in a keen way. After a pause*): Look here, Harry, tell me something. Does she ever take you into her bedroom?

HARRY: Sssh! How did you guess? That's part of our secret doings.

LOUISE: I see. So you do secret things together during the morning, down there! I might have guessed it. She looks that sort!

HARRY: She's very nice. And she treats me well. She's taught me really nice little things. I enjoy them all. But she says I must never, never talk about them. They're secrets just between her and me.

LOUISE: Let's hope to heaven her husband doesn't get to hear about them.

HARRY: She says he wouldn't mind. He doesn't like her anymore. He doesn't kiss her, she says. He only kisses other women – much younger women.

Penny suddenly comes out of her room. She is in a nightgown, with a dressing-gown over it.

PENNY: Mummy, did you hear all that noise outside? I believe someone has been hurt down in the basement.

LOUISE: Were you looking out of the window? Did you see who it was running off?

PENNY: I looked out. I've been looking out for the past few minutes – but couldn't see anything. I heard Tim's voice, though. He seems to be talking to Mrs. Baxton. I wonder if she was assaulted in any way.

LOUISE: What sort of way?

PENNY: Oh, I don't mean indecently. She's much too much of a fright for that. I meant an ordinary cosh assault. I hear she has jewellery.

They hear footsteps thumping up the stairs. Tim comes in.

LOUISE: What happened, Tim?

TIM: Hooliganism. Hooliganism as usual. And this is supposed to be a respectable neighbourhood!

LOUISE: It wasn't Helen and her crowd, was it?

TIM: I don't think so – though I wouldn't be surprised. They all ran off after kicking an ash-bin down into the basement area and nearly frightening the wits out of Mrs. Baxton.

HARRY: Naughty, naughty, naughty.

LOUISE: Harry, you'd better go and get your blanket and things and get settled in bed. (*She moves to the divan and begins to strip it of its covering. She folds up covering*) Penny, back in your room.

Harry goes out at left.

PENNY: Did they assault Mrs. Baxton, Timmy dear?

TIM: Did you hear what your mother said! Get back to your room.

LOUISE: Go on, Penny. Go on. No idiotic questions! Get out!

PENNY: Poor me. I can't even ask polite questions now. Life can be hard for intelligent teenagers! (*She goes out, back to her room*)

Tim goes to his writing-table and seats himself before his typewriter.

LOUISE: Are you going to go on working, Tim?

TIM: May as well. Helen hasn't come in yet, you know!

LOUISE: I'm sick of talking to Helen. I've told her dozens of times she must try to be home by ten, at the latest.

TIM: Talk! Sick of *talking* to her! Why don't you stop talking and *do* something about it!

LOUISE: What would you like me to do? I can't tie her down to a chair in the flat here, can I?

TIM: No. But you can manhandle her a bit, though. Give her a sound whacking once or twice, and she'll begin to take notice and come in earlier.

LOUISE: Tim dear, you puzzle me. I thought you were all against violence. Isn't that what you say in your novels? That people who commit violence against the human person and property should be treated as vermin and exterminated?

TIM: I know I preach that – but I think I've stipulated that there is constructive violence and destructive violence. The violence committed by your cosh-boys and thugs and smash-and-grab raiders is malicious violence. That's the destructive kind. But spanking a child for its own good. That's the constructive kind. And I wish schoolteachers as well as parents could take that to heart.

LOUISE (*laughing*): You're so deadly serious! Why can't you relax a little, darling? (*Giving his head a brief, affectionate pat*) You're too tense and obsessed. That's what's spoiling your writing. You make your heroes just what you are. That's why they seem so unsympathetic. (*Stopping by his desk and gesturing to a pile of scripts*) Look at those last three novels you did. In every one of them you've depicted a hero who was anti-social, who simply ranted and preached against the decadence of our present-day world. No reader is going to want to stomach a hero like that.

TIM: But don't my heroes speak the truth? That's the point. Don't I put into their mouths honest, irrefutable arguments against the weak, stinking sentimentality that permeates the whole fabric of our liberal, democratic thought! Tell me if I don't!

LOUISE (*laughing*) See! There you are! On your soapbox again. Why must you *preach*, Tim? You can't change people by preaching at them in novels. Or in plays, for that matter. Shaw used to do a lot of it in his plays – and did he change anything?

Harry, in pyjamas, carrying pillow and blankets, comes in and goes to the divan. He arranges the bedclothes and settles down under them.

LOUISE (*with a glance at Harry*): By the way, Tim, do you know what Harry has been telling me? (*Lowering her voice*) That Newby woman on the ground floor has been enticing him into her bedroom.

TIM: No! Since when? (*He is amused*) This is interesting. When did it begin?

LOUISE: Very recently, it seems. He's been doing her shopping for her.

TIM (*laughing*): That's rich. Good for Harry! Shows he's got enterprise!

LOUISE: Strange how you don't seem to preach against sex in your books. Aren't you against vice and immorality?

TIM: Sex is a normal function. I have nothing against it.

LOUISE: Yes, but what about vice and immorality?

TIM: Oh, I disapprove of that – but there's no need for me to preach against it. God knows, we're inhibited enough as it is in this country.

LOUISE: But you look on sex-criminals as vermin, don't you?

TIM: The worst kind of vermin. I'd have no mercy in exterminating them if I were in charge of running the country.

LOUISE: Ssssh! Don't let me set you off. When last have you seen Grace?

TIM: You're rather clumsy at changing the subject. (*Pacing about*) I'd shoot every one of them out of hand. That's what's wrong with us. We coddle these monsters – can't even hang them – and we don't think of the victims. The poor young children who get raped and strangled. How would you like to have a policeman arrive at your door and tell you a child of yours has been raped and strangled? Would you want to trot out a lot of simpering cant about maladjustment and environment to excuse the man who was responsible for such a crime? These psychologists with their bookish theories get me mad. They're born that way, these sex-criminals. It's heredity. They've got a kink. They're no use to society. They should be ruthlessly wiped out as you'd wipe out fleas and lice.

LOUISE: Oh, Lord! Oh, Lord! Darling, I wasn't merely trying to change the subject to divert you from your favourite topic. I really wanted to know when you last saw Grace.

TIM: Why? Why the sudden interest in Grace?

LOUISE: Certain things have been coming to my ears. Tell me, Tim, is she still keen on you?

TIM: Look here, what are you hinting at now?

LOUISE: You haven't answered my question yet. When last have you seen her?

TIM: Four or five days ago. I took her out last Saturday.

LOUISE: The theatre?

TIM: Yes. Graham Greene's *The Potting Shed*.

LOUISE: Did she enjoy it.

TIM: In her fashion, I suppose she did. The usual sarcastic comments, of course.

LOUISE: What sort of sarcastic comments? Doesn't she like Graham Greene?

TIM: She said that in future she'd be glad if I took her to the theatre and not to High Mass.

LOUISE: Somehow my spirit hasn't taken to her. She certainly isn't the kind of person *I* would have chosen for you as a girlfriend.

TIM: (*chuckling and slapping her behind*): You're jealous. Confess!

Penny suddenly opens her room door and pushes out her head.

PENNY: I'm jealous too!

LOUISE: Penny, aren't you in bed yet?

PENNY: No, I was eavesdropping on you and Tim. Isn't that the word?

HARRY (*raising his head and wagging a finger at Penny*): Naughty! Naughty!

LOUISE: Penny, back into the room!

PENNY: It's only my head that's out of the room. If the rest of me were out, Tim might think me indecent. My nightgown is very thin.

TIM: See! See the colour of her mind! A nymphomaniac in embryo!

LOUISE (*laughing*): But, dear, you've just told me don't object to sex. Why do you let Penny's sexy nonsense upset you?

He says nothing. He begins to drum with his fingers on the table.

PENNY: He can't answer that, Mummy. My instinct about him is right.

LOUISE: That will do, Penny! Into bed – this minute! And I mean this minute!

Penny gives a teasing whistle, kisses her hand and vanishes.
A silence. Tim continues to drum with his fingers on the table.

TIM (*suddenly*): Why are you asking me about Grace? You said something about things coming to your ears. What things?

LOUISE: Never mind.

TIM: What's the mystery about? Or is it something I know already?

LOUISE (*a trifle distractedly*): Never mind, never mind! It doesn't matter. (*Another brief silence*)

TIM: I'm seeing her on Monday.

LOUISE: Taking her out again?

TIM: No. She's coming here. She's going to read what I've written of this new thing and give me her views.

LOUISE: That'll be interesting. Decidedly interesting.

TIM: I don't like the way you say that. You sound very significant.

LOUISE: Think so? Oh, well, I must be going to bed.

TIM: Helen isn't home yet.

LOUISE (*snappishly*): You've said that before!

TIM: And I'm saying it again.

LOUISE (*flaring up*): What do you want me to do? Go out and search the whole of Shepherd's Bush for her?

TIM: You're going to regret this casual attitude of yours, Louise.

LOUISE: Oh, for Gods sake, don't be such a bore!

TIM: I don't care! I'm going to continue to be a bore. And I say you're going to regret it. That girl should be watched! *And* disciplined!

LOUISE: You're not only a crashing bore – but you have a filthy mind!

TIM: I'll keep it, damn you! And I'll go on saying it – again and again! One night Helen won't come home. Do you hear me? One night she won't come home.

LOUISE: You're mad, Tim! Twisted and mad! Quite, quite mad! (*She goes into the room through door at left, slamming the door after her*)

Almost at once, Penny appears at the room door opposite. She stands on the threshold, in her nightgown only – no dressing-gown over it.

PENNY: I heard the fireworks between you and Mummy.

TIM: Back to bed! Back to bed, blast you!

PENNY (*whistling*): Phew! You do sound savage! How do you like my nightgown?

Tim stares at her, his hands clenching. The silence grows prolonged.

PENNY: Very thin, isn't it? Very transparent. But I'm only thirteen, so you shouldn't be shocked.

TIM (*breathing hard*): Little bitch! Little *bitch*!

PENNY (*giggling*): Not yet. At present I'm only a little *witch*! (*Waggles her fingers at him, kisses her hand and vanishes into the room*)

HARRY (*raising his head and wagging his finger at the closed door*): Oh! Oho! Naughty... naughty Penny!

TIM: Bitch!... Bitch!... *Bitch*! (*Last 'bitch' almost in a whisper*)

He keeps staring at the closed door, his hands still clenched hard.

Curtain on Act One

ACT TWO
Scene One

Monday evening. Supper is just over, and Louise is taking out the dirty cups and plates. A table for supper was laid about mid-stage.

Tim is at his typewriter. In an easy chair, Bill sits with the evening paper. On her stomach, on the carpet, lies Penny doing a French exercise. At his table, Harry is drawing the figure of a man on a large square piece of paper. He is using crayons.

In an easy chair, not far from Bill, sits GRACE BENTON-MEARNS, *Tim's girlfriend. She is about twenty-eight, medium height, brown hair and a fairly good figure. Her face is pretty but is spoilt by a certain superciliousness, a certain acidity of expression. She is smoking and reading a batch of MS. folios – part of Tim's new novel.*

There is a silence, until Harry suddenly looks around and says:

HARRY: I'm going to come and help you wash up, Louise.

LOUISE: Don't bother, Harry. I'll manage alone.

HARRY: No, I'll help you. As soon as I've drawn the legs.

Louise goes out with the plates.

BILL: What are you drawing, Harry?

HARRY: The picture of a happy man. (*He holds up the paper to show him*) See! This is his stomach here, and this green spot here is the poison he's just drunk. Half a glass of poison.

Bill chuckles, wagging his head. There is no other comment.
Silence again. Louise comes in again and collects more plates.

HARRY: Don't be afraid, Louise. I'm going to come and help you with the washing up. I liked the supper you gave us. The salami was nice.

LOUISE: Thanks, Harry. By the way, is anyone having coffee?

GRACE: Not for me. I don't think I'll bother, thank you.

LOUISE: Oh, it's no bother.

BILL: How about some Worthington, Grace?

GRACE: Not just at the moment, Bill.

LOUISE: Tim?

TIM: Hallo! (*Turning with a slight start*)

LOUISE: Coffee?

TIM: No, thank you, Louise.

PENNY: I'll have some, Mummy.

Louise glances at her, hesitates, glances about – then abruptly leaves the room, and we sense that there is some tension in the air.

BILL (*after a pause*): I notice I wasn't asked if I wanted coffee.

PENNY: Why didn't you speak up when Mummy asked at first?

BILL: Ssssh! You go on with your French exercise.

HARRY: Louise didn't ask me because she knows I never have coffee.

Bill begins to whistle softly behind his paper.

GRACE (*breaking the silence*): There should be a hyphen here, I think.

TIM (*turning and leaning towards her as she shows him*): Where?

GRACE: Here. "Middle-aged". There's always a hyphen.

TIM: Yes. Quite right. Put a tick in the margin for me.

(*He turns back to the typewriter and continues to tap at it. And silence returns*)

PENNY (*breaking the silence*): What's the past participle of "*Combattre*"?

BILL: *Combattre*. To fight or struggle. I remember that verb.

PENNY: Go on. What's the past participle?

BILL: Oh well, that's easy. *Combatté* of course.

PENNY: I don't think that's right.

BILL: What's wrong with it?

PENNY: It's not conjugated like "*donner*".

BILL: I can't help you, then.

Silence again. Harry suddenly rises, crosses over to Tim with his picture.

HARRY: Timmy, would you mind looking at my picture and telling me if I'm doing it right.

TIM: Not at all, Harry. Let's see. (*Taking the picture*) Ah-h-h-h! Yes, this is beginning to look like something.

HARRY: See the poison in the stomach?

TIM: Yes. Yes, I can see it. Very clearly done. You're improving.

HARRY: I want to draw his heart now, but I'm not sure what colour I should use. What do you think, Tim?

TIM (*rubbing his chin as he considers*): H'm. Well, let's see… What about a nice pink? Have you got pink among those crayons?

HARRY: Yes. Yes, I have pink.

TIM: Good. Well, you go and draw a nice pink heart.

HARRY: With just a little touch of green in the middle of the pink to show where the poison has reached?

TIM: That's it! Poison in the heart. Perfectly logical. Go and do that, Harry.

Harry hurries back to his table to continue drawing.

BILL (*rising suddenly*): Blast! (*Throws down the newspaper and goes to the drinks-cabinet and pours himself a glass of Worthington*) This is more like it! (*He takes a sip, then raps his nail against the bottle to attract Grace's attention. Grace glances round at him. In dumb-show he points to the bottle, and she shakes her head*)

PENNY (*who has slyly observed this incident*): She told you before she didn't want any.

BILL (*glaring at her*): Are you supposed to be doing your lessons or not?

Penny makes no reply. She bends assiduously over her exercise-book and begins to whistle softly.

BILL (*returning to his chair with glass of beer in hand*): Stop that whistling. You can't do French and whistle.

PENNY: Lucky Helen! She must be doing a lot of whistling where she is now.

BILL: Where is Helen?

PENNY: Skiffling, as usual.

BILL: But where? Where?

TIM (*turning his head suddenly*): In Tottenham.

BILL: In Tottenham? Who does she know in Tottenham?

TIM: It's a competition. She's gone with a party.

BILL: How do you know? Did she tell you so?

TIM: When I arrived home at half-past six she was going out. I asked her where she was going, and she told me.

BILL: I never knew about it.

PENNY: You're a careless father.

BILL: Cut that out, Penny!

Tim goes on typing. Bill sips his beer, fidgeting, glancing at Grace. Louise comes in. She has brought no coffee for Penny.

PENNY: Where's my coffee, Mummy?

LOUISE: I wasn't in the mood to make any. Go and make it yourself if you really want it.

PENNY (*giggling*): Everybody is in a queer mood this evening – except Uncle Harry and yours truly.

BILL: Louise, did you know Helen was planning to go to Tottenham for a skiffle competition?

LOUISE: I think I did hear her saying something about it. (*She lights a cigarette*) Why do you ask?

BILL: Nothing, nothing.

PENNY (*chanting*): Happy, happy Helen! How I wish I were Helen!

BILL: Did she say what time she'd be home, Louise?

LOUISE: No. I didn't even know it was this evening she was going.

PENNY: I dare say she'll be home by one o'clock.

HARRY (*starting*) Ooops! Ooops! Ooops! What o'clock is it? Timmy what's the time?

TIM: Five past nine, Harry. Why? What's the matter?

HARRY (*rising*): I've just remembered. It's a secret, Timmy. I've got to go somewhere (*He begins to put away his crayons*) I should have been there by nine. Nine o'clock.

They all stare at him.

LOUISE: Where have you got to be by nine, Harry?

HARRY (*glancing furtively about him*): It's a secret. A dead secret. But I'll tell you if you promise to keep it secret. Will you?

PENNY: We promise, Uncle Harry. Tell us.

HARRY: It's Mrs. Newby on the ground floor. She asked me to go down to keep her company this evening. She said I could come about nine. She has some nice lemonade for me, she says. And some buns she's made herself.

LOUISE: But her husband!

HARRY: He's in Birmingham. He went there this morning, and he won't be back until Friday. She's all alone for the next few days. She said, 'Harry, you must come and keep me company. Please, dear. You can tell them you went for a walk. Tell them, anything, but you must come and keep me company in the evenings while Bob is away! Our little secret, Harry. Our lovely little secret!' Yes, that's what she said to me – and she's so nice. I mustn't disappoint her. She might even take me into her bedroom again and teach me to do those nice little things again. I can't talk about *those*! Those are really very, very secret!

Bill and Penny laugh out loudly – but the others keep serious faces. Tim coughs ostentatiously, evidently amused but refusing to smile.

LOUISE: I can't see anything funny in that.

BILL: I should say it's bloody funny! Harry, old man, you're developing.

LOUISE: This is becoming just a little too much. Harry, sit down and go on with your drawing. You're not to go down to that woman.

HARRY: But she'll be disappointed, Louise.

LOUISE: Let her be disappointed.

TIM: This is where I interfere again. Harry, do you want to go down to keep Mrs. Newby company?

HARRY: Yes, Timmy, I'd like to.

TIM: Then go. Get along.

LOUISE: Tim, I'm his sister – and he's not responsible for himself.

TIM: We're all responsible for him – and it happens I'm very fond of him. I'm not going to stand aside and see you spoil his fun.

BILL: He's right, Louise. Let Harry go down and have some fun. He deserves a little recreation now and then.

LOUISE: But it's immoral.

TIM: Good God! Did you hear that, Grace? In February 1958 – in a flat in Holland Park!

GRACE (*unruffled, glancing up from the Ms.*): I think you need a comma here, darling.

TIM: Where?

GRACE (*showing him*): Here. After "contemptuous".

HARRY (*glancing from Louise to Tim, then to Bill*): Must I... can I... am I to go down?

PENNY: Daddy said yes. Tim said yes. What are you waiting for?

LOUISE: Go on, Harry. Go on. This is February 1958. You're in the first floor flat in Holland Park. That excuses anything. Go down to your lady friend on the ground floor. Don't take any notice of me. Go! Go!

Harry moves to the door, pauses as he opens it, then looks at Louise.

HARRY: Louise, I have lots of whang in me. Lots of whang. (*He goes*)

PENNY (*applauding*): Good for Uncle Harry!

BILL: Shut up, you! Shut up!

LOUISE: I'm going to bed. (*Moving towards bedroom door*)

BILL: Oh, don't be such a cold blanket. Have some Worthington.

LOUISE: That's an idea – but I'll have it alone in the pub round the corner.

BILL: Who do you think you'll be hurting?

LOUISE (*pausing at the bedroom door*): Not *you*. Oh, I'm not such a fool!

BILL: Cut out the hysteria! Blimey! I'm getting sick of your tantrums.

LOUISE (*with a bitter laugh*): The trouble is you think you're clever. A pity you won't realise it's only you who think so.

BILL: And what is that remark supposed to refer to?

LOUISE: I'll leave that for you to guess. (*She goes into the room*)

PENNY: The beginning of a Grand Mystery! (*In a chanting voice*)

TIM (*turning suddenly – to Grace*): Grace, I've changed my mind. I think we'd better go out.

GRACE: Go out where?

TIM: Anywhere. An espresso. We'll have some coffee or something.

PENNY (*chanting*): The plot takes a new turn!

BILL: Look, Tim, this flat is yours. Don't let us chase you out. If you want some peace and quiet I'll go out.

TIM: Keep your hair on, sergeant-pilot. The whole lot of you combined couldn't chase me out of here if I didn't want to go.

GRACE: Well, the truth is, Tim, I'm not in the mood to go anywhere. I'd planned to sit here and read this thing through. I'm lazy as hell this evening.

TIM: No argument. My mind is made up.

PENNY: Strong, masterful man!

BILL: For God's sake, shut your mouth, Penny!

Louise, in overcoat, emerges from room and goes out.

TIM (*rising and moving slowly towards his room door*): You can go on reading in the meantime. I've got to shave first.

BILL: Didn't you shave this morning?

TIM: I was late. Overslept. Couldn't do a thorough job. (*He goes out into his room through door at left*)

A silence. Bill has tense, and is staring at Grace. Then to Penny:

BILL: Penny, run out and buy me some fags. (*Holding out ten-shilling note*)

PENNY: I was expecting it. (*Springing up*)

BILL: What the devil do you mean by that?

PENNY: Nothing. Just being idiotic. Don't you like me to behave my age? (*She takes the note and dashes for the door*)

BILL: Penny!

PENNY (*pausing*): Yes?

BILL: Buy twenty Players – at the espresso. Don't try to work any of those slot-machines. They're not always reliable.

PENNY: I understand. And I'll be as long as I can in coming back. Isn't that what you want, too?

BILL: Look, what the hell? (*But she has already darted out*)

Grace laughs.

BILL: What are you laughing at?

GRACE: Something that Louise hinted at not many minutes ago.

BILL: What was that?

GRACE: About you thinking how clever you are.

He says nothing. Begins to pace about.

GRACE: You're not clever, you know, Bill.

BILL (*stopping suddenly, glaring*): One day I'm going to strangle you.

GRACE: It would be nice to have you try.

BILL (*coming close to her*): I know. You'd enjoy me rough-handling you, wouldn't you? That's what Tim does to you, I suppose.

GRACE: You'd better lower your voice, or he might overhear you.

BILL: I'm getting to a point I'm beginning not to care who knows how I feel about you.

GRACE: Louise and Penny already suspect.

BILL (*staring at her – after a pause*): I phoned you up today, but they said you were busy.

GRACE: I told them to say that. I guessed it was you who rang.

BILL: I only wanted to ask you to lunch with me.

GRACE: We've got a very good canteen at the British Council, Bill. I'm not at all keen on lunching anywhere else.

BILL: Special meals of culture for the cultivated only. Is that what you mean?

GRACE: Don't be tiresome. (*She suddenly fumbles in her handbag*) By the way, I thought I'd better bring this. I can't accept it. (*She hands him a silver cigarette case*)

BILL: But it was your birthday. I heard Tim mention...

GRACE: Yes, but I don't want a birthday gift from *you*, Bill.

BILL: Stiffening up on me all of a sudden now, eh?

GRACE: I think it's time to put an end to this nonsense. I made it clear from the outset that there could never be anything between us.

BILL: That's a lie. It's weeks you've been giving me the come-hither look.

GRACE (*shuddering*): What a vulgar way you have of expressing yourself!

BILL: Just the kind of remark I'd expect from a bishop's daughter who works at the British Council!

GRACE: For God's sake, don't be so pathetic!

BILL: Anyway, you can't deny it. You did give me some encouragement. Every time Tim's back's been turned you've shown plain you wanted to do a little flirting with me on the side.

GRACE: I admit that your attentions did flatter me, Bill – and I suppose I'm naturally flirtatious. But it's an exaggeration to say that I encouraged you.

BILL: Even when you let me kiss you the other night! You wouldn't call that encouragement, would you?

GRACE (*shrugging*): Oh, that was mere curiosity to see what technique you would employ.

BILL: And you didn't like my technique, I take it?

GRACE: To be frank, no. When you kissed me that night I realised you're not my kind of man.

BILL: What is your kind of man?

GRACE: Let's not go into that, if you don't object.

BILL: Have a mind I can guess. I'm too soft for you. I try too hard to be a gentleman. Blimey! What a mixed-up world! You'd think a bishop's daughter would appreciate a man who dishes out a kid-glove treatment – but no. Oh, no. It's a caveman she wants. Only the rough stuff gives her a thrill.

GRACE: You seem unusually perceptive this evening.

BILL: So you admit it! It's the rough stuff you like. Tim knocks you around – and you like it.

GRACE: Very well. Since you want me to shock you, I'll shock you. I like it. I love it.

He stands and stares at her. Then Tim calls out from his room.

TIM: I'll be out in a minute, Grace! (*Off*)

GRACE: Very well, darling!

BILL (*after a pause*): You disgust me.

GRACE: I'm not surprised. Naked candour often proves disgusting.

BILL (*abruptly walking off towards hallway door*): I'm going out. I'll retch if I remain here a minute longer.

GRACE: Go to your local and get drunk. It'll help.

He opens the door – and Penny is there, as though just about to enter.

PENNY: Your cigarettes. (*She holds out a pack of cigarettes to him*)

BILL: Just back?

PENNY: Not exactly. Here's your change. I took sixpence for my trouble. The usual commission. (*She gives him the change and comes in*)

BILL (*hesitating and staring at her*): Look here, were you…?

PENNY: Yes?

BILL: Never mind. (*He shuts the door and is heard going downstairs*)

PENNY (*advancing towards Grace*): Nice and mild outside this evening.

GRACE: You seem to have returned with remarkable promptitude.

PENNY: That's right. Can't you guess?

GRACE: Guess what?

PENNY: I wanted to listen outside the door.

GRACE: Oh, I understand now.

PENNY (*seating herself on the carpet right before Grace and looking up at her*): I heard most of the conversation.

GRACE: I hope you were entertained.

PENNY: Yes – but there's another word, too. Help me out.

GRACE: Edified?

PENNY: Yes, that's it. I was entertained *and* edified. I learn a lot from listening to conversations I'm not supposed to hear.

GRACE: Good for you.

PENNY (*giggling and regarding her quizzically*): You're not so cool, after all.

GRACE: Cool?

PENNY: Don't you know what Mummy calls you? The cool breeze of culture from the British Council.

GRACE: That's a neat description!

PENNY: But not a true one. I'd say you were a *warm* breeze. Very warm.

GRACE: Thanks!

PENNY: In fact, there's a better word for it. Help me out. They use it when talking about some female film-stars.

GRACE: Sultry?

PENNY: That's it! Sultry. You're a great help, I must say! A few more evenings in your company and I'll have a smashing vocabulary.

Grace rises and begins to wander around, just a trifle perturbed but trying desperately to preserve her supercilious calm.

PENNY: I suppose you know you have a rival in me.

GRACE: What I do know is that you have been making yourself particularly obnoxious to Tim.

PENNY: Did he tell you that?

GRACE: Yes, he's mentioned it more than once.

PENNY: Don't take him too seriously.

GRACE: From what I've seen of you, I can well believe it.

PENNY: Careful! You and I are of the same sort, you know!

GRACE: The same sort?

PENNY: I like the rough stuff, too. I love it. From *men*, I mean!

GRACE: In a moment I'm going to lose my temper with you.

PENNY: You mustn't do that. I'd hate having to black your eyes. (*She rises and they stand staring at each other*)

GRACE: How old are you, child?

PENNY: I'm always being asked that question. I don't have to ask you your age. I know it. You're twenty-eight – and you don't look a minute younger.

GRACE: You are going to come to a sticky end long before you're twenty-eight.

PENNY: I'm always being told that, too.

GRACE: And with good reason, I think.

PENNY: I wonder if I should tell *you* something.

GRACE: What something?

PENNY: Something really serious.

GRACE: Better not. The effort might melt the jelly in your head.

PENNY: Just for that reason I shall tell you.

GRACE: Get the agony over, then – quickly.

PENNY: What a sneering thing you are! British culture doesn't seem to have done you any good.

GRACE: If you persist with that fizzy joke you'll soon find yourself suffering from flatulence.

PENNY: Help me out again. I don't know that word.

GRACE: When you grow up will be time enough to know what it means.

PENNY: Score one to you! But let me tell you what I was going to tell you. Do you know when it was I first fell hard for Tim? It was the night he first had you.

GRACE: Don't you think you're going a little too far?

PENNY: No I don't think so. In fact, I'm not even at the first milestone. Let me go on quickly before you drop down in a faint. Well, you know why I fell for him that night? It was the way he handled you – like a real he-man. In this very room. Remember the night? Daddy and Mummy and Uncle Harry were at Granny's in Maida Vale, and Helen, too, as usual, was out somewhere. Only I was at home, but you thought I was in my room sound asleep. But I wasn't asleep. I was listening to you and Tim *and* peeping at you.

GRACE: Playing Peeping Tom, in short!

PENNY: I'm a girl. Peeping Penny would sound better.

GRACE: You seem to have no shame at all.

PENNY: There can be no shame in love and war. I thought you knew the old saying.

GRACE: It sounds to me more like your own.

PENNY: All right, all right. Don't – what's the word? Don't put me off the track. I was telling you. I peeped and I listened, and I got everything straight in my mind about you and Tim. It was a real education – better than any they can give me at school. Tim, that night, took you by force. But he didn't want to take you by force. He wanted to take you gently. But you behaved in such a way that he *had* to take you by force. You *wanted* him to. You would have *died* if he hadn't taken you by force. Now isn't that the truth? Can you deny that?

GRACE (*after a brief pause*): I never deny what I know to be the truth.

PENNY (*clapping hands*): Good for you! You're braver than I'd thought!

At this point, Tim comes in from his room, all ready to go out.

TIM (*glancing from one to the other*): What's going on in here between you two?

PENNY: Big cat and little cat scratching at each other.

TIM: Making yourself as overbearing as possible, Penny?

GRACE: What understatement!

PENNY: I was telling her a few truths I've discovered about her.

TIM (*ignoring her*): Where's your coat, Grace? In the hallway?

GRACE: Yes I left it there. Ready to go?

TIM: Yes. Come on.

PENNY: I hope you don't run into Daddy. He left here in a fierce mood. He said he was disgusted with Grace.

TIM: What do you mean? What's this now?

GRACE: Come on, Tim. Come on. Ignore her.

PENNY: Poor Timmy! You don't even suspect she's been carrying on with Daddy, do you? Or do you?

GRACE: You little demon! You little… (*She rushes at Penny and slaps her face. Penny hits out at her in retaliation. Tim grabs Penny, and they begin to wrestle, Penny screaming*)

PENNY: Let go of me, Tim! Let go! Let me get at her!

TIM: Keep yourself there! You stay there! (*As he shakes her and pushes her down into an easy chair, she tries to spring up, but he pushes her down again*) Hear what I say! You stay there!

PENNY (*remaining in the chair, glaring at Grace who is now at the door*): You wait until I get you alone, you stinking hypocrite!

Tim, hands clenching and unclenching, stares at her, then turns and begins to move towards Grace.

PENNY: (*suddenly chuckling*): Thanks for the rough-handling, Timmy. I love it. This is only the beginning of things between us.

Tim pauses at the door, stands still and stares hard at her – then he and Grace go out.

Curtain on Act Two, scene one.

ACT TWO
Scene two

The same evening, 11.30
Penny is in an easy chair reading one of Tim's typescripts – the novel he is working on
now, and the same script Grace has been reading. Beside her on the floor is a large dictionary.
Every now and then she raises her head and glances quickly towards the door, as though on
alert lest she be surprised by anyone entering.

PENNY (*frowning suddenly*): "Ambiguous" I don't think I know the meaning of
  that... (She *reaches down and takes the dictionary, begins to look for "ambiguous"*)
  H'm... "Uncertain; indistinct; doubtful in meaning"... Good, I think I twig
  that alright. (She *shuts the dictionary, puts it down on the floor and carries on reading*)
      The silence is resumed. Then the telephone rings. The telephone is in the hallway.
  She springs up and goes out, but does not shut the door, so we can see and hear her as
  she answers the phone.
PENNY: Hallo. Park 26... What? Montgomery? Oh, Lord, no! This is not the
  number you want. Nobody called Montgomery lives here. (*She hangs up,*
  exclaiming) Blast!

She comes in again and settles down in the easy chair with the script. She becomes engrossed,
her head bending lower and lower. She giggles now and then. Then abruptly the hall doorway
opens and Tim comes in. She springs up and makes a dash for the writing-table to put
down the script – then realises she is too late.

PENNY (*sighing as she puts down the script*): Oh well! You've certainly caught me
  red-handed this time!
TIM: What have you been doing with that script?
PENNY: Reading it, of course.
TIM: Reading it?
PENNY: Yes. I can read, you know. Some things they *have* managed to teach me
  to do at school.
TIM: Which script is that, by the way? I hope... (*As he moves towards the writing-*
  table)
PENNY: It's the one you're working on. The one darling Grace was reading.
TIM: Look here, is this a new practice of yours?
PENNY: No it isn't. It's an old habit. I've read all your others. I liked best the
  one called THE BRAVE BUT DAMNED. Remember how the heroine got raped
  and shot through the chest by the homicidal sex maniac? That was really
  exciting. I lapped it up.
TIM: Heredity. It *must* be heredity. I'm *convinced* it's heredity.
PENNY: What's that now?
TIM: The stronger of the two influences – that's what heredity is. Your sister
  Helen was brought up in the same household. She was exposed to precisely
  the same way of life as you were. It's my old theory! Heredity is what does
  it. Not environment. Environment my grandmother! You were born that
  way! We are all what we were born! And to hell with the psychologists!
PENNY: Do you hear me arguing with you?

TIM: But look, is it just curiosity? Why do you want to read my writings?

PENNY: Yes – curiosity, I suppose. But I like reading. And your books are just what I like to read. Lots of sex and violence and interesting conversations.

TIM: What do you mean by interesting conversations?

PENNY: Conversations about sex and violence. I find them very edifying.

TIM: Don't talk nonsense. I'm sure the conversations my characters carry on must be far above your head. You don't understand a word of them.

PENNY: I don't find them so baffling. And I use a dictionary for the words that stump me.

TIM: But how can you...? All right, all right. I give up. Anyway, don't let me come and find any of my scripts dog-eared. I'm very particular about that sort of thing.

PENNY: It hasn't happened yet, has it? And it won't. You stupid man! Let's talk about something else. Where's the she-dragon? Was she too mad with me to come back here?

TIM: If you had some sense of good taste, you'd refrain from referring to what happened earlier this evening.

PENNY: Quite right! Score one to you!

TIM: Where's your Uncle Harry? Hasn't he come in yet?

PENNY: Not yet. Still down there with Mrs. Newby. Those "nice little things" she's teaching him to do must be very, very nice this evening.

TIM: Bill and Louise?

PENNY: They, too, haven't come in yet – and it's half-past eleven. The pubs are closed. See what a wicked family we are!

TIM: Stop showing off and go to bed.

PENNY: Are you going to bed now?

TIM: No, I'm going to read.

PENNY: Why not sit and talk to me?

TIM: What I have in mind to do is give you a talking to.

PENNY: Fire away. You can spank me, too, if you like. I give you my full permission.

TIM: Really, I've met infuriating children, but you...

PENNY: I'm different from them all. I'm the most ambiguous child you've ever met.

TIM: The most what?

PENNY: Ambiguous. It's the newest big word I've learnt. I read it in your novel, and I looked it up in the dictionary. "Uncertain; indistinct; doubtful in meaning". Don't I seem like that to you?

TIM (*chuckling*) You're too damned conceited, if you ask me!

PENNY: Not more than Grace. Oh, sorry! Bad taste!

TIM: Have you been trying your hand at some detective work? How did you know about her and your father?

PENNY: It was only a matter of keeping my eyes open. I can be very nosey with my eyes when I want.

TIM: And with your mouth, too!

PENNY: Did you have a row with her about it when you were out?

TIM: No. We neither of us referred to the matter.

PENNY: For the whole time you were out together?

TIM: Yes. Why?

PENNY: Phew! Talk about English reserve! That really takes the cake!

TIM: Run off to bed! Run off to bed! (*He settles down in an easy chair with a book*)

PENNY (*seating herself on the arm of his chair and stroking his hair*): Go to bed and miss a wonderful chance like this?

TIM: What wonderful chance?

PENNY: Of being alone with you in the flat as we now are.

TIM: You're trying my patience, Penny.

PENNY: Not your patience. Your manly strength. You're fighting to resist me, aren't you? (*Stroking his hair still*)

TIM (*brushing her hand off*): I've told you before! Don't maul me about!

PENNY (*not daunted*): Can't you see what I'm trying to do?

TIM: What? What are you trying to do?

PENNY: I'm trying to make you lose your temper so that you can give me a taste of your constructive violence.

TIM (*staring at her*): Where did you hear that phrase? I don't remember ever using it in your presence.

PENNY: I read it only a few minutes ago in your novel there. Geoffrey the hero has lost his temper with Beatrice the heroine, so he threw her down on a divan and gave her a taste of constructive violence.

TIM: See what I told you! You haven't understood a word of what you read!

PENNY: But you made it quite clear what kind of violence was constructed on the divan.

TIM (*springing up*): This is monstrous! Really monstrous!

PENNY: What's monstrous?

TIM: This – this talk of yours! A girl your age has no right to talk like this.

PENNY: For goodness sake, don't make so much of my age. I'm fourteen next May. That's in three month's time.

TIM: Even if you were fifteen it would still be utterly incongruous!

PENNY: Help me out. I don't know that word.

The telephone rings, and she dashes off to answer it.

PENNY (*visible and audible through the doorway at the phone*): Hallo... Oh, that you, Mummy?... What?... No, Daddy hasn't come in yet... Uncle Harry? No, not yet. He's still with his lady friend on the ground floor... No, Helen hasn't come yet... Yes, Timmy has come... What?... No, he didn't bring her back with him. She must have been scared I'd give her a beating... What?... A beating, I said... No, I won't go into details. It would be in bad taste... Where did you go to?... Oh, the cinema... All alone?... But it's getting on for twelve... In an espresso? All by yourself? But why?... What?... No I don't know where Daddy is. He hasn't rung up... All right, hurry up and come, there's a dear! (*She hangs up and returns to the sitting room*)

PENNY: Can you believe it? Mummy went to the cinema – all alone – and then she sat in an espresso drinking coffee – all alone – for more than an hour. And why? Just because she didn't want to come home and find Grace with you.

TIM: Did she say so?

PENNY: Not in plain language – but it was easy to guess from the questions she asked me.

TIM: You will keep working that instinct of yours overtime, eh?

PENNY: Not at all. I just keep it ticking over. At the minute, for instance, it's telling me something very interesting.

TIM: Oh, shut up!

PENNY: At the minute it's telling me you aren't really in love with Grace.

He glances at her – then says nothing and becomes engrossed in his book.

PENNY: See! No answer. You know I'm speaking the truth.

She wanders about the room. There is a pause.

PENNY: I feel Daddy is really in love with her – but not you.

He still makes no comment. Ignores her, reading.

PENNY: The only kind of woman you can love is the kind who is honest and plain-spoken and not afraid to tell you about your faults. I'm sure you haven't met her yet. Or perhaps you have. (*Touching her chest*) perhaps she's right here.

He chuckles, shakes his head indulgently, but otherwise takes no notice.

PENNY: Another thing about you my instinct keeps telling me. You're always fighting with yourself. It's a kind of fight between the English gentleman part of you and the natural part of you. I believe, in the end, the natural part of you will win.

She approaches and stands close to him, smiling down at him.

PENNY (*musingly*): The twisted man. That's what Mummy calls you. Not to me, though. To me you seem just a sweet, soft-hearted old thing who likes to bark his head off at people to make them believe he's a big strong brute with fine ideas for changing the world.

TIM (*gazing at the ceiling*): Patience!... Patience!...

PENNY (*mimicking him; gazing up, too*): Strength!... Strength!... (*She giggles, bends and kisses him on the forehead. At this instant, the door opens and Harry comes in, just in time to witness the kiss.*)

HARRY: Not like that! Not like that! Susan didn't kiss me on the forehead. She kissed me on the mouth.

TIM: So you're back, Harry!

PENNY: Who is Susan, Uncle Harry? Is that Mrs. Newby's name?

HARRY: Yes. That's her name. And she's asked me to call her Susan from tonight. Oh, I spent a lovely evening with her. But I mustn't say a word about it! It's very, very, *very* secret. The little things we did! Ooops! Ooops! Ooops! (*He hugs himself ecstatically*)

PENNY: Why didn't you spend the whole night with her?

HARRY: Well, I would have stayed longer, but we heard Bill singing "Roll out the barrel", so she said I'd better run off at once. She was afraid Bill might have made trouble.

TIM: Is Bill outside there now? Has he come back?

HARRY: Yes, we heard him singing in the street. *"Roll out the barrel".*

Penny runs to the hallway door and opens it, and they hear footsteps coming up the stairs and a voice singing.

PENNY: It sounds like him all right.

Bill appears. He is drunk, but stops singing at once on sight of Penny.

PENNY: Don't stop singing. It isn't quite midnight yet.

BILL (*swaying slightly, morosely*): Whadsthisabout? Whadareyoudoing? Should be in bed... Little girl. Where'sh your mother?

PENNY: Not back yet – but she'll soon be here. She phoned.

TIM: Ran into some of your drinking friends, sergeant-pilot?

BILL: Yesh. Old drinking friendsh. Faithful friendsh. Where'sh Louish? (*He advances cautiously into the room. He does not stagger.*)

PENNY: I told you she's not back yet.

BILL: Full of tantrumsh. Getting shick of Louish and her tantrumsh.

TIM: Bed, bed! That's the place for you, sergeant-pilot!

BILL: How's violence, squadron-leader?

TIM: To bed, to bed! (*Waving him off*)

BILL: Exterminated any human vermin in my absence?

PENNY: You're a bit tight, sergeant-pilot.

BILL: Hey! You! You! Penny! Have reshpect for me – y'hear me? Resh... Reshpect. Go to bed.

HARRY: Go to bed, Penny. It's very late.

BILL: Harry... You! (*With a guffaw*) Shpent a good time with Mrs. – what'sh her name? Mrs. Newby? Enjoyed yourself, Harry?

HARRY: Very, very, *very* much, Bill. It was lovely!

BILL: Immoral, Louish shays. Bad fellow. But it'sh all right. Tim shays it'sh all right. *He* should know.

PENNY: What are you trying to hint at now?

BILL: Sssh! Didn't speak to you. Where'sh Grace? Tim, where'sh Grace?

TIM: Home by now, I should hope.

PENNY: Tim came back without her.

BILL: I suppose she told you... Told you about ush. Her and me.

TIM: We didn't discuss you, Bill.

PENNY: The whole time they were out together – they never said a word about the disgraceful affair.

BILL: You! You! (*pointing shakily at her*) Shut up! Dishrespectful... Have no right...

HARRY (*pointing at her*): Go to bed, Penny. Naughty. Very naughty.

TIM: I think we should all go to bed. Harry, go and get your blankets and things.

HARRY: Yes, Timmy. (*He goes obediently*)

BILL: Haven't finished talking to you, Tim. Got a lot to talk about.

TIM: Put it off for tomorrow.

BILL: No. Tonight. Now.

TIM: All right. What's it?

BILL: What did you talk about with Grace-sh when you went out?

TIM: Generalities, chiefly. And about my writing. Why?

BILL: Trying to fool me? No use. Can't fool me. You talked about her – and me. Didn't you? She told you about me.

TIM: No, we did not discuss you, Bill. Look here, if you want to know the truth, I was aware of it before. I've known for quite a while what's been going on between you and Grace.

BILL: Cor blimey! No! Did y'hear that? Penny, did y'hear that? He was aware... He knew.

PENNY: Not surprising. You gave yourself away in lots of little ways.

BILL: Blimey! (*Turning again to Tim*) You knew and you never batted an eyelid! Ish that it, Tim? Ish that what you want me to believe, squadron-leader?

TIM: Let's not go into that now, Bill.

BILL: Shee! Hear him? "Let's not go into that now, Bill". Just like her. Just like Grace-sh. Birds of a feather. English gentleman and English lady. (*Mimicking*) Begad! Some thingsh are not talked about, old boy, what! Shimply not done, old boy!

PENNY: That sounds very silly! You don't really know Tim.

BILL: You! You! Keep your trap closed!

PENNY: I won't. You're always scolding Tim because he writes and talks about killing off criminals – and you're much worse with this silly social talk of yours. I prefer hearing about criminals than about who is a gentleman and who isn't.

BILL: Cheeking me off, hey! Shee! No reshpect for me. Only a railway clerk. Ashamed of me. It'sh Timmy you'd have preferred for a father. Come on. Admit it. It'sh Timmy...

TIM: For God's sake, stop this idiocy! Get to bed, Bill!

PENNY: He! He'll never go to bed until he's told us about the hard days he spent as the son of a bus-driver. You should know him by now, Tim.

TIM: None of that, Penny! None of that!

PENNY: All right, all right. It's in bad taste. Don't bother to tell me.

Harry comes in with blankets and pillow, and proceeds to strip divan and make up his bed. He is in pyjamas.

BILL (*pacing about unsteadily*): Mixed-up world. Blimey! What a mixed-up world! (*Stopping abruptly and staring at Tim*) Tim, why the hell did you invite me to share thish flat with you? What was behind it? What did you have in mind?

TIM (*sighing*): Bill, I want to read.

BILL: I'm sherious. Tell me. I want to know. I'm drunk – but I know what I'm shaying. Why did you ask me to share thish flat? You didn't have to ask me. That day we ran into each other in the Strand...

TIM: That was nearly two years ago. Haven't you got used to the idea of being in the flat?

BILL: Yesh. But I've always wanted to know *why* you asked me here. You didn't have to ask me and my family to come...

TIM: Don't be an ass. Didn't you tell me you were cramped and unhappy in your mother's flat in Maida Vale. Wasn't it natural I'd suggest you come and share this place with me? I told you it was far too big for me, and that I didn't mean to keep it all to myself. What's on your mind now? Is it sheer cussedness that makes you ask these questions?

BILL: Why didn't you ask one of your own kind? That's what worries me. Why *me*? Me, Bill Harrow, a nobody?

PENNY: But you were in the R.A.F. with Timmy, weren't you, Daddy? You risked your lives together. Isn't that good enough reason for his wanting you to live in the same flat?

TIM (*springing up*): I'm sick of this discussion. I'm going to bed.

BILL: Wait, wait! Tell me thish, Tim. Did you give Grace a birthday present?

TIM: What? Birthday… Why should that concern you?

BILL: Have a reason for asking. Tell me. Did you give her anything?

TIM: As it happens I did – yes. What of it?

BILL: And – and did she accept it?

TIM: Why shouldn't she?

BILL: Nothing, nothing. (*Gives a bitter laugh*)

TIM: You don't seem too right in the head this evening, Bill.

BILL: It'sh all right. (*He moves towards the door left*) I'm a fool.

TIM (*chuckling*): Tell me something new, sergeant-pilot.

BILL (*halting*): There's a name for you, too, squadron-leader.

TIM: What's that?

BILL: Never mind.

TIM: No, let's hear it. It may be important.

BILL: Ugly name… But I won't mention it.

TIM (*rather tensely now*): Let's hear it. Come on. Out with it!

PENNY: Don't take any notice of him, Timmy. He only wants to be nasty.

BILL: You shut your trap, Penny!

TIM: I give you permission, Bill. Let's hear the name for me.

BILL: Forget it. Going to bed…

TIM: No, I'd like to hear it. I'm anxious to hear it.

BILL (*taking the silver cigarette case from a pocket*): Shee thish? I gave it to Grace-sh… For her birthday. Thish evening she hands it back to me. Won't accept it. And you know why? I'm not good enough. Not good enough and – and too soft. Trying too hard to be a gentleman. Public schoolboys haven't got to try to be gentlemen. They're gentlemen already – no they can behave like cavemen when it suits them. I'm not a caveman. I'm not a sadist! I don't thump her about and manhandle her when she gets fractious. Hear that? I'm not a sadist! That'sh the word! Hear it! I'm not violent, so she can't even accept a birthday present from me. Blimey! What a mixed-up world! (*He dashes the cigarette case to the floor, turns and goes into the room, slamming the door after him*)

A moment of silence. Then:

HARRY: Bill is very angry.

PENNY: That word you used, Tim… Envir… Environment. Do you think it's environment that's turned Daddy into what he is? Or would you say he was just born that way?

TIM: Just born that way. If he'd been a public schoolboy like me he'd be soured because he didn't have a title.

PENNY: And suppose he'd been born with a title?

TIM: If he'd been born an earl or a viscount he'd have been grumbling because he wasn't a duke. If he'd been born a duke he'd have felt hurt because he wasn't born into royalty. And by heavens, I'm willing to lay my head down that if he'd been born into royalty he'd have cursed his luck because he wasn't God.

PENNY (*giggling*): I believe you're right.

TIM: I know I'm right. Some people are just born that way. They can't help it.

HARRY: I was born liking poison. Isn't that true, Timmy?

TIM: Yes, Harry.

The telephone rings. Penny dashes out into hallway and answers it.

PENNY: Hallo... Yes... Who? Helen?... No, she hasn't come home yet. Who is that? ... Bertie... Oh... To Edgware? ... Oh, I see. A rock-and-roll dance... Is the competition in Tottenham over?... I see... In a car... No, she's not here yet... (*She hangs up and comes back into the sitting room*)

TIM: Who was that?

PENNY (*shrugging*): Some one of Helen's boyfriends.

TIM: What did he want?

PENNY: He wanted to know if Helen had come home yet.

TIM: Why should he want to know that?

PENNY: Don't ask me.

TIM: Didn't I hear you say something about Edgware?

PENNY: Yes. He said she left him and the others and went off to Edgware in a car with another boy.

TIM: What for?

PENNY: A rock-and-roll dance.

TIM: At this hour! And who is this other boy she's gone with?

PENNY: I don't know, Timmy. Bertie didn't mention his name.

TIM: Some damned teddy-boy, I suppose.

Penny mimes a man's hands closing around a throat. A slow, deliberate performance.

TIM: What's that for?

PENNY: That's how he is going to strangle her – after raping her.

TIM: I don't think that's very funny.

PENNY: One thing English you haven't got, Tim, is a sense of humour!

TIM (*chuckling*): All right, all right. I suppose not.

At this instance, the door opens and Louise comes in.

PENNY: Hurrah! Here's the midnight wanderer! The poor wronged wife!

LOUISE: Who has wronged me?

PENNY: The drunk man in there (*pointing to bedroom*). Your husband.

LOUISE: Has your father come in?

PENNY: Your husband is my father, isn't he? Don't ask unnecessary questions, dear Louise.

LOUISE: You sound as if you've been drinking.

PENNY: No, I'm bad, but I haven't reached that stage of – what's the word? Help me, Timmy.

TIM: Degradation.

PENNY: That's it. I must remember it!

HARRY: Did you enjoy yourself, Louise? (*He is under the bed clothes*)

LOUISE: Yes, Harry. Did you?

HARRY: Oh, lovely! Lovely! (*Hugging himself*)

LOUISE (*sniffing*): One day, if your mind does grow up, you'll think differently. You'll see sex in a different light.

TIM: Then let's hope to God his mind doesn't grow up!

LOUISE: What are you reading? *Crime and Punishment*? Or *Crime and Extermination*?

TIM (*chuckling*): Something just as good. *The Cruel Sea*.

LOUISE: So Bill came home drunk?

TIM: Stinkingly.

PENNY: Violently.

LOUISE: What do you mean violently?

PENNY (*pointing at the cigarette case*): He sent that smashing to the floor. Hurled it down with violence.

LOUISE (*picking it up*): What is this? I can't say I know it.

PENNY: Birthday present to darling Grace – but it was refused.

LOUISE: Is that true, Tim? Did he give this to her?

TIM: So he said – yes.

LOUISE: Didn't she tell you?

TIM: No.

LOUISE: What a fool! I'm not surprised she wouldn't take it.

TIM: Why are you not surprised?

LOUISE: She's not his type. You know that yourself.

TIM: Type! What is a type? There are no types – only individuals. I've told you that before, Louise.

LOUISE: Anyway, you know what I mean. She's an empty, hypocritical person.

PENNY: And the daughter of a bishop!

TIM: People are more complicated than you think. Perhaps it's because she's such an empty, hypocritical person that she appeals to Bill.

LOUISE: Yes, but *he* doesn't appeal to her. I could have told him that from the outset.

HARRY (*raising his head*) Susan says I appeal very strongly to her.

TIM: If I were you, Louise, I wouldn't be complacent. My advice to you is to keep your eye on the situation.

LOUISE: But tell me something. How do *you* feel about it? Doesn't it upset you to know she's been flirting with Bill behind your back?

TIM (*laughing briefly*): I'm too much of a cynic to be upset.

PENNY: He doesn't love Grace, Mummy. Can't you see that?

LOUISE: I believe you're right.

TIM: Then what are you making a fuss for?

LOUISE: Really, I wish I could understand you!

PENNY: I do – perfectly.

LOUISE: Nobody asked your opinion, Penny. Keep out of this.

The telephone rings.

PENNY: Heavens! That phone! This is the fifth or sixth time it's rung for the evening! (*She dashes out to answer it. They gaze casually at her as she lifts the instrument*) Hallo, hallo! Who's that now?... What?... Oh, it's you again, Bertie? ... No, she hasn't come in yet... What? Not at the dance? Where is she then?... Oh... Tough luck on you! Too bad!... Everybody seems to be in an unfaithful mood tonight... Can't explain. It wouldn't be in good taste... Worried? Too bad! I wouldn't let it worry me if I were you. Never worry over a woman, Bertie...

LOUISE: Penny, what is all this about?

PENNY (*into the phone*): Oh, she'll turn up before long, I suppose. And if I were you I'd give her a good sound spanking. Women like to be spanked by their men, Bertie... No... No... All right – but don't be worried... Cheerio! (*She hangs up*)

LOUISE: Who was that on the phone, Penny?

PENNY (*approaching*): Bertie. Helen's boy friend who took her to the skiffle competition in Tottenham.

LOUISE: And what did he want to know?

PENNY: This is the second time he's phoned. He wanted to know if Helen had come home.

LOUISE: But didn't she go with him?

PENNY: Yes, but she has been unfaithful to him.

LOUISE: What do you mean by that?

PENNY: He says she left the party and went off to Edgware with some boy. Said she was going to a rock-and-roll dance.

LOUISE: What boy is this? Hasn't he a name?

PENNY: Bertie doesn't seem to know his name. Very flashily dressed, he says. But that's telling us nothing, because they're all flashily dressed, even Bertie himself.

LOUISE: Did she go off in a car?

PENNY: Yes. The boy had a car.

TIM: I keep warning you, but you don't take any notice of me.

PENNY: We can only hope he's not a raping, strangling boy.

LOUISE: Stop that talk, Penny! It's most unbecoming!

HARRY: Susan says I'm fast becoming her dearest sweetheart!

TIM (*springing up*): Penny, where was that boy speaking from?

PENNY: Who? Bertie?

TIM: Yes.

PENNY: Edgware. He went there to look for Helen.

TIM: What exactly did he say?

LOUISE: Why the sudden cross-examination?

TIM: All right, all right. I'm speaking to her. Come on, Penny. Let's hear. What did Bertie tell you?

PENNY: Just what I've said. Helen left the party in Tottenham and went off with this strange boy in his car.

TIM: He told you that the first time he phoned, didn't he?

PENNY: That's right. Why?

TIM: I want to get it straight. Your mother may not be concerned – but I am. I have sufficient interest in you people to care what happens to Helen.

LOUISE: My God! What a sanctimonious prig you can sound like sometimes!

TIM: Go on. Call me all the names you like. Penny, I'm talking to you. What did Bertie tell you when he phoned again? Did he go to Edgware to search for Helen?

PENNY: Yes. He went to the dance-hall where the rock-and-roll affair was taking place. But she wasn't there. Nobody had seen her, it seems.

TIM: So that means she has probably gone for a drive somewhere with the strange boy!

PENNY: It won't be the first time she's been for a drive with a boy at night.

TIM: I won't deny that for a moment.

PENNY: And I hope you're not trying to fool yourself she's a virgin. I can tell you she's definitely not.

LOUISE: Penny, how dare you say a thing like that!

PENNY: I dare to say it because it's the truth, Mummy!

TIM: Good show! Good show!

PENNY: I knew you'd approve, Timmy dear. You're always saying that the truth is what matters above everything else.

TIM: Certainly, certainly. Anyway, let's continue. What else did this Bertie boy say? What did he do when he discovered she wasn't at the rock-and-roll dance?

PENNY: He said he was worried and wanted to report the matter to the police – but I told him not to bother, that she's turn up before long. I told him he must never worry over women.

TIM: We heard you say that. But did he say if the others at the party were with him? How did he get to Edgware? By bus or car?

PENNY: He said some other boy took him in his car. A strange boy.

LOUISE: They must be a very wealthy lot, these boys. They all seem to have cars.

TIM: That struck me, too. And you know what I'm beginning to think? These strange "boys" Bertie mentioned are probably American servicemen on the rampage from one of the camps or depots in the vicinity. They always have cars at their disposal, these Americans.

PENNY: Oh well! Not a bad thing! Perhaps Helen will marry one of them and go to Hollywood. She's pretty enough for the films.

TIM: I'm getting worried. I don't like it at all.

LOUISE: If you want to torture yourself with morbid thoughts you can go ahead. I'm making a beeline for bed.

HARRY (*raising his head*): Susan's bed is very comfortable.

TIM: Go to bed. Go to bed. After midnight, and your daughter isn't home – but what does it matter to you?

LOUISE: If I didn't know you well I'd give you a piece of my mind, you know, Tim!

TIM: Get away! Get away. Go in to your bed.

PENNY: I'll stay up and keep you company until Helen comes in, Timmy.

TIM: Thanks, but I'd prefer you to go to bed, too.

The telephone rings. Penny makes to dash off, but Tim darts after her and grabs her.

TIM: Wait! I'll answer that myself. (*He goes out into the hallway to the phone. They gaze at him as he lifts up the instrument*) Hallo! Yes. That's right. Who is that speaking?... Bertie?... I'll take the message. I'm a friend of the family. I stay in the same flat... What, speak slowly. You're babbling too excitedly. I can't make out a word you're saying?... What?... I see... Yes... Where?... Your friends made a search, you say?... In a nearby park?... Yes... I see... I see... (*A longish pause*) Very well. You wait there. I'll take a taxi and come as quickly as I can... (*He hangs up*)

LOUISE: What is it, Tim? What is it?

TIM: Bertie's friends made a search in a nearby park. They've found her handbag. And one of her shoes,

Curtain. End of Act Two, Scene Two.

ACT THREE

The following evening. 9.45
Louise sits in an easy chair knitting. Penny is on the floor with an essay. Harry is at his table building a tower with his blocks. There is silence until Harry's tower, too tall, crashes.
HARRY: Too high, always too high.
Another silence. Harry begins to build again.
HARRY: What's the time, Louise?
LOUISE: A quarter to ten.
HARRY: I promised Susan to go down and have a glass of wine with her at ten o'clock.
No comment from Louise. Silence again. Harry builds. His tower crashes.
HARRY: Too high, always too high.
LOUISE: Harry, for God's sake!
HARRY: What's it, Louise? Have I done something wrong?
LOUISE (*with a sigh*): No, no. It's all right. Go on with your building.
HARRY: I can stop it if it annoys you.
LOUISE: No, no. Go ahead. It's just... My nerves are a bit... oh, well!
HARRY: I understand. Poor Helen. No news yet if they've found her?
LOUISE: No.
Silence again. Harry puts away his blocks.
HARRY: I think I'll do a little drawing instead. (*He pulls out a drawer in the table and takes out his drawing paper and crayons*)
PENNY: How do you spell "incongruous", Mummy?
LOUISE: I-N-C-O-N-G-R-U-O-U-S. What are you writing?
PENNY: An essay.
HARRY: Louise, do you think they'll find any poison in her?
LOUISE: What?
HARRY: In Helen. Do you think they'll find any poison in her stomach?
LOUISE: No, Harry. I don't think they will.
HARRY: Poor Helen! I wonder why she left one shoe behind.
Louise gets up. Throws down her knitting distractedly and begins to pace.
HARRY: Where's Bill, Louise?
LOUISE: He's gone to the police station.
HARRY: To hear if there's any news?
LOUISE: Yes.
HARRY: Of course, she might not be dead. They might have taken her away in a car to some house in the country. Don't you think so, Louise?
LOUISE: I don't know what to think, Harry.
The telephone rings. Penny gets up to go, but Louise stops her.
LOUISE: I'll answer it. (*She goes out to the phone*) Hallo... Yes, I'm Mrs. Harrow... No... No, I think you phoned before, and I told you I'm not in the mood for any interviews... Yes, I have a photograph of her, but I'm not eager to see her picture in the papers... Yes, that is my last word on the matter. Good night! (*She hangs up and returns into the room*) I'm sick of these newspaper men.
PENNY: What did he want?
LOUISE: The usual thing. A sensational story with intimate frills. An exclusive interview with the mother of the missing girl.

PENNY: Tim wasn't so wrong in some of the things he's said. He said civilised society pretends to abhor violence, but the millions who read what the sensational press publishes prove that violence is their real god. They worship it in secret.

LOUISE: I can't say I like this interest of yours in Tim's ideas.

PENNY: His ideas are far more honest than yours. You are one of the hypocrites who think its the right thing to behave like a namby-pamby.

LOUISE: I suppose you've been reading his manuscripts?

PENNY: Yes, I've read everything he's written.

LOUISE: I suspected as much. Anyway, that sort of thing is going to stop.

PENNY: Who's going to stop it?

LOUISE: Circumstances will. We're not remaining in this flat.

PENNY: So you're going to move out on Tim?

LOUISE: Yes, we're going to move out – as soon as I can find another place.

PENNY: Simply out of spite, I suppose?

LOUISE: What do you mean by that?

PENNY: Because his words have come true – about Helen.

LOUISE: We should have moved out of here a long time ago. I've never liked his outlook – and his views.

PENNY: Of course you wouldn't. He makes you feel too guilty.

LOUISE: Under his influence you seem to be developing into a lovely little monster.

PENNY: Under the influence of you and Dad I've developed into something much worse – if influence does count at all.

LOUISE: Oh, you think the influence of other people doesn't count?

PENNY: No. I believe as Tim does – that heredity does most of the work on us. We're born what we are!

LOUISE (*laughing*): Your own words refute your belief, for you are simply echoing him. On your own you couldn't have such ideas.

PENNY: Don't fool yourself. I feel what I do deep inside me. Tim has only given me the words to express myself. Eventually, I'd have discovered for myself all he's teaching me.

HARRY: Do you know where Timmy has gone to, Penny?

LOUISE: He's gone with Grace to see some film she recommended. He ought to be back any minute now.

HARRY: What sort of a film? A film about a poisoner?

PENNY: I don't think so, Uncle Harry.

LOUISE: Look what he's done to your Uncle Harry. Harry never had this obsession with poison until we came to stay with Tim.

HARRY: What's that, Louise?

PENNY: That's the silliest thing I've ever heard. Before we came to stay with Tim, Uncle Harry used to be obsessed with rats. I can remember perfectly how he'd always be asking if anyone had any rats in their pockets. Was Tim responsible for the rat obsession, too?

HARRY: Yes, I remember! That's true. I was very fond of rats. That place we used to stay at, Louise – we used to hear rats in the wainscotting – and I loved to hear them! They used to squeak like tiny babies crying for their mothers. Oh, I loved rats – but now I love poison better. Much, much better!

LOUISE: Anyway, I'm getting out of here. I'm sick to death of this atmosphere
   of typewriters and manuscripts and highbrow argument.
HARRY: Are we going to go and leave Timmy? You don't mean that, Louise?
PENNY: That won't stop me from coming to see him.
LOUISE: I believe you have a wanton streak in you, child.
At this instant, Tim and Grace come in.
HARRY: Here's Timmy! Timmy, I'm going to miss you. I'm going to miss you a lot!
TIM: Miss me? What do you mean?
GRACE: Hallo, Louise!
LOUISE: Hallo, Grace!
HARRY: Hasn't Louise told you, Timmy? She says we're going away from here.
   We're going to leave you.
TIM: She said that, did she? That's news to me.
LOUISE: Why don't you shut up, Harry? Go on with your drawing!
PENNY: But you did say it, didn't you? Why haven't you the courage to say it
   again now that Timmy's here?
LOUISE: I'm your mother, Penny. I won't have you speak to me like this!
PENNY: You've always let me speak to you like this. Isn't it too late now to try
   to break me of the habit?
*A silence. Louise paces agitatedly. Tim goes to the writing table and toys with scripts. Grace
settles herself into an easy chair with a cigarette.*
GRACE: No news from the police yet, Louise?
LOUISE: No. Bill has gone to the station to inquire.
HARRY: Did they find any poison in her handbag, Louise?
Louise makes no reply. Only paces.
HARRY: Timmy, did they find any poison in Helen's handbag?
TIM: No, Harry. No poison.
HARRY: I was wondering. I suppose this is not a poisoning case. It's just an ordinary
   coshing.
Silence again. No one makes any comment.
HARRY: Some very bad fellow must have done it. A cosh-boy or a thug or a
   strangler. I hope they kill him off when they find him.
LOUISE: I think I'll go to bed.
PENNY (*sniffing*): Always going in to bed when you can't face anything.
Louise rushes at her and slaps her head.
PENNY (*unmoved*): It's true, though. And you know it's true. You run away.
LOUISE: What am I running away from now? Tell me!
PENNY: I don't need to tell you. I'm sure you know.
LOUISE: You see that, Tim? See what a fine job you're making of her!
TIM: Me?
LOUISE: Yes, you! You say Bill and I are indifferent parents – and what have
   you been doing! Inoculating her with your bilious hate! It's your influence
   that's got her precocious like this.
PENNY: That's stupid! Stupid!
TIM: Damned stupid!
GRACE: I wouldn't say it was so stupid, Tim. Perhaps you don't realise the insidiously
   morbid effect you have on people.

TIM: On people! On you, too, I assume?

GRACE: Yes, on me, too.

PENNY (*rushing up to Tim and gripping his arm*): Don't listen to her, Tim dear. She's like Mummy. Soft and sentimental, in spite of her acid airs. She has no guts.

HARRY: No whang!

LOUISE: Yes, hang on to his arm! See where he's going to lead you before long! The signs are all there!

TIM: What the hell are you getting at now, Louise?

LOUISE: Do I have to go into details?

TIM: You must! I insist. Where do you think I'm threatening to lead her?

PENNY: Ignore her, Timmy. Just ignore her!

TIM: I'm not going to ignore this. I've got to get to the bottom of it. Tell me Louise. What's this you're trying to hint at?

LOUISE (*laughing*): You're getting angry. That alone gives you away.

TIM: I have every right to get angry. You should know my temperament by now. I don't lie supine and let people walk on me.

LOUISE: Of course not. It's a wonder you haven't drawn your automatic pistol on me yet.

HARRY: Timmy wouldn't shoot you, Louise. Only the cosh-boys and the thugs and the stranglers.

LOUISE: You had better not talk too confidently, Harry. One day he might decide you're a specimen of human vermin and put a bullet in you.

TIM: By God, I could kill *you* for that!

PENNY: What a dirty thing to say! You ought to be ashamed of yourself, Mummy!

LOUISE: Haven't you advocated in your writings that the mentally ill should be wiped out?

TIM: That's a gross distortion! I particularly stipulated that the mentally ill who show *homicidal* tendencies should be got rid of, never that people like Harry should be killed off. Good God! Why, I'm fonder of Harry than any of you in here. Many's the time I have to protect him against you and Bill. He may be mentally backward but he's a most loveable human creature. Why should I want to put a bullet into him!

GRACE: I've told you more than once, Tim, that what you write will always be misunderstood by present-day society, It's your own fault. You are out of tune with the spirit of the times. Louise wouldn't be the only one to draw distorted conclusions from the opinions you express in your books. Nine people out of ten would.

TIM: Go on. Lecture me. I can take it. I'm accustomed to it.

LOUISE: Of all the egotistic upstarts I've met! You take the prize!

HARRY: Susan says that one day I may win a prize for my drawings. I showed her a picture I drew of a man smiling a poisonous smile.

Penny goes to the writing-table and begins to turn the pages of the dictionary.

TIM: What are you doing there, Penny?

PENNY: I'm looking up the meaning of "egotistic"?

Tim utters a bark of laughter, slapping his thigh.

GRACE: You're not quite right in the head, you know, Tim

LOUISE: I always knew he was mad. The only unfortunate thing is that there is method in his madness. And its a catching madness. (*Pointing at Penny*) She has caught it from him.

PENNY: "Egotistic"... "Showing egotism; self-important; conceited." (*She turns and points at Grace*) That's you to a T! If Timmy is self-important and conceited it's you he's caught it from!

GRACE: I can afford to ignore you!

PENNY: I know you can. You didn't ignore me last night, though, when I let the cat out of the bag about you and Daddy!

TIM: Penny! Penny!

PENNY: I don't care if it's in bad taste. With creatures like her you have to be crude! And talking of that, there's the rejected cigarette case on the mantelpiece! Daddy left it there in full view.

Tim begins to laugh again. He paces away. Pauses and toys with cigarette case, then puts it down again on the mantelpiece.

LOUISE: You see that, Grace! He agrees with her! Approves of her!

GRACE (*quietly*): I know he does.

TIM (*flashing round upon her*): And you know why I agree with her, don't you? Because she's right! It may be impolite to say, but she's right. If there's one thing I respect it's honesty. There was a time when I thought you did, too. That's what attracted me to you. You said it was your policy never to deny what you know to be the truth–

GRACE (*interrupting*): And don't I still say that?

TIM: Yes – but for effect only! Without a single spark of sincerity. You say it merely to strike a pose. For sheer braggadocio...

HARRY (*urgently to Penny*): Look up "braggadocio" quickly, Penny, and see if it's the name of a poison!

TIM: When we first met, I said to myself: "Here's someone, at last, who doesn't fall into the conventional pattern of civilised hypocrisy". But how dismally wrong I was! You're no better than any of the rest of them. Put you to the stern test, and you crumble up. You takes sides with the sentimental namby-pambies...

LOUISE: Me, for example! Thanks!

TIM (*continuing*): Rough-handle you in bed, and you melt with delight – but hold a mirror before you in the bright light of the sitting-room, with other people present, and you quail and blush. You daren't look yourself in the eye. You give yourself superior airs to make everyone feel you're contemptuous of the orthodox, but you aren't clever enough to bring it off. You only fool hypocrites like yourself.

LOUISE: Why have you continued being friendly with her if this is how you feel about her?

TIM: Ask her why – but I don't think she'll tell you. It's too intimate.

Grace says nothing. Wanders about vaguely, a little distractedly.

LOUISE: Sometimes I really wonder if you're human.

PENNY: Only Uncle Harry and I don't have to wonder. We know he is.

HARRY: Timmy treats me very nicely. Better than anyone else – even Susan.

The telephone begins to ring. Penny makes to go but Louise stops her.

LOUISE (*hurrying towards the hallway door*): I'll answer it.

HARRY: It may be news about Helen. Perhaps they found her in a farmhouse drinking milk with the farmer.

LOUISE (*at the phone*): Hallo... Oh, is that you, Mother?... No, Bill is still at the police station... No, Mother, no news yet... What?... No, it wasn't an American, after all. Bertie said it was some man in a sports coat... Yes, I know, I know, but it's too late to say that – and you yourself knew that she had a latchkey. You never told her you didn't like the idea, did you?... That was in your time. You can't compare these days with these... Yes, I know. Tim would agree with you. Discipline. Discipline doesn't mean the same these days as it did in your time...

Tim utters a bark of laughter.

LOUISE (*still into phone*): Yes, I know, Mother. Tim says that too. But nowadays we're more enlightened, thank God. We don't approve of canings in school – especially for girls...

TIM: God Lord no! (*As though quoting from a modern textbook*) The teacher-pupil relationship ought to be one of trust and friendship. Corporal punishment is a relic from a less enlightened age! So say all the best textbooks! (*With a contemptuous bark of laughter*)

LOUISE (*still into the phone*): Very well, Mother. I daresay we'll have to agree to differ. Bill and I have never believed in slapping and thumping our children...

PENNY: Only when you're in a temper! Tell her! Tell her how you slapped my head only a few minutes ago, you awful fibber!

LOUISE: (*still into phone*): What?... No, it's only Penny shouting at me... Very well, Mother, I'll give you a ring the minute we hear anything definite. (*She hangs up*)

HARRY: Was it news about Helen from Bill's mother, Louise?

LOUISE: No, Harry. Bill's mother was enquiring if *we* had any news.

PENNY (*to Harry*): And at the same time lecturing her daughter-in-law on old-fashioned methods of child-control!

LOUISE: Penny, go to bed!

PENNY: It's only ten o'clock. Why should I?

LOUISE: Because I say you must. Is that good enough?

PENNY: Suppose I say it's unreasonable to ask me to go to bed now?

LOUISE: Why unreasonable?

PENNY: Because most nights I go to bed at midnight and after, and you don't say a word about it – and tonight of all nights I have a right to stay up late, because at any minute we may hear something about Helen.

TIM (*with a bark of laughter*): Logic! Can't deny it! Logic!

LOUISE: So, you're siding with her, Tim?

TIM: Yes. In a manner of speaking, I am. She's on solid ground.

LOUISE: Didn't I hint it few moments ago? The signs are all there!

TIM: What signs?

GRACE: For heaven's sake, don't start that up again!

PENNY: You keep out of this! Let Tim and Mummy hammer it out alone.

TIM: Come on, Louise. We got sidetracked the last time. Tell me all about it. Reveal the dark secret!

GRACE: Tim, don't you think we ought to go out again?

TIM: No.

GRACE: Really, I can't stand quarrels! They do something to me.

PENNY: No guts, that's why!

HARRY: No whang!

TIM: It's not my habit to run away.

LOUISE: Heard that? Heard that, Grace? Penny said that, too, a little while ago.

PENNY: What did I say?

LOUISE: About running away. You accused me of wanting to run away because I said I was going to bed. You and Tim are saying and acting your parts in such a way that even a fool will be able to put two and two together and know what's happening.

TIM: Go on. We're getting somewhere, at last. Don't stop.

Grace clicks her tongue in disgust and wanders to the writing-table. She takes up one of Tim's scripts and settles down in an easy chair with it.

TIM: (*glancing at her*): That's right. You keep out of the way.

LOUISE: I'm sick to death of this haranguing and haranguing.

HARRY (*urgently to Penny*): Look up "haranguing" in the dictionary, Penny.

TIM: It means a dignified and pompous quarrel, Harry. Not quite the same as a vulgar cat-and-dog row.

PENNY: That should suit Mummy all right – with her suburban upbringing!

Louise rushes at her to slap her, but Tim intervenes and catches her arm.

TIM: Now, don't forget what you told your mother-in-law on the phone. You don't hit your children. Not in these enlightened times! It isn't done, Louise. Come on, steady yourself and tell me what's on your mind. Bill had a dark secret about me, too, but he succeeded in spitting it out last night. He called me a sadist. What's weighing on your soul now? What's the dirty word you're too polite to shout at me? Get it out. Grace won't mind. She's not half as inhibited as you fancy she is.

LOUISE: You behave very much as if you suspect what I'm thinking.

TIM: Perhaps I do suspect – but I want it brought into the open. I prefer everything to be in the open.

LOUISE: Are you sure it isn't shame and guilt that makes you so anxious for me to say what's on my mind? Some people are like that, you know. It gives them relief when their sins are brought into the open. You may be one of that kind.

GRACE: Look, before you get involved in anything too desperate, let me read a few passages from this thing for you, Louise!

TIM: Read what? Is that my new novel?

GRACE: Yes. Do you mind if I read something for Louise?

TIM: I do. Put it down. I didn't ask for a reading of my work.

PENNY: Let her read out what she wants to read, Timmy! It'll be interesting to see what *she* finds amusing.

HARRY: Is it something about arsenic, Grace?

GRACE: In one way of looking at it, Harry – yes. Very poisonous, indeed!

TIM: Look here, put that script down, Grace! (*Striding up to her*) Give it to me!

PENNY (*intervening, holding his arm*): Please, Timmy! Be a sport! Let her read out whatever she thinks she ought to. It'll be a good chance to prove how big a hypocrite she is. She's always said she agrees with what you write. Well, let's see! Go on, Grace. Read!

TIM: All right. Fire away. Let's hear!

GRACE (*with a sneering chuckle*): Very well. And no interruptions, please. Not a word of comment until I finish! (*Turning the folios of the script*) Here we are. This is Godfrey, the hero speaking. The scene is a cocktail party in a publisher's flat, and he's holding forth to a superannuated lady novelist and a publisher who had a passion for cats and canaries. He tells them: "Strength, vigilance, discipline – these are the biggest needs of our age. Those are the things we need to counteract the morbid sentimentalism that has spread throughout the whole nervous system of our civilisation during the past half-century or so. Our energy and devotion nowadays are misdirected. Instead of being more concerned about *human* safety, we get all worked up about our 'poor dumb friends'. Old ladies are coshed and robbed, young girls are raped and strangled, bank clerks are clubbed and bound and gagged. What are we doing to protect such people from the cold-blooded activities of thugs and louts? It's always a sign of over-ripeness in any society when animals are given more affection than we give to our fellow-humans. When you think of the energy and devotion that civilised men and women today are lavishing on canaries and poodles and cats – my God, don't you consider it a frightful waste? The world might be a much better place if we directed such energy and devotion towards human beings rather than dumb animal pets. In England, the police aren't even allowed to carry firearms. The thugs and louts can carry Bren guns if they feel like it. They are always armed to the teeth. But you and me and the police mustn't dare carry a penknife as a means of self-defence. We move heaven and earth to take care of dogs and cats and the dear little budgerigars in their cages, but we do nothing about effectively ridding ourselves of the vermin of our species who prey upon ordinary decent folk" (*Glancing up, turning towards Louise*) How does that impress you, Louise?

LOUISE: Need I say? In the same way that it should impress any balanced, human person. I'm passionately fond of animals myself.

PENNY (*dancing and clapping her hands*): Trapped! Trapped! We've got Mummy trapped now, Timmy!

LOUISE: What's this now? Who is trapped?

PENNY: You! You are trapped! Tell her, Grace! She thinks *you* feel as she does. She thinks *you* disapprove of what Tim has made Geoffrey say. Tell her!

LOUISE: I'm afraid this is getting beyond me. Grace, what point are you trying to make?

GRACE: She's right, Louise. I don't disapprove. I agree with every word Tim has put into his character's mouth. But I read that passage with a purpose. I read it to illustrate what a hopeless fool Tim keeps making of himself.

TIM: All right. Stop hedging, and tell us plainly. Have I or have I not made my character speak the truth? That's what we want to know. Tell us how you feel about that!

GRACE: Of course you have. The truth – yes. You damned idiot! But that's just it! Are you really so utterly naive as to think that the novel-reading public wants the truth? Ninety percent of the people who read novels and go to see plays *hate* the truth! The truth makes them fidget and squirm. It's desperately uncomfortable; it's ugly and upsetting. My God! Even a moron should know that!

TIM: Very well. I'm a moron. And as you're so clever, tell me what the ninety percent of the public who read novels and see plays do want.

GRACE: Harmless euphemisms. Comforting fantasies. Pleasingly decked-out half-truths. Provocative little idylls. Murder mysteries with the murderer *always* brought to justice. Naughty but not nasty bedroom escapades. That's what they want. Anything spicy and amusing that doesn't seem to conflict with the current conception of what is humane, liberal, democratic. The honest, stark truth as you portray it in your writing sounds Fascistic – and that could never be popular today. Why, good Lord, you've only got to whisper the words "strength", "discipline" and everyone wants to jump down your throat and call you a Nazi or a Fascist, no matter how firmly you may be convinced that the Nazis and the Fascists were a bunch of thugs and criminals. These are days when it's considered disgraceful to be strong and disciplined, didn't you know? You must be weak – meek and mild – and then you're considered liberal and democratic. A civilised person. A Christian. You must be a pacifist. You must loathe the H-bomb, and leave the manufacture of such a horror to your potential enemies. You must make yourself as defenceless as you can, so that when the time comes your enemy can walk over you and impose his will. That's the kind of world we're living in, and if you had a grain of sense you'd know that what you write doesn't stand a chance of being published. Yet you go on and on and on spilling out the raw truth on page after page. A damned imbecile is what you are!

A pause. They are all silent, a bit stunned. Then Harry murmurs:

HARRY: A lot of whang in that. Nice juicy cyanide.

The door opens and Bill enters. He looks tense, a bit dazed.

LOUISE: Bill!

Bill seems not to hear her. He walks slowly towards Tim. He grabs Tim by the coat-front.

BILL: You were right. Bloody right!

LOUISE: Bill! Bill! what's it? What has happened? Have they... Have they found...?

BILL (*ignoring her*): You were right, Tim. I take back everything I've said to you. (*He releases Tim and turns off, trembling, agitated*)

A pause. They stare at him. Then Louise exclaims hysterically:

LOUISE: Bill, what is it? What is it? The police... Have they found her?

BILL: Yes. They've found her.

LOUISE (*with a sob*): You mean...? Is she...? For God's sake, tell us what has happened, can't you?

BILL: She is dead.

LOUISE: Oh my God!

BILL: Marks on her throat. They found her in a wood... Her clothes torn off.

Louise throws herself into an easy chair, sobbing.

BILL: (*grabbing Tim's coat front again*): What did you tell us squadron-leader? What did you say in your novels? That we should exterminate them clinically, painlessly? Christ! Human vermin! That's where I disagree with you, squadron-leader.

Painlessly? Christ! Let me put my hands on the bastard who did that to Helen. *He* wouldn't be painlessly exterminated. He'd writhe and writhe before I squashed the life out of his guts! (*He releases Tim, turns off and paces agitatedly*)

Grace gets up and approaches him, grips his arm.

GRACE: Take it easy, Bill.

BILL: Take it easy! I've done that already. We've all taken things too easy – that's our big trouble. How many times we haven't read in the paper of people being attacked and murdered – but it was somebody else, so we didn't concern ourselves. We took it easy. It was easy to talk about crime and delinquency and teddy-boys as if it was just a highbrow topic for writers and parsons and social welfare workers to argue about. It was so easy for us to turn upon Tim and call him ugly names because he talked about wiping out the bastards. But now we know for ourselves what it's like to have someone close to us, right in our midst, raped and done to death. Now we can see what Tim was getting at. Twisted we called him. Twisted! Blimey! It's *we* who were being twisted!

TIM (*gripping Bill's arm*): Never mind, old man. When it comes to being twisted, the whole of what we call our western world is screwed up into a knot. It's not only you people in this flat. Helen is dead. She is beyond our help. But this fellow who's responsible for her death is alive – and he's going to get free legal aid when he's caught. He's going to be tried, given every chance of defending himself in a court of law – and at the end of it he won't even be hanged. Oh, no! Nowadays we don't hang murderers. How cruel and barbarous! How uncivilised! We put them in prison, so that perhaps one day they may be able to escape. This fellow who's raped and strangled Helen may one day do it all over again to some sixteen year-old girl. We can't kill him off when we catch him. No we must leave him alive to give him the chance to repeat the trick. That's what our world has come to. It's screwed up tight in a knot of sentimentality. That's the true sickness we're suffering from today. Sentimentality. We stink with sentimentality.

LOUISE (*raising her head*): I prefer sentimentality to brutishness, all the same!

PENNY: Brutishness! Who was more a brute than the man who attacked Helen? I suppose you call him sentimental! Soft and tender!

LOUISE: Two wrongs don't make a right!

BILL: Blimey! For Christ's sake!

TIM: Heaven save us from these suburban platitudes!

LOUISE: Hear that! Hear that, Grace! Suburban! The same word Penny flung in my face only a few minutes ago!

PENNY: And what if I did? Tim is right. It's people like you who are spoiling the world for us. It's jellyfish like you who cause wars!

TIM: Penny! Penny!

PENNY: I'm getting sick of Mummy, Tim! Sick of her wailing and whining. She's crying her eyes out because of what's happened to Helen – but what's the use of crying! The thing is to get busy as you say and wipe out all these dirty beasts that go round coshing post-office men and robbing mailbags and attacking even old people. What's the use of crying and talking about two wrongs not making a right! That doesn't help. If only I could get my hands on that beast! That dirty, dirty beast who killed Helen! (*She turns off, pressing her hands to her face with a sob*)

HARRY (*approaching and hugging her*): Never mind, Penny. Never mind. The police will catch him.

BILL: And what will the police do to him! Lock him up!

TIM (*gripping his arm*): All right, Bill. Look, come and have a drink. I think you need it. (*Leads him over to the drinks cabinet. Pours a whisky for him*) Louise? A drink?

LOUISE: No. No thank you. The next thing you'll be telling me is that I want to drink to escape.

BILL: Oh don't be so petty!

LOUISE: I was born petty. Ask Tim and he'll tell you it's heredity. Anyway, Bill, understand this. I'm getting out of this flat.

BILL: Getting out and going where?

LOUISE: Anywhere. I don't care where. I can't stay here after what has happened to Helen.

PENNY: Why not be truthful and tell him it's just spite! That's all it is, Daddy. She wants to spite Tim because Tim's words have come true.

LOUISE: You see the virago she's turning into, Bill!

BILL: I don't see it! She sounds as if she's hit the nail on the head. You're only saying this because you feel sore we didn't take notice of Tim's warnings. If you had any decency you'd get off your high horse and admit we've been bloody poor parents.

LOUISE (*hysterically*): I admit nothing like that! Nothing! And if you want to know, it may be for *her* good I want to get her out of here! (*Pointing at Penny*)

PENNY: For my good! How do you make that out? Let's hear!

TIM: The big, dark secret. Twice for this evening you've got sidetracked, Louise. Don't let's put you off this time. Spit it out!

LOUISE: You think everyone is a fool but you. I don't write. I don't know about Freud and Adler, but I see what I see, and I can put two and two together.

PENNY: And make forty!

TIM: All right, Penny! All right! Look here, Louise, cut out this talk about Freud and Adler. Where human relations are concerned, scientific knowledge doesn't count for one jot – at least in my estimation. What counts, *I* believe, is common sense. And that's something you have to be born with. It's the intuition of the poet and creative artist. It's the infallible know-how some of us have, whether we're artistic or inartistic. An ignorant peasant may have it, and the most learned college professor sadly lacking in it. She has it! (*Pointing at Penny*) Yes, Penny has it! She calls this instinct – but it's the same thing!

LOUISE (*with a bitter laugh*): I have my own views about her "instinct"!

PENNY: Hear that, Daddy! That's intended to be a dirty remark!

LOUISE (*screaming at her*): Your instinct *is* dirty! That's what I mean! You little wanton! Not fourteen yet and your mind is like a sewer.

GRACE: I'm going. I really can't stand any more of this.

HARRY: Have a Worthington, Grace!

TIM (*to Grace*): Sit down and stop being affected. (*To Louise*) Come on, Louise! We're hot on the trail now. Spill it out!

The telephone begins to ring. Penny makes to dash off to answer it, but Tim catches her arm.

TIM: Leave it! Let it ring! *This* time we're not going to be sidetracked. Come on, Louise! Speak up!

LOUISE (*moving towards the hallway door*): I'm going to answer the phone.

TIM (*holding her back*): Let it ring, blast it! To hell with it! You stay here and tell us what's on your mind. Now! This instant!

Pause. The phone rings and rings. Then Penny breaks the silence of voices.

PENNY: She hasn't got the nerve!

TIM: She's going to tell us.

The phone rings and rings.

GRACE: This is maddening, maddening. That phone!

TIM: We're waiting, Louise. You said it may be for Penny's good that you leave this flat. Tell us why you said that.

LOUISE: Very well. Because I don't trust you with her – that's why.

TIM: Aha. It's coming out.

PENNY: Coming out?

The telephone stops ringing.

HARRY: It might have been the police ringing up.

TIM: Go on. You're telling us, Louise. You don't trust me with Penny.

LOUISE: No. I don't.

BILL: What the hell is this now, Louise?

LOUISE: It's just what I say. I don't trust him with Penny. Because I've seen the way he looks at her.

PENNY: See what a sewer *her* mind is, Daddy! Watch it how it oozes!

TIM: Quiet, Penny! Go on, Louise. How do I look at her? Tell me.

LOUISE: I don't have to go into details about that. *You* know what I mean. You can try to brazen it out, but you don't fool me.

GRACE: Louise, I think your imagination is running away with you.

LOUISE: Then you think wrong! I have my instinct, too.

PENNY: What a miserable pussyfoot you are! I'll tell you what she wants to say, Grace! I'll tell you what she hasn't got the guts to say in plain language. She wants to tell us that Tim has his eye on me. That he'd like to follow me into my room and rape me. She wants to tell us that Tim may do to me just what some dirty beast has done to Helen! She wants to say that Tim himself might be a specimen of human vermin who needs to be exterminated.

LOUISE: Thank you, Penny. Yes, that is what I wanted to say. I hadn't the courage to say it, I admit.

A pause. Rather tense. Then Louise looks at Tim.

LOUISE: Well, Tim? And what have *you* to say. Do you deny it?

TIM (*after a pause*): No, Louise. I don't. It is the truth. It is the absolute truth. Does that satisfy you?

Another pause. Then suddenly Grace moves towards the door, saying:

GRACE: I'm going.

She as suddenly pauses at the mantelpiece, and takes up the cigarette case.

GRACE: Oh, this cigarette case… I think I'll accept it, after all, Bill. (*She continues to move towards the door*)

Bill glances in a sort of panicked manner, uncertain, from one to the other of them, then:

BILL: I'll come to the station with you, Grace.

GRACE: Thanks.

She and Bill go out together.

A pause. Then Louise, without a word, goes out – goes into her room.

HARRY: Oh, I've just remembered! What's the time, Penny? Tim?

TIM: A quarter past ten, Harry.

HARRY: Ooops! And I promised Susan to have a glass of wine with her at ten o'clock. I must be off. (*He begins to move towards the door, then pauses, turns and comes swiftly to Tim*) A little poison, please, Timmy? A little poison for me to drink before I go down to Susan?

Tim solemnly goes through the mime of giving him poison (as in Act One)

HARRY: Ah-h-h-h! That's nice! I love to drink poison! It does me good. Thanks, Timmy. (*He begins to move towards the door again, but again pauses, turns and comes back to Tim*) Timmy, I won't go and leave you. I won't desert you. You've been too good to me. (*He smiles, taps Tim on the shoulder lightly and then goes out*)

PENNY (*sighing*): Well!... Once again, Tim, we've been left alone together.

Tim says nothing. Sits in an easy chair drumming with his fingers on the arm of the chair.

PENNY: It must be fate that we're always being left together like this. Though it isn't the same tonight. Tonight is different... Tonight... I just can't believe it... Helen... I just can't believe that Helen... (*She presses her hands to her face with a muffled sob, and there is a longish pause. Then she removes her hands and looks at him. Moves towards him and squats on the floor before him*)

Tim continues to drum with his fingers on the arm of the chair. He stares through her, grim, tense.

PENNY: Tonight, I *feel* different. I feel I must stop being precocious and start behaving in a really grown-up manner.

Pause. Tim still says nothing. Sits tense.

PENNY: I shan't tease you anymore. It was unfair to you, the way I've been teasing you. (*She stares up at him, seriously, earnestly*) Tim, tell me something. Do you still believe in my instinct?

TIM: Firmly.

PENNY: Good. Then I'm going to tell you something my instinct has found out about you. That gun you carry all the time in your hip pocket – you carry that not so much because you are afraid of being attacked, but because you are afraid of yourself. You've been afraid that you might have lost control of yourself one day and committed an act of destructive violence – to somebody like me, perhaps. That means you would have had to look on yourself as a specimen of human vermin. You yourself would have turned into the very creature you abhor and preach against. And you would have had to kill yourself – put a bullet in your head. Isn't my instinct right?

He makes no response. Just stares through her, drumming with his fingers...

PENNY: I know I'm right. But I'll tell you something that should put your mind at ease. For the very reason that you *could* control yourself all this time, even though I've tempted you so badly, shows that you have strength – strength and discipline – and that's why you haven't done anything horrible. That's why you're *not* a specimen of human vermin. It's the weak people – the people who have no discipline over themselves – who lose control and do horrible things – cosh people, rape and strangle, and murder and rob. But you're not like that. You were born strong – and you'll always be strong. See how I've been working my instinct overtime? It's a hardworking instinct. Tough and strong – just like you.

A pause. Still no response from him.

PENNY: I must go on writing my essay – but before I go on there's something else I ought to say. In three years and three months from now I'll be seventeen. I'll be something for marrying… What's the word? Help me out. It begins with E…

TIM: Eligible.

PENNY: Yes. That's it! Eligible. I'll be eligible for marrying – though, of course, I won't really be able to have my own say legally until I'm twenty-one. I hope I'm right. Isn't that right?

TIM: Quite right.

PENNY: Well, look here, what about waiting for me, Tim? What about waiting until I'm seventeen and then let's get married? I think we'll make a good team, don't you? Two honest people – I with my instinct telling me just how to go right and you with your strength and discipline. What do you say? Will you wait for me?

Still no response from Tim – though he gives the faintest of smiles.

PENNY: I'm serious. Only three years and three months to wait – and if Mummy and Dad make any objections we'll just run off to Japan or Mexico and leave the whole lot of them here to stew in their weakness. What do you say?

Still no response from Tim. A pause.

PENNY (*earnestly, almost with a sob of seriousness*): Timmy, I want your answer. Please. I'm serious. Don't treat me as if I'm a silly little girl. Tell me. Do you think you can wait?

TIM (*stirring slightly and nodding*): Yes. Yes. I believe I can. In fact I'm certain I shall.

CURTAIN
End

POETRY

FAREWELL TO A WOMAN

Peccaries rampaging
Are not more savage than these weeks
That have snapped upon our heels
And coveted our midnight peaks
So that now we must part as the bugle peals.

Soon, woman, I shall be old
And you to me but a shadow
Accidental in the past:
A breeze blowing through my memory
cold –
A still-life incident
Of heated days
That seared our limbs and went.

Night winds did moan
And the rains were cruel, woman,
But the earth together we have known
In our breathing raptures,
In our labour of living,
In the passion of our species,
Desperate in taking and giving,
When, cooling, we panted at the futile sky.

Soon, woman, I shall be dry
And you to me but a symbol
Mysterious in the past:
A ghost china-fragile
Dusted with Time's patina –
And I no longer virile,
But brooding on the thunder gone:

And the sorrow of men succeeding the storm
And thus and thus…
To the twilight of death.

EPITHALAMIUM

Trembled we have in the wind,
In the damp, in the fury of the night.
Reclined have they in the warmth,
In the perfumed security of the home.
The fear of the dark we have known
And the startling crack of a twig,
The roar, the whirl and the hiss of rain.
While on a couch
In the safety of a drawing room
They have murmured and yawned
In ascetic content.
Trembled we have in the heat
Of unrestrained rapture,
In the cool, in the starry purple of night,
And kissed in the settling dew;
We of the Earth.
Chaste and controlled have they sat
In the warmth
Under the static lights of the home,
While we have roamed
In primeval gloom,
But in joy without bound;
We of the Earth:
Incorrect, incorrigible, immoral.
They of the drawing-room:
Correct, proper, and clean in thought.
Indeed!
Gentlemen, a toast to the bride!
To the bridegroom!
To the drawing-room!

COLONIAL ARTIST IN WAR-TIME.
A POEM.

Overture:

Reality is actuality produced
Into the vital abstract:

When the rice-men are reaping
The sackies intersperse cheeping.

Objective events and objective thought
Tangled with the essence of dreams:

When the war-planes are droning
Coconut palms make dulcet moaning.

Things moved, welded and wrought
And the inner-singing trend of carried out schemes:

Ships in convoy bring we mails
Despite torpedoes which are worse than gales.

1.
And how now are we to live?
In baffled armistice with our mind and dreams?
Or stealthy in conflict with our scenes? –
Our vicarious spectacles – Hamburg was bombed last night –
The Duce, bulging man, is in Albania to fight:
To direct the rush of blood in successful gouts.

Or shall we daze our frame,
Shall we sink our movement in apathetic respiration,
Shall we take the strands of imagery out the light –
The white light, the blue light, the green light
Reflected from our tropic landscape? This tame,
This andante scene of breeze and sun and mud,
Where, where is the chaos of the droning light:
The flash, the yell, the groans and splintered glass?

Hear the voice: the chalk-crisp voice –
Last night the R.A.F. for choice
Rained T.N.T. and fire on Wilhelmshaven –
White, orange, red flames they left – and blue:
That was the power-station – or the gas-works.

Two of our aircraft failed to return.

And how now are we to live?
In baffled turmoil with desire, duty and our dreams?
Or stealthy with bowed mind to our blues and greens? –
Our itching reason spawning new reversive theories –
Manna for the mind's upkeep – how many calories?
Self-sacrificial dung for the soul – or nectarine?

Tell us how to live.

Watch the green eye a-wink in the brown mahogany,
Hear the voice: the Oxford chalk-drawled voice:
Yesterday a new contingent came
Eager-shouting for the Martian game.
Were we with them
When their shouts in implication braved the air?
"For England! For Freedom! For Democracy!"
Khaki-ed, bristling and without fear –

But were we there?

2.
White clouds drift in puffs of A.A. shells,
Making leisured defiance at God's tropic blue.

Whose God?
Mine, Britain's or the Duce's? Or nobody's at all?
"I'm a jealous God," the trade-wind saith,
"Bearing Hitler's 'planes in my northern partner-wraith,
To England's shores and England's factories –
And you – you artist, produce your prophilactories
Against guilt of inactivity!"

Say I: "Did I make the war?
Did I crouch in evil on this calm Guiana coast
And lure the eye of Mars to glare and roast
My fellow-Britishers and fellow-earthy-men
So that I might produce diversion glamoured, gilt and-pearled
For my poetic fancy-world?"

3
In the dark-green cabbage palms
I hear my mind in elevation a-muttering,
Questioning for fears, for motives and for qualms;
But the wisdom of a hundred years involved in palms
Is not enough for this matter of a war;
For this matter of a creator's conscience a-guttering

Like a candle eclipsed by the glare of Hamburg
Seen (so the pilots said) a hundred miles afar.

Our creation-point circles in mid-air,
But not to centre upon the target –
No objective in the Rhine: no tensioned fear
Of white ghosts wavered, up-and-all-ways wavered.

Why are we not up there?

Tell us how to live.

You there in the Saxon north,
Tell me if to silt your bodies in putrescent hate,
To brew a murder-gleam in your soul's deep inner eye,
To hatch gas-schemes of mustard-scorching death
For our enemies of the Ruhr and Rhine
Will give you joy in abundant thunder, and will sate
Your spirits earnest-seeking for the truth beyond the sky,
Will bring you all the flooded glow of peace
You writhe, you splutter, you groan to drink as wine –
Wine to soothe your war-wondering, war-tattered,
War-sobbing, war-working, trembling days and raided nights.

Or tell me if to love beneath the cabbage palm,
Amid the coconut sun-glittering fronds, in shade
And to see the human race in sighs and rapture-panting
Heralding new units for the future rage,
If this, instead of hate, will sprinkle on our souls the dew of calm;
If this awesome welding of the male and female made
With singing breath of earth and limbs blind-rhythmed
Will settle wars, mind-storms and write upon the page
The alpha-cypher of solution, of evolution, revolution,
Of mankind's morning yearning, midday sweating, evening dreaming.

My mind zooms again to fronded dark green;
I hear it in elevation a-muttering,
Questioning for opinions, outlooks and a stable scene;
But the wisdom of a hundred years involved in palms
Is not enough for this matter of a man and woman;
For this matter of love and hate co-struggling
In the mountain-rains of Albania,
In the factories of steel-hammering Coventry,
In London's battered grey, in Petain's cowering France;
So once again
Our creation point circles in mid-air
To centre upon the truth-filled target –

Objective on the earth: in the human fair
Of wars and roundabouts and births; orgasm and demise.

Why are we philosophizing here ?

Tell us how to live.

4.

Triumphal moments sometimes soaringly materialize
To here, far-separated haven from the furnace-glow:
Moments making greener, silver-greener
Moonlight-glimmer in trees that never heard of foe:
Moments bringing to serene savannah atmosphere serener.

Graf Spee scuttled! Hail *Ajax*! Hail *Achilles!*
Exeter still kicking! Kicking hard!

See the sunlight glitter gold, gold, golder!
Hear the trade-wind hum bold, bold, bolder!
Watch creek-water black-lulling in mysterious flow,
Jumbie flitting pale-green past the *mucca-mucca*;
Hear the outboard motorboat: steady chukka-chukka.

Three hundred Britishers off the stinking Nazi hulk!
Watch the *Altmark* barbarian-bullies how they sulk!

Ave Cossack! Te salutamus!

Oh, were that we were there!

Inspired moments sometimes ringingly etherealize
Our starry, purpled evening sky:
Moments dreaming on the piebald moth-wing
Out the ether deathless, deathless: ever not to die –
Words of Winston, flames from F.D.R. sing and sing.

"Give us the tools and we'll finish the job!"

See the starlight winking white, white, whiter!
Hear the crickets cheet bright, bright, brighter!
Watch the creole faces in the red-dust lane;
Baccoo wailing for raw meat behind a gloomed back-door;
Hear the radio's percolating hum: the world's deep roar.

"The British need 'planes. From America they will *get* 'planes!
The British need food. From America they will *get* food!

Conjure Gettysburg with Lincoln there! Hail F.D.R.!

This time – *this* time we were there!

Mumbling from the wings I heard:
"This is jingo-jingo, rabid jingoism;

Mesmerized, poor fellow, by British propaganda-curd
So much jingo-jingo, heroic jingoism."

Let the mumblings cross the stage from wing to exit-wings;
Truth may smell of jingo-batics,

But truth above the balloon-barrage to infinity sings
And never deigns to sniff on Heil-heil-heil-obatics.

Avaunt, barbarians!
Attila's day is not today;
No Fuehrer-fury will hinder us upon our way;
No "Heils!" and Piazza-puffing will dismay;
No Gestapo keep free men at bay!

Hit, hit, hit us, Hitler,
Put the Duce in your pocket and let him nip, nip, nip us, Hitler;
We'll keep our civilized wit.
For you're both in for a fit, fit, fit, Hitler.

5.

Our mind is a lonely drum
Amid an orchestra of rustling trees;

The flat brown mud is dumb,
But not so the yellow-breasted kiskadees;

Our lips posture in appeal
To that dense and knowledged *cookerit* palm;

But its shadows are mean to reveal,
And our ears sense no balm.

Once we craned our sight to the moon –
Moon over dark-brown stream –
But it spun a circle in our conscience,
And grinned all round and round
And showed its fullness as a moon.

"Over there – the north, the north, I mean –
Not the Corentyne savannah cow-sleepy-mild –
They're using all my glamour for the night;
They're zooming over Bremen, Hamburg and the Ruhr:
It's me, you see, making their targets better seen."

Tell us, Mars, the rendez-vous,
Tell us the setting of your corpse-curtained drama,
Duly censored by the blue curve of Space
(Full whereabouts would be useful to the enemy).
In the fired northern air (not the exact front or place)?
In Britain and the Rhine – or off Finisterre?
Or deep perhaps within the sluggish drift
Of these brown-watered streams,
Within the hum and buzz of insects – cheet! Tiff-tift!
Inter-preying insects
Upon each other's abbreviated scheme for living?

Is this your drama: the insects?
Or the men in Spitfires?
The men in funeral-pyres?
The men in overalls? Or the children flayed?
The women-corpses in totalitarian death?
(Civilians are in this, too. They are undismayed)
Or me in creation wriggling in my wicker-seat?
(Wicker-seats squeak like Nazi pigs).
Or just the metal – raw material refined into tanks –
Clashing in an awful frictioned heat?

                          6.

I met a woman on the burnt-earth lane
One midnight when the moon was on the wane:

An East Indian woman moving laden home,
Vegetables on her head and baby-bulging belly like a sideways dome.

And portently my soul mumbled from its anticipated grave:
"In twenty years this belly-bulge may be a brave

When nations once again make somersault and rave;
But you, of course, being an artist, cannot help to save

Either now or then your country, because you'd fain
Make images and mango-coloured dreams in imaginative rain."

I met a negro fellow casual-talking,
And he wagged and wagged his forty-greying head;
"In de las' war," he said,
"Ah serve in Palestine, Ah serve in German East,
An' den we went to Egypt,
An' we serve dere till de whole t'ing ceased."

In Palestine.
In German East
And Egypt in the Middle East –
Why did the tinsel of these name-sounds
Make a white rebound like bright sand-mounds
Revealing Wavell's tanks all battle-caterpillared?

Scherzo:

What! What say you?
Oh, no, not true!

Sidi Barrani has been taken! – Our troops
Are surrounding Bardia! – How many prisoners? – oh, whoops!
Ten, twenty thousand flabbergasted dagoes
Are streaming gunless toward the Sphinx – oh, goops!
Oh, silly, silly Betty Boops!
Watch them in the newsreel!
Eating a weary, weary sandstorm meal!

All those macaroni-eating dagoes!

Tobruk tumbling, too?
Tobruk making old Ansaldo rue?

But Benghazi will give us trouble
Benghazi will not crumble into rubble.

What! What say you?
Oh, no, not true! Not true!

Our troops have taken Benghazi now?
Woe, woe, Ansaldo! Oh, what a wow!

Finale:

When the celebration-bottle pops and clinks,
When the Hurricanes roll
The final victory roll
And the army-drums in continuation roll

And the jungle-thunder augments the roll with its primeval roll:
Roll roll roll – the Empire, Europe and the world a-roll –
The trade-wind, humming in imitation-roll,

Murmurs to our soul:

"Did you – did you artist enroll?"

Teach us to live.

Teach us where reality moves profound,
If actual things abound
In red conflicting horror objectively achieved,
In frontiers welded, moved and wrought –
By Dictators bombed, twisted, thwarted, sent to naught,
Or with the labouring lovers in their rhythmed prelude:
Ecstasy and sighs for the coming human scene:
Climax producing fodder for the distant tragedies;
Or merely in the tangled torture of an artist's dreams,
With obbligato of coconut fronds a-sizzling;
The rice-men in earnest reaping
And the sackies' inner cheeping;
In the warm-chill rain prosaically a-drizzling,

Teach – adjust us for living.

New Amsterdam,
British Guiana, March 16, 1941.

MOOD OF FEBRUARY 11ᵀᴴ 1940

Our bodies like powder
And the warm wind
Spirited through our pores
And our flesh that is not quite seen
Because it is dust
In the warm wind here...
The thick wind with clouds
Coming overhead and pillowing into
Woollen grey and white
But mostly grey on white
And our flicker of visions...
Our imagery in the dust.

The day makes to near noon
So let us trudge on through the heat
And feel the padded wind
Going through our brave limbs
And all the imagery
That cannot be dispelled
Because our bodies are sometimes flesh and urge
And not always powder
And the wind cannot always cool
The excitement of our imagery.
So let us trudge on
Trudge on through the heat
And sound heroic grunts
And swing our lean limbs
Against the glare of the near-noon
And let us feel that our bodies
Are hard like metal grounded

For grounded metal may cloud
The agitation of our imagery
And keep our minds on railroads
That parallel into a waiting goal...
A goal receptive to our bodies
That are sometimes warm and wanting
And not always cool like dust.

REALITY

Reality is a steely, bitter wind;
It numbs the scent of saffron flowers,
Veiling the blue of bluebells
Softly poised,
Cool in compassion of this morning's dew.
Cigarette smoke is incense to this body;
It pierces a myriad sweetened tunnels
Deep beyond the lungs and heart.

But reality, a steely, bitter wind,
Filters through a million myriad funnels,
Galling the incense
Gritting the lungs and heart.
And even the looming realness of this face,
Serene o'er with beauty tulip-pink,
Chills and sadly wilts
As though a shroud of phantom lace
Had blown against its simple solidness.
For, yes;
Reality is a steely, bitter wind.

FOR ME – THE BACK-YARD

Play your Carnival, play your masque,
Dance with your Country Club set,
Hop, jump at your midnight fete;
For these things I'll never ask –
Take them all and leave for me
The back-yard scene at dusk:
The haze of blue wood-smoke,
Morning mist amid mango leaves
And the nancy-story fantasies
That the cries of kiskadees
From long, long ago evoke.

Keep your calypsos and your steel-bands!
Wiggle your hips and waggle your hands!
For me the good soft tingling dew
And mottled shadows beneath a guava tree,
The glimmer, the dim mysterious hue,
Of coconut fronds – spider hands
Immobile, immeshed in the filigree,
The plaited pattern, of star-apple and plum,
Breadfruit and mango – and the perpetual hum
Of all the insects hidden in jumbie-lands:
The magic a waning moon can weave; set free.

Let the saxophones quark and wail!
And pianos thump a jiving jumbled tale!
For me the ruby warmth in sunshine,
The haphazard tracery of this wild vine,
Coconuts a-sizzling,
Water-vapour in the air,
A red cock crowing, the clatter of a pail,
The swift white drift
Of clouds in the cool trade wind,
A whiff of rice and salt-fish cooking
And of earth, dank, dark and bare.

Keep your serge suit, collar and tie!
Asparagus, lentils, your high-falutin apple-pie!
Keep your respectability; I don't care!
For me the sun, the dew, the leaves, the wind –
And why should I even spurn
These little ragged clumps of fern
And the rickety latrine standing near
The old grey-trunked tamarind!
Assuredly for me – the naive back-yard
Where *bajak* ants, without hypocrisy, troop by
And no gentlemen politely smile and lie.

DOVE ON GASPAREE

To go on holiday,
expecting quiet banalities
and to hear the solitary moan
of this mysterious bird
subtly among dry-weather shrubs…
"I haunt the noon," it calls to you,
"the evening and the noon…
Far away or near,
I haunt the evening and the silence of your room."

To hear this bird whose portentous rue
is laden with the spawn
of cooled desires reconceived
and the sum of yesterday's fancies…

"For the dead I utter a rune,
for the far-buried dead; a rune
for Apodaca and his burning ships
and for poor Chacon, too –
even the galleons under the moon –
a rune… a rune…"

To hear this bird,
and watch spider-webs frail
against volcanic rock,
nostalgic as old lattice-work
viewed beyond the four-poster's tester-rails…
"Soon for you – oh, not too long,
but soon for you,
a touch on the shoulder – a tap;
the skeleton-finger, fool –
for all of you… soon."

To hear this lonely bird,
and to watch in the green and rippling bay
a boat's noon-white sails,
is to evoke the unpredictable –
ghosts that sleep
in cocoon-quiescence
amid the stillness of this island-day…"

"A rune… a rune for you…"

IN THE BEGINNING – NOW – AND THEN

In the beginning was the Work,
and the Work was made ice and rock
fragment without words or logic –
out of the cooling of tall fires.
A few bare strands beckoned
the prime response to swimming cells,
and all the cells waited
for the bigger beckonings to come:
the dark winds within dappled stirrings,
swirl of swift lights and greater glooms,
sudden nodules, softly spurted blades –

Then the gash of silence;
a hush of hidden pullulation,

Red twilight,
unheard blasts,

Before the first protozoa
bubbled, paused, headed
the horn-summons of the Spirit

and become Life.

Lo and woe!
The Work launched, committed,
swelled and suspired,
and the Spirit urged
subordination of Matter
and sounded the first drone of strife:
sad, but needed, friction,
for without strife, without friction,
ice would have remained ice,
rock rock, silence silence.

Some strands turned fishes,
large and serrate, crooked;
small with tails and barbed whips.
Small fishes envied large fishes;
large fishes pounded on small fishes
much-pursued fishes took to land,
hardened, changed, arranged new schemes, but

never without a muttering,
always with a clamour,

For in struggle lies salvation,
survival and ever painful,
warm regeneration –

and to the weaker, without doubt,
must come annihilation.

So to the armoured saurians,
the half-bats and quarking monsters
amid the mist and swamp and rocks;
the Flesh was being distilled;
the Flesh fumed and stank;
the Flesh crowed and capered
and snarled and groaned – bowed
to the blind Mind behind all urge.

Lo and woe!
And here today stands the Work,
after a multitude of trumpets,
shaken by catacombal drums.
Here today is the Flesh
elegantly fashioned; today
infinite refinements;
extravaganzas of colour;
sounds of cacophonous dolour;
aberrant fancies in paint, stone,
mime and word.

Oh, lo and woe!

The Work advances,
defeating, destroying itself
even while it distils
more and more complex elixirs.
The Work goes on and on,
as it was in the beginning,
as it is with us now,
and in far tomorrows will be:
the aspiring, struggling, heated,
self-defeating,
undefeatable Work.

PITCH-WALK MOOD

When I loll on this green bench,
savannah-grass behind me and the hills,
and view going by
the cavalcade of many-tinted faces,
each mobile with its spate of dreams,
I sometimes wonder at the destiny
that cooped within frail fleshly cases
such vital, vivid entities:

hates, loves, stupidity and greed –
at the purpose, the wandering streams
that feed the ever-surging need
for life and more life
and still more pullulatating life;
at the fertilizing of the seed
that curves the belly of this girl;
the naivety of this olive tot
with dusky cheek and tender hand –
another fool, perhaps, who knows?
Or will he, in twenty years,
with pen or voice contumely hurl
upon his fellows now mewling, too,
and slash awake a thousand fears
to quicken the leaven of his native land?–

Yes, who knows?
Who knows the purpose,
the livid formula, of life,
or the reason for our morbid strife?
And don't you sometimes wonder why we fuss
over piddling coins and rustling slips?

And to what end?

When does the cavalcade reach the final bend,
and what vista lies beyond the bend?
Angel-wings among the clouds weaving,
or the sinners' hell?
or, for like atheist me – just *dunkel Abend?*
Perpetual, perpetual dark evening!

So what! This bench is green,
like the grass where insects procreate unseen,
and the hills – ah, what a noble looming screen!
Let's forget the faces, boy,
and breathing deep,
not wonder what they mean.

MEDITATIONS OF A MAN SLIGHTLY DRUNK

I came, and they drunkened me lightly
With a medley of liquors.
There was falernum,
There were literary disagreements,
Poetical dissonances.
Yes, but chiefly there was rum.

They talked to me of stanzas,
The ancient and the very modern.
They broached even painting,
Haggled about form,
Over Epstein concorded with reverence.
Yes, but chiefly there was rum.

We jabbered of pendulums,
Pendulums that swung like my vision.
They gesticulated and bawled –
Ranting about matter,
Eulogizing imagery.
Yes, but never forgetting the rum.

We slashed at Swinburne,
And we justly kicked old Kipling.
We grimaced dreadfully at Pater,
How we hacked poor Donne,
And sniffed at Rupert Brooke!
Though, always, always, mind,
There was the rum!

THE VIRGIN

I sat one afternoon and watched
A virgin pass,
A virgin, poor lass,
Withering slowly on her Dead Sea shore,
Where the tide of years had lapped before
And left her now to plod,
Alone, alas –

OCTOBER SEVENTH

In me I am troubled,
For the night is stilled,
This moon a lone, dim globe;
In me I am filled
With unsettling passions
That itch as a woollen robe;
For the night is warm –
Yea, stilled and weird,
And I am troubled.

This night did I see Eugenie,
Eugenie this night was sad,
Yea, troubled,
For the trees did see me a cad,
The trees that were quiet
In this unbreathing night.

Yes, in me I am troubled,
By some hungry want
That stirs in the hollow of me,
And will haunt,
Will haunt me long after
This night with my passion,

This night is warm and stilled,
Hath been brushed aside,
In my usual fashion,
With a smile and a chuckle –
And my empty laughter.

ISLAND TINTS

Sound is a special kind of trembling
garnered by a waiting tympanum, and,
through the distilling process of a brain,
translated into endless wraiths and portents –
or merely reportorial communication.
Colour, too, is a special kind of trembling
but garnered by a retina. "I sometimes
think that never blows so red the rose", or
"far from these carrion kites that scream below"
are specimens of colour – the kind of colour
which exists as colour only because
it has been converted into mirrors and mirages
through the machinery of intoxication
set into motion by the optic nerves
of lucubrating, vacillating homo sapiens.

Accept an invitation to adventure
with this specific tremor: to explore
the labyrinths – tumble into valleys –
of fantasy and satire and seeming lunacy.

Colour is a squirming, sur-realistic thing.
Colour contains a hooked and awkward
Dada-istic sting.

Our eyes, weighted still with sleep,
can watch, unfevered and detached,
a cloud-pencil floating clear above
the dawn – of a solemn umber tint,
horizontal, and so suggestive of
contentment and quiescence. (But
this is the hour of deception,
of muffled contemplation and inaccurate
speculation). It awaits the cue
to write off the night,
is alert for the word to act,
for the word still unheard –
the word that crouches in the outer Void
where, presumably, Gautama Buddha swirls,
an entity dissolved, diffused – Jesus,
perchance, and Confucius, too –
unshackled from the passions
of an earthly *karma*, unjoined forever
from scintillating *maya*; from the hundred-
thousand manifestations of make-believe,

awaits the sign to redecorate the east
with tints of violet known alone,
perhaps, to flowers that, in solitude,
enrich some brambled dusk – a version
of yellow or of red that the sting-ray
exclusively has observed in submarine
fastnesses, and in rock-caves that
howl beyond the breakers on a hoodoo shore;
other subtler, ephemeral hues existing –
you and I will never know – beyond yonder line
of mangrove-mud and distant, secret *courida* trees:
a palm-berry crimson, or cobalt
in an orchid's belly, high up the Canje;
not quite crimson and not quite
cobalt, but just rare, very rare
indefinable tints: vibrations that
no eye – not even Picasso's – can
decide for sure as this or that;
sound and colour in hybrid assonance,
but beyond the power of Gertrude Stein
to amalgamate and synthesise.

Or merely the old and ordinary tints –
fresh within the morning's chill,
though antique: the antique gamboge welling
out of the flame of the antique mauve
welded in stealth to the mystery
of purple and the gloom of indigo – indigo,
mayhap, that is an echo steeped
in the last sunset's lapis lazuli:
a spiritual hue in which the peace of trees
alone may dwell and pass all understanding.
The old tints viewed a thousand mornings
from the walls of Ur and Babylon – yea,
and Sumer – and even before, by the dinosaur
and plesiosaur. (Unwelcome they may have been
for the pterodactyl, still hungry
from a vain nocturnal hunt, flapping haunted wings,
but gaunt, lizard-wise, toward the sepia
sanctuary of a slimy cave; in there
are monsters green and ultramarine –
griffons with fiery eyes, fretted tails
whose quarks make avalanching thunder
on a fabled landscape; a landscape harsh
and run amok with humps; concave where
swamps subsided in a greying stench
and left a saffron grin of slush

edged with gravel gnarled but of a pure,
fresh, brilliant burnt-sienna brown).

Colour is a gnashing, pristine thing.
Colour possesses an acrid bark and
a crisp, elusive wing.

Recline and watch a change of hues –
the range from dark – a tint debatable
merely because it is dark – to rose-madder
(tincture of gentian), thence to the
murky blue of corrosive sublimate always
recalling newspaper suicides, and to bright pink –
sea-shells on Worthing beach, Barbados –
or that more significant pink – the pink
of Caucasian skin: complexion of
a ruling people (God bless the Secretary
of State for the Colonies!). Glance beyond
the wing-tip of our droning machine
at the naive and ragged cumuli, for now
we proceed ten thousand foot above
incipient day. Through the misted void
we can observe with casual awe
(we are sophisticated travellers)
the verdured humps of our island fade –
that island Columbus, in a religious moment,
named after God the Father, the Son
and the Holy Ghost; though Columbus
did not see it from a nimbus-edge.

It has faded, and only dawn militates
upon a sea coal-black with height,
and our machine lows in defiance –
a bull lowing at an infinite savannah
to boost its courage, to insulate its ego
against the curdling solitude
of a brinkless waste.

Presently, a phantom arm appears
reaching out from amidst the warring brume,
and soon spreading back to reveal
the body remote but real: of a nebulous shade,
though, with lessened height, dullish blue
changing into dullish green.
A body hirsute with drought; shaggy
and shamed into such a hue
as only concoction on a painter's palette

can arrive at: Prussian blue – a fleck
fused with a greater fleck of yellow-ochre
and an invading smear of crimson lake,
resulting in a greenish brown that
sits static in our optic dreams.

A body stern with ancient rock, but
ancient rock sombre after aeons
of pyrotechnic riot; mollified by trees.
A mere, yet momentous, interruption
in a dark-blue sea – one of a crescent
of momentous interruptions. A body
cautiously crumbled – a trifle corroded
on the skin; bearing a brave patina
where palms, nutmegs and tufted canes
may sprout and spread an economic mantle
for the wrangling over and the tangled
shouts of raucous, rowing humankind.

A body, as seen today from aloft,
stacked with many eyes; carmine, terra-cotta,
buff and brown; and in shape rectangular;
results of the constructive manipulations –
just habitations – of irrepressible,
depressible, competitive humankind.

The name grins in concrete letters
on the airport building – *Grenada* it grins
above a cluster of living grins
on faces sallow, sienna, coffee-brown:
faces weighted with a glut of smugness;
faces mounted on a plinth of bygone planters;
moulded on coals of Gallic heat,
tempered with a Saxon frost.
Faces, very-near-white, near white,
not-so fair, light-olive, most
emphatically olive, pale brown,
and some crowned with kinky hair, to boot!
For dat Zambesi – oh, dat river!
It never, it never was a lady!
It got a past, it deep, it deep and shady!
Shut, shut you' eyes and watch
a belaboured legion rasping chains,
surviving jungle-treks, slave-ship stench –
thus, lo! unwittingly, we have slithered
down the prickly, aromatic vale
of miscegenation, sociology and discrimination:

a theme as inevitable in these isles
as the sight of shadowed hills.

Colour is a swirling, dynamic thing.
Colour has a turgid skin and a mumbled,
suspicious buzzing.

But out of it and return
to serious contemplations
of the rainbow's permutations
(for the time for rhyme is near).
Here's a clutter of fishes in a seine:
dozens, hundreds, blue and scarlet-lake,
some spotted amber – here, there a lemon flake;
rock-hine, queen-mullet and silvery snappers,
all vicious, cold and toothy flappers –
jumping, flapping, jumping, clumped together,
in the dripping seine, for hell and leather!

Please watch them – coloured fishes all –
occupied, preoccupied, with dying
on Grand Anse beach: a spattering,
hopping, magnificent, glittery animation
preceding death.

To die like a speckled fish in a seine,
your pink, raw gills in burning pain,
engaged in jitters on a flat, white beach,
the cool, green waves far out of reach,
seems an ignoble way to beguile
a brown-faced audience – even for a while.
But this audience knows the growling ache
that only deflated stomach's make.
This is an audience clad in rags,
not inured to mincing, highbrow gags.
This audience dwells in roof-torn shacks,
having never worn sharkskin slacks,
nor an evening-suit and gold shirt-studs,
or a corsage of Marechal Neil rose-buds,
and so to them this piscine show
signifies the wherewithal to make life go,
to keep the thick, vermillion blood a-glow.

Now, turn, and having gazed
upon that priggish little town
aloofly red and buff and raised
on steepish hills, a shop-worn crown,

wonder at the kind of ghosts
that left behind such rusty folk
as move among the stony walls and posts
of this town that never woke,
this town that moulders in a trance,
merged in a smug religious pall,
where Wesleyans frown upon the dance
and all young men have heard the Call.

Oh, yea, oh, yea!
All is proper, English, insipid-gay.
No dragons, no dragons here
for brave St George to slay!

And so to bend and peep
through a wall cracked with streams
that have their source in Grand Etang –
no bottom, they say, to this lake,
will ever be found by knave or brave.
But come! To peep beyond the cracks:
cracks not really stream (that
was our sur-realistic fancy rumbling
as Grand Etang once rumbled, for
it behaved in antique times
as did Stromboli, Etna or Pelee).

Peeping, we can note
that afternoon tea is over,
and the ladies now are smiling
sweet and bleary smiles.
Sallow, olive, pale-brown ladies
more refined than Great-grandpa Mac
or Great-grandpa Harris of early times.
Well-bred ladies on a nutmeg isle,
as good as those in Glasgow, Brighton
or Cornwall, only that their hair, alas!
Their Hair is Not so Good;
dat shady, shady Zambesi – oh, dat river!
It simply, it simply will not be denied!

"You," says one lady gazing coyly
at the dregs of an empty cup,
"will have a letter. So say
the leaves." And to another:
"You – I see a dark man, Mary,
in your life. Now, dear! Beware!"

Colour is a queer, satiric thing.
Colour holds an acid hiss, and functions with
a clownish spring.

Of high colour, that lady over there!
She directs her chin at the innocent sky,
and states in effect to you and me
of umber, humbler hue! "Me? I'm sorry,
but I simply do not mix with him and her
who do not coincide with me in shade!
Oh, no my dear! These niggers
are too presumptuous. You see
my hair? Good hair! You see
my skin? Fair skin? You see
my nose? High nose!" Of high,
high colour, that lady over there!

Colour is a phantom, fascinating thing,
a futile, fumbling thing,
emits a perverse, perverted ring.

Our eyes, weighted with approaching sleep
can watch, unfevered detached,
many a hooded wraith float through
the night – a solemn cavalcade of
Caribs, Frenchmen, English, and
the dark Zambesi exiles a-whimpering…
Du Parquet is among them, and
the sinister Hugues in company
with the planter – the coloured planter,
Julien Fédon… The drought-dry hills
are haunted, and if we listen we can hear
the midnight shrieks at Grenville:
Fédon hauls the townsfolk from their sleep
to cut their throats for the Brigands'
War is on – and that was 1795, long after
those falling, vanishing gouts of sound
from brown men leaping into space…
"Death," they scream, "death before capture!"
And the Frenchmen watch unblinking.
"Death before capture!" scream
the Leapers, leaping always,
and the Frenchmen shudder and exclaim:
"Mon dieu! C'est insupportable!
Quels hommes! Quels sauteurs!"
The echo goes on and on
to now: Morne des Sauteurs!

But where are they today, these wraiths?
With Gautama Buddha dissolved, diffused?
With Jesus and Confucius in the outer Void?
Or are they shackled still to *karma*,
awaiting their cue to return
to this scene of scintillating *maya*,
to rejoin the stream of make-believe?

Our eyes, weighted with approaching sleep,
can watch a cloud-duster floating in the west.
The decorations, one by one, imperceptibly,
are being rubbed out – liquidated
at the order of the Voice unheard.
The sea smiles back deep violet hues,
orange and a gaudy red.

The hills behind us strive
to spin a reticule of blue,
but the spiritual tint will not
be lured – no lapis lazuli;
no lapis lazuli tonight!
The peace of trees has passed
and will not return to be examined,
analysed – and understood.
This is the murmured swan-song,
the suspired perdendosi,
the bowing out in uncertainty:
muffled contemplation, inaccurate
speculation; trapped within mirrors
and mirages, flickering in the cogs –
the machinery of intoxication…

The sea roars remotely…
a car toots in the twilight…
and that –
that must have been
a green jumbie
hissing.

Colour has a soft-toned tread…
this blue, this vague red
dwell with the dead.

FOR BETTER THINGS!

Tomorrow's sunrise can't simulate to-day's,
nor to-day's breeze lure back the fragrance
that was yesterday's; nor the sun's rays
that whitened our minds – the live thoughts, the vagrants
strayed from nowhere to heat and depress our dreams
impinge upon these our diverse days,
or add one fork of fire to our current schemes:
yearning into space for a star that's not there,
seeking the golden-egged goose that never lays.

For better things, better men and better ways,
for better houses – no bugs or lice,
better work – no strikes, no wish to laze,
politicians sincere and men without vice,
Lebensraum for all who shout for elbow-room
and art for art's sake on which to gaze,
food a-plenty and never a cause for gloom,
reaching into space for the real star that's there!
finding the golden-egged goose that always lays!

Ask me how to shape these better things,
ask me where to find these better men;
if they're hiding in the palaces of kings
or in some foul beggar's miserable den.
Ask me about all those houses without bugs,
ask me about the politicians, the work –
the work without strikers lazers, bums or thugs
and the art and the food a-plenty,
and the star and the golden-egged goose.

Ask me, but I can't tell you where you'll find them
all I can tell you is about guns
and big armies with other armies to stem,
one thrusting here while the other runs.
Ask me, but I can't tell you of better things
than warplanes, bombs and *Flammenwerfers,*
torpedoed men with crushed legs and battered heads
fire-bombs flaring, people blown up in their beds.

Those are the best things I have to tell,
for about what other things the future brings
when I ask myself I only hear a knell.

So don't ask me.
Ask the stars for better things!

[This poem is one incorporated in the text of the latest book, Better Things!
It's a war novel and this poem was supposed written by the hero who is a poet.]

EVENING AT STAUBLES TRINIDAD

For Ruthie

The lateness makes it ruby:
Sunshine chalking soft gold
On the soft receptiveness of mosquito-mesh,
And penumbra-ed shadows of coconut fronds
Soft, too –, like X-Ray fingers
Shifting filmy and cool on mosquito mesh.

A benign pleasantness,
An unusual breeze,
Rushing through the twitter of afternoon birds
And over the green roofs – from the red roofs
Of Gaspar Grande – from Centipede Island –
And the lonely Pattos –
Over the bay with green-clear water in sparkles:
Unhurrying glass-green water all choppy
In sunshine ruby with lateness.

And the milk of mist mysterious
On the mountains of Venezuela:
A fairyland already chilled with evening,
Purple and mesmerized in the grey north-west;
Cowering tombs, you feel –
Andean crypts that were dream-cities
Bearing a patina of dead escapades –
Ghost-galleons of the Skull-and-Bones
And sunken men and trove –
Sulky beneath the indigo feather of night
Reaching out from the Spanish Main.

POET CREATING

To Ruth

Oh My Poor Old Brain.
Why must I create and create?
What Lernian Hydra with unresting mania
Impels my pen, compels my mind
To feed and feed and sate
Its many mouths – its all-hungry yearning bellies?
To root, delve, to rummage and to find
This thought, that truth, this hue and tint
Until the very wracked timbre of my being
Reels and quivers like a noisy mint,
Coining words and dreams and potent jellies?–

And no peace, no peace for me –
No cooling wind, no shade of tamarind tree
To give me respite from this surging thing;
No wizard-wand from out the burning day
To touch my spirit and wake me free.

TO THE MEMORY OF KEN JOHNSON

(*For Ruth – In secret memory of our furious argument on the backdam on Tuesday evening, 1941*)

Cabbage palms are more pleasant than bombs:
The depth of solemn green
And soft sizzle of fronds in twilit air;

Dull barrage in the night
And the drone and careen
Of metal pencils overhead – here, now over there –
Dorniers gaming with the shifting prongs of white
Cannot pullulate such abundant peace
As these afternoons on our Guiana coast
Drifting with a saffron glow,
Making way in leisured release
For the naivety of cool moonlight;

No can incendiaries ignite more glory
Than the moon in tinsel fragments on the river –

Pause and ponder on our lot.

We here whose only vivid story
Is the story of flambouyants red and fragrant-hot
And the sun on burnt-earth country lanes;
We here, who without fear and qualms,
Powder cool our-lungs with tropic breeze
And suck smug-serene the juice of canes:
Lounge and listen to the rustle of our palms;

Pause – and for an instant change the site.

Ponder on the misty-distant north and forget the mirth;
Watch men stride through the yellowed flashing night:
Laugh and defy and dance from Portsmouth to Perth –
A gush of flame – thud and splinters – anguished gout of earth!

Forget the palms and the white clouds in the sky:
Red country lanes and the contented sigh –

And think of now and then –

How now and then –
Here in this street – there in that cafe –
Now and then,
One of them jolts and falls:

One of these daring men.

JUST BETWEEN US

(In memory of last night at Betty's)

We saw them as we walked:
Street-lights turned in magic-sparkling pearls in evening air –
Ruth, with shifting moods, delectable, and myself.
And we heard them as we talked:
The rabble in creole-jabber along the street.

Sitting in a tiny friendly parlour,
We listened to night-noises blue and vague outside:
Ruth, full of whimsy, delectable, our friends and I;
A strange bird gurgling and some jumbie-sigh,
As we talked of omens, past things, present, people who had died.

And once we paused to crane our ears
For sounds from out the purple dark: the goblin-dreaming trees;
Distant guitar-thrumming and patter of fleeting fears;
On our way home watched Sirius and the paler stars
Sprinkle radium honey-dust like night-time ghosts turned bees.

Ruth, full of hopes and schemes, delectable, and myself.

(1941)

DEATH IN PROSPECT

Dimly...
Suave...
But so deadly soon –
The maimed and the mean and the brave;
And when the Gaunt Man treads – clip-clop,
When auricle and ventricle halt and pump,
And, halting, pump and pump – and stop:

Let there be soft fanfare.

Down into the glass-green sea,
Quick into ashes with electric fire,
Or if they settle what is left of me
With just the dank earth-worms-
With all the common fellows in the mire,

I shall not care,

For I shall be a rustling in the gloom;
A shadowed breathing in a room –
And how I shall smile to watch
The same old drumming pageant onward move:
Birth at dawn;
Babies into warriors, into poets, into gun-men –
To trumpet-blaze at noon;
And the clerks in their groove –

The dull and the beauteous and the brave –

Unto evening
Approaching like a purple rumour then:
Dimly...
Suave...
But so deadly soon.

(1941)

REALITY AT MID-DAY

Times happen when our minds dwell upon decay;
Rottenness at our door and within our den,
A rat grey in the sunshine dead
And skins of fruit in an alleyway –
The stink and uncertainty in the doings of men:
Quarrels, intrigues, the gossip with which we're fed;

Times happen when our minds are warped with strain:
Awaiting and dreaming and loving; and waiting
A haven of quiet, some far retreat –
A turmoil like serpents and wasps in the brain:
Things surging, heroic flights, despair and things hunting,
So that sighs and chuckles merge and strange pulses beat;

Times, too, when our bodies long, to crack asunder
Dampened and fevered, hungry for that or this:
The unique companion, the love that is real –
And the pitch of life rolls to a desperate thunder:
A too screaming conflict – a stammer of death, existence and bliss
So that thought grows numb and tingling nerves cause to feel;

Yes, times happen like this –
Happen like this when reality looms stark,
When illusions have been flogged into whimpering things,
When eventide visions have become dust in the glare of day –
When living is no more a leaf-green, cycling lark,
When the morning wren no longer honey-tone sings
And when,
Yes, when the swan-song of youth is heard
Coming, winging in the trade-wind
Not too far – not too far away.

MAZARUNI ROCKS

A dog howling recalls primeval mists
And a time of rocky earth without animalcula,
So that chunks of Mazaruni rocks piled in a pyre
Welded in greys and the blues and blacks
Of twilight-aeons: an age of gestating silence
Leave our minds in the void thinking
Of brutal conflict and cathartic fire –
Fire distilling silica and diabase from bones,
Blood, protoplasm and the hairs of unborn men
Which, rasped crystalline compact in utter cruelty,
Steeped in the acid guts of deathless unions,
Torn and gashed and shaken cataclysmically,
Knew only storm and panting; rabid licence.

Now we can merely gape at this massed oneness
Composite of greys and the blues and blacks
Of twilight-aeons: an age of brume –
A stolid testament of haze and gestating silence.

AFTERNOON REFLECTIONS

If we could fly through time –
Five, ten years in the sough of a breath inhaled –
And light a top the silvered hills
We try in vain to climb;
If we could dust away the sundown red
And smear upon the east the sunrise pink,
The blare of ochre, the morning tints
Of the dreamed day: the yearned for hour;

If one could shut one's eyes
And in a pregnant humming second
Open them again upon huge splashes of gold:
Barrels of silver and ivory jewels
And a panorama of undulating green:
Dark brown streams and dimly whispering wooded haunts
And small red bungalows: just a few

If we could make things cease to linger:
Bombs and armies and dictators,
Guns, U-boats and the winging squadrons –
The Panzer units, too –

All at the gesture of one slim finger.

ESSAYS

NEW AMSTERDAM

New Amsterdam is a town from which many have escaped, never to return. Yet it is a lovely little town. From the middle of the estuary, when you are on the ferry-steamer, the town really has a picture postcard look. The two steeples of the principal churches, the Anglican and the Presbyterian, jut up like clean, white flower-pistils out of the reds and pinks and greyish-whites and the greens that go to make up a sort of limp bouquet spread out along the eastern bank of the river. Cabbage and coconut palms and samaan trees, mango trees and sandbox trees, innumerable flowering shrubs, go to make up the greens, and the pinks and reds and greyish-whites are the wooden cottages, one-storey and two-storey, with their red-painted roofs, or, in some cases, shingled or of plain corrugated iron that looks blueish-grey from a distance. A peaceful, pleasing sight New Amsterdam makes from mid-estuary, and with the amber-tinted water of the river in the foreground, and the bright-blue sky of a dry-weather day overhead, it is more than a peaceful, pleasing sight. It is a technicolour photographer's dream.

When the ferry-steamer draws nearer to the town, however, the mudflats begin to show up, and these are not so pleasing a sight. They are ugly –riddled with crab-holes, overgrown in places with straggly grass and weedlike plants – and right at the edge of the lapping water, they look soft and slimy, and you can imagine yourself sinking with a horrible squelch waist-deep...

Mud has been the enemy of New Amsterdam for decades. In the eighteenth century, Crab Island was a tiny mud-bank in the middle of the river-mouth, decorated with a few courida trees. But with the years, it grew and grew in size until today it is well over a mile long and a quarter of a mile in width. On the eastern side, the channel between it and the mainland has grown so shallow from silting that at low tide you can wade across it. And while Crab Island grew in size, the mud that helped to build it up also helped to build up the mud-flats alongside the town. As the mud-flats grew wider, the stellings had to be extended outwards, and today the ferry stelling is a quarter of a mile in length, and could be longer than this, for the ferry steamer often touches bottom when the tide is low.

In Dutch days – that is, before 1803 – New Amsterdam was the capital town of the colony of Berbice which was a separately governed territory. In fact it was not until 1831 that Berbice was officially combined with its neighbours of the West – Demerara and Essequibo – and the whole territory dubbed British Guiana.

In the last decade of the eighteenth century, when Abraham van Imbyze van Batenburg held court at Colony House, in the northern part of the town, social life in New Amsterdam was at its peak. The plantations, despite the crippling effects of the slave insurrection of 1763, were in a flourishing state, and the port was active; ocean-going ships came and went as freely as they did in Georgetown, sixty miles west along the coast, at the mouth of the Demerara River.

New Amsterdam is very near to the jungle. You can feel the mystery of unknown tracts of land simply by staring east towards the Canje Creek. There it is all bush where once plantations had flourished. The Canje Creek is really a river well over one hundred miles long – but in Guiana rivers are such large scale affairs that a stream simply a hundred miles long and hardly three hundred yards across at the mouth, as is the Canje, is dismissed as a mere creek. The Essequibo is so wide near the mouth that you cannot see across from one bank to another, and there are large cultivated islands in the estuary. The Berbice is two and a half miles wide between New Amsterdam and Rosignol on the west bank. The Demerara is three-quarters of a mile wide at its mouth. The Essequibo has its source in Brazil, six hundred miles away from the coast. The Berbice is four hundred miles long.

THE CANJE

The Canje branches off on the eastern bank of the Berbice, near Crab Island, and soon after you pass the steel swing-bridge that spans the stream about a quarter of a mile from its mouth, the water turns a deep Vandyck brown, markedly different from the amber, muddy tint of the Berbice and of the lower section in the vicinity of the bridge. Along its bank you see the slim trunks of the mucca-mucca – a fantastic-looking plant seven or eight feet in height with large, arrow-shaped leaves that could be nodding goblin-heads in the uncertainty of a moonlit night. And clumps of what we call missouri grass float down perpetually on the tide. These clumps often carry strange flowering plants in their midst, and insects not usually seen on the coast – occasionally, camoodies, as water boa-constrictors are called in Guiana, can be seen coiled up slyly among the dense weedy clutter of a floating clump. As a boy, I could never resist peering intently at each clump as it drifted past, on the alert for what I might see hidden among these moving chunks of jungle.

During the early nineteen-thirties I used to take long walks along the road that leads to Sandvoort – a narrow road built up of burnt earth. My purpose was simply to get away for a few hours from the stultifying dullness of the town and savour something of the jungle atmosphere of the district. Motor traffic and the occasional shops and cottages of the residents frequently destroyed the illusion of a primeval setting, but here and there I came upon spots where terrain offered to my view only straggly trees – courida chiefly – and swampy rain savannah. I always paused at these spots, sometimes to tease an alligator lying a short distance from the road by throwing pebbles at it. It would bare its teeth and utter croaking sounds, and sometimes make vicious snapping noises as a pebble landed near its snout. And sometimes I would come to a halt and peer cautiously at a black labaria snake lying still in the middle of the red road, then move as cautiously round it and halt again and wait until it had wiggled its way into the grass bordering the road. They are venomous, but do not attack. Only if you tread on them will they strike out. The brown labaria is supposed to be more venomous, and though it does not attack without provocation, it is more touchy than the black.

The peasants along this road live quiet unsensational lives, like peasants in most parts of the world. They are small farmers and cow-minders, Negro as well as East Indian, though for the most part, Negro. And it is the Negroes, descendants of the slaves of the old Dutch plantations, who are occasionally responsible for the little excitement Sandvoort experiences. A number of them indulge in the illicit manufacture of rum – known as bush-rum or bushy – and these moonshiners are sometimes raided by the police, who, however, seldom succeed in catching the culprits red-handed. Bush-rum moonshiners are an extremely loyal group, and their lookout system is excellent. And they have the jungle as an ally. Their stills are generally so well concealed that discovery is not easy.

There are two villages in Berbice county famous for bush-rum – Sandvoort on the lower Canje and Ithaca on the west bank of the Berbice. Ithaca is far more isolated than Sandvoort and the peasants here are militant in their outlook. If the police venture in the district to make a raid they go in strength and well armed. Ithaca is several miles south of the large sugar plantation, Blairmont, and the road that leads to it is not one suited to motor vehicles.

One of the most fascinating experiences, as a boy, was for me to watch the Ferry Bridge, as the steel bridge that spans the Canje Creek is called, being opened to allow schooners to pass up stream on their way to the stellings of the sugar-estates a few miles east or down stream on their way out to sea. Sometimes molasses ships passed through, black metallic-looking monsters that belched even blacker smoke from their funnels. The bridge is about a mile north of New Amsterdam, and not far from the grounds of the Mental Hospital – the only mental institution in British Guiana.

OF CASUARINAS AND CLIFFS
AN ESSAY

WITH a gesture of blasé desolation, an artist in Barbados once said to me: "There's nothing here to paint." And he wagged his greying head and smiled on: "There's just nothing in Barbados to paint."

Two days before when the 'plane was circling to descend and I was seeing for the first time what it looked like, the panorama spread out beneath me at once sent my thoughts to Degas. I said to myself that this might have been a pattern done in pastel by Degas – all these patches of dull greens and browns and soft middle tints. And later, in the car on the way from Seawell, looking around at the gradually undulating countryside, with an old windmill here and a grey stone church there, decrepit shingled cottages and new modern bungalows and, every now and then, a glimpse of too-blue-to-be-true blue sea and fishing-boats I thought that the difficulty of a painter would be not to find something to paint but to wonder what to paint first.

Have you ever found yourself in such a state of uncertainty about something that you not only began to experience a feeling of being baffled but even felt restless and irritable? This was my reaction to casuarinas, for I found them peculiar trees. In something I am writing I have described them as "odd trees… not of the earth", meaning that they lack a spirit of material reality. I don't agree with the popular view that they make weeping sounds. They don't. The sounds they make, I think, are the key to the mystery they inspire. If we could discover what sound it is they make – whether a moaning or a soughing or a swishing or a breathing note too low or too high to register on human ears with any intelligibility – then I think we would have happened upon the secret of their elusiveness and singular charm. I have never yet seen trees that, for me, so defied definition. Sometimes they look quite futile and flimsy, fingering about against the sky, and at other times they don't seem like trees at all, for they have no leaves. What they have appears from a distance like a hairy, indefinite fur that makes you think you might be gazing upon an elaborate mass of fungus that accidentally became attached to a group of slim poles stuck up, haphazard, in the ground. At other times they loom up unexpectedly like ragged, diffused daubs on the distant horizon. Or, on the other hand, you might be approaching one of them when the sun strikes it in such a fashion that it becomes a thing of tantalizing chiaroscuro, wispy and elfish and secretive, casting feathery shadows on the brown film of needles strewn on the ground around its trunk.

From the beach at Cattlewash you can look toward the south-east and see far away a long row of casuarinas high up, unreal and remote along the line of a ridge, the name of which I don't know, except that it is not far from Hackleton's Cliff where the lonely coconut palm stands out as though it were a weather-sign erected and stuck up there against the clouds by the rocky gods of the Scotland District. When its fronds are sharply visible you know that the weather is fine up there on the cliff; when they are hazed you know that a drizzle is falling, and when they vanish you know that heavy rain-clouds are lowering or that a driving sheet of misty rain is attacking the cliff.

I was very much impressed by the aloof, threatening air of this cliff. I think its name suits it remarkably: Hackleton's Cliff. I can't imagine a name more hard and forbidding. Viewed from Bathsheba, this cliff looks not only aloof, threatening, hard and forbidding, but it exudes also an umber dignity: a calm, stolid austerity that you might associate with a figure from Victorian times. Mr. Gladstone, perhaps – or that character of Dickens's, Mr. Gradgrind. Often in gazing up at it from Shepherd's I would feel something in me going out to it with a familiar secrecy as though it were a personality I could communicate with. It seemed to me to have a psyche of intelligence: a knowingness that involved Time and Geology.

But, then, all the terrain in this district inspires one this way.

On the way to Martin's Bay you look up on the right of you, and huge craggy rocks, pitted and gnarled, keep leaning down at you as though poised there specially in waiting for the split moment when you of all people will pass under them. And when the moment does arrive and you pass under one of them you glance up in half-troubled expectancy, waiting to hear some terrible mystic revelation, or, failing that, a grumbling avalanche of sound before the whole mass thunders down on the pathway in an awful blot-out of consciousness.

On the left, those far below you, which the sea smashes against in a constant savagery of ghostly spray, seem less mystic than the ones above you on the right. Those down there seem less possessed of a silent, watching aloofness. They look like monsters on platforms: elemental creatures, jagged-black-toothed, snarling back and defying the blue-green power wantonly attacking them hour upon hour, night and day. You cannot help admiring them. Watching them sometimes, you feel a little belligerent, a little heroic. "I", you tell yourself, "might be a general, and out there – ranged all along out there – are my invincible forts defying the enemy. Perhaps losing by inches – crumbling imperceptibly. But fighting. Grimly. Giving back crashing blow for crashing blow. Stopping them."

Have you ever slept alone in an empty cottage at Martin's Bay, with moonlight on your feet coming in through salt-blurred windowpanes? And a skylight-window rattling as windows are supposed to rattle in haunted houses? But this cottage I mean was, somehow, not in the least ghost-inspiring. It had all the requisite effects, so to speak, but for some reason I felt nothing but a quiet, safe peace sleeping in it. Perhaps it was because there were no spiders. I had taken the lamp all over and searched for spiders which I fear even more than snakes and lions. But, to my amazement, there was not even a wisp of cobweb anywhere. The walls were shiny and sticky from the sea-salt in the air, and perhaps this is the reason why there was not a single verminous insect in the place. All the same, in its way, it was an odd cottage. The peace it inspired, at times, seemed too conscious, too deliberate, and, to my forever morbid imagination, too sinisterly complete.

But not being a character in a ghost story I had nothing strange happen to me. I was up at five-thirty and went out on the beach where fishermen pointed out to me the Well Pit. Just a small patch of water that looks more blue-green than the rest of blue-green water around it. A few jutting rocks mark the spot, too, and foam. The fishermen said that boats had been known to have been sucked down there and never seen again. And when I asked how deep the Well Pit was they told me that its depth had never been fathomed, making me think at once that here would be just the setting for some tale with a tragic end. Imagine your central character plunging into this rough, foaming pool and being never seen again. But plunging would be too melodramatic. And swimming out would be too much like the sentimentality of Miss Florence Barclay in her novel, *Boy*. It would have to be some other way.

But while we are deciding what way, it might not be bad to hark back –just by way of symmetry – to what my artist friend said. "There's nothing here to paint," he said to me, with a gesture of blasé desolation, and wagged his greying head and smiled on: "There's just nothing in Barbados to paint."

Perhaps not. So much depends upon what we are looking for to paint. There are some people who say that Barbados is too much like England and too little like Barbados to be typically West Indian. One clever fellow even told me that English schoolboys ought to be sent to Barbados so that they might learn something about the English, while another fellow amended this by adding: "You mean learn something about the English as the English used to be. In the seventeenth century."

For me, however, I have no argument to brew. I'm content that, paintable or not, English or truly West Indian in spirit, the island (as you might have observed) did give me a little to write about.

CARNIVAL CLOSE-UP

This morning no piercingly chilly drifts of water-vapour flooded down from the hills to make the citizens of Port of Spain snuggle deep into blankets. This morning, unlike other mornings, it was cloudy and warmish. Beyond the thin, wistful crowing of cocks that patterned the greyish outside, I was aware of a sound not always heard at this time of day. The rumble of distant drums. It contrasted vividly with the cock-crowing and the general stillness of things. To my morbid and, I fear, rather martial imagination, it might have been the ominous thunder of artillery. All through my fitful dozing I kept listening to it. Then the clanging toll of the bell at St. Patrick's Church roused me finally. The six o'clock Angelus. It was still ringing when the distant drums took on a sudden alarming animation. In a dramatic crescendo they seemed to billow through the morning air, and all at once hubbub and riot had come.

Jour ouvert – or, as they say in patois, Jou'vert. Yes, the day has opened and from my window I watched the first steel band come clattering and tinkling and clanging along the street. Windows everywhere opened, other sleepy faces looked out. The clouds had lightened, and here and there a spot of pink and a spot of yellow was showing as though in reflection of the colours which so abruptly had bespattered the street.

A straggly group they were, with old biscuit-tins, paint-pots, dustbins, motorcar parts, old bugles, sticks and shack-shacks. They pranced and tramped and hopped and sang, some of them masked, some of them with faces painted in hideous hues, some of them in ragged bathrobes, some in costumes, pirate, clown, priest or any old popinjay might have claimed for his own. *Cela ne fait rien*. This morning it is old Masque. You don't have to care what you wear. After twelve o'clock today, and tomorrow, Mardi Gras – that's when you'll fish out your special costumes and blossom out afresh to startle the world.

And so, for the time being, through the streets – (Tee-bam! Tong, Bimbam!) trams and trolley-buses are held up in intricate traffic jams, but nobody cares. The bands must go through. Neither passengers nor pedestrians are in a hurry this morning. Everybody is in a bubbly, light-hearted mood. The pavements are dotted with confetti. Confetti specks the hair and the shoulders of people going to work and masqueraders alike. The offices and shops are open, but the shop-assistants and office-folk are at windows and doors watching the antics of the passing bands. The thump and clatter of drum and metal, the blare of trumpets and the wail of voices flame up between the looming close-packed buildings of Frederick Street. Work? You making joke, boy! Today is Carnival, oui!

The pavements are lined with spectators, and it is difficult to thread your way through the jostling mass of humanity. Tullum is on sale in trays – and ginger-beer and sugar-cake and pistachio; souse and black pudding. A band goes past, and as the instrumental part of it comes directly abreast of you, you feel the clang and clash of metal deep in the pit of your stomach; you literally taste as well as hear it, and this is not mere exaggeration.

I saw a robber "hold-up" people on foot and in cars at the point of a wooden dagger and pistol.

Rebels in black shirts and tights creep stealthily along, in the middle of the street, with menacing postures at approaching trams. Painted devils hop and gyrate and whoop and whistle, and African warriors in full battle regalia thrust spears at invisible enemies. A doctor, gowned as though for an operation, hurries by, Gladstone bag and stethoscope in hand. "All day, all night play you' masque!" and 'Ah went down Donkey city" ... and "Lal Fung Lee... Low See Ay..."

On and on to noon.

Then the lorries came out. Andrews Liver salts... Top-Notch Rum... Rediffusion... Coca-cola... the *S.S. Alcoa* Pageant... Jive Roosters... West Indian Artists... "Jump in de line and shake you' body-line!" chorus costumed girls crammed tight in the lorries as they drone past, and you can believe me, the girls never fail to illustrate the advice contained in their refrain. Hips waggling, breasts a-joggle, heads nodding, arms waving, they bawl out their chorus to the tune and rhythm of a calypso.

Meanwhile, pageants and competitions are taking place on the Savannah, and the Queen of Carnival is being crowned. Robinson Crusoe, with parrot and sheepskin umbrella, strolls across an improvised stage followed by Jonah in the whale's belly and a human coca-cola bottle. Midnight-raiders, Red Indians, rebels, robbers, the Red Army, Axis war criminals under escort – all parade before applauding crowds in the Turf Club grandstand. The calypsonians and the steel-bands colour the air with jolting splashes of rhythm and such a fantastic kaleidoscope of harmonies as only an abstract painter could portray adequately in terms of visual colour.

The Control Board came in for many digs, sly and direct. One boy went straight to the point and arrayed himself to represent what he labelled himself to be: "The Confusion Board". He wore patches of cotton marked *No Rice, No Tea, No Salmon, No Cheese, No Suits*, and a number of other noes relating to controlled articles. I saw another fellow in a band with a placard on his back that read: "We eat the flour and wear the bag."

On and on, through the night.

Tuesday morning. The riot goes on. The masqueraders are tireless. Sleep is a forgotten necessity. More and more bands materialize, and the streets by noon have become rivers of agitated colour that torrent through the warm day in an ever-swelling roar of madness. Nothing can check the tides of milling, bedecked humanity, nothing can still the clash and clamour of metal, the whoop and whistle of Red Indians, sooty-faced devils, the shrieks and hoots of fantastic sailors and soldiers, the soaring voices of singing clowns and columbines and dragons, the guttural howl of a lone rebel or a lone robber. The human form goes through every conceivable contortion – arms and legs wave and whirl and writhe; torsos curve and sway and lurch; heads nod and shoulders, hips and breasts contribute a shivering obligato; it is a symphony of mime and motion, with variations so infinite, your vision blurs from very bewilderment.

In Woodford Square, a masked, costumed lady of voluptuous build, embraced me lovingly. "I was wishing to meet you," she murmured huskily.

"You were?" I said.

"I'm Doris," she nodded. "Come along with me to the Hotel de Paris."

But I was out for pictures not pleasure, so I put something in her purse, made her pose for a picture along with a friend who had strolled up, snapped her and proceeded.

An African warrior yells wildly and lunges at you. Cracked trumpets and crazy trombones add dissonance to the din... "Ole sport!" the creole voices cry. "Ole spote!... Ole spoh-h-ht!"... "Doctor, me belly a hurt me! Doctor, gimme an injection..."

Everywhere I looked a sprinkling of khaki figures met my eye. American soldiers with cameras. White-clad sailors, too – with cameras. Marines – with cameras. Puerto Rican soldiers stamped and whirled and writhed like any of the rebels and devils. Spanish now and then jolted the ear, making new cacophony in an already indescribable din.

And still the melee goes on. Flags and banners slash blue, red, green segments out of space, and confetti drizzles down from balconies in diffused showers, speckling heads and shoulders that bob and shake in unheeding abandon. Everywhere is colour, colour. Colour splotches the grey of walls, the black asphalt, the drab sides of trolley-buses and trams. Faces are black and red with paint, or red and brown, or pink and yellow. Blue silk shimmers in the sun, and orange silk, and emerald silk and purple silk. The rainbow in shamed into buff neutrality... "Lai Fung Lee... Low See Ay..."

And so on to dusk and evening. The drums thump on, the paint-pots and old iron clang and tinkle through the dark.

Midnight. The Monarch of Mania issues his mandate.

"All right, children! All you go home now! Fun done, yes! Till nex' Jou'vert!"

The drumming and the shouting fade with a suddenness that's almost grotesque – they leave a wondering gap in your awareness.

But the voices and shuffling footsteps linger on – weary footsteps heading toward the dawn of Ash Wednesday. Carnival is over.

MASQUERADERS

Not masqueraders, but masquerades – that's what we called them. And for me, as a boy, they constituted the big feature of Christmas (after, of course, Santa Claus). It was Masquerades that made the Christmas of my youth a fascinating, even a pleasantly frightening, season. Yes, it frightened me when I was a boy, this custom of men in masks and elaborate costumes parading in bands in the street, beating drums and playing flutes,

"Masquerades", our nurse had often warned my sister and myself, "sometimes put children into a bag and take them away." Even without this warning, however, it would have given us a terrifying thrill to watch the fantastically garbed figures go by, hopping and leaping and miming in a manner that could excusably have put fear into an adult.

Yet Christmas in New Amsterdam would have been an intolerably dull business had it not been for the Masquerades. Indeed, to us children, the word was synonymous with Christmas and nothing but Christmas.

Throughout the whole season the alarm continually flared. "Masquerades!" … "Drums! Masquerades are coming down the street!"

And my sister and I, as though in the toils of some fatal enchantment, would go scampering off to take up our posts of vantage behind the drawn blinds in the gallery.

Long before I reached adulthood, the Masquerades had vanished. Up to when I left British Guiana in 1941 the flutes were still trilling at Christmas – but in rum-shops and dance-halls, accompanied sometimes by the deep bark of euphoniums or "sousaphones", or the wail of saxophones. Why were there no more Masquerades? Was it that their peculiar magic could not hope to survive the harsh glare of "progress"?

ROMANTIC PROMENADE

A DIVERTISSEMENT IN MINOR CHORDS

For myself, I know it is merely an expression of the romantic in me, though I have no doubt that a few will probably want to quibble and attribute it to a variety of mysticism. Whatever it may be, however, the simple fact still stands that, when strolling along the pitch walk that borders the Grand Savannah of Port of Spain, I often find myself indulging in a pastime peculiar to my solitary moments in the open air – that of endowing trees or buildings with a living intelligence and human emotions. The more striking the tree or building – which is to say, the more dramatic its appearance against the sky – and the more antiquated its mien, the more am I inclined to impregnate it with animate properties.

For example, there is that huge, gnarled giant which stands at a point roughly equidistant between All Saints Church and the Turf Club paddocks. I have no idea what sort of tree it is, but it looks a cross between a silk cotton and an oak – or what I conceive an oak must look like, for I have never seen one save in a picture. It towers fully seventy feet into the air and the spread of its branches must shelter an area well over an acre; its roots protrude above the ground around it in small irregular humps that, from a distance, appear like boulders embedded in the turf.

I do not need to be a botanist to estimate the age of this tree; I simply *know* that it must be well over a hundred years old – and the instant this occurs to me my imagination gropes back with whimsical tendrils into the middle of the nineteenth century, and I begin to wonder at the rumours of men and events that must have settled during thousands of afternoons within the silent bulk of sap and wood upon which I am gazing now on a mild, pink-skied evening in 1946.

Wagner was still a young man and struggling in 1846, and five years later Bismarck was just entering the diplomatic service. And perhaps a scrap of newspaper discarded by a seafaring gentleman and wafted across the grassy sward toward the Peschier sugar plantation might have informed a lonely young sapling of the death of Balzac.

Who can tell what varied segments of history, wide and narrow, the sapling had not garnered to itself and aloofly smiled upon throughout the decades that had converted it into this majestic colossus? Who can guess what dreams and memories are not simmering, even at this instant, deep within those tight-packed rings of wood that go to form a trunk? That is the kind of thing I mean when I speak of endowing trees or buildings with a living intelligence and human emotions, and, to many, I doubt not, it will seem a distinctly puerile occupation. How much more profitable would it not be for me, instead, to contemplate the magnificent residences of Queen's Park West with an eye to estimating how many thousands of dollars this one or that one must have cost its owner and speculating as to my own chances of acquiring one of them so that I could resell it at, say, twice what I paid for it, or, perhaps – by George! Why couldn't I get a mortgage on it so as to enable me to purchase a cocoa estate in the

Maracas Valley. The price of cocoa has jumped from $13.90 to $23.15 on Wall Street. What a golden opportunity!

Which, of course, proves how values differ!

Fashioned as I am, I cannot, for instance, see myself appraising in monetary terms an edifice like the Roman Catholic Archbishop's Palace, that crimson-and-yellow scar on the landscape; whose Norman battlements seem so ludicrously vulgar and anachronistic in a fresh coat of post-war paint! And the blue-grey stolidity of Queen's Royal College takes my fancy not into the sphere of big business but into the thunder and lightning of four decades. "1904" is the date on the facade, and I reflect that in that year I was not yet born but that my father must have been a young man seriously and respectably contemplating the question of matrimony.

1904… 1914… Well, yes, I was in the world in 1914 – but just a mewling little oaf who was not even aware that there was a man with fiercely turned-up moustaches who had dreams of watching the Teutonic goose-step in the streets of London. And this building was ten years old, quietly staring across the Savannah at the wooded hills. How many distant growls of thunder had it hearkened to since 1904? How much rain had lashed against its walls? Had the clock-tower whimpered in terror when lightning sizzled out of a slate-grey noon sky?

In 1907?… That was the year of the earthquake in Kingston, Jamaica. Had the news caused its foundations any qualms of apprehension?

And by the way, where now are all those irresponsible boys who frolicked and cat-called at each other within its shadow – in 1908? In 1912? … In 1916? … Some, we know, are wagging greying heads over manufacturers' price-lists; others summing up gravely in the matter of Rex versus John Smith. A few are M.B.Es, and a larger few Principal Clerks or Deputy Chiefs. The sons of some of them are on the football field at this very moment. And the sons of a few are buried with the debris of Lancasters and Spitfires in the soil of Europe.

Whenever the clock strikes there is always a long and portentous pause between the chimes and the hour-strokes; age is already attacking the mechanism. Or could it be that the old clock, fraught with much disillusionment, hesitates to record the passing of another hour of time in dread for what tomorrow may bring? I have even noticed that a hoarse wheezing accompanies each rich deep stroke. Again, a mechanical defect, of course. Or could it be that forty years of densely water-vapoured winds blowing down from the purple hills have begun to chill the breath that seeps through these ageing stones? Just a romantic hypothesis – like all of the others about thunder and lightning, Balzac, historical segments and what not of which you have been reading this past minute or two. For so, you see, happens to be my way of viewing the scenery when I am strolling on the pitch walk. Idiotic or not, there is no help for it. Blame it on the conspiring chromosomes from which I sprang.

VAN BATENBURG OF BERBICE

One day in Montreal, early this year, I received a letter from a lady who had read my novel *Children of Kaywana* – Mrs. Olive van Batenburg Palmer of Westmount, Montreal. She was interested to know whether I could tell her anything of Governor van Batenburg of Berbice colony, who, she said, was an ancestor of hers.

As I had just completed the second volume in the British Guiana historical saga I am engaged on – the volume that treats of the period 1763-1803 – I had recently had cause to do some research in respect to van Batenburg, so was able to supply her with what little information I had unearthed, only to discover that what she had, in turn, to supply to me was of a much more colourful nature and of extreme value to me. After a pleasant evening at the home of this lady, during which her husband, a doctor, related how he had accidentally, during the war, happened upon the ruins of Batenburg Castle, the seat of the old Batenburg family, I left with a document which, for me, proved very exciting. It was the copy of a letter written in the early nineteenth century by an anonymous army medico and which had been handed down in the family, having come into Mrs. Palmer's possession through an aunt.

I asked Mrs. Palmer's permission to publish it as I felt that it was something that ought not to be kept merely to myself but should be made available to other students of West Indian history. Following is the letter, or, to be precise, the extract which has survived:

> I have lately had the opportunity of making several boat excursions with Col. Gomnel and others of the officers to New Amsterdam and have had the honour of being presented to Governor and Madame van Batenburg of whose hospitality and polite attention I cannot express myself in terms of sufficient praise. They have kindly invited me to take up my abode at the Government House during my stay in the Colony, but I have to comment that my duties at the hospital will not allow me to avail myself of so flattering and agreeable an accommodation. The Government House is beyond all comparison the handsomest and most spacious edifice I have yet seen in South America. It is built near the river with the front commanding the water, the other the town. At the entrance is a handsome flight of steps leading to a spacious hall which extends across the building throughout its whole depth. At the upper end of the hall an open double staircase leads up to another large room which also runs across the centre of the building, having the window of one end looking to the town and those of the other end to the river. At the sides of this room and opening into are the different apartments occupying the four angles of the building. From this construction a free current of air is present in the great centre room, and all the other apartments by communicating with it kept pleasantly cool.
>
> We have lately made a party from the fort and spent two most pleasant days, one at the Governor's, the other with Mr. Blair, a rich planter residing

at a short distance down the coast on the opposite shore of the river. At
the Governor's a dance and fête were given in the evening to the slaves
and we were extremely delighted to see with how much of real happiness
they enjoyed themselves. They assembled in the great hall of the
Government House having a violin with the fife and drum for their band.
The Governor and his lady, his sister, several gentlemen of the colony
and our party from the fort attended as spectators and were all amazed
and gratified. Madam van Batenburg, who is studious to promote the
comfort of her sable throng, cordially participated in their mirth and
by her cheerfulness and vivacity added new wings to the festive hours.
Recollection brought to my memory that every slave had not Governor
van Batenburg for a master nor Madam van Batenburg for a friend, for
which she truly is to those who serve her in bondage.

In the course of the evening a circumstance arose which had nearly
interrupted the order and harmony of the fête, but it terminated with only
affording to the Governor a pleasant and factious opportunity of convincing
us of his intimate knowledge of the English language. In the midst of the
dance three officers, who were not of the party invited ,and who had been
devoting rather freely to the rosy god, came reeling abruptly into the hall.
One of them with the busy officiousness of inebriety insisted upon introducing
the others to Madam van Batenburg, but he had forgotten his English, or
in the confidence inspired by wine was ambitious to display his knowledge
of French and then addressed only in the latter language, speaking it so
incorrectly that it was difficult to understand what he meant to say. Alarmed
at his reeling and stammering, Madam van Batenburg begged to be protected
lest he should stumble against her and true enough, at this moment, the
poor Captain fell sprawling at her feet and narrowly escaped knocking her
down. He had now to make his apologies which were likewise attempted
in bad French, too bad to be understood. During all this his companions
were reeling about the middle of the hall, but regardless of them he continued
to persecute Madam van Batenburg with his bad French and ever insisted
upon her or Mademoiselle van Batenburg joining with him in the dance.
"Venez, venez, Madam," said he. "Il faut danser. Voulez-vous viens danser
avec moi?", but finding he could not prevail with either of the ladies, he
suddenly turned from them. Madam van Batenburg, feeling surprised at
our intoxicated Captain speaking to her only in bad French, mentioned it
as remarkable that he did not utter one syllable of English. When the Governor
hearing the observation replied, "That, my dear, is not strange at all, that
the Captain should not speak English tonight. On the contrary, it is highly
proper and correct. You know he is a British officer." "True," said Madame
van Batenberg, "and that is expressly the reason he should not. It would
be disloyal in a British officer to clip the King's English."

On another occasion, this agreeable Dutchman gave a similar proof of
his close acquaintance with our language. One day as they were sitting over
their wine, he and an officer of the Navy debated respecting some property
which the Governor considered private, and the officer as public; each
maintained his opinions with amicable warmth, neither yielding to the other.
In the evening, a ball was given to the party at the Governor's House and
in the mirthful dance the officer, perhaps a little elevated by the debate,
took Madam in his arms and saluted her. The Governor observing it, instantly
called out with emphasis: "Very well, Captain, do you not consider that
private property, either?"

Perhaps few foreigners who have not resided long in England have acquired a more just idea of the spirit of our language. The Governor is a pleasant, well informed man and a social companion. His address is genteel, his manners cultivated, his mind is highly liberal and in his conduct he obtains general respect and esteem. His door is always open to his friends. The officers are frequently invited to his table, and he kindly allows them to consider his house their home. Madam van Batenburg is cheerful and entertaining. Her disposition is lively and animated. She sings very sweetly and in conversation is sprightly and affable.

By way of a postscript, I might mention that Governor Abraham Jacob van Imbyze van Batenburg died in Barbados on the 10th November, 1806, while passing through on his way to England. This event is reported in *The Barbados Mercury and Bridgetown Gazette* of Tuesday November 11th, 1806. Van Batenburg was buried in the churchyard of St. Michael's cathedral, but, for some reason, the tombstone gives the date of his death as 9th October, 1806. This date is definitely incorrect.

COLOUR, CLASS AND LETTERS

IF I WERE asked to write about British Caribbean literature for a public in, say, Trinidad, all I should need to do would be to plunge straight into my subject – name and discuss the few poets who have come into being within the past three decades or so and comment on the works of the novelists who, all in a rush, tumbled into the literary world of Britain during the past eight years. If I said that John Hearne's purpose seems to be to concentrate solely on portraying coloured middle-class life in Jamaica and that Samuel Selvon has a special flair for depicting East Indian peasant life in Trinidad, it would be necessary for me to elaborate on these statements purely on a literary basis. For an English or American audience, however, I should first of all have to make it clear what I meant by "coloured middle-class," and I can well imagine somebody asking: "Why do you say *East* Indian peasant life? Aren't you talking about West Indians?"

I am always stressing this: before anyone in Britain or North America can understand the literature being produced in the British Caribbean, the social and ethnological history of the region must first be examined and grasped. And I say "examined" with deliberation, for I don't think it essential that a deep study of the subject should be made. A mere outline picture ought to be quite sufficient, and this is what I should like to give before turning to the literary side of things.

The original inhabitants of the Caribbean islands and mainland territories were Indians – Caribs, Arawaks, Macusi, Warraus, Wapisiana, to name the chief tribes. The Spaniards who first established themselves in the region slaughtered the Indians wholesale. Some records say that they treated the Indians as big game hunters in Africa today treat lions and zebra; they hunted and killed them for the sport of it. The Caribs and Macusi, the most warlike of the tribes, in turn hunted and killed or captured the peaceable Arawaks, Warraus and Wapisiana. Sometimes the Caribs were hired as mercenaries by European governors or military men. Later, the Dutch in Guiana frequently called upon the Indians to aid the military in putting down rebellions staged by the Negro slaves on the plantations, and also to pursue runaway slaves. The Indians were never made slaves in the Dutch and British colonies. Apart from keeping the Negroes in order in times of crisis, they hunted and fished and kept the planters supplied with *labba* and tapir and venison and the freshwater fish of the rivers. But they dwindled rapidly, especially in the islands. Their own internal wars helped in this process, and the Europeans continued to massacre them. By the nineteenth century the Indians were almost extinct in the islands, and in Guiana only a few straggling tribes persisted far in the interior.

As in the American states, the Europeans and their Negro slaves took over as the principal inhabitants of the islands and the mainland territories whose coasts had been put under cultivation. The West Indies became known as the Sugar Islands, though coffee and cotton were also cultivated, especially in Guiana. The French and the

Dutch and the English fought to retain their hold on the territories won in the earlier days, the French sometimes wresting a colony or two from the Dutch, the English wresting it away from the French, and then the Dutch receiving it back through some treaty signed in Europe, only perhaps a year or two later having to surrender it to a British Naval squadron.

Meanwhile, the planters lived in high style, not much bothered by the frequent changes of national status. Their Negro serfs, though sometimes rebellious, imbibed the language and ways of the Europeans. When slavery was abolished in the British Empire in 1838, the Negroes of the British Caribbean were primitives only insofar as education and economic status were concerned. Socially, they were European in outlook; they dressed like their planter masters, ate the same food, and had the same ambitions of possessing land and making their way up in the world.

Both the Dutch and the British in the Caribbean acknowledged the value of the white blood in the veins of mulattoes, and invariably such people had received their freedom without much trouble long before 1838. The result was that society acquired a middle stratum of people of mixed blood. These "free people," proud of their infusion of white blood, set themselves up as hucksters, peddlers and artisans, and insisted on being known as "coloured," as distinct from "Negro" or "black." They cultivated a snobbery of their own, looked up with awe at the whites and looked down upon the black men, strove to better themselves socially and economically and culturally. The whites, though regarding them as inferiors, supported and encouraged the notion that they were above the Negroes in status—an attitude quite different from that of the whites of America, who dubbed as Negro every individual known to possess a drop of Negro blood, no matter how fair-complexioned he was, or European in appearance. In the Caribbean a coloured man could hope to graduate out of the ranks of the coloured and marry into a white family and so forget his "dark" past, despite the fact that his pedigree might be known to all. Prejudice has always existed in the Caribbean, and still exists, but it is covert rather than overt. Only the utterly vulgar would raise his voice to discuss the racial origins of his neighbour.

When emancipation came in 1838, the planters faced the urgent problem of labour. The Negroes had acquired a deep antipathy for field work; now freed, they turned to the towns and sought work as porters, stevedores and house servants. Some began to compete with the coloured hucksters and set up roadside provision barrows, or stalls in the marketplace; some learned trades and became carpenters, masons and tinsmiths; some simply squatted on the land and attempted to live like ladies and gentlemen of leisure, in imitation of their old planter masters.

After many tumults and setbacks, and quarrels with the Home Government, the planters eventually were allowed to bring in Portuguese from Madeira. Few of these, however, could stand up to field labour, and yellow fever mowed them down. The survivors deserted the fields and set themselves up as peddlers and small shopkeepers. Their living standards were low, and their readiness to accept small profits made them hated. Soon they had entrenched themselves in commerce, and were becoming wealthy as rum-shop owners and pawnbrokers. The truth is that they were a hard-working people, and lacked the grandiose notions of high-style living that the Negroes and coloured people had absorbed from the Dutch and English planters.

Next to come were the Chinese, also a practical, hard-working people, and soon these, too, were prospering in commerce, though not in quite the same style as the

Portuguese; they mostly remained small shopkeepers, and ran gambling-houses-cum-opium-dens and cook-shops (as slum restaurants are called).

Both the Chinese and Portuguese kept to themselves, the individuals within each group supporting one another loyally. The Chinese, too, were hated by Negroes and coloured, but not with the same intensity. The Portuguese were hated for a double reason – their cut-throat commerce and their Roman Catholicism,

Between 1845 and 1917 hundreds of thousands of immigrants poured in from India. Today more than 40 per cent of the population of British Guiana is Indian, and nearly 40 per cent of Trinidad's population is of the same stock. (To differentiate between them and the aboriginal Indians, they are called *East* Indians.) Poor, uneducated, cringing, these Indians formed another group looked down upon by the older inhabitants – white, Negro and coloured. They were dubbed "coolies," and to this day are called coolies, even though, like the Portuguese and Chinese, they eventually insinuated their way into commerce and the professions and even into politics. (The leading political figure today in British Guiana is Dr. Cheddi Jagan, a Communist-minded East Indian.)

To the hotchpotch of races and nationalities was added another little group – the Syrians, who came in fairly large numbers to Jamaica, Trinidad and British Guiana during the early part of the present century. They came as peddlers and tradesmen in textiles, and today are as wealthy as the Portuguese.

The Negroes and coloured people have struggled along in their soap-bubble tradition of planter-grandiosity, and today most of the Negroes are still artisans and labourers and messenger-boys, postmen and policemen; the coloured middle-class continue to be accountants, doctors, lawyers, business executives, shop-assistants, merchants and typists.

In 1954, the book-critic of *Time,* reviewing a novel of mine, said: "It shows what happens when the laws of the jungle are replaced by the codes of the suburbs, and it portrays with grimness the lives of coloured people whose worship of ancestral ju-jus has changed into keeping up with the Joneses." It was obvious that this writer knew little of Caribbean coloured people, otherwise he could not have implied that the coloured society of this region has only recently forgotten "the laws of the jungle."

Travel writers from the north have taken pains to highlight the "superstitions" of the natives, giving such practices as *voodoo* and *obeah* far more importance than they deserve. So far as I am aware, only in Haiti is *voodoo* strongly rooted. In other territories *obeah* is something heard of as, in England and America, the average citizen would hear of, say, quack spiritualists or fortune-tellers. Only a few ignorant peasants believe in it – and, with education, these are becoming fewer and fewer.

There is no one national tradition among British West Indians. Each island or territory developed socially in accordance with the strongest of the conflicting European influences at work within it. Thus St. Lucia is markedly French, not only in the patois French spoken by most of its peasants but also in its religious and secular attitudes. Trinidad is strongly Catholic, too, but not to the same extent as St. Lucia; and its Gallic flavour is considerably diluted by Spanish and Anglo-Saxon elements. Further, the East Indians and Portuguese and Chinese complicated matters; they brought new foods, new customs, new outlooks – and new conflicts. British Guiana should be Dutch in outlook, but British ideas swamped those of the Dutch, and the result is something British but not quite. For, again, the influx of East Indians,

Portuguese and Chinese produced modifications and nuances. Barbados has been uninterruptedly British since 1625, and because of this – also because no East Indians, Portuguese or Chinese went there – it is the most English of the islands. Many of the peasants still make use of Elizabethan expressions like "brave" (for "handsome") and "peradventure." You hear: "Very well, mistress," instead of "Very well, ma'am." In Trinidad every servant says: "Madam" – and it sounds like "Madame."

Why, the northerner might ask, since the British West Indies has been for so long in the civilized melting pot, has literature been so slow to emerge? The answer is easy: economics. Talent in all the arts has always been there, but has never blossomed because of poor financial support. Writers, painters, musicians, sculptors have all had to be content to give their talents second place, and earn livings as shop assistants, office clerks or government servants. There has never been (and there still is not) a publishing concern to which an aspiring novelist could send his book; the London publishers are 4,000 miles away and those in New York, much nearer, learn of Caribbean writers only when they appear in England. There has never been an orchestra to perform the works of a promising composer, no picture gallery (or group of private individuals) to support the efforts of an embryo Gauguin or Rodin. The daring few who felt they *must* make good as artists left their Caribbean homes and went to Britain. Those who compromised and remained home have made their mark in a restricted way, despite the shackles of their bread-and-butter jobs, but their success will be appreciated only by the small circle of those who know them through intimate local contact.

Up to 1942, there was only one poet in the region of any worth: Arthur J. Seymour, a civil servant of British Guiana, then suddenly came Frank Collymore, a schoolmaster of Barbados, who has produced some of the most lyrical atmospheric verse featuring the Barbados scene that has ever appeared in print. Then Derek Walcott, a schoolteacher of St. Lucia, startled us all by pouring out in quick succession two volumes of strong, stark poetry bearing the undoubted stamp of genius – and this at the age of nineteen.

The first novels of any significance appeared in the nineteen-thirties – C. L. R. James's *Minty Alley,* which treated lyrically of barrack-yard (slum-yard) life of Port of Spain, and Alfred Mendes' *Pitch Lake,* a picture of Portuguese family intrigues within a creole frame, and *Black Fauns,* by the same author, which, like *Minty Alley,* treated of the slum scene in Port of Spain. All three works were brought out in England. Neither James nor Mendes has produced anything more, the Trinidad civil service claimed Mendes, and James entered politics.

James, a Negro, wrote in English, his mother tongue. There was no language difficulty for him, for he had been brought up in a British colony under British influences. Mendes, though a Portuguese, spoke only English, and received a thoroughly British education, so of necessity had to write in English. There is no "native" language in Trinidad, though a few of the peasants do speak a patois French not dissimilar to that spoken in St. Lucia,

No other novel by a West Indian writer appeared until 1941 when my own *Corentyne Thunder* was published in London amidst the chaos of the blitz. In those days no British Guianese would have cared to be called a "West Indian." British Guiana is a mainland colony, and therefore, felt the Guianese (and some still feel so), not to be classed with "a mere string of little islands in the Caribbean." Nevertheless, the colony's background, both politically and socially, is extremely close to that of the Caribbean islands, and it has never bothered me that I have been classed a West Indian writer. *Corentyne Thunder* was about the poor East Indian peasants who farmed and kept cows on the Corentyne Coast (extending west from the mouth of the Corentyne River). The reviews were good, but the book was smothered by the war – so much so that when my second novel, *A Morning at the Office,* appeared in 1950 it was greeted as "a first novel."

Two years before, in 1948, had come Victor Reid's *New Day.* Reid, a Jamaican journalist, wrote this historical novel in Jamaican dialect. It is a lyrical dialect, and Reid has an excellent poetic fancy, but to readers unfamiliar with Jamaican dialect (and only Jamaicans are familiar with it) *New Day* proved difficult.

The appearance of *A Morning at the Office,* a study of Trinidad society, seemed to trigger a chain reaction, In swift succession came not only one novel a year by myself but also two works by George Lamming, *In the Castle of My Skin* and *The Emigrants,* which were part fiction and part autobiography (Lamming is from Barbados). Then followed Samuel Selvon's *A Brighter Sun* and *An Island Is a World,* both of which are pungent, down-to-earth stories dealing with East Indian peasant life in Trinidad. Selvon comes of Trinidad peasant East Indian stock.

Roger Mais of Jamaica died in 1955, but left behind him at least two powerful novels published in the early fifties – *The Hills Were Joyful Together* and *Brother Man.* His work is strongly dramatic, and he knew how to tell a story that could hold the interest from beginning to end. His characters, all peasant types, are clearly drawn and entirely real.

Space does not remain in this article to discuss in detail the aims (or apparent aims) of all the Caribbean writers who have suddenly whizzed into the British literary scene within the past eight years, but this can be said of them: as might be expected from their background, they are by no means a single-purpose group. As one English critic put it recently: "They are as varied technically as they are racially. It is their variety, their vigour, their individual treatment of unhackneyed material, which distinguish them from many of the more superficially accomplished but less adventurous and less promising of their English contemporaries."

To this I can add only that it is the complex nature of their social origins, and the conflicting loyalties involved in the scheme of their race, class and economic status, which dictate that each must tread his own lone-wolf path of literary expression.

Some Caribbean Writers

Jan Carew. *Black Midas.* Secker & Warburg. Novel by a British Guianese. It describes the diamond mines in the interior of British Guiana, as well as the low-life of Georgetown, the capital.

John Hearne. *Stranger at the Gate.* Faber & Faber. A novel of middle-class life in Jamaica.

George Lamming. *In the Castle of My Skin.* The Viking Press. The author is a Barbadian (half white and half Negro). His book is a combination of autobiography and fiction, written in poetic prose.

Roger Mais. *The Hills Were Joyful Together.* Jonathan Cape. A story of low-life in Jamaica by a writer of near-white stock. Roger Mais died in 1955.

Edgar Mittelholzer. *Children of Kaywana.* John Day. *Hubertus.* John Day. *The Old Blood.* Doubleday. A family saga incorporating the history of British Guiana from 1611 to 1953.

V. S. Naipaul. *The Mystic Masseur.* Deutsch. A comic novel about East Indians in Trinidad. The author, himself a Trinidad East Indian of peasant stock, is a graduate of Oxford and now lives in England.

Samuel Selvon. *Brighter Sun.* The Viking Press. Novel about East Indian peasant life in Trinidad by an East Indian brought up in the creole tradition.

V.S. Reid. *New Day.* Alfred A. Knopf. Novel treating of a nineteenth century historical event, in Jamaica. The author, a journalist, writes in Jamaican dialect.

ROGER MAIS

Having never had much use for middle-class hypocrisy and sentimentality, I care nothing for the convention which rules that one should speak only good of the dead. I shall praise or damn a man as I think he deserves, whether he be dead or alive. So it may be taken for granted that what I say here about Roger Mais is what I sincerely felt quite a little time before I heard that he was even ill. In fact, in a letter to Henry Swanzy in October last, a copy of which I still have on my files, I said: "I'm convinced Mais has the right idea about writing fiction. When he gets over this 'proletarian' phase, it will be interesting to see what he does."

News of his death affected me in much the same manner as did the death of Philip Pilgrim, some ten or eleven years ago. Another highly talented West Indian artist gone – and we can ill spare such men! Death is a cockeyed economist.

I have never met Mais personally, but I know his work. His short stories always struck me as being outstanding, and his novel *The Hills were Joyful Together*, when I read it two years ago, left no doubt on me that here was no fumbling, amateurish talent doomed to fizzle out in a short while. I can say with perfect truth that this novel of Mais's was the first I had read by a West Indian which had held my interest from cover to cover, and which, in my opinion, contained all the ingredients that a good novel should.

I am never weary of pointing out to people who ask me that, as I see it, a good novel is one which succeeds in three basic things: telling a story that holds the interest, depicting credible characters, and creating a strong atmosphere of place. In *The Hills* the story is not only gripping but powerful and dramatic. The characters all live and can be believed in as human beings. The atmosphere of place is rich; at times, overwhelmingly so. Added to this, there is a lyrical quality about the prose that delights the ears.

When I saw *Brother Man* announced, I suspected another "proletarian" novel – and when the book came into my hands, I found that my suspicions had been justified. I began the work with a groan, expecting a mere repetition of *The Hills* – but before I had read a chapter I had begun to succumb to Mais's magical manner, and *Brother Man* held me to the last sentence. It was repetition with a difference!

Again, as in *The Hills*, story, characterisation and atmosphere are strong, but, unlike the previous book, the tragedy is touched with a deeper pathos. The central character, Brother Man, dominates the book as no character, not even Surjue, did in *The Hills*. In the hands of a lesser artist, this character could easily have been a caricature or a figure of intolerable sentimentality; the actuality that emerges is a creature not only credible but one for which the reader cultivates a definite affection. There must be few people in this part of the world who are unaware of the impatience I feel for religion and religious fanaticism; it is expressed in almost everything I write. Yet for not a single instant did I feel myself out of sympathy with Brother Man. He was too human.

We shall never be able to prove it, but some intuition tells me that Mais could have treated middle-class characters with the same understanding and depth as he did his proletarians. His scope as an artist was big enough, and it seems a pity that he could not have set his hand to writing novels at an earlier period of his life. He certainly had the right idea about writing fiction. He was no airy, impractical experimenter, and realised that however "poetic", however strange and highbrow a novel might be, if it lacks a good story, if the characters don't live, and if the atmosphere is poor, it is a failure.

Basically, as a novelist, Mais was sound, and, given another ten or fifteen years, I feel certain, would have produced a body of work of solid literary worth.

LITERARY CRITICISM AND THE CREATIVE WRITER

This – I have good reason to believe – will be mainly about literary criticism and its benefit, or lack of benefit, to the creative writer. It will probably be a bit garrulous and rambling, for that happens to be my mood of the moment. I like indulging my moods. By way of illustration, it will be necessary for me to refer to one or two of my own literary experiences, though it is a necessity I abhor, for I have always preferred, and still prefer, the detached, impersonal treatment. I am of the strict belief, however, that it is chiefly through one's own experiences that the soundest judgments are arrived at. I might even go so far as to say that I consider it a good thing to be self-opinionated, to be more influenced by one's own individual summings-up on people and things than by the findings of others.

I recall – not maliciously but with smiles made kindly and indulgent through the mellowing of time – a certain journalist with whom I often came to literary grips in the early days in New Amsterdam. He was a gentleman forever in fear of offending, who loved doing homage to those in high places, who preferred to praise rather than administer a salutary drubbing, and who dreaded standing alone in expressing an opinion. His favourite phrase was "It is the consensus of opinion". Indeed, he wrote as though he had carried out a private Gallup Poll on every occasion before taking up his pen.

I remember, too – in Trinidad this time – another gentleman, a sub-editor, who suffered from a somewhat different type of malady. His took the form of overcautiousness – an overcautiousness verging on neurosis. This is the sort of thing that often happened: I would submit an article which, provided it was not *too* vitriolic – it often was – he would accept. But before it was published he would summon me to his office for "a friendly chat", in the course of which he would (with a continuous friendly smile) point out where one or two "minor amendments" might not be amiss. Would I object, he would suggest, if he inserted "a little phrase" here or "just a word" there? Not wishing to have my article turned down (it was bringing me in five dollars), I would protest but agree. The result of these conferences was as follows. Let us, for the sake of argument, say that I had written in my article something like this: "Mr. Jones is an ass. Mr. Brown is a renowned idiot, and Mrs. Green a nincompoop." Profound truths, incidentally, of which the public ought to be made aware. Anyway, this is how my statements (after sub-editing) would read in print: "Mr. Jones, it might appear, is an ass. Mr. Brown, it would seem, is a renowned idiot, and Mrs. Green, it could be said, a nincompoop."

The point I am trying to make is that I consider such writing bogus, and I am not concerned here with bogus writing or the writers who produce it. I am addressing this to writers of integrity – creative writers who really want to produce creations that are honest and free of polite or hypocritical evasions and sham language. I am addressing the writer who feels that the poem or short story or novel he is bringing to life is emphatically *his own* and not a pastiche of half-veiled cribbings from the works of other writers, not a collection of cautious clichés – or even sensational clichés – intended to impress but, in actuality, drab or unconvincing. I am not addressing the writer who believes in expressing "the consensus of opinion". I am speaking to the writer who loves his own ideas, who respects his own opinions, and is determined, if the heavens cave in, to say what, deep in his heart – or in his reason – he feels to be the truth about people and things.

And now for the question I want to pose. Forgetting the aesthetic aspect of the subject and forgetting the profound and involved – and often obscure – opinions adduced by such people as Mr. T. S. Eliot and Mr. D. S. Savage (in *The Withered Branch*, an excellent book, incidentally), what, from a strictly down-to-earth, practical point of view, is the use of criticism to any creative artist and, more especially, the literary artist? Without criticism, I readily admit, the artist would be like a man sealed up in a glass case and left severely to himself in the middle of a public park; even assuming that he could arrange for the requisite ventilation and other means of keeping alive, and even assuming he were satisfied to be stationary indefinitely, observing what went on outside his prison with the keenest interest, he would eventually be overcome by the utter silence, the lack of stimulating commentary from without. So egotistic is the species that without the stimulus of criticism, be it favourable or adverse, the human spirit would wither. Yet, apart from mere stimulus, where is the actual gain to the artist?

To simplify the matter somewhat. Here is a poem, here a short story, here a novel, produced by a man or woman of poor, middling or high talent. And here come our critic who takes it to bits and tells us where it flops and where it succeeds. Mr. Smith's poem is poor in imagery, is lacking in depth of feeling and universality of spirit. Mr. Jones's short story reveals a talent for characterization but is faulty in construction. Miss Brown's novel is a penetrating study in human relations, but her dialogue is a little stilted and unnatural. These are the views of Mr. I. M. A. Nabob in *Bim* or the *Observer*, and Mr. Nabob ought to know what he is talking about, for he is among the Top Five Critics in the country.

The following week, however, we read in *Caribbean Quarterly* or *The Sunday Times* that Mr. Smith's poem is a masterpiece of imagery, profundity and universality of spirit. Mr. Jones's short story is delightfully constructed but is poor in characterization, while Miss Brown's novel is noteworthy for its sparkling dialogue though rather flat as a study of human relations. And these are the findings of Mr. B. I. G. Panjandrum, also of the Top Five.

Now, where does our creator stand ? How do Smith and Jones feel? And Miss Brown ? How should they feel? What must Mr. Smith think when he reflects upon the respective remarks of Messrs. Nabob and Panjandrum? Is his poem a failure or a masterpiece? Should he toss a coin to decide it? Heads – Nabob! Tails – Panjandrum! How is Mr. Jones to make up his mind whether he is good at characterization and bad at construction, or the reverse? If his characterization is poor, then he ought to do something about it. But there it is, Mr. Nabob thought he has a talent for characterization. If his construction is faulty, then he must strive to do better in this respect. But didn't Mr. Panjandrum say that his story is delightfully constructed?

What complicates matters still more is that Messrs. Nabob and Panjandrum – though I may seem to be poking fun at them – really do know something about literature. They are both sound critics. No reputable journal will employ a critic who lacks a thorough knowledge of his subject, at least not in England and America and Europe (and, I would like to hope, not in British Guiana or the West Indies). This being the case, then, the creative writer cannot afford to reject out of hand what has been said about his work. Unless he is a producer of popular tripe and writes solely to make a living, being entirely insensible to aesthetic values, the views of the critics are bound to make some impression upon him, and if he happens to be a very sensitive individual he may even feel that he should take to heart what has been said – with, perhaps, damaging results. Indeed, since the best of the critics insist on expressing such completely conflicting views, what effect can their pronouncements have on the creator but to confuse him?

Added to the critics who actually appear on the stage, so to speak, there are the backstage critics – the publishers' readers and literary advisers, the pundits in editorial offices, the editors of literary reviews – the men who give "advice" to creative writers and those business it is to sift the not-so-good from the very-good, and, accordingly, decide whether the would-be writer makes his bow or remains in backstage obscurity. Very important gentlemen, these, but, like their brothers in the limelight, they are human, each with his particular likes and dislikes. They differ just as fiercely as the public critics. What one may consider venom another may deem the choicest venison.

A Morning at the Office was turned down by seven of the most reputable London publishers, one of whom said in a brief note to me : "Our feeling is that the material has not been worked into a novel, quite successfully". Yet, shortly after, the editor of a well-known literary review said this in a letter: "I found it most absorbing and a considerable technical achievement." In America the MS. was rejected by two of the leading publishing houses. One said: "It was a worthy attempt and an interesting one, but I don't believe that the results can be called entirely satisfactory. There are too many loose threads in your tapestry, too much disproportion of effect and an insistence on the theme of social inequality that is out of all proportion with its conclusiveness and cogency."

Very well. Suppose I were the "very sensitive" kind of individual referred to above. Suppose I had not been the nasty, self-opinionated ogre I am, what would have happened? I should have decided that the whole thing was beyond me, just too baffling for words, and I should probably have taken the MS. and given it a nice, quiet decent cremation. Not, I admit, that this would have constituted a major loss to the world of literature, but remembering the hysterical praise that hailed the book's appearance in print, what could I feel about the *seven* publishers who had turned it down? What faith could I put in the opinions of the editors and publishers readers who had pronounced against it? Indeed, wouldn't I be justified in thumbing my nose even at the critics who were so lavish in their eulogy?

Shadows Move Among Them, despite the overwhelming critical success it won in both England and America, was turned away by two of the most distinguished London publishers and two old-established American firms; the editor of one of the latter would have accepted it if I had agreed to alter the work and give it a sweet, neat, slick Hollywood ending (of course, I wouldn't agree). Mr. Leonard Woolf, one evening in December, 1950, shook his head dismally at me, between cocktails, and said: "No, I really think you've gone off the rails this time." And some months later, Miss Marghanita Laski was saying in the *Observer*: "A novel of unexceptional merit". And Mr. C. P. Snow in *The Sunday Times* : "It is a bad book".

How does all this, then, reflect on literary criticism as a whole? Had Mr. Jones or Mr. Smith or Miss Brown been subjected to my experiences, what conclusions would he or she have come to? Must the creative writer take the critic seriously? Must he look upon critics as people whose opinions deserve careful and constructive consideration? And if so, which group of critics should he heed? The ones that slate him, or the ones that praise him? How is he to decide which are giving him good and useful advice and which misleading him? Since critics are really just ordinary human beings with temperaments that vary, with individual idiosyncrasies, how is the creative writer to know that the remarks directed at his work are the result of calm and detached judgment and not of personal taste – or distaste ?

It would be easy for me to end by saying to Messrs Smith and Jones, take my advice and write as you please. Enjoy yourself with words, expressing what ideas you want to express, and how you want to express them, and treat the critics as academic entertainers to divert rather than edify you. But that would be to set myself up as an arbiter of the creative writer's outlook. I should, be guilty of just what I am quarrelling with the critics for doing. Therefore my final word must be: Ignore me!

THE TORMENT OF TECHNIQUE

Looking back on the years when the postman always brought the heavy package or the thick envelope, I've often thought it a great pity there wasn't among my acquaintances some really nasty-minded literary critic who could have said to me with utterly frank brutality: "Look here, all this you're doing is quite wrong-sided. No editor or publisher will look at it, and the reason why he won't is because..." and here he would go on to enumerate with cold-blooded lack of reserve the flaws he detected in my work, dissecting and analysing with ruthless detachment, and not caring two hoots how much it hurt me.

It would have hurt me – I'm sure of that – but I still like to think of the great good it would have done me, the new tricks of technique I would have learnt overnight, the valuable time and labour it would have saved me. In this I'm probably not singular. There must be few writers who don't look back upon their period of initiation and think: "If only I could have been taught *then* what I know now." And I should be surprised if there aren't a great many – I know I am one – who don't add the thought: "And if only I could learn now what I'll know in ten years time." It may be trite to say it, but so dismally true: you no sooner congratulate yourself that you know all there is to learn when with the next book, or short story, some new little trick or device – some new way of shaping a phrase or achieving some particular effect – bobs up, and compels you to mutter: "Now, why didn't I realize before it could have been done *that* way?"

With all this in mind, however, I'm still one of those who believe that writing cannot be taught. Every writer, I feel, must in his own fashion find his salvation. Which does not mean, nevertheless, that those who believe they have found theirs cannot indicate the obstacles they encountered on their way to the goal – and I say "goal" in a purely material sense, meaning the cheques that every writer setting forth dreams of. For it would be difficult to say when a writer has reached his aesthetic goal; I'm certain no writer of integrity ever imagines he has reached it, and perhaps for the simple reason that he can conceive of no such goal.

One of the things I used to find most frustrating in the good old bad days was the habit many how-to-do-it writers had of stating what should and should not be done if you wanted to be a successful writer, but not *illustrating* their do's and don'ts. It is because of this that I thought it might be better for me, instead of trying to lay down the law in pompous pundit fashion, to deal with a few practical problems in writing and try to show how I would overcome them. Note I emphasise I, because I am aware that, in writing, there are dozens of different ways of overcoming any one difficulty, each way depending upon the individual manner, temperament, whim, or what you will, of the particular writer concerned. The point I'm trying to make is that my way will not necessarily be the only effective one. In fact, I should not advise any beginner to imitate my way, or that of any other writer. The most I ask the beginner to do here is to observe me at work on two or three stories by aspiring writers and take note of the mechanics of technique involved in my attempt to improve them.

The stories I have chosen are from two West Indian magazines which are doing a lot of good work in encouraging new writers in that part of the world. Most of the stories published in the particular issues I have before me are fairly well constructed, but where they fail is in the quality of the writing and general effectiveness.

In one, entitled "Fish Story", the author tells of the death of a peasant boy by drowning, and her narrative skill is irreproachable; she can tell a story. But though the tale occupies only a thousand words, I found no less than ten clichés – an average of one to every paragraph in the whole piece. Here are some of them: "It had been a gruelling day, trying to find Willie's body" (the opening sentence)... "All afternoon they had stood there, a couple of hundred strong"... "He was a fellow with a shining black face"... "The dreadful, heart-wrenching crying of a woman bereft"... "a little thatched hut leaning crazily to one side"... "She crouched, gibbering like an idiot" ... "An ear-splitting din that sent shivers down my spine."

Few beginners realize how easy it is to let devitalized phrases like these spoil a good narrative. I myself did it when I started out so I ought to know. But what's the remedy? Well, this is how I personally learnt to tackle the matter. I read over every sentence of my story, slowly, paragraph by paragraph, and asked myself as I go along: "Does this sound very facile"? "Does it sound as if it could have been done by a 'practised' writer?" If the answer is yes, then I am suspicious; there must be a cliché in it. So I read over the paragraph in doubt carefully, challenging every syllable and comma – and suddenly there it is! Cliché!

I'd passed it over two or three times before without noticing it. A worn-out, hackneyed expression, dovetailed neatly amidst the rest of my sentence and so "just right" in context that it was not surprising I had failed to spot it. What a pity to have to hack it out, for the sentence reads so quickly! But there can be no pity where good writing is concerned, so it must go.

But then comes the question. How else can I say it?... "A gruelling day"... "a woman bereft"..."a couple of hundred strong". And so the torment begins. But being determined to get it right, I persist.

First "a gruelling day". Well, why not simply "a strenuous day"? Or "a trying day"? No, not "trying". A day could be trying without involving physical effort... But what is the matter with "strenuous?" It's a straightforward word, simple and yet carrying the idea of effort plus ordeal. Very well. Then let it be "a strenuous day".

Now, for the next: "a woman bereft" ... And at this stage another aspect of the matter comes to my awareness, "The dreadful, heart-wrenching crying of a woman bereft." Apart from containing a cliché, isn't this a little over-written? Why so many "expressive" epithets? Suppose I'd said: "And Maggie in her little room behind the kitchen was crying – a desperate inconsolable kind of crying." Far less sensational, far less florid, yet effective. And what is more, I've cured two ills at once: ... cliché and over-writing.

Next, "a couple of hundred strong". Well, what about striking out "strong"? No "a couple of hundred" has an unfinished sound. Not quite right, somehow. So, after more thought: Well, suppose we forget the whole phrase "couple of hundred strong" and say: "All afternoon they had stood there, about two hundred of them." That seems all right. Clear, unmistakable in its meaning.

Having one by one rid the thing of its bogus phrases. I pause, for the memory of that patch of over-writing lingers. Another going-over is indicated. This time the hunt will be for over-writing instead of clichés. And not until I have satisfied myself that everything florid and superfluous has been eradicated will I feel that I have done a good piece of work.

To tackle the problem of over-writing I will take another story – a story called "The Cupboard", which is a study in the supernatural.

In this kind of story it will be found that the soft-pedal approach can be far more effective than too much emphasis on what is sensational. "The Cupboard" suffers all through from over-writing; there is too much use of words like "horror", "menace", "ghostly". Paradoxical as it may be, these are the words that should be carefully avoided if you are writing a tale of this sort. A supernatural story calls for restraint; suggestion and understatement are essential in obtaining the required effects.

Here is a paragraph from "The Cupboard" which is typical of many others in this tale: "I had sensed the room. An atmosphere of dread, of foreboding, of horror was around me. In that room some wretched human being had gone through agony beyond bearing. It encompassed me – it was all about me. My brain was numbed, beads of sweat stood upon my forehead because of it. The suffering that had been endured in that bare, wretched room was so indelibly impressed upon its atmosphere that to senses capable of its perception the terror of it lived again. And more and more as I sat there, unable to move, my psychic sense was drawn to the cupboard…"

And now to work on it. First of all, the thing is too verbose. It needs more condensation. Added to this it is loud and unsubtle. The sophisticated reader shakes his head and smiles, realising that the writer is trying too hard to impress him. Now, there are many ways of treating such a passage. It could be broken up into shorter, staccato sentences and made more tense, more tight. Its could be treated lyrically – that is, in longish sentences, following each other with a dirge-like rhythm and gradually building up an atmosphere of horror and uncertainty. Anyway, had I to do it, this is what I would have settled for:

"I looked about the room, feeling, somehow, that all was not right. It could almost have been that some human creature had suffered here – suffered terribly. After a moment, I was certain. I could feel his suffering as though it were a cloud, invisible but stifling, that hung about me. Definitely uneasy now, I began to move about, still looking around me, alert for I could not say what. And then I halted. Turned and looked at the cupboard…"

Reading this over, it seems a great improvement. Indeed, I assure myself, perfect. So I pat myself on the back and put it away. But when I come back to it after an hour or two I begin to see flaws. No, it is not an perfect as I had thought. For instance "all was not right" followed so soon by "It could almost have been" has an unpleasing ring. "All" and "almost" create a repetitious sound effect.

So I proceed to score out "It could almost have been". I must think up a new way of shaping that bit. Ah! A little idea. The word "shaping" gave me the clue. So I write in the new new clause… And continue to hunt for more flaws. Three more come to my notice, and I attend to these. And now here is the final result:

"I looked about the room, feeling, somehow, that all was not right. In me a belief wanted to take shape that some human creature had suffered here – perhaps terribly. After a moment I was certain. I could feel his suffering as though it were a cloud, invisible and stifling, that drifted beside me, alert for what I could not say what. And then I halted. Turned and stared at the cupboard…"

Note what has happened. For "It could almost have been" I have substituted "In me a belief wanted to take shape," and this is the idea I had: the phrase "take shape", though apparently used innocently in an idiomatic sense, also subtly suggests something ghostly coming into being – "taking shape". Remember, every word counts when building up atmosphere of this sort. The purpose is to chill the reader by the sheer magic of words. Note, too, that I have changed "suffered terribly" to "perhaps terribly". "Perhaps" is a word of doubt; it gives added uncertainty to the situation. Then in the very next sentence (almost equivalent to a soft gasp) I am certain. A minor but sharp surprise has been sprung upon the reader... Then instead of "hung about me" note I've substituted "drifted about me." Again, the ghostly notion. Later for "Turned and looked" I thought it better to say "Turned and stared". Sixteen words before I had used "looking"; to avoid repetition and also to produce a more impressive effect "stared" was just the word I wanted. "Stared" suggests that there was something (though unnamed) there to see – something, possibly terrifying.

The temptation to go on like this, analysing and shuffling and piecing together, could easily lead me into many thousands of words, so I must restrain myself and before ending this, deal with just one more instance where the beginner often finds that he has slipped into a puddle of weak writing.

The fault involved in this third instance may be termed lack of a sense of the true value of words, and to illustrate my point I have taken this passage from a story called: "He wanted 'em different":

"In the course of a split second her world had changed with the forceful relentlessness of an amused fate. Her lovely peach bloom colouring had drained to a pale moon-wan lifelessness of shock. Only her lips remained rosy like a scarlet thread of silk on snow."

Now, here we see the opposite of cliché-writing – the absurd opposite. No one could possibly accuse the writer here of using worn-out phrases; in fact, she has gone to great pains to be fresh and vivid. But the trouble is that her respect for words was poor, and, in revenge, the words defeated her.

She begins, ironically, enough, with a cliché – "In the course of a split second" – then as though subconsciously aware of having erred somewhere on the banal side, follows this up with highly coloured exaggerations. Now, can we think of relentlessness as forceful? Possibly, but it is a bit of a strain. Something that is relentless, we know, is something unyielding, merciless and so forth, but we are dealing with a negative quality, remember, and "forceful" is a very positive word, hence to tack on a positive word to one that is obviously negative in significance at once strikes the critical reader as being lopsided. Again, can a world change with relentlessness? Yes, feasibly – and there is nothing really wrong in putting it like this. But it isn't *effective* writing. After all, "one's world" is a passive abstraction. *Influences* can be relentless in changing it. So when we speak of one's world changing what we really mean is not that this world is changing itself in an active sense but that some force or set of forces outside it is acting upon it and altering the setup that already exists.

However, to complicate matters further, this writer has added "of an amused fate". All at once we realize that in the torrent of her unrestraint she has switched the responsibility for the relentlessness to "fate" and not merely fate but an *amused* fate. The effect produced at this stage can only be one of incoherence, and the reader is forced to shake his head and pass on, registering as he does so one emphatic bad mark.

To add incoherence to incoherence, we go on to read that "Her lovely peach bloom colouring had drained to pale moon-wan lifelessness of shock". To try to analyse this would prove too agonizing, so we must pass on to the next statement: "only her lips remained rosy like a scarlet thread of silk on snow". Now, here is where the writer did not pause to exercise her sense of logic, for it should have been obvious to her that, poetic licence or no poetic licence, a scarlet *thread* of silk on any quantity of snow would be invisible except to a microscopically keen eye, which, of course, defeats the whole intention of the imagery.

The moral to be drawn from this, then is try to be as simple and "uncomplicated" as you can in saying whatever you want to say. Never attempt to indulge in purple flights of language until you are perfectly sure of yourself – and when you do feel sure you probably won't make such attempts. Few beginners realize that "purple passages" are very often written not by conscious straining but out of an easy sincerity of purpose.

And to end, I think that that would be a good word of advice: Be sincere every time you try to write anything, and the struggle will seem not half so tough.

FOLLOWED BY AD. LIB. DISCUSSION with EDGAR MITTELHOLZER, NORMAN RAE and VIDIA NAIPAUL

AT 43: A PERSONAL VIEW OF THE WORLD

Human beings have invented innumerable ways of escaping from reality, and by reality I want to make it clear that I mean not the ultimate spiritual reality the Orientals speak of, but reality as represented by the unpleasant things that afflict us, such as war and the fear of war, money and domestic worries, ill health, social ostracism and social maladjustment, to name a few. Some humans continue escaping until death, leading a sham-happy existence, superficially satisfying but, at depth, bleak with despair. Some – and these are much rarer – refuse to escape, decide with determination to "face out" the unpleasant and "find a solution", and either achieve a compromise that brings them an uneasy peace of mind or suffer defeat – a defeat that results in untimely death or a mental home. Among the latter group are to be found a few cranks who, lacking the capacity to sustain a faith in anything, even in the concomitants of despair, and supported by what I can only describe as an awareness of the ironies of living, fluctuate between uneasy peace of mind and defeat: a limbo state that is neither happiness nor unhappiness – a sort of Dead Sea mood of perpetual detachment.

At forty-three, I have reason to believe that I can be numbered among these cranks, and it is in this Dead Sea mood of perpetual detachment that I have decided to take stock of myself and define my outlook on the world as I see it at the moment.

For months past I have been wanting to do this, but kept brushing it aside as a task that called for too much pompous effort. The itch, however, remained; indeed, it has almost assumed the proportions of a neurosis, so I have made up my mind to do it, and to do it in a spirit of chilly, dispassionate honesty, for only in this way can I really be free of it.

I shall begin with people – the way I see people as a whole – after which I shall tackle institutions and flail about ruthlessly and recklessly amidst the idols men have set up to worship. For me, the human species did not come clearly into focus until I was nineteen. I was at this age when an elderly gentleman, an old friend of the family, but one who had rejected respectable society, introduced me to Oriental philosophy and Yoga. He was the first human being who gave me a feeling of genuine awe – awe of mankind. Outwardly, himself no impressive specimen – he was careless in dress and habits – he, nevertheless, was highly intelligent and intensely sincere. To listen to him logically and earnestly rending to bits orthodox beliefs and conventions was, to me, a feat to marvel at. Here, I told myself, was a big intellect, the human spirit – lo and behold! – at its highest. Here was a real instance of the triumph of Spirit over Flesh.

And I became a practising Yogi.

But not for longer than eight or nine months. For it soon came upon me that quite a number of people, not excluding the people in my own home, were not big intellects nor necessarily examples of the human spirit at its highest. Indeed, very painfully I discovered that I could find no one (save my old friend) who was interested in conquering the Flesh so that the Spirit might finally be released from mortal rebirth, from mortal pain and suffering. And not only could I find no one interested in doing this, but I also realized that there was no one who even wanted to sympathize with my new way of living. Dieting? Rhythmical breathing? Physical posturing? Contemplation? No smoking, no drinking, no fleshly pleasures? Only mad men, I was told, lived like that. Certainly not normal, civilized beings.

So finding Yogi existence too uncomfortable to be worth the lack of co-operation from those around me, and finding also (please don't fail to note the honesty) that the pleasures of the world were not so bad as I had ascetically wanted to think, I stopped being a Yogi and began trying to be, if not a normal, at least an individual civilized being.

In the process of this policy-change, however, something vital happened to me. My view of people altered. After this, human beings were, for me, merely human beings: beasts with overdeveloped brains who, because of their overdeveloped brains, had acquired the ability to lord it over the beasts that wandered in the bush. Human beings, as I now saw them, were beasts who had succeeded in taming themselves sufficiently to enable them to fashion an elaborate, but not necessarily sensible, system of behaviour.

Quite a lot, naturally, can happen between nineteen and forty-three – quite a lot did, though the modifications in my outlook, I must dismally report, have been superficial. Basically I still feel as I did in my post-yogi period. I still see human beings as self-tamed beasts who suffer from an excess of egotism. Yet I have noted a number of things that have made me think very hard. For instance, no matter what foul thoughts I harboured about the species, I simply could not help being supremely impressed by some of the edifices they have created. The Paris Opera House, the Trocadero, The Rockefeller Center, the General Pulaski skyway have given me a deep respect for the men who conceived and built them. And I have to admit that I have been greatly moved by a lot of the music I have heard – the *Seventh Symphony* of Beethoven, *Scheherazade*, *The Ring of the Nibelungs* among a great number of others. Also some pieces of sculpture have left a definite mark on my imagination: Rodin's *John the Baptist*, Epstein's *Adam*, and *The Annunciation*. Some literature, too: *The Rubaiyat of Omar Khayyam*, T.S. Eliot's *Four Quartets*. All these and others have made me pause whenever I found myself too ready to despise the species, too ready to brand the whole of mankind ignoble.

Nevertheless, I should be dishonest if I said that I love the human species. There are two things in particular for which I cannot forgive mankind, no matter in what liberal a mood I might find myself. They are sex and religion. Men have taken sex, a natural function, and, by an attitude of mind, converted it into something obscene so that today – yes, today when we are supposed to be highly enlightened – even the human body is an object of shame and may not be freely exposed. I cannot pardon this, nor can I pardon the fact that men have sustained a belief in myths that ought long ago to have been consigned to a primitive past. I consider it a matter for shameful reflection that men, to this day, should have allowed these myths to influence their behaviour patterns, and that men, in 1953, can still seriously contend that faith in these myths, including faith in a mythical god, can solve world problems of an economic and political nature. Prayer! "This week is a week of prayer for peace." How many times haven't I read that in my daily newspapers. No matter if I live to a hundred I shall never be able to reconcile such attitudes toward sex and religion with genuinely enlightened, civilized beings. This is partly why, without any intention of being cynical, but in all sincerity, I refuse to recognize our present-day world as truly civilized. I feel that sex "morality" and an adherence to formalized religion stamp people as savages, and my frank opinion of our world today is that the men and women I see about me are barbarians who have pretentiously dubbed themselves civilized.

2.

No doubt it will be attributed to my self-confessed crankiness, but I cannot tolerate ceremony of any kind; I become impatient with anything that savours of ritual or formality. Kind friends have suggested to me that it is probably a psychological reaction resulting from the years between thirteen and nineteen when I was subjected to a surfeit of religious ritual. I was confirmed in the Church of England at thirteen, and for the six years following this elaborate ceremony – the church in my home town is very High Church – was an acolyte garbed in cassock and lace-frilled cotta, marching in processions with lighted candles, holding the priest's cope, serving at the altar. The explanation, however, is not as simple as that. My hatred of ceremony derives from my passionate love of truth. I am obsessively devoted to truth. Be it unimaginably lovely or unspeakably horrible, I demand the truth. It is my belief that if men could be persuaded to stand up to the uncamouflaged truth, we should be well on the way to achieving a genuinely civilized world. Face things as they are: the pleasant and the nauseous alike. It is the evading of the nauseous, the escaping from what is uncomfortable and loathsome that I disapprove of, because I feel that such an evasion, such an escape, comprises a false attitude; the ugly horror remains, whether we try to delude ourselves about its existence or not. But to recognize it, to stare it down, is to have the advantage of it.

In every form of ceremony, hypocrisy or insincerity of some sort is involved. Only a spontaneous act can be sincere and unhypocritical. Any act or series of acts that is planned or prearranged in accordance with a set pattern dictated by tradition, custom or religion must of necessity constitute a sidetracking of the truth. It is a false attitude.

Now, there are ceremonies and ceremonies. The act of saying good morning is a ceremony. Secretly, I may think Jones or Smith well deserving of an excruciatingly miserable morning, but I still nod and smile and wish him good morning. This kind of ceremony, however – this kind of hypocrisy – I readily excuse, because I look upon it as a concession to good manners. Casual ceremony is part of the general stuff of courtesy, and I am fanatically on the side of courtesy. Anything that helps to bring out the humane, the compassionate, the tolerant in us I am enthusiastic about. The ceremony I am bitterly opposed to is the kind that calls for deliberate, planned thinking. Ceremony aforethought. Funerals which are lugubrious exhibitions of bell-tolling, wreaths, organ music and corteges, black and purple garb. "Oh, death, where is thy sting?" says the reverend gentleman at the graveside. Yet from the fuss that's being made one could be excused for thinking it was a stab. The same goes for weddings which I consider ostentatious displays that merely afford Mrs. Smith the opportunity of showing Mrs. Jones what a grand splash she can give on behalf of her daughter. How many of the guests at a wedding, I wonder, send their gifts in a spirit of real sincerity! And the toasts that bridegrooms and bestmen torture themselves to memorize – can these be said to come from the heart?

Religious ceremony I consider even more stultifying in its effect upon the outlook of the man or woman who is seeking a life of genuine civility. I can conceive of nothing more damaging to one's sense of truth than a series of church services and "feast days" extending from Christmas to Christmas in monotonous repetition. December after December Christ is born, a few months later made to suffer in the wilderness, crucified and resurrected. Year after year the same carols, the same lugubrious sentiments, the same exclamations of ecstatic joy are spewed forth in a world of "highly enlightened human beings", and we are expected – intelligent people, mind – to find this sincerely moving, sincerely convincing and sincerely inspiring. Church leaders blame "the times in which we live" when their congregations fall off. It never occurs to them that the reason might be that the imaginations of some members of their flocks have become sated and dulled by the repetitious ritual that is served up Sunday after Sunday, Christmas after Christmas, Easter after Easter; it never strikes them that perhaps the few "faithful" who still attend services may be so limited in imagination, so drilled into a habit – a habit approved by custom and generations of past pious, respectable folk, hence "safe", even "estimable" in the eyes of their living fellows – that it would disturb their sense of cosy security to stop going to church. Nor does it occur to the parsons that it might well be that many among their loyal flocks do not sing hymns and pray to God because they really believe in what they are doing but because they have failed to put to good use the everyday stuff of life in the "ugly" world outside the church, and, through fear and lack of confidence in themselves as human beings, must perforce seek solace in a world of make-believe.

When asked if I believe in God my answer is always a prompt "No." And please remember the spirit of "chilly, dispassionate honesty" in which I am writing this – I repeat it here. Emphatically no. There are times, I admit, when I deem it unfortunate that I was not born with a capacity to delude myself, times when – and I am not being ironical – I envy people who can submerge themselves in the fairy-tale atmosphere of religion and derive comfort – and bliss. Think, I would reflect, if I could have sidetracked what I consider to be the truth of things and, in a spirit of genuine faith in God, entered a church, knelt in a pew and allowed myself to be swallowed up in the lovely, peaceful half-gloom, muttering prayers which I honestly believed were being heard by God, feeling that Jesus Christ was beside me; what a beautiful, comforting respite it would be from the drabness, the stupidity, the greed, the envy, the snarling rapaciousness I had left outside in the street! (Yes, I have not judged hastily. I have put myself in the place of people who are religious. In fact, in my teens I was religious – obsessively so. Those six years between thirteen and nineteen I went through the whole process of prayer, hymn-singing and elaborate ritualism – and I believed in what I was doing – believed until I began to think). These feelings of regret, however, never last longer than a few seconds, for inevitably the stern, chill universe impinges upon my awareness, and I know that should I walk into the path of a thundering Mack truck no fairy-tale would save me from death. I remember that the laws of life and death are simple. Two members of a species, male and female, copulate and a new member of that species comes into being. A physical act; not a fairy-tale act. And when the body dies that, too, is an act performed in the sphere of the physical. The body decomposes. Horrible but true. And no matter, I tell myself, what lovely myths the overdeveloped human brain may weave around the realities of life and death, the laws of nature are uncaring. Disobey certain laws – defy gravity and throw yourself out of a third-storey window – and death results. Obey certain laws – feed yourself, protect yourself against fire and cold – and you survive. This, as I see it, is the truth.

I think it lovely that the human imagination should evolve fairy-tales around the realities of existence. Life would be dismal without fairy-tales – and the little ceremonies, the little gestures of goodwill, that go with the courteous conduct of beings who aspire to be better than the beasts of the bush. But I believe that fairy-tales should be kept in their place – like pictures and novels and poetry and music. And ceremonies which have degenerated into mechanical, insincere occasions of ostentation or false sentiment should be eradicated. Such things should not be allowed to influence the practical, down-to-earth existence of truly enlightened, intelligent beings.

3.

The nearest I have ever come to feeling I was among truly civilized people was in South Devon, England, where I spent two successive summer holidays at an hotel called Sheplegh Court. Three miles from the nearest tiny village, and set amidst about fifty acres of wooded grounds, this is a Naturist hotel. Here the guests do not have to wear clothes. Bedroom doors and bathroom doors need not be closed for "privacy". A male may go into the bathroom and shave and at the same time carry on a casual conversation with a lady having her bath only two yards away. And believe it or not, the lady never faints or reaches for her towel with a shrill cry of outraged "modesty". At this hotel one can play lawn tennis, badminton, ping-pong, swim in a pool and engage in archery – all in the nude. And it may seem odd, but I witnessed no instance of rape, no orgies of "licentiousness" – no "immorality" at all. I swam, played tennis and badminton and ping pong, and sometimes sat in the sun and wrangled over art and literature and politics with my fellow guests – among them a university professor, a squadron-leader of the Royal Air Force, a chemist from the Midlands, the wife of a journalist, a young actress just out of drama school, a Church of England cleric – and the fact that we were without a thread of clothing on our bodies did not make us stammer or fidget or want to hide our faces behind our hands. Before coming to this hotel we had, for some unaccountable reason, admitted to ourselves the loathsome truth that we were in possession of sex organs and that these organs had been naturally acquired – like our noses and ears and hands and feet. And perhaps it was because we had resigned ourselves in advance to this horrible knowledge that we were able to enjoy the sense of genuine freedom that we did – freedom from clothes that restricted the movements of the body and prevented the sun from doing full benefit to our systems, freedom from the prohibitions of the world beyond the grounds of this haven – the world where women shrieked when surprised unclothed, and men recoiled with gasps – or used binoculars to watch skimpily-clad women parading on a beach.

In Victorian times it was considered immodest, indecent – indeed, immoral – for a lady to reveal an ankle. Nowadays the exposure of knees and thighs has attained drab respectability. Why? If morality forbade a show of ankles in 1890 it ought to do the same in 1953; if not something is the matter: there must be a false element in this morality. It must prove that morality, where sex is concerned, is merely an attitude of mind that shifts in accordance with the individual and his situation – which reveals it as a hoax. A virtue that is valid does not lose its validity with the lapse of time or the change of man's estate.

If people in an hotel in South Devon, and in the many Naturist sun-camps scattered over England, can conduct themselves in a reasonable and decorous manner, even though nude, and if in 1953 it is conventional and respectable for a female to reveal her knees and thighs when this could not be done in 1890, then it seems feasible to assume that a world of thinking, refined beings should already have discarded the mystery and humbug with which sex has been surrounded in the past. It seems to me feasible that sex should by now have come to be regarded as a normal, healthy bodily function – and treated as such. Instead, despite skyscrapers, television, jet-bombers and all the other indications of "advancement" and "progress", sex is still being whispered about, is still a subject for shame. Newspapers and magazines are still forbidden to print words or pictures that are "too frank". Sex is still a subject for "off-colour" stories. The authorities lay down set rules – in the name of "public morals" – as to what can and cannot be exhibited or spoken on radio, television, stage and screen!

Call it crankiness if you like, but I shall still say it: I can visualize a superstitious, ignorant bushman keeping up a cramping system of taboos and prohibitions around the subject of sex, but I honestly cannot visualize a civilized man doing this.

4.

Not very often, but sometimes, I am asked: "What are your political views?" And my answer is always: "I have none." Why? Because I am still looking for the perfect political party. I have observed, up to this age of forty-three, only political self-seeking, political greed for power, and political corruption in various forms and odours. I have not met – or read of – a politician who impressed me that he was sincerely concerned with the welfare of mankind, or even of the particular nation he represented. Though I must pause. After brief reflection, chin in hand, I find I can recall one. Just one. Franklin D. Roosevelt. But not another could I name without sacrificing my integrity. I will say, however, that I believe others have existed and may even exist today, unknown to me, but I also believe that these individuals were and are so rare that I can safely disregard them when forming my own personal estimate of politics and politicians.

One thing I never fail to point out when drawn into a discussion on politics. It is this: so long as politicians don't try to interfere in what the people think and say I can tolerate them, because I realize that politicians are necessary; a body of men must take care of the management of the country. Having pointed this out, however, someone inevitably rebuts: "But there are politicians who try to interfere in what the people think and say. It's like that in Russia." My reply is: "Exactly. That is why I have never been able to sympathize with the rulers of the Soviet Union and their methods." Then a voice snaps: "What about the witch-hunt in the U.S.?" And so the argument is on.

For me, however, the issues remain simple. All the talk of peace doves and world peace conferences, all the talk of equality and brotherhood of men could not win me over to Communism so long as I know that I would have to live under a state of things where a Party is going to try to dictate to me what I should think and say, and put me under arrest when I "deviate". And as for the witch-hunt in the United States, my personal view is: why should the Communist countries have a monopoly on witch-hunting? People who talk idealistically about "our democratic rights" always forget that a ruthless enemy has no respect for the rights of other people. To permit such an enemy to function freely in a democratic state must inevitably mean the downfall of that state. Idealism won't stop a determined, cold-blooded enemy. Then what would have become of "our democratic rights"? They would be a pipe-dream of the past!

I believe that (apart from sex and religion) much of my low opinion of present-day mankind may be traced to my subconscious knowledge that there are millions of people feeble-minded enough to be gulled by the patently puerile kind of propaganda that is served up by Communist agents. It certainly doesn't speak well for the commonsense coefficient of a large mass of people, and it proves that even big "specialized" brains – I am thinking of our well-known Communist scientists and artists – need not necessarily be intelligent in the broad sense of the word.

In any event, I must state frankly that politics have never interested me very much. I like to keep well informed about world affairs, but no matter how I try I shall never be able to get enthusiastic over any political cause. The very thought of political activity of any sort makes me yawn. Politics, law and accountancy are the three subjects that from adolescence to now have seemed to me outstandingly dull.

Patriotism, too, is something for which I have never been able to generate much warmth, but in this case there are definite reasons involved.

I feel that patriotism has been the basic cause of most of the miserable conflicts the world has witnessed, and I agree with Clive Bell when he says in his book, *Civilization*: "A highly civilized person can never unquestioningly accept the ethics of patriotism. Indeed, the civilized person will tend to think less and less in terms of groups; the conception of 'his country' as an entity with interests distinct from those of the rest of the world will gradually lose precision in his eyes".

To me, patriotism is so much bigoted sentimentality. I can understand a warm attachment to the region of one's birth and upbringing; it is inescapably human to be sentimental about the sights and incidents of one's childhood and adolescence. But where sentiment – and I am not against sentiment, mind – lapses into sentimentality is when we begin to puff out our chests and say: "My country is the best in the world. I will die for it." This is not sentiment but sentimentality, and herein, I feel, lie the seeds of war. As far back as I can recall, I have always preferred to view things in universal rather than regional terms. Possibly it was because I felt such a prisoner in my home town with its cramping respectability that I rebelled so early against provincialism and threw out my sympathies into the wider world into which I yearned to escape. In my novels I write most often about my native British Guiana merely because it is the locale I know best, having lived there from infancy to the age of thirty-two; not because I feel it is the most marvellous country in the world. Should I live long enough in Timbuctoo to absorb the ways of its people and its individual atmosphere, I should begin to write about Timbuctoo.

I could live and be at ease in any part of the world, provided conditions were tolerably civilized. This rules out places like South Africa and the southern states of America, which I do not consider tolerably civilized. Intermingled with my Swiss-German, French and English bloods there is African, and though I can think of not a single occasion on which I have ever been discriminated against or humiliated because of this circumstance, I am perfectly aware that I would not be so fortunate in Johannesburg or Miami. This is why I shall have to die without seeing these places, for I should not relish being insulted by barbarian inferiors with pink skins, however authentic the pink. I prefer to think of myself as a member of the world's human community rather than as a native or national of any particular country. Officially I am British, but within me I think of myself as belonging to no race or nation. In the *Times Literary Supplement* of London a correspondent once credited me with Dutch blood; I wrote a letter refuting it. A Swiss society in New York invited me to dine at the Waldorf-Astoria and I declined, pointing out that while I am partly descended from a Swiss family, I have never even visited Switzerland, this country being as foreign to me as Siberia or Togoland. A kindly disposed acquaintance asked me to co-operate in giving him some material for an article he wanted to write on me for a magazine called *Ebony*; he wanted to write of me as "a negro author". I declined, pointing out that I did not consider myself a negro. I have long ago faced the awful truth that I am, by accident of birth, a human mongrel. And having faced it and forgotten it, it has ceased to bother me. I feel no stigma of "disgrace". When I fill in forms I put "Mixed" under "Race", and which official can say me nay.

I am well aware that in North America the practice is to dub as negro any person (no matter how European in appearance) who is known even as far back as six or seven generations to possess some negro blood in his pedigree. This does not concern me; I cannot hold myself responsible for the childish fallacies of the North American continent. If I took these seriously I should have to look upon half the population of southern Europe as negro. For where did the swarthy French Provençals, Spaniards, Italians and Portuguese acquire their swarthiness but from Africa? And perhaps (when research has progressed sufficiently in North America) the day may yet come when we shall read of "Pushkin, the negro poet who wrote in Russian", and "Alexandre Dumas, that negro novelist, author of *The Three Musketeers*." But that is in the future; for the time being, Pushkin, by the grace of North America, remains a Russian poet and Dumas a French novelist.

5.

One thing I have never wanted to be, and that is a social reformer through the medium of my pen. The world, I have long discovered, cannot be reformed by words, written or spoken, and the reason for this, I feel, is that the vast majority of people possess too low an intelligence to grasp, by means of verbal explanation, that sentimentality and superstition are seriously damaging factors. Education – the education of whole communities of children – is the only hope for mankind, but because, at present, the teachers themselves are cluttered up with sentimentality and superstition the same stultifying myths will continue to be passed down from one generation to another. The leaven of the intelligent few is always swamped so completely that it is allowed virtually no chance to spread and work with any appreciable effect. In a recent novel of mine, *The Weather in Middenshot*, one of my characters says: "What we need is an education free of religious bias and based on the elements of courtesy... No community thoroughly schooled in the graces of courtesy would want to seek war as a solution to our problems. Instead of instilling into our children a fear of God and a love of this same intangible God, instead of filling their imaginations with superstitious myths, suppose we taught them to be courteous for the sake of being humane... A doctrine of simple good conduct can be taught to every man and woman of every race and nation and be comprehended. But can we say that it would be as easy to convince men of every race and nation of the correctness of this or that particular religious attitude?... Why must we attempt to be decent creatures for the sake of God instead of for the sake of our own practical good?"

The views of this character are my own as well. I feel that the world has suffered enough because of a blind faith in myths and legends. I think it is time to discard these and face the realities of our existence in a sensible, enlightened and practical manner. It is time, I feel, to stop escaping into soap bubbles when the problems of living seem too great a burden to bear. Soap bubbles eventually burst.

These are my honest views, but I know that if I blared them day and night through every loudspeaker on the earth it would make no difference to the way of life that now exists. My purpose, as stated in the beginning, was simply to define in a spirit of chilly, dispassionate honesty what I feel about the world as I myself see it at the age of forty-three, and I think I have done this. But not for an instant do I imagine that anything I have said will have the slightest effect on other people's outlooks. A writer can indicate what he feels will make a better world, but the moment he begins to hope that he can change the way of the world by what he writes, he has ceased to be a realist.

INTELLECTUAL SISSIES

In every serious book I attack directly or obliquely the attitudes of our so-called liberal intellectuals – especially in respect to the coddling of dangerous criminals. I feel that this is one of several manifestations of the 'rot' in our society, the effeteness of our intelligentsia.

My argument is that decent people – the non-criminal section of society which struggles so hard to make this world a place worth living in – have a right to be protected, and effectively protected, against thugs, psychopathic or non-psychopathic. Almost every instance of criminal violence nowadays is excused on grounds of 'diminished responsibility' or mental derangement of some kind, and the culprit, accordingly, let off lightly so that inevitably he repeats his beastliness and claims further victims among decent people. This, I am convinced, is a wrong-sided attitude and stems from weakness. It is a false and hypocritical humanism which can show more sympathy for psychopaths and dangerous characters than for their victims and prospective victims. I shall keep on hammering away at this theme, no matter how unpopular it makes me with the critics and our Left Wing sissies.

The man with the unfashionable views is novelist Edgar Mittelholzer. He is sometimes spoken of as a leader of the West Indian group of writers that has gained prominence since the war but this is inaccurate. Firstly, they are hardly a 'group' in the literary sense. Secondly, Mittelholzer is not a West Indian. He was born in New Amsterdam, British Guiana. He did live for a time in Trinidad but has been permanently settled in Britain since 1956, now living in Farnham, Surrey, with his wife whom he met at the Writers' Summer School (which they still attend each year).

He has produced 19 novels of immense variety in a very short time. We asked him whether he regarded each book as completely individual or whether he felt his work as a whole fell into some kind of pattern:

I do regard every book as something 'completely individual'. I don't like repeating myself in respect of theme and setting, and try to vary my books as much as I can. This, roughly, is how I view the matter: though my books must differ one from another in theme, setting, and even treatment, my serious books must always be threaded through with my own individual philosophy.

It takes this form: Life, I feel, functions on the principle (whether we like it or not) that the strong overcomes the weak; this is true of every form of life. Human society, through an over-civilising process, tends at a certain stage to jettison the essential virtues of strength and discipline, and this results not only in decadence but in eventual defeat and annihilation. Hence, I preach: only through strength and discipline can we be saved.

There come moments when I feel I must take a holiday from 'seriousness' and then I plunge into a book that is more or less a lightweight attempt at fantasy or comedy or mystery or the supernatural (to wit, *Of Trees and the Sea, My Bones and My Flute, A*

Tinkling in the Twilight, *The Weather Family* and *Eltonsbrody*). My serious work can be said to be divided into two classes – the purely sociological (*A Morning at the Office*, *The Life and Death of Sylvia* and *A Tale of Three Places*) and the sociological-philosophical (*Shadows Move Among Them*, *The Kaywana Trilogy*, *The Weather in Middenshot*, *The Mad Macmullochs* and *The Piling of Clouds*). Yet it may be noted that the latter group, though serious in conception, do not adhere strictly to any set treatment. *Shadows Move Among Them* contains elements of fantasy as well as comedy, and so do *The Weather in Middenshot* and *The Mad Macmullochs*. The Kaywana trilogy is an historical saga. This illustrates what I said above about trying to vary my books as much as I can in order to avoid repetition and monotony.

Into which category does your new book, The Wounded and the Worried, *fall?*

It's one of my 'serious' books, and it's the first time that I have ever attempted to treat my beliefs of an Other World nature seriously. Since the age of 19 I have been a convert to Oriental Occultism but I have always been cautious not to bring this theme into the open in a novel because I know how sceptical most people are in this sphere. It's so difficult to be convincing when writing on psychic phenomena and Occult beliefs. However, I've done my best in this book. It probably will not be my last word on the subject.

Have you a regular writing routine?

Yes. I sit down at my desk at about 3 p.m. and work for about three hours; sometimes four or five, depending upon how easy or difficult any particular day's task happens to prove. I do this every day, without fail, from Monday to Friday. I plan to take my Saturdays and Sundays off but when I'm in the middle of a book and the heat of creation has me in its toils, I break this rule and simply have to do a little work on Saturdays and Sundays. I usually do about a thousand words every day (I set that as my minimum) but more often than not I get 1,500 or even 2,000 done in a day, especially when the book is far advanced and things are boiling up towards a climax.

Have you any strong views on trends in fiction today?

Well, I feel that the tendency seems to be one of turning capers, in style and treatment, rather than a concentration on revealing depths of character and telling an interesting story. The *avant-garde* boys (and girls) seem determined to be anti-everything traditional (anti-story, anti-hero, anti-sense). The result, in many cases, is chaotic nonsense that can have only a brief vogue. I feel that eventually the solid plot-and-character novel will come back.

    The Cruel Sea is the best novel that has been published during the past two decades, and though Monsarrat's other novels have not come up to this one by long chalks, I find him always a fascinating story-teller. My other favourite novelist is Iris Murdoch. I think she combines all the qualities that, for me, make a novel worthwhile: well-drawn characters, a plot-line you can follow, atmosphere, a clear style entirely lacking in affectation, and often a delicious touch of fantasy.

SOURCES

FICTION

Creole Chips (New Amsterdam: Lutheran Press, 1937).
The Adding Machine (Kingston: The Pioneer Press, 1954).

SHORT STORIES

'Miss Clarke is Dying', *BIM,* Issue: 5, Feb 1945.
'Something Fishy', *BIM*, Issue: 6, Dec 1945.
'Breakdown', *BIM*, Issue: 6, Dec 1945.
'Samlal', *BIM*, Issue 7, 1946.
'The Cruel Fate of Karl and Pierre', *BIM*, Issue: 8, 1947.
'Jasmine and the Angels', *Caribia*, 1946/47.
'West Indian Rights', *Caribia,* 1947/48.
'The Pawpaw Tree', *BBC Caribbean Voices*, Script 97, 1947.
'The Burglar', *BBC Caribbean Voices*, Script 202, 1948.
'Tacama', *BIM*, Issue: 9, 1948.
'We Know Not Whom to Mourn', *BIM*, Issue: 10, June 1949.
'Sorrow Dam and Mr Millbank', *BBC Caribbean Voices*, 1949.
'Mr Jones of Port of Spain', *BIM*, Issue: 11, Dec 1949.
'The Amiable Mr Britten', *BIM*, Issue: 12, June 1950.
'A Plague of Kindness', *BBC Caribbean Voices*, Script 567, 1950.
'The Sibilant and Lost', *BIM*, Issue: 13, Dec 1950.
'Wedding Day', *BIM*, Issue: 14, June 1951.
'Portrait with a Background', *BIM*, Issue: 18, June 1953.
'Only a Ghost We'll Need', *BIM*, Issue: 17, Dec 1952.
'Hurricane Season', *BIM*, Issue: 20, June 1954.
'Towards Martin's Bay', *BIM*, Issue: 21, Dec 1954.
'Gerald', *BIM*, Issue: 23, Dec 1955.
'Heat in the Jungle', *BIM*, Issue: 26, Jan-June 1958.
'Herr Pfangle', *BIM*, Issue: 32, Jan-June 1961.

WRITING FOR CHILDREN

'Poolwana's Orchid', Unpub. circa 1951: Herman Mittelholzer/Gail Calthrop
    Private Collection

DRAMA

'The Sub-Committe', *BIM*, Issue: 15, Dec 1951.
'Before the Curtain Rose', *BIM*, Issue: 28, Jan-June 1959.
'Village in Guiana', Unpub. circa 1959: Herman Mittelholzer/Gail Calthrop Private
    Collection
'Borderline Business', Unpub. circa 1959: Herman Mittelholzer/Gail Calthrop
    Private Collection
'The Twisted Man', Unpub. circa 1958: Herman Mittelholzer/Gail Calthrop Private
    Collection

POETRY

'Farewell to a Woman', *Chronicle Xmas Album*, Georgetown, 1939.
'Epithalamium',*Caribia*, 1945.
Colonial Artist in War-time (Georgetown: Argosy, 1941).
'Mood of February 11th 1940', in *Best Poems of Trinidad*, 1943.
'Reality', in *Best Poems of Trinidad*, 1943.
'For Me – the Backyard', *Kyk-over-Al*, 1946.
'Pitch-walk Mood', BIM, Issue: 7, 1946.
'Dove on Gasparee', in *Papa Bois* (Trinidad: Port of Spain Gazette, 1947)
'Island Tints', in Papa Bois (Trinidad: Port of Spain Gazette, 1947).
'In the Beginning – Now – and Then',*BIM*, Issue: 13, Dec 1950.
'Meditations of a Man Slightly Drunk', *Kyk-over-Al*, 1954.
'The Virgin', *Kyk-over-Al*, 1954.
'October 7th ', *Kyk-over-Al*, 1954.

UNPUBLISHED POEMS

'For Better Things', Unpub. circa1941: Ruth Wilkinson Collection.
'Evening at Staubles, Trinidad', Unpub. 1941: Ruth Wilkinson Collection.
'Poet Creating', Unpub. 1941: Ruth Wilkinson Collection.
'To the Memory of Ken Johnson', Unpub. 1941: Ruth Wilkinson Collection.
'Just Between Us', Unpub. 1941: Ruth Wilkinson Collection.
'Death in Prospect', Unpub. circa 1930s/early 1940s: Ruth Wilkinson Collection.
'Reality at Mid-Day', Unpub. 1941: Ruth Wilkinson Collection.
'Mazaruni Rocks', Unpub. 1941: Ruth Wilkinson Collection.
'Afternoon Reflections', Unpub. 1941: Ruth Wilkinson Collection.

ESSAYS & PERSONAL WRITING

'New Amsterdam', in *My Lovely Native Land* (London: Longman Caribbean, 1971).
'Canje', in *My Lovely Native Land* (London: Longman Caribbean, 1971)
'Of Casuarinas and Cliffs', BIM, Issue: 5, Feb 1945.
'Carnival Close-up', *BBC Caribbean Voices*, Script 96, 1947.
'Romantic Promenade', BIM, Issue: 8, 1947.
'Literary Criticism and the Creative Writer', *Kyk-over-Al*, 1952.
'Masquerades', *Kyk-Over-al*, 1955.
'Van Batenberg of Berbice', *BIM*, Issue: 19, Dec 1953.
'Roger Mais', *Kyk-over-Al*, 1955.
'The Torment of Technique',*BBC Caribbean Voices*, Script 1158, 1956.
'At 43, A Personal View of the World', Unpub. circa 1953: Lucille Mittelholzer Collection.
'Color, Class and Letters', *The Nation*, 1959.
'The Intellectual Cissies',*Books and Bookmen* (UK), Aug 1962.

Corentyne Thunder
ISBN: 9781845231118; pp. 248; pub. 1941, 2009; price, £8.99

Ramgolall, an old Indian cow-minder, has punished himself to save money and has built a sizeable herd. His first daughter is the long-established mistress of a well-to-do white planter. Their son, his grandson, Geoffry, light-skinned and ambitious, seems destined for success. But when Geoffry becomes involved with Kattree, his daughter by a second marriage, Ramgolall's world begins to fall apart.

This classic work of West Indian fiction, first published in 1941, is much more than a pioneering and acute portrayal of the rural Indo-Guyanese world; it is a work of literary ambition that creates a symphonic relationship beween its characters and the vast openness of the Corentyne coast.

This beautiful new edition, with a cover by Bernadette Persaud, features an introduction by Mittelholzer scholar Juanita Cox.

A Morning at the Office
ISBN: 9781845230661; pp. 210; pub. 1950, 2010; price £9.99

From four minutes to seven, when the aspiring black office-boy, Horace Xavier, opens up the premises of Essential Products Ltd in Port of Spain in 1947 and leaves a love poem in the in-tray of the unattainable, high-brown Nanette Hinckson, to noon when the poetic Miss Jagabir is the last to leave for lunch, the reader is privy to the interactions and inner feelings of the characters who make up the office's microcosm.

Expatriate English, Coloured Creoles of various shades, Chinese, East Indians and Trinidadian Blacks (and a sympathetically presented gay man), all find ample scope for schemes and fantasies – and wounded feelings when they think their positions on the scale of colour and class are being incorrectly categorised, or when those at the bottom are reminded of their position.

Enlivened by the inventive device of "telescopic objectivity" and a humane comedic touch, Mittelholzer's classic novel of 1950 challenges the present to declare honestly whether his news is old.

With an introduction by Raymond Ramcharitar.

Shadows Move Among Them
ISBN: 9781845230913; pp. 358; pub. 1951, 2010; price, £12.99

When Gregory Hawke, a burnt-out case from the Spanish civil war, seeks refuge at the remote utopian commune his uncle, the Reverend Harmston, has set up among the local Amerindians one hundred miles up the Berbice River, he finds a society devoted to "Hard work, frank love and wholesome play".

Apparently free-thinking and ecologically green before its time, Gregory finds much in Berkelhoost to attract him, particularly when his pretty cousin Mabel shows an unmistakeable interest. But there is an authoritarian side to the project that alarms Gregory's democratic instincts and it is this which makes it impossible to read the novel, first published in 1951, without seeing elements of prophecy – of the fate of the People's Temple commune at Jonestown in Guyana in 1978.

No such dreadful end awaits the generality of the communards, but in this most inventive of Mittelholzer's novels there are darker notes beneath the generally comic tone.

With an introduction by Rupert Roopnaraine.

The Life and Death of Sylvia
ISBN: 9781845231200; pp. 366; pub. 1953, 2010; price, £12.99.

When Sylvia Ann Russell's louche and philandering English father is murdered in scandalous circumstances, she soon discovers that for a young woman with a black mother, 1930's Georgetown is a place of hazard. This is a world where men seek either respectable wives from "good" families, or vulnerable young women to exploit. Here the fall from respectability to prostitution at the Viceroy Hotel can be all too rapid.

The Life and Death of Sylvia is a pioneering and affecting novel of social protest over the fate of women in a misogynist world – and a richly imagined study of character, that inhabits Sylvia's psyche with great inwardness. But Mittelholzer's ambition extends beyond character and protest. His goal is to present Sylvia's individual fate as cosmically meaningful, both when she redeems herself by reclaiming her own story through writing, and by making her story part of the larger patterns of sex and death, creativity and decay, sound and silence that he composes in this onwards surging "Georgetown symphony" of life.

With an introduction by Juanita Cox

My Bones and My Flute
ISBN: 9781845232955; pp. 206; pub. 1955, 2015; price, £9.99

Only when he is on board the steamer halfway to their remote destination up river in Guyana does Milton Woodsley realise that there is more to Henry Nevinson's invitation to spend time with his family in their jungle cottage. Milton, an artist, thinks he has been invited to do some paintings for Nevinson, a rich businessman, and possibly be thrust into the company of their daughter, Jessie. But when the Nevinsons mention a flute player that no one else can hear, Woodsley begins to glean that there is more to their stay.

Told in Woodsley's sceptical, self-mocking and good-humoured voice, the tension rises as the cottagers' sanity and lives are threatened by psychic manifestations whose source they must discover before it overwhelms them.

Mittelholzer subtitled his 1955 novel "A Ghost Story in the Old-fashioned Manner", and there is more than a hint of tongue-in-cheek in this thoroughly entertaining work, though it rises to a pitch of genuine terror and has serious things to say about the need to exorcise the crimes of slavery that still echo into the present in the relationship between the light-brown, upper-class Nevinsons and their black servant, Rayburn. Amongst the barks of baboons, rustles of hidden creatures in the remote Berbice forests, Mittelholzer creates a brilliantly atmospheric setting for his characters and their terrified discovery that this is not a place where they can be at home.

Edgar Mittelholzer's ghost story, written in the old fashioned manner, still chills over sixty years after it was first published. With an extensive and loving introduction by Kenneth Ramchand, *My Bones and My Flute* is offered to a new generation of readers.

In the Eye of the Storm: Edgar Mittelholzer, Critical Perspectives
Edited by Juanita Cox
ISBN: 9781845231286; pp. 352; pub. April 2018; price, £19.99

In the 1950s and early 1960s no Anglophone Caribbean novelist had a higher profile and was more praised than Edgar Mittelholzer.

He was the first Caribbean writer to earn his living from writing and his earlier novels in particular found enthusiastic reviewers in the UK and USA. But after his suicide in 1965 his reputation sank and until Peepal Tree began republishing his earlier writing in 2007, for several decades, none of his books were in print. This collection of essays charts both the way Mittelholzer's work was read in the 1960s, 70s and 80s, and shows how a contemporary generation of critics is rediscovering his real merits – the quality of his prose, his literary ambition and the ways in which at least some of Mittelholzer's ideas about the Caribbean speak to a postnationalist generation.

The essays in this collection explore Mittelholzer's treatment of race and the divided person, of sexuality, history, heredity and the charge that he wrote pornography. More recent essays discuss his formal inventiveness in exploring analogies for musical forms, the leitmotiv in his fiction. and the diversity of genres he employs in his short stories. Contributors include A.J. Seymour, Michael Gilkes, Joyce Sparer and an important biographical essay from Mittelholzer's widow, Jacqueline Ward. More recent critics include Keith Jardim, J. Dillon Brown, Juanita Cox and Jeremy Poynting on Mittelholzer's short stories.

The collection is edited by Juanita Cox, whose research on Mittelholzer's life and writing has played an important role in the rediscovery of this important Caribbean writer.

All Peepal Tree Press titles are available from the website
www.peepaltreepress.com
with money back guarantee, secure credit card ordering
and fast delivery throughout the world at cost or less

Contact us at Peepal Tree Press, 17 King's Avenue, Leeds LS6 1QS
Tel: +44 (0) 113 2451703; E-mail: contact@peepaltreepress.com